T0043955

NOVA SCOTIA
& ATLANTIC
CANADA

Welcome to Nova Scotia & Atlantic Canada

Bordered by the sea, Canada's easternmost provinces share an appealing, low-key vibe as well as striking natural beauty. Nova Scotia's capital, Halifax, is the region's largest city. Elsewhere, coastal towns dot the landscape, adding mellow charm with weathered wharves and lighthouses. You can visit Prince Edward Island's Green Gables sites, hike around New Brunswick's Bay of Fundy, or marvel at Newfoundland's spectacular parks. As you plan your travels, please confirm that places are still open and let us know when we need to make updates by writing to us at editors@fodors.com.

TOP REASONS TO GO

★ **Marine marvels:** Whales, seabirds, icebergs, and the planet's highest tides.

★ **Coastal scenery:** Drives such as the Cabot Trail reveal beautiful ocean vistas.

★ **Historic sites:** The Vikings, French, and British all left their mark here.

★ **Beaches:** Sandy strands for swimming, pebble-strewn coves, surfers' favorites.

★ **Succulent seafood:** Lobster, oysters, salmon, and scallops don't come any fresher.

★ **Traditional music:** Listening to Celtic or Acadian tunes is a memorable experience.

Contents

Chapter 1

EXPERIENCE NOVA SCOTIA AND ATLANTIC CANADA

15 ULTIMATE EXPERIENCES

Nova Scotia & Atlantic Canada offer terrific experiences that should be on every traveler's list. Here are Fodor's top picks for a memorable trip.

1 Lunenburg, Nova Scotia

"Timeless" is a word that's justifiably applied to the South Shore's signature port town. Hundreds of colorful 18th- and 19th-century buildings line the steep streets of its historic core, a UNESCO World Heritage Site. *(Ch. 3)*

2 Gros Morne National Park, Newfoundland

The stellar scenery encompasses a fjord, glacier-carved Western Brook Pond, and the Tablelands, a rock massif created millions of years ago. *(Ch. 6)*

3 Bay of Fundy, New Brunswick

Fundy's tides—the highest in the world—rise and fall twice daily with dramatic results. You can watch the waters peak and ebb at the Hopewell Rocks. *(Ch. 4)*

4 *Anne of Green Gables, Prince Edward Island*

On PEI it's hard to avoid a certain redheaded orphan. For fans of the 1908 novel *Anne of Green Gables,* the sites around Cavendish are much-loved ground. *(Ch. 5)*

5 Beaches, Prince Edward Island

Lapped by the warmest waters north of the Carolinas, PEI's pebbly shores and sandy crescents attract swimmers, sun worshippers, and bird-watchers. *(Ch. 5)*

6 Cabot Trail, Nova Scotia

Cape Breton's winding highway by the ocean proves the journey is more important than the destination: it's often called one of the most gorgeous roads on earth. *(Ch. 3)*

7 Seafood

Lobster, scallops, oysters, salmon, and more: whether you dine at casual waterfront shacks or in fine dining rooms, sublime fresh seafood tops the menu. *(Ch. 3–6)*

8 Halifax, Nova Scotia

The province's capital manages to feel at once traditional and trendy. Atlantic Canada's largest city is built around the world's second-largest natural harbor. (Ch. 3)

9 Confederation Trail, Prince Edward Island

Following a former railroad bed, this gently graded bike path crosses the island, winding past green fields, red clay cliffs, sandy beaches, and the blue sea. *(Ch. 5)*

10 Golf, Prince Edward Island

PEI is said to have more golfing options per square mile than anywhere else in Canada, with 30-plus courses, some quite scenic, open from May through October. *(Ch. 5)*

11 Icebergs, Newfoundland

Icebergs weighing 100,000 to 200,000 tons may still serenely float offshore in Notre Dame Bay from June through early July, but climate change has significantly reduced the chance of sightings. *(Ch. 6)*

12 L'Anse aux Meadows, Newfoundland

A UNESCO World Heritage Site, this is where you'll find the remains of a 1,000-year-old Viking encampment, the earliest evidence of European settlement in North America. *(Ch. 6)*

13 The Confederation Bridge, New Brunswick

The longest bridge in the world that goes over ice-covered waters, the 18-mile engineering marvel takes you from New Brunswick to Prince Edward Island. *(Ch. 4)*

14 St. Andrews-by-the-Sea, New Brunswick

Century-old homes and manicured gardens give this resort village a genteel vibe, but proximity to the Bay of Fundy means there are options for outdoor adventure. *(Ch. 4)*

15 Lighthouses

Lighthouses are a charming staple across the region, with over 160 in Nova Scotia alone. The most photographed is Peggy's Point Lighthouse in Peggy's Cove. *(Ch. 3)*

WHAT'S WHERE

1 Nova Scotia. Nova Scotia is the land of lighthouses and lobster traps: throw a dart at the map and you'll likely hit one or the other. But there are inland highlights, too, like sylvan orchards of the Annapolis Valley, the dramatic highlands of Cape Breton, and the vast wilderness of Kejimkujik National Park. There are also historic sites of national importance—Fort Anne, Port-Royal, and the Melanson Settlement. If you're looking for urban amenities, the capital—hip, historic Halifax—is the largest city in Atlantic Canada and has the broadest range of dining and nightlife options.

2 New Brunswick. Fronted by the Bay of Fundy, New Brunswick is a fine place to witness the action of the planet's highest tides as they rise and fall a phenomenal 48 feet twice daily. Beyond the bay, the province boasts rivers, mountains, and dense forests, the latter covering some 15 million acres, or 85 percent of the total area. All of this nature offers abundant adventure opportunities—plus three rich cultures

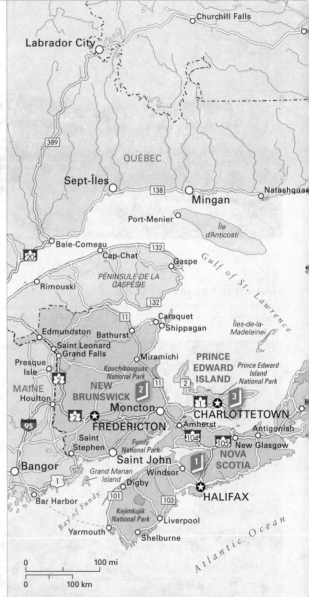

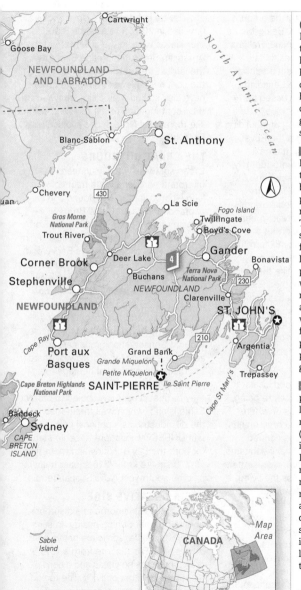

(English, French, and First Nation) and more than four centuries of history. Moncton is the largest city, while the capital, Fredericton, has historic buildings at its core, a splendid art gallery and a lovely riverside setting.

3 Prince Edward Island. PEI is rightly nicknamed the "Gentle Island" because it's generally prettier and more pastoral than its neighbors. The province's rich red soil supports thriving farms, which produce large quantities of potatoes, while its sandy warm-water beaches and nostalgia-inducing towns are a magnet for vacationers. Being largely flat, Canada's smallest province is also hugely popular with cyclists and golfers.

4 Newfoundland. The province of Newfoundland and Labrador is rugged and remote (Newfoundland sits alone in the North Atlantic; Labrador is tucked into northern Québec on the mainland). It's also relatively cold, which allows for the possibility of iceberg-watching in summer, though sightings have dwindled of late, with global warming taking the blame.

Nova Scotia and Atlantic Canada Today

THE ECONOMY

The economic outlook in Halifax remains bright, as demonstrated by the amount of construction downtown. Being the de facto capital of Atlantic Canada, Halifax is the regional center for health care and education (which gives it a strong white-collar presence); the Canadian navy's Atlantic fleet is also based here (thus adding a lot of "sailor blue"). As a port city, it is home to Irving Shipbuilding Inc., which is working with the Royal Canadian Navy to develop the next class of combat vessels. Unfortunately, the picture isn't so rosy elsewhere. St. John's, with its offshore oil industry, is impacted by local and global trends affecting oil prices. Rural areas, meanwhile, are struggling throughout the region. Heritage industries still form their economic backbone: farming is one, forestry and its offshoots (like the pulp-and-paper business) is another. Fishing, of course, also counts because seafood here isn't merely a menu staple—along much of the coast, it provides residents' livelihood. Not surprisingly, tourism in such spots is especially important.

THEIR ROOTS

In today's fast-changing world locals might not be sure where they're going, but they are very conscious of where they came from. Mi'Kmaq communities continue to honor traditions handed down from the land's original inhabitants, and the legacy of early European settlers is equally apparent. Witness the living culture of Francophone Acadians, who proudly fly their own Stella Maris flag in parts of Nova Scotia, New Brunswick, and PEI. Their *joie de vivre* tinges everything from the instruments they play to the delicacies they devour (think spoons and *rappie* pie respectively). On Cape Breton, conversely, descendants of Scots who arrived centuries ago still nibble oatcakes and step-dance to Celtic fiddle music. African Canadians celebrate their past at the Black Loyalist Heritage Centre in Birchtown, Nova Scotia: unveiled in 2015, it recalls the 3,000 former slaves who, in the aftermath of the American Revolution, made Birchtown the largest free settlement of its kind on the continent. Newer immigrant groups have also staked their claim, showcasing their contributions to the region at events like the annual Nova Scotia Multicultural Festival.

THE GREAT OUTDOORS

Urban sprawl is virtually unheard of around here, and huge tracts of land—particularly in Newfoundland and Labrador and central New Brunswick—remain undeveloped. Generously sized civic green spaces (picture Halifax's Point Pleasant Park or Saint John's Rockwood Park) are plentiful as well, so it's easy for outdoorsy sorts to find a place to play. Fresh-air fans regularly lace up hiking boots, pick up paddles, hop on bikes, lob golf balls, and grab fishing gear. All their energy isn't expended on exercise, though. Conservation groups are active across the region, and locals work hard to preserve their natural heritage for future generations. This explains why they have successfully lobbied to protect Sable Island (which was threatened by the oil industry) as a national park, and to win UNESCO Biosphere Reserve status for both the Bay of Fundy and more than 13,770 square km (5,316 square miles) of pristine southwest Nova Scotian terrain.

THEIR CREATIVE SIDE

Atlantic Canada is home to a disproportionate number of high-quality artisans and craftspeople: some are native born, others are CFAs ("come from aways") drawn by inspiring vistas and a comparatively low cost of living. The region abounds with potters, painters, and pewterers, as well as practitioners of folk disciplines such as quilting, wood carving, and rug hooking—many of whom give traditional motifs an updated twist. These creative types can be found in city centers and quiet rural locales. Notable among the latter is Newfoundland's remote Fogo Island, where an extraordinary, übermodern arts colony featuring studios and residency programs was built from scratch by the Shorefast Foundation. But they can also be found in postsecondary institutions because several schools (including a New Brunswick craft college and a Nova Scotia university devoted to art and design) lend the scene academic cred and added prestige.

FINE FOOD

Long before the Slow Food and Eat Local movements gained momentum, folks here tended to be locavores. Now a matter of preference, it was once a matter of necessity. In cities, "local" was all that you could buy fresh. In the countryside, where people fished, raised, picked, or otherwise procured their own food, it was all that was available. Yet the down-home diet has never presented any great hardship since stellar seafood is prevalent across all four provinces; and, in Newfoundland especially, game gets added to the list (if you have never tried moose burgers or caribou medallions, here's your chance!). Factor in a cornucopia of farm produce, plus a bounty of wild berries and local maple syrup, and you have the makings for memorable meals. Visitors can sample these at a range of innovative eateries and old-school restaurants. Want to learn to prepare them yourself? Nova Scotia's award-winning Trout Point Lodge offers gourmet cooking vacations.

LOCAL LIBATIONS

Like all Canadians, those on the Atlantic coast are crazy about Tim Hortons coffee. (Forget that mocha-choca latte: the standard order here is Timmie's large double-double—shorthand for a big cup of Joe with two creams and two sugars.) Starbucks also has a presence in the major cities too, as well as a growing number of independent coffee shops, some of which also roast the beans they use. Residents, however, are always ready to imbibe something stronger. And they don't just drink it: they make it, too. Nova Scotian wine is a case in point. Samuel de Champlain and his thirsty French crew planted the former colony's first grapevines back in 1611. Today the wine industry adds more than C$200-million a year to the provincial economy with around 20 vineyards and wineries occupying some 20,000 acres of vines, and Nova Scotia has even been granted its own appellation (Tidal Bay, a crisp white that was introduced in 2012). The number of grape growers and boutique wine producers is also increasing almost annually, the newest of the bunch being Lightfoot & Wolfville Vineyards, which aims to become the first certified biodynamic winery in the province. Thanks to a mild microclimate, most local wineries are concentrated in the lovely Annapolis Valley, and several (including Domaine de Grand Pré, Luckett Vineyards, and Sainte-Famille Wines) organize regular tours and tastings. New Brunswick also has around 20 wine producers, and the provincial government is investing in the development of the industry, while Prince Edward Island has five local wineries. The already significant number of craft breweries, distilleries, and cider producers is growing apace throughout the Atlantic Provinces and is well worth investigating. Some offer tours and tastings—local tourist offices will have details—and all can be discovered in the region's pubs.

What to Eat and Drink in Atlantic Canada

BLUEBERRY GRUNT

If you have a sweet tooth, try a traditional blueberry grunt—a sweet, summertime dessert made from fresh Atlantic Canada blueberries. Essentially a cobbler, the "grunt" is made from sweet biscuit dough, and is best served with a big scoop of vanilla ice cream.

SOLOMON GUNDY

Pickled herring, or solomon gundy as it's known here, is well known throughout the world, but it's especially popular in Atlantic Canada. Soft, fat slices of herring are pickled in a jar with onions. This is not a rare delicacy, so the best place to sample some is a local grocery store.

FIDDLEHEADS

If you are in New Brunswick in May, sample the local delicacy, fiddleheads. Named for their resemblance to the curl at the end of a violin head, these ferns grow along local streams and riverbeds. Locals forage for them, and you'll find them on some restaurant menus.

LOBSTER

It's always lobster season somewhere in Atlantic Canada, which means that wherever and whenever you go, there will be a chance to feast on fresh lobster. Summer is the best time to catch a traditional lobster supper, notably on Prince Edward Island, where, in addition to regular restaurants, vast dining halls open specifically to serve lobster suppers for an all-in price. Lobster rolls, however, are popular year-round; shredded lobster meat on warm buttered hot dog buns are served on boardwalks across the region.

NEWFOUNDLAND SCREECH

Originally a Jamaican rum, Newfoundland Screech became popular thanks to the tradition of being "screeched in" at Christian's Bar on George Street in St. John's, Newfoundland. In this ritual, visitors recite the Creed, kiss a real cod fish, then down a shot of screech, thus become an honorary Newfoundlander (even the late Anthony Bourdain joined this club).

BLUE DOT RESERVE STEAK

Blue Dot is the trademark steak of Prince Edward Island, and you can taste the flavorful, well-marbled, AAA-grade beef at nearly any restaurant on PEI. One of the reasons PEI beef is so good is because of the island's rich, fertile soil; thanks to this, it's even been dubbed "Canada's Food Island."

Fresh Atlantic Canada lobster

MAPLE SYRUP

As the frost fades and the temperature rises in March, sap starts running on the maple trees in eastern Canada. For a few precious weeks, the sap is collected, boiled, and turned into maple sugar, maple syrup, maple taffy, and other maple treats created by sugar shack owners throughout the region. If you're lucky enough to visit New Brunswick or Nova Scotia during maple season, head to a sugar shack and sample the products directly. New Brunswick is second only to Québec in the amount of maple syrup produced, and a visit to a sugar shack might include the chance of enjoying a pancake breakfast–with syrup, of course.

CINNAMON ROLLS

Acadian cuisine shares many flavors and techniques with its French-Canadian neighbors, and one sweet example can be found in *pets de soeurs*, literally translated as "nun's farts" (yes, nun's farts). These traditional cinnamon rolls are also known by other names that are equally as puzzling, including *bourriques de viarges*, or virgins' belly buttons.

TIDAL BAY WINE FROM ANNAPOLIS VALLEY

Established in 2012, the Tidal Bay white wine appellation is unique to Nova Scotia, and contains only Nova Scotian grapes. Acidic and fresh, the distinct flavor is an excellent companion to seafood. There are several wineries in Nova Scotia's Annapolis Valley that produce Tidal Bay, and many ways to visit them, including wine bus tours.

PRINCE EDWARD ISLAND OYSTERS

The oyster industry on PEI has exploded in recent years as new forms of aquaculture enable the salty bays that surround Canada's smallest province to overflow with cultured oyster beds. Malpeque oysters are still the most famous, but all have a clean flavor and sweet finish.

What to Buy in Atlantic Canada

LOCAL JAM

Thanks to bogs and marshes filled with wild berries, local jam is a constant in Atlantic Canada. Wild partridgeberries make a popular sour-tart jam while bakeapple jam is harder to find but very tasty. Crowberries, squashberries, and blueberries round out the list of the province's wild berries.

WOODEN PENS

Those looking for a souvenir straight from a PEI forest can buy a handmade wooden pen from Watts Tree Farm, which are sold in select shops throughout the island. Pieces of firewood from about 20 types of trees are sized, shaped, sanded, shellacked, waxed, and turned into these one-of-a kind gifts.

HONEYCOMB MITTENS

The Fogo Island Shop says the traditional Newfoundland honeycomb stitch signifies a good catch for fishermen, and luck or plenty for everyone else. Honeycomb mittens in every color combination and fabric are sold across the province—even in random gas stations and convenience stores.

SEA SALT

Thanks to its proximity to the ocean, Atlantic Canada is known for its sea salt. The most famous company, Maritime Salt Makers of Canada, produces solar-dried sea salt, some smoked with applewood chips; their products are sold in various retailers and wineries in Nova Scotia. Other local sea salt is sold across the region, by everyone from artisan companies to large commercial operators.

FOGO ISLAND QUILTS

Nothing says Fogo Island quite like a handmade heritage quilt celebrating the textile arts. On the internationally popular but remote island, you are sure to find crazy quilts, strip quilts, Rob Peter to Pay Paul quilts, and more, all hand-woven by local artisans. Every pattern has a story, so be sure to take the time to hear it. Because of the work that goes into making them, these quilts tend to be an investment that typically cost hundreds (even thousands) of dollars, so consider starting small; there are ornament-size mini-quilts that hang from twine.

SUSTAINABLE CAVIAR

For an ethical indulgence, consider Canadian caviar produced in Carters Point, New Brunswick. Acadian Sturgeon and Caviar farms Atlantic and shortnose sturgeon, and works with a small commercial fishery on the Saint John River to harvest a limited number of wild fish each year. The smoked sturgeon pâté also travels well (although you might have trouble taking

Products from Maritime Salt Makers of Canada

smoked fillets over the border). A New Brunswick Atlantic sturgeon farm is now supplying caviar to restaurants and shops across Canada.

SEAWEED GIN

Seaweed gin made by the Newfoundland Distillery Company has unexpectedly captivated the masses. Drinking a Newfoundland Distillery's multi-award-winning gin flavored with seaweed has been likened to "being in an ocean mist." Lightly flavored with dulse (seaweed) harvested from the Grand Banks and proudly full of local juniper, this craft gin offers subtle hints of the sea. Summer visits to the distillery in Clarke's Beach mean gin, vodka, and aquavit can be sampled alongside locally sourced plates of sourdough bread, chutney, cheese, charcuterie, and smoked salmon. If you can't make it to the distillery, select bars and restaurants serve the line of spirits; you can also find it sold at various liquor stores in Newfoundland and Nova Scotia.

RECYCLED ROPE CRAFTS

Driving through the region's various fishing communities, especially in Nova Scotia and Newfoundland, you'll see piles of frayed rope that did serious ocean time and are waiting to be transformed into hand-woven door mats, baskets, bowls, and centerpiece-size wreaths. Craft shops are great hunting grounds for these beautiful handmade products. On Cape Breton polythene fishing rope found on local beaches is recycled into sturdy woven doormats.

LABRADORITE JEWELRY

Named after a major mining discovery near the Inuit community of Nain in Labrador, labradorite is the province's official mineral and shines in a beguiling kaleidoscope of blues and greens. Artisans sell their pieces throughout St. John's.

Best Outdoor Adventures in Atlantic Canada

THE BAY OF FUNDY TIDES, NEW BRUNSWICK

The Bay of Fundy is home to the world's highest tides and the Hopewell Rocks, gorgeous rock formations that resemble flowerpots thanks to centuries of tidal erosion. You can walk the ocean floor before and after low tide, and watch high tide from the observation deck.

SEA KAYAKING IN NOVA SCOTIA

Paddling a kayak through the relatively sheltered waters of Nova Scotia is a treat. The best place is Peggy's Cove, a coastal region where you can explore fishing villages, islands, inlets, and beaches from your kayak. You might get lucky and spot whales, seals, eagles, and even tuna.

WHALE-WATCHING IN NEW BRUNSWICK

Humpback, minke, and finback whales are all found in the waters of NB, along with the occasional endangered North Atlantic right whale, plus porpoises, seals, and seabirds. Numerous companies offer boat trips to spot the whales.

PUFFIN SPOTTING IN NEWFOUNDLAND

There's a reason the Atlantic puffin was named the provincial bird of Newfoundland—nearly 95% of North America's puffins breed here every spring after wintering at sea. The Witless Bay Ecological Reserve is puffin central, and multiple operators offer boat trips to visit. The Elliston Puffin Viewing Site also offers views from land.

DEEP-SEA FISHING IN PRINCE EDWARD ISLAND

You don't need to know how to fish or even want to eat your catch to enjoy kicking back for a few hours on the water with a fishing adventure. Deep-sea fishing charters around PEI might involve sharks, bluefin tuna, cod, or mackerel. Lobster tours are a popular alternative if you want to see how lobster, mussels, and oysters are harvested.

ICEBERG HUNTING IN NEWFOUNDLAND

Although Canada's youngest province has long been a hot spot for iceberg tourism, the term "hot spot" is now relevant in a different way. Global warming has significantly decreased the number of floating icebergs that make their way past its shores, but boat trips are still possible when they do hove into view.

CANOING IN KEJIMKUJIK NATIONAL PARK, NOVA SCOTIA

The 147-square mile Kejimkujik National Park consists of a number of

Puffins in Newfoundland

waterways originally used by the Mi'Kmaq tribe for thousands of years. The best way to explore the park is to follow in their footsteps and explore the area by canoe, where you can travel past ancient petroglyphs carved into the rocks ashore. You're also likely to spot beavers, owls, loons, white-tailed deer, and other wildlife.

BIKING THE CONFEDERATION TRAIL, PRINCE EDWARD ISLAND

Originally the island's main railway, the Confederation Trail stretches for 470 km (292 miles), extending to almost the complete length of PEI and accessible to walkers and cyclists alike. Multiple companies offer bike tours of this relatively gentle and level pathway,

which is part of the Trans Canada Trail. Cycle past a charming collection of old-fashioned villages, gorgeous coastlines, and rolling hillsides.

HIKING IN GROS MORNE NATIONAL PARK, NEWFOUNDLAND

Newfoundland's most popular UNESCO World Heritage Site, Gros Morne is the second largest national park in Canada and home to a stunning collection of outdoor beauty. Popular hiking and boating tours can take you through the gorgeous fjord that divides the park, the second highest peak in the province, and the Tablelands, a unique, desertlike rock formation created by colliding tectonic plates. This fascinating exposure of mantle rock is rarely seen on the earth's surface.

SHIPWRECK HIKES IN NEWFOUNDLAND

The waters here are littered with shipwreck sites; many are located under the ocean, but a few are in shallow enough waters that you can spot the wrecks during hikes at low tide. Several companies offer guided seaside hikes; popular locations include Chamber Cove and Bear Cove Point.

Best Historic Sites in Atlantic Canada

ALEXANDER GRAHAM BELL NATIONAL HISTORIC SITE, NOVA SCOTIA
The famed Scottish-born inventor decided to settle down on Cape Breton Island amid its rolling hills. His former home-turned-museum offers a unique glance at his most interesting innovations and achievements.

SIGNAL HILL, NEWFOUNDLAND
A trip to Newfoundland's capital city, St. John's, is not complete without a visit to Signal Hill, where Guglielmo Marconi received the world's first transatlantic wireless signal from Poldhu, Cornwall, in 1901. The location offers self-guided hikes with city and ocean views; depending on the time of year, you might be able to see whales and icebergs.

KINGS LANDING, NEW BRUNSWICK
About a half-hour outside Fredericton is the 300-acre living museum known as Kings Landing, where visitors can enjoy hands-on historical exhibits and workshops. While it was never an actual settlement, it still gives a fascinating depiction of life at various points throughout the province's history.

PROVINCE HOUSE NATIONAL HISTORIC SITE, PEI
Right in the middle of Charlottetown, Province House is the place where Canada was born. In 1864, it was the location of the Charlottetown Conference, a meeting that led to the Canadian Confederation in 1867, which united the British colonies of Canada, Nova Scotia, and New Brunswick into one country.

FORTRESS OF LOUISBOURG, NOVA SCOTIA

Located on Cape Breton Island, the Fortress of Louisbourg is more than just a museum. Based on an incredible body of historic documents, it's an entire settlement re-created to depict life in the 1700s, when the French ruled this part of Canada. Everyone here is in character, from the waitresses at Grandchamp House to the parading soldiers.

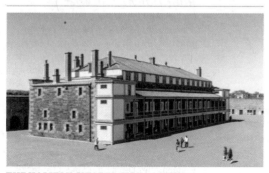

L'ANSE AUX MEADOWS NATIONAL HISTORIC SITE, NEWFOUNDLAND

By many accounts, the first visitors to North America were the Vikings, who sailed from Greenland to this remote area over 1,000 years ago. Immerse yourself in the re-creation of a Viking encampment amid the stunning scenery.

THE HALIFAX CITADEL, NOVA SCOTIA

Step inside the guarded walls of Halifax's most important fortification. Built upon a naturally occurring geological feature, the 19th-century fort offers multiple visitor experiences, including ghost tours. It's also a great place to just relax with a picnic.

Ministers Island barn

MINISTERS ISLAND, NEW BRUNSWICK

On Ministers Island, near St. Andrews by-the-Sea, you can visit the summer home of Sir William Van Horne, former president of the Canadian National Railway. The island is a utopia, with beautiful buildings, gardens, and a massive barn where Van Horne kept Clydesdale horses.

THE CANADIAN MUSEUM OF IMMIGRATION AT PIER 21, NOVA SCOTIA

Housed at the pier that was the first port of call for many Canadian immigrants, this Halifax museum is a tribute to the story of Canadian immigration. It celebrates its positive, challenging, and sometimes uncomfortable chapters over the years.

BLACK LOYALIST HERITAGE CENTRE, NOVA SCOTIA

At the end of the 1700s, Nova Scotia had the largest free Black population in North America. Here in Birchtown, outside of Shelburne, you can explore a digital copy of the Book of Negroes, where the names of 3,000 Black Loyalists were recorded.

What to Read and Watch

FALL ON YOUR KNEES BY ANN-MARIE MACDONALD

This sprawling, multigenerational saga follows the members of the Piper family, whose lives are as stormy as their Cape Breton Island home. The novel, set in the late-19th and early-20th centuries, chronicles how secrets, tragedy, and ambition have influenced the complex bonds that tie the members of this troubled clan together.

ANNE OF GREEN GABLES BY LUCY MAUD MONTGOMERY

This beloved children's book tells the story of an orphan girl named Anne who's mistakenly sent to two adult siblings to help out around their farm on Prince Edward Island. *Anne of Green Gables* (and the numerous sequels that follow) account her many adventures as she explores her newfound home.

THE SHIPPING NEWS BY E. ANNIE PROULX

After the deaths of his parents and his abusive wife, Quoyle agrees to his aunt's suggestion that he and his two daughters move from upstate New York back to their family's ancestral Newfoundland home. In the small coastal town, Quoyle finds a job reporting on the ships in the local port as he works to figure out what it means to start his life over.

STAR IN THE STORM BY JOAN HIATT HARLOW

Maggie loves her dog, a Newfoundland named Sirius, more than anything. So when her small town on the coast of Newfoundland outlaws all non-herding canines, Maggie and her family decide to keep Sirius a secret. But when a steamer wrecks during a terrible storm and Sirius is one of the few who would be able to rescue the people aboard, she's faced with a difficult choice.

COME FROM AWAY

In the days following the terrorist attacks of September 11th, 38 planes were grounded in the small town of Gander, Newfoundland. This Broadway hit tells the true story of the 7,000 stranded passengers and crew, and the generosity of the local residents who opened up their homes (and their hearts) to the unexpected visitors.

MY ANCESTORS WERE ROGUES AND MURDERERS

Anne Troake explores her own family history with the controversial practice of seal hunting in this 2005 documentary. Troake explores how the practice initially attracted controversy and, via interviews with family members, works to dispel what she sees as misconceptions about the nature of the hunt.

MAUDIE

Based on the life of Nova Scotian folk artist Maud Lewis, the 2017 film *Maudie* follows its titular character as she strives to make her own way in the world, in spite of the fact that her family views her as practically helpless.

HIGH TIDE AT NOON

In this 1957 film, a young woman named Joanna returns to a small island off the coast of Nova Scotia where most of the residents work as lobster fishermen and finds herself faced with three suitors. Eventually impoverished Joanna is forced to flee and leave her beloved island home behind.

CLOUDBURST

This raucous 2012 road comedy follows Stella and Dot as they make their way to Canada after Dot's granddaughter tricks her into being put in a nursing home. The pair hightail it north, where same sex marriage is legal, in order to legalize their 31-year relationship.

Chapter 2

TRAVEL SMART

Updated by
Penny Phenix

★ **CAPITALS**
Halifax, NS; Fredericton, NB; Charlottetown, PEI; St. John's, NL

POPULATION
2,446,674

LANGUAGES
English, French

$ **CURRENCY**
Canadian dollar

AREA CODE
506, 709, 902, 782

⚠ **EMERGENCIES**
911

DRIVING
On the right

ϟ **ELECTRICITY**
120-240 v/60 cycles; plugs have two or three rectangular prongs

TIME
One hour ahead of New York except Newfoundland, which is an hour-and-a-half ahead

WEB RESOURCES
www.novascotia.com; www.tourismnewbrunswick.ca; www.tourismpei.com; www.newfoundlandlabrador.com

LABRADOR

CANADA

NEWFOUNDLAND

ST. JOHN'S

PRINCE EDWARD ISLAND

NEW BRUNSWICK

CHARLOTTETOWN

FREDERICTON

UNITED STATES

NOVA SCOTIA

HALIFAX

ATLANTIC OCEAN

Know Before You Go

The Atlantic Canadian provinces appear as mere blips on a map compared with the rest of Canada, but in reality, the region is incredibly large. Travelers often make the mistake of trying to jam-pack their itinerary to fit it all in, but driving times can be very long, so be sure to plan your trip accordingly.

YOU SHOULD PACK FOR EVERY SEASON.

You will not need to pack your swimsuit if you're visiting Atlantic Canada during the winter months, unless it's for use in an indoor swimming pool. The weather is consistently cold, remaining below freezing for long periods, and there can be massive amounts of snow. This is good news for winter sports enthusiasts, of course, and there are plenty of opportunities for skiing, skating, and snowmobiling. Assuming you're visiting in the busiest spring or summer months, you'll want to pack a few extra layers as well as rain gear (although umbrellas often don't fare well in the windy coastal areas). Fall tends to be cooler, but with temperatures ideal for hiking and getting outdoors, and there are likely to be some lovely sunny days to highlight the spectacular autumn colors.

WATCH OUT FOR MOOSE.

As they say in Newfoundland and Labrador, put your moose eyes on. Although Prince Edward Island is exempt from this issue, the risk of running into moose while driving throughout the other Atlantic Canadian provinces is a real issue. In Newfoundland, you'll find road signs informing visitors of how many moose/vehicle collisions have already happened this year, and the numbers are nearly always high. Moose are hard to see at night (and especially at dusk), and their uniquely long-legged stature means they'll collapse heavily onto your windshield if you drive into one. But don't let that frighten you off. Just stay aware of your surroundings, and if you're driving with a passenger, ask them to be vigilant, especially at dusk.

EACH PROVINCE IS CULTURALLY UNIQUE.

Despite their proximity, each of the Atlantic Canadian provinces boasts unique cultures and traditions. In Nova Scotia and New Brunswick, Acadian history is important. If you're visiting in August, you can celebrate Acadian Day; otherwise, visit the Grand-Pré National Historic Site in Nova Scotia, which was once home to the largest Acadian settlement in the Bay of Fundy. Prince Edward Island is more straightforwardly Canadian; it's the birthplace of the Canadian Confederation, and Charlottetown's Province House National Historic Site is an important landmark. So is Green Gables Heritage Place from the beloved book series *Anne of Green Gables*. In Newfoundland and Labrador, experience the cod fisheries that shaped the province for hundreds of years by doing a little cod jigging yourself. Soak up the Celtic influences through musical performances and chatting with locals. The accent is strikingly similar to Scottish and Irish accents, and Newfoundlanders have their own dialect (complete with its own dictionary). The first native peoples were here long before anyone else, with tribes that include the Innu, Mi'Kmaq, and Beothuk. Keep an eye out for Mi'Kmaq Pow Wow celebrations, or visit one of the many educational sites in the region like Metepenagiag Heritage Park in New Brunswick.

YOU'RE GOING TO EAT A LOT OF SEAFOOD.

People from around the world flock to Nova Scotia to sample the province's lobster, and you can't go home without trying the region's famous lobster roll. The same goes for New Brunswick: travel anywhere along the Bay of Fundy or Acadian coasts, and you'll find plenty of places doling out affordable seafood. Prince Edward Island is world renowned for its oysters, thanks to its many cold water bays that provide ideal harvesting conditions. You'll find oysters on just about every seafood menu around the province and in all varieties and flavors. In Newfoundland and Labrador, cod is king. Look for the traditional dishes, like cod au gratin or fish and brewis (pronounced "brews," it's a type of hard bread, or "hart tack"). Don't shy away from the cod tongues or cheeks either—they're served with fried *scruchions* (crunchy salted pork fat).

ADVENTURE LOVERS WILL BE HAPPY.

At first glance it may seem like the ultimate destination for those wishing to relax and recharge, but Atlantic Canada is built for adventure lovers. Some of Canada's most remote and wild country is here, including in Labrador and the Torngat Mountains. If you're a hiker, the Long Range Traverse in Gros Morne National Park, Newfoundland will take you on a multiday journey through fjords, marshland, and mountains. In New Brunswick, the Bay of Fundy is home to the highest tides in the world, with 160 billion tons of seawater flowing in and out each day (that's enough to fill the Grand Canyon twice over). To experience it, visit the Hopewell Rocks at both low and high tide, or explore the Fundy National Park. In Nova Scotia, try tidal bore rafting on the Shubenacadie River. But if you'd prefer two feet firmly planted on the ground, you must hike the Skyline Trail in Cape Breton. And although Prince Edward Island is known as the gentler island, it's not without its thrills. The 270 miles of the flat Confederation Trail is ideal for cyclists and hikers.

TRAVELING THROUGH RURAL AREAS CAN BE TRICKY.

The rural areas of Atlantic Canada can be tricky to navigate, so proper preparation is key to a safe and easy trip. Keep in mind that driving times can be long, and sometimes gas stations are few and far between. Make sure you set out for the day with a full tank of gas, and pack plenty of snacks for the drive. Not all areas have cell phone service either. If you're depending on your phone's GPS to get around, you may want to pick up a basic map at any gas station or visitor center. Generally, though, the locals will be more than happy to point you in the right direction should you need it.

YOU'RE GOING TO HEAR A LOT OF CELTIC MUSIC.

As much as the sea is a part of Atlantic Canadian life, so is music. The traditional music in the region draws from Celtic influences, and you won't have to search long to experience it. Walk down any busy street in cities like St. John's, Halifax, Charlottetown, and Fredericton, and you're bound to hear fiddle and accordion ditties pouring out of bars and pubs. Other genres are just as popular, and the large music community spread throughout the four provinces is impressive. If you want to fully immerse yourself into the local arts scene, pick up a free local paper and dive right in.

YOU SHOULD BOOK EVERYTHING AHEAD OF TIME.

Most visitors travel to Atlantic Canada during the summer, which means higher volumes of traffic and lower accommodation availability. This isn't a place where you can do a spur-of-the-moment trip (at least not in peak season). If you're arriving between early June and September, you'll want to book your accommodations well in advance. The same goes for ferry schedules and even popular activities like whale-watching or iceberg viewing. In Newfoundland and Labrador, there's a particular shortage of car rentals. If possible, book at least six months in advance if you plan on renting one for a road trip in the region. But overall, don't be afraid of all this legwork. The reward of traveling around Atlantic Canada is well worth the effort.

Getting Here and Around

Air

Many visitors arrive to the region by flying into Halifax. Flying time to Halifax is 1½ hours from Montréal, 2 hours from Boston, 2½ hours from New York, and 6 hours from London. The flying time from Toronto to both Charlottetown and St. John's is about 3 hours; a flight from Montréal to St. John's takes 2 hours. Visitors from New York can expect a four-hour flight to St. John's, while Bostonians can expect a three-hour trip to Newfoundland and Labrador's capital. Inside the Atlantic provinces, a jump from Halifax to Charlottetown or Moncton takes only about 30 minutes, while a trip from Halifax to St. John's takes about 90 minutes.

Departing passengers at all major airports must pay an airport-improvement fee (AIP)—C$35 for passengers traveling outside the province or C$22 for inter-provincial flights, plus a security fee before boarding (up to C$14.25 for round-trip flights within Canada and C$24.21 for international ones), though these are usually rolled into the ticket price.

Air Canada and its partners (including Air Canada Express and Air Canada Rouge) dominate the national airline industry, serving every major city in the region as well as many smaller centers. WestJet, the main competitor, serves select cities both within Atlantic Canada and elsewhere on the continent, while Porter Airlines, a comparative upstart, flies direct to Halifax from Ottawa, Montréal, and St. John's with connections to other locales. Two newer national discount carriers—Flair Air and Swoop—are now giving the established brands a run for their money.

Regional carriers like PAL Airlines connect Newfoundland and Labrador with destinations in other Atlantic Canadian provinces and also in Québec. Contact regional travel agencies for charter companies. Halifax's airport is 40 km (25 miles) northeast of downtown, and ground transportation takes 30 to 45 minutes, depending on traffic.

AIRPORTS

The largest airport in the area is Halifax Stanfield International Airport (YHZ) in Nova Scotia. Smaller regional airpots include J.A. Douglas McCurdy Sydney Airport in Sydney, NS; Saint John Airport in Saint John, NB; Great Moncton International Airport in Moncton, NB; Fredericton Airport in Fredericton, NB; Charlottetown Airport in Charlottetown, PEI; St. John's International Airport in St. John's, NL; and Gander International Airport in Gander, NL.

🚢 Boat

Car ferries provide essential transportation on the east coast of Canada, connecting Nova Scotia, New Brunswick, PEI, and Newfoundland. Bay Ferries Ltd. sails from Portland, Maine, to Yarmouth at least five times per week from early June to early October. Service is by high-speed catamaran, and crossings take 5½ hours. The same company sails the *Fundy Rose* between Saint John, New Brunswick, and Digby year-round. There is at least one round-trip per day—typically two from mid-May to mid-October—and the crossing takes approximately 2 hours and 15 minutes. Weather permitting, from May through late December, Northumberland Ferries operates between Caribou, Nova Scotia, and Wood Islands, Prince Edward Island, making the 75-minute trip several times each day. Marine Atlantic operates daily year-round between North Sydney and Port aux Basques, on the west coast of Newfoundland. Thrice-weekly service between North Sydney and Argentia, on Newfoundland's east coast, is offered from late June through mid-September. Advance reservations are nearly always required for these ferries.

🚌 Bus

If you don't have a car, you'll likely have to rely on bus travel in Atlantic Canada, especially when visiting the many out-of-the-way communities that don't have airports or rail lines. Buses usually depart and arrive only once a day from any given destination. Maritime Bus provides regional service throughout Nova Scotia, New Brunswick, and PEI, while DRL serves Newfoundland. Tickets may be purchased in advance, but—capacity-wise—it isn't usually necessary to do so.

🚗 Car

Driving is the easiest and often quickest way to get around the region. Your own driver's license is acceptable in Atlantic Canada for up to three months, and the national highway system is excellent. It includes the Trans-Canada Highway, the longest in the world—running about 8,000 km (5,000 miles) from Victoria, British Columbia, to St. John's, Newfoundland, with ferries bridging coastal waters at each end.

If you're coming from the U.S., drivers must carry owner registration and proof of insurance coverage, which is compulsory in Canada. The Canadian Non-Resident Inter-Provincial Motor Vehicle Liability Insurance Card, available from any U.S. insurance company, is accepted as evidence of financial responsibility within the country. The minimum liability coverage in New Brunswick, Newfoundland and Labrador, and Prince Edward Island is C$200,000; in Nova Scotia, it's C$500,000. If you're driving a car that is not registered in your name, carry a letter from the owner that authorizes your use of the vehicle. The U.S. Interstate Highway System leads directly into Canada along Interstate 95 from Maine to New Brunswick, and there are many smaller highway crossings between the two countries as well (⊕ *www.cbsa-asfc.gc.ca*).

GASOLINE

Because Canada uses metric measurements, gasoline is always sold in liters with one gallon equaling about 3.8 liters. The cost is regulated by provincial governments and can change weekly, often by zone. (You can expect to pay C$1.47 per litre—or US$4.39 per gallon—in Halifax for mid-grade unleaded gas.) For up-to-date per-liter prices, check the individual governmental websites.

RULES OF THE ROAD

Speed limits, always given in kilometers, vary from province to province, but are usually within the 90- to 110-kph range outside cities. (As a mile equals 1.6 km, that translates into 50 to 68 mph.) Radar-detection devices are illegal, and speed limits are strictly enforced. Depending on where you are and how far over the limit you go, speeding tickets can start in the C$200 range and rise quickly.

By law, you are required to wear a seat belt. Children must also be properly

Getting Here and Around

restrained regardless of where they're seated. Those under 40 pounds must be strapped into approved child-safety seats. Even children over 40 pounds are legally required to use child seats if they are less than 57 inches tall or under a set age (8 in Newfoundland and Labrador, 9 in New Brunswick and Nova Scotia, 10 in PEI). This rule does not apply, however, if you're visiting from outside Atlantic Canada and driving your own vehicle, provided it complies with the child-restraint safety laws of the province or country where the car is registered.

Drinking and driving (anything over 0.08 blood-alcohol level) is a criminal offense. In the Atlantic provinces, however, there are also serious penalties—including license suspension and vehicle confis-cation—if you're found to have a 0.05 blood-alcohol level. Road-block checks are not unusual, especially on holiday weekends.

Another no-no is using a handheld cell phone while driving. All four provinces have banned the practice. Other regula-tions, such as those concerning headlight use and parking, differ from province to province. Some have a statutory require-ment to drive with your headlights on for extended periods after dawn and before sunset. Parking rules are set by individ-ual municipalities. In Halifax, tickets for violators are common and start at C$30 if paid within the first seven days, C$35 after that.

🚢 Cruise

Every season, from mid-April to early November, cruise ships sailing up from New England, and in some cases across the ocean from Europe, arrive in Atlantic Canadian waters. In terms of traffic,

Halifax is hands down the most popular port of call, annually receiving more than 170 ships representing major lines such as Royal Caribbean, Holland America, Princess, Silversea, Carnival, Crystal, and Cunard.

Saint John (New Brunswick) expects around 100 cruise ships in 2022, while Charlottetown (PEI), and Sydney (Nova Scotia) each receive about 75 cruise ship calls annually. Cruise ships are also an emerging element of the Newfoundland and Labrador tourism sector. Right now, the province plays host to a relatively small number of major lines, and they must first dock at either Corner Brook or St. John's; however, there are another 30-odd outports all over the province that attract smaller, more intrepid operators like Adventure Canada or Lindblad Expe-ditions (a National Geographic Society partner).

🚆 Train

VIA Rail, Canada's Amtrak counterpart, provides rail service to Atlantic Canada, but it's limited to an overnight Mon-tréal-to-Halifax trip, called The Ocean, which runs three times per week. The train stops in a dozen Nova Scotian and New Brunswick communities along the way, among them Truro, Amherst, Moncton, and Miramichi. There are two service classes: Economy Class, which features an upright seat with foot- and head-rest, and Sleeper Class Plus, which can cost three times as much but includes a bedroom cabin, meals, access to the panoramic Park Car, and compli-mentary educational activities in peak season (mid-June to mid-October).

Essentials

🏃 Activities

Atlantic Canada is an outdoor lover's dream, with plenty of opportunities for hiking, biking, horseback riding, fishing, kayaking, and whale-watching thanks to its 10 national parks and multiple reserves and provincial parks. The gorgeous beaches along the coasts offer a variety of water-based options, from sailing to surfing; New Brunswick in particular offers some of the warmest waters in the northeast thanks to the Gulf Stream. Newfoundland is well known for its icebergs, which are fun to spot on sailing tours.

🍴 Dining

The Atlantic provinces are a preferred destination for seafood lovers. Excellent fish and shellfish are available in all types of dining establishments. There's also a big emphasis on local ingredients, with everything from fruit, vegetables, and meat being raised and/or foraged locally. While there are a few fine dining restaurants, mostly in the major cities, even these tend toward the casual. Some of the best food in the region can be found at seaside shacks and unassuming eateries. In smaller, more remote towns, there might only be a handful of restaurants available, many of which are attached to hotels. In many of these towns, expect places to close up shop early (sometimes as early as 8 pm). If you plan to arrive late to a destination, be prepared to eat beforehand; it isn't uncommon for there to be zero restaurants or grocery stores open past 10 pm.

Restaurant reviews have been shortened. For full information, visit Fodors. com.

What It Costs In Canadian Dollars			
$	$$	$$$	$$$$
RESTAURANTS			
under C$12	C$12– C$20	C$21– C$30	over C$30

➕ Health and Safety

COVID-19

COVID-19 brought travel to a virtual standstill for most of 2020 and into 2021, but vaccinations have made travel possible and safe again. However, each destination (and each business within that destination) may have its own requirements and regulations. Travelers may expect to be asked for proof of vaccination, to continue to wear a mask in some places and to obey any other rules (and non-vaccinated travelers may face certain restrictions). Given how abruptly travel was curtailed at the onset of the pandemic, it is wise to consider protecting yourself by purchasing a travel insurance policy that will reimburse you for cancellation costs related to COVID-19. Not all travel insurance policies protect against pandemic-related cancellations, so always read the fine print.

🛏 Lodging

In Atlantic Canadian cities, you may choose between luxury hotels (whether business-class or boutique-y), moderately priced modern properties, and older ones with fewer conveniences but more charm. Options in smaller towns and in the countryside include large full-service resorts, small privately owned inns, bed-and-breakfasts, and a diminishing number of roadside motels.

Essentials

Accommodations will generally cost more in summer than at other times (except in places, such as ski resorts, where winter is high season) and should be booked well in advance for peak periods. A special event or festival that coincides with your visit might fill every room for miles around. Inquire about special deals and packages when making reservations. Big-city hotels that cater to business travelers often offer weekend packages. Discounts are common when you book for a week or longer, and many urban hotels offer rooms at up to 40% off in winter.

Rental cottages are common in the Atlantic provinces, especially Nova Scotia and Prince Edward Island. Many of them are privately owned but used by the family for only a few weeks each summer. That leaves week after week available for rental potential, with most owners leaving the booking to an online agency or enterprising neighbor. Start your house hunting by visiting reliable commercial websites or search under "Where to Stay" at the official provincial tourism websites.

Hotel reviews have been shortened. For full information, visit Fodors.com.

What It Costs In Canadian Dollars			
$	$$	$$$	$$$$
HOTELS			
under C$125	C$125–C$174	C$175–C$250	over C$250

🍸 Nightlife

Nightlife in these four provinces are pretty low-key, with the major cities having decent bar scenes (especially if they're home to a university). Irish and Scottish pubs in particular are great choices here, thanks to the colorful history of Celtic settlers. Be on the look-out for "kitchen parties," which combine Celtic music and dancing. Newfoundland in particular is known for its partying; in St. John's, you can become an honorary Newfoundlander by taking part in a "screech-in," which consists of reciting the "Screecher's Creed," kissing a cod, and taking a shot of Screech Rum.

Locally produced wines, ranging from young table wines to excellent vintages, are offered in most licensed restaurants and are well worth trying. Provincially owned liquor stores, as well as private outlets, are operated in Atlantic Canada. Stores selling alcohol are permitted to be open on Sunday (typically from noon or 1 until 5 pm). But provinces like Prince Edward Island allow certain outlets to open on that day in peak months only. Sunday aside, most liquor stores open at 10 am and close at 9 or 10 pm. For a list of government-operated stores (including private "agents" who sell beer through convenience stores in Newfoundland and Labrador), check out the website for each province.

🌐 Passport

Citizens of the United States need a passport or other WHTI-compliant document to reenter their country when returning by air from Canada. Passports, passport cards, or other WHTI-compliant documents are also required for adults crossing the border by land or sea, though children under age 16 may continue to do so using only a U.S. birth certificate. Check with U.S Customs and Border Protection (🌐 *www.cbp.gov/travel*) for full details.

📺 Performing Arts

Cities like Halifax, Saint John, Fredericton, and St. John's have pretty decent theater scenes, but the region shines with its live music, especially in the Celtic and Acadians traditions.

💲 Tipping

Tips and service charges are not usually added to a bill in Canada. In general, tip 15% of the total bill (before tax). This goes for waiters and waitresses, barbers and hairdressers, and taxi drivers. Porters and doormen should get about C$2 a bag. For maid service, leave at least C$2 per person a day (C$3 in luxury hotels).

🇺🇸 U.S. Embassy/Consulate

The U.S. embassy—like all other foreign embassies—is in Ottawa, Ontario (the nation's capital). There are also seven U.S. consulates in Canada, including one in Halifax.

🪪 Visa

Visas are not currently required for U.S. citizens traveling to Canada. Visa requirements for non-American travelers differ by country.

📅 When to Go

HIGH SEASON

July and August, when long, warm days let you fully enjoy attractions and activities, are the most popular months to visit Atlantic Canada. Beaches beckon in summer, sites open their doors for extended hours, and outfitters go full tilt, offering both easy and extreme outdoor adventures. As an added bonus, seafood is freshest during those sunny days (or at least it seems so when you're eating at a waterside café) and the calendar is packed with festivals. Nights can get cool, even in the summer (St. John's in particular can be uncommonly cold all year-round). However, crowds during this time are at their highest, and you need to make travel and hotel reservations far in advance, or else things will be booked up.

LOW SEASON

Although many outlying inns and eateries close for the coldest months, there is a lot to do in Atlantic Canada during the winter. Snowmobilers and skiers can chill in northern New Brunswick, which gets as much as 157 inches of snow annually. The rest of the region is typically blanketed by some amount of snow throughout winter, so driving conditions might be dangerous, but you will avoid the crowds. Due to the Gulf Stream, Halifax is relatively moderate in winter.

VALUE SEASON

Fall brings bountiful harvests, excellent whale-watching, and of course, brilliant foliage. The trees, which start turning in late September, are at their most dazzling in October, and events like Cape Breton's Celtic Colours International Festival are scheduled to coincide with the vivid displays. Autumn can last well into November, with warm, clear days and crisp nights. March and April are the months for maple syrup and north-bound migratory birds, but the weather is often frosty and wet. Late spring, though, is delightful. Apple trees bloom, wildflowers reappear, seasonal tourism operators reopen, and the visitor-to-local ratio remains low.

Helpful French Phrases

BASICS

Yes/no	wee/nohn	Oui/non
Please	seel voo play	S'il vous plaît
Thank you	mair- **see**	Merci
You're welcome	deh ree- **ehn**	De rien
Excuse me, sorry	pahr- **don**	Pardon
Good morning/ afternoon	bohn- **zhoor**	Bonjour
Good evening	bohn- **swahr**	Bonsoir
Good-bye	o ruh- **vwahr**	Au revoir
Mr. (Sir)	muh- **syuh**	Monsieur
Mrs. (Ma'am)	ma- **dam**	Madame
Miss	mad-mwa- **zel**	Mademoiselle
Pleased to meet you	ohn-shahn- **tay**	Enchanté(e)
How are you?	kuh-mahn-tahl-ay **voo**	Comment allez-vous?
Very well, thanks	tray bee-ehn, mair- **see**	Très bien, merci
And you?	ay voo?	Et vous?

NUMBERS

one	uhn	un
two	deuh	deux
three	twah	trois
four	**kaht**-ruh	quatre
five	sank	cinq
six	seess	six
seven	set	sept
eight	wheat	huit
nine	nuf	neuf
ten	deess	dix
eleven	ohnz	onze
twelve	dooz	douze
thirteen	trehz	treize
fourteen	kah- **torz**	quatorze
fifteen	kanz	quinze
sixteen	sez	seize
seventeen	deez- **set**	dix-sept
eighteen	deez- **wheat**	dix-huit
nineteen	deez- **nuf**	dix-neuf
twenty	vehn	vingt
twenty-one	vehnt-ay- **uhn**	vingt-et-un
thirty	trahnt	trente
forty	ka- **rahnt**	quarante
fifty	sang- **kahnt**	cinquante
sixty	swa- **sahnt**	soixante
seventy	swa-sahnt- **deess**	soixante-dix
eighty	kaht-ruh- **vehn**	quatre-vingts
ninety	kaht-ruh-vehn- **deess**	quatre-vingt-dix
one hundred	sahn	cent
one thousand	meel	mille

COLORS

black	nwahr	noir
blue	bleuh	bleu
brown	bruhn/mar- **rohn**	brun/marron
green	vair	vert
orange	o- **rahnj**	orange
pink	rose	rose
red	rouge	rouge
violet	vee-o- **let**	violette
white	blahnk	blanc
yellow	zhone	jaune

DAYS OF THE WEEK

Sunday	dee- **mahnsh**	dimanche
Monday	luhn- **dee**	lundi
Tuesday	mahr- **dee**	mardi
Wednesday	mair-kruh- **dee**	mercredi
Thursday	zhuh- **dee**	jeudi
Friday	vawn-druh- **dee**	vendredi
Saturday	sahm- **dee**	samedi

MONTHS

January	zhahn-vee- **ay**	janvier
February	feh-vree- **ay**	février
March	marce	mars
April	a- **vreel**	avril
May	meh	mai
June	zhwehn	juin
July	zhwee- **ay**	juillet
August	ah- **oo**	août
September	sep- **tahm**-bruh	septembre
October	awk- **to**-bruh	octobre
November	no- **vahm**-bruh	novembre
December	day- **sahm**-bruh	décembre

USEFUL PHRASES

Do you speak English?	par-lay **voo** ahn- **glay**	Parlez-vous anglais?
I don't speak ...	zhuh nuh parl pah ...	Je ne parle pas ...
French	frahn- **say**	français
I don't understand	zhuh nuh kohm- **prahn** pah	Je ne comprends pas
I understand	zhuh kohm- **prahn**	Je comprends
I don't know	zhuh nuh say **pah**	Je ne sais pas
I'm American/ British	zhuh sweez a-may-ree- **kehn** / ahn- **glay**	Je suis américain/ anglais
What's your name?	ko-mahn vooz a-pell-ay- **voo**	Comment vous appelez-vous?
My name is ...	zhuh ma- **pell** ...	Je m'appelle ...
What time is it?	kel air eh- **teel**	Quelle heure est-il?
How?	ko- **mahn**	Comment?
When?	kahn	Quand?
Yesterday	yair	Hier
Today	o-zhoor- **dwee**	Aujourd'hui

Tomorrow	duh- **mehn**	Demain
Tonight	suh **swahr**	Ce soir
What?	kwah	Quoi?
What is it?	kess-kuh- **say**	Qu'est-ce que c'est?
Why?	poor- **kwa**	Pourquoi?
Who?	kee	Qui?
Where is …	oo ay	Où est …
the train station?	la gar	la gare?
the subway station?	la sta- **syon** duh may- **tro**	la station de métro?
the bus stop?	la-ray duh booss	l'arrêt de bus?
the post office?	la post	la poste?
the bank?	la bahnk	la banque?
the … hotel?	lo- **tel**	l'hôtel …?
the store?	luh ma-ga- **zehn**	le magasin?
the cashier?	la **kess**	la caisse?
the … museum?	luh mew- **zay**	le musée …?
the hospital?	lo-pee- **tahl**	l'hôpital?
the elevator?	la-sahn- **seuhr**	l'ascenseur?
the telephone?	luh tay-lay- **phone**	le téléphone?
Where are the …	oo sohn lay	Où sont les …
restrooms?	twah- **let**	toilettes?
(men/women)	(**oh**-mm/ **fah**-mm)	(hommes/femmes)
Here/there	ee- **see** /la	Ici/là
Left/right	a goash/a draht	A gauche/à droite
Straight ahead	too drwah	Tout droit
Is it near/far?	say pray/lwehn	C'est près/loin?
I'd like …	zhuh voo- **dray**	Je voudrais …
a room	ewn **shahm**-bruh	une chambre
the key	la clay	la clé
a newspaper	uhn zhoor- **nahl**	un journal
a stamp	uhn **tam**-bruh	un timbre
I'd like to buy …	zhuh voo- **dray ahsh**-tay	Je voudrais acheter …
cigarettes	day see-ga- **ret**	des cigarettes
matches	days a-loo- **met**	des allumettes
soap	dew sah- **vohn**	du savon
city map	uhn plahn de **veel**	un plan de ville
road map	ewn cart roo-tee- **air**	une carte routière
magazine	ewn reh- **vu**	une revue
envelopes	dayz ahn-veh- **lope**	des enveloppes
writing paper	dew pa-pee- **ay** a **let**-ruh	du papier à lettres
postcard	ewn cart pos- **tal**	une carte postale
How much is it?	say comb-bee- **ehn**	C'est combien?
A little/a lot	uhn peuh/bo- **koo**	Un peu/beaucoup
More/less	plu/mwehn	Plus/moins
Enough/too (much)	a-say/tro	Assez/trop
I am ill/sick	zhuh swee ma- **lahd**	Je suis malade
Call a …	a-play uhn	Appelez un …
doctor	dohk- **tehr**	docteur
Help!	o suh- **koor**	Au secours!

Stop!	a-reh- **tay**	Arrêtez!
Fire!	o fuh	Au feu!
Caution!/Look out!	a-tahn-see- **ohn**	Attention!

DINING OUT

A bottle of …	ewn boo- **tay** duh	une bouteille de …
A cup of …	ewn tass duh	une tasse de …
A glass of …	uhn vair duh	un verre de …
Bill/check	la-dee-see- **ohn**	l'addition
Bread	dew panh	du pain
Breakfast	luh puh- **tee** day-zhuh- **nay**	le petit-déjeuner
Butter	dew burr	du beurre
Cheers!	ah **vo**-truh sahn- **tay**	A votre santé!
Cocktail/aperitif	uhn ah-pay-ree- **teef**	un apéritif
Dinner	luh dee- **nay**	le dîner
Dish of the day	luh plah dew **zhoor**	le plat du jour
Enjoy!	bohn a-pay- **tee**	Bon appétit!
Fixed-price menu	luh may- **new**	le menu
Fork	ewn four- **shet**	une fourchette
I am diabetic	zhuh swee dee-ah-bay- **teek**	Je suis diabétique
I am vegetarian	zhuh swee vay-zhay-ta-ree- **en**	Je suis végétarien(ne)
I cannot eat …	zhuh nuh puh pah mahn- **jay**	Je ne peux pas manger de …
I'd like to order	zhuh voo- **dray** ko-mahn- **day**	Je voudrais commander
Is service/the tip included?	ess kuh luh sair- **veess** ay comb- **pree**	Est-ce que le service est compris?
It's good/bad	say bohn/mo- **vay**	C'est bon/mauvais
It's hot/cold	say sho/frwah	C'est chaud/froid
Knife	uhn koo- **toe**	un couteau
Lunch	luh day-zhuh- **nay**	le déjeuner
Menu	la cart	la carte
Napkin	ewn sair-vee- **et**	une serviette
Pepper	dew **pwah**-vruh	du poivre
Plate	ewn a-see- **et**	une assiette
Please give me …	doe-nay- **mwah**	Donnez-moi …
Salt	dew sell	du sel
Spoon	ewn kwee- **air**	une cuillère
Sugar	dew **sook**-ruh	du sucre
Waiter!/Waitress!	muh- **syuh** / mad-mwa- **zel**	Monsieur!/ Mademoiselle!
Wine list	la cart day vehn	la carte des vins

Great Itineraries

Nova Scotia, 7 Days

Don't let the fact that Nova Scotia is Canada's second-smallest province fool you. Driving will likely take longer than you expect.

DAY 1: HALIFAX

Spend your first full day in **Halifax.** Explore the many downtown and waterfront attractions, which include the dynamic Canadian Museum of Immigration at Pier 21, the Maritime Museum of the Atlantic, and the huge Halifax Seaport Farmers' Market, full of local food and craft vendors. Leave time to linger on the harborfront boardwalk, perhaps taking a boat trip, and enjoying a meal at one of the city's fine restaurants. Be sure to have a fun evening out in one of the many pubs.

DAY 2: PEGGY'S COVE TO LUNENBURG

Get up early to beat the crowds to **Peggy's Cove.** Head west from Halifax via Quinpool Road and follow Highway 3 for 4 km (2½ miles), then turn onto Route 333, the Lighthouse Route. After about 36 km (22 miles), turn left onto Peggy's Point Road. Take in the views and the photo ops then, at the first sight of an approaching tour bus, head down to the "Holy Trinity" of South Shore towns: Chester, Mahone Bay, and Lunenburg. Rejoin the 333 from Peggy's Cove, and on meeting Route 103, go left and continue to **Chester,** a sailing center that's home to Canada's largest keel racing regatta each year, and a good place for a coffee break at Julien's Pâtisserie, Bakery, and Café and perhaps a visit to the Ross Farm Living Museum of Agriculture or a boat trip to the Big and Little Tancook Islands. From here, it's about a 20-minute drive, still on Route 103, to lovely **Mahone**

Bay, considered one of Canada's most beautiful towns. After lunch and boutique browsing or a paddle around the calm waters, it's about a half-hour drive on Route 103 to **Lunenburg,** where you can visit the Fisheries Museum and sign up for one of the boat tours departing from its dock. Next, drive on to the Liverpool area (an hour away), where you'll stop for the night.

DAY 3: KEJIMKUJIK NATIONAL PARK

Depending on your preferences, you can dedicate the morning to blissful beaches, with several excellent options in the Liverpool area, or immediately veer northwest on Highway 8, which connects Liverpool to Annapolis Royal, a 90-minute drive. Hikers can dally en route at **Kejimkujik National Park and Historic Site,** but history buffs might prefer to drive straight through, thereby allowing more time to visit the heritage sites in and around **Annapolis Royal** and **Wolfville,** just over an hour's drive east of Annapolis Royal on Highway 1. Spend the night at a cozy inn in town.

DAY 4: PICTOU

After checking out the Grand Pré National Historic Site or the Domaine de Grand Pré vineyard, both just east of Wolfville, continue on the pretty drive cross-country to **Pictou,** via Route 236, which will take about two hours. There you can visit the Hector Heritage Quay living history site, where the Scots landed in 1773, and the Nova Scotia Museum of Industry. Afterward, take a dip in the strait's warm, salty water. Check what's on at the DeCoste Entertainment Centre that evening before spending the night at the Auberge Walker Inn.

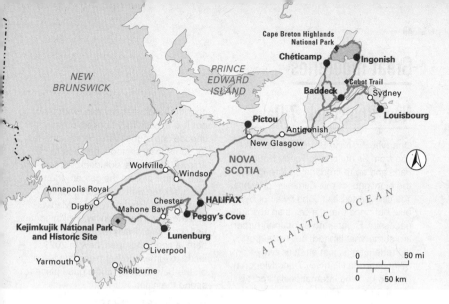

New Brunswick • Prince Edward Island • Nova Scotia • Cape Breton Highlands National Park • Chéticamp • Ingonish • Cabot Trail • Baddeck • Sydney • Louisbourg • Pictou • Antigonish • New Glasgow • Wolfville • Windsor • Nova Scotia • Annapolis Royal • Digby • Chester • Mahone Bay • Halifax • Peggy's Cove • Kejimkujik National Park and Historic Site • Lunenburg • Liverpool • Yarmouth • Shelburne • Atlantic Ocean

0   50 mi

0   50 km

DAY 5: CHÉTICAMP TO INGONISH

On the Sunrise Trail, head east on the Trans-Canada Highway (104) via Antigonish to Port Hasting, which will take about 1 hour and 15 minutes. From here, follow the 107-km (67-mile) Ceilidh Trail (Highway 19), passing through music-loving Mabou on the way to **Chéticamp**, about another 1 hour and 50 minute drive. Stop here for lunch at Le Gabriel and a whale-watching cruise, then take the **Cabot Trail** north, looping around **Cape Breton Highlands National Park.** The cliff-hugging trail ranks among the world's most dramatic and beautiful drives and at the right time of year you can often see whales breaching the waves offshore. There may be time for a scenic hike along the way, with a number of trails to choose from. After about 100 km (64 miles), you'll arrive in **Ingonish** to spend the night.

DAY 6: BADDECK

Continue south on the Cabot Trail to meet the Trans-Canada (105), where you'll turn right and continue to **Baddeck** to explore the fascinating Alexander Graham Bell National Historic Site and perhaps get out on the lovely Bras d'Or Lake. Spend the night in Baddeck, with dinner at the congenial Baddeck Lobster Suppers and, if it's July or August, a ceilidh at St. Michael's Parish Hall.

DAY 7: LOUISBOURG

Get an early start for the 80-minute drive to **Louisbourg.** Take the Trans-Canada (105), then Highway 125 Peacekeepers Way to bypass North Sydney. On the approach to Sydney, turn onto Highway 22 Louisbourg Highway. Devote the morning to the reconstructed 18th-century French fortress, a National Historic Site that played an important role in Canadian history, where costumed reenactors bring that history to life. After lunch, backtrack to Sydney, then follow Highway 4 along the southern shore of Bras d'Or Lake to Port Hawkesbury and return to Halifax, about a five-hour drive.

Great Itineraries

New Brunswick, 7 Days

One week in New Brunswick can take you from Saint John to Fundy National Park, and on to Fredericton, giving you the highlights of this Canadian province. You can get to Saint John by air or by bus, but once there, a car is an absolute necessity. Flights into Saint John Airport are somewhat limited, but the airport in Fredericton is just an hour away from Saint John via Highway 7, and Moncton Roméo Leblanc International Airport is about 90 minutes' drive southwest of Saint John via Highway 1.

DAY 1: SAINT JOHN

Start in **Saint John,** steeped in English and Irish traditions and rich in history and art. Explore the characterful old streets of the city's historic downtown (called "uptown"), and take in the provincial museum; then visit the Reversing Falls Rapids just to the west where, as the tide comes in, the river's water is pushed back upstream. In the evening, there may be live entertainment on the waterfront Market Square or in nearby pubs, and there are several good places to eat.

DAY 2: ST. ANDREWS BY-THE-SEA TO FUNDY BAY

Explore the resort town of **St. Andrews by-the-Sea,** which is an hour's drive west on Highway 1, plus a turn onto Route 127 for the final stretch. This lovely little town, a designated National Historic District, has plenty of art, crafts, history, nature, and seafood, so take a leisurely stroll along picturesque Water Street to see what's on offer. Whale-watching tours leave from the wharf, off Water Street; kayaking and scuba diving are also available. Before walking or driving up King Street to the outstanding **Kingsbrae Garden,** check whether the excellent Savour in the Garden restaurant will be open for lunch that day and whether or not it is already fully booked; otherwise choose one of the Water Street eateries for some local seafood, perhaps to be enjoyed on a waterside deck. After lunch take a stroll around the garden, then backtrack through Saint John, taking Route 1 then Route 111 to St. Martins and the **Fundy Trail Parkway**, which continues through to **Fundy National Park**. From here, a connector road, new in 2021, leads to Alma, another pleasant village on the Bay of Fundy, and a good place to spend the night.

DAY 3: CAPE ENRAGE TO HOPEWELL CAPE

Hop on Route 915, east of the park, which hugs the coast for the 15-minute drive to **Cape Enrage,** where you can visit a working lighthouse, enjoy a cup of seafood chowder, and try out ziplining or rock climbing. Another 30-minute drive will bring you to the unmissable **Hopewell Cape,** where the Fundy tides have sculpted gigantic rocks into flowerpot formations that turn into islands at high tide. Try to time your visit for low tide and you can stroll on the ocean floor among the rocks, but be sure to check what time the tide is due to turn; otherwise view from above and perhaps see how quickly the tide rushes in or out.

DAY 4: MONCTON

Head to **Moncton,** about a half-hour drive from Hopewell Cape, still on Route 114 as it follows the water to the northwest. This bustling city, a microcosm of New Brunswick culture, offers another place to experience the Fundy tides, in the form of the famous tidal bore, which pushes the river in a great surge (times are posted near the best viewing point). Another natural phenomenon awaits, at any time of day, at Magnetic Hill, on the edge of town, where, in addition to

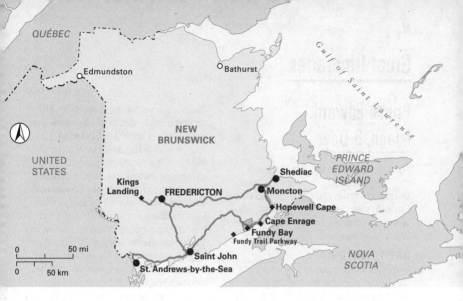

seemingly freewheeling uphill in your vehicle, there's also a zoo and various amusements for kids. Allow time for a visit to **Resurgo Place** for its engaging displays relating the city's history.

DAY 5: SHEDIAC

After spending the night in Moncton, head northwest out of town via Highway 15 then Highway 11, about a 25-minute drive, to explore the area around **Shediac,** famous for its lobsters and the wide golden sands of Parlee Beach. The town of Shediac is attractive, with waterfront areas and a nice Main Street, but it can get clogged with traffic in high season (summer). Plan to stay overnight here, to allow plenty of time for the beach and to explore the town after the day-trippers have departed.

DAY 6: KINGS LANDING TO FREDERICTON

Depart early in the morning for a two-hour drive back east to **Kings Landing Historical Settlement,** where a collection of old buildings, populated by interpreters in costume and in character, is a faithful depiction of life in a loyalist settlement on the river in the 19th century. Then continue on Route 102 for the 20-minute drive to **Fredericton,** a great stopping place and

the seat of the province's government. Dine at MOCO, then take an evening stroll along the riverside path and onto the old railroad bridge. If it's getting dark by this time, look back toward the rear of the Beaverbrook Art Gallery—from the exact right spot, there's a partial view of the illuminated star exhibit, Salvador Dali's *Santiago El Grande*.

DAY 7: FREDERICTON

On your final day, don't miss the Historic Garrison District in Fredericton, with 18th-century former military quarters and a grassy area often used for festivals. Be sure to do a bit of shopping on Queen and King streets too before making the hour drive back to Saint John for your departure.

Great Itineraries

Prince Edward Island, 5 Days

The smallest Canadian province can still keep you plenty busy for five days. During this time, you can explore Prince Edward Island and fall in love with its beauty, its charm, and its Anne of Green Gable quirkiness.

DAY 1: VICTORIA

Begin your Island escape by making the 10-minute drive across the Confederation Bridge from the mainland to Borden-Carleton. The PEI section of the Trans-Canada Highway begins here and continues through Charlottetown to the Wood Islands Ferry Terminal on the southern shore. But, once through the town of Crapaud, look for a branch right by the white St. John the Evangelist Anglican Church with a tall spire that goes onto a minor road, PE-116 (Nelson Street). Head south for your first stop, 22 km (14 miles) east of Borden-Carleton, in Victoria, one of the Island's quaintest little communities.

From **Victoria**, turn right by the lighthouse onto the causeway that crosses the Westmoreland River estuary and continue along the shore of the bay, eventually turning left, still on PE-116 to reach Hampton. Turn right at the stop sign to rejoin the Trans-Canada Highway and continue on to Charlottetown. Here you'll have time to see key city sights and catch a performance of *Anne of Green Gables: The Musical* at the Confederation Centre before bedtime.

DAY 2: CAVENDISH

Continuing the Anne of Green Gables experience, take the 41 km (25 mile) cross-Island drive to the area that has been dubbed the **Green Gables Shore**—aka northern Queens County—for the quintessential PEI sun-and-sand experience. Landing in **Cavendish**, you can lounge on the beach (or take advantage of the educational programming that might include sandcastle building, yoga, or a *ceilidh*) in **Prince Edward Island National Park**; make a pilgrimage to the Green Gables farmhouse (Anne's fictional home); then indulge in some cheesy but fun amusements along the Route 6 strip, otherwise known as Cavendish Road. Logistics: From Charlottetown, head west on Highway 2, signposted Summerside, as far as Hunter River, then go north on Highway 13, a journey of around 45 minutes.

DAY 3: GEORGETOWN

Take the 109-km (68-mile) drive east to **Georgetown** in Kings County. You can reach Georgetown by heading back down Highway 13 for 5 km (3 miles) before turning left onto Line Road, signposted North Rustico. In 3 km (2 miles) turn right onto Rustico Road (Highway 6), signposted Charlottetown, and stay on this road as far as Brackley Beach. Here, turn right on Highway 15 for 4½ km (3 miles), then turn left to rejoin Highway 6. On meeting Highway 2, turn left (St Peters Rd, aka Veterans Memorial Highway) and continue for 29 km (18 miles) before turning right on Highway 321 for Georgetown. This should take about 1½ hours.

Take a stroll through this classic waterside town, which has one of the deepest harbors in North America, then sign on for one of the two-hour, up-close seafood encounters run by Tranquility Cove Adventures: clam digging, starfish hunting, or a deep-sea fishing expedition. From Georgetown, it's a 41-km (26-mile) drive south to **Wood Islands,** where you can catch a ferry to Pictou, on the mainland of Nova Scotia. Just keep in mind

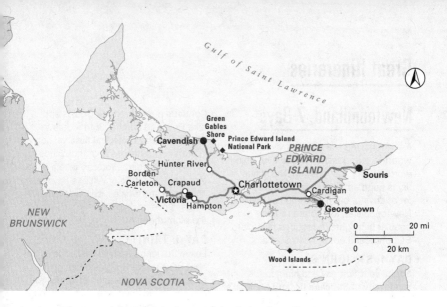

that from May to early November, the last one leaves at 7:30 pm. Note that this route can essentially be done in reverse if you're entering the Island by way of the Northumberland Strait ferry.

DAY 4: SOURIS

Stay in the **Georgetown** area, in which case check whether there's anything on at the highly regarded Georgetown Playhouse, which stages theatrical works and Small Halls Festival concerts. Alternatively, you can move up to **Souris.** Either place makes a good base for discovering some of the east coast's picturesque lighthouses and their stunning views, notably those at Souris East, East Point, Panmure Head (aka Panmure Island), and Cape Bear.

DAY 5: ISLAND EXPERIENCES

Investigate one of the island "experiences" that will put you directly in touch with some aspect of island life. You can spend half a day with a local fisherman hauling and baiting lobster traps, engage in some guided beachcombing culminating in a clam boil, or work with a local farmer or artisan (www.tourismpei.com/pei-experiences).

Logistics: From Georgetown, take Highway 3 back to Pooles Corner and pick up Highway 4. Going south will bring you to Montague where you can pick up Highway 17 leading to Panmure Island. Highway 4 north leads to Dingwells Mills, where Highway 2 east will take you to Souris, about a 35-minute drive. From here Highway 16 hugs the coast around the East Point. At the end of your stay, retrace your route back to Montague, then pick up Route 315 to Wood Islands for the ferry to Nova Scotia. If you plan to take the Confederation Bridge to New Brunswick, take Highway 2 east from Souris (or from St. Peters Bay if you've followed Route 16 around the cape) as far as Charlottetown, then Highway 1 east to Bordon Carleton.

Great Itineraries

Newfoundland, 7 Days

Newfoundland is a huge province, where it is impossible to see everything worthwhile in just one trip. This itinerary is quite ambitious, and involves a lot of driving, but it takes you all over Newfoundland, and to the region's most popular highlights. It requires flying into St. John's and out of Nova Scotia.

DAY 1: ST. JOHN'S

Spend your first day and night in the capital city of **St. John's** (fly into St. John's airport) and take advantage of the town's abundance of history, culture, and live music. The latter, particularly in the city's pubs, is strong on Irish culture but also features folk, rock, and other genres. George Street is at the heart of the entertainment scene. Check out the local shops and restaurants, take time to chat up the locals, or, if the weather is bad, head to the Rooms Museum and Gallery, where you can take in interactive displays about the history of Newfoundland, see amazing art in the galleries, and enjoy a great meal looking out over the harbor. For an even better view, head up to the **Signal Hill National Historic Site**, with sweeping views out over the Atlantic and a memorial to Marconi in recognition of the first ever transatlantic wireless signal that gave the hill its name.

DAY 2: CAPE SPEAR TO WITLESS BAY

Visit **Cape Spear**, a 20-minute drive from St. John's and the most easterly point in North America—arrive before dawn and you'll be the first on the entire continent to see the sunrise. From Cape Spear, drive through Petty Harbour where you can stop for lunch, visit the mini-aquarium, go ziplining, or just take a stroll along the prettiest little wharf in the province.

Continue out toward the Goulds and take Route 10 another 30 minutes to the **Witless Bay Ecological Reserve,** home in summer to hundreds of thousands of nesting seabirds. You can take a boat tour from Bay Bulls or Witless Bay for a chance to see whales, seabirds, and icebergs. Drive back to St. John's to spend the night there.

DAY 3: TRINITY

Leave St. John's early to make the three-hour drive to the Bonavista Peninsula and the picturesque town of **Trinity**. You can join the historic walking tour through town or simply walk around on your own (be sure to check out the paths that lead up over the town for beautiful views). For your best chance to see whales, even in the shoulder seasons, book a boat tour with the highly knowledgeable operators of Sea of Whales. Spend the night here.

DAY 4: GANDER

Find your way back down to the highway and head west to **Gander** (about a two-hour drive) where you can tour the famous airport from *Come From Away*—the movie and hit Broadway musical based on events here on 9/11—and have a flight of beer at a local brewery for lunch. Base yourself here for the night, and if you're feeling up to it, take the 45-minute ferry out to Fogo Island, where you can tour the unique art communities and eat dinner at the extraordinary Fogo Island Inn (if you can afford to stay the night there, you should definitely do so).

DAYS 5-6: GROS MORNE NATIONAL PARK

The next day is another long drive, but trust us, it's worth it as soon as you see the rugged beauty of this place. Drive west to **Gros Morne National Park** (1½ hours on Route 340 to the highway, then 2½ hours on the Trans-Canada Highway

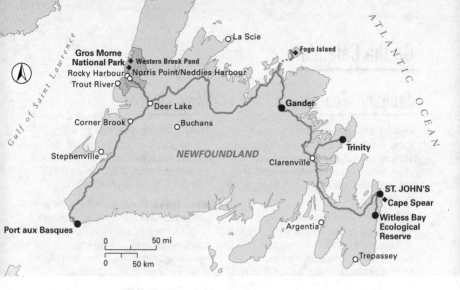

to Deer Lake, and another hour to Rocky Harbour/Norris Point on Route 430). Stay in Rocky Harbour that night if you want a more lively scene, or pick Norris Point or Neddies Harbour for a quieter retreat. Make sure to stop in at the visitor center as you exit the highway to Rocky Harbour/Norris Point to get your Parks Canada passes (C$10), maps, and consult the staff for help with planning your hikes and sightseeing for the next day.

Gros Morne National Park features some of the most spectacular scenery in Canada's Atlantic Provinces. Hike up Gros Morne Mountain (the trailhead is 7 km (4 miles) south of Rocky Harbour on Route 430), or if that seems too daunting, take the shorter, easier walk to scenic **Western Brook Pond** for a boat trip through the iconic landlocked fjord. The trail head is 26 km (16 miles) north of Rocky Harbour on Route 430, and you must park and hike from here for about 45 minutes on a gravel road to get to the boat dock. Make reservations well in advance with Bon Boat Tours (C$66). The company also offers day-long hiking tours (C$295) through pristine Gros Morne wilderness, beginning with a boat-ride across the "pond."

DAY 7: PORT AUX BASQUES

On your last day, drive to **Port aux Basques**, where you will take the overnight ferry to North Sydney, Nova Scotia to catch a flight home. The ferry is run by Marine Atlantic, and you will need a reservation in advance (⊕ www.marineatlantic.ca); it is $114.19 each way for car and pickups up to 20 feet plus C$43.79 per adult, but you will also need to reserve a place to sleep on board. Two-person berths start at an additional C$127. Canada's Harmonized Sales Tax (HST) is not levied on passenger and vehicle rates, but it is added to accommodations and onboard purchases.

On the Calendar

January–February

Jack Frost Winterfest, PEI. An outdoor snow kingdom is among the attractions at this mid-February festival in Charlottetown, which features extreme sledding, a disco skate, live music, fireworks, and an ice bar.

Frostival, NB. Over four weekends mid-January to mid-February more than 150 events in and around Fredericton include the Shivering Songs Music Festival, skating, skiing, ice carving, and shows at the Playhouse. ⊕ *frostival.ca.*

March–April

Atlantic Festivals of Music, NS. Mount Saint Vincent University in Halifax hosts one of Canada's finest music festivals over three days in late April, with an international lineup. ⊕ *www.atlanticfestivals.com.*

St. Patrick's Day. Maritimers of Irish descent celebrate their homeland's patron saint with much enthusiasm on March 17, and everyone else joins in.

Maple Capital of Atlantic Canada Festival. In New Brunswick, when the sap is rising in the sugar maple trees, there are tours, meals, fireworks, and other celebrations of maple syrup. ⊕ *tourismnewbrunswick.ca/maple-syrup.*

May–June

Festival of Small Halls, PEI. It's worth planning a trip to Prince Edward Island around this superb and intimate festival, spread over more than two weeks in mid-June. ⊕ *www.smallhalls.com.*

Trails, Tales & Tunes, NL. In mid-May picturesque Norris Point, in Newfoundland's Gros Morne National Park, hosts concerts, art exhibits, storytelling, culinary events, guided walks, hikes, and bike rides. ⊕ *www.trailstalestunes.ca.*

Apple Blossom Festival, NS. In Nova Scotia's Annapolis Valley the apple orchards put on a spectacular floral display and more than a dozen communities host celebratory events and tours. ⊕ *www.appleblossom.com.*

Fredericton Marathon. In more ways than one this is the longest-running event of its kind in the Maritimes, taking place along a scenic riverside route. ⊕ *www.frederictonmarathon.ca.*

July–August

Highland Games, Antigonish. The biggest and oldest Highland Games outside of Scotland is a week-long celebration with pipe bands, Highland dance, ceilidhs, and caber-tossing. ⊕ *www.antigonishhighlandgames.ca.*

Area 506. One of New Brunswick's signature events sees two days of music on the Saint John waterfront, along with a multicultural shipping container "village" housing artists, artisans, entrepreneurs, and food vendors. ⊕ *area506.ca.*

Newfoundland and Labrador Folk Festival. The province's biggest traditional music festival takes place in St. John's in early August, with acts for everyone from grandparents to teenagers and young families. ⊕ *nlfolk.com.*

Cavendish Beach Music Festival. Prince Edward Island goes a little bit—actually, a lot—country during this early July festival: Luke Bryan, Taylor Swift, and Lady Antebellum have all been past headliners. ⊕ *cavendishbeachmusic.com.*

September—October

Celtic Colours International Festival. This nine-day Cape Breton event, held when the fall foliage colors are at their most spectacular, showcases the finest local and international Celtic musicians and dancers. ⊕ *celtic-colours.com.*

International Shellfish Festival. Charlottetown's four-day festival in mid-September promises all kinds of seafood, celebrity chefs, fishing excursions, cooking demos, and other themed events. ⊕ *peishellfish.com.*

Harvest Music Festival. More than 400 world-class musicians of many genres perform at 100 concerts on 20 stages in downtown Fredericton over six days. ⊕ *www.harvestjazzandblues.com.*

November—December

Silver Wave Film Festival. Feature films and documentaries that have been filmed in the province and produced by New Brunswick filmmakers are among the screenings showcased. ⊕ *swfilmfest.com.*

Charlottetown Christmas Festival. From mid-November through mid-December, this festival includes the Indigenous Artisans Christmas Market and a Victorian Christmas Market, plus entertainment. ⊕ *www.tourismpei.com.*

Merry and Bright. The MUN Botanical Garden hosts the Merry and Bright Festival on a Friday in early December, when its gardens glow with Christmas lights and hot chocolate and fires keep visitors warm. ⊕ *www.mun.ca/botgarde.*

Contacts

✈ Air

Charlottetown Airport. ☎ *902/566-7997* ⊕ *flyyyg. com.* **Gander International Airport.** ☎ *709/256–6677* ⊕ *www.ganderairport. com.* **Greater Moncton Roméo LeBlanc International Airport.** ☎ *506/856–5444* ⊕ *www.cyqm.ca.* **Halifax Stanfield International Airport.** ⊠ *Halifax* ☎ *902/873–4422* ⊕ *halifaxstanfield. ca.* **St. John's International Airport.** ☎ *506/638–5555* ⊕ *stjohnsairport.com.*

🚢 Boat

Bay Ferries, Ltd. ☎ *877/762–7245* ⊕ *www. ferries.ca.* **Marine Atlantic.** ☎ *800/341–7981* ⊕ *www. marineatlantic.ca.* **Northumberland Ferries.** ☎ *877/762–7245* ⊕ *www.ferries.ca.*

🚌 Bus

DRL. ☎ *888/263–1854* ⊕ *www.drl-lr.com.* **Maritime Bus.** ☎ *800/575–1807* ⊕ *maritimebus.com.*

🚗 Car

Insurance Bureau of Canada. ☎ *902/429–2730, 844/227–5422 within Atlantic Canada* ⊕ *www. ibc.ca.*

🚢 Cruise

Adventure Canada. ☎ *800/363–7566* ⊕ *www.adventurecanada.com.* **Cruise Halifax.** ☎ *902/426–8222* ⊕ *www. cruisehalifax.ca.* **Cruise Newfoundland and Labrador.** ☎ *709/738–7530* ⊕ *cruisetheedge.com.* **Lindblad Expeditions.** ☎ *800/397–3348* ⊕ *www.expeditions. com.*

🇺🇸 U.S. Embassy/Consulate

U.S. Consulate. ⊠ *Purdy's Wharf, 1969 Upper Water St., Halifax* ☎ *902/429–2480* ⊕ *ca.usembassy. gov/embassy-consulates/ halifax.* **U.S. Embassy.** ⊠ *490 Sussex Dr., Ottawa* ☎ *613/688–5335* ⊕ *canada.usembassy.gov.*

🚆 Train

VIA Rail Canada. ☎ *888/842–7245* ⊕ *www. viarail.ca.*

📍 Visitor Information

Newfoundland and Labrador Tourism. ☎ *800/563-6353* ⊕ *www.newfoundlandlabrador.com.* **Nova Scotia Tourism.** ☎ *902/742–0511, 800/565–0000* ⊕ *www. novascotia.com.* **Tourism New Brunswick.** ☎ *800/561–0123* ⊕ *www. tourismnewbrunswick.ca.*

Chapter 3

NOVA SCOTIA

3

Updated by
Lola Augustine Brown

⊙ Sights	🍴 Restaurants	🛏 Hotels	💼 Shopping	🍸 Nightlife
★★★★★	★★★★☆	★★★☆☆	★★☆☆☆	★★☆☆☆

WELCOME TO NOVA SCOTIA

TOP REASONS TO GO

★ **The coastline.** There are postcard-perfect fishing villages and sprawling sandy beaches. The water is inviting, too, for kayaking, sailing, or whale-watching.

★ **Seafood.** This province is shaped liked a lobster claw, a happy coincidence because the lobster here is so delicious. Mussels and oysters are also plentiful, and Digby lays claim to the world's finest scallops.

★ **Crafts.** Nova Scotians—from the rug-hookers of Cape Breton to the students of Halifax's Centre for Craft & Design—create high-quality products.

★ **Celtic and Acadian culture.** Cape Breton "kitchen parties" combine music and dancing, allowing you to sample the region's rich Celtic culture. For a French-tinged alternative, substitute a rollicking Acadian soirée.

1 **Halifax.**

2 **Peggy's Cove.**

3 **Chester.**

4 **Mahone Bay.**

5 **Lunenburg.**

6 **Liverpool.**

7 **Kejimkujik National Park and Historic Site.**

8 **Shelburne.**

9 **Barrington and Cape Sable Island.**

10 **Yarmouth.**

11 **Point de l'Église (Church Point).**

12 **Digby.**

13 **Long Island and Brier Island.**

14 **Annapolis Royal.**

15 **Wolfville.**

16 **Windsor.**

17 **Sherbrooke and Sherbrooke Village.**

18 **Antigonish.**

19 **Pictou.**

20 **Tatamagouche.**

21 **Springhill.**

22 **Amherst.**

23 **Cape Chignecto and Cape d'Or.**

24 **Parrsboro.**

25 **Five Islands.**

26 **Truro.**

27 **Cape Breton Island.**

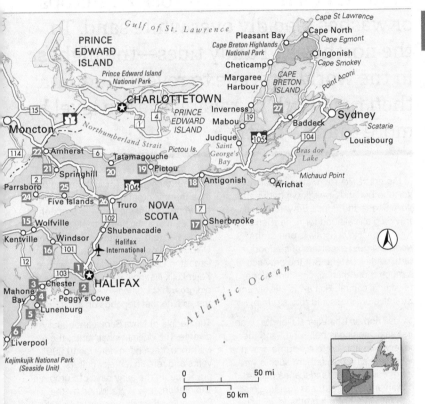

For many, Nova Scotia evokes images of seascapes. To the south and east, the Atlantic crashes against rocky outcrops or washes placidly over white sand. To the northwest, Fundy tides—the highest in the world—recede to reveal mudflats, then rush back in, raising the sea level by more than 50 feet.

To the north, warm, relatively shallow Northumberland Strait flows between Nova Scotia and Prince Edward Island, providing a livelihood for fishermen on both sides. Nova Scotia is one of the world's largest exporters of seafood, particularly lobsters. But the province is much more than its coastline alone; its coastal capital, Halifax, is a lively and attractive business and tourism hub.

It was Thomas Chandler Haliburton who first said "seeing is believing," and the observation applies to his home province because it's hard to fathom such a variety of cultures and landscapes packed into an area smaller than West Virginia without witnessing it firsthand. Within the perimeter drawn by that convoluted coastline lie the rolling farmlands of the Annapolis Valley, which yields vintner's grapes, apples, corn, peaches, and plums. In the middle of the province, dense forests are interspersed with blueberry patches, cranberry bogs, and, in spring and summer, open fields of wildflowers—purple and blue lupines, yellow coltsfoot, pink fireweed—that blanket the ground with color. In Cape Breton are highlands that rival Scotland's, rugged rock-rimmed inlets, woodlands that provide spectacular fall foliage, and mountains that plunge dramatically down

to meet the waves. Throughout the province there is great biodiversity, including a number of endangered and threatened species that are being actively protected. In the western arm, the Southwest Nova UNESCO Biosphere Reserve, the second largest in Canada, includes the remote Kejimkujik National Park, which protects old-growth transitional woodland and all the wildlife that depends on it.

The people of Nova Scotia are equally diverse. The original inhabitants, the Mi'Kmaq, have been here for 10,000 years and remain a major cultural presence. In the early days of European exploration, they were joined by the French and English who settled on the shores and harvested the sea. Later, waves of immigrants came: Germans in Lunenburg County; Highland Scots displaced by their landlords' preference for sheep; New England Loyalists fleeing the American Revolution; freedmen or escaped slaves; then Ukrainians, Poles, West Indians, Italians, and Lebanese drawn to the industrial centers of Halifax and Sydney. Most recently, Nova Scotia welcomed thousands of Syrian refugees fleeing conflict.

That multicultural mélange accounts for the fact that you'll see Gaelic signs in Mabou and Iona, an abundance of excellent Syrian restaurants in remote communities, and Francophones proudly flying their own tricolor flag in Acadian communities along the western Fundy coast, and places such as Chéticamp in Cape Breton. It also helps explain why Nova Scotians, who originally hailed from so many different places themselves, are so famously hospitable to "people from away."

Planning

When to Go

Spring comes late in Nova Scotia: trees don't get leafy until mid-May, and it takes until mid-June for temperatures to heat up. As a result, many find July and August to be the ideal months here, but even then, come prepared. Bring a raincoat for morning fog and showers, a sweater to keep the ocean breezes at bay at night, and your bathing suit for the blazing sun in between. Autumn has its own charm: September has warm days, refreshingly cool nights, and hot events like Halifax's Atlantic Film and Atlantic Fringe festivals. Late September through October is peak time for foliage fans. The downside is that wildlife cruises, cycling tours, and kayaking outfitters generally operate only from mid-June through September. Keep in mind, too, that outside major tourist centers, many resorts, inns, and B&Bs close after Canadian Thanksgiving (Columbus Day in the United States) and don't reopen until Victoria Day in late May. Some shops, restaurants, and sites are also seasonal.

Planning Your Time

Nova Scotia covers 55,280 sq km (21,344 sq miles), and is a long narrow province that's about 750 km (470 miles) from end to end and about 200 km (124 miles)

from north to south at its widest point. Halifax, the provincial capital, about halfway along the southern mainland shore, is the best place to start your trip. It's a lively city with a great waterfront, lots of history, and good shopping and entertainment. From here, highways 103 and 101 encircle the eastern section of the region, with picturesque fishing communities along the coast and a French region on the northern Fundy shore. Inland are the lovely, agricultural Annapolis Valley, the Wolfville wine region, and dense forests dotted with lakes, including the Kejimkujik National Park and Cloud Lake Wilderness Area. The night sky is particularly clear for stargazing here.

West of Halifax, Highway 7 gives access to the south shore, a ragged coastline with a succession of beaches that are great for surfing, before turning north to meet with the Trans-Canada Highway (104), which offers a quick route along the northwest of the province through New Glasgow and Antigonish. For a more leisurely exploration of the Northumberland Strait coast, take Highway 6 from Amherst, near the New Brunswick border. And then there's beautiful, unforgettable Cape Breton, an island linked to the western end of the mainland by a causeway. Several tourist routes guide visitors to the best the island has to offer. The Ceilidh Trail starts at the causeway and follows the west coast, leading to the world-famous Cabot Trail, which invariably features on lists of "most scenic places in the world." This follows the coast for much of its length, taking in the Cape Breton Highlands National Park and several good whale-watching spots before looping back down to Baddeck. Here the Bras d'Or Lakes Scenic Drive explores this great "inland sea." The Fleur de Lis Trail, leading east from the causeway to historic Louisbourg, takes in fishing villages and beaches with an Acadian vibe, while the Marconi Trail goes from Louisbourg north to Glace

Bay, with sights like the location of the first-ever radio waves, sent by Guglielmo Marconi himself.

Getting Here and Around

AIR

Halifax's Stanfield International Airport is Atlantic Canada's largest airport and major gateway, with flights from the United States via New York (LGA), Boston, and Newark, and from overseas via London (Heathrow and Gatwick) and Glasgow in the United Kingdom, Frankfurt in Germany, Paris in France, and Reykjavik in Iceland. Ground transportation into Halifax takes from 30 minutes. Limousine and taxi services and car rentals are available on-site. Halifax Transit operates its MetroX 320 service to and from the airport every 30 minutes at peak times (6–9 am and 3–6 pm), otherwise hourly; the fare is C$3.50. Exact fare is required, and change is available at the Security Administration Office on the ground level. Maritime Bus also operates a shuttle service from the airport to Halifax and Dartmouth. An Airport Express shuttle bus service is available to Dalhousie and St. Mary's universities and hotels in Halifax and Dartmouth (fare for both shuttle services is C$22 one-way, C$40 round-trip). Regular taxi fares into Halifax are C$63 each way. If you book ahead with Halifax Share a Cab, the fare is around C$32, depending on your time of arrival, but you must share your cab with another passenger; call ahead, before 8 pm, to book your appointment.

Visitors proceeding on to other destinations in Nova Scotia, or onward to New Brunswick and Prince Edward Island, can get connections via the Maritime Bus network of routes. Cape Breton–bound travelers short on time can also fly into Sydney's J.A. Douglas McCurdy Airport (YQY).

AIRPORTS Halifax Stanfield International Airport. ⊠ *1 Bell Blvd. Extension, Enfield* ☎ *902/873–4422* ⊕ *www.hiaa.ca.* **J.A. Douglas McCurdy Sydney Airport.** ⊠ *280 Silver Dart Way, Sydney* ☎ *902/564–7720* ⊕ *www.sydneyairport.ca.*

BUS

Long-distance bus service to Nova Scotia is limited. Maritime Bus runs the length of the Trans-Canada Highway from Rivière-du-Loup, Québec, through New Brunswick to Truro and Halifax, North Sydney, and Kentville. It can also get you to Nova Scotia from Prince Edward Island. Seats must be reserved in advance. Buses between Halifax and Sydney are also run by Nova Shuttle (C$70 one-way, C$130 round-trip).

CONTACTS Maritime Bus. ☎ *800/575–1807* ⊕ *maritimebus.com.* **Nova Shuttle.** ☎ *902/435–9686, 800/898–5883* ⊕ *www. scotiashuttle.ca.*

CAR

The only overland route to Nova Scotia crosses the Isthmus of Chignecto: a narrow neck of land that joins the province to New Brunswick. The Trans-Canada Highway (Highway 2 in New Brunswick) becomes Highway 104 in Amherst, the first town on the Nova Scotia side of the border. From there you can make it to Halifax, connecting to Highway 102 at Truro, in two hours. If you're headed to Cape Breton via New Glasgow and have time to spare, you can head east from Amherst on Route 6 to cross the isthmus and follow a scenic drive along the coast of Northumberland Strait.

FERRY

Car ferries connect Nova Scotia with New Brunswick, Prince Edward Island, Newfoundland, and Bar Harbor, Maine. Bay Ferries cross the Bay of Fundy from Saint John, New Brunswick, to Digby, Yarmouth to Bar Harbor; Northumberland Ferries provide service from Wood Islands on Prince Edward Island, to Caribou; Marine Atlantic makes the crossing between Port aux Basques or Argentia, Newfoundland, to North Sydney.

CONTACTS Bay Ferries Ltd.. ☎ *877/762–7245 reservations, 506/649–7777 Saint John Terminal, 902/245–2116 Digby Terminal* ⊕ *www.ferries.ca.* **Marine Atlantic.** ☎ *800/341–7981 reservations, 800/897–2797 customer relations* ⊕ *www.marineatlantic.ca.* **Northumberland Ferries.** ☎ *800/565–0201 Caribou and Wood Islands terminals, 877/762–7245 reservations* ⊕ *www.ferries.ca.*

TRAIN

VIA Rail offers overnight service from Montréal to Halifax three times a week. The trip takes about 23 hours and 20 minutes. An economy seat costs C$209.25 including tax and luggage allowance. A sleeper cabin for two with a shower costs C$756.54, including tax and luggage allowance.

CONTACTS VIA Rail. ☎ *888/842–7245* ⊕ *www.viarail.ca.*

Discounts and Deals

The Nova Scotia Museum Pass grants you admission to 27 facilities—including popular picks like Halifax's Maritime Museum of the Atlantic, Lunenburg's Fisheries Museum of the Atlantic, and Cape Breton's Highland Village—as many times as you want for a full year. Priced at C$46.85 for adults and C$92.65 for a family of four, the pass is an excellent value. Call ☎ *800/632–1114*, go to ⊕ *museum.novascotia.ca/our-museums/ museum-pass*, or visit any provincial museum for details.

Outdoor Activities

Hiking, biking, and horseback-riding routes make inland exploring a breeze; kayak and canoe routes let you splash out with ease; and there are snowmobile and cross-country skiing options, too. The province's trail site (⊕ *trails.gov.ns.ca*) will put you on the right path.

Motorists can sample Nova Scotia's sensational scenery by following any of the province's 11 Scenic Travelways. There are five in Cape Breton and six on the mainland, all clearly identified by roadside signs with icons that correspond to route names. Nova Scotia Tourism's encyclopedic *Doers and Dreamers Guide* has the lowdown (☎ *902/425–5781 or 800/565–0000*). The two best places for whale-watching are on the Bay of Fundy, from Digby down to Digby Neck, in Cape Breton on Pleasant Bay, or in Chéticamp. There are other spots to go whale-watching (Halifax, for instance), but the chances of sightings aren't as great.

In addition to the commercial outdoor-activities outfitters listed throughout the chapter, the following organizations are also valuable resources: **Canoe Kayak Nova Scotia** (☎ *902/377–2962*); **Nova Scotia Golf Association** (☎ *902/468–8844*); **Nova Scotia Trails Federation** (☎ *902/425–5450*); **Sail Nova Scotia** (☎ *902/425–5450*); and **Surfing Association of Nova Scotia** (⊕ *sans@surfns.com*).

Restaurants

The eating has always been good in Nova Scotia. The ocean's bounty lured the first Europeans across the Atlantic, and seafood remains a prime attraction for visitors today. From Halifax's high-end restaurants to the most casual coastal café, seafood is treated with the utmost respect. Many Nova Scotian chefs are committed to sourcing locally—you only have to visit one farmers' market here to appreciate the range and quality of the ingredients available to them. Generally speaking, eating out is not a stuffy affair in Nova Scotia. Even the finest dining destinations tend to be relatively casual, though you'd likely want to change out of your shorts before entering the swankiest places. One of the classic gastronomic experiences, of course, is to simply don a plastic bib and get to work on a fresh-cooked lobster within sight of the boat that delivered it from the sea. You can also follow the Taste of Nova Scotia Chowder Trail (⊕ *www.tasteofnovas-cotia.com/chowder-trail-2*), featuring 58 places to enjoy a nourishing bowl.

Restaurant reviews have been short-ened. For full information, visit Fodors. com.

Hotels

Nova Scotia is famous for its picturesque, historic bed-and-breakfast inns, of which there are many spread across the prov-ince's cities, towns, harbors, and country-side. Most B&Bs preserve the heritage and style of the buildings they occupy but come fully equipped with modern requirements such as Wi-Fi, flat-screen TVs, and updated bathrooms. It's worth doing some research, though, if modern conveniences are important to you—there are a few establishments that really do want to transport you back in time. As for hotels, most major chains have a presence, and every town of any size will have an acceptable motel or two on the outskirts. Nova Scotia is also renowned for the friendly welcome it extends to visitors, and this holds true for all types of accommodations. Far from being a cliché, there is a widespread and genuine desire to please that goes well beyond issuing a routine "have a nice day."

Hotel reviews have been shortened. For full information, visit Fodors.com.

What It Costs In Canadian Dollars			
$	**$$**	**$$$**	**$$$$**
RESTAURANTS			
under C$12	C$12–C$20	C$21–C$30	over C$30
HOTELS			
under C$125	C$125–C$174	C$175–C$250	over C$250

Tours

Multiday packaged bus tours to and within Nova Scotia are available through Atlantic Tours.

Atlantic Tours
BUS TOURS | In addition to multiprovince tours in Atlantic Canada, this company offers two Cape Breton tours. One is a three-day trip that includes whale-watch-ing, and the other is a four-day tour taking in the Celtic Colours International Festi-val. They also have a two-day, one-night South Shore Getaway, taking in Peggy's Cove, Lunenburg, and Mahone Bay. ☎ 902/423–7172, 800/565–7173 ⊕ *www. atlantictours.com* ✉ *From C$819.*

Visitor Information

CONTACTS Nova Scotia Tourism.
☎ 902/742–0511, 800/565–0000 ⊕ *www. novascotia.com.*

Halifax

1,240 km (770 miles) east of Montréal; 1,137 km (705 miles) northeast of Boston; 275 km (171 miles) southeast of Moncton, New Brunswick

Surrounded by natural treasures and glo-rious seascapes, Halifax is an attractive and vibrant hub with noteworthy historic and modern architecture, great dining and shopping, and a lively nightlife and festival scene. The old city manages to feel both hip and historic. Previous generations had the foresight to preserve the cultural and architectural integrity of the city, yet students from five local universities keep it lively and current. It's a perfect starting point to any tour of the Atlantic provinces, but even if you don't venture beyond its boundaries, you will get a real taste of the region.

It was Halifax's natural harbor—the second largest in the world after Sydney,

Australia's—that first drew the British here in 1749, and today most major sites are conveniently located either along it or on the Citadel-crowned hill overlooking it. That's good news for visitors because this city actually covers quite a bit of ground.

Since amalgamating with Dartmouth (directly across the harbor) and several suburbs in 1996, Halifax has been absorbed into the Halifax Regional Municipality, and the HRM, as it is known, has around 431,000 residents. That may not sound like a lot by U.S. standards, but it makes Nova Scotia's capital the most significant Canadian urban center east of Montréal.

There's easy access to the water, and despite being the focal point of a busy commercial port, Halifax Harbour doubles as a playground, with one of the world's longest downtown boardwalks. It's a place where container ships, commuter ferries, cruise ships, and tour boats compete for space, and where workaday tugs and fishing vessels tie up beside glitzy yachts. Like Halifax as a whole, the harbor represents a blend of the traditional and the contemporary.

GETTING HERE AND AROUND

For those not arriving by air into Halifax's Stanfield International Airport, public transportation to the city is somewhat limited. VIA Rail offers "The Ocean" service from Montréal three times a week. The journey takes 23 hours and 20 minutes, and fares range from C$209.25 for an economy seat to C$756.54 for two people in a twin cabin with shower. Maritime Bus offers service to Halifax from New Brunswick and Prince Edward Island, with stops at a number of places along the Trans-Canada Highway and links from certain major towns not along the Trans-Canada. By car, the Trans-Canada Highway heads south across the New Brunswick border, where it changes from Highway 2 to Highway 104. At Truro, Highway 102 branches off for Halifax.

Halifax is an intimate city that's large enough to have the trappings of a capital, yet compact enough to be explored with ease. Because most sites are comparatively close, walking is a good way to get around. The caveat is that streets connecting the waterfront to Citadel Hill are steep. If you're not prepared for a nine-block uphill hike, take a bus or grab a cab. Metro Transit operates comprehensive bus and ferry services. Fares are C$2.75 per ride or C$24.75 for 10 tickets. Regional Express route buses (C$4.25), which have limited stops, are designed for commuters. You'll need the exact amount because drivers don't carry change. Transfers are valid for up to 90 minutes and may be used on any route. Taxi rates begin at C$3.20 and increase by C$1.70 per km (from 5% to 10% more if traffic is heavy; extra charges are made for additional passengers and bulky luggage; a crosstown trip should cost from C$7 to C$8, depending on traffic). You can usually hail a taxi downtown or pick one up at a hotel stand. Otherwise, call **Casino Taxi** or **Yellow Cab.**

TAXI AND BUS CONTACTS Casino Taxi.
✉ *Halifax* ☎ *902/429–6666, 902/425–6666* ⊕ *www.casinotaxi.ca.* **Metro Transit.**
☎ *902/490–4000, 311 within Halifax* ⊕ *www.halifax.ca/transit.* **Yellow Cab.**
✉ *Halifax* ☎ *902/420–0000* ⊕ *www. yellowcabhalifax.ca.*

TOURS
BOAT TOURS
Metro Transit Commuter Ferry

BOAT TOURS | An affordable alternative to a Murphy's tour is to take the ferry from the boardwalk terminal at Lower Water Street across the harbor to downtown Dartmouth. Inaugurated in 1752, it's North America's oldest saltwater ferry service and offers a 20-minute ride across the harbor to Dartmouth.
✉ *Lower Water St.* ☎ *902/490–4000, 311 within Halifax* ⊕ *www.halifax.ca/transit* 🎫 *C$2.75 each way.*

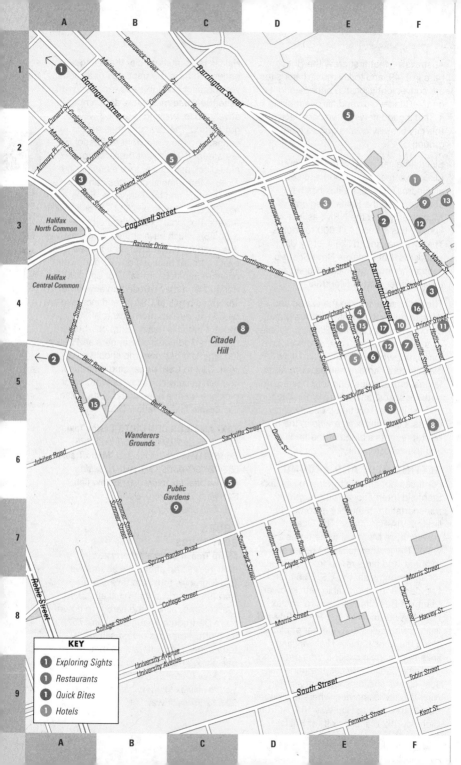

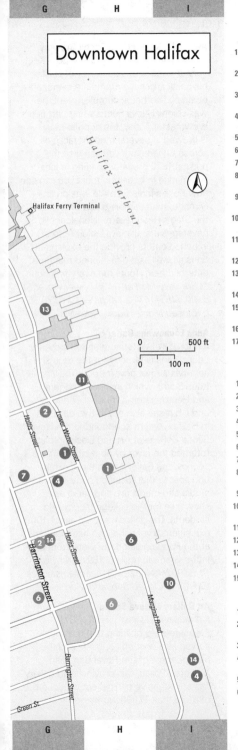

Downtown Halifax

Halifax Harbour

Halifax Ferry Terminal

Halifax Harbour

Hollis Street
Lower Water Street
Barrington Street
Hollis Street
Marginal Road
Barrington Street
Green St.

| 0 | 500 ft |
| 0 | 100 m |

Sights ▼

1 Alexander Keith's Nova
Scotia Brewery **G6**
2 Anna Leonowens
Gallery **E3**
3 Art Gallery of
Nova Scotia **F4**
4 Canadian Museum of
Immigration at Pier 21....**I9**
5 Casino Nova Scotia **E2**
6 Discovery Centre **H7**
7 Government House..... **G6**
8 Halifax Citadel National
Historic Site **D4**
9 Halifax
Public Gardens...........**C7**
10 Halifax Seaport Farmers'
Market **I8**
11 Halifax Waterfront
Boardwalk............... **G5**
12 Historic Properties **F3**
13 Maritime Museum of the
Atlantic................... **G4**
14 Mary E. Black Gallery **I9**
15 Nova Scotia Museum of
Natural History.......... **A5**
16 Province House.......... **F4**
17 St. Paul's
Anglican Church......... **F4**

Restaurants ▼

1 The Bicycle Thief **H6**
2 Da Maurizio **G5**
3 Dharma Sushi............ **F5**
4 Five Fishermen........... **E4**
5 The Foggy Goggle **B2**
6 The Henry House **G8**
7 Highwayman **F5**
8 Hop Scotch
Dinner Club............... **F5**
9 Lower Deck............... **F3**
10 Mary's
African Cuisine........... **F4**
11 McKelvie's................ **F4**
12 The Press Gang.......... **F4**
13 Salty's **F3**
14 Stories **G7**
15 The Wooden Monkey ... **E4**

Quick Bites ▼

1 Café Aroma Latino...... **A1**
2 The Cheeky Neighbour
Diner **A5**
3 Dee Dee's Ice Cream... **A2**
4 Flynn's Dairy Bar &
Convenience **G6**
5 Indochine Banh Mi...... **C6**
6 Le French Fix
Pâtisserie................. **E4**

Hotels ▼

1 Halifax Marriott
Harbourfront **F2**
2 The Halliburton.......... **G7**
3 Hotel Halifax............. **E3**
4 Prince George Hotel..... **E4**
5 Sutton Place Hotel
Halifax..................... **E5**
6 Westin
Nova Scotian........... **H8**

Murphy's The Cable Wharf

BOAT TOURS | FAMILY | Narrated tours include bus tours throughout Halifax, including their partner company Ambassatour's hop-on, hop-off service aboard double-decker buses and trips to outlying communities like Peggy's Cove and Lunenburg. Murphy's also runs the broadest selection of boat tours, sailing various vessels from mid-May to late October, among them a 130-foot schooner, a 45-foot sailing yacht, and a Mississippi-style stern-wheeler. Murphy's even has an amphibious Harbour Hopper for those who want to tour by land and water. Dinner cruises and party boats are also available, and private charters can be arranged. ⊠ *1751 Lower Water St.* ☎ *902/420–1015* ⊕ *murphysonthewater. com* 🎫 *From C$34.50.*

VISITOR INFORMATION

CONTACTS Discover Halifax. ⊠ *Halifax* ☎ *902/422–9334, 877/422–9334* ⊕ *www.discoverhalifaxns.com.* **Halifax Waterfront Visitor Information Centre.** ⊠ *Sackville Landing, 1655 Lower Water St.* ☎ *902/424–4248* ⊕ *discoverhalifaxns. com.*

⊙ Sights

Africville Museum

HISTORY MUSEUM | Until the 1960's, a century-old African Nova Scotian community resided in Africville. Forced out by the city to make way for industrial development, the residents scattered and the community broken. After an apology in 2010, some of the land was given over to the building of this museum and a memorial park. Open since 2012, this museum tells the stories of Africville and its people and is housed in a replica of the original church that served the community. The park offers beautiful views out over the Halifax Harbor. ⊠ *5795 Africville Rd.* ☎ *902/422–1116* ⊕ *africvillemuseum.org* 🎫 *$5.75* ⊙ *Closed Sun. and Mon.*

Alexander Keith's Nova Scotia Brewery

HISTORIC SIGHT | Although Alexander Keith served three terms as mayor of Halifax, his political achievements are overshadowed by another accomplishment: he was colonial Nova Scotia's first certified brewmaster. Today, the popular beer is brewed in several modern facilities across Canada, but you can visit the original 1820 brewery building, a local landmark. On hour-long tours you can see how Keith's India Pale Ale was originally made, then sample a pint or two in the Stag's Head Tavern. (Nonalcoholic beverages are also available.) Actors in period outfits provide the explanations as well as old-fashioned maritime entertainment. Tours run every half hour. ⊠ *Brewery Market, 1496 Lower Water St.* ☎ *902/455–1474* ⊕ *keiths.ca* 🎫 *C$29.95* ⊙ *Closed Mon.–Thurs., Nov.–May.*

Anna Leonowens Gallery

ART GALLERY | Victorian wunderkind Anna Leonowens is famous for the time she spent as a royal governess in Thailand (then Siam), which inspired Rodgers and Hammerstein's musical *The King and I*, but she also spent two decades in Halifax, where she founded the Nova Scotia College of Art and Design. It later returned the favor by opening the Anna Leonowens Gallery, with three exhibition spaces that focus on contemporary studio and media art, and serve as a showcase for the college faculty and students. The gallery mounts about 100 exhibitions a year and also has offshoots at the Port Loggia on the waterfront and in the Granville mall. ⊠ *1891 Granville St.* ☎ *902/494–8223* ⊕ *theanna.nscad.ca* 🎫 *Free* ⊙ *Closed Sun. and Mon.*

Art Gallery of Nova Scotia

ART MUSEUM | FAMILY | In an 1867 Italianate-style building that previously served as a post office, bank, and the headquarters of the Royal Canadian Mounted Police, this provincial art gallery has an extensive permanent collection of more than 17,000 works—so many

The iconic Town Clock, housed in a 19th-century Palladian building, is located within Halifax Citadel National Historic Site.

that there are also two floors of gallery space within the neighboring Provincial Building. Some are primarily of historical interest; others are major works by contemporary Canadian painters like Christopher Pratt, Alex Colville, and Tom Forrestall. The gallery also has a major collection of Annie Leibovitz photographs. The gallery's heart, however, is an internationally recognized collection of maritime folk art by artists such as wood-carver Sydney Howard and painter Joe Norris. The Provincial Building annex also contains the actual home of the late painter Maud Lewis (Canada's answer to Grandma Moses), whose bright, cheery paintings cover the tiny structure inside and out. ✉ 1723 Hollis St. ☎ 902/424–5280 ⊕ www.artgalleryofnovascotia.ca 🎫 C$12; Free Thurs. 5–9 pm ⏱ Closed Mon.–Weds.

★ Canadian Museum of Immigration at Pier 21

HISTORY MUSEUM | FAMILY | Affectionately dubbed "Canada's Front Door," Pier 21 served as the entry point for nearly a

million immigrants—refugees, evacuees, war brides, and others—between 1928 and 1971, and in a country where the population is only slightly more than 36 million, it's a significant number. It's now a national museum, honoring the huge contribution that these immigrants have made to Canada. Personal and often very moving stories have been collected from immigrants, offering insight into their quest for a new life and the success (and occasional failure) of the system. The Scotiabank Family History Centre is often buzzing with new generations of Canadians discovering their genealogy, while temporary exhibitions highlight issues such as asylum seekers, peace through diversity, and the foreign cultures that continue to enrich Canadian life. The museum also offers a work experience and mentoring program to help ease newly arrived immigrants into the workplace—your guide might have his or her own personal immigration story to tell. ✉ 1055 Marginal Rd. ☎ 902/425-7770, 855/526-4721 ⊕ www.

The Halifax Citadel, erected between 1826 and 1856 on the city's highest hill, dominates the skyline.

pier21.ca ✉ *C$14.50* ✆ *Closed Mon. and Tues., Dec.–Mar. and Mon. in Apr.*

Casino Nova Scotia

CASINO | Right on the waterfront, the casino has a full range of gaming tables and hundreds of slots. There's entertainment, too, mostly provided by tribute bands and C-listers on their way up—or down. Patrons must be 19 or older. ✉ *1983 Upper Water St.* ☎ *902/425–7777* ⊕ *casinonovascotia.com.*

Deadman's Island

CITY PARK | This tiny spit is the final resting place of almost 200 American prisoners of war who died while imprisoned in Halifax during the War of 1812. The U.S. Department of Veterans Affairs unveiled a memorial in 2005 to honor the men, who died of communicable diseases such as smallpox and were buried in mass graves. Over time, the island, now a park, has become naturally linked to the mainland, so you can walk to it without getting your feet wet. ✉ *Halifax ✈ 6 km (4 miles) west of downtown. On Purcells Cove Rd. near Melville Cove, look for*

Deadman's Island sign at Pinehaven Dr. ✉ *Free.*

Discovery Centre

SCIENCE MUSEUM | FAMILY | Halifax's interactive science center is an exciting place for children, and keeps many a parent enthralled, too. Galleries exploring energy, health, flight, and oceans use fascinating and fun interactive displays to bring science to life, ranging from the mysteries of the deep and the science of flight to how our brains and bodies work. In the Innovation Lab, various new ideas are explored with the help of expert staff, while younger children and toddlers engage their brains and their imaginations in the Just for Kids! gallery. There's also a dome theater with live star shows and movies. ✉ *1215 Lower Water St.* ☎ *902/492–4422* ⊕ *thediscoverycentre.ca* ✉ *C$15; Dome Theatre $2* ✆ *Closed Mon. and Tues.*

Fairview Lawn Cemetery

CEMETERY | This cemetery is the final resting place of 121 victims of the *Titanic*. The graves are easily found, in a graceful arc of granite tombstones. One—marked J. Dawson—attracts particular attention from visitors. Alas, it's not the fictional artist played by Leonardo DiCaprio in the 1998 film, but James Dawson, a coal trimmer from Ireland. Nineteen other victims are buried in Mount Olivet Catholic Cemetery and 10 in the Baron de Hirsch Jewish Cemetery. The Maritime Museum of the Atlantic has an exhibit about the disaster. Fairview Lawn also includes many graves of victims of the Halifax Explosion. ⊠ *3720 Windsor St., 3 km (2 miles) northwest of downtown.*

Government House

GOVERNMENT BUILDING | Built between 1799 and 1805 for Sir John Wentworth, the Loyalist governor of New Hampshire, and his racy wife, Fannie (Thomas Raddall's novel *The Governor's Lady* tells their story), this elegant house has since been the official residence of the province's lieutenant governor—the Queen's representative. Its construction of Nova Scotian stone was engineered by a Virginian Loyalist, Isaac Hildrith, and it's North America's oldest consecutively occupied government residence because the White House, while older, was evacuated and burned during the War of 1812. Half-hour guided tours are offered in July and August, and the Lieutenant Governor's Garden Party in June is open to the public. ⊠ *1451 Barrington St.* ☎ *902/424–7001* ⊕ *www.lt.gov.ns.ca/ government-house* 🎫 *Free* 🕑 *Closed Sept.-June.*

★ Halifax Citadel National Historic Site

MILITARY SIGHT | FAMILY | Erected between 1826 and 1856 on Halifax's highest hill, the Citadel still dominates the skyline and, as Canada's most-visited National Historic Site, remains a magnet for tourists. The present Citadel, with its dry moat and stone ramparts, was the fourth defensive structure to be built on the site, and formerly was linked to smaller forts and gun emplacements on the harbor islands and the bluffs above

Halifax and the *Titanic* ◉

When the *Titanic* sank in 1912, Halifax became the fabled ship's final destination. Being the closest major port, it was the base for rescue and recovery operations. Emergency-response skills honed in the aftermath of the sinking were put to use five years later. In December 1917, two ships collided in Halifax Harbour, one of them loaded with explosives. The event sparked the greatest man-made explosion before Hiroshima, leveling part of the city and claiming nearly 2,000 lives.

the harbor entrance. You can visit the barracks, guardroom, and powder magazine before heading for the parade ground to watch reenactors, sporting kilts and tall feather "bonnets," practice their drills. Tours help bring the history of the fort and the city to life throughout the day in high season, but the best time to visit is just before noon when the Noon Gun is fired—a tradition since 1857. The Citadel is also home to the Army Museum, with excellent exhibits and a War Art Gallery. ⊠ *Citadel Hill, 5425 Sackville St.* ☎ *902/426–5080* ⊕ *www.pc.gc.ca/en/ lhn-nhs/ns/halifax* 🎫 *C$12 July and Aug.; C$8 early May, June, Sept., and Oct.; rest of year free (grounds only)* 🕑 *Closed Nov.–early May, except grounds.*

Halifax Public Gardens

GARDEN | FAMILY | One of the oldest formal Victorian gardens in North America, this city oasis had its start in 1753 as a private garden. Its layout was completed in 1875 by Richard Power, former gardener to the Duke of Devonshire in Ireland. Gravel paths wind among ponds, trees, and flower beds, revealing an astonishing variety of plants from all over the world.

The centerpiece is an ornate gazebo-like bandshell, erected in 1887 for Queen Victoria's Golden Jubilee, where free Sunday afternoon concerts take place at 2 from mid-June through mid-September. Grab a coffee and a treat at Uncommon Grounds Cafe, which is housed in the historic Horticulture Hall. The gardens are open year-round and a pleasure in every season. ⊠ *Bounded by Sackville, Summer, and S. Park Sts. and Spring Garden Rd.* ⊕ *halifaxpublicgardens.ca* ⌧ *Free.*

Halifax Seaport Farmers' Market

MARKET | Green in more ways than one, this waterfront weekend market that hosts more than 250 local farmers, food producers, and artisans is one of Canada's most eco-friendly buildings. Noteworthy features include wind turbines, solar-energy and water-conservation systems, and a "biowall" that allows natural ventilation. There's a wonderful array of fresh produce and crafts, and the international backgrounds of many vendors make it particularly interesting, with some unique offerings. Sampling and shopping opportunities abound, though aside from Saturday not every vendor is out in force (unless a cruise ship is in). Don't confuse this venue with Brewery Square's Historic Farmers' Market, whose vendors didn't want to move here. Both claim to be the country's oldest farmers' market—and in a way, they both are. ⊠ *1209 Marginal Rd.* ☎ *902/492–4043* ⊕ *www.halifaxfarmersmarket.com.*

★ Halifax Waterfront Boardwalk

PROMENADE | **FAMILY** | Running from the Canadian Museum of Immigration at Pier 21 to Casino Nova Scotia, this photogenic 3-km (2-mile) footpath offers backdoor access to the Historic Properties, the Marine Museum of the Atlantic, and the Discovery Centre. Newer landmarks such as Purdy's Wharf (site of Halifax's two grandest skyscrapers) and Bishop's Landing (an attractive complex with condos and shops) are on the route; while others, including the Seaport Farmers' Market and the cruise-ship terminal, are only a few minutes' walk away. Shops and restaurants line the section between Sackville Landing and the Historic Properties, and in peak season, festivals and events, ice-cream peddlers, and street performers do, too. The water, however, remains the real attraction. To get out on it, take one of the many boat tours that depart from the boardwalk's Cable Wharf. ⊠ *Halifax.*

Historic Properties

HISTORIC DISTRICT | This series of restored waterfront warehouses dates from the days when trade and war made Halifax prosperous. They were built by such raffish characters as Enos Collins, a privateer, smuggler, and shipper, whose vessels defied Napoléon's blockade to bring American supplies to the Duke of Wellington. The buildings have since been taken over by shops, offices, restaurants, and pubs, including those in Privateer's Warehouse. Seven of them, all erected between the late 18th and early 19th century, have been designated as National Historic Sites. ⊠ *1869 Upper Water St.* ☎ *902/422–4424* ⊕ *historicproperties.ca.*

Maritime Museum of the Atlantic

OTHER MUSEUM | **FAMILY** | The exhibits in this waterfront museum, housed partly in a restored chandlery, include small boats once used around the coast, as well as displays describing Nova Scotia's proud sailing heritage. The most memorable ones, though, are devoted to the *Titanic* and the Halifax Explosion. The former includes the ship's only surviving deck chair. Also on display are a section of wall paneling, a balustrade molding and part of a newel from the dual curving staircase, a mortuary bag, and the log kept by a wireless operator in Newfoundland on the night the ship sank. In the Halifax Explosion exhibit, newspaper accounts and quotes from survivors are poignantly paired with everyday objects recovered from the rubble. Other exhibits cover the Canadian Navy, sailing ships, the Age of Steam, and shipwrecks. On the wharf outside is the hydrographic steamer CSS *Acadia,* permanently moored here after a long life of charting the coasts of Labrador and the Arctic, and museum-ticket holders can board for tours from May through September. Be sure to say hello to the museum's resident talking rainbow macaw, Merlin. ⊠ *1675 Lower Water St.* ☎ *902/424–7490* ⊕ *maritimemuseum. novascotia.ca* ⊡ *C$5.15* ⊘ *Closed Mon. Nov.–Apr.*

Mary E. Black Gallery

ART GALLERY | Between Pier 21 and the Seaport Farmers' Market, the exhibit space of the Nova Scotia Centre for Craft and Design, home of the Mary E. Black Gallery, presents shows of pottery, jewelry, textiles, metalwork, and other innovative, high-end crafts. The center also holds classes, including one- and two-day workshops, from fall through spring. ⊠ *1061 Marginal Rd., Suite 140* ☎ *902/492–2522* ⊕ *www.craft-design.ns. ca* ⊡ *Gallery free; workshops individually priced* ⊘ *Closed Mon. and Tues.*

Nova Scotia Museum of Natural History

SCIENCE MUSEUM | **FAMILY** | This is the place to learn about fossils and dinosaurs, as well as the flora and fauna prevalent in Nova Scotia today. It's also home to star exhibit Gus, a friendly Gopher Tortoise born in the 1920s, who is usually out and about around 3:30 pm. The Nature Centre is home to other live creatures, including snakes, frogs, and insects. The museum has a program of daily events and hosts major traveling exhibits as well as nature talks, walks, and workshops that appeal to all interests and ages. ⊠ *1747 Summer St.* ☎ *902/424–7353* ⊕ *naturalhistory. novascotia.ca* ⊡ *C$6.30.*

Point Pleasant Park

CITY PARK | **FAMILY** | Most of the city's former fortifications have been turned into public parks, including this one, which encompasses 186 wooded acres on a headland south of downtown with walking trails and seafront paths. The major military installation here is a massive round tower dating from the late 18th century, but the greatest threat the park ever faced came from Mother Nature. In September 2003, Hurricane Juan tore through, uprooting or damaging 75,000 trees (about 75% of the park's total) in a matter of hours, in the process leaving present-day parkgoers the same harbor views that must have inspired its use as a military command post in the first place. Having been nurtured since the storm, Point Pleasant is again immensely popular with strollers, joggers, and dog walkers. It's the perfect vantage point from which to watch ships entering the harbor, and in summer it's the site of Shakespeare by the Sea performances. ⊠ *5718 Point Pleasant Dr.* ☎ *902/490–4700* ⊡ *Free.*

Province House

GOVERNMENT BUILDING | Charles Dickens proclaimed this structure, now a National Historic Site, "a gem of Georgian architecture." Erected in 1819 to house Britain's first overseas self-government, the sandstone building still serves as the meeting place for the provincial legislature. The politicos' proceedings are notoriously dull, but the free tours of the building in July and August yield many interesting tidbits. Self-guided tours are available year-round. ⊠ *1726 Hollis St.* ☎ *902/497–6942* ⊕ *nslegislature.ca/content/tours* ⊡ *Free* ⊘ *Closed weekends Sept.–June.*

St. Paul's Anglican Church

CHURCH | Opened in 1750, this is Canada's oldest Protestant church and the burial site of many colonial notables. It played a pivotal role during the 1917 Halifax Explosion, as the vestry was used as a makeshift hospital. Evidence of the damage done to the building can be seen in the still-broken Explosion Window and debris embedded above the Memorial Doors. Designated as a National Historic Site, St.

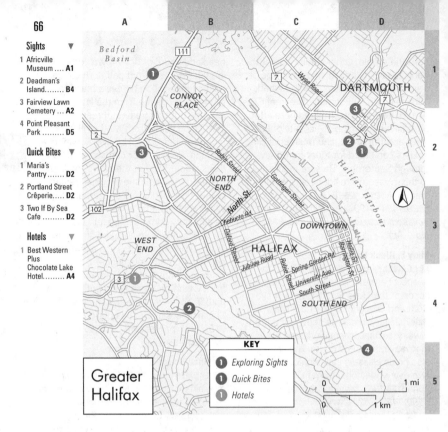

Greater
Halifax

KEY

1 Exploring Sights

1 Quick Bites

1 Hotels

Paul's remains an active church. A pew is always reserved for Queen Elizabeth at Sunday morning services, and other out-of-town worshippers are welcome as well. Free guided tours available May through October. ✉ *1749 Argyle St., on the Grand Parade* ☎ *902/429–2241* ⊕ *st-paulshalifax.org* ⊘ *Closed Sun., except for 10 am service.*

🏖 Beaches

Rainbow Haven Beach Provincial Park

BEACH | FAMILY | For ocean swimming, this sand and cobble beach is the closest serviced option to Halifax, although it's a 30-minute drive from downtown, and the area near the channel should be avoided when the tide is going out because of strong rip currents. Lifeguards, on duty in July and August, set out markers to indicate the dangerous areas. Elsewhere,

Rainbow Haven is safe and great for families. The beach is free for day use, and there is a campground (fee) with its own swimming area. Change houses are available, and boardwalks aid accessibility. The beach's access road closes at 8 pm, so plan your time accordingly. **Amenities:** food and drink; lifeguards; parking (free); showers; toilets. **Best for:** swimming; walking. ✉ *2249 Cow Bay Rd., Cole Harbour* ✛ *Off Bissett Rd. (Rte. 322), 8 km (5 miles) east of Quigley's Corner* ⊕ *parks. novascotia.ca.*

🍴 Restaurants

The Bicycle Thief

$$$$ | INTERNATIONAL | Casual, boisterous, and hugely popular, this place has a patio right on the waterfront—on the landward side, look for the "tree" of old bicycles stacked outside. The lengthy menu slants

Italian but also features meat-heavy main courses, all with interesting accompaniments that incorporate the finest Nova Scotian ingredients. **Known for:** reservations usually needed; good cocktails and wide range of wines by the glass; great views over the waterfront. $ *Average main: C$33* ⊠ *Bishop's Landing, 1475 Lower Water St.* ☎ *902/425–7993* ⊕ *bicyclethief.ca.*

Da Maurizio

$$$$ | ITALIAN | This Northern Italian restaurant is a classic big-night-out choice. Subdued lighting, elegant furnishings, fresh flowers: all the details have been attended to, and ditto the food, which is impressive and satisfying. **Known for:** high prices that are worth the expense; decadent desserts; well-informed and friendly waitstaff. $ *Average main: C$32* ⊠ *1496 Lower Water St.* ☎ *902/423–0859* ⊕ *damaurizio.ca* ⊗ *Closed Sun. No lunch.*

Dharma Sushi

$$ | JAPANESE | Tasty sushi, fresh sashimi, feather-light tempura, gyudon, and teriyaki dishes that are among the authentic Japanese dishes that are artfully presented here on the extensive menu. Seating is available both inside the pint-size eatery and, in summer, out on a small street-front patio, and takeout is another option. **Known for:** plenty of options for those who don't like "raw" sushi; good value; friendly and efficient service. $ *Average main: C$20* ⊠ *1576 Argyle St.* ☎ *902/425–7785* ⊕ *dharmasushi.ca* ⊗ *Closed Sun. No lunch Sat.*

Five Fishermen

$$$$ | SEAFOOD | Installed in a heritage building across from the Grand Parade, this restaurant is splurge-worthy. While classics like oysters Rockefeller and seared scallops never disappoint, inventive seafood dishes such as lobster-crusted haddock and a 6-pound flash-fried lobster tower elevate the menu. **Known for:** fascinating history and ghostly occurrences; exciting cocktails and impressive wine list; separate vegetarian and vegan menu. $ *Average main: C$35* ⊠ *1740 Argyle St.* ☎ *902/422–4421* ⊕ *fivefishermen.com* ⊗ *No lunch.*

The Foggy Goggle

$$ | CANADIAN | They call it "comfort food with attitude" and it's certainly struck a chord with locals and visitors, who flock to this bar to fill up on freshly made dishes like lobster mac and cheese, ribs roasted in root beer, and Foggy Spuds (roasted potatoes with chopped bacon, corn, and red onion, sautéed in a rich cream sauce and topped with cheese). There are lighter choices and vegetarian options, too. **Known for:** very good service; 14 beers on tap and innovative cocktails; open until 1 am on Friday and Saturday. $ *Average main: C$14* ⊠ *2057 Gottingen St.* ☎ *902/444–1414* ⊕ *thefoggygoggle.ca.*

The Henry House

$$ | BRITISH | At this pub in what was once the house of a prominent Canadian politician, Haligonian brewers uphold beer-making traditions dating back to 1754, and you can sample the results, along with craft and bottled beers from beyond the city. The food is impressive, too—especially the Nova Scotia salt cod fishcakes and beer-battered fish-and-chips. **Known for:** excellent craft beer; wide range of seafood specialties; great tiered patio in summer. $ *Average main: C$16* ⊠ *1222 Barrington St.* ☎ *902/423–5660* ⊕ *www.henryhouse.ca* ⊗ *Closed Mon. and Tues.*

★ Highwayman

$$$ | SPANISH | This small, on-trend restaurant and bar serves a seafood-heavy Spanish-inspired menu and delicious cocktails. There's a selection of oysters on ice, as well as other chilled and cured seafood and meats, classic Spanish tapas, and bar snacks that make for a perfect evening of grazing, but also a menu of hearty pasta and meat dishes should you require something more robust. **Known for:** exceptional and friendly service; seafood tower served with a

Local Flavors 🍴

Nova Scotia's verdant landscapes and churning seas provide a feast for the eyes and one for the table as well. Residents contend that the best meals are made using local ingredients—Lunenburg lobster, Digby scallops, Atlantic salmon, Annapolis Valley apples—and generations-old recipes. If you're serious about discovering down-home favorites, seek out dishes with curious names like Hodge Podge (a summer staple of beans, peas, carrots, and baby potatoes, cooked in cream), Solomon Gundy (a pickled-herring pâté), *rappie* pie (a hearty Acadian dish usually of chicken, with dried, shredded potatoes), and blueberry grunt (a steamed pudding made with Nova Scotia's finest berries). For more sophisticated fare, check out the fine-dining establishments in Halifax and the southern part of the province that put their own spins on Nova Scotian classics, preparing time-honored dishes with contemporary flair. The province's annual free *Taste of Nova Scotia: Culinary Adventure Guide*will help you find them.

For local libations, try a beer (or two) from the growing number of microbreweries. The Craft Brewers Association of Nova Scotia (🌐 *nscraftbeer.ca*) currently lists 50, including brewpubs, and nine of them are in Halifax: 2 Crows, Gahan House, Garrison, Good Robot, Granite, North Brewing Company, Propeller, Rockbottom, and Tidehouse. The rest are evenly spaced across the province, and all draw on the history of the region and produce distinctive ales, lagers, stouts, and other brews. Local wines are gaining in popularity and reputation as well, with 19 wineries listed by the Winery Association of Nova Scotia (🌐 *winesofnovascotia.ca*). And what better way to cap a Nova Scotian dinner than with a dram of the acclaimed Glen Breton (🌐 *www.glenoradistillery.com*), North America's original single-malt whiskey. (Nova Scotia may mean "New Scotland," but you still can't call it "Scotch" unless it's actually produced in Scotland.) In Gaelic, they call single malt *Uisge beatha* ("the water of life"); sip some Glen Breton, and you'll know why. Glenora is just one of 12 distilleries in the province, alongside the Authentic Seacoast Distilling Company in Guysborough, Barrelling Tide in Port Williams, Caldera in River John, Coldstream Clear in Stewiacke, Halifax Distilling Company, Ironworks in Lunenburg, Compass in Halifax, Steinhart in Arisaig, Still Fired in Annapolis Royal, Teaghlach Ross in Waverley, Raging Crow in North River, and Tipping Point in Chester.

dozen oysters; fun, lively atmosphere. [$] *Average main: C$22* ✉ *1673 Barrington St.* ☎ *902/407–5260* 🌐 *highwaymanhfx.com* 🕘 *Closed Sun. No lunch.*

★ Hop Scotch Dinner Club

$$$$ | CANADIAN | Started as a pop-up restaurant by some of the city's most creative chefs, Hop Scotch has evolved into one of the city's most sophisticated dining rooms where incredible food and inventive cocktails are to be eagerly anticipated on each visit. The small menu changes often in order to showcase the best in seasonal, local ingredients, and brunch is always amazing. **Known for:** fantastic curated wine list; intimate and classy dining experience; delectable desserts such as their s'more tart.

A stroll along the waterfront boardwalk, lined with shops, seafood restaurants, and museums, is a Halifax must.

$ *Average main: C$32* ✉ *1537 Barrington St.* ☎ *902/420–9626* ⊕ *hopscotchdinnerclub.com* ✪ *Closed Mon. and Tues. No lunch but brunch on weekends.*

Lower Deck

$$ | **CANADIAN** | History surrounds you in Privateer's Warehouse, where two eateries share old stone walls and hand-hewn beams. The main-floor pub sticks to pub grub, which is served at long trestle tables; the patrons here consider ale an entrée, so you can just order a beer and join the fun. **Known for:** live music every night in the pub; house-made burgers; very lively atmosphere. $ *Average main: C$17* ✉ *Historic Properties, 1887 Upper Water St.* ☎ *902/425–1501* ⊕ *lowerdeck. ca.*

Mary's African Cuisine

$$ | **AFRICAN** | Delicious African stews— beef, goat, curry chicken, eggplant— with tasty sides such as *jollof* rice and *enjera* bread are served in Mary's friendly downtown restaurant. **Known for:** Mary makes her own fresh juices; plenty of vegetarian and gluten-free options; huge portions. $ *Average main: C$12* ✉ *1701 Barrington St.* ☎ *902/404–3144* ⊕ *marysafricancuisine.com* ✪ *Closed Mon.*

McKelvie's

$$$$ | **SEAFOOD** | In a handsome 1906 firehouse across from the Maritime Museum of the Atlantic, McKelvie's is that rare find that hits the sweet spot between upscale and down-home. Though all the menu mainstays are here, from oysters Rockefeller to surf and turf, the best bets are the contemporary twists on seafood classics. **Known for:** historic building; signature fish and lobster platters; great location for waterfront attractions. $ *Average main: C$33* ✉ *1680 Lower Water St.* ☎ *902/421–6161* ⊕ *mckelvies.com* ✪ *No lunch Sat.-Sun.*

★ The Press Gang

$$$$ | **CANADIAN** | Easily one of the city's hippest upscale establishments, the Press Gang prepares fish and meat with equal panache, with wines from the well-stocked cellar. A four-course tasting menu (C$160 for two) is also offered. **Known for:** Thursday whiskey night;

romantic date night favorite; exceptional array of oysters. $ *Average main: C$39* ✉ *5218 Prince St.* ☎ *902/423–8816* ⊕ *the-pressgang.ca* ⊘ *No lunch.*

Salty's

$$$ | **SEAFOOD** | Overlooking Privateer's Wharf on the harbor, Salty's wins the prize for best location in Halifax. Steaming bowls of shellfish stew and curried scallops crown a menu sure to satisfy seafood lovers, though there are also meat and pasta options. **Known for:** separate gluten-free menu; incredible view; choose-your-own lobsters from the live tank. $ *Average main: C$22* ✉ *Historic Properties, 1877 Upper Water St.* ☎ *902/423–6818* ⊕ *saltys.ca.*

★ Stories

$$$$ | **CANADIAN** | In the very elegant dining room of the historic Haliburton Hotel, just a few exquisitely set tables set the scene for a sophisticated meal. The menu is short, but is carefully devised to cater to various tastes, and everything, including inventive accompaniments, is very well executed. **Known for:** separate area for small groups; refined formal atmosphere; top quality ingredients. $ *Average main: C$33* ✉ *Haliburton Hotel, 5184 Morris St.* ☎ *902/444–4400* ⊕ *www.storiesdining.com* ⊘ *Closed Sun. and Mon. No lunch.*

The Wooden Monkey

$$$ | **ECLECTIC** | This fun, funky spot attracts health-conscious diners with its macrobiotic and organic food, locally brewed beer and wines, and fair-trade coffee. Aside from being good for you, though, the food here is also just plain good. **Known for:** healthy children's menu; wide selection on the menu; environmentally sound sourcing of ingredients. $ *Average main: C$23* ✉ *1707 Grafton St.* ☎ *902/444–3844* ⊕ *www.thewooden-monkey.ca.*

☕ Coffee and Quick Bites

Café Aroma Latino

$$ | **LATIN AMERICAN** | Come to this fab spot to grab breakfast where they serve authentic Central and South American dishes in a cozy location. **Known for:** churros and ice-cream dessert; delicious arepas and empanadas; tiny attached Latin grocery store. $ *Average main: C$15* ✉ *5780 North St., North End* ☎ *902/444–8393* ⊕ *cafearomalatino.com* ⊘ *Closed Mon.*

The Cheeky Neighbour Diner

$$ | **CANADIAN** | Specializing in superb breakfasts and upscale comfort foods for lunch and dinner, this fun and quirky spot is worth lining up for on weekends. **Known for:** decent kids' menu; chicken and waffle breakfasts; selection of premium poutines. $ *Average main: C$15* ✉ *6024 Quinpool Rd.* ☎ *902/474–4152* ⊕ *cheekyneighbour.com* ⊘ *Closed Mon. and Tues.*

Dee Dee's Ice Cream

$ | **ICE CREAM** | Every lick of the small-batch artisan ice cream made at Dee Dee's is pure pleasure whether you opt for classic vanilla, banana cardamom, Mexican chocolate, or one of the many other flavors on offer. **Known for:** long lines in hot weather; ice-cream sandwiches made with fresh baked cookies; excellent affogato with your choice of ice-cream flavor. $ *Average main: C$5* ✉ *5668 Cornwallis St.* ☎ *902/407–6614* ⊕ *deedees.ca* ⊘ *Closed Sun.*

Flynn's Dairy Bar & Convenience

$ | **ICE CREAM** | Home to ridiculous milkshakes topped with cotton candy and slices of birthday cake or cheesecake, as well as stacked cones and a massive selection of international candy, Flynn's is a delight. There's also a branch in the Hydrostone neighborhood. **Known for:** snack foods from all over the world; over-the-top milkshakes; rare candy and breakfast cereals. $ *Average main:*

C$10 ✉ *1365 Hollis St.* ☎ *902/406–0334* 🌐 *flynnsexotic.com.*

Indochine Banh Mi

$ | **VIETNAMESE** | Traditional Vietnamese subs, noodle soups and bowls, fusion tacos, and more at this fast-service spot just across from the Halifax Public Gardens. **Known for:** authentic banh mi subs; tasty bubble tea smoothies; plenty of vegetarian, vegan, and gluten-free options. [$] *Average main: C$10* ✉ *1551 South Park St.* ☎ *902/407–1222* 🌐 *indochine.ca.*

Le French Fix Pâtisserie

$ | **FRENCH** | Decadent pastries and excellent coffee are to be had at this authentic French bakery in the heart of downtown. **Known for:** perfectly flaky croissants; hazelnut eclairs that melt in your mouth; colorful and delicious macarons. [$] *Average main: C$4* ✉ *5233 Prince St.* ☎ *902/497–5308* 🌐 *www.lefrenchfix.com* 🕘 *Closed Sun.*

Maria's Pantry

$$ | **ITALIAN** | House-made pasta rules at this tiny café where a talented young chef creates dishes based on his *nonna* Maria's recipes brought over from the Abruzzo region of Italy. **Known for:** authentic pizza slices to go; everything made in-house; cozy, neighborhood feel. [$] *Average main: C$14* ✉ *17 Prince St., Dartmouth* ☎ *902/407–2029* 🌐 *mariaspantry.ca* 🕘 *Closed Sun.-Tues.*

Portland Street Crêperie

$ | **EUROPEAN** | Here you'll find sweet and savory crepes with unexpected fillings such as garlic mashed potato, or pesto with goat cheese and chicken, as well as classic flavors. **Known for:** the Darkside fudge brownie dessert crepe; ice-cream served in bubble-waffle cones; gluten-free buckwheat crepes. [$] *Average main: C$9* ✉ *55 Portland St., Dartmouth* ☎ *902/466–7686* 🌐 *portlandstreetcreperie.com.*

Two If By Sea Café

$ | **CAFÉ** | This fun local café's slogan is "Eat Butter," so it's no surprise that their massive buttery croissants are amazing, and freshly roasted beans from the coffee roastery next door—Anchored—means that the caffeinated drinks are perfect, too. **Known for:** fun, young vibe; always delicious croissant of the week; vegan ginger molasses cookies. [$] *Average main: C$5* ✉ *66 Ochterloney St., Dartmouth* ☎ *902/469–0721* 🌐 *twoifbysea.cafe.*

Hotels

Best Western Plus Chocolate Lake Hotel

$$$ | **HOTEL** | **FAMILY** | A lakeside location, friendly staff, and range of room types make this a good alternative to downtown lodgings, and it's less than 5 km (3 miles) from the heart of the city. **Pros:** right on Chocolate Lake, with water access; some drive-up rooms; good food, including buffet breakfast. **Cons:** breakfast buffet area is a bit cramped; some rooms are rather small; outside of downtown area. [$] *Rooms from: C$179* ✉ *250 St. Margaret's Bay Rd.* ☎ *902/477–5611, 800/780–7234 reservations* 🌐 *chocolatelakehotel.com* 🛏 *142 rooms* 🍴 *Free Breakfast.*

Halifax Marriott Harbourfront

$$$$ | **HOTEL** | Built low to match the neighboring ironstone buildings, this waterfront hotel is convenient to the Historic Properties and the boardwalk. **Pros:** one of the restaurants has a waterfront patio; only hotel right on the harbor; deals and value-added packages available. **Cons:** charge for enhanced high-speed Wi-Fi; some rooms could use upgrading; parking is pricey. [$] *Rooms from: C$299* ✉ *1919 Upper Water St.* ☎ *902/421–1700, 800/943–6760* 🌐 *www.marriott.com* 🛏 *352 rooms* 🍴 *No Meals.*

★ The Halliburton

$$$ | HOTEL | Three early-19th-century town houses were cleverly combined to create Halifax's original boutique hotel, a couple of blocks from the waterfront and Spring Garden Road shopping. **Pros:** breakfast included; great on-site restaurant; elegant historic buildings. **Cons:** no elevator; some rooms far from reception; some parking is a block away. Ⓢ *Rooms from: C$199* ✉ *5184 Morris St.* ☎ *902/420–0658, 888/512–3344* ⊕ *www.thehalliburton.com* ⇌ *29 rooms* ⏍ *Free Breakfast.*

Hotel Halifax

$$$ | HOTEL | FAMILY | The Hotel Halifax, in a good downtown location, is a popular choice for both business and leisure travelers, with spacious, attractive rooms—many of which have water views. **Pros:** friendly and helpful staff; pleasant pool area and fitness center; restaurant doesn't charge corkage for Nova Scotia wine purchased elsewhere. **Cons:** uphill walk from the waterfront; extra fees for phone calls, parking, and other amenities add up; drivers will need to get directions to the attached parking garage. Ⓢ *Rooms from: C$219* ✉ *1990 Barrington St.* ☎ *902/425–6700, 1833/357–8155* ⊕ *hotelhalifax.ca* ⇌ *295 rooms* ⏍ *No Meals.*

Prince George Hotel

$$$ | HOTEL | A huge gleaming lobby and open-aspect sitting areas with some fun features, like a giant chair and modern art, welcome you to this fine hotel. **Pros:** lots of restaurants and bars in surrounding streets; plenty of business services including free Wi-Fi; covered walkways connect to shops and entertainment. **Cons:** steep climb up from the waterfront; breakfast and parking are not always included; parking garage can be confusing. Ⓢ *Rooms from: C$219* ✉ *1725 Market St.* ☎ *902/425–1986, 800/565–1567* ⊕ *www.princegeorgehotel.com* ⇌ *201 rooms* ⏍ *No Meals.*

★ Sutton Place Hotel Halifax

$$$$ | HOTEL | As the first five-star hotel in Nova Scotia, this new property delivers European-style luxury and modern amenities—including smartphone app-controlled air-conditioning, heat, and lights—in the heart of downtown Halifax. **Pros:** bathrobes and luxurious extras in every room; exceptional levels of service; fantastic location in heart of downtown. **Cons:** location can be noisy as it's close to several bars; parking can be expensive; no pool or spa. Ⓢ *Rooms from: C$329* ✉ *1700 Grafton St.* ☎ *902/932–7548* ⊕ *suttonplace.com/halifax* ⇌ *362* ⏍ *No Meals.*

Westin Nova Scotian

$$$$ | HOTEL | FAMILY | Close to the train station, Seaport Farmers' Market, cruise ship harbor, and Cornwallis Park, this imposing heritage hotel provides top-notch business services and good amenities for leisure guests, including a serene pool. **Pros:** plenty of parking; half the rooms have harbor views; beautiful historic architectural detailing. **Cons:** some bathrooms are cramped; soundproofing can be an issue in rooms near elevators; on southern edge of the action. Ⓢ *Rooms from: C$259* ✉ *1181 Hollis St.* ☎ *902/421–1000, 888/627–8553* ⊕ *www.thewestinnovascotian.com* ⇌ *310 rooms* ⏍ *No Meals.*

🍸 Nightlife

Native Haligonians are, by nature, a convivial lot. Factor in the seafaring types any thriving port attracts and a large contingent of students, and you'll see why this is such a sociable city. Because of the premium put on fun, it can sometimes be difficult to draw the line between dining and entertainment options. In many cases, whether an establishment functions primarily as a restaurant or club depends on your definition—and the time of day.

BARS AND MUSIC CLUBS

Bearly's House of Blues and Ribs

LIVE MUSIC | This dimly lit tavern's name gives music and food equal billing, but the outstanding blues artists the place books makes clear where its loyalty lies. You can catch an act every day except Monday, stand-up comedy (8:30) followed by killer karaoke (at 10) on Wednesday, and a Sunday blues jam at 8:30. The cover charge, when there is one, is usually C$5, but can be up to C$10, depending on the band. ✉ 1269 Barrington St. ☎ 902/423–2526 ⊕ www. bearlys.ca.

Old Triangle

LIVE MUSIC | A traditional Irish alehouse, the Old Triangle reels in patrons with better-than-average pub food and pints of Guinness, then keeps them fixated with live Celtic music every night. Traditional open sessions take place on Sunday afternoon and Tuesday evening. ✉ 5136 Prince St. ☎ 902/492–4900 ⊕ oldtriangle. com.

Seahorse Tavern

LIVE MUSIC | Now in a great new location, with the Marquee Ballroom upstairs, the Seahorse continues to draw an eclectic indie crowd for late-night music. The two spaces showcase the very best in local, national, and international music. Cover charge is usually around C$7 to C$15, but some nights are free. ✉ 2037 Gottingen St. ☎ 902/423–7200 ⊕ thesea- horsetavern.ca.

The Split Crow

LIVE MUSIC | Halifax's oldest watering hole (its earliest incarnation opened in 1749) has an old-time ambience and a full menu heavy on finger foods and deep-fried seafood. Nevertheless, it's the beer/band combination—nightly and on Saturday afternoon—that accounts for the bar's enduring popularity. ✉ 1855 Granville St. ☎ 902/422–4366 ⊕ split- crow.com.

✪ Performing Arts

CONCERTS

Dalhousie Arts Centre

ARTS CENTERS | The Rebecca Cohn Auditorium at Dalhousie University's Arts Centre hosts a full program of perfor- mances, including touring national and international entertainers—recent shows have ranged from Rufus Wainwright and Mavis Staples to comedian Billy Connolly and various tribute bands—and opera and classical concerts featuring Sympho- ny Nova Scotia. ✉ 6101 University Ave. ☎ 902/494–3820, 800/874–1669 ⊕ dal.ca/ dept/arts-centre.html.

THEATER

Neptune Theatre

THEATER | The country's oldest profes- sional repertory playhouse—it opened in 1915—is also the largest in Atlantic Cana- da, with a main stage and studio theater under one roof. It presents year-round performances ranging from classics to comedy and contemporary Canadian drama, plus occasional concerts. ✉ 1593 Argyle St. ☎ 902/429–7070, 800/565– 7345 ⊕ neptunetheatre.com.

★ Shakespeare by the Sea

THEATER | From July through early Sep- tember, actors perform works by the Bard and others in Point Pleasant Park, at the southern end of the Halifax penin- sula. The natural setting—dark woods, rocky shore, and ruins of fortifications— provides a dramatic backdrop. Perfor- mances take place from Tuesday through Sunday at 7 pm, with an improv night on Mondays (weather permitting) and you can arrive up to two hours before to secure a good spot (at least 30 minutes before is recommended). ✉ Cambridge Battery, Point Pleasant Park, Point Pleasant Dr. ☎ 902/422–0295 ⊕ shake- spearebythesea.ca ⌦ C$20 donation suggested; reserved seating C$25; chair and blanket rentals C$2 each.

🍽 Shopping

BOOKS

Bookmark

BOOKS | This friendly independent bookstore has been serving the reading public for almost 30 years, with an excellent range of fiction, nonfiction, and local-interest books. ✉ *5686 Spring Garden Rd.* ☎ *902/423–0419* ⊕ *www.bookmarkreads. ca.*

CRAFTS AND GIFTS

Argyle Fine Art

ART GALLERIES | This funky small gallery focuses on emerging to mid-career Atlantic Canadian artists and always carries a selection of highly affordable pieces mixed in with more expensive ones. You'll also find a selection of ceramics, jewelry, and artsy greeting cards. ✉ *1559 Barrington St.* ☎ *902/425–9456* ⊕ *argyle-fineart.com.*

Inkwell Modern Handmade Boutique

OTHER SPECIALTY STORE | Bright and fun store that sells letterpress artwork and stationery, as well as modern handicrafts—many of which are made by local artists. This is the perfect place to pick up cool and unique gifts that reflect Halifax's artistic vibe. ✉ *2011 Brunswick St.* ☎ *902/405–8309* ⊕ *inkwellboutique.ca.*

Jennifer's of Nova Scotia

CRAFTS | Tempting Jennifer's sells pottery, glass, handmade soaps, hooked mats, ceramics, pewter, and other craft items made in Nova Scotia by nearly 30 artisans. ✉ *5635 Spring Garden Rd.* ☎ *902/425–3119* ⊕ *www.jennifers.ns.ca.*

FOOD

Peace by Chocolate

CHOCOLATE | Tareq Hadhad arrived in Nova Scotia as a Syrian refugee in 2015 and started up this successful chocolate business with his family, becoming the subject of a book and subsequent movie. Originally based in small-town Antigonish, this flagship store on the Halifax waterfront sells a selection of boxed chocolates and tasty bars, many printed with messages of hope. ✉ *1741 Lower Water St.* ☎ *902/421–9176* ⊕ *peacebychocolate.ca* ⊗ *Closed Thurs.*

SHOPPING COMPLEXES AND MALLS

Bishop's Landing

MALL | An attractive small complex of shops, condos, and a marina, Bishop's Landing contains worth-a-peek jewelry, fashion, handmade candies and rum cakes, Halifax's best wine store, and other boutiques. ✉ *1475 Lower Water St.* ⊕ *bishopslanding.com.*

Historic Properties

NEIGHBORHOODS | A pleasant place to stroll through some of the city's oldest buildings, this delightful complex also houses interesting shops and restaurants. ✉ *1869 Upper Water St.* ⊕ *historicproperties.ca.*

★ Hydrostone Market

NEIGHBORHOODS | This block-long building, a Parks Canada Federal Heritage Site and recipient of a Nova Scotia Built Heritage Award, lures shoppers to the city's North End with all sorts of one-of-a-kind items. Flattened by the Halifax Explosion in 1917, the market site and surrounding area were rebuilt in a charming English-garden style using hydrostone—aka concrete. Shops of note include Made in the Maritimes Artisan Boutique for fine crafts, Lady Luck Boutique for jewelry and accessories, and L.K. Yarns for yarns and needlecraft accessories. After browsing, break for lunch at Julien's Patisserie Bakery & Café or enjoy a fabulous dinner at the Ostrich Club. ✉ *5515–5547 Young St., between Isleville and Gottigen Sts., North End* ⊕ *hydrostonemarket.ca.*

🏃 Activities

BIKING

I heart bikes

BIKING | Housed in a converted shipping container on the Halifax Waterfront, this hip young company offers a series of bike and e-bike tours of the city that showcase the very best of the city's architecture and neighborhoods, as well as places that only locals go (CA$74.50). Rentals of bikes and e-bikes start at $25 per hour, and you can also rent trailers for hauling kids, as well as other equipment such as panniers for longer rides. ⊠ *1507 Lower Water St.* ☎ *902/406–7774* ⊕ *iheartbikeshfx.com* ⊙ *Closed Oct.-June.*

CANOEING
St. Mary's Boat Club
CANOEING & ROWING | Beautiful century-old homes dot the placid Northwest Arm, and the bench of a canoe is definitely the best seat from which to view them. On weekends from June through September, St. Mary's loans canoes on a first come, first served basis, for a maximum of one hour to adults 18 years and older and to younger certified canoeists; they also have some stand-up paddleboards. There's no charge, and the boat house is open from 11 am, with the last canoe pickup at 6 pm. Safety equipment is provided. ⊠ *1641 Fairfield Rd.* ✛ *Off Jubilee Rd., below Connaught Ave.* ☎ *902/490–4538* ⊕ *www.halifax. ca/recreation/facilities-fields/rec-centres/ st-marys-boat-club.*

GOLF
Glen Arbour Golf Course
GOLF | FAMILY | Natural features, including elevation changes and mature woodlands, lakes, and streams, make the 18-hole championship course here a scenic and memorable experience, culminating in the featured hole (the 18th), a 565-yard downhill par 5 with a dazzling view. The club also has a nine-hole, par-3 course designed for novices, with holes from 50 to 135 yards, and offers junior golf camps for ages 8–15. ⊠ *40 Clubhouse La., Hammonds Plains* ☎ *902/835–4653* ⊕ *www.glenarbour.com* ⊠ *Championship Course, C$65–C$110; Executive Course, C$15 for 9 holes, C$30 for 18 holes; junior golf camp C$300/week* ⅄ *Championship Course:*

18 holes, 6850 yards, par 72; Executive Course: 9 holes, 1688 yards, par 27 ⊙ *Closed early Oct.–Apr.*

Granite Springs Golf Club
GOLF | This lush, semiprivate course, an easy drive west of downtown Halifax, overlooks Shad Bay. It progresses across rolling hillsides with granite outcroppings, water features, and sand traps. Fairways are narrow, calling for accurate shots, but four sets of tees cater to different levels of golfing ability. ⊠ *4441 Prospect Rd., Bayside* ☎ *902/852–3419* ⊕ *granitespringsgolf.com* ⊠ *C$45–C$60* ⅄ *18 holes, 6401 yards, par 72* ⊙ *Closed mid-Oct.–Mar.*

HIKING
McNab's Island Provincial Park
HIKING & WALKING | At the mouth of Halifax Harbour, this island appeals to adventuresome spirits. Accessible only by boat, it has 14 km (9 miles) of wooded trails and birding sites, plus a 19th-century fort. Several companies provide water taxis or tours from different Halifax locations (see McNab's website for list). The trip takes 25 minutes from the Halifax boardwalk. There is no drinking water available on the island, so you must bring your own. Guided tours are available from the Friends Of McNab's Island Society for the price of their boat ride. ⊠ *Halifax* ☎ *902/434–2254 (evenings only)* ⊕ *mcnabsisland.ca.*

Sir Sandford Fleming Park
HIKING & WALKING | FAMILY | This 95-acre park, free and very accessible, but open only mid-April to mid-November, has a 2.8-km (1¾-mile) trail, with views across the Northwest Arm to Point Pleasant Park on the opposite shore. Marked by an impressive stone tower called the Dingle (open in summer), it's named for the inventor of standard time zones, who summered on the property and donated it to the city in 1912. ⊠ *260 Dingle Rd.* ✛ *Follow signs off Purcell's Cove Rd.* ⊕ *novascotia.com/see-do/attractions/ sir-sandford-fleming-park-the-dingle.*

SEA KAYAKING

East Coast Outfitters

KAYAKING | This outfitter rents kayaking equipment and offers instruction and guided excursions from May through September. Half-day, full-day, and shorter midday and sunset tours are available, and there's the option to have a customized tour or just rent a kayak. ✉ *2017 Lower Prospect Rd., Lower Prospect* ✛ *Follow Rte. 333 toward Peggy's Cove, turn left on Terence Bay Rd. and continue for 9 km (5½ miles)* ☎ *902/852–2567, 877/852–2567* ⊕ *eastcoastoutfitters.com* 🖃 *Tours from C$59; rentals from C$20 per hr.*

SWIMMING

Chocolate Lake

SWIMMING | **FAMILY** | In July and August, from 11 am to 5 pm, lifeguards supervise this lake, just off the Northwest Arm, that's popular for swimming. The name doesn't mean that the water is delicious, but rather comes from a former chocolate factory on the site. Although it's in a residential area, the lake is surrounded by trees, giving it a secluded feel, and there's a nice beach. Water quality is tested weekly. ✉ *2 Melwood Ave.*

Peggy's Cove

48 km (30 miles) southwest of Halifax.

Peggy's Cove is the home of Canada's most photographed lighthouse. As you wind along the edge of St. Margaret's Bay, woodlands eventually give way to rugged outcroppings that were deposited when the last glaciers swept through. On one side, massive granite boulders stand semi-erect in scrubby fields; on the other, they lie prone, creating the granite shelf on which Peggy's Cove is perched. The hamlet itself consists of little more than a Lilliputian harbor with a tiny wooden church, a cluster of shingled houses, and some salt-bleached jetties. What distinguishes Peggy's Cove, though, is the

solitary lighthouse towering over a slab of wave-blasted rock; while it's not open to the public, it's well worth seeing from a distance just for the photo op. Just don't be tempted to venture too close to the edge—many an unwary visitor has been swept out to sea by the mighty surf that sometimes breaks here. (Repeat this mantra: dark rocks are wet rocks, and must be avoided.) A brand-new accessible viewing platform means that everyone can enjoy the view. In addition to navigating the rugged terrain, you'll have to contend with the crowds in summer—750,000 tourists descend annually. To avoid them in July and August, plan to arrive early or late in the day.

GETTING HERE AND AROUND

There is no public transportation to Peggy's Cove. Travelers based in Halifax can drive here by taking either Exit 2 or Exit 5 from Highway 103 onto Highway 333. The former is mostly inland while the latter runs along St. Margaret's Bay. The ideal scenario, though, is to go via one and return via the other. At Peggy's Cove you can drive almost to the base of the lighthouse, but you'd do better to park in the spacious public lot below and make the three-minute walk up to this Canadian icon. Bus tours from Halifax are another option.

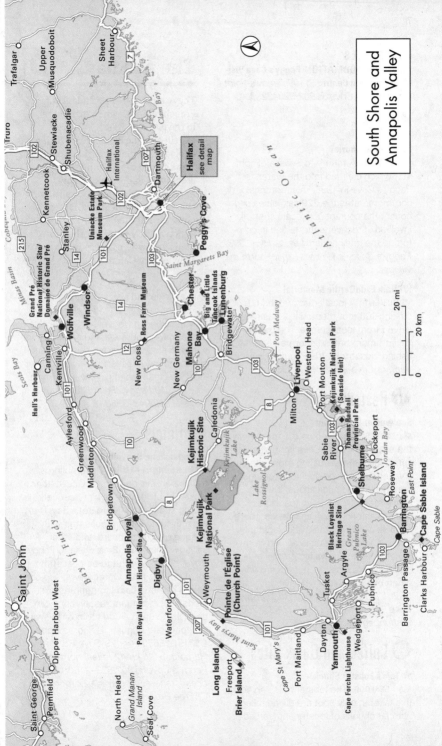

South Shore and Annapolis Valley

ESSENTIALS

VISITOR INFORMATION Peggy's Cove Visitor Information Centre. ✉ *109 Peggy's Point Rd., Peggy's Cove* ☎ *902/823–2253.*

[👁] Sights

Swissair Memorial

MONUMENT | A tribute to Swissair Flight 111, which crashed into the waters off Peggy's Cove in 1998, this memorial commemorates the 229 casualties and honors the courageous local fisherfolk involved in recovery efforts and in comforting the grieving families. ✉ *Hwy. 333, Peggy's Cove* ✥ *1½ km (1 mile) north of village.*

William E. deGarthe Memorial

MONUMENT | A local artist created the striking 100-foot memorial, a bas-relief carved from local granite. The memorial commemorates fishermen and the fishing industry. ✉ *109 Peggy's Point Rd., Peggy's Cove* ✥ *Off Hwy. 333.*

🍴 Restaurants

Sou'wester Restaurant

$$$ | **SEAFOOD** | Poised on the rocks near the base of Peggy's Cove lighthouse, this sprawling 180-seat dining room serves a variety of seafood, including orange brandy shrimp and scallops, lobster dinners, and Down East specialties such as salt-fish hash and beans. There are also chicken, steak, and vegetarian options, and breakfast is served from 8:30 to 11 am. **Known for:** great views; traditional local dishes; lots of crowds when bus tours are in. [$] *Average main: C$25* ✉ *178 Peggy's Point Rd., Peggy's Cove* ✥ *Off Hwy. 333* ☎ *902/823–2561* 🌐 *shoppeggyscove.com.*

☕ Coffee and Quick Bites

★ **Tom's Lobster Shack**

$$$ | **SEAFOOD** | The lobster rolls served at this takeout-only spot are divine, filled with fat chunks of lobster and served with a pickle and potato chips on the side. Order a classic (with celery and mayo), cajun (spicier version of the classic), or naked (pure lobster) and sit by the water to enjoy. **Known for:** salted caramel chocolate pate dessert; fast, friendly service; ice-cream cones. [$] *Average main: C$21* ✉ *110 Peggys Point Rd., Peggy's Cove* ☎ *902/943–3950.*

The Acadians [👁]

The Acadians are descendants of French colonists who settled here in the 1600s. In 1755, they were expelled by the British for refusing to pledge allegiance to the Crown. Some eluded capture and slowly crept back, many making new homes in New Brunswick and along this shore of Nova Scotia. Others, however, migrated south to another region held by France at the time: Louisiana, where their name was shortened to Cajun.

🛏 Hotels

★ **Oceanstone Seaside Resort**

$$$$ | **B&B/INN** | **FAMILY** | Resembling a traditional seaside hamlet, Oceanstone's cluster of buildings sits picturesquely on the shore of St. Margaret's Bay. The attractive interiors are accented with antique pine, barn board, and other salvaged materials. **Pros:** close to Peggy's Cove, but far enough to be peaceful; most options have water views; eco-conscious owners. **Cons:** sometimes hosts weddings; restaurant reservations can be tricky to get; can be too cold to swim except in late August. [$] *Rooms from: C$315* ✉ *8650 Peggy's Cove Rd., Indian Harbour* ✥ *3½ km (2 miles) north of Peggy's Cove* ☎ *902/823–2160,* 🌐 *www.oceanstoneresort.com* 🛏 *22 rooms* 🍴 *Free Breakfast.*

In addition to its famous lighthouse, Peggy's Cove is also known for its stunning coastal vistas.

Activities

Boat excursions are available around Peggy's Cove from spring through fall.

Peggy's Cove Boat Tours

WILDLIFE-WATCHING | FAMILY | Tours lasting from 1 to 2½ hours are offered daily, June through October, with prices ranging from C$30 to C$45. Options include a sightseeing and marine life tour; a puffin, birds, and seal tour; a sunset tour; and a full-moon tour. Lobster dinner cruises and deep-sea fishing are also available. ⊠ *Government Wharf, Peggy's Cove* ☏ *902/541–9177* ⊕ *www.peggyscoveboattours.com.*

Chester

64 km (40 miles) west of Peggy's Cove.

Although Chester is a short drive west of Peggy's Cove, you'll be forgiven for thinking you've taken a wrong turn and ended up in Maine or Massachusetts. New England planters settled the site in 1759, and their numbers were later bolstered by Loyalists escaping the American Revolution and Boston Brahmins who simply wanted to escape the city in summer. Thanks to the clapboard saltboxes and Cape Cod–style homes they left behind, Chester still calls to mind a classic New England community. Most visitors are content to explore its tree-shaded lanes or make forays into the surrounding countryside. Yachtsmen invariably stick close to the water.

GETTING HERE AND AROUND

There is no public transportation to Chester. From Halifax it's a 68-km (42-mile) drive via NS–103 and NS Trunk 3 W, or a slightly longer, much slower, meandering drive along St. Margaret's Bay Road, NS–213, and NS Trunk 3 W.

Sights

Big and Little Tancook Islands

ISLAND | Out in Mahone Bay, 8 km (5 miles) out from Chester, these scenic islands have trails for hiking and biking, and provide great bird-watching and photography opportunities. There are sandy beaches, too, one of which is great for fossil hunting. Reflecting its part-German heritage, Big Tancook claims to have the best sauerkraut in Nova Scotia. The ferry from Chester runs four times daily Monday through Thursday, six times on Friday, and twice daily on weekends. The 50-minute ride costs C$7 round-trip (cash only). ✉ *Chester* ☎ *902/275–7885 ferry information* 🌐 *tancookcommunitynews.com.*

Ross Farm Museum
FARM/RANCH | FAMILY | A restored 19th-century farm illustrates the evolution of agriculture from 1600 to 1925. The animals are those found on an 1800s farm—draft horses, oxen, and other heritage breeds—and traditional activities such as blacksmithing and spinning are demonstrated. Hands-on programs are regularly scheduled for kids who'd like to help out with the chores. The Peddler's Shop here sells items made in the community. ✉ *4568 Rte. 12, New Ross* ✣ *30 km (18 miles) northwest of Chester via NS Trunk 3 E* ☎ *902/689–2210, 877/689–2210* 🌐 *rossfarm.novascotia.ca* 🎟 *C$10; free Sun. 9:30–11 am* 🕓 *Closed Mon. and Tues. mid-Oct.–late Apr.*

SENSEA Nordic Spa
OTHER ATTRACTION | Soak away your troubles overlooking the Chester Basin at Nova Scotia's first Nordic spa, with massage and treatment rooms set in a cluster of geodomes and wooden structures containing saunas and steam rooms. There's an on-site restaurant, where you can take a light meal by the fireside, or you can have refreshments delivered to your hammock or chosen relaxation area using a QR code. Online advance bookings are highly recommended, especially if you want a massage or treatment as well as to use the water circuit. ✉ *40 Sensëa Rd., Chester* ☎ *902/800–9033* 🌐 *sensea.ca* 🎟 *Spa pass CA$57.50, massages from CA$120.*

🍴 Restaurants

Fo'c'sle Tavern
$$ | CANADIAN | This rustic midtown spot—a former store, stable, and Nova Scotia's oldest rural inn, dating to 1764—is full of natural pine and local art, and its staff and clientele treat regulars and newcomers like kin. In the windowed front section, a woodstove keeps things warm on chilly nights, and year-round you can order from a menu that's strong on seafood and comfort food. **Known for:** craft beers on tap; live music some nights of the week; weekend brunches with lots of choices. $ *Average main: C$17* ✉ *42 Queen St., Chester* ☎ *902/275–1408* 🌐 *www.focslechester.com.*

The Rope Loft
$$$ | SEAFOOD | Housed in one of Chester's oldest buildings, with 200-year-old hand-hewn beams and plenty of original features, this dockside restaurant and pub offers excellent seafood, steaks, and pasta dishes in the most picturesque of locations. With decks right on the harbour, the views here can't be beat. **Known for:** great spot to watch boats sailing by; superb pan seared scallops; being family friendly. $ *Average main: C$25* ✉ *36 Water St., Chester* ☎ *902/275–3430* 🌐 *ropeloft.com* 🕓 *Closed Weds.*

☕ Coffee and Quick Bites

The Kiwi Cafe
$$ | CAFÉ | This bright and friendly spot is a Chester community hub, and is a great spot to grab breakfast, lunch, or just coffee and a treat. Everything served is fresh, locally sourced where possible, and absolutely delicious. **Known for:** excellent mimosas; large bright and sunny patio; outstanding haddock and lobster chowder. $ *Average main: C$12* ✉ *19 Pleasant St., Chester* ☎ *902/275–1492* 🌐 *www.thekiwicafe.com.*

Hotels

Mecklenburgh Inn

$$ | B&B/INN | Nautical touches abound in this heritage B&B at the top of one of Chester's main streets. **Pros:** the sailor innkeeper can arrange boating trips; complimentary gourmet breakfast; claw-foot tubs in three rooms. **Cons:** one bathroom, while private, is not en suite; books up a year ahead for Race Week; two blocks from the water. $ *Rooms from: C$169* ⊠ *78 Queen St., Chester* ☎ *902/275–4638, 866/838–4638* ⊕ *www. mecklenburghinn.ca* ⊗ *Closed Jan.–Apr.* ↪ *4 rooms* ⦿ *Free Breakfast.*

🎭 Performing Arts

Chester has long had a vibrant arts scene and several cultural festivals are held throughout the summer months. Although the much-loved and historic Chester Playhouse suffered a devastating fire in 2021, visitors can still enjoy a full program from the Playhouse held in community halls and venues throughout Chester until the building is restored (⊕ *chesterplayhouse.ca*).

👜 Shopping

Amicus Gallery

ART GALLERIES | Fine art, jewelry, stained glass, and other crafts by Maritimes artisans can be found here, along with the owner Paula MacDonald's own pottery made in her on-site studio. ⊠ *20 Pleasant St., Chester* ☎ *902/275–2496* ⊕ *www. amicusgallery.ca.*

Jim Smith Fine Studio Pottery

CERAMICS | The earthenware pottery at this studio is as cheerful as the bright yellow-and-green building on the front harbor in which it's housed. ⊠ *Corner of Duke and Water Sts., Chester* ☎ *902/275–3272* ⊕ *www.jimsmithstudio. ca* ⊗ *Open by appointment.*

Mahone Bay

24 km (15 miles) west of Chester.

Three vintage churches along a grass-fringed shoreline set a tranquil tone for this pastoral town that wraps around a sweeping curve of water. Of course, life here wasn't always so serene. Mahone Bay was once a thriving shipbuilding center. Before that, it was popular with pirates and privateers. In fact, Mahone Bay was named for the type of low-lying ship they used: it's a corruption of the French word *mahonne* (a low-lying bargelike boat).

Mahone Bay's outdoor pleasures include kayaking into secret coves or around the many islands, including Oak Island, reputedly a favorite haunt of the notorious Captain Kidd. Modern-day treasure hunters are better off onshore, perusing the galleries and studios along Main Street and environs. Although Mahone Bay has a population of just 1,100, it supports an enviable assortment of craftspeople.

GETTING HERE AND AROUND
There is no public transportation to Mahone Bay. To drive here, leave Highway 103 at Exit 10, turning onto NS–3.

ESSENTIALS
VISITOR INFORMATION Mahone Bay Visitor Information Centre. ⊠ *165 Edgewater St., Mahone Bay* ☎ *902/624–6151, 888/624–6151* ⊕ *www.mahonebay.com.*

👁 Sights

Mahone Bay Museum

HISTORY MUSEUM | Housed in one of the delightful old buildings in this pretty little town, the museum contains interesting displays about the long history of Mahone Bay and some of the people who shaped its future. The collection includes boatbuilding items and models, ceramics, household antiques, and a display relating the story of the first settlers who arrived in the 1750s. Museum volunteers can also arrange tours by appointment. ✉ *578 Main St., Mahone Bay* ☎ *902/624–6263* 🌐 *mahonebaymuseum.com* 🎟 *Free (donations welcome)* 🕒 *Closed Mon.–Weds. Closed early Oct.–late May and random days in Sept. (call ahead for details).*

🍴 Restaurants

Mug & Anchor Pub

$$ | **CANADIAN** | **FAMILY** | Take in a view of the bay from inside this old, British-style alehouse, or enjoy waterside dining on the back deck. The menu includes basic pub fare, such as fish-and-chips and steak and ale pie. **Known for:** picturesque location; lobster rolls and scallops; great selection of local beers on tap. [$] *Average main: C$15* ✉ *643 Main St., Mahone Bay* ☎ *902/624–6378* 🌐 *facebook.com/themugandanchorpub.*

Rebecca's Restaurant

$$$ | **CANADIAN** | **FAMILY** | Head to Rebecca's for freshly prepared, flavorful, and beautifully presented dishes. Creamy seafood chowder is a popular starter, while hearty and interesting mains include inventive seafood, meat, and vegetarian choices (vegan on request). **Known for:** lovely view over the water; local free-range meat and eggs; gigantic and delicious made-from-scratch desserts. [$] *Average main: C$26* ✉ *619 Main St., Mahone Bay* ☎ *902/531–3313* 🌐 *www.rebeccas-restaurant.ca* 🕒 *Closed Thurs.*

🛍 Shopping

Amos Pewter

CRAFTS | Inside a former boatbuilding shop that dates to 1888, the artisans at Amos Pewter design and create pewter items using traditional methods. Jewelry, sculptures, tableware, and pewter renditions of shells and other natural objects are among the items for sale, along with a new original-design Christmas ornament each year. Interpretive displays explain the history of pewter and Amos Pewter's involvement with the "Econo-museum Network," which emphasizes traditional skills. If watching the artisans at work gets your creative juices flowing, you can participate in the Hands-On Experience (C$5), and take home what you make. ✉ *589 Main St., Mahone Bay* ☎ *800/565–3369* 🌐 *www.amospewter.com.*

The Biscuit Eater Cafe and Books

BOOKS | Housed in a period building, used books line floor-to-ceiling shelves in rooms filled with overstuffed chairs and antique furniture. There's also a great selection of new books by local and Canadian authors. The cafe is quite lovely, serving afternoon tea as well as truly delicious baked goods and excellent coffee. ✉ *16 Orchard St., Mahone Bay* ☎ *902/624-2665* 🌐 *www.thebiscuiteater.com.*

🏃 Activities

Salty Dog Sea Tours

BOAT TOURS | Join super friendly and knowledgable Capt. Tony on a tour of Mahone Bay, where exploring the mysteries of Oak Island, as seen on the TV show *The Curse of Oak Island!*, is always on the itinerary. As the boat is covered, tours can run even on rainy days. ✉ *36 Treasure Dr., Mahone Bay* ☎ *902/300-4108* 🌐 *saltydogtours.com* 🎟 *C$60* 🕒 *Closed Nov.-mid-May.*

Lunenburg

14 km (9 miles) south of Mahone Bay.

This remarkably preserved town has a colorful past and some *very* colorful buildings, a combo that earned it a UNESCO World Heritage Site designation. The British probably had something more staid in mind when they founded Lunenburg in 1753, but the German, Swiss, and French Protestants recruited to settle here put their own stamp on it. The result? Rainbow-hue houses characterized by the "Lunenburg Bump": a detailed dormer over the front door. Naturally, locals didn't spend *all* their time on home improvements. By the 1850s they'd transformed the town into a world-class fishing and shipbuilding center. Today, blacksmiths and dory builders continue to work on the waterfront and, appropriately, the Fisheries Museum of the Atlantic is the top attraction. An in-the-middle-of-it-all location, plus a growing supply of fine lodging, dining, shopping, and touring options, makes Lunenburg one of the best bases for a Nova Scotia vacation.

GETTING HERE AND AROUND

When the Beatles sang about "the long and winding road," they might have had the Lighthouse Route in mind. The curvy back roads that make up most of it hug the South Shore from Halifax to Yarmouth and are undeniably scenic, but a shorter option is to get to Lunenburg via Highway 103, using Exit 10 or Exit 11; either exit will take about the same amount of time, but Exit 11 has nice views around Mahone Bay. Once you're in town, walking is the way to go, provided you're not daunted by the steep hill.

TOURS

Lunenburg Town Walking Tours

WALKING TOURS | Landlubbers can get their exercise on one of the guided strolls conducted by this company, with a lively narrative of local history, folklore, and personal stories from the guides. The Essential Lunenburg tour is each day at 10 am and 2 pm, June through October, and the Haunted Lunenburg tour is each evening at 8:30 pm June through September, 7:30 pm in October. ⊠ *Lunenburg* ☎ *902/521–6867* ⊕ *www. lunenburgwalkingtours.com* ☜ *C$25* ☉ *Closed mid-Oct.–early Apr.*

ESSENTIALS

VISITOR INFORMATION Lunenburg Visitor Information Centre. ⊠ *11 Blockhouse Hill Rd., Lunenburg* ☎ *902/634–8100, 902/634–3656, 888/615–8305* ⊕ *www. lunenburgns.com.*

👁 Sights

DesBrisay Museum

HISTORY MUSEUM | FAMILY | Artifacts dating back to the mid-19th century, including rare photographs of local shops, factories, and shipyards, are among the holdings of this museum of Lunenburg County history. There's also a folk-art gallery, a First Nations gallery, and the Kidology Korner, with toys and games from pre-technology days. Walking trails wind from behind the museum building through nearby parkland. ⊠ *130 Jubilee Rd., Bridgewater* ☎ *902/543–4033* ⊕ *desbrisaymuseum.ca* ☜ *Free.* ☉ *Closed Sun. and Mon.*

★ Fisheries Museum of the Atlantic

HISTORY MUSEUM | FAMILY | Flanked by sailing ships and painted a brilliant red, this museum on the Lunenburg waterfront strikes a dazzling pose. An aquarium features 14 tanks with native species and tidal touch tanks, and there are themed films in the Ice House Theatre, daily activities, and three floors of displays about shipbuilding, whaling, and other maritime endeavors. Demonstrations cover topics such as sail-making, boatbuilding, and dory launching, and dockside you can visit a restored 1938 saltbank schooner and a 1962 steel-hulled trawler. The *Bluenose II,* the province's sailing ambassador, is also based here. Built in 1963, it's a faithful replica of the original *Bluenose,* the Lunenburg-built schooner prominent during the 1920s and 1930s as the North Atlantic fleet's fastest vessel, which sank in 1946 after striking a reef. ⊠ *68 Bluenose Dr., Lunenburg* ☎ *902/634–4794, 866/579–4909* ⊕ *fisheriesmuseum.novascotia.ca* ☜ *C$12* ☉ *Closed Oct.–mid-June.*

Did You Know?

Lunenburg has always had deep ties to the sea. It was once a major shipbuilding center and it also boasted one of the largest fish processing plants in North America. You can learn about its rich maritime history at the Fisheries Museum of the Atlantic, housed in a large red waterfront complex.

Wile Carding Mill Museum

HISTORY MUSEUM | Life became easier for the locals after this mill opened in 1860, greatly reducing the time needed to card (process) wool. On a visit here you can view the restored mill, glean fascinating facts from engaging guides about its working days, and try your hand at carding wool and spinning yarn. ✉ *242 Victoria Rd., Bridgewater* ☎ *902/543–8233* 🌐 *cardingmill.novascotia.ca* 🎟 *Free* 🕑 *Closed Oct.–May.*

🍴 Restaurants

The Beach Pea Kitchen and Bar

$$$ | **MEDITERRANEAN** | Owned by esteemed local chef Martin Ruiz Salvador, each thoughtful dish embraces fresh, local produce and meat, as well as incredible seafood. The Mediterranean-inspired menu elevates mussels and scallops to another level, their pasta is all handmade, and service is exceptional. **Known for:** great selection of Nova Scotian beers and wines; tender grilled octopus; scallop and rabbit risotto. [$] *Average main: C$26* ✉ *128 Montague St., Lunenburg* ☎ *902/640–3474* 🌐 *beachpeakitchen.com* 🕑 *No lunch.*

★ **Grand Banker Bar and Grill**

$$$ | **CANADIAN** | With a focus on fresh produce and local seafood, the Grand Banker is a great spot for a tasty lunch or dinner overlooking the harbor whether you're in the mood for wings and a craft beer, lobster mac 'n' cheese, or rack of lamb. There's an impressive selection of Nova Scotian wines, and you can order a five 2-ounce glass sampler for C$22, as well as a cocktail list that embraces locally distilled liquors. **Known for:** fun, lively atmosphere; seafood-packed chowder; local craft brews. [$] *Average main: C$25* ✉ *82 Montague St., Lunenburg* ☎ *902/634–3300* 🌐 *grandbanker.com.*

★ **Salt Shaker Deli and Inn**

$$ | **INTERNATIONAL** | In a gorgeous location by the water, this restaurant is much more than just a deli, with a long menu that includes an award-winning chowder, gourmet sandwiches, hand-rolled, thin-crust pizzas, inventive burgers with an international slant, and plenty of vegetarian choices. In the evening, chef Martin Ruiz Salvador adds a short dinner menu to the options, with dishes like scallop linguine and fisherman's stew. **Known for:** local Nova Scotian wines; good range of expertly prepared dishes; waterfront patio overlooking the harbor. [$] *Average main: C$20* ✉ *124 Montague St., Lunenburg* ☎ *902/640–3434* 🌐 *saltshakerdeli.com.*

The South Shore Fish Shack

$$$ | **SEAFOOD** | Head here for great fish-and-chips, juicy scallops, or a lobster roll. Two patios overlook the water, and there's indoor seating too. **Known for:** massive burgers; fast service; selection of ciders. [$] *Average main: C$22* ✉ *108 Montague St., Lunenburg* ☎ *902/634–3232* 🌐 *southshorefishshack.com.*

☕ Coffee and Quick Bites

No. 9 Coffee Bar

$ | **BAKERY** | This adorable café serves excellent coffee and a range of baked treats that you can enjoy in their antique-furniture-filled parlor or leafy backyard patio. **Known for:** great place to hide away with a book; tons of vintage charm; great vegan treats and desserts. [$] *Average main: C$6* ✉ *135 Montague St., Lunenburg* ☎ *902/634–3204* 🌐 *facebook.com/no9coffeebar.*

Sweet Treasures Confectionery

$ | **ICE CREAM** | The aroma of freshly made waffle cones makes it hard to walk on by this little store selling delicious homemade ice cream and fudge. **Known for:** fun selection of international candy; fresh strawberry ice cream; huge scoops piled high. [$] *Average main: C$5* ✉ *110 Montague St., Lunenburg* ☎ *902/634–4949* 🌐 *facebook.com/SweetTreasuresconfectionery.*

Hotels

Lunenburg Arms Hotel & Spa

$$ | **HOTEL** | It's rare to find hotel-style amenities in small-town heritage properties, but this place has them, including a full-service spa. **Pros:** choice of good restaurants nearby; mid-hill location; complimentary use of spa's steam shower and hot tub. **Cons:** some rooms are small; rather sparse breakfast buffet; not on the waterfront (but there are views). *[$] Rooms from: C$134 ✉ 94 Pelham St., Lunenburg ☎ 902/640–4040, 🌐 lunenburgarmshotel.ca 🛏 24 rooms 🍴 No Meals.*

Lunenburg Inn

$$ | **B&B/INN** | This luxurious lodging has rooms that are spacious and furnished with antiques. **Pros:** take-one, leave-one book exchange; friendly, warm owners; delicious breakfasts with home baking. **Cons:** not all rooms have a balcony; a bit outside the main tourist area; street can be noisy. *[$] Rooms from: C$169 ✉ 26 Dufferin St., Lunenburg ☎ 902/634–3963, 800/565–3963 🌐 www.lunenburginn.com 🕒 Closed late Oct.–Mar. 🛏 7 rooms 🍴 Free Breakfast.*

Pelham House Bed & Breakfast

$$ | **B&B/INN** | **FAMILY** | Close to downtown, with a veranda overlooking Lunenburg Harbour, this circa-1906 sea captain's home is decorated in homey, country style. **Pros:** suite works well for families; great breakfasts included with rates; owners fluent in English, French, and Spanish. **Cons:** ceiling fans rather than air-conditioning; resident dog not great for people with pet allergies; no grounds to speak of. *[$] Rooms from: C$135 ✉ 224 Pelham St., Lunenburg ☎ 902/634–7113, 800/508–0446 🌐 www.pelhamhouse.ca 🛏 3 rooms, 1 suite 🍴 Free Breakfast.*

Shopping

Block Shop Books

BOOKS | **FAMILY** | Run by authors and book enthusiasts, this independent bookstore has a hand-picked selection with a focus on fiction, poetry, small press, graphic novels, young adult, and children's books. They run writing workshops in addition to a monthly book club, and also host author readings and book signings. *✉ 125 Montague St., Lunenburg ☎ 902/634–4015 🌐 blockshopbooks.ca.*

Bluenose II Company Store

CRAFTS | Official merchandise from the ship *Bluenose II* is sold here, along with other quality crafts. You can pick up all kinds of nautical memorabilia, from a splendid model of the *Bluenose* to a jaunty cap, and there's art, clothing, pewter crafts, and much more. *✉ 121 Bluenose Dr., Lunenburg ☎ 902/640–3177, 855/640–3177 🌐 www.bluenose2store.ca.*

Dots and Loops

CRAFTS | This bright and spacious store stocks crafts, ceramics, and affordable artworks from emerging Canadian artists, as well as fun and funky giftware and apparel. *✉ 183 Lincoln St., Lunenburg ☎ 902/634-3282 🌐 dotsandloops.ca.*

Ironworks Distillery

WINE/SPIRITS | Load up on liquid souvenirs here. Named for the old marine blacksmith's shop it occupies, Ironworks produces hand-distilled vodka from Annapolis Valley apples and luscious liqueurs from local berries. Tours (C$35 per two-person booking) are offered Wednesday to Sunday mid-May–early September. *✉ The Blacksmith's Shop, 2 Kempt St., Lunenburg ☎ 902/640–2424 🌐 ironworksdistillery.com.*

Peer Gallery

ART GALLERIES | On Lunenburg's gallery row, this contemporary artist-cooperative gallery represents more than a dozen artists and has been recognized by the provincial government for its contribution to local art and culture. *✉ 166 Lincoln St., Lunenburg ☎ 902/640–3131 🌐 peer-gallery.com.*

🏃 Activities

Lunenburg Bike Shop

BIKING | FAMILY | Both bike rentals and guided cycling tours customized to suit participants' abilities and interests are available here. Rentals range from C$25 for a half-day to C$175 per week. Tours cost C$80 per group for a half-day and C$160 for a full day, not including bike rental. If you bring your own bike, they offer certified maintenance and repairs. And if you want to look the part, cycling apparel is available for purchase. ⊠ *169 Montague St., Lunenburg* ☎ *902/521–6115* ⊕ *lunenburgbikeshop.com.*

Lunenburg Ocean Adventures

FISHING | The thrill-seeker activities this outfitter makes possible include deep-sea and shark fishing and diving to explore various wrecks and East Point Reef. Boats depart from the Fisheries Museum of the Atlantic. ⊠ *68 Bluenose Dr., Lunenburg* ☎ *902/521–0251* ⊕ *lunenburgoceanadventures.com* 🍽 *Fishing C$60; shark fishing from C$1,500 per day; call for diving prices* 🌣 *Closed Oct.–mid-May.*

Lunenburg Whale-Watching Tours

WILDLIFE-WATCHING | FAMILY | Whales, seals, and other marine life are the star attractions of these tours. The three-hour trips depart four times daily, from May through October, from the Fisheries Museum Wharf. You can arrange for bird-watching excursions and tours of Lunenburg Harbour, too. ⊠ *62 Bluenose Dr., Lunenburg* ☎ *902/527–7175* ⊕ *novascotiawhalewatching.com* 🍽 *C$70* 🌣 *Closed Nov. to May.*

Pleasant Paddling

KAYAKING | FAMILY | Guided kayak excursions include a four-hour trip to view a seal colony (C$87), paddling to a secluded beach on one of the islands (C$72), full-day coastal tours (C$125), and moonlight tours (C$65). Multiday tours range from C$650 to C$1,595. Two-hour stand-up paddleboard tours around Whynot Island cost C$55. Kayak rentals are priced from C$35 for a single kayak for two hours to C$95 per day for a double. Stand-up paddleboards range from C$38 for two hours to C$78 for a full day and come with safety gear and a map. ⊠ *245 The Point Rd., Blue Rocks* ☎ *902/541–9233* ⊕ *pleasantpaddling.com* 🌣 *Closed mid-Oct. to May.*

Star Charters

SAILING | FAMILY | From June through October, two-hour sailing trips take place aboard a 48-foot wooden ketch; you may even get the chance to take the helm or help raise the sails. ⊠ *Fisheries Museum Wharf, 124 Bluenose Dr., Lunenburg* ☎ *902/634–3535 June–Oct., 877/386–3535* 🖂 *info@novascotiasailing. com* ⊕ *novascotiasailing.com* 🍽 *C$45* 🌣 *Closed Nov.–May.*

Liverpool

69 km (43 miles) southwest of Lunenburg.

In recent years, a paper mill has been Liverpool's economic mainstay, but between the American Revolution and the War of 1812, privateering was the most profitable pursuit. New Englanders who had turned on their former neighbors with a vengeance founded the town in 1759. Armed with a "Letter of Marque" from the British Crown, they made a booming business out of seizing American ships and the valuable cargo they carried. Depending on which side you were on, such activity was interpreted as political expediency or legalized piracy. Each July, the town celebrates its notorious past with its Privateer Days festival.

GETTING HERE AND AROUND

There is no public transportation to Liverpool. By road, it's off Highway 103 at the White Point Connector, then a left turn onto White Point Road. The town is small and easily walkable.

ESSENTIALS

VISITOR INFORMATION Liverpool Visitor Information Centre. ✉ *32 Henry Hensey Dr., Liverpool* ☎ *902/354–5421* ⊕ *www. regionofqueens.com/visit.*

◉ Sights

Fort Point Lighthouse Park

LIGHTHOUSE | This is one of Canada's oldest surviving lighthouses, located on the site where Samuel de Champlain and Sieur de Monts landed in 1604. Inside, the Port of the Privateers exhibit recounts the lighthouse's decades of stalwart service, from its completion in 1855 until 1989, when operations ceased. Even if the lighthouse isn't open when you arrive, there are interpretive signs outside, and the views of Liverpool Harbour from the park are splendid. ✉ *21 Fort Point La., off Main St., Liverpool* ☎ *902/354–3456,* ☒ *Free* ⊗ *Closed early Oct.–mid-May.*

Kejimkujik National Park–Seaside

NATIONAL PARK | One of the last untouched tracts of coastline in Atlantic Canada, this park has isolated coves, broad white beaches, and imposing headlands, all of which are managed by Kejimkujik National Park and Historic Site (just plain "Keji" to locals or the linguistically challenged). A hike along a 6-km (4-mile) trail reveals a pristine coast that's home to harbor seals, eider ducks, and many other species. To protect nesting areas of the endangered piping plover, parts of St. Catherine's River Beach (the main beach) are closed to the public from late April to early August. ✉ *Port Joli* ⊹ *Off Hwy. 103, 25 km (16 miles) southwest of Liverpool* ☎ *902/682–2772* ⊕ *www.pc.gc.ca* ☒ *C$6.*

Rossignol Cultural Centre

HISTORY MUSEUM | FAMILY | A refurbished high school is now home to this eclectic center that contains three art galleries, an artist-in-residence, and six museums—including one devoted entirely to outhouses. Among the varied offerings are a trapper's cabin, an early-20th-century drugstore, 50 stuffed-wildlife exhibits, and a complete wood-paneled drawing room brought over from an English manor house. ✉ *205 Church St., Liverpool* ☎ *902/354–3067* ⊕ *facebook.com/ rossignolculturalcentre* ☒ *C$5* ⊗ *Closed mid-Sept.–mid-June.*

Thomas Raddall Provincial Park

BEACH | FAMILY | With four migratory seabird sanctuaries nearby, this 1,600-acre park is a great spot for birding, and it has some good hiking trails. Or you could just stretch out on one of the white-sand beaches. Occasional organized activities include family fun days, a sand sculpture contest in September, and stargazing. ✉ *529 Raddall Park Rd., East Port l'Hebert, Liverpool* ☎ *902/683–2664* ⊕ *www. novascotiaparks.ca* ☒ *Free* ⊗ *Closed early Oct.–mid-May.*

◉ Beaches

Summerville Beach Provincial Park

BEACH | FAMILY | The Liverpool area has easy access to some of the South Shore's best beaches, and this one has more than a kilometer of fine, pale-color sand. Backing the beach is a dune system that shelters nesting sites for piping plovers—a clue to the location's uncrowded tranquility—and beyond this are salt marshes. Make sure to stick to the designated paths here. The shallow water makes Summerville ideal for families, and near the beach is a picnic area with tables that have sunshades. **Amenities:** parking (free); toilets. **Best for:** solitude; sunset; swimming; walking. ✉ *7533 Hwy. 3, Summerville Centre* ⊹ *14½ km (9 miles) southwest of Liverpool* ⊕ *www.novascotiaparks.ca* ☒ *Free.*

🛏 Hotels

Quarterdeck Beachside Villas & Grill

$$$$ | **RESORT** | **FAMILY** | Built just above the high-water mark on the edge of the Summerville Beach Provincial Park, the accommodations here include quality villas, each with a furnished deck and propane fireplaces, and many with full kitchens. **Pros:** terrific beach; recreation center includes an 18-seat theater; restaurant offers room service and takeout. **Cons:** cooking aromas can linger in the units with a kitchen; some units have only a shower, no tub; restaurant is closed from mid-October to mid-May. $ *Rooms from: C$299* ✉ *7499 Hwy. 3, Port Mouton* ✛ *15 km (10 miles) west of Liverpool* ☎ *902/683–2998, 800/565–1119* ⊕ *www.quarterdeck.ca* ⇆ *15 villas, 36 rooms* ⦿ *No Meals.*

🏃 Activities

Rossignol Surf Shop

SURFING | The shop rents boards and wet suits and conducts two-hour surfing lessons for adults and one-hour lessons for children ages 9–12 (reservations recommended) at Summerville Beach. ✉ *White Point Beach Resort, 75 White Point Rd., White Point* ✛ *10 km (6 miles) south of Liverpool* ☎ *902/350–6053* ⊕ *www.rossignolsurfshop.com* ⛱ *Board rentals from C$25; wet-suit rentals from C$25; adult lessons C$95.*

Kejimkujik National Park and Historic Site

67 km (42 miles) northwest of Liverpool; 45 km (28 miles) southeast of Annapolis Royal.

This inland woodsy area, within the UNESCO Southwest Nova Biosphere Reserve, attracts campers, canoeists, hikers, bird-watchers, and cyclists.

GETTING HERE AND AROUND

You'll need a car to get to the park, which is off Highway 8 between Liverpool and Annapolis Royal. Just south of Maitland Bridge, the Kejimkujik Main Parkway heads east into the park from the highway.

👁 Sights

★ Kejimkujik National Park

NATIONAL PARK | **FAMILY** | You'll have to veer inland to see this 381-square-km (147-square-mile) national park, which is about halfway between the Atlantic and Fundy coasts. The Mi'Kmaq used these gentle waterways for thousands of years, a fact made plain by the ancient petroglyphs carved into rocks along the shore. You can explore "Keji" on your own or take a guided interpretive hike—perhaps spying beavers, owls, loons, white-tailed deer, and other wildlife along the way. Guided paddles and children's programs are also available in summer, and leaf peepers can see the deciduous forests blaze with color in autumn. Designated a Dark Sky Preserve by the Royal Astronomical Society of Canada, the park conducts nighttime programs for stargazers. ✉ *Kejimkujik Main Pkwy., Maitland Bridge* ✛ *Off Hwy. 8* ☎ *902/682–2772 seasonal visitor center, 888/773–8888 information center* ⊕ *www.pc.gc.ca* ⛱ *C$6.*

🛏 Hotels

★ Mersey River Chalets and Nature Retreat

$$ | **RESORT** | Swimming, paddling, hiking, and bedtime bonfires fill the agenda at this 375-acre wilderness resort 5 km (3 miles) north of Kejimkujik National Park. **Pros:** cross-country skiing offered in winter; wide variety of activities available; excellent accessibility for wheelchair-bound guests. **Cons:** no on-site restaurant; minimum stays for chalets and log house; sometimes hosts weddings and large groups. $ *Rooms*

Spend a serene day amid pristine nature–keep an eye out for beavers and white-tailed deer–in Kejimkujik National Park.

from: C$135 ✉ *322 Mersey River Chalets Rd. E, Caledonia* ✛ *Off Hwy. 8, 44 km (27 miles) south of Annapolis Royal, 75 km (47 miles) north of Liverpool* ☎ *902/682–2443, 877/667–2583* ⊕ *www.mersey-riverchalets.ns.ca* 🛏 *9 chalets, 5 tipis, 4 lodge rooms, 1 log house* 🍽 *No Meals.*

🏃 Activities

Whynot Adventure Outfitters

KAYAKING | Also known as Keji Outfitters, this company inside Kejimkujik National Park rents bicycles, paddleboards, kayaks, canoes, and camping gear from mid-May through mid-October. Guided trips and shuttle services are also available. ✉ *Kejimkujik National Park, Kejimkujik Main Pkwy., Jakes Landing* ☎ *902/682–2282* ⊕ *www.whynotadventure.ca* 💲 *Kayak rentals from C$23 for 2 hrs; stand-up paddleboards from C$30 for 2 hrs.*

Shelburne

67 km (42 miles) southwest of Liverpool.

Shelburne, about two-thirds of the way down the Lighthouse Route, has a frozen-in-time appearance that many travelers love. It was settled after the American Revolution, when 10,000 Loyalists briefly made it one of the largest locales in North America—bigger than either Halifax or Montréal at the time. A smaller, temporary influx of Americans changed the face of Shelburne again in 1994, when film director Roland Joffe and crew arrived to shoot his version of *The Scarlet Letter*. The movie, starring Demi Moore, was an unequivocal mess, but the producers helped tidy up the town and raise awareness about its rich architectural heritage. Today's waterfront district looks much as it did when it was laid out in the 1780s, and many of the existing structures date from that period.

GETTING HERE AND AROUND

There is no public transportation to Shelburne. If you're driving from the Halifax direction, turn off Highway 103 at Exit 25 and follow Woodlawn Drive and then King Street. From the Yarmouth direction, you can take Exit 27 or Exit 26. Once in Shelburne, you'll find it pleasant to stroll around.

ESSENTIALS

VISITOR INFORMATION Shelburne Visitor Information Centre. ✉ *31 Dock St., Shelburne* ☎ *902/875–4547.*

Sights

★ Black Loyalist Heritage Site
HISTORY MUSEUM | When Shelburne's population exploded after the Revolutionary War, Black Loyalists were relegated to land 7 km (4½ miles) northwest of town. The community they created—Birchtown, named for the British general who oversaw their evacuation from New York—became the biggest free settlement of African Americans in the world. Birchtown's virtually forgotten story was told in Lawrence Hill's award-winning novel *The Book of Negroes*, adapted for a CBC TV miniseries in 2015 and filmed locally, and its founders are now honored at this site, which includes a national historic monument, a 1½-km (1-mile) interpretive trail, and the modern Heritage Centre that features a multimedia presentation, archaeological relics, and a genealogical research facility (some of the docents there are descendants of the Black Loyalists). ✉ *119 Old Birchtown Rd., Birchtown* ✥ *Off Hwy. 103, Exit 27* ☎ *902/875–1310* 🌐 *blackloyalist.novascotia.ca* 🎟 *Monument and trail free; museum C$10* ⏲ *Heritage Centre closed weekends mid-Oct.–late May.*

Shelburne Museum Complex
HISTORY MUSEUM | **FAMILY** | On Shelburne's historic waterfront, big-ticket attractions include three properties operated by the Shelburne Historical Society. The **Ross-Thomson House and Store** is reputedly the oldest surviving (and from the looks of it, best stocked) general store in North America, restored to its 1820s appearance. Shelburne once had a thriving boatbuilding industry turning out the traditional dories that were the mainstay of the fishing fleet. At the former waterfront workshop that houses the **J.C. Williams Dory Shop,** you can watch artisans craft new ones using old-fashioned techniques. Rounding out the trio, the **Shelburne County Museum** provides an overview of area history. There are tours of the historic district and a lively program of events and activities for all ages. ✉ *20 Dock St., Shelburne* ☎ *902/875–3219* 🌐 *www.shelburnemuseums.com* 🎟 *From C$5* ⏲ *Closed mid-Oct.–May.*

Restaurants

Boxing Rock Taproom
$$ | **CANADIAN** | The menu isn't huge at this funky taproom, but the charcuterie boards, sandwiches, and pizza—all of which showcase local produce—do go perfectly with this craft brewery's tasty beers. You can sit out on the spacious patio or inside, and there's even an axe-throwing studio on-site to make your evening a little more entertaining. **Known for:** offers private beer and food pairing experiences; occasional live music; being a fun, vibrant local hangout. [$] *Average main: C$12* ✉ *218 Water St., Shelburne* ☎ *902/494–9233* 🌐 *shop.boxingrock.ca.*

Hotels

Cooper's Inn
$$$ | **B&B/INN** | **FAMILY** | Built in 1784 and variously occupied by mariners, merchants, and the barrel maker (aka the cooper) for whom it is named, the inn is known for hospitality and comfortable and attractive guest rooms. **Pros:** breakfasts are cooked to order; lovely location with water-view garden; some rooms have massage chairs. **Cons:** staircase is

rather narrow; no air-conditioning; only breakfast is served on-site. $ *Rooms from: C$189* ✉ *36 Dock St., Shelburne* ☎ *902/875–4656, 800/688–2011* ⊕ *www.thecoopersinn.com* ⊗ *Closed mid-Oct.–Jun.* ⇌ *8 rooms* ⦿ *Free Breakfast.*

⚡ Activities

Candlebox Kayaking

KAYAKING | Half-day, full-day, and three-day kayaking tours are available, exploring around and beyond Shelburne Harbour, including a trip to McNutts Island with a hike to the lighthouse. Sea- and whitewater-kayak coaching is also offered. Prices range from C$55 to C$165 for half- to full-day tours; a three-day trip, including meals and camping equipment, costs C$595. Coaching starts at C$125 for a four-hour introduction to kayak rolling. ✉ *107 Water St., Shelburne* ☎ *902/637–7115* ⊕ *www.candleboxkayaking.com.*

Barrington and Cape Sable Island

48 km (35 miles) south of Shelburne.

Cape Sable Island—not to be confused with Sable Island, way out in the Atlantic—is a sleepy spot just off the beaten path, known for its contribution to the province's seafood harvest. You'll find colorful fishing boats afloat in Clark's Harbour. There are fine sandy beaches as well, one of which, Hawk Beach, offers excellent bird-watching and views of the 1861 Cape Sable Island Lighthouse.

GETTING HERE AND AROUND

Cape Sable Island is Nova Scotia's most southern point, located south of Shelburne and accessed via the short Cape Sable Island Causeway (NS–330 South). Barrington is on the mainland side of the causeway along Highway 3.

◉ Sights

Barrington Woolen Mill

FACTORY | Built in the 1800s, with a heyday around the turn of the 20th century, this historic water-driven mill provided the raw material for woolen clothing. It was eventually preserved as a museum in the late 1960s, and today visitors can view the interior and learn about the process. ✉ *2368 Hwy. 3, Barrington* ☎ *902/637–2185 Cape Sable Historical Society* ⊕ *woolenmill.novascotia.ca* ⊠ *Free* ⊗ *Closed Oct.–May.*

Old Meeting House Museum

HISTORY MUSEUM | The oldest meeting house in Canada, retaining its sturdy box pews and pulpit, was built by "Planters" from Cape Cod during the 1800s. Guided tours include stories of the early settlers and their lifestyle. ✉ *2408 Hwy. 3, Barrington* ☎ *902/637–2185* ⊕ *meetinghouse.novascotia.ca* ⊠ *Free* ⊗ *Closed Oct.–May.*

Seal Island Light Museum

LIGHTHOUSE | It may be a replica and only half the height of the original, but this 35-foot red-and-white lighthouse looks authentic enough, and the light on the top still carries out the original purpose. In addition, it contains a display of fascinating seafaring artifacts, including the Fresnel lens used between 1902 and 1978. The view from the top is worth the climb. ✉ *2422 Hwy. 3, Barrington* ☎ *902/637–2185* ⊕ *capesablehistoricalsociety.com* ⊠ *C$5* ⊗ *Closed mid-Sept.–mid-June.*

Western Counties Military Museum

MILITARY SIGHT | Dating from 1843, Barrington's old courthouse now houses this museum, with an impressive collection of military memorabilia ranging from 17th-century cannonballs to items from the two world wars and the Korean War. It includes uniforms, medals, and a large collection of photographs. Most evocative of all are the personal stories of local people who served. ✉ *2401 Hwy.*

3, Barrington ☎ 902/637–2185 ⊕ www.
capesablehistoricalsociety.com ⊘ Closed
Oct.–May.

Yarmouth

98 km (61 miles) west of Shelburne.

Yarmouth's status as a large port and its
proximity to New England accounted for
its early prosperity, and today the town's
shipping heritage is still reflected in its
fine harbor, marinas, and museums. The
ferry service from Maine makes this an
obvious destination for U.S. travelers, and
the handsome Victorian architecture and
a pleasantly old-fashioned main street
make it worth a visit. Since the Evangeline Trail and Lighthouse Trail converge
here, Yarmouth also allows easy access
to the Acadian villages to the north or the
Loyalist communities to the south.

GETTING HERE AND AROUND

If you're coming from or via Maine, the
high-speed CAT Bar Harbor–Yarmouth
ferry service operated by Bay Ferries
Limited (⊕ www.ferries.ca; check
website for schedules and prices), offers
a pleasant way to travel. Within Nova
Scotia, Mariner Shuttle Co links Halifax
to Yarmouth on Mon., Weds., and Fri.
departing Yarmouth at 7 am and Halifax
between 1–3 pm (depending on where
you want to be picked up). Fare each way
is C$105. If you're driving, Yarmouth is
at the eastern end of Highway 103 along
the South Shore and Highway 101 along
the Fundy coast. For getting around, a
new bus service follows a circular route
around the town for a flat rate of C$3 per
day or C$15 per week.

ESSENTIALS

**VISITOR INFORMATION Yarmouth
Visitor Information Centre.** ⊠ 228 Main
St., Yarmouth ☎ 902/742–5033 ⊕ www.
yarmouthandacadianshores.com.

◉ Sights

Art Gallery of Nova Scotia (Western Branch)

ART GALLERY | This is the gallery's satellite
location. As with the flagship in Halifax,
this one is housed in a heritage building
and has a broad mandate, yet it's at
its best when showcasing the works
of regional artists. The branch exhibits
art from the main gallery's permanent
collection and mounts temporary shows
of folk art and other disciplines. Family Sunday and children's workshops
occasionally take place. If you plan to
visit both branches, keep your receipt—it
will give you a reduction on the second
admission fee. ⊠ 341 Main St., Yarmouth
☎ 902/749–2248 ⊕ www.artgalleryofno-
vascotia.ca ☒ C$6.

Cape Forchu Lighthouse

LIGHTHOUSE | It isn't the South Shore's
most photogenic lighthouse—the one
at Peggy's Cove wins that award—but
this one scores points for its dramatic
vistas and the dearth of other cam-
era-clutching tourists. Erected in 1962
on the site of an earlier lighthouse, the
concrete structure rises 75 feet above
the entrance to Yarmouth Harbour. The
adjacent keeper's quarters house a small
museum with interactive exhibits, a
fully equipped light-keeper's workshop,
a restaurant serving seafood and local
craft brews, and a gift shop. ⊠ 1856
Cape Forchu Rd., off Hwy. 304, Cape
Forchu ☎ 902/740–1680 ⊕ capeforchu.
com ☒ CA$6.75 to climb the lighthouse
⊘ Closed Oct. to May.

Firefighters' Museum of Nova Scotia

HISTORY MUSEUM | FAMILY | A good rainy-
day destination, this museum recounts
the history of firefighting in the province
through photographs, uniforms, and
other artifacts, including vintage hose
wagons, ladder trucks, and an 1863
Amoskeag Steamer. Kids will especially
enjoy this spot—after checking out the
toy engines, they can don a fire helmet
and take the wheel of a 1933 Bickle

Pumper. ✉ *451 Main St., Yarmouth* ☎ *902/742–5525* 🌐 *firefightersmuseum.novascotia.ca* 🎟 *C$5.*

Yarmouth County Museum & Archives
HISTORY MUSEUM | One of the largest collections of ship paintings in Canada resides here, along with exhibits of household items, musical instruments (including rare mechanical pianos and music boxes), and other items that richly evoke centuries past. There's even a Norse runic stone dating back to Viking transatlantic explorations around AD 1000. The museum has a preservation wing and an archival research area, where local history and genealogy are documented. Next door is the **Pelton-Fuller House,** summer home of the original Fuller Brush Man, which is maintained and furnished much as the family left it. The museum offers guided tours of a third building in high season: the **Killam Brothers Shipping Office**. Located at 90 Water Street, it recalls a long-standing family business that was established here in 1788. ✉ *22 Collins St., Yarmouth* ☎ *902/742–5539* 🌐 *yarmouthcountymuseum.ca* 🎟 *C$5* 🕒 *Closed Sun. June–Sept. Closed Sun. and Mon. Oct.–June.*

🍴 Restaurants

Gaia Global Kitchen
$$ | **INTERNATIONAL** | This funky spot that started out as a food truck offers an eclectic and tasty menu that runs from jerk chicken bowls to butter chicken poutine to fish-and-chips. The dining room doubles as a gallery space, adding to the vibrant atmosphere. **Known for:** tasty banh mi sandwiches; vegan, vegetarian and gluten-free options; fun and friendly staff. [$] *Average main: C$18* ✉ *222 Main St., Yarmouth* ☎ *902/881–2627* 🌐 *gaiaglobalkitchen.com* 🕒 *Sun. and Mon.*

Rudder's Seafood Restaurant and Brew Pub
$$ | **SEAFOOD** | As its name implies, this hopping waterfront spot serves the expected fish dishes along with pub grub like steak with seafood and fries and Acadian rappie pie, all of which can be washed down with ales handcrafted on-site. Seating is inside a converted warehouse supported by 18th-century beams or, in fine weather, at picnic tables on the wraparound deck. **Known for:** waterfront location in the heart of downtown; beer brewed on the premises; traditional pub menu with lots of choices. [$] *Average main: C$20* ✉ *96 Water St., Yarmouth* ☎ *902/742–7311* 🌐 *ruddersbrewpub.com.*

☕ Coffee and Quick Bites

Edna's Bakeries Ltd.
$ | **BAKERY** | This delightfully old-fashioned bakery supplies traditional Maritimes brown bread to all the restaurants in the area and is the best spot to grab sticky pecan buns, ginger snaps, date squares, and other retro baked goods. **Known for:** treats just like Grandma used to make; amazing cheese loaf; local flavor. [$] *Average main: C$4* ✉ *3151 Evangeline Trail, Yarmouth* ☎ *902/649–2080* 💳 *No credit cards* 🕒 *Closed Sun.* ☞ *Cash only.*

Honey Bee Deli and Ice Cream Parlor
$ | **ASIAN** | Initially known for having the best ice cream around, this fun spot expanded into serving excellent sushi and has become an appealing option for lunch or dinner as well as dessert. **Known for:** wide selection of bubble teas; decadent ice cream cupcakes; perfect Korean fried chicken. [$] *Average main: C$8* ✉ *409 Nova Scotia Trunk 1, Yarmouth* ☎ *902/748–0900* 🌐 *honeybeesorders.ca* 💳 *No credit cards* 🕒 *Closed Mon.*

JoAnne's Quick-n-Tasty
$ | **CANADIAN** | Devotees swear by the hot lobster sandwich at this retro diner—indeed, Haligonians have been known to make the three-hour trek just to dine on the creamed crustacean concoction that was supposedly invented here. Laminated tables, vinyl banquettes, and bright

lights greet you, and it all looks much as it did circa 1960. **Known for:** early closing time of 7 pm; retro lunchtime spot; excellent lobster and other seafood. $ *Average main: C$12* ✉ *490 Hwy. 1, 4 km (2½ miles) northeast of Yarmouth, Dayton* ☎ *902/742–6606* ◯ *Closed Dec.–Feb.*

Perky Owl Coffee

$ | **CAFÉ** | This locals' favorite is known for superb espresso drinks and baked goods, as well as a great selection of soups, sandwiches, and hot lunch entrées. There are a number of musical instruments in the café that guests are encouraged to pick up and play. **Known for:** buttermilk-biscuit breakfast sandwiches; best lattes for miles around; friendly and welcoming atmosphere. $ *Average main: C$8* ✉ *255 Main St., Yarmouth* ☎ *902/881–2140* ⊕ *perkyowlcoffee.ca* ◯ *Closed Sun.*

🛏 Hotels

Lakelawn B and B Motel

$$ | **B&B/INN** | A very distinctive former mansion is at the heart of this property, and contains four bed-and-breakfast rooms, with additional motel-style rooms in two attached wings. **Pros:** friendly bilingual owner; great for ferry passengers; rates almost halved in off- season. **Cons:** picnic area is also the smoking area; some areas in need of an update; some bathrooms have a shower but no tub. $ *Rooms from: C$139* ✉ *641 Main St., Yarmouth* ☎ *902/742–3588* ⊕ *www. lakelawnmotel.com* ⤹ *25 rooms* ⧫⦿⧫ *Free Breakfast.*

★ Trout Point Lodge

$$$$ | **RESORT** | A large and spectacular log building houses this remarkable wilderness eco-resort, where guests can get away from it all without sacrificing luxury, excellent food, or top-notch amenities. **Pros:** large and luxurious rooms; environmentally sound without sacrificing comfort and amenities; wood-heated hot tub and sauna beside the river. **Cons:** Wi-Fi

can be patchy; no cell phone coverage; very long and bumpy access via dirt road. $ *Rooms from: C$550* ✉ *189 Trout Point Rd., East Kemptville* ⊕ *Off East Branch Rd. and Hwy. 203, 40 km (25 miles) northeast of Yarmouth* ☎ *902/761–2142* ⊕ *www.troutpoint.com* ⤹ *13 suites* ⧫⦿⧫ *No Meals* ☞ *No children under 14.*

🛍 Shopping

Hands On Crafts

CRAFTS | Local artisans make all the cool jewelry, knitwear, birch-bark soap, and other items sold at this downtown co-op. ✉ *314 Main St., Yarmouth* ☎ *902/742–3515* ⊕ *facebook.com/HandsOnCrafts.*

Yarmouth Farmers' Community Market

MARKET | This Saturday morning market is the perfect spot to pick up local produce and handicrafts, as well as tasty treats that you can eat out by the waterfront. ✉ *15 Hawthorne St., Yarmouth* ⊕ *www. yarmouthfarmersmarketns.com.*

The Yarmouth Wool Shoppe

CRAFTS | For a gift or something to keep you warm on chilly Nova Scotian evenings, this local institution, open since 1883, has you covered. Much of the inventory consists of high-end imported items from England, Ireland, and Scotland, including duffel coats, mohair throws, cashmere shawls and sweaters, Harris tweed caps, Guernsey fisherman-knit sweaters, and tartan robes. The Nova Scotia Duck Tolling Retriever T-shirts are another local find. If you'd rather create your own garment, they also have knitting yarns. ✉ *352 Main St., Yarmouth* ☎ *902/742–2255.*

Pointe de l'Église (Church Point)

70 km (43 miles) north of Yarmouth.

As small as they are, you still can't miss the communities that collectively make up the Acadian Shore. Each one on this stretch, beginning roughly in Beaver River and ending in St. Bernard, seems to have a surplus of Stella Maris flags, a disproportionately large Catholic church, and a French-speaking populace with an abiding passion for *rappie* pie, a hearty chicken stew with shredded potatoes. Church Point, called Pointe de l'Église by Francophones, tops the rest on all three counts.

GETTING HERE AND AROUND
There is no public transportation to Pointe de l'Église. By car, it's on Highway 1, the Evangeline Trail, which follows the coast parallel to Highway 101. Coming from the west, take Exit 29 onto Little Brook Road, then go north on the Evangeline; from the east, take Exit 28 onto the Evangeline at St. Bernard.

◉ Sights

Church Point Lighthouse and Le Petit Bois
LIGHTHOUSE | A faithful replica of the former lighthouse and keeper's quarters not only offers incredible views and information panels, it's also staffed by a marine biology interpreter, who is a mine of information about the ecology of the offshore waters and the history of the lighthouse. The local university carries out bird-banding, tracking, and nesting projects here. Informative tours along the beach and guided nighttime walks are also available (the latter booked through the Visitor Information Centre). Encircling the lighthouse and its hinterland, Le Petit Bois trail network threads through woodland, marshland, and along coastal paths. ⊠ *150 Lighthouse Rd., Pointe de l'Église* ☎ *902/769–2345* ⊕ *www.lepetitbois.ca* ⊙ *Closed Sept.–June.*

Rendez-vous de la Baie
OTHER ATTRACTION | An arts and cultural complex that tries to be all things to all people—and succeeds—the Rendez-vous de la Baie serves locals, tourists, and students. Housed in a

contemporary structure on the Université Sainte-Anne campus, the center has as its highlight the **Acadian Interpretive Centre and Museum,** whose exhibits provide an evocative overview of Acadian culture and history. The Rendez-vous complex also includes an art gallery that shows contemporary works, a theater for live and media presentations, an Internet café that hosts events, and a visitor information center. The gift shop at the interpretive center carries an excellent selection of Acadian music. ⊠ *Université Sainte-Anne, 23 Lighthouse Rd., Unit 1* ☎ *902/769–2345* ⊕ *rendezvousdelabaie.ca* ⊙ *Closed Sat and Sun. Closed Nov.–Apr.*

St. Mary's Church (Église Ste-Marie)
CHURCH | The *église* for which this village is named stands proudly on the main road overshadowing everything around it. That's hardly surprising given that it is the largest wooden church in North America. Completed in 1905, St. Mary's is 190 feet long by 185 feet high, and the steeple, which requires 40 tons of rock ballast to keep it steady when ocean winds blow, can be seen for miles. The church is a registered museum with a stunning interior, two exhibit rooms housing a collection of vestments, and a souvenir shop that sells religious articles. Bilingual guides give tours regularly in summer and off-season by appointment. ⊠ *1713 Hwy. 1* ☎ *902/769–2832* ⊕ *www.museeeglisesaintemariemuseum.ca* ☒ *C$2 recommended donation* ⊙ *Closed Nov.–mid-May.*

⑪ Restaurants

★ La Cuisine Robicheau
$$ | SEAFOOD | Firmly established as the best place to eat along this stretch of the coast, La Cuisine Robicheau overlooks the ocean and specializes in seafood and Acadian cuisine. The excellent *pâté à la râpure* (rappie pie) is usually the first thing to sell out, so come early. **Known for:** BYO wine policy; early closing at 7

pm; intimate dining experience, with five individually styled areas. [$] *Average main: C$20* ✉ *9651 Hwy. 1* ☎ *902/769–2121* 🌐 *www.lacuisinerobicheau.ca* 🕓 *Closed Mon. and Tues.*

Hotels

Havre du Capitaine
$ | **HOTEL** | Within easy reach of both Pointe de l'Église and Yarmouth, this low-rise lodging along the Evangeline Trail has sea views and modern, good-size rooms. **Pros:** friendly service; nice lodgelike feel to the lounge area; lovely views. **Cons:** no air-conditioning; only three rooms have Jacuzzis; breakfast a little disappointing. [$] *Rooms from: C$75* ✉ *9118 Hwy. 1, Meteghan* ☎ *902/769–2001* 🌐 *www.havreducapitaine.ca* 🛏 *20 rooms* 🍴 *Free Breakfast.*

Digby

35 km (22 miles) northeast of Pointe de l'Église/Church Point.

Digby is underappreciated: people tend to race to or from the ferry connecting it with Saint John, New Brunswick. Yet there is quite a bit to the town, including a rich history that dates to the 1783 arrival of Loyalists and an appealing waterfront. Then, of course, there are the legendary Digby scallops. The world's largest in-shore scallop fleet docks in the harbor, and the plump, sweet "fruits of the sea" unloaded here are deemed to be delicacies everywhere. Come, if you can, for the Digby Scallop Days festival in early August. There are other fish in the sea though, and while walking along the waterfront, you can buy ultrafresh halibut, cod, and lobster—some merchants will even cook your purchase for you right on the spot. You can also sample Digby chicks (aka salty smoked herring) in local pubs or buy them from fish markets.

GETTING HERE AND AROUND

Bay Ferries Ltd. sails the *Fundy Rose* between Saint John, New Brunswick, and Digby year-round. There is at least one round-trip per day—two per day mid-May to mid-October and in December—and the crossing takes about two hours 15 minutes. If you are already in Nova Scotia, you'll need to drive here on Highway 1, the Evangeline Trail, or Highway 101 (which are the same road as you approach Digby). Take Exit 26. The town itself is easily explored on foot.

ESSENTIALS

VISITOR INFORMATION Digby Tourist Bureau. ✉ *110 Montague Row, Digby* ☎ *888/463–4429, 902/245–5714.*

Sights

Admiral Digby Museum
HISTORY MUSEUM | The town, county, and this museum are named for Britain's Rear Admiral Robert Digby, who during the American Revolution helped evacuate Loyalists to Nova Scotia following the British surrender of New York City. You can learn a little bit about the admiral and a fair amount about Digby County history viewing the artifacts, paintings, and maps displayed here. ✉ *95 Montague Row, Digby* ☎ *902/245–6322* 🌐 *admiraldigbymuseum.ca* 🎟 *By donation* 🕓 *Closed Sun.*

Restaurants

Fundy Restaurant
$$$ | **SEAFOOD** | **FAMILY** | A waterfront location with stunning harbor views and great seafood make this a prime spot in Digby to sample the world-famous local scallops as well as lobster, salmon, Bay of Fundy halibut, and a few nonseafood dishes for good measure. The lunch menu is lighter and includes chowder, sandwiches, fish-and-chips, and a crispy "seaburger," plus a kids' menu with plenty of choices. **Known for:** good place to watch the Fundy tide come in or go out;

seafood samplers; extensive gluten-free menu. [$] *Average main: C$22* ✉ *34 Water St., Digby* ☎ *902/245–4950* 🌐 *www.fundyrestaurant.com.*

★ **Sydney Street Pub and Café**

$$$ | **SEAFOOD** | **FAMILY** | You don't have to dine on the waterfront in Digby to enjoy great seafood and good views, and this friendly pub offers both. Just uphill from the main street, its two-story deck has great sea views, and the menu mostly features local seafood that couldn't be any fresher. There are other choices, too, including vegetarian and vegan options, and any dish can be downsized for children. **Known for:** local beer, coffee, and live music; expertly cooked local scallops; beautifully restored historic building. [$] *Average main: C$23* ✉ *14 Sydney St., Digby* ☎ *902/245–1066* 🌐 *www.sydneystreetpub.ca* 🕒 *Closed Sun.–Tues.*

🛏 Hotels

Admiral Digby Inn

$$ | **B&B/INN** | A few minutes' drive from the ferry terminal, this friendly inn has a variety of accommodations, all with a water view. **Pros:** nice amenities; very convenient for the ferry; panoramic sea views. **Cons:** there are better restaurants in the town; not within walking distance of the town; beds are very firm. [$] *Rooms from: C$129* ✉ *441 Shore Rd.* ☎ *902/905–6331* 🌐 *www.digbyhotels.com* 🔑 *47 rooms* 🍴 *No Meals.*

Digby Pines Golf Resort and Spa

$$$ | **RESORT** | **FAMILY** | Complete with walking trails, lavish gardens, and Annapolis Basin views, this casually elegant 300-acre property offers myriad comforts. **Pros:** beautiful grounds; kids under five eat free; no charge for Digby shuttle service. **Cons:** rooms are in need of an update; some rooms and bathrooms are small; nearest beach is small, rocky, and across the road. [$] *Rooms from: C$175* ✉ *103 Shore Rd., Digby* ☎ *800/667–4637* 🌐 *www.digbypines.ca* 🕒 *Closed mid-Oct.–May* 🔑 *84 rooms, 6 suites, 31 cottages* 🍴 *No Meals.*

Long Island and Brier Island

About 46 km (40 miles) southwest of Digby.

You don't just stumble across these islands—reaching them requires a commitment. It's well worth the effort because Long Island and Brier Island are surrounded by water rich in plankton, which attracts a variety of whales along with harbor porpoises, seals, and abundant seabirds. Bring your binoculars.

GETTING HERE AND AROUND

First, follow Highway 217 down to the end of Digby Neck, a narrow peninsula separating St. Mary's Bay and the Bay of Fundy, to the hamlet of East Ferry. From there hop a five-minute ferry for Tiverton, Long Island. If you're going on to Brier Island, take a second, eight-minute ferry ride onward from Freeport, Long Island, to Westport. Brier Island Ferry links the two islands. Ferries must scuttle sideways to fight the ferocious Fundy tidal streams coursing through the narrow gaps. They operate hourly, year-round, at a cost of C$7 for each ferry (cash only) for the round-trip for car and passengers.

🛏 Hotels

Brier Island Lodge and Restaurant

$$ | **HOTEL** | Atop a bluff at Nova Scotia's most westerly point, this three-building complex commands a panoramic view of the Bay of Fundy. **Pros:** excellent seafood restaurant; discounts on whale-watching and nature tours; on-site gift shop. **Cons:** Wi-Fi not always reliable; main lodge rooms lack ocean views; motel-quality rooms. [$] *Rooms from: C$149* ✉ *557 Water St., Westport* ☎ *902/839–2300,*

800/662–8355 ⊕ www.brierisland.com
⊘ Closed Nov.–Apr. ⌨ 38 rooms.

🏃 Activities

★ Brier Island Whale and Seabird Cruises

WILDLIFE-WATCHING | FAMILY | Of several
operators of seasonal boat tours, this
is best. On thrice-daily trips, from early
June until mid-October, you travel out
of Westport on the MV *Mega Nova,*
with researchers who collect data for
international organizations. A portion of
the fare funds further research. The same
company also offers adrenaline-fueled
Zodiac excursions five times daily from
mid-May through mid-October. ✉ 223
Water St., Westport ☎ 902/839–2995
⊕ www.brierislandwhalewatch.com
🖃 Tours from C$50.

Mariner Cruises Whale & Seabird Tours

RAFTING | FAMILY | Narration by an onboard
naturalist makes this operator's cruises
(from 2½ to 4½ hours) a solid choice.
Boats depart Westport daily from mid-
June to mid-October. ✉ 325 Water St.,
Westport ☎ 902/839–2346, 800/239–
2189 ⊕ www.novascotiawhalewatching.
ca 🖃 C$49.

Ocean Explorations Whale Cruises

WILDLIFE-WATCHING | FAMILY | Tom Good-
win, a marine and wildlife biologist, con-
ducts well-regarded trips in fast-paced,
open-top Zodiacs to view whales and
other marine life. ✉ Hwy. 217, opposite
old ferry wharf, Tiverton ☎ 902/839–2417,
877/654–2341 ⊕ www.oceanexplora-
tions.ca 🖃 C$85.

Annapolis Royal

37 km (23 miles) northeast of Digby.

Annapolis Royal's history spans nearly
four centuries, and the town's bucolic
appearance today belies its turbulent
past. One of Canada's oldest settlements, it was founded by the French in
1605, destroyed by the British in 1613,
rebuilt by the French as the main town
of Acadia, and then fought over for the
better part of a century. Finally, in 1710,
New England colonists claimed the town
and renamed it in honor of Queen Anne.
There are approximately 150 historic
sites and heritage buildings here, including the privately owned DeGannes-Cosby
House, the oldest wooden house in
Canada (built in 1708), which happens to
sit on St. George, Canada's oldest street.

As if it didn't have enough history on its
own, Annapolis Royal is also the ideal
starting point for excursions to Port Royal, the place where European settlement
of Canada began.

GETTING HERE AND AROUND

There is no public transportation to
Annapolis Royal. To drive here, take the
Evangeline Trail or Highway 101 to Exit
22. If you are traveling from the east,
Highway 201 is also an option.

ESSENTIALS

**VISITOR INFORMATION Annapolis Royal
Visitor Information Centre.** ✉ Annapolis
Tidal Power Plant, 236 Prince Albert
Rd., Annapolis Royal ☎ 902/532–5454
⊕ www.annapolisroyal.com.

👁 Sights

Annapolis Royal Farmers' and Traders' Market

MARKET | On Saturday morning from 8
to 1 mid-May through mid-October and
also on Wednesday from 10 to 2 in July
and August, the best place in Annapolis
Royal to stock up on picnic supplies is
the farmers' market, which sets up on
lower St. George Street across from the
King's Theatre. Expect artisanal bread,
cured meats, homemade sweets, and
preserves, plus fresh Annapolis Valley
produce. Local artisans attend, too, and
there's live entertainment. Most vendors
accept cash only. ✉ Lower St. George
St., Annapolis Royal ⊕ www.annapolis-
royalfarmersmarket.com.

Step back in time during a visit to Port Royal National Historic Site, a replica of a 1605 French trading post.

Annapolis Royal Historic Gardens

GARDEN | Like everything else in this town, the plants here are a blast from the past—17 heritage-theme acres represent different eras and include a glorious Victorian garden, a knot garden, a typical Acadian house garden, and a 2,000-bush rose collection with about 250 varieties. The main season is May through October, but the gardens are accessible year-round, although they are not maintained November through April. ⊠ 441 St. George St., Annapolis Royal ☎ 902/532–7018 ⊕ www.historicgardens. com ⊑ C$15 ⊗ Closed Oct. to May.

Fort Anne National Historic Site

MILITARY SIGHT | Gazing over the grassy knolls, it's hard to believe that this fort qualifies as the "most attacked spot in Canadian history" or that those knolls are actually nearly 400-year-old earthwork ramparts built up, in part, with rubble and blood. First fortified in 1629, the site preserves what is left of the fourth military edifice to be erected here, an early-18th-century gunpowder magazine

and officers' quarters. The latter now houses a small museum, and anyone who believes a picture is worth 1,000 words should be sure to see the massive Heritage Tapestry displayed inside. Its four meticulously detailed panels depict four centuries of local history and as many local cultures. Special events at the fort include reenactments and Mi'Kmaq cultural presentations. ⊠ 323 St. George St., Annapolis Royal ☎ 902/532–2397 May–Oct., 902/532–2321 Oct.–May ⊕ pc. gc.ca/en/lhn-nhs/ns/fortanne ⊑ C$4 ⊗ Closed early Oct.–mid-May.

Historical Association of Annapolis Royal

HISTORIC DISTRICT | Because Annapolis Royal flip-flopped between the French and English so many times, the past here is a complicated affair, but the members of the historical association are happy to walk you through it. They've developed a series of high-season strolls led by guides dressed in typical 18th-century fashion. This is an entertaining way to learn more about the historic significance and cultural heritage of the region. Options include daytime tours of the National Historic District and sites associated with the Acadian Experience. The wildly popular Candlelight Graveyard Tour of Canada's oldest English cemetery (at Fort Anne) takes place at 9:30 pm several times a week in June and every night from July through October. Reservations for tours aren't necessary, but call or check the website for times. The association has put together a self-guided walk pamphlet for visitors who'd rather wander independently. ✉ *Annapolis Royal* ☎ *902/532–3034* 🌐 *www.tourannapolisroyal.com* 🎟 *C$15* 🕒 *Closed mid-Oct.–June.*

★ Port Royal National Historic Site
HISTORIC SIGHT | **FAMILY** | Downriver from Annapolis Royal is this reconstruction of Sieur de Monts and Samuel de Champlain's fur-trading post. The French set up shop here in 1605—two years before the English established Jamestown—making this the first permanent European settlement north of Florida. Port Royal also set other New World records, claiming the first tended crops, the first staged play, the first social club, and the first water mill. Unfortunately, it didn't have the first fire department: the original fortress burned down within a decade. At this suitably weathered replica, which is ringed by a log palisade, you're free to poke around the forge, inspect the trading post, pull up a chair at the dining table, or simply watch costumed interpreters perform traditional tasks in the courtyard. The heritage of the Mi'Kmaq people, who assisted the early settlers, can be explored in a wigwam. ✉ *Annapolis Royal* ✣ *Hwy. 1 to Granville Ferry, then left 10½ km (6½ miles), following signs for Port Royal* ☎ *902/532–2898 May–Oct., 902/532–2321 Oct.–May* 🌐 *pc.gc.ca/en/lhn-nhs/ns/portroyal* 🎟 *C$4* 🕒 *Closed early Oct.–mid-May.*

🍴 Restaurants

Bistro East
$$$ | **INTERNATIONAL** | Offering seafood, steaks, pasta and pizza, the food at this dinner-only spot is consistent and delicious, with many ingredients locally sourced. The atmosphere is warm and friendly, and the service is top-notch. **Known for:** pastas freshly made in-house; chocolate mousse topped with whipped cream; excellent fresh seafood dishes. [$] *Average main: C$24* ✉ *274 St. George St., Annapolis Royal* ☎ *902/532–7992* 🌐 *bistroeast.com* 🕒 *Closed Mon. and Tues. No lunch.*

Sachsen Cafe & Restaurant
$$ | **GERMAN** | This authentic German bakery and café is much loved for its delicious strudels, cookies, and other European-style baked goods. It's also a great spot for lunch or early dinner of bratwurst, schnitzel, and other German specialties (or just a pretzel or sandwich if you're looking for something lighter). **Known for:** friendly, welcoming owners; closes early (6 pm, 6:45 pm on Sat.); mouthwatering schnitzel sandwich. [$] *Average main: C$17* ✉ *358 St. George St., Annapolis Royal* ☎ *902/532–1990* 🌐 *germanbakery.ca.*

🛏 Hotels

The Bailey House
$$ | **B&B/INN** | This immaculately restored Georgian home on North America's oldest streetscape has a great location on the waterfront and retains many quirky original features. **Pros:** lovely garden; only B&B in town on the water; really good breakfasts. **Cons:** no Wi-Fi in the coach house; some strict rules; no air-conditioning. [$] *Rooms from: C$170* ✉ *150 St. George St., Annapolis Royal* ☎ *902/532–1285* 🌐 *www.baileyhouse.ca* 🛏 *5 rooms* 🍽 *Free Breakfast.*

Queen Anne Inn

$$$ | **B&B/INN** | A beautiful Victorian building that's rimmed with gardens may not be out of the ordinary in Annapolis Royal, but what really distinguishes this inn is the consistent quality of the guest rooms, all generously proportioned and handsomely decorated. **Pros:** helpful hosts; family-friendly; in-room extras include bathrobes. **Cons:** a 10-minute walk from the center of town; closed off-season; lots of stairs. [$] *Rooms from: C$179* ✉ *494 St. George St., Annapolis Royal* ☎ *902/532–7850, 877/536–0403* 🌐 *www.queenanneinn.ns.ca* 🕐 *Closed Nov.–Mar.* 🛏 *12 rooms* 🍴 *Free Breakfast.*

Performing Arts

King's Theatre

CONCERTS | Drama, concerts, comedy, and independent films are among the offerings at this intimate but up-to-date venue that opened in 1921 as a movie house. ✉ *209 St. George St., Annapolis Royal* ☎ *902/532–7704* 🌐 *www.kingstheatre.ca.*

Shopping

Lucky Rabbit & Co

CRAFTS | This collection of artisans in a heritage home showcases ceramic works, leather goods, jewelry, and other fine locally made crafts. ✉ *15 Church St., Annapolis Royal* ☎ *902/532–0928* 🌐 *luckyrabbitandco.com.*

The Woven Basket Boutique

CRAFTS | This bright and modern store stocks beautiful clothing, purses, and hats, but also carries locally made handicrafts, apparel, jewelry, and carefully curated gift items. ✉ *258 St. George St., Annapolis Royal* 🌐 *thewovenbasketboutique.square.site.*

Wolfville

114 km (71 miles) east of Annapolis Royal.

Settled in the 1760s by New Englanders, Wolfville is a fetching college town with ornate Victorian homes (some of which have been converted into B&Bs), a lively arts scene, and several fine restaurants. Established in 1838, Acadia University and its handsomely groomed hillside campus dominate the town, and the student population rivals that of the residents. The natural setting is impressive, too: after all, the fields here are fertile enough to support a thriving wine industry. That's due partly to a mild microclimate and partly to an elaborate system of dikes built by the Acadians in the early 1700s to reclaim arable land from the unusually high tides. They can still be viewed along many of the area's back roads. The original Acadians didn't get to enjoy the fruits of their labor, but their legacy lives on at nearby Grand-Pré.

GETTING HERE AND AROUND

Maritime Bus offers daily service on its Halifax–Kentville route, with bus stops at Acadia University (Horton Avenue) and the Mud Creek Mini Mart (Skyway Avenue). If you're driving, the Evangeline Trail runs right through town, and Highway 101 runs along the southern edge—take Exit 10 or Exit 11.

ESSENTIALS

VISITOR INFORMATION Wolfville Visitor Information Centre. ✉ *11 Willow Ave., Wolfville* ☎ *902/542–7000, 877/999–7117* 🌐 *www.wolfville.ca.*

TOURS

Magic Winery Bus

SPECIAL-INTEREST TOURS | For those driving around the region, here is a perfect solution for visiting some of Nova Scotia's finest wineries with the freedom to enjoy tastings along the way. This London-style double-decker bus offers a hop-on, hop-off service to five of the best vineyards

in the Wolfville area, with about one hour to enjoy all that's on offer before the bus comes around again to take you to the next. The bus departs from Wolfville Visitor Information Centre, and the price includes transportation, a professional guide, and a glass of wine at each winery. ⊠ *Wolfville Visitor Information Centre, 11 Willow Ave., Wolfville* ⊕ *www. magicwinerybus.ca* ☏ *C$60.*

◉ Sights

Acadia University Art Gallery
ART GALLERY | Temporary exhibitions here are devoted to established and up-and-coming artists, and there's a permanent collection strong on maritime and Inuit art, works on paper, and works by women artists. It amounts to more than 3,000 works, though not all are on display. ⊠ *Beveridge Arts Centre, 10 Highland Ave. at Main St., Wolfville* ☎ *902/585–1373* ⊕ *gallery.acadiau.ca* ☏ *Free* ⊗ *Closed Mon.*

★ Domaine de Grand Pré
WINERY | With award-winning vintages and sigh-inducing Fundy views, a stop at Domaine de Grand Pré is doubly pleasing. Vineyard tours and tastings are offered twice daily, at 11 am and 4 pm; reservations are not required (but call ahead to confirm they are happening on any given day). They take about 45 minutes, but you'll likely want to linger on the picturesque 10-acre property, so plan to have a meal at Le Caveau Restaurant or sip a glass of wine under the pergola. Live Music under the Vines events take place on certain evenings in July and August, weather permitting, and other events are detailed on the website. ⊠ *11611 Hwy. 1, Wolfville* ✛ *3 km (2 miles) east of Wolfville* ☎ *902/542–1753, 866/479–4637* ⊕ *grandprewines.ns.ca* ⊗ *No tours mid-Oct.–mid-May.*

Grand Pré National Historic Site
HISTORIC SIGHT | Added to UNESCO's list of World Heritage Sites in 2012, this site commemorates the expulsion of the Acadians by the British in 1755. The tragic story is retold at the visitor center through artifacts and an innovative multimedia presentation that depicts *Le Grand Dérangement* from both a civilian and military perspective. The latter is shown in a wraparound theater that's modeled on a ship's interior. A bronze statue of Evangeline, the title character of Longfellow's tear-jerking epic poem, stands outside a memorial stone church that contains Acadian genealogical records. The manicured grounds have a garden, apple orchards, a duck pond, and, appropriately enough, French weeping willows. ⊠ *2205 Grand Pré Rd., Grand Pré* ✛ *Off Hwy. 1 (Evangeline Trail), 5 km (3 miles) east of Wolfville* ☎ *902/542–3631* ⊕ *experiencegrandpre.ca* ☏ *C$8* ⊗ *Closed early Oct.–mid-May* ⚷ *pc.gc.ca/en/lhn-nhs/ns/ grandpre.*

Hall's Harbour
TOWN | You'll see one of the best natural harbors on the upper Bay of Fundy and some of the highest tides *anywhere* in Hall's Harbour, a small community about 30 km (18 miles) northwest of Wolfville via Kentville and Highway 359. Go for a walk on a gravel beach bordered by cliffs, try sea kayaking, or seek out the artisans whose studios open here during summer months. The small Red Fish House Museum, with local artifacts, is open in summer. ☎ *902/678–7001* ⊕ *www. hallsharbour.org.*

Harriet Irving Botanical Gardens
GARDEN | These 6-acre gardens are devoted mainly to indigenous plants from the Acadian Forest Region. Nine native habitats are displayed, and there's also a medicinal and food garden, a beautiful walled garden, and a conservatory. ⊠ *32 University Ave., Wolfville* ✛ *Entry through K.C. Irving Environmental Science Centre* ☎ *902/585–5242* ⊕ *botanicalgardens. acadiau.ca* ☏ *Free.*

Robie Tufts Nature Centre

NATURE SIGHT | Many Wolfvillians will tell you that the best show in town is watching swifts—aerobatic birds that fly in spectacular formation—descend on the Tufts Centre's oversized chimney at dusk on summer evenings. The venue is named in honor of the late ornithologist, author, and longtime resident who published *Birds of Nova Scotia* in 1961. The illustrated tome is still considered the bible for birders in the province, and Tufts had lots of material to work with because Nova Scotia, being located on the Atlantic flyway, is an important staging point for migratory species. Birders can tick several off their "must-see" list without straying too far from Wolfville. Each summer as many as half a million sandpipers and plovers flock to Evangeline Beach near Grand Pré to gorge on the Minas Basin's nutrient-rich mudflats before continuing nonstop to South America. Winter, meanwhile, brings hundreds of regal bald eagles to Sheffield Mills, northeast of Kentville. ⊠ *117 Front St., Wolfville* ⊕ *www.wolfville.ca/robie-tufts-nature-centre*.

🍴 Restaurants

★ Church Brewing

$$ | **CANADIAN** | Housed in a converted stone church complete with stained glass windows, Church Brewing produces tasty beers and has a fabulous menu of upscale pub grub with a farm-to-table focus. There's a huge patio out front that overlooks the hustle and bustle of Main Street, and there's often live music in the evenings and on the weekends. **Known for:** reservations recommended in the summer; fun and friendly atmosphere; Church Burger. Ⓢ *Average main: C$16* ⊠ *329 Main St., Wolfville* ☎ *902/542–2337* ⊕ *churchbrewing.ca*.

Hall's Harbour Lobster Pound & Restaurant

$$ | **SEAFOOD** | If you're in the neighborhood during lobster season, this site is well worth a visit. It's one of the largest lobster holding facilities in Canada, storing live lobsters in temperature-controlled pounds until they can be packed and shipped to international destinations. **Known for:** waterfront dining room; pick your own lobster; live lobsters for sale. Ⓢ *Average main: C$20* ⊠ *1157 W. Halls Harbour Rd., Halls Harbour* ☎ *902/679–5299* ⊕ *www.hallsharbourlobster.com* ⊘ *Closed late Oct.–early May.*

★ Le Caveau

$$$ | **ECLECTIC** | The restaurant at the Domaine de Grand Pré vineyard has been showered with accolades, including being named "one of the world's 20 best winery restaurants" by *Wine Access Magazine*. Aside from the excellent wines, the interesting menu features local seafood, game, meat, and vegetarian options. **Known for:** inventive combinations of top-quality ingredients; lovely patio shaded by grapevines; excellent wine list. Ⓢ *Average main: C$28* ⊠ *11611 Hwy. 1, Grand Pré* ☎ *902/542–7177* ⊕ *grandprewines.ns.ca/restaurant/*.

🛏 Hotels

Blomidon Inn

$$ | **B&B/INN** | Teak and mahogany furnishings, marble fireplaces, Victorian-style wallpaper, and a painted ceiling mural all add to the ambience at this 1887 sea captain's mansion. **Pros:** the stand-alone Perth Cottage offers maximum privacy; central location in walking distance to most attractions; several rooms have Jacuzzis and propane fireplaces. **Cons:** only a cold breakfast buffet; some rooms on third floor and there's no elevator; dinner reservations recommended even for guests. Ⓢ *Rooms from: C$169* ⊠ *195 Main St., Wolfville* ☎ *902/542–2291, 800/565–2291* ⊕ *www.blomidon.ns.ca* ⮡ *30 rooms* ⦿ *Free Breakfast.*

Farmhouse Inn Bed and Breakfast

$$ | **B&B/INN** | In a pleasant shipbuilding village amid lovely countryside, this 1860 B&B is perfect for outdoor enthusiasts.

Pros: complimentary beverages and sweets always available; surrounded by good hiking country; open year-round. **Cons:** breakfast room can seem a bit crowded at times; removed from Wolfville's restaurants; a bit old-fashioned for some. $ *Rooms from: C$139* ✉ *9757 Main St., Canning* ✣ *15 km (10 miles) north of Wolfville* ☎ *902/582–7900, 800/928–4346* 🌐 *www.farmhouseinn.ca* 🛏 *6 rooms* 🍴 *Free Breakfast.*

Tattingstone Inn

$$ | **B&B/INN** | Amid large gardens, this inn has an interesting history and many exceptional features, including the delightful conservatory, where delicious breakfasts are served. **Pros:** peaceful; Jacuzzi tubs in some rooms; pleasant atmosphere. **Cons:** not all rooms are spacious; some rooms may not suit those with mobility issues; a bit of a walk to downtown. $ *Rooms from: C$145* ✉ *620 Main St., Wolfville* ☎ *902/542–7696, 800/565–7696* 🌐 *www.tattingstoneinn.com* 🛏 *12 rooms, 2 suites* 🍴 *Free Breakfast.*

Shopping

Annapolis Cider Company

OTHER FOOD & DRINK | Local apples are used to create a range of tasty, award-winning ciders, which you can sample on-premises or ready-bottled to take with you. ✉ *388 Main St., Wolfville* ☎ *697–2707* 🌐 *drinkannapolis.ca.*

Tangled Garden

FOOD | This fairytale-like store where flowers and herbs dry in bunches hanging from the ceiling sells jams, jellies, and vinegars made on-premises, as well as delicacies such as rose ice cream. You can tour the acres of delightful gardens and a seven-circuit flower labyrinth for C$10. ✉ *11827 Nova Scotia Trunk 1, Grand Pré* ☎ *90/542–9811* 🌐 *www.tangledgarden.ca* ⏲ *Closed Jan.–Apr. Garden closes late-Oct.*

Activities

Blomidon Provincial Park

HIKING & WALKING | **FAMILY** | This park on the shores of the Minas Basin has four main trails that collectively cover 14 km (9 miles). The beach is accessible at low tide, but be sure to check the tide tables; the water comes back in quite rapidly. The 1.6-km (1-mile) Lookoff Trail yields especially fine cliff-top vistas. ✉ *3138 Pereau Rd., Cape Blomidon* ✣ *Off Hwy. 101, 31 km (19 miles) north of Wolfville* ☎ *902/582–7319* 🌐 *www.novascotiaparks.ca.*

Windsor

25 km (16 miles) southeast of Wolfville.

Windsor has much in common with Bridgewater on the South Shore in that both are historic towns that have evolved into regional service centers. One marker of Windsor's history is King's-Edgehill School. Founded in 1788, it is the oldest independent school in the British Commonwealth. The countryside around Windsor is pretty, particularly in autumn, and Haligonians often make the 66-km (41-mile) drive to the "Gateway of the Annapolis Valley" for its Pumpkin Festival.

GETTING HERE AND AROUND

When driving from east or west, take Exit 6 off Highway 101.

ESSENTIALS

VISITOR INFORMATION Windsor Visitor Information Centre. ✉ *Colonial Rd., Windsor* ✣ *North off Hwy. 101, Exit 6* ☎ *902/798–2690.*

Sights

Fort Edward National Historic Site

MILITARY SIGHT | Despite a devastating fire in 1897, some evidence of Windsor's earliest days remains at Fort Edward, which, dating from 1750, is the oldest blockhouse in Canada. ✉ *67 Fort Edward St., Windsor* ☎ *902/798–2639 July and Aug., 902/798–4706 West Hants Historical Society, Sept.–June* 🌐 *www.pc.gc.ca* 🎟 *Free* ⏲ *Closed Sun., Mon., and early Sept.–mid-June.*

Haliburton House Museum

HISTORIC HOME | This was once home to Judge Thomas Chandler Haliburton (1796–1865), a lawyer, politician, historian, and, above all, humorist. Hugely popular in his own day, Haliburton inspired Mark Twain and put Nova Scotia on the literary map with *The Clockmaker,* a book that used a fictional Yankee clock peddler named Sam Slick to poke fun at provincial foibles. Although you may not be familiar with Haliburton's name, you surely know some of the phrases he coined. The Windsor wordsmith gave us expressions like "quick as a wink," "it's raining cats and dogs," and "the early bird gets the worm." Themed programs and events are offered throughout the summer.

Thomas Haliburton is also remembered for making the first recorded reference to hockey—the sport that was "born" here in the early 1800s. Fittingly, the Windsor Hockey Heritage Museum (☎ *902/798–1800,* 🌐 *www.birthplaceofhockey.com/museum*) resides at Haliburton House, and several rooms contain items from the collection. These include antique skates, hand-carved sticks, wooden pucks, trophies, team uniforms, and photographs. ✉ *414 Clifton Ave., Windsor* ☎ *902/798–2915* 🌐 *www.haliburton-house.novascotia.ca* 🎟 *C$4* ⏲ *Closed early Oct.–May.*

Uniacke Estate Museum Park

HISTORIC HOME | This country mansion was built in about 1815 for Richard John Uniacke, attorney general and advocate general to the admiralty court during the War of 1812. Now a provincial museum, the Georgian-style house is preserved in its original condition, right down to the antique furnishings. Seven walking trails wend through the large lakeside property. There are picnic tables and a small tearoom in the former basement kitchen of the house. The access road is gated, and the gates are locked at dusk. ✉ *758 Hwy. 1, Mount Uniacke* ✥ *30 km (19 miles) east of Windsor* ☎ *902/866–0032* 🌐 *uniacke.novascotia.ca* 🎟 *Museum C$4* ⏲ *Closed Mon. and early Oct.–May.*

🍴 Restaurants

Winegrunt

$$ | **INTERNATIONAL** | Every dish offered on the small, creative menu is perfectly executed whether it's a French classic like Boeuf Bourguignon or a charcuterie board. There's a huge selection of local wines to try, as well as an international wine list, and often live jazz in the evenings. **Known for:** staff are very knowledgeable on wines; lively, fun atmosphere; locally sourced ingredients in food offerings. [$] *Average main: C$16* ✉ *43 Water St., Windsor* ☎ *902/472–2863* 🌐 *winegrunt.com* ⏲ *Closed Mon.—Weds.*

🛏 Hotels

Clockmakers Inn

$$ | **B&B/INN** | A distinctive 1894 building with original features houses this appealing inn on the Evangeline Trail that offers a range of services and room styles. **Pros:** two bicycles available for guest use; family-friendly; garden playground. **Cons:** front rooms susceptible to traffic noise; outside of town; private bathroom for one room is not en suite. [$] *Rooms from: C$129* ✉ *1399 King St., Windsor* ☎ *902/792–2573, 866/778–3600* 🌐 *www.theclockmakersinn.com* 🛏 *8 rooms* 🍽 *Free Breakfast.*

🎭 Performing Arts

Mermaid Theatre of Nova Scotia

THEATER | **FAMILY** | Puppets and performers retell classic and contemporary children's stories here. The troupe's home base is the 400-seat MIPAC (Mermaid Imperial Performing Arts Centre) adjacent to its Gerrish Street headquarters, but catching a show can be tricky because of the hectic worldwide touring schedule. If you can't time your trip to coincide with a play date, you can still marvel at Mermaid's props and puppets, as several floors filled with them are open for public viewing. ⊠ *132 Gerrish St., Windsor* ☎ *902/798–5841* ⊕ *www.mermaidthea-tre.ca* ✉ *By donation.*

Sherbrooke and Sherbrooke Village

187 km (122 miles) northeast of Halifax.

Established by the French in the middle of the 17th century, this little town prospered briefly on the back of a gold rush in the late 19th century, and it's something of a thrill to know that 80% of Sherbrooke's gold is still buried underfoot. Today, however, it's better known for the Atlantic salmon that rush up St. Mary's River (though you can't fish for them) and for the excellent Sherbrooke Village open-air museum. The town makes a good base for exploring the rugged coastline.

GETTING HERE AND AROUND
There's no public transportation to Sherbrooke. From Halifax, drive east on Highway 107, then Trunk 7 E, via Musquodoboit Harbour and Sheet Harbour. If you're coming from the Northumberland Shore, head for New Glasgow and take Highway 347 south, turning onto Trunk 7 W for the last 20 km (12 miles) or so.

 Sights

Sherbrooke Village
MUSEUM VILLAGE | FAMILY | Most visitors come to Sherbrooke to see this living-history museum, set within the contemporary town. It contains more than two

dozen restored buildings (including an operating water-powered sawmill) that re-create life during the town's heyday. Between 1860 and 1914, this was a prime shipbuilding, lumbering, and gold-rush center. These days, costumed interpreters and artisans recapture the bustle by demonstrating blacksmithing, weaving, wood turning, soap making, and similar skills. Special events, such as old-fashioned Christmas and courthouse concerts, are held throughout the year. ⊠ *42 Main St., Hwy. 7, Sherbrooke* ☎ *902/522–2400, 888/743–7845* ⊕ *sher-brookevillage.novascotia.ca* ✉ *C$19.95* ⊙ *Closed Tues. and Weds. Seasonal from early Oct.–mid-May (except Christmas events).*

 Beaches

Port Bickerton Lighthouse Beach Park
LIGHTHOUSE | Hiking trails and a boardwalk lead to a sandy beach here, but the park's main attractions are its two lighthouses, which share the lofty bluff above. One is still working; the other, built in the early 1920s, houses the Nova Scotia Lighthouse Interpretive Centre, which recounts the history, lore, and vital importance of the province's lights. **Amenities:** none. **Best for:** swimming, surfing. ⊠ *640 Lighthouse Rd., Port Bickerton* ⊹ *Off Hwy. 211, about 32 km (20 miles) east of Sherbrooke* ☎ *902/364–2007* ⊕ *www.portbickerton-lighthouse.ca* ✉ *Entry to lighthouse site C$3* ⊙ *Lighthouse Interpretive Center closed Oct.–June.*

🛏 **Hotels**

Liscombe Lodge Resort
$$$ | RESORT | FAMILY | In a superb natural setting, with a choice of lodge rooms or secluded chalets and cottages, this place pairs an away-from-it-all location with a wide range of activities. **Pros:** live music on Saturday nights; fun packages and free experiential programs; great

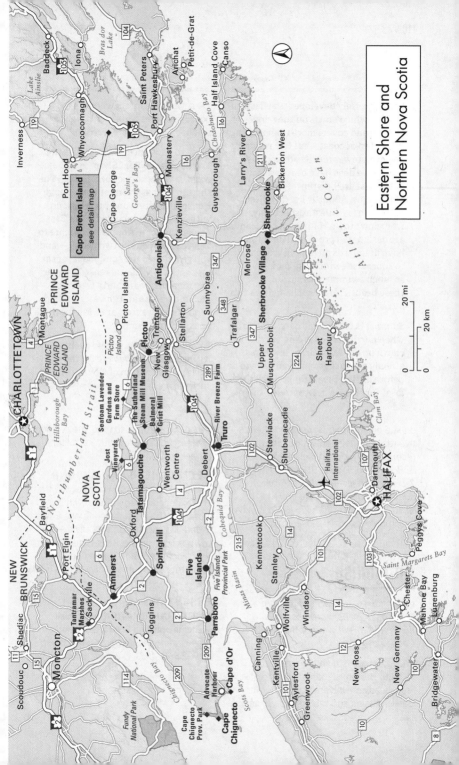

Eastern Shore and Northern Nova Scotia

Surf's Up Down East

Being sparsely developed, the Eastern Shore—which starts on the fringes of Halifax and covers more than 200 km (125 miles) of coast—has few residents and even fewer tourist attractions. But it sure does have beaches. Two of the best are Lawrencetown and Martinique. About 27 km (17 miles) and 57 km (35 miles), respectively, from downtown Halifax, both strands are designated provincial parks and have lifeguards on duty in season to supervise swimming. Yet it's not so much swimmers as surfers that these beautiful, wave-blasted beaches attract.

Summer is prime time here, especially when northward-tracking hurricanes churn up the Atlantic, so if you've already got surf gear all you have to do before hitting the water is check the local surf forecast. Otherwise, there are several outfitters who rent or sell boards and wet suits (you'll want a suit because the water is cold).

Close to Lawrencetown Beach is the **Kannon Beach Surf Shop** (☎ 902–471–0025; ⊕ *www.kannonbeach.com*). The shop, in the basement of MacDonald House, also offers one-hour lessons, with equipment included, from C$55 per person for a group of 10 or more to C$95 each for one or two people—and you get to keep the equipment for the rest of the day. Rentals cost C$40 per day for a surfboard and a wet suit, including boots and gloves; stand-up paddleboard rentals are C$30 for three hours or C$50 per day.

For more information and event listings, visit the website for the Surfing Association of Nova Scotia (⊕ *surfns.com*).

on-site dining options. **Cons:** no alternative restaurants nearby; poor cell-phone reception; somewhat isolated location. Ⓢ *Rooms from: C$229* ✉ *2884 Hwy. 7, Liscomb Mills* ✛ *27 km (17 miles) southwest of Sherbrooke on Hwy. 7* ☎ *902/779–2307, 800/665–6343* ⊕ *www. liscombelodge.ca* ☉ *Closed mid-Oct.– Apr.* ➲ *59 rooms* ⦿ *Free Breakfast.*

Antigonish

61 km (38 miles) north of Sherbrooke; 115 km (71 miles) northeast of Truro; 55 km (34 miles) west of the Canso Causeway.

Pretty Antigonish, on the main route to Cape Breton Island, is home to St. Francis Xavier University, a center for Gaelic studies and the first coeducational Catholic institution to graduate women. The campus also has several cultural attractions.

GETTING HERE AND AROUND
Maritime Bus offers a daily service from Halifax, connecting at Truro with buses from New Brunswick and Prince Edward Island. Driving couldn't be easier—the town is right on the Trans-Canada Highway (Highway 104). Coming up from Sherbrooke, you need Nova Scotia Trunk 7 E.

ESSENTIALS
VISITOR INFORMATION Antigonish Visitor Information Centre. ✉ *c/o Antigonish Library, 283 Main St., Antigonish* ☎ *902/863–4921* ⊕ *www.visitantigonish. ca.*

Sights

Bauer Theatre

PERFORMANCE VENUE | During the school year, the Bauer is home to Theatre Antigonish, a nonprofit community company that presents classic and contemporary works. Its Green Room Lounge features improv comedy on certain Saturday nights, with admission by donation. ✉ *St. Francis Xavier University, West St., off Hwy. 104, Antigonish* ☎ *902/867–3333* 🌐 *www2.mystfx.ca/theatre-antigonish* 🎫 *C$20.*

StFX Art Gallery

ART GALLERY | St. Francis Xavier University's campus art gallery mounts a dozen exhibits of mostly contemporary works each year and hosts talks with regional and other artists. ✉ *103 Bloomfield Centre, 1st fl., Antigonish* ☎ *902/867–2303* 🌐 *mystfx.ca/art-gallery* 🎫 *Free* 🕒 *Closed Mon. and Tues.*

Restaurants

Gabrieau's Bistro

$$$ | **ECLECTIC** | **FAMILY** | Gabrieau's has earned a place in Antigonish hearts with its pleasant interior and an epicurean yet affordable menu that includes seafood, meat dishes, pasta, tapas, sushi, and various vegetarian dishes. There are also luscious desserts, and the wine list impresses, too. **Known for:** special occasion cakes made to order; wide range of dishes; friendly and efficient service. [$] *Average main: C$25* ✉ *350 Main St., Antigonish* ☎ *902/863–1925* 🌐 *www.gabrieaus.com* 🕒 *Closed Sun. and Mon. No lunch Sat.*

★ **The Townhouse**

$$$ | **ECLECTIC** | A locals' favorite serving craft beer, cocktails, and upscale modern food. Oysters, salt-cod fish cakes, and *moules marinière* showcase local seafood, and there's an excellent selection of carnivorous and vegetarian dishes to choose from. **Known for:** interesting vegan options; fun, warm, and friendly atmosphere; offers local beer tasting flights. [$] *Average main: C$22* ✉ *76 College St.* ☎ *902/863–2248* 🌐 *antigonish-townhouse.com* 🕒 *Closed Mon.*

Hotels

Antigonish Victorian Inn

$$ | **B&B/INN** | Turn-of-the-20th-century Victorian style—but with modern amenities—reigns at this beautifully restored turreted mansion. **Pros:** delicious hot breakfast; just a short walk from the town center; open year-round. **Cons:** third-floor rooms have sloped ceilings; room size varies widely; not all options have en suite bathrooms. [$] *Rooms from: C$180* ✉ *149 Main St., Antigonish* ☎ *902/863–1103, 800/706–5558* 🌐 *www.antigonishvictorianinn.ca* 🛏 *12 rooms* 🍴 *Free Breakfast.*

Shopping

Red Sky Gallery

ART GALLERIES | Small contemporary gallery showcasing works by local artists with covetable prints, ceramics, and jewelry for sale. ✉ *320 Main St., Antigonish* ☎ *902/863–8000* 🌐 *redskygallery.ca* 🕒 *Closed Sun. and Mon.*

Activities

Antigonish Landing Trail

HIKING & WALKING | A 4-km (2.8-mile) walking trail along the shoreline of Antigonish Harbour borders a large tidal marsh and wildlife sanctuary teeming with ospreys, bald eagles, and other birds. There are two elevated platforms for superb views. To find the trailhead, park at the Antigonish Heritage Museum, on East Main Street, then cross the railroad tracks and bear right on Adam Street. Bring drinking water and watch out for poison ivy. ✉ *Trailhead at end of Adam St., Antigonish* 🎫 *Free.*

Pictou

74 km (46 miles) northwest of Antigo-nish; 66 km (41 miles) northeast of Truro.

Many people come to Pictou for the sole purpose of catching the ferry onward to Prince Edward Island (it departs from Caribou, just minutes away), but the town itself is lovely, with a revitalized waterfront centered on a very different vessel. In 1773 an aging cargo ship named the *Hector* arrived here carrying the initial load of Scottish Highlanders, making Pictou the "Birthplace of New Scotland." Each year in early July to mark the close of this region's fishing season, the raucous Pictou Lobster Carnival features lobster-boat races, trap-hauling contests, and, of course, a chance to eat the tasty crustaceans.

GETTING HERE AND AROUND

The Wood Islands Ferry from Prince Edward Island will land you in Pictou, but that's the only public transportation there is. The ferry runs from May through late December, with a minimum of three sailings a day, and up to nine in peak season. The fare for a vehicle, including passengers, is C$67.50; walk-on passengers pay C$17. Driving to Pictou is via the Trans-Canada Highway (Highway 104), branching onto Highway 106 for the last stretch.

TOURS

Pictou Island Charters

GUIDED TOURS | The charter company operates ferry service between Caribou and Pictou Island. ⊠ *Pictou* ☎ *902/497–5974* ⊕ *www.pictouislandcharters.ca* ⊠ *Ferry C$5.*

Sights

Hector Heritage Quay

HISTORIC SIGHT | A 110-foot fully rigged replica of the *Hector* is moored here, and (although under renovations until 2023) you can go aboard to see how early immigrants traveled. The handsome post-and-beam interpretive center recounts the story of the first hardy pioneers (33 families plus 25 unmarried men) who arrived aboard the original vessel in 1773, and the flood of Scots who followed them. The site also has working blacksmith, rigger, and carpentry shops. ⊠ *33 Caladh Ave., Pictou* ☎ *902/485–4371* ⊕ *facebook.com/shiphector* ⊠ *C$5* ⊘ *Closed mid-Oct.–late May.*

Nova Scotia Museum of Industry

HISTORY MUSEUM | FAMILY | Your own job may be the last thing you want to think about while vacationing, but if you're curious about those the industrious locals have traditionally held, Stellarton, just 20 km (12 miles) from Pictou, is worth a detour for this museum that brings our industrial heritage to life with daily demonstrations in the machine shop, sawmill, and print shop. Like factory and mine workers of old, you can punch in with a time card and then get straight to work. Hands-on exhibits will show you how to hook a rag mat, print a bookmark, operate a steam engine, or pack chocolates into a moving box on an assembly line. Interactive computer exhibits explore multimedia as a tool of industry, and some 30,000 industrial artifacts are on display, including Canada's oldest steam locomotives. The kids' train gallery is a hit with very young children. ⊠ *147 N. Foord St., Stellarton, Pictou* ⊕ *Off Hwy. 104, Exit 24* ☎ *902/755–5425* ⊕ *museumofindustry.novascotia.ca* ⊠ *C$9.*

Beaches

Melmerby Beach Provincial Park

BEACH | FAMILY | One of Nova Scotia's most popular beaches, Melmerby has a boardwalk, picnic tables, and some of the warmest water north of the Carolinas. Beaches straddle both the inner and outer edges of this horseshoe of land, the inner portion a glorious stretch of white sand. Swimming is safe here unless winds are high, when strong currents develop. The supervised area (in July and August) is clearly marked. Beware of poison ivy in the sand dunes and, between mid-July and early August, jellyfish in the water. **Amenities:** food and drink; lifeguards; parking (free); showers; toilets. **Best for:** swimming. ✉ *6280 Little Harbour Rd.* ✥ *About 30 km (18 miles) east of Pictou* 🌐 *parks.novascotia.ca.*

Hotels

★ The Scotsman Inn

$$ | B&B/INN | A registered Heritage Property built in the 1860s, this centrally located inn, a block from the waterfront, is furnished with antiques and original oil paintings. **Pros:** some rooms have water views; barn storage for bikes and motorbikes; very helpful and hospitable hosts. **Cons:** lots of stairs but no elevator; limited check-in times, but accommodations can be made by prior arrangement; fireplaces not operational. [$] *Rooms from: C$140* ✉ *78 Coleraine St., Pictou* ☎ *855/770–1433* 🌐 *www.scotsmaninn.com* 🕒 *Closed mid-Nov.–mid-May* 🛏 *10 rooms* 🍴 *Free Breakfast.*

Performing Arts

deCoste Performing Arts Centre

ARTS CENTERS | The center presents a summer-long program of concerts, dinner theater, comedy, pipe bands, Highland dancing, and ceilidhs with Gaelic music and dance. Past headliners have included acts ranging from k.d. lang to the Scottish Symphony Orchestra. ✉ *99 Water St., Pictou* ☎ *902/485–8848, 800/353–5338* 🌐 *decostecentre.ca.*

Shopping

Water Street Studios

CRAFTS | This artisans' co-op sells a wide range of crafts, many of which are handcrafted in the Maritimes. Items include hand-dyed and natural yarns, felted woolen items and knits, weaving, blankets, pottery, stained glass, jewelry, and woodwork. ✉ *110 Water St., Pictou* ☎ *902/485–8398* 🌐 *waterstreetstudio.weebly.com.*

Activities

Jitney Trail

HIKING & WALKING | The Jitney is a 5-km (3-mile) paved water's-edge route around Pictou Harbour to Brown's Point that puts you in sight of marine life, birdlife, and working wharves. Hikers and bikers frequent it, and there are benches and picnic tables along the way. ✉ *Pictou* ✥ *Off Caladh Av.* 🌐 *www.novascotia.com/see-do/trails/jitney-walking-trail-the-great-trail-trans-canada-trail/6163.*

Tatamagouche

54 km (33½ miles) west of Pictou.

Though it only has about a thousand residents, tiny Tatamagouche is a force to be reckoned with. Canada's second-largest Oktoberfest (*nsoktoberfest.ca*)—a boisterous event complete with sausages, schnitzel, and frothy steins of beer—takes place here each fall. Summer brings strawberry and blueberry festivals, lobster, and chowder suppers. On the waterfront, Creamery Square is the hub of the town with a museum complex, a farmers' market, and a center for the arts with a small theater. Within a 10-minute drive of Tatamagouche you have the opportunity to visit two historic mills.

GETTING HERE AND AROUND

There is no public transportation to Tatamagouche. If you're driving on the Trans-Canada Highway (Highway 104), go north at Truro via Highway 311; heading west from Pictou or east from Amherst, Highway 6 along the coast is the way to go.

👁 Sights

Balmoral Grist Mill

HISTORY MUSEUM | Built in 1874, this is one of the few water-powered mills still operating in Nova Scotia, now serving as the centerpiece of a small museum. You can observe milling demonstrations and walk the site's 1-km (½-mile) trail. ⊠ *660 Matheson Brook Rd., Denmark* ☎ *902/657–3016* ⊕ *balmoralgristmill. novascotia.ca* ⊠ *C$4* ⊗ *Closed early Oct.–May.*

Jost Vineyards

WINERY | The Jost winery produces wines from an astonishing number of varietals, consistently winning awards for its ice wine, a sweet affair made from grapes left on the vines until frost has "iced" them. You can taste wines year-round at the store here, roam the scenic vineyards, and enjoy a delicious lunch at the on-site Seagrape Café which specializes in fresh, local produce that compliments their wines perfectly. ⊠ *48 Vintage La., Malagash* ✛ *17 km (11 miles) northwest of Tatamagouche via Hwy. 311* ☎ *902/257–2636, 800/565–4567* ⊕ *jostwine.ca.*

★ Seafoam Lavender Gardens and Farm Store

FARM/RANCH | Wander the acres of fragrant lavender at this beautiful farm and pick up a range of homemade lavender products including tasty oatcakes, skin care products, soap, honey, and bath goodies at the farm store. ⊠ *3768 Highway 6* ☎ *902/536–3366* ⊕ *lavender-canada.com.*

The Sutherland Steam Mill Museum

HISTORIC SIGHT | Dating from 1894, this mill participated in the transition from water to steam power. Steam engines allowed greater flexibility about location—mills no longer *had* to be near a river or other water source—and provided more raw power to run factory machinery. Workers at the Sutherland mill manufactured useful wooden items ranging from carriages and sleds to wooden bathtubs, and you'll see hundreds of examples displayed inside, along with tools of the trade, some of which were ingeniously repurposed from other uses. Interesting demonstrations and hands-on activities sometimes take place in July and August. ⊠ *3169 Denmark Station Rd., Denmark* ✛ *Off Hwy. 326* ☎ *902/657–3365* ⊕ *sutherlandsteammill. novascotia.ca* ⊠ *C$4* ⊗ *Closed Mon. and early Oct.–May.*

Tatamagouche Heritage Centre

HISTORY MUSEUM | Creamery Square is the hub of activity in Tatamagouche, and this waterfront heritage center on the square has gathered together several museums that were previously dotted around town. Located in a former dairy facility, the center appropriately includes the **Creamery Museum,** with butter-making equipment and related displays. The **Sunrise Trail Museum** traces Tatamagouche's Mi'Kmaq, Acadian, French, and Scottish roots through interactive displays. The **Anna Swan Museum** relates the story of local giantess Anna Swan (1846–88), who grew to the height of 7 feet 11½ inches. Finally, the **Brule Fossil Centre** preserves 290-million-year-old fossil tracks that were discovered nearby in 1994. Demonstrations on boatbuilding and butter making are regularly staged. This is also the site of a Saturday-morning farmers' market from February through December. ⊠ *39 Creamery Rd., Tatamagouche* ☎ *902/657–3449* ⊕ *tatamagoucheheritagecentre.ca* ⊠ *C$6* ⊗ *Closed Mon.-Fri. Closed early Oct.–mid-May.*

☕ Coffee and Quick Bites

Tatamagouche Ice Creamery

$ | ICE CREAM | The gourmet hard ice creams and milkshakes made by this ice cream shop are heavenly whether you opt for dreamy strawberry or vanilla, or go with a more adventurous flavor. Expect long lines in the summer, but from the first lick you'll know it was worth the wait. **Known for:** can sell out early in the day; uses fresh local ingredients; interesting flavors like lavender and basil. [$] *Average main: C$8* ✉ *271 Main St.* 🌐 *tatamagoucheicecreamery.com* 🕒 *Closed Mon.-Thurs.*

Hotels

Train Station Inn

$$ | B&B/INN | Sleep in an 1887 train station or one of eight beautifully converted cabooses parked on the tracks outside, with authentic railroad memorabilia throughout. **Pros:** memorable gift shop; the Trans-Canada Trail runs alongside the property; close to the water. **Cons:** no Wi-Fi in the cabooses; dining car and café not always open; air-conditioning in railcars only. [$] *Rooms from: C$159* ✉ *21 Station Rd., Tatamagouche* ☎ *902/657–3222, 888/724–5233* 🌐 *www.tatatrainstation.com* 🕒 *Closed late Oct.–Apr.* 🛏 *10 rooms* 🍴 *No Meals.*

Nightlife

Tatamagouche Brewery

BREWPUBS | The taproom of this popular organic craft brewery is a great place to sample brews while seated on the patio overlooking Main Street (or inside). Besides having a great selection of beers on tap to suit all tastes, there's live music on the weekends and on some summer weeknights. No food is served, but you're welcome to order in from other local businesses such as the butcher shop next door that makes excellent sandwiches. ✉ *235 Main St., Tatamagouche* ☎ *902/657–4000* 🌐 *tatabrew.com.*

Shopping

Earltown General Store

FOOD | This charming general store is owned by a young family who've created a gorgeous space to pick up fresh-baked-in-store bread, locally made jerky, produce, and all manner of locally sourced goodies from chocolates to maple syrup. There's an ice-cream kiosk open through the summer months, too. ✉ *5556 NS-311, Tatamagouche* ☎ *902/657–9001* 🌐 *facebook.com/downtownearltown.*

Sara Bonnyman Pottery

CERAMICS | Here you can watch the shop's namesake potter herself at work, producing mostly tableware and also hooked rugs. In July and August informal tours are given. Visitors are also welcome to explore the large gardens. ✉ *326 Maple Ave. (Hwy. 246), Tatamagouche* ☎ *902/657–3215* 🌐 *www.sarabonnyman-pottery.com.*

Activities

The Butter Trail

HIKING & WALKING | Named for the creamery it backs onto, this is part of the Trans-Canada Trail system. The 25-km (15-mile) multiuse path follows the reclaimed railbed that the Train Station Inn's cabooses once traversed, and along the way are parks, impressive bridges, and fine views of the bay. ✉ *Tatamagouche* 🌐 *novascotia.com/see-do/trails/butter-trail-and-shortline-trail/6487.*

★ **Seafoam Lavender Company & Gardens**

FARM/RANCH | Wander among the rows of fragrant lavender at this gorgeous farm, then stop at their farm store to pick up all manner of lavender-infused items including tasty oatcakes, bath goodies and soaps, honey, skin care, and aromatherapy oils. ✉ *3768 Highway 6, Tatamagouche* ☎ *902/536–3366* 🌐 *lavendercanada.com* 🎟 *Free.*

Springhill

75 km (46½ miles) west of Tatamagouche.

If you're not going to be visiting Cape Breton, Springhill (on Highway 2) is worth a stop because it gives you a second chance to sample Nova Scotia's music-and-mining combo. This town was both the birthplace of acclaimed singer Anne Murray and, before that, home to the ill-fated coal mine immortalized in "The Ballad of Springhill" (aka "Springhill Mining Disaster") by Peggy Seeger and Ewen McColl. The mines closed in 1962, but Springhill is still using them—as a source of geothermal energy.

GETTING HERE AND AROUND

There is no public transportation to Springhill. By road, it's just west of the Trans-Canada Highway (Highway 104) between Oxford and Amherst; take Exit 5 onto Highway 142.

◉ Sights

Anne Murray Centre

OTHER MUSEUM | The likable Springhill-born, part-Acadian pop singer spread her tiny wings and flew away to worldwide fame and fortune, but she still celebrates her roots—and her hometown pays tribute to her illustrious career—at this repository of costumes, gold records, photographs, and other artifacts. Diehard fans can record a (virtual) duet with Murray, providing instant bragging rights to having performed with a partner who has sold more than 55 million albums to date and received four Grammy and 31 Juno awards. ☒ *36 Main St., Springhill* ☎ *902/597–8614* ⊕ *www.annemurraycentre.com* ☒ *C$10* ☾ *Closed mid-Oct.–mid-May.*

Springhill Miners Museum

MINE | The site of several tragedies, the Springhill coalfield gained international attention in 1958 when an earthquake created a "bump" that trapped mine workers underground (75 of them died), but today at this museum you can descend into a mine under safer circumstances. Some of the guides are retired miners who provide firsthand accounts of their working days. Children under five are not admitted. ☒ *145 Black River Rd., Springhill* ✛ *Off Hwy. 2* ☎ *902/597–3449*

⊕ *facebook.com/SpringhillMinersMuseum* ☒ *C$10* ☾ *Closed mid-Oct.–mid-May.*

Amherst

33 km (21 miles) northwest of Springhill.

Amherst is a quaint, quiet town with a central location, but from the mid-1800s to the early 1900s, it was a bustling center of industry and influence. Four of Canada's Fathers of Confederation hailed from Amherst, including Sir Charles Tupper, who later became prime minister. From Amherst, Nova Scotia's Sunrise Trail heads toward Northumberland Strait, and the Glooscap Trail runs west through fossil country. Amherst is a mere 7 km (4 miles) from New Brunswick and 55 km (34 miles) from the Confederation Bridge, which connects the Maritimes mainland to Prince Edward Island.

GETTING HERE AND AROUND

Maritime Bus provides daily service from Halifax to Amherst, where the bus stop is at the Circle K on South Albion Street. It takes a little over three hours and the fare is C$41.75 one way. Maritime also operates bus service from Fredericton (C$53.25; four hours) and Moncton (C$14.25; one hour). Although the train station is closed, you can disembark here from trains on the Montréal–Halifax route, but, with only three trains per week, it's not a very useful option. Amherst is on the Trans-Canada Highway (Highway 104), just south of the Nova Scotia–New Brunswick border; take Exit 3 or Exit 4. The town itself has no public transit system.

ESSENTIALS

VISITOR INFORMATION Amherst Visitor Information Centre. ☒ *90 Cumberland Loop, Amherst* ☎ *902/667–0787* ⊕ *www. amherst.ca/visitors.html.*

👁 Sights

Joggins Fossil Centre

NATURE SIGHT | On the Glooscap Trail, 35 km (22 miles) southwest of Amherst and 70 km (43 miles) northeast of Cape Chignecto, Joggins is famous for Coal Age fossils that were embedded in sandstone, then uncovered through erosion caused by Fundy's surging tides. You can spy them outside, in the sea cliffs, or inside the center. Also a UNESCO World Heritage Site, this striking museum has a large, well-curated collection of specimens dating back some 300 million years, along with interesting displays outlining the region's geological and archaeological history. The admission fee includes a half-hour guided beach tour; two-hour guided cliffs tours take place daily in peak months; and an in-depth four-hour tour occurs on certain weekends in June, July, and August. Reservations are essential for the two-hour and four-hour tours. Bear in mind that the beach is reached by a steep slope and staircase, over boulders and watercourses. ✉ *100 Main St., Joggins* ☎ *902/251–2727 guided tour reservations, 888/932–9766* ⊕ *www.jogginsfossilcliffs.net* 💲 *C$10.*

Tantramar Marshes

NATURE SIGHT | Spanning the Nova Scotia–New Brunswick border and covering more than 20,000 acres, the Tantramar Marshes stretch from Amherst up to Sackville and are alive with incredible birdlife and other wildlife. The name comes from the French *tintamarre* (meaning din or hubbub) because of the racket made by vast flocks of wildfowl. The Tantramar is a migratory route for hundreds of thousands of birds and a breeding ground for more than 100 species. ✉ *Amherst.*

🛏 Hotels

Amherst Shore Country Inn

$$ | **B&B/INN** | With a 600-foot private beach and 20 acres of lawns and gardens overlooking Northumberland Strait, this inn has an interesting range of lodging options. **Pros:** lovely view over gardens to the sea; tranquil location; outstanding dining. **Cons:** fixed evening mealtime; dinner menu selections must be made prior to arrival; most accommodations are away from the inn. 💲 *Rooms from: C$160* ✉ *Hwy. 366 (Tyndal Rd.), Lorneville* ⊹ *32 km (20 miles) northeast of Amherst* ☎ *902/661–4800, 800/661–2724* ⊕ *www.ascinn.ns.ca* ⊗ *Closed Mon.–Weds. Nov.–May* 🍴 *11 rooms* 🍽 *No Meals.*

Cape Chignecto and Cape d'Or

105 km (65 miles) southwest of Amherst.

Two imposing promontories—Cape Chignecto and Cape d'Or—reach into the Bay of Fundy near Chignecto Bay.

GETTING HERE AND AROUND

There is no public transportation to the capes. From the Trans-Canada Highway (Highway 104) at Amherst, you need to head southwest via Highways 302, 242, and 209. Highway 209 loops around a peninsula, with turnoffs for both capes.

👁 Sights

Advocate Harbour

TOWN | This little fishing community is set on a Bay of Fundy natural harbor that loses all its water at low tide. A delightful coastal walk here follows the top of an Acadian dike that was built by settlers in the 1700s to reclaim farmland from the sea. Nearby is rocky Advocate Beach, which stretches for about 5 km (3 miles) east from Cape Chignecto and is noted

Cape Chignecto, with its rocky promontory, is one of many scenic points on the Bay of Fundy.

for its monumental supply of tide-cast driftwood.

Age of Sail Heritage Museum

HISTORY MUSEUM | Exhibits spread out over several buildings trace the history of the Fundy region's shipbuilding and lumbering industries, and the museum has an archive and genealogical-research area. The main displays are in the restored 1854 Methodist church. The Wind and Wave Building is shaped to resemble an inverted half-model of a ship, and you can also view a blacksmith shop, a boathouse, and a lighthouse. Be sure to take a stroll on the boardwalk along the wharf. A cute café serves light meals—chowder, lobster rolls, sandwiches, and the like. ✉ *8334 Hwy. 209, Port Greville* ☎ *902/348–2030* ⊕ *www. ageofsailmuseum.ca* 🖾 *C$5* ⊙ *Closed Nov.–Apr. and Tues. and Wed. May, June, Sept., and Oct.*

Cape Chignecto Provincial Park

NATURE PRESERVE | Miles of untouched coastline, more than 10,000 acres of old-growth forest harboring deer, moose, and eagles, and a variety of unique geological features are preserved in Nova Scotia's largest provincial park. It's circumnavigated by a 51-km (31-mile) hiking trail along rugged cliffs that rise 600 feet above the bay, and there are other trails of varying lengths. Wilderness cabins and campsites are available. ✉ *1108 W. Advocate Rd., Advocate Harbour* ⊹ *Off Hwy. 209* ☎ *902/392–2085, 902/254–3241 off-season* ⊕ *www.novascotiaparks.ca* 🖾 *Free.*

Cape d'Or (*Cape of Gold*)

TRAIL | The explorer Samuel de Champlain poetically, but inaccurately, named Cape d'Or—there's copper in these hills, not gold. The region was actively mined a century ago, and at nearby Horseshoe Cove you may still find nuggets of almost pure copper on the beach, along with amethysts and other semiprecious stones. Cape d'Or's hiking trails border the cliff edge above the Dory Rips, a turbulent meeting of currents from the Minas Basin and the Bay of Fundy punctuated by a fine lighthouse, which has a viewing deck with telescopes. ✉ *Cape d'Or* ⏲ *Lighthouse closed Nov.–mid-May.*

🍴 Restaurants

Wild Caraway Restaurant & Café
$$$ | **CANADIAN** | The young proprietors of this eatery are enthusiastic about using local products in their cuisine. Casual but quality options like lobster rolls, fish cakes, quiche, and a daily pasta are served at lunch, while dinners are more sophisticated. **Known for:** use of local and foraged ingredients; great location overlooking the wharf; original recipes with international elements. [$] *Average main: C$29* ✉ *3721 Hwy. 209, Advocate Harbour* ☎ *902/392–2889* 🌐 *wildcaraway.com* ⏲ *Closed Tues. and Wed. No lunch Mon. Call for off-season hrs.*

🛏 Hotels

The Lighthouse on Cape d'Or
$$ | **B&B/INN** | Before automation, two lighthouse keepers manned the light on rocky Cape d'Or, and their cottages have been transformed into a small inn with unparalleled views of the Minas Basin. **Pros:** congenial common room; unique and fun setting; warm hosts. **Cons:** two rooms share a bathroom; breakfast not included; requires a rather steep walk on the final stretch. [$] *Rooms from: C$145* ✉ *Cape d'Or* ✥ *Off Hwy. 209, 6 km (4 miles) from Advocate Harbour* ☎ *902/670–8314* 🌐 *www.capedor.ca* ⏲ *Closed Nov.–Apr.* 🛏 *4 rooms* 🍴 *No Meals.*

🏃 Activities

NovaShores Adventures
KAYAKING | **FAMILY** | These kayak and stand-up paddleboarding tours explore the unspoiled coast of Cape Chignecto on the Bay of Fundy daily from mid-May through mid-October. Prices for a day tour are C$129; two- and three-day options are also available. ✉ *37 School La., Advocate Harbour* ☎ *902/392–2222, 866/638–4118* 🌐 *www.novashores.com* ⏲ *Closed mid-Oct.–mid-May.*

Parrsboro

55 km (34 miles) east of Cape d'Or.

Parrsboro, the main town on the north shore of the Minas Basin, is a hot spot for rock hounds and fossil hunters.

GETTING HERE AND AROUND

There is no public transportation to Parrsboro. By road, it's on Highway 2, which can be accessed from the Trans-Canada Highway (Highway 104) near Amherst, Springhill, or Truro.

👁 Sights

Fundy Geological Museum
NATURE SIGHT | **FAMILY** | Not far from the Minas Basin, where some of the oldest dinosaur fossils in Canada have been found, this museum showcases 200-million-year-old specimens alongside other mineral, plant, and animal relics. The opportunity to peer into a working fossil lab and to see bright interactive exhibits (like the Bay of Fundy Time Machine) give this museum real kid appeal. On Friday and Saturday in July and August, the curator leads fascinating two- to four-hour field trips through the surrounding area, but you need your own transportation because most don't start at the museum. ✉ *162 2 Island Rd., Parrsboro* ☎ *902/254–3814* 🌐 *fundygeological.novascotia.ca* 🎟 *From C$8.50* ⏲ *Closed Tues. mid-May–mid-Nov. Closed Sat. and Sun. mid-Nov.–mid-May.*

Minas Basin
NATURE SIGHT | The cliffs that rim the Minas Basin are washed by the world's highest tides twice daily: the result is a wealth of plant and animal fossils revealed in the rocks or carried down to the shore. ✉ *Parrsboro.*

Nova Scotia Gem and Mineral Show

NATURE SIGHT | The combination of fossils and semiprecious stones makes Parrsboro a natural place to hold this long-established show (the first was in 1966) during the third weekend of August. In addition to dozens of exhibitors, the event includes themed demonstrations and geological field trips. Experts are on hand to identify any treasures you turn up. ✉ *Lions Arena, King St. and Western Ave., Parrsboro* ☎ *902/254–3814 Fundy Geological Museum* 🌐 *facebook.com/nsgemshow.*

Ottawa House-by-the-Sea Museum

HISTORIC HOME | Although fossils have become Parrsboro's claim to fame, this harbor town was also a major shipping and shipbuilding port, and its history is chronicled here. The house, which overlooks the Bay of Fundy, is the only surviving building from a 1700s settlement. It was later the summer home of Sir Charles Tupper (1821–1915), a former premier of Nova Scotia and briefly the prime minister of Canada. Those with roots in Nova Scotia can research their ancestors in the genealogical archives. Occasional special events might include music, afternoon teas, or model railroads. ✉ *1155 Whitehall Rd., 3 km (2 miles) south of downtown, Parrsboro* ☎ *902/254–2376* 🌐 *www.ottawahouse-museum.ca* 🎟 *By donation* 🕒 *Closed Tues. and Weds. Closed Oct.–mid-May.*

Partridge Island

ISLAND | Semiprecious stones such as amethyst, quartz, and stilbite can be found at Partridge Island, 1 km (½ mile) offshore and connected to the mainland by an isthmus. The 1½-km (1-mile) Partridge Island Trail can be followed from the beach up to a lookout tower on the high point. ✉ *Off Whitehall Rd., Parrsboro.*

🛏 Hotels

Gillespie House Inn

$$ | **B&B/INN** | Colorful gardens border the driveway leading up to this 1890 home that is convenient to Parrsboro but also a great choice for active visitors—the hosts can organize golfing, kayaking, and hiking experiences for you. **Pros:** eco-friendly, including some solar power; impeccable rooms; customized packages available. **Cons:** not all bathrooms are en suite; property's friendly dogs will not suit those with allergies; continental breakfast is the only meal served. [$] *Rooms from: C$139* ✉ *358 Main St., Parrsboro* ☎ *902/254–3196* 🌐 *www.gillespie-houseinn.com* 🕒 *Closed Nov.–Apr.* 🔑 *7 rooms* 🍴 *Free Breakfast.*

Maple Inn, Parrsboro

$$ | **B&B/INN** | Two Italianate homes built in 1893 have been combined to form this charming inn within walking distance of downtown Parrsboro and the waterfront. **Pros:** complimentary home-brewed afternoon tea; full breakfast included; theater, food, and activity packages available. **Cons:** fixed breakfast time; potential floral-wallpaper overload; no elevator. [$] *Rooms from: C$145* ✉ *2358 Western Ave., Parrsboro* ☎ *902/254–3735, 877/627–5346* 🌐 *www.mapleinn.ca* 🕒 *Closed Nov.–Apr.* 🔑 *8 rooms* 🍴 *Free Breakfast.*

Parrsboro Mansion Inn

$$ | **B&B/INN** | Although this 1880 home, set far back on a 4-acre lawn, presents an imposing face, it's bright and modern inside. **Pros:** heated pool; German breakfast buffet; host is a massage therapist (on-site treatment room). **Cons:** soundproofing could be better; one-week minimum stay from mid-October to mid-June; rooms are not actually in the mansion. [$] *Rooms from: C$150* ✉ *3916 Eastern Ave., Parrsboro* ☎ *902/254–2585, 866/354–2585* 🌐 *www.parrsboroman-sion.com* 🔑 *4 rooms* 🍴 *Free Breakfast.*

✈ Performing Arts

Ship's Company Theatre

THEATER | Top-notch plays, comedy, and a concert series are presented from July through September at this three-stage facility. At its heart is the *Kipawo,* a former Minas Basin ferry that was transformed into the original floating theater in the 1980s. ✉ *18 Lower Main St., Parrsboro* ☎ *902/254–2003, 800/565–7469* ⊕ *www.shipscompanytheatre.com.*

⛷ Activities

Spirit Reins Ranch

HORSEBACK RIDING | FAMILY | Both experienced horseback riders and complete novices will find trail riding to suit their abilities, with scenic rides through countryside or along the beach and packages that include fossil tours and picnics. Lessons and summer horse camps for children are also available. Trail rides range from 1 to 4½ hours. ✉ *432 Prospect Rd., RR1, Parrsboro* ☎ *902/254–3138, 902/254–4262* ⊕ *www.spiritreinsranch. com* 🍽 *From C$65.*

Five Islands

25 km (15½ miles) east of Parrsboro.

Located between Parrsboro and Truro, Five Islands is one of the most scenic areas along Highway 2, with spectacular views of the Bay of Fundy. According to Mi'Kmaq legend, these islands were created when the god Glooscap threw handfuls of sod at Beaver, who had mocked and betrayed him.

GETTING HERE AND AROUND
There is no public transportation to Five Islands. Highway 2 can be accessed off the Trans-Canada Highway (Highway 104).

⊙ Sights

That Dutchman's Cheese Farm

FARM/RANCH | FAMILY | Known for his Gouda and other delicious cheeses that are found on menus across Nova Scotia, you can visit the Dutch-style farmhouse of "That Dutchman" to sample his cheeses or buy Dutch candy and clogs, and wander the beautiful gardens that double as a petting zoo. There's a large duck pond, baby goats to feed, angus cows, donkeys, and miniature potbellied pigs along the trail through gardens. ✉ *132 Brown Rd.* ☎ *902/647–2751* ⊕ *www. thatdutchmansfarm.com* 🍽 *CA$4.25 to tour gardens.*

⏱ Beaches

Five Islands Provincial Park

BEACH | On the shore of Minas Basin, the park has lofty sea cliffs, a beach for combing, trails for hiking, and mudflats for clam digging. Interpretive displays reveal the area's intriguing geology—semiprecious stones, Jurassic-period dinosaur bones, and fossils can all be found within the park's 1,500 acres. You can learn about geology and other topics, among them astronomy, rock hounding, and tidal-pool exploration, during complimentary programs offered during high season (check the website). Because the water recedes nearly a mile at ebb tide, you can walk on the ocean floor, though you'll have to run back mighty fast when the tide turns. That's precisely the goal of 2,000 or so participants in the Not Since Moses 10K Race (⊕ *www.notsincemoses.com*), an early-August event of (almost) biblical proportions. **Amenities:** parking (free); showers; toilets. **Best for:** swimming; walking. ✉ *618 Bentley Rd., Hwy. 2, Five Islands* ☎ *902/254–2980* ⊕ *parks.novascotia.ca* 🍽 *Free.*

An aerial view of Truro, a centrally located town along the Trans-Canada Highway.

Truro

91 km (57 miles) east of Parrsboro.

Truro's central location places it on many travelers' routes: this is rightly called "The Hub of Nova Scotia" because if you're driving down the Trans-Canada Highway, you'll have to pass by. In recent years the town has grown considerably, supporting a number of new restaurants, cafés, and community events. There's a large farmers' market every Saturday from mid-May to the end of October.

GETTING HERE AND AROUND

Truro is on the Trans-Canada Highway (Highway 104). Maritime Bus can get you here from Halifax in just under 2 hours (C$25.56), with several buses daily, or from various points in New Brunswick (Fredericton, 5½ hrs, C$68.06) and Prince Edward Island (Charlottetown, about 3½ hrs, C$56.98; requires one transfer).

◉ Sights

River Breeze Farm

FARM/RANCH | FAMILY | For up-close appreciation of local produce, this farm has pick-your-own strawberry and raspberry fields in summer and Atlantic Canada's largest corn maze in the fall. The place turns decidedly scary from late September to Halloween, when "Fear Farm" is haunted by gruesome characters (real live actors) in the maze and a haunted house. ✉ *660 Onslow Rd., Truro* ⊕ *Upper Onslow, off Hwy. 102, Exit 14A* ☏ *902/895–6541* ⊕ *www.riverbreeze.info* 🎟 *From C$10.*

★ Victoria Park

CITY PARK | FAMILY | At 3,000 acres, this park on the edge of downtown has wooded hiking trails, a viewpoint, a winding stream, two waterfalls, public tennis courts, and an outdoor (heated) pool. Even if you're not staying in Truro, this park can be a good pit stop for car-weary travelers: kids especially will enjoy the pool, water spray park, picnic pavilion, and playground. Energetic visitors can climb the 175 steps of the Jacob's Ladder fitness staircase. The Railyard mountain biking park at the top of Victoria Park has 35-miles of cross-country trails, some with platforms, jumps, and other advanced features, as well as a skills track that's popular with kids and adults. ✉ *Park Rd., off Brunswick St., Truro* ☎ *902/893–6078* 🌐 *victoriaparktruro.ca* 🎫 *Park free; pool C$4.*

🍴 Restaurants

★ Bistro 22

$$$ | **CONTEMPORARY** | Rich farmland fringes Truro, and the menu makes the most of the fabulous produce grown around here. The 32-seat eatery has an upscale-casual feel and a small but mighty menu. **Known for:** intimate, welcoming atmosphere; bistro classics on the menu; extensive choice of Nova Scotia wines. [$] *Average main: C$21* ✉ *16 Inglis Pl., Truro* ☎ *902/843–4123* 🌐 *www.bistro22.ca* 🕒 *Closed Sun. and Mon. No dinner Tues. and Wed.*

NovelTea Coffeehouse and Bakery

$ | **BAKERY** | This adorable locals' favorite café is filled with floor-to-ceiling bookcases and housed in a heritage building. They offer a fun selection of tasty caffeinated drinks named for literary characters, decadent baked goods, sandwiches, and salads. **Known for:** warm, friendly, and cozy atmosphere; scrumptious cheesecakes with varied toppings; inventive drinks menu. [$] *Average main: C$8* ✉ *604 Prince St., Truro* ☎ *902/301–5912* 🌐 *ntbookstorecafe.ca.*

★ Sugar Moon Farm

$$ | **CANADIAN** | **FAMILY** | This sugar camp, store, and pancake house in the Cobequid Mountains, about 30 km (19 miles) north of Truro off Highway 311, is Nova Scotia's only year-round maple destination. You can tour the working facility and hike the sugar woods. **Known for:** rib-sticking breakfasts; sweet maple coffees; hiking trails just outside the restaurant. [$] *Average main: C$16* ✉ *221 Alex MacDonald Rd., Earltown* ☎ *902/657–3348, 866/816–2753* 🌐 *www.sugarmoon.ca.*

🛏 Hotels

Belgravia Bed & Breakfast

$$ | **B&B/INN** | This bright, beautiful heritage home in downtown Truro offers four comfortable rooms, a pool, and patio set in pretty gardens. **Pros:** charming old house; fantastic central location in quiet neighborhood; gourmet breakfasts and home baking. **Cons:** very much a family home (some may love this); some may find the decor in rooms old-fashioned; one room is smaller than others. [$] *Rooms from: C$125* ✉ *5 Broad St., Truro* ☎ *902/893–7100* 🌐 *www.belgravia.ca* 🍽 *Free Breakfast.*

Suncatcher Bed and Breakfast

$$ | **B&B/INN** | Rooms at this modest B&B are cheerful and bright: ditto for owner Ruth Mailloux, who knows the province from stem to stern and will happily advise you about itineraries and attractions. **Pros:** cozy furniture on the patios overlooking gardens; knowledgeable host; spacious rooms. **Cons:** might be too intimate for some; has friendly dog, con if allergic; a slight distance from Truro proper. [$] *Rooms from: C$155* ✉ *25 Wile Crest Ave., North River* ☎ *902/893–7169, 877/203–6032* 🌐 *www.suncatcherbnb.com* 🛏 *2 rooms* 🍽 *Free Breakfast.*

🎭 Performing Arts

Marigold Cultural Centre

CONCERTS | This sweet 208-seat theatre and gallery space hosts plays, concerts, and cultural events showcasing regional performers (as well as amateur and local theatre groups). Concerts range from popular Canadian folk artists to Celtic bands to cover bands and on occasion you get to see these performers in a much more intimate setting than they might usually play. ✉ *605 Prince St., Truro* ☎ *902/897-4004* ⊕ *marigoldcentre.ca.*

🛍 Shopping

My Home Mercantile

CRAFTS | Besides stocking their own line of seriously cool Nova Scotia-themed hoodies and tees, this gorgeous boutique stocks a huge range of gifts, cards, and food items from local makers. ✉ *10 Inglis Pl., Truro* ☎ *902/843-5899* ⊕ *my-homemercantile.com.*

Thrown Together Pottery and Art

ART GALLERIES | The owner's clay creations are created in the studio here and sold in the on-site shop alongside works by more than 20 other local artisans. There are also classes and workshops, but advance booking is highly recommended. ✉ *37 King St., Truro* ☎ *902/895–9309* ⊕ *www.throwntogetherpottery.com.*

🏃 Activities

Shubenacadie River Adventure Tours

WHITE-WATER RAFTING | FAMILY | On these adrenaline-inducing, 90-minute to three-hour Zodiac inflatable-boat trips, you ride the waves created by the famous Fundy tides as the waters surge upstream, then enjoy a barbecue. The intensity of the tides determines the intensity of your ride; call or check the company's website to find out when your trip will be (relatively) mellow or fierce. There are also thrilling ziplines on-site. ✉ *10061 Hwy. 215, South Maitland* ☎ *902/261–2222, 888/878–8687* ⊕ *www.shubie.com* 🎟 *From C$85.*

Cape Breton Island

Cape Breton Island's reputation rests on simple pleasures and heartfelt hospitality. Spectacular scenery doesn't hurt either, and the very best of it is found on the Cabot Trail, a scenic 298-km (185-mile) stretch of road, winding along ocean-side cliffs. This rugged terrain made the Highland Scots, who settled here in the 18th century, feel right at home, and their influence remains obvious: North America's first single-malt whiskey distillery is on Cape Breton, as is its only college devoted to Gaelic language, arts, and culture. Elsewhere on the coast you'll find Francophone villages full of Acadian joie de vivre, plus historic attractions like the mighty Fortress at Louisbourg, which bear witness to the area's long-standing French presence. Bras d'Or Lake—a vast, almost landlocked inlet of the sea occupying the entire center of Cape Breton—is still home to ancient Mi'Kmaq communities, yet it appeals equally to an international contingent of boaters who come to cruise the lake's unspoiled coves and islands. And golfers are very excited about the Cabot Cliffs and Cabot Links courses, hailed as among the best in the world.

Judique

30 km (18 miles) north of the Canso Causeway; 75 km (47 miles) northeast of Antigonish.

Like so many Cape Breton communities, Judique is only a little clutch of buildings with Highway 19 running straight through as the main street. Nevertheless, the presence of **the Celtic Music Interpretive Centre** makes Judique an essential destination for anyone interested in the island music scene. Need some fresh air before getting back in the car and continuing up the Ceilidh Trail? The coastal area around Judique is good for hiking (a portion of the Trans-Canada Trail threads through) as well as swimming. For an offshore experience, consider taking a tour out of Little Judique Harbour.

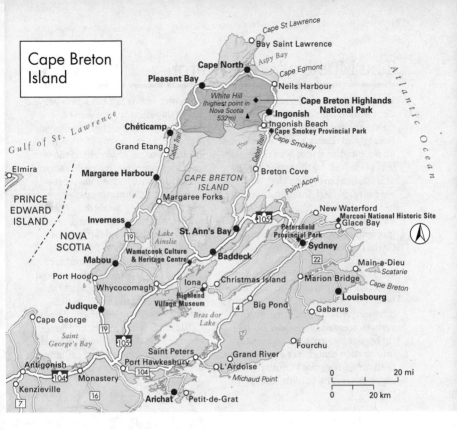

Cape Breton Island

Cape St Lawrence
Bay Saint Lawrence
Aspy Bay
Cape North
Cape Egmont
Pleasant Bay
Neils Harbour
White Hill
(highest point in
Nova Scotia
532m) ▲
Cape Breton Highlands
National Park
Ingonish
Chéticamp
Ingonish Beach
Cape Smokey Provincial Park
Grand Etang
Cape Smokey
Gulf of St. Lawrence
Margaree Harbour
Breton Cove
CAPE BRETON
ISLAND
Point Aconi
Elmira
Margaree Forks
PRINCE
EDWARD
ISLAND
New Waterford
Marconi National Historic Site
Inverness
105
Glace Bay
Lake
Ainslie
St. Ann's Bay
Petersfield
Provincial Park
NOVA
SCOTIA
19
Sydney
Wamatcook Culture
& Heritage Centre
Baddeck
Mabou
22
Main-a-Dieu
Port Hood
Iona
Christmas Island
Marion Bridge
Scatarie
Whycocomagh
Highland
Village Museum
Cape Breton
Judique
4
Big Pond
Louisbourg
Cape George
Bras d'or
Lake
Gabarus
19
Saint
George's Bay
105
Fourchu
Saint Peters
Grand River
Antigonish
Port Hawkesbury
L'Ardoise
104
104
Michaud Point
Kenzieville
Monastery
16
7
Arichat
Petit-de-Grat

Gulf of St. Lawrence

Atlantic Ocean

Cabot Trail

0   20 mi
0   20 km

GETTING HERE AND AROUND

There is no public transportation to Judique. By road, it's on the Ceilidh Trail (Highway 19)—a left turn at the traffic circle over the Canso Causeway.

👁 Sights

Celtic Music Interpretive Centre

OTHER MUSEUM | Packed with interactive exhibits detailing the fine points of Cape Breton music, the center also has an archive with classic recordings and oral history interviews. Visitors eager to pick up a fiddle and bow can play along to a video tutorial. If you'd rather just listen, that's no problem: there are plenty of ceilidhs, demonstrations, music workshops, and other events here, all listed on the website. ✉ *5471 Hwy. 19, Judique* ☎ *902/787–2708* 🌐 *www.*

celticmusiccentre.com ✉ *From C$6* ⊘ *Closed (except for Sun. Ceilidh) mid-Oct.–early June.*

Mabou

28 km (17 miles) northeast of Judique.

The village of Mabou is very Scottish (Gaelic-language signs attest to it), and the residents' respect for tradition is apparent in everything from the down-home meals they serve to the music they so exuberantly play; arguably the best place to sample both is at the Red Shoe.

GETTING HERE AND AROUND

There is no public transportation to Mabou. It's on the Ceilidh Trail.

The Music of Cape Breton

Weaned on old-time Scottish tunes, Cape Breton Island's traditional musicians are among the world's finest—and there's a widely held belief (in Scotland, too) that here the music was preserved, by the better players at least, in a purer form than in the old country itself. In summer you can hear local musicians play at festivals, concerts, and, of course, *ceilidhs* (pronounced KAY-lees). The word, Gaelic for "visit," derives from the days when folks would gather in a neighbor's kitchen for music, stories, and step dancing (you might also hear the term "kitchen party"). Today ceilidhs have evolved into public events that visitors are welcome to join. Bulletin boards, newspapers, and visitor information centers are a good source for listings. Inverness County, which encompasses the Ceilidh Trail, is the epicenter of activity, but wherever you are in Cape Breton, you won't be too far from the music. There's additional information online too at 🌐 *www.inverness-ns.ca*. Any night of the week in peak season, you'll also be able to attend a square dance somewhere in Inverness County. Propelled by virtuoso fiddling, locals of every age whirl through taxing "square sets," shaking the floor and rattling the rafters in the process. The highlight of the musical calendar is undoubtedly the Celtic Colours International Festival, held every October at the height of the island's spectacular fall-colors season. It gathers together Celtic musicians, singers, and dancers from around the corner and around the world for concerts and ceilidhs across the region.

Beaches

West Mabou Beach Provincial Park

BEACH | **FAMILY** | A wide sweep of sandy beach backed by a dune system is the standout feature of this 530-acre park on Mabou Harbour. The only public-access beach in the area, it also has a fishpond, a picnic area, and change rooms, but its status as a protected natural environment prevents any further development and preserves its peaceful quality. Behind the beach are 12 km (7½ miles) of hiking trails, through agricultural land and marshes, that have fine views. **Amenities:** parking (free); toilets. **Best for:** swimming; walking. ✉ *1757 Little Mabou Rd., Mabou* ✣ *Off Hwy. 19* 🌐 *www.novascotiaparks.ca* 🎫 *Free.*

Restaurants

★ **Red Shoe**

$$$ | **CANADIAN** | **FAMILY** | More than a mere pub, this Cape Breton institution has evolved into an attraction, in part because it is owned by four of the Rankins, Canada's most celebrated singing siblings. Expect the usual pub favorites: fish-and-chips, pulled pork sandwiches, grilled salmon, and mussels steamed in ale, garlic, and bacon. **Known for:** above-average pub food and good selection of beers; great music featuring the finest local fiddlers and step dancers; very busy, often with a line to get in. [$] *Average main: C$25* ✉ *11533 Hwy. 19, Mabou* ☎ *902/945–2996* 🌐 *redshoepub.com* 🕒 *Closed mid-Oct.–late May.*

Hotels

Duncreigan Country Inn
$$ | **B&B/INN** | With its harborside deck and peaceful location, the inn provides a great place to unwind after a day spent exploring Cape Breton. **Pros:** might hear some live music from the innkeeper; lovely tree-shaded deck; open year-round. **Cons:** buildings are replicas; trees block some harbor views; no restaurant on-site. [$] *Rooms from: C$165* ✉ *11409 Rte. 19, Mabou* ☎ *902/945–2207, 800/840–2207* 🌐 *www.duncreigan.ca* 🛏 *8 rooms* 🍴 *Free Breakfast.*

Glenora Inn & Distillery
$$$$ | **B&B/INN** | North America's first single-malt whisky distillery adjoins this whitewashed inn north of Mabou, making it easy to sample a wee dram of Glen Breton Rare. **Pros:** twice daily ceilidhs June through October; some ground-level rooms have their own patio; beautifully wooded property bisected by a brook. **Cons:** pub and restaurant may not be open in May; road to chalets is steep and tricky to navigate at night; expensive. [$] *Rooms from: C$259* ✉ *13727 Hwy. 19, Glenville* ☎ *902/258–2262, 800/839–0491* 🌐 *www.glenoradistillery.com* 🕒 *Closed mid-Oct.–mid-May* 🛏 *28 rooms* 🍴 *No Meals.*

Performing Arts

Strathspey Performing Arts Centre
ARTS CENTERS | Concerts, plays, and musicals are presented at this arts center that is also one of the many venues for the annual Celtic Colours Festival. ✉ *11156 Hwy. 19, Mabou* ☎ *902/945–5300* 🌐 *facebook.com/StrathspeyPerformingArtsCentre.*

Activities

Mabou Highlands
HIKING & WALKING | The Cape Mabou Trail Club, a volunteer organization, maintains 30 km (18 miles) of nature trails, 17 in total, on this mountain range. Gaelic-speaking immigrants from Scotland settled this region of plunging cliffs, isolated beaches, rising mountains, and glens, meadows, and hardwood forests, and some of the trails follow tracks made by carts traveling to and from the pioneer settlements. Today the area is so hauntingly quiet that you might halfway expect to meet the *sidhe,* the Scottish fairies, capering on the hillsides. Trail maps can be purchased from local retailers or viewed online. ✉ *Mabou* 🌐 *www.capemabouhiking.com.*

Inverness

22 km (13 miles) north of Mabou.

Major investment from the Cabot Cape Breton resort, which has two of Canada's best golf courses, has helped lift this former coal mining community into one of Cape Breton's most upmarket areas for visitors. Sat on the shores of the almost mile-long white sand Inverness Beach, with excellent restaurants and fun attractions close by, Inverness makes a great stop on your Cape Breton itinerary for golfers and non-golfers alike.

GETTING HERE AND AROUND

There is no public transportation to Inverness. It's on the Ceilidh Trail.

Sights

Inverness Miners' Museum
HISTORY MUSEUM | Housed in a former railway station, this small museum has a range of artifacts relating to the community's coal mining past and the everyday life of the miners and their families, along with an antique-filled study room and film screenings. Volunteers offer personalized guided tours. ✉ *62 Lower Railway St., Inverness* 🌐 *invernessminersmuseum.com* 🎟 *C$5* 🕒 *Closed Oct.–May.*

Inverness Raceway

OTHER ATTRACTION | Harness racing has been happening here since 1926, and the Wednesday and Sunday races held throughout July and August are about as traditional as you get. This is the perfect spot for local color, and placing bets is pretty fun even if your horse doesn't come in! ✉ *112 Forest St., Inverness* ☎ *902/258–3315.*

🍴 Restaurants

Route 19 Brewing

$$$ | **CANADIAN** | Besides an excellent selection of beers brewed on the premises, this eatery serves up a seafood-heavy menu that truly hits the spot whether you're going for perfectly battered fish-and-chips, chicken burger, or poutine. The dining room is bright, modern, and airy, and the vibe is fun. **Known for:** excellent selection of local craft ciders and wines; fat, juicy, perfectly prepared lobster rolls; huge patio with ocean views. [$] *Average main: C$25* ✉ *16030 Central Ave., Inverness* ☎ *902/550–2739* 🌐 *route19brewing.com* 🕒 *Closed Mon. and Tues. No lunch.*

🛏 Hotels

★ **Cabot Cape Breton**

$$$$ | **RESORT** | Easily the most luxurious stay on Cape Breton Island, the contemporary and beautifully designed lodge rooms and golf villas at this resort are exceptional. **Pros:** central location; exceptional levels of service; luxurious touches like L'Occitane bath products. **Cons:** need advance reservations for golf and rooms; parties of golfers can be loud in restaurants; more expensive than other island accommodations. [$] *Rooms from: C$615* ✉ *18 Cabot La., Inverness* ☎ *902/258–4653, 855/660–6243* 🌐 *cabotcapebreton.com/resort* 🕒 *Closed mid-Oct.–May* 🛏 *72 rooms, 19 villas* 🍽 *No Meals.*

🏃 Activities

★ **Cabot Cliffs and Cabot Links Golf Courses**

GOLF | Canada's only true links courses have turned Cape Breton into an international golf destination, rated among the world's best by publications like Golf Digest. Cabot Cliffs, perched atop 80-foot cliffs with stunning views, was designed by the impressive team of Bill Coore and Ben Crenshaw. Set along the rugged Cape Breton seashore near Inverness, Cabot Links, designed by Rod Whitman, is both challenging and stunningly scenic. Superb lodging and dining options for both are part of the Resort at Cabot Links. These are walking-only courses, so no buggy rentals. ✉ *15933 Central Ave., Inverness* ✣ *22 km (14 miles) north of Mabou on Cabot Trail* ☎ *902/258–4653, 855/728–6886* 🌐 *www.cabotlinks.com* 🎟 *Each course C$120–C$295 (discounts for resort guests and Nova Scotia residents)* ⛳ *Cabot Cliffs: 18 holes, 6764 yards, par 72; Cabot Links: 18 holes, 6854 yards, par 72.*

Margaree Harbour

32 km (20 miles) north of Inverness.

Aside from pleasant pastimes like hillside hiking and saltwater swimming (Whale Cove and Chimney Corner are the locals' top picks for the latter), the Margaree area promises world-class fly-fishing. Margaree Harbour not only marks the point where the Ceilidh Trail joins the Cabot Trail, it also sits at the mouth of the Margaree River: a designated Canadian Heritage River known for legendary salmon runs.

GETTING HERE AND AROUND

There is no public transportation to Margaree Harbour. It's just north of where the Ceilidh Trail meets the Cabot Trail, so is accessible cross-country from Baddeck as well as up the coast.

Sights

Margaree Salmon Museum

HISTORY MUSEUM | Exhibits at this unassuming and yet widely renowned museum are proudly old-school, which seems fitting because they're housed in a former one-room schoolhouse. On display are all manner of fishing tackle, photographs, hand-tied flies, and other memorabilia related to salmon angling on the Margaree—check out the rod that once belonged to a wartime British spy who shared fly-fishing tips with Hermann Goering. Visitors can watch videos, study models of the river, and peek into the fish tank. ✉ *60 E. Big Intervale Rd., North East Margaree* ☎ *902/248–2848* 🌐 *www.margareens.com/margaree_salmon.html* 🎫 *C$2* ⏲ *Closed mid-Oct.–mid-June.*

Restaurants

★ **Dancing Goat Cafe & Bakery**

$ | **BAKERY** | This fabulous bakery opens at 7:30 am for breakfast, great coffee, and tasty treats. Their sandwiches and soups are excellent, and stocking up on cookies and oatcakes to take with you is highly advised. **Known for:** warm and friendly staff; sandwiches made with fresh baked bread; delicious selection of cheesecakes. [$] *Average main: C$9* ✉ *6289 Cabot Trail Rd., Margaree Harbour* ☎ *902/248–2727* 🌐 *facebook.com/DancingGoatCafe* ☞ *Closes at 4 pm every day.*

Hotels

Normaway Inn and Cabins

$$ | **B&B/INN** | Set on 500 acres in the Margaree Valley, this inn has rooms full of country character, hiking trails on the doorstep, and a music venue in a converted barn that rings with the sound of live traditional music from top Cape Breton fiddlers; performers sometimes play "unplugged" in the parlor, too. **Pros:** delicious, locally sourced food; bucolic setting; central to island touring loops. **Cons:** some rooms are tucked in under the roof; about 25-minute drive from Margaree Harbour; not luxurious (but doesn't aspire to be). [$] *Rooms from: C$129* ✉ *691 Egypt Rd., Margaree Harbour* ☎ *902/248–2987, 800/565–9463* 🌐 *www.thenormawayinn.com* ⏲ *Closed Nov.–May; cabins available off-season by arrangement* 🛏 *27 rooms* 🍴 *No Meals.*

Activities

The Margaree has two fishing seasons: the early-summer run, which opens annually on June 1, and the fall run, from mid-September through October, which coincides with the peak foliage period. Salmon-fishing licenses cost about C$64 per week for anglers who don't live in Nova Scotia. Before planning a fishing trip, check the latest catch-and-release regulations, imposed in 2015 amid concerns about declining stocks in Margaree and other rivers.

Margaree Salmon Association

FISHING | The association is heavily involved in salmon conservation and habitat restoration, and has put together a pamphlet, available on its website, outlining Margaree River fishing etiquette. In addition to the fishing advice, the pamphlet lists the names and contact information of guides who know the river well and can help you catch that trophy-size salmon. The guides typically charge C$175–C$350 per day. ✉ *Margaree Harbour* ☎ *902/248–2555 general information* 🌐 *www.margareesalmon.org.*

Chéticamp

25 km (16 miles) north of Margaree Harbour.

In Chéticamp, an Acadian enclave for more than 200 years, Francophone culture and traditions are still very much alive. That's why the Gaelic-inflected lilt in locals' voices is replaced by a distinct

French accent. (You might be greeted in French but can respond in English—most residents are bilingual.) Size is another distinguishing factor because, with population of about 3,000, Chéticamp feels like a major metropolis compared to other Western Shore communities. The landscape is different, too. Poised between mountains and sea, Chéticamp stands exposed on a wide lip of flat land below a range of bald green hills, behind which lies the high plateau of the Cape Breton Highlands. Commercial fishing is the town's raison d'être, but rug hooking is its main claim to fame, a fact reflected in local attractions and shops. So pause to peruse them before racing into the adjacent national park.

GETTING HERE AND AROUND

There is no public transportation to Chéticamp. By road, it's on the Cabot Trail just south of the Cape Breton Highlands National Park.

ESSENTIALS

VISITOR INFORMATION Chéticamp Visitor Information Centre. ✉ *Les Trois Pignons, 15584 Cabot Trail, Chéticamp* ☎ *902/224–2642* 🌐 *www.cheticamp.ca.*

Sights

Les Trois Pignons Cultural Center

HISTORY MUSEUM | The center, which contains the Elizabeth LeFort Gallery, displays samples of the rugs, tapestries, and related artifacts that helped make Chéticamp the World Rug Hooking Capital. Born in 1914, Elizabeth LeFort created more than 300 tapestries, some of which have hung in the Vatican, the White House, and Buckingham Palace. (One standout depicting U.S. presidents is made from 11 km [7 miles] of yarn!) Les Trois Pignons is also an Acadian cultural and genealogical information center. ✉ *15584 Cabot Trail Rd., Chéticamp* ☎ *902/224–2642* 🌐 *www.lestroispignons.com* 🎟 *C$7* 🕓 *Closed late-Oct.–mid-May.*

Restaurants

★ L'Abri

$$$ | **FRENCH** | Classic French cuisine with Acadian heart, this beautiful restaurant is filled with antiques and raw wood, with views out over the crashing ocean. Every carefully prepared dish is spectacular, from Acadian fricot to salt cod gratin to their upscale burger. **Known for:** sophisticated atmosphere in an unexpected location; impressive selection of whiskeys; their Basque cheesecake with berry preserves. [$] *Average main: C$29* ✉ *15559 Cabot Trail Rd., Chéticamp* ☎ *902/224–3888* 🌐 *labri.cafe* 🕓 *Dinner only Mon. to Weds.*

Coffee and Quick Bites

Mr. Chicken

$$ | **CANADIAN** | This fun locals' favorite serves tasty and well-seasoned fried and roasted chicken, burgers, and fried foods. There's also an attached ice-cream parlor. **Known for:** oceanfront location with picnic tables; delicious roast chicken poutine; huge portions and fast service. [$] *Average main: C$12* ✉ *15546 Cabot Trail Rd., Chéticamp* ☎ *902/224–2975.*

Shopping

Freya and Thor Gallery & Café

ART GALLERIES | This bright and modern gallery showcases local folk art woodcarvings, screenprinting, jewelry, and all manner of made-in-the-Maritimes handicrafts. Some say that the attached café serves the best coffee in Cape Breton, and once you try their baked goods you'll want to grab a few extras for the road. ✉ *15856 Cabot Trail, Chéticamp* ☎ *902/224–1831* 🌐 *freyaandthor.ca.*

Cape Breton Highlands National Park, brimming with waterfalls, wooded valleys, and steep cliffs, is a hiker's paradise.

🏃 Activities

On whale-watch cruises departing from Chéticamp's government wharf, you can see minkes, humpbacks, and finbacks in their natural environment.

Captain Zodiac Whale Cruise
WILDLIFE-WATCHING | FAMILY | The operators of these cruises aboard Zodiac vessels are so confident you'll spot a whale—finbacks, humpbacks, minkes, and pilots are the ones most sighted—that they'll refund your money if you don't. Trips take place daily from early July through late August. ⊠ *15407 Cabot Trail Rd., Chéticamp* ⊕ *www.novascotiawhales.com* ☎ *From C$59.*

★ Gypsum Mine Trail
HIKING & WALKING | An easy 2.6 km (1.6 mile) round-trip hike along a gravel trail through pretty woodland and across a river delivers you to a turquoise lake that was once a gypsum mine. The lake is a beautiful swimming spot that stays warm into October, and if you use the anchored rope provided you can clamber up to a viewpoint that shows the entire lake and thousands of trees around it (which is extra spectacular in the fall). ⊠ *Cheticamp Back Rd., Chéticamp.*

Le Portage Golf Club
GOLF | The beautiful but formidable holes at Le Portage overlook the Gulf of St. Lawrence. Course designers Robert and David Moote incorporated 60 sand bunkers, which together with the area's heavy winds provide no end to challenges no matter your skill level. ⊠ *15580 Cabot Trail Rd., Chéticamp* ☎ *902/224–3338, 888/618–5558* ⊕ *www.leportagegolfclub.com* ☎ *C$75–C$110* 🏌 *18 holes, 6777 yards, par 72.*

Cape Breton Highlands National Park

5 km (3 miles) north of Chéticamp; 108 km (67 miles) north of Ingonish.

Encircled by one of the world's most scenic driving routes—the glorious, partly coast-hugging, switchback Cabot Trail—this beautiful national park rises from sea level to forested mountaintops, with stunning views, wilderness hiking, and a wealth of wildlife and plants. Fall colors here are nothing short of breathtaking.

GETTING HERE AND AROUND
There is no public transportation to the park. The Cabot Trail loops around it, past the western entrance, at Chéticamp, and the eastern one, at Ingonish.

◉ Sights

★ Cape Breton Highlands National Park
NATIONAL PARK | A 950-square-km (366-square-mile) wilderness of wooded valleys, barren plateaus, and steep cliffs, Cape Breton Highlands National Park stretches across northern Cape Breton from the gulf shore to the Atlantic. High-altitude bogs here are home to wild orchids and other unique flora. Moose, eagles, deer, bears, foxes, bobcats, and coyotes call this home, and your chances of spotting wildlife improve if you venture off the main road and hike one of the trails at dusk or dawn. The park has 26 hiking trails, ranging from a few yards to a lookout point to 12-km (7½-mile) treks to salmon pools or to a remote cove, and guided hikes are among various activities on offer. A permit or pass is required for entering sections of the Cabot Trail within the national park and for use of the facilities; there are additional fees for camping, fishing, and golf. Full details are available at the gateway information centers. ⊠ *Entrances on Cabot Trail near Chéticamp and Ingonish, 37639 Cabot Trail, Ingonish* ☎ *902/224–2306,* *902/224–3814 bookstore* ⊕ *www.parks-canada.ca* ⊠ *C$8.*

Pleasant Bay

41 km (26 miles) north of Chéticamp.

Because it's about halfway around the Cabot Trail, Pleasant Bay is a convenient place to stop. Local fishermen catch lobster in spring and snow crab in summer. The water yields much bigger creatures, too, and it could be said that whales here outnumber people. Of course, that isn't hard considering the population is just about 350.

GETTING HERE AND AROUND
There is no public transportation to Pleasant Bay. By road, it's on the Cabot Trail just as it briefly emerges from the northwest boundary of the Cape Breton Highlands National Park.

◉ Sights

Gampo Abbey
RELIGIOUS BUILDING | Nova Scotia is a center of Shambhala Buddhism, and though Shambhala International is headquartered in Halifax, this abbey is its monastic heart. Finding the site high above the sea, however, requires more than soul searching. From Pleasant Bay, a spur road creeps along the cliffs to Red River; beyond that, a gravel road twists and turns for some 3 km (2 miles) before reaching the broad, flat bench of land on which the monastery sits. You can tour the abbey and wander through some of its 230 acres to visit a small shrine and grotto. If the abbey is closed for a retreat or other event, continue down the road for about ½ km (¼ mile) to see the Stupa of Enlightenment, a large and elaborate shrine dedicated to world peace. ⊠ *1533 Pleasant Bay Rd., Chéticamp* ☎ *902/224–2752* ⊕ *gampoabbey.org.*

Whale Interpretive Centre

SCIENCE MUSEUM | FAMILY | Visitors who like to stay on dry land while observing sea life should stop by here. Exhibits and models inside the center's modern structure explain the unique world of whales, dolphins, and porpoises, and there's a life-size model of a pilot whale. Using zoom scopes on the whale-spotting deck, you may catch a close-up glimpse of the many different species that often frolic just off-shore. ⊠ *104 Harbour Rd., Pleasant Bay* ☎ *902/224–1411* ⊕ *whale-interpretive-centre.business.site* ✉ *C$5* ⊘ *Closed Oct.–May.*

🛏 Hotels

★ True North Destinations

$$$ | RESORT | The ultimate glamping experience, these large and tastefully outfitted geodomes overlooking the bay come complete with king-size beds and pull-out sofas, and bathrooms with a shower. **Pros:** boardgames and condiments are provided; unbelievable views from skylight above; kitchens are fully equipped. **Cons:** lack of soundproofing means you can hear neighbors; only half the domes are ocean front with unobstructed views; book out a year in advance. 💲 *Rooms from: C$250* ⊠ *23241 Cabot Trail Rd., Pleasant Bay* ☎ *833/223-6637* ⊕ *truenorthdestinations.ca* ⊘ *Open Sat. and Sun. only Nov.-May* 🍴 *10* 🍽 *No Meals.*

🏃 Activities

Captain Mark's Whale & Seal Cruise

RAFTING | FAMILY | Sightings of whales (minke, finback, or pilot whales, hopefully, all three) are guaranteed on tours, from June through mid-September, aboard inflatable Zodiac boats. Expect to also see seals and birdlife, expertly explained by Captain Mark. ⊠ *Harbour Rd., off Cabot Trail, Pleasant Bay* ☎ *902/224–1316, 888/754–5112* ⊕ *www.*

whaleandsealcruise.com ✉ *From C$65* ⊘ *Closed mid-Oct.–May.*

Cape North

30 km (19 miles) east of Pleasant Bay.

This is where explorer Giovanni Caboto (aka John Cabot) made land in 1497. Not only does Cape North still feel like a new discovery, it also provides access to locales that are even more remote, like Bay St. Lawrence and Meat Cove.

GETTING HERE AND AROUND

There is no public transportation to Cape North. By road, it's at the northernmost point on the Cabot Trail.

🏖 Beaches

Cabots Landing Provincial Park

BEACH | This long, sandy beach remains untouched by modern development, other than the picnic tables on the adjoining grassland. It's a great place for beachcombing and pondering the journeys of First Nations boatmen who once set out from here to paddle to Newfoundland. A cairn in the park, commemorating the purported arrival of John Cabot from England in 1497, offers further historical insights, but the jaw-dropping views of Aspy Bay and the surrounding wilderness area provide the best reasons to come here. **Amenities:** parking (free). **Best for:** solitude; walking. ⊠ *1904 Bay St. Lawrence Rd., Bay St. Lawrence* ✛ *2 km (1 mile) north of Four Mile Beach Inn* ⊕ *parks.novascotia.ca/content/cabots-landing* ✉ *Free.*

🛏 Hotels

Channel Breezes Bed and Breakfast

$$ | B&B/INN | On Aspy Bay, just off the Cabot Trail and with glorious sea and mountain views and two beaches just a short walk away, this cozy bed-and-breakfast makes a great base for exploring the North Cape. **Pros:** comfortable beds; one

room has a private balcony; sitting room with mini-refrigerator for guests. **Cons:** some rooms on smaller side; communal breakfasts don't suit everyone; rather remote. $ *Rooms from: C$155* ⊠ *706 Dingwall Rd., Dingwall* ☎ *902/285–0650* ⇨ *4 rooms* ⏐○⏐ *Free Breakfast.*

Activities

Cabot Trail Adventures
KAYAKING | FAMILY | Based in Dingwall, which neighbors Cape North, this outfitter offers kayak and cycling tours, kayak and bike rentals, and half- and full-day guided hikes, from May through October. ⊠ *299 Shore Rd., South Harbour, Dingwall* ☎ *902/383–2552* ⊕ *www.kayakingcapebreton.ca* ⊠ *Tours from C$85; rentals from C$35* ☉ *Closed Oct.–Jun.*

Captain Cox's Whale Watch
RAFTING | Tours in a speedy Zodiac set out three times daily in July and August, and twice daily mid-to-late June and in September from Bay St. Lawrence Wharf. Tours last between 2 and 2½ hours, and if you don't see a whale, you get another trip for free. ⊠ *Bay St. Lawrence Rd., off Cabot Trail, Bay St. Lawrence* ☎ *902/383–2981, 888/346–5556* ⊕ *www. whalewatching-novascotia.com* ⊠ *C$45.*

Oshan Whale Watch
RAFTING | FAMILY | The C$45 charge for a 2½-hour trip on a working lobster boat is a bargain, and this outfitter offers a 100% refund if you don't spot any whales and are unhappy with your trip. They're such a likable crew that it's highly unlikely you will step off the boat without a smile on your face though. ⊠ *3384 Bay St. Lawrence Rd., Bay St. Lawrence* ☎ *902/383–2883, 877/383–2883* ⊕ *www.oshan.ca.*

Ingonish

35 km (22 miles) southeast of Cape North.

The western gateway to the Cabot Trail, Ingonish is one of the leading vacation destinations on Cape Breton, largely because it's home to the much-touted Keltic Lodge Resort and adjacent Highland Links golf course. The spot is actually comprised of five villages—Ingonish proper, Ingonish Centre, Ingonish Beach, Ingonish Harbour, and Ingonish Ferry. Poised on two bays and divided by a long narrow peninsula, all together they cover about 16 km (10 miles).

GETTING HERE AND AROUND
There is no public transportation to Ingonish. By road, it lies on the eastern section of the Cabot Trail.

Sights

Cape Smokey Provincial Park
HIKING & WALKING | The park that caps the 984-foot Cape Smokey Peak has a challenging 10-km (6-mile) round-trip coastal trail that is breathtaking in more ways than one. Hiking it takes about four hours. There are also picnic tables and lookout points—and great skiing if you come in winter. ⊠ *40301 Cabot Trail Rd., Ingonish* ⊕ *parks.novascotia.ca/content/cape-smokey* ⊠ *Free.*

Restaurants

★ Salty Rose's & the Periwinkle Café
$$$ | CANADIAN | FAMILY | This beautiful café filled with art and vintage furniture serves tasty breakfasts, sandwiches, and delectable baked goods, as well as perfect espresso drinks. With a focus on fresh and local, you'll find snowcrab and lobster rolls on the menu, as well as produce from the gardens out back. **Known for:** ocean views from their patio; the Brekkie sandwich with lobster; warm, friendly atmosphere. $ *Average main:*

C$23 ✉ 36056 Cabot Trail Rd., Ingonish ☎ 902/202–2431 🌐 saltyrosesandtheperiwinklecafe.com 🕓 Closed Tues. and Weds. Closed Nov.–May.

Coffee and Quick Bites

Bean Barn Cafe
$$ | **BAKERY** | Perhaps the best place on the island to grab a slice of pie, this bakery always has a huge selection of sweet treats as well as excellent sandwiches and decent coffee too. The café is pretty tiny, but there's a patio and picnic tables outside. **Known for:** great spot to grab takeout as you're leaving Ingonish; sky-high cream pies; delicious cinnamon rolls. [$] *Average main: C$12 ✉ 36743 Cabot Trail Rd., Ingonish 🌐 beanbarn.ca 🕓 Closed Weds.*

Hotels

Lantern Hill & Hollow
$$$$ | **B&B/INN** | **FAMILY** | Hearing the surf is no problem at this intimate property because the six cottages are just steps from a private 3-km (2-mile) beach that is ideal for quick dips and nightly bonfires; firewood and beach toys are supplied. **Pros:** fresh contemporary style; gorgeous and well-maintained property; convenient location. **Cons:** very light housekeeping; self-catering only; no meals provided. [$] *Rooms from: C$300 ✉ 36845 Cabot Trail, Ingonish Beach, Ingonish ☎ 902/285–2010, 888/663–0225 🌐 www.lanternhillandhollow.com 🕓 Closed mid-Oct.–late May 🛏 10 suites 🍴 No Meals.*

Keltic Lodge Resort and Spa
$$$$ | **RESORT** | **FAMILY** | Spread across the sea cliffs, this resort has glorious views of Cape Smokey and the surrounding highlands. **Pros:** gorgeous location; breakfast is included; lots to do. **Cons:** expensive; could use a makeover; standard of service, though friendly, can be patchy. [$] *Rooms from: C$389 ✉ 383 Keltic Inn Rd., Middle Head Peninsula, Ingonish Beach ☎ 902/285–2880, 800/565–0444 🌐 www.kelticlodge.ca 🕓 Closed mid-Oct.–mid-May 🛏 84 rooms 🍴 Free Breakfast.*

Activities

Highlands Links
GOLF | Perennially ranked as one of Canada's top courses, Highlands was designed by Stanley Thompson, who dubbed it "the mountains and ocean" course. It's a delight to play, with many challenges presented in the land or prevailing winds—even if you think a shot looks easy, it's unlikely that it will be, so be prepared. Over the past few years work has been done to open up the views, so you can now see the ocean from 11 holes. *✉ Cape Breton Highlands National Park, 247 Keltic Inn Rd., Ingonish Beach ☎ 902/285–2600, 800/441–1118 🌐 www.kelticlodge.ca/golf 🎟 C$75–C$135 ⛳ 18 holes, 6592 yards, par 72.*

St. Ann's Bay and Around

Extends for 65 km (40 miles) from Ingonish south to St. Ann's.

Continuing down the Cabot Trail from Ingonish, you'll skirt St. Ann's Bay where communities are of the blink-and-you'll-miss-it variety. Other than North America's only Gaelic college, there are few actual attractions, but there are fun outdoor opportunities and some of Atlantic Canada's most distinctive shops.

GETTING HERE AND AROUND

There is no public transportation to the St. Ann's Bay area. By road, approach from the north on the Cabot Trail; from the south take the Trans-Canada Highway (Highway 105, aka "Mabel and Alexander Graham Bell Way") north from Baddeck, then turn onto Highway 312, and continue through Englishtown.

👁 Sights

Gaelic College of Celtic Arts and Crafts

COLLEGE | Being home to direct descendants of the Gaelic pioneers, St. Ann's Bay is a logical site for this college, established in 1938 with a mission to promote and preserve the settlers' heritage. And mission accomplished, because today the campus provides a crash course in Gaelic culture. For instance, after learning about Scottish history in the Great Hall of Clans (particularly the Highland Clearances that sparked a mass exodus of Scots to the New World during the 18th century), you can view a short Gaelic-language film, then discover traditional disciplines like weaving and dancing at interactive stations. Not surprisingly, music at the college is especially noteworthy. Week-long summer-school courses—as well as occasional weekend workshops—focus on topics such as bagpiping and fiddling. The college hosts lunchtime and Wednesday-evening ceilidhs in summer and in fall it's a key site for the Celtic Colours Festival. ☒ 51779 Cabot Trail Rd., St. Ann's, St. Ann's ☎ 902/295-3411 ⊕ gaeliccollege.edu ☒ Great Hall of the Clans C$10; ceilidhs from C$15 ⊙ Closed early Oct.–mid-May.

🛍 Shopping

Gaelic College of Celtic Arts and Crafts Gift Shop

CRAFTS | Filled with Celtic and clan-related items—crafts, books, clothing, and music—this shop has a custom-kilt maker on-site. ☒ 51779 Cabot Trail Rd., St. Ann's ☎ 902/295-3411 ⊕ gaeliccollege. edu/visit/craft-shop.

Glass Artisans Studio & Gallery

CRAFTS | Gorgeous glassware—be it stained, painted, blown, or fused—is sold here. There are also glass-blowing demonstrations. ☒ 45054 Cabot Trail, North Shore ☎ 902/929-2585 ⊕ www. glassartisans.ca.

Leather Works by Jolene

LEATHER GOODS | Butter-soft purses in beautiful, bright hues, pet collars, wallets, bags, and nifty items for the home are the specialties here, all crafted in the adjoining workshop. ☒ 45808 Cabot Trail, Indian Brook, St. Ann's ☎ 902/929-2414 ⊕ www.leather-works.ca.

Piper Pewter

CRAFTS | Much of the lead-free pewter giftware and jewelry created here and on display in the bright showroom is inspired by Celtic designs. ☒ 46112 Cabot Trail, Indian Brook, St. Ann's ☎ 902/929-2227 ⊕ www.piperpewter.com.

Sew Inclined

WOMEN'S CLOTHING | Need a new outfit, or something to top off the one you're wearing? Fashions and theatrical hand-made hats in almost every imaginable style and fabric are crafted here by milliner and costume designer Barbara Longva. ☒ 41819 Cabot Trail, Wreck Cove ☎ 902/929-2259, 902/929-2050 ⊕ www. sewinclined.ca.

Wildfire Pottery

CERAMICS | Cool clay creations, many of them in the shape of area animals, are the specialty here. ☒ 44546 Cabot Trail, North Shore ☎ 902/929-2315 ⊕ www. wildfirepottery.ca.

🏃 Activities

North River Kayak Tours

KAYAKING | Guided excursions are conducted by this outfitter. A light lunch is included in the half-day tour, and full-day tours include a hot lunch of fishcakes and homemade beans and bread on the beach. Basic rentals are also available. ☒ 644 Murray Rd., North River Bridge ✛ 40 km (25 miles) northeast of Baddeck via Cabot Trail ☎ 902/929-2628, 888/865-2925 ⊕ www.northriverkayak. com ☒ Tours from C$74 ⊙ Closed mid-Oct.–mid-May.

Baddeck

20 km (12 miles) southwest of St. Ann's.

Baddeck has enough down-to-earth amenities (like a grocery store) to make it a service center, and enough charm to make it a tourist destination. The population is only about 1,000 residents but the town's larger-than-usual concentration of lodgings, restaurants, and shops attracts motorists who are ending (or starting) a Cabot Trail trek. Boaters also come to explore Bras d'Or Lake. The most competitive among them raise anchor during Regatta Week, Baddeck's main event, which begins the first Sunday in August at the Bras d'Or Yacht Club (☎ 902/295–2107).

GETTING HERE AND AROUND

Maritime Bus serves Baddeck with one bus daily. The journey from Halifax takes about 5½ hours and costs C$75.30 one way; the time from Truro is about 3½ hours and the fare is C$58.63. Baddeck is on the Trans-Canada Highway (Highway 105).

BOAT TOURS

Amoeba Sailing Tours

BIRD WATCHING | FAMILY | Take a tour aboard a sleek schooner, lasting from 90 minutes to two hours, which views bald eagles and the Alexander Graham Bell Estate. Trips depart daily at 11, 2, and 4:30 from June to mid-October, with an extra sailing at 6:30 pm in July and August. ✉ *Baddeck Wharf, Baddeck* ☎ *902/295–7780* ⊕ *www.amoebasailingtours.com* ☞ *C$30.*

Donelda's Puffin Boat Tours

BIRD WATCHING | FAMILY | The Bird Islands, 2 km (1 mile) from the entrance to Bras d'Or Lake, are the breeding grounds for Atlantic puffins, as well as other seabirds and gray seals. To see them, sign up for one of these narrated nature cruises. Boats depart daily from Englishtown, about 28 km (17 miles) northeast of Baddeck. ✉ *1099 Hwy. 312,*

Englishtown ✛ *Just before Englishtown Ferry* ☎ *902/929–2563, 877/278–3346* ⊕ *www.puffinboattours.ca* ☞ *From C$47* ☯ *Closed late Sept.–mid-May.*

SUP Baddeck

KAYAKING | Stand-up paddleboards can be rented here daily, for C$20 per hour. ✉ *368 Shore Rd., Baddeck* ☎ *902/295–0710* ⊕ *www.facebook.com/supbaddeck.*

ESSENTIALS

VISITOR INFORMATION Baddeck Visitor Information Centre. ✉ *454 Chebucto St., Baddeck* ☎ *902/295–1911* ⊕ *www.visit-baddeck.com.*

👁 Sights

★ Alexander Graham Bell National Historic Site

HISTORY MUSEUM | FAMILY | This very engaging site pays homage to the many inventions and humanitarian work of Alexander Graham Bell. Inside the main building, films, photos, artifacts, and models provide a window into his ideas for creating telephones, man-carrying kites, airplanes, and a record-setting hydrofoil boat (a full-scale replica of which dominates one exhibit hall). A kid's corner hosts demos and hands-on activities for aspiring young inventors. Bell spent large blocks of time, from 1886 until his death in 1922, at his Baddeck estate—Beinn Bhreagh, Gaelic for "beautiful mountain." His home (which is still owned by the family), and some spectacular scenery, can be seen from the roof of the National Historic Site that bears his name. ✉ *559 Chebucto St., Baddeck* ☎ *902/295–2069* ⊕ *pc.gc.ca/en/lhn-nhs/ns/grahambell* ☞ *C$8* ☯ *Closed Nov.–late-May.*

★ Highland Village Museum

MUSEUM VILLAGE | FAMILY | The 43-acre "village" is set high on a mountainside with a spectacular view of Bras d'Or Lake and narrow Barra Strait. Its 11 historical buildings (among them a forge, a school, a church, and a barn filled with heritage

Learn more about the Scottish-born inventor of the telephone at the Alexander Graham Bell National Historic Site in Baddeck.

breeds of livestock) were assembled from all over the province to depict the Highland Scots' way of life, from their origins in the Hebrides to the present day. Costumed animators who tackle daily chores lend the village a further touch of authenticity and are always on the ready to give an impromptu Gaelic lesson. Interactive programs include games and activities for children. There's a gift shop on-site as well as a Genealogy and Family History Center (open by appointment) that may be of interest to anyone with Cape Breton blood in their veins. In the off-season, the gift shop remains open weekdays when the rest of the site is closed. ⊠ *4119 Hwy. 223, Baddeck* ⊹ *Go south from Baddeck on Trans-Canada Hwy. (105) to Aberdeen, then take Rte. 223 east toward Iona for 23 km (14 miles), taking Little Narrows ferry en route* ☎ *902/725–2272, 866/442–3542* ⊕ *highlandvillage.novascotia.ca* ⊠ *C$11* ☉ *Closed mid-Oct.–May, except Sydney cruise ship days.*

Uisge Bàn Falls Provincial Park

WATERFALL | The focal point of this park, 14½ km (9 miles) north of Baddeck, is a forested 1½-km (1-mile) round-trip trail to a much-photographed 50-foot-high waterfall (*uisge* is Gaelic for "water"). ⊠ *715 N. Branch Rd., Baddeck Forks, Baddeck* ☎ *902/662–3030 Parks & Recreation Division* ⊕ *www.novascotiaparks.ca* ⊠ *Free.*

Wagmatcook Culture & Heritage Centre

INDIGENOUS SIGHT | The center spotlights the ancient history and rich traditions of the Mi'Kmaq people, with aboriginal guides providing interpretations and cultural entertainment, including drumming and song performances on Monday, Wednesday, and Friday in July and early August. The restaurant here serves traditional foods (such as moose and eel), as well as more contemporary fare, and a crafts shop sells items made by members of this First Nations community. ⊠ *10765 Hwy. 105, 16 km (10 miles) west of Baddeck, Baddeck* ☎ *902/295–2999,* ⊠ *Free (fees for some services); donations are welcome.*

🍴 Restaurants

Baddeck Lobster Suppers

$$$$ | **SEAFOOD** | For superfresh seafood and views overlooking Bras d'Or Lake, head for this former legion hall. There are just four options on the main-course menu—lobster, planked salmon, snow crab, and grilled steak—each of which can also come as a fixed-price feast with unlimited mussels, seafood chowder, homemade rolls and biscuits, desserts, and nonalcoholic beverages (yes, all of these items are unlimited). **Known for:** no reservations, so there may be a line outside; jovial atmosphere; all-you-can-eat starters and sides deals. [$] *Average main: C$36* ✉ *17 Ross St., Baddeck* ☎ *902/295–3307* 🌐 *www.baddecklobstersuppers.ca* 🕒 *Closed mid-Sept.–May. No lunch.*

The Freight Shed

$$$ | **SEAFOOD** | Fresh local seafood is what this waterfront eatery is known for, but they also do a great breakfast, hearty burgers and various other entrées. Prices are a little high, but that's common for Baddeck and the food is well prepared and tasty. **Known for:** huge waterfront patio; great selection of local craft beers; juicy lobster rolls. [$] *Average main: C$29* ✉ *2 Jones St., Baddeck* ☎ *902/295–1389* 🌐 *facebook.com/thefreightshed.*

🛏 Hotels

Inverary Resort

$$$ | **RESORT** | **FAMILY** | Rooms are distributed between several buildings dotted around this 11-acre lakeside resort, with options including cottages, suites, efficiency units, and a modern building. **Pros:** nice grounds and lake views; very family-friendly; walking distance to town. **Cons:** some rooms could do with an update; reduced services November through May; breakfast not included. [$] *Rooms from: C$180* ✉ *368 Shore Rd., Baddeck* ☎ *902/295–3500, 800/565–5660* 🌐 *inveraryresort.com* 🔑 *134 rooms* 🍽 *Free Breakfast.*

🎟 Performing Arts

The Baddeck Gathering Ceilidhs

MUSIC | Featuring traditional music and dancing, ceilidhs are held at St. Michael's Parish Hall every evening from July to late August, starting at 7:30. The hall opens at 5 for ticket sales, or you can be sure to get in by phoning ahead for a reservation. ✉ *6 Margaree Rd., Baddeck* ☎ *902/295–7663* 🌐 *www.baddeckgathering.com* 🎫 *C$15.*

🛍 Shopping

Flying Kite Artisan Shop

CRAFTS | This bright and airy store stocks a huge range of crafts from local artisans, including jewelry, apparel, jams, leather goods, prints, and photography as well as books by local authors. Most items are trendy rather than traditional, and this is a great place to pick up neat souvenirs. ✉ *507 Chebucto St., Baddeck* ☎ *902/295–3424* 🌐 *www.flyingkiteshop.ca.*

🏃 Activities

Bell Bay Golf Club

GOLF | In addition to panoramic views from nearly all its holes, the club has a highly regarded golf school and one of the largest practice facilities in Eastern Canada. Thomas McBroom, responsible for several dozen courses in Canada, along with some in Europe and the Caribbean, designed Bell Bay, and its wide fairways and large greens are well kept. It's suitable for novices, but also has some challenges for more experienced players. ✉ *761 Hwy. 205, Baddeck* ☎ *902/295–1333, 800/565–3077* 🌐 *www.bellbaygolfclub.com* 🎫 *C$80–C$120* 🏌 *18 holes, 7013 yards, par 72.*

Sydney

77 km (48 miles) east of Baddeck.

If you come directly to Cape Breton via plane, ferry, or cruise ship, Sydney is where you'll land. If you're seeking anything resembling an urban experience, it's also where you'll want to stay: after all, this is the island's sole city. Admittedly, it is not the booming center it was a century ago when the continent's largest steel plant was located here (that era is evoked in *Fall on Your Knees,* an Oprah Book Club pick penned by Cape Bretoner Anne-Marie MacDonald). However, Sydney has a revitalized waterfront and smattering of Loyalist-era buildings that appeal to visitors. Moreover, it offers convenient access to popular attractions in the region—like the Miner's Museum in nearby Glace Bay (named for the *glace,* or ice, that filled its harbor in winter), the Fortress at Louisbourg, and beautiful Bras d'Or Lake.

GETTING HERE AND AROUND

Sydney is on the Marconi Trail, one of the province's main driving routes, and it has Cape Breton's only real airport. There are year-round air connections via Halifax on Air Canada/Jazz and seasonal ones (from May through October) via Toronto on WestJet. Scheduled flights to the French-held islands of St-Pierre and Miquelon also run. Marine Atlantic operates ferries between Newfoundland and North Sydney, about 20 km (12 miles) north, year-round. Maritime Bus can get you here from many places in Nova Scotia, New Brunswick, and Prince Edward Island, though connections will need to be made for some routes. From Halifax it's straight through, with a daily departure at 3 pm; the journey takes nearly seven hours, and the one-way fare is C$89.20.

ESSENTIALS

VISITOR INFORMATION Sydney Visitor Information Centre. ⊠ *Joan Harriss Cruise Pavilion, 74 Esplanade, Sydney*

☎ *902/539–9876* ⊕ *www.sydney.cape-bretonisland.com.*

Sights

Cape Breton Miners' Museum

MINE | Here you can learn about the difficult lives of the local men whose job it was to extract coal from undersea collieries. After perusing the exhibits, you can don a hard hat and descend into the damp, claustrophobic recesses of a shaft beneath the museum with a retired miner who'll recount his own experiences toiling in the bowels of the earth. The 15-acre property also includes a replica village that gives you a sense of workers' home life, and it has a theater where the Men of the Deeps choir, a world-renowned group of working and retired miners, performs on certain evenings in summer. ⊠ *17 Museum St., Glace Bay* ✛ *Quarry Point, 20 km (13 miles) east of Sydney* ☎ *902/849–4522* ⊕ *www.minersmuseum.com* 🖾 *C$18* ⊘ *Closed mid-Oct.–late May, except by appointment.*

Casino Nova Scotia

CASINO | At the casino you can try your luck at slot machines, test your skill at gaming tables, or simply settle in to enjoy the live entertainment—assuming you're at least 19 years old, the legal gambling (and drinking) age in Nova Scotia. ⊠ *525 George St., Sydney* ☎ *902/563–7777, 866/334–1114* ⊕ *www.casinonovascotia.com.*

Marconi National Historic Site

HISTORIC SIGHT | On a spectacular headland, this site commemorates the spot at Table Head where, in 1902, Guglielmo Marconi built four tall wooden towers and beamed the first official wireless messages across the Atlantic Ocean. An interpretive trail leads to the foundations of the original towers and transmitter buildings. The visitor center has large models of the towers as well as artifacts and photographs chronicling the radio pioneer's life and work. ✉ *15 Timmerman St., Glace Bay* ✣ *23 km (14 miles) northeast of Sydney; follow signs from Hwy. 255* ☎ *902/295–2069, 902/842–2530 summer* 🌐 *www.pc.gc.ca* 🎫 *Free* 🕒 *Closed early Sept.–June.*

Peterfield Provincial Park

CITY PARK | Take a hike through history at this park on the south arm of Sydney Harbour. Initially developed as the private domain of David Matthews, a onetime mayor of New York City who remained loyal to the crown during the War of Independence, its 56 acres are laced with trails. ✉ *1126 Westmount Rd., Westmount* ✣ *Off Hwy. 239* ☎ *902/662–3030 Nova Scotia Provincial Parks* 🌐 *www.novascotiaparks.ca* 🎫 *Free.*

🍴 Restaurants

Flavor Downtown

$$ | **CONTEMPORARY** | In a city where deep fryers reign supreme, this small eatery is a welcome find. The haddock is poached, the scallops seared, the prawns tossed in pesto sauce—and Flavor's flavors shine through. **Known for:** healthy meals to go; wide range of gluten-free and vegan dishes; interesting sandwich fillings. [$] *Average main: C$20* ✉ *16 Pitt St., Sydney* ☎ *902/562–6611* 🌐 *www.cbflavor.com* 🕒 *Closed Sun. No dinner.*

Governor's Pub and Eatery

$$$ | **CONTEMPORARY** | **FAMILY** | Sydney's first mayor, Walter Crowe, once lived in this Victorian home, built in the late 1800s. The restaurant, with hardwood floors, a fireplace, and high ceilings, is known for fresh seafood and hand-cut steaks, though there are lighter options such as salads, wraps, and burgers. **Known for:** pub offers plenty of local color; bustling and welcoming atmosphere; decks on both levels overlooking the harbor. [$] *Average main: C$25* ✉ *233 Esplanade, Sydney* ☎ *902/562–7646* 🌐 *governorseatery.com.*

★ Kiju's

$$$ | **INTERNATIONAL** | Located in a conference center on the Membertou First Nation's urban reserve, this spacious dining room serves up inspired global cuisine using fresh, local ingredients with many dishes having an Indigenous twist—and you can order a prix fixe three-course First Nation menu (CA$45) that changes with the seasons. Regular menu items range from lamb chops perfectly cooked with a pistachio pesto to a delicately spiced curry paella. **Known for:** traditional luskinikn bread served with molasses; award-winning coconut cream pie; huge, heated patio. [$] *Average main: C$29* ✉ *50 Maillard St., Sydney* ☎ *902/562–6220* 🌐 *kijus.com* 🕒 *Closed Sun.*

☕ Coffee and Quick Bites

Doktor Luke's

$ | **CAFÉ** | This fun and funky coffee house is the perfect spot for an expertly prepared latte, fresh-baked goods, and a little conversation with the locals. **Known for:** really good decaf; sweet, friendly staff; fun vibe. [$] *Average main: C$8* ✉ *54 Prince St., Sydney* ☎ *902/270–5800* 🌐 *doktorlukes.com.*

JJ's Plant Based Eats

$ | **VEGETARIAN** | This cozy café is Cape Breton's first vegan eatery and serves up inventive and tasty dishes. **Known for:** friendly, warm service; the seitan donair with coconut donair sauce; amazing roast potatoes as a side. [$] *Average main: C$11* ✉ *54 Prince St., Sydney* 🌐 *facebook.com/jjsplantbasedeats* 🕒 *Closed Sun.*

🛏 Hotels

Cambridge Suites Hotel

$$$ | **HOTEL** | **FAMILY** | You can put yourself in the center of Sydney's waterfront action by staying at this comfortable all-suites hotel. **Pros:** great location and views; free continental breakfast buffet;

pet-friendly. **Cons:** decor is rather dull and dated; conventional room style; other people's pets are sometimes audible. [$] *Rooms from: C$179* ✉ *380 Esplanade, Sydney* ☎ *902/562–6500, 800/565–9466* 🌐 *www.cambridgesuitessydney.com* 🛏 *147 suites* 🍴 *Free Breakfast.*

Performing Arts

Joan Harriss Cruise Pavilion

ARTS CENTERS | More than just a port for the many cruise ships that dock here each year, the pavilion is a popular entertainment venue, too. Its main stage and lighthouse stage host many musical acts, especially during events like Sydney's nine-day Sydney Harbour Front Festival in August and the 10-day Celtic Colours International Festival in October. Even if you're not arriving by ship, the pavilion is easy enough to find: just look for the 60-foot fiddle that towers outside it. ✉ *74 Esplanade, Sydney* ☎ *902/564–9775* 🌐 *www.sydneyport.ca.*

Shopping

★ The Cape Breton Centre for Craft and Design

CRAFTS | Showcasing the work of more than 80 traditional and cutting-edge Cape Breton artisans in its airy gallery, the center, which houses on-site studios for pottery, weaving, and glass- and jewelry-making, also hosts hands-on workshops that are open to craft aficionados. Pick up a copy of the Artisan Trail Map here to find more studios elsewhere. ✉ *322 Charlotte St., Sydney* ☎ *902/270–7491* 🌐 *www.capebretoncraft.com.*

Cape Breton Farmers' Market

MARKET | The vendors at this vibrant Saturday morning market sell everything from local honey, produce, and baked goods to hand-crafted jewelry, ceramics, and photography. There's also a food hall where you can pick up excellent Indian and Korean cuisine to enjoy mid-shop, as well as sweet treats and coffee. ✉ *15 Falmouth St., Sydney* ☎ *902/564–9948* 🌐 *capebretonfarmersmarket.com.*

Louisbourg

35 km (22 miles) south of Sydney.

Though best known as the home of the largest historical reconstruction in North America, Louisbourg is also an important fishing community with a lovely harbor front.

GETTING HERE AND AROUND

There is no public transportation to Louisbourg. By road it's about a two-hour drive from the Canso Causeway, via Highway 125 then (at Exit 8) Route 22.

ESSENTIALS

VISITOR INFORMATION Louisbourg Visitor Information Centre. ✉ *7495 Main St., Louisbourg* ☎ *902/733–2321* 🌐 *www.louisbourg.ca.*

Sights

★ Fortress of Louisbourg National Historic Site

HISTORIC SIGHT | **FAMILY** | This may be Cape Breton's—or even Nova Scotia's—most remarkable attraction. After the French were forced out of mainland Nova Scotia in 1713, they established their headquarters here in a walled, fortified town at the mouth of Louisbourg Harbour. The fortress was captured twice (by New Englanders in 1745 and by the British in 1758), and after the second attack it was razed, a critical factor in ending France's dream of a North American empire.

In the 1960s, archaeologists rebuilt a fifth of the fortress, using the original plans. From June through mid-October, costumed interpreters well versed in the history of the site convincingly re-create the era with military drills, cannon-firing, and general day-to-day activities of the 18th-century inhabitants. The three inns serve food prepared from 18th-century

The Fortress of Louisbourg, a former French fort captured by the British in 1758, is now a living history museum.

recipes. Free guided tours are given in high season, and events—including themed dinner theaters and archaeological programs—make a visit even more memorable. An off-season visit, without all these activities, can paint an even more compelling picture of life here 300 years ago. ✉ *265 Parks Service Rd., Louisbourg* ☎ *902/733–3552* 🌐 *pc.gc.ca/en/lhn-nhs/ns/louisbourg* 🎫 *C$18 late June–mid-Oct., C$8 mid-Oct.–late June; guided tour C$4.*

🍴 Restaurants

Spoondrift Café & Gift Shop

$$ | **CANADIAN** | This bright and airy diner specializes in seafood dishes, steaks, and casual dining favorites with a cozy, down-home style. There aren't many options for dining in Louisbourg, but this place makes up for that. **Known for:** can get busy; truly excellent seafood chowder; warm, friendly service. [$] *Average main: C$18* ✉ *7541 Main St., Louisbourg* 🌐 *facebook.com/spoondriftcafe* 🕓 *Closed Mon.*

🛏 Hotels

Cranberry Cove Inn

$ | **B&B/INN** | This cozy cranberry-hued house, built in 1904, overlooks the harbor and is just a short drive from the Fortress of Louisbourg. **Pros:** historic charm; cooked breakfast included; impeccable rooms. **Cons:** lots of patterned wallpaper might not please everyone; Wi-Fi is spotty in some rooms; no elevator for three-story building. [$] *Rooms from: C$119* ✉ *12 Wolfe St., Louisbourg* ☎ *902/733–2171, 800/929–0222* 🌐 *www.cranberrycoveinn.com* 🕓 *Closed Nov.–Apr.* 🛏 *7 rooms* 🍽 *Free Breakfast.*

Louisbourg Harbour Inn Bed & Breakfast

$$ | **B&B/INN** | The central location of this grand, former sea captain's residence means it's just a few minutes' walk to the Louisbourg Playhouse, Main Street, and the harbor. **Pros:** historic style without being overfussy; cooked breakfast included; lovely views. **Cons:** two-night minimum for the best room; several rooms are small; breakfast is the only

meal available on-site. 💲 *Rooms from: C$135* ✉ *9 Lower Warren St., Louisbourg* ☎ *902/733–3222, 888/888–8466* 🌐 *www.louisbourgharbourinn.com* 🕒 *Closed early Oct.–early June* 🛏 *7 rooms* 🍽 *Free Breakfast.*

★ North Star Suites

$$$ | **HOTEL** | Built to resemble an oversized beach house, this stylish waterfront property is the closest to the Fortress of Louisbourg, with an enticing view across the bay. **Pros:** Fortress entrance just down the road; private pebble beach; owned by TV design stars Colin and Justin. **Cons:** some distance from center of town; limited restaurant menu off-season; not all units have ocean views. 💲 *Rooms from: C$195* ✉ *15 Commercial St. Extension, Louisbourg* ☎ *902/733–2080, 888/374–8439* 🌐 *www.hellonorthstar.ca* 🕒 *Closed mid-Oct.–mid-May* 🛏 *19 rooms* 🍽 *No Meals.*

Performing Arts

Louisbourg Playhouse

ARTS CENTERS | You can take in traditional Cape Breton music and other entertainments nightly at the Louisbourg Playhouse, a 17th-century-style theater that was modeled after Shakespeare's Globe. Originally constructed as part of the Disney movie set for *Squanto: A Warrior's Tale,* the venue was donated to the community in 1994 after filming wrapped. ✉ *11 Aberdeen St., Louisbourg* ☎ *902/733–2996, 902/733–3838 tickets* 🌐 *louisbourgplayhouse.ca.*

Arichat

154 km (95 miles) southwest of Louisbourg.

Arichat is the principal village on Isle Madame: the largest island in a 44-square-km (17-square-mile) archipelago of the same name, which sits at Cape Breton's southernmost tip. Known for its friendly Acadian culture and many secluded coves and inlets, Arichat has a deep harbor that made it an important fishing, shipbuilding, and trading center during the 19th century. Some fine old buildings from that period still remain. The two cannons overlooking the harbor were installed after John Paul Jones sacked the village during the American Revolution.

GETTING HERE AND AROUND

One of the best ways to experience Isle Madame is on foot. Try Cape Auguet Eco-Trail, an 8½-km (5-mile) hiking trail that extends from Boudreauville to Mackerel Cove and follows the rocky coastline overlooking Chedabucto Bay, with interpretive panels about the early days of immigration along the way. Another good half-day hike leads to Gros Nez, the "large nose" that juts into the sea. The island also lends itself to biking, as most roads glide gently along the shore.

Sights

LeNoir Forge Museum

HISTORY MUSEUM | This restored 18th-century French blacksmith shop occupies a handsome stone structure on the waterfront. In its 19th-century heyday, it supplied parts to local shipbuilders, and a barn on-site today has seafaring memorabilia. There's also a genealogy center and gift shop. ✉ *708 Veterans Memorial Dr., Arichat* ✣ *Off Hwy. 206* ☎ *902/226–9364* 🌐 *imhs.ca* 🎟 *Free, donations welcome* 🕒 *Closed late Oct.–June. Open Tues.–Fri. in June and Sept. Open Tues.–Sat. in July and Aug.*

Chapter 4

NEW BRUNSWICK

Updated by
Penny Phenix

◉ Sights	🍴 Restaurants	🛏 Hotels	🛍 Shopping	🍸 Nightlife
★★★★☆	★★★☆☆	★★☆☆☆	★★☆☆☆	★★☆☆☆

WELCOME TO NEW BRUNSWICK

TOP REASONS TO GO

★ **Whale-watching.** Double the fun of the Bay of Fundy by getting out onto the water to view several types of whales, plus seals, porpoises, and seabirds.

★ **Acadian culture.** Attractions such as Le Pays de la Sagouine or Acadian Historical Village on the Acadian Coastal Drive portray the French heritage of the region. Hear the distinctive accent at Dieppe Farmers' Market.

★ **Food and drink.** Enjoy freshly caught salmon, scallops, and lobster, organic produce and meat (including buffalo) from local farms, and some highly regarded local wines and craft beers.

★ **Hiking.** New Brunswick's provincial and national parks have amazing hiking trails and plenty of great spots to contemplate the gorgeous scenery or watch birds from an ocean cliff.

★ **Swimming.** New Brunswick is blessed with beaches, rivers, and lakes; you can choose from water that's cold or warm, fresh or salty.

1 Saint John.

2 St. Andrews by-the-Sea.

3 Grand Manan Island.

4 Deer Island.

5 Campobello Island.

6 St. Martins.

7 Fundy National Park.

8 Cape Enrage, Hopewell Cape, and Nearby.

9 Moncton and Dieppe.

10 Dorchester and Memramcook.

11 Sackville.

12 Shediac.

13 Bouctouche.

14 Kouchibouguac National Park.

15 Miramichi.

16 Shippagan.

17 Caraquet.

18 Edmundston.

19 Grand Falls.

20 Florenceville-Bristol.

21 Hartland.

22 Woodstock.

23 Kings Landing Historical Settlement.

24 Mactaquac Provincial Park.

25 Fredericton.

26 Village of Gagetown.

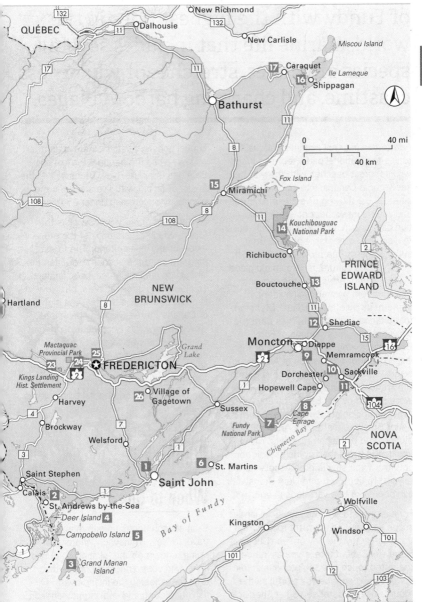

Stunning scenery, vast forests, and world-class attractions characterize New Brunswick. Topping the list is the Bay of Fundy, with the highest tides in the world, marine life that includes several species of whales, stretches of wilderness coastline, and charming harbor villages.

Add to this national and international historic sites, national parks teeming with wildlife, great beaches with the warmest seawater in Canada, vibrant towns and cities, and a thriving diversity of cultures, and you might wonder how the population can remain so utterly laid-back, but that's just another facet of New Brunswick's charm. The province, with a rich First Nations culture, is also an old place in New World terms, and the remains of a turbulent past are still evident in some of its quiet nooks. Near Moncton, for instance, wild strawberries perfume the air of the grassy slopes of Fort Beauséjour, where, in 1755, one of the last battles for possession of Acadia took place, with the English finally overcoming the French. Other areas of the province were settled by the British; by Loyalists, American colonists who chose to live under British rule after the American Revolution; and by Irish immigrants, many seeking to avoid the famine in their home country. If you stay in both Acadian and Loyalist regions, a trip to New Brunswick can seem like two vacations in one.

For every gesture in the provincial landscape as grand as the giant rock formations carved by the Bay of Fundy tides at Hopewell Cape, there is one as subtle as the gifted touch of a sculptor in a studio. For every experience as colorful as the mountains of lobster served at Shediac's annual Lobster Festival, there is another as low-key as the gentle waves of the Baie des Chaleurs. New Brunswick is the luxury of an inn with five stars and the tranquility of camping under a million.

At the heart of New Brunswick is the forest, which covers 85% of the province—nearly all its interior. The forest contributes to the economy, defines the landscape, and delights hikers, anglers, campers, and bird-watchers, but New Brunswick's soul is the sea. The biggest of Canada's three Maritime provinces, New Brunswick is largely surrounded by coastline. The warm waters of the Baie des Chaleurs, Gulf of St. Lawrence, and Northumberland Strait lure swimmers to their sandy beaches, and the chilly Bay of Fundy, with its monumental tides, draws breaching whales, whale-watchers, and kayakers.

Planning

When to Go

Each season brings unique reasons to travel to New Brunswick. Winter means skiing, snowmobiling, skating on public rinks, and cozy dinners. Spring is the time for canoeing the inland rivers, fishing, picking and cooking fiddleheads, viewing waterfalls engorged by melting snow, and watching the province come alive.

Summer is peak tourist season, and the beaches attract thousands of sun worshippers. The resort towns of Fundy, including Alma, St. Andrews, and St. George, get busy, too. It's a good time to trek up to the lighthouse at Cape Enrage. Summer festivals abound, and the province's two national parks, Fundy and Kouchibouguac, as well as its Stonehammer UNESCO Global Geopark, are filled with nature lovers.

Fall means country fairs, harvest suppers, and incredibly beautiful scenic drives to enjoy autumn foliage. Fall colors are at their peak from late September through mid- to late October. The Autumn Foliage Colours Line (800/268–3255) provides daily updates on which drives are best, and Tourism New Brunswick's website has a map (updated weekly) that shows the best leaf-peeping opportunities.

Planning Your Time

A good way to tour New Brunswick is to follow one of the five scenic drives into which the province is divided: The River Valley Scenic Drive follows more than 500 km (310 miles) of road along the St. John River; the Fundy Coastal Drive has potential views of whales and wildlife in the region of the Bay of Fundy; the Acadian Coastal Drive offers sandy beaches, picturesque villages, and vibrant culture; the Miramichi River Route is home to salmon fishing and folk festivals; and the Appalachian Range Route has serene mountain vistas and beautiful bays. The Fundy Coast is perhaps the most popular area, and many prefer to spend most of their time there. Overnight in lively, historic Saint John, the only city on the Bay of Fundy; Alma, the little coastal town that services Fundy National Park; or in Moncton, which, while not on the coast, is in easy reach and has some good

restaurants, shopping, and fun amusements for children.

Getting Here and Around

AIR

New Brunswick has three major airports: Greater Moncton Roméo LeBlanc International Airport, Saint John Airport, and Fredericton Airport.

CONTACTS Fredericton International Airport. ⊠ *2570 Rte. 102, Fredericton* ⊹ *About 10 min east of downtown Fredericton* ☎ *506/460–0920* ⊕ *yfcfredericton.ca.* **Greater Moncton Roméo LeBlanc International Airport.** ⊠ *777 Aviation Ave., Dieppe, Moncton* ⊹ *Off Hwy. 15 about 10 km (6 miles) northwest of central Moncton* ☎ *506/856–5444* ⊕ *cyqm.ca.* **Saint John Airport.** ⊠ *4180 Loch Lomond Rd., Saint John* ⊹ *About 18 km (11 miles) northeast of downtown Saint John* ☎ *506/638–5555* ⊕ *www.saintjohnairport.com.*

BOAT AND FERRY

Bay Ferries Ltd. runs from Saint John, New Brunswick, to Digby, Nova Scotia, and back once or twice a day, depending on the season. Passenger fares are C$41–C$51 per adult one way or C$67–C$87 round-trip, C$117–122 for a car, and C$9.50 per foot for a motorhome or car with trailer.

The year-round 20-minute ferry crossing from L'Etete, on mainland New Brunswick, to Deer Island is a free service operated by Coastal Transport for the government of New Brunswick. From Deer Island, East Coast Ferries Ltd. runs services to Campobello, New Brunswick, and Eastport, Maine, from June through September. On the Campobello route, the fares are C$16 for a car and driver, and C$4 for each adult passenger. For a motorhome and car with trailer the fare is C$1.50 per foot, plus a fuel surcharge of C$10. The crossing takes about 30 minutes. On the Eastport route, the fares

4

New Brunswick PLANNING

are C$13 for a car and driver and C$4 for each adult passenger. On both routes the fare for motorcycles is C$8, and a fuel surcharge of C$4 is also applied. Foot passengers pay C$5.

Coastal Transport has up to seven crossings per day from Blacks Harbour to Grand Manan from late June through mid-September and four crossings per day the rest of the year. Round-trip fares, payable on the Grand Manan side, are C$35.80 for a car and C$12 for an adult. A one-way crossing takes about 1½ hours.

CONTACTS Bay Ferries Ltd.. ✉ *170 Digby Ferry Rd., Saint John* ☎ *506/694–7777 Saint John Terminal, 888/249–7245 reservations* ⊕ *www.ferries.ca.* **Coastal Transport.** ☎ *506/662–3724, 855/882– 1978* ⊕ *www.coastaltransport.ca.* **East Coast Ferries Ltd..** ✉ *Deer Island Point Rd.* ☎ *506/747–2159, 877/747–2159* ⊕ *www. eastcoastferriesltd.com.*

BUS

Maritime Bus runs buses within the province and to destinations in Nova Scotia, Prince Edward Island, and Québec. Routes include the length of the Trans-Canada Highway from Québec to the Nova Scotia border and beyond, branching off to Prince Edward Island just south of Sackville. Another route heads up the Acadian Coast from Shediac to Campbelton, and there's a loop south from Oromocto, near Fredericton, to Saint John and Sussex. Tickets must be reserved. Be aware, though, that some stops are on the edge of town and might be inconvenient for passengers trying to get downtown.

CONTACTS Maritime Bus. ✉ *77 Canada St., Moncton* ☎ *506/854–2023* ⊕ *www. maritimebus.com.*

CAR

New Brunswick is the largest of the Atlantic provinces, covering nearly 78,000 square km (30,000 square miles): around 320 km (200 miles) north to south and 240 km (150 miles) east to west. Unless you plan to fly into one of the hubs and stay there for your visit, you'd be wise to have a car. There's a good selection of car-rental agencies, but book early for July and August, and be aware that debit cards may not be accepted (thus you'll need a credit card); call or visit the websites to search for pickup and drop-off locations throughout the province (bear in mind that rentals from airports carry a surcharge).

From Québec, the Trans-Canada Highway (Route 2, marked by a maple leaf) enters New Brunswick at St-Jacques and follows the St. John River through Fredericton and on to Moncton and the Nova Scotia border, with a branch crossing the Confederation Bridge to and across Prince Edward Island. From Maine, Interstate 95 crosses at Houlton to Woodstock, New Brunswick, where it connects with the Trans-Canada Highway. Those traveling up the coast of Maine on Route 1 cross at Calais to St. Stephen, New Brunswick, or via the Fundy Islands car ferries. New Brunswick's Route 1 extends through Saint John and Sussex to join the Trans-Canada Highway near Moncton.

A well-designed, well-marked system of provincial scenic drives takes you to most of the places in New Brunswick that you'd want to go. Begin in the south, on the phenomenal Fundy Coastal Drive (watch for the lighthouse-on-a-cliff logo). At the upper end of the bay it connects with the Acadian Coastal Drive (the logo is a white starfish on a red background), which hugs the gentle eastern shore. In the middle of the Acadian Drive is a bit of a detour for the Miramichi River Route (a jumping salmon logo). The Acadian Drive eventually meets the Appalachian Range Route (mountains logo), which takes you across the rugged northern part of the province, where the hardwood ridges ignite in a blaze of color in fall, and then connects with the River Valley Scenic

Drive (a fiddlehead logo), which runs down the entire western side of the province and back to Saint John, on the Fundy Coastal Drive.

Route 7 joins Saint John and Fredericton. Fredericton is connected to Miramichi by Route 8. Route 15 links Moncton to the eastern coast and to Route 11, which follows the coast north to Miramichi, around the Acadian Peninsula, and up to Campbellton.

CRUISE SHIP

Saint John has been welcoming cruise ships for more than 30 years and has two modern cruise terminals that in 2020 welcomed 92 cruise ships from 15 different cruise companies between April and November, bringing 200,000 passengers (the city population is 70,000, or 128,000 in the metro area). Entertainers help to create a festive atmosphere, local artisans and vendors set up tented markets, and tour operators have kiosks where you can sign up for various excursions. In 2021, the Port Authority was provided with around $1.75 million for the "container village" project, in which containers will be rented to local businesses, retail shops, hospitality companies and vendors and there will be a stage for live performances, a bar lounge, and a plaza. The harbor has also been dredged to allow for larger ships to visit regardless of the state of the tides. City-center sights are within walking distance of the terminals, and tour buses give access to those that are farther afield. Saint John Transit offers a two-hour tour for C$30 per adult and $15 per child aged six to 15, and the Big Pink buses charge C$56.94 a day for their hop-on, hop-off service. Taxi fares range from C$8 to C$15 within the city center, plus C$0.50 to C$1 for each additional passenger. For exploration outside the city by taxi, a trip to St. Martins, for example, would cost about C$120 and St. Andrews by-the-Sea would be about C$200.

TRAIN

Train travel options in New Brunswick are limited: VIA Rail offers a thrice-weekly passenger service from Montréal to Halifax on the Ocean route, stopping in New Brunswick at Campbellton, Bathurst, Miramichi, and Moncton, with request stops at a number of smaller towns along the route. The Montréal to Moncton economy fare is C$175 each way. There is no train service to the cities of Saint John or Fredericton.

CONTACTS VIA Rail. ✉ *77 Canada St., Moncton* ☏ *888/842–7245 toll-free in North America, 506/857–9830 Moncton* ⊕ *www.viarail.ca.*

Restaurants

You can eat extremely well in New Brunswick, with many restaurants sourcing top-quality ingredients from local farmers, fishermen, and artisan producers. At the top end are some of Canada's finest restaurants, such as Little Louis in Moncton and Savour in the Garden in St. Andrews by-the-Sea. Clos, on Moncton's Main Street, is another fine-dining spot combining local ingredients with international flavors. The 11th Mile in Fredericton is a chic place with a small-plates menu that's great for sharing, and Edmundston's Café Lotus Bleu has a range of healthy and delicious, beautifully presented vegetarian dishes. With its open kitchen and creative small plates, Origines: Cuisine Maritime is worthy of a special trip to Caraquet, while in Saint John, the Port City Royal restaurant uses only local products, including house-cured meats, pickles and vegetables, and has a ramen night on Wednesdays.

Restaurant reviews have been shortened. For full information, visit Fodors.com.

Hotels

Just about every kind of lodging experience is available in New Brunswick, including a plethora of high-end bed-and-breakfasts, rental properties, a smattering of boutique hotels, and, lording it over them all, the superbly renovated historic Algonquin Resort in St. Andrews by-the-Sea—part of the Marriott Autograph Collection. When it comes to chain hotels, all the North American names have a good presence in or around the major cities, but the Delta Hotels by Marriott group is the cream of the crop, offering high standards of accommodations, superb restaurants, well-trained and very welcoming staff, and attractive room rates. The one in Fredericton also has a gorgeous riverside location. The renowned Maritimes welcome is also much in evidence in the province's best bed-and-breakfasts, offering cozy (and sometimes luxurious) lodgings, often in historic homes, and plenty of inside information on the local area. There are some novel choices too, including treehouses, plastic bubbles in dark-sky reserves, tipis, chuckwagons, and lighthouses. You can even sleep in a cell of a former prison, now a nice bed-and-breakfast establishment. In peak season and during major festivals and events, rooms are snapped up quickly, so it's wise to book as far in advance as possible. Outside peak season many of the bed-and-breakfasts and rental properties are closed, although those in the cities tend to stay open year-round.

Some of the bed-and-breakfasts that are closed may consider accommodating guests staying for several nights, and rental properties may be available during the winter sports season, so it's always worth asking.

Hotel reviews have been shortened. For full information, visit Fodors.com.

What It Costs In Canadian Dollars

	$	$$	$$$	$$$$
RESTAURANTS				
	under C$12	C$12–C$20	C$21–C$30	over C$30
HOTELS				
	under C$125	C$125–C$174	C$175–C$250	over C$250

Tours

Whale-watching, sea kayaking, bird-watching, scuba diving, garden tours, vineyard and winery tours, city culinary tours, river cruising, golfing, fishing, skiing, and snowmobiling are just a few of New Brunswick's alluring experiences. Also, bicycling in particular is a great way to tour New Brunswick. B&Bs frequently have bicycles for rent and so do most bicycle shops. Two favorite biking areas in the province are the 33 km (20 miles) of country roads on Grand Manan Island (you can rent bikes here from Adventure High) and the Quoddy Loop, which goes around Passamaquoddy Bay and the western mouth of the Bay of Fundy. Fredericton has more than 120 km (75 miles) of multiuse trails, including one that goes alongside and across the river, Moncton has a trail alongside the Petitcodiac River, and there's the 500 km (300-mile) Veloroute on the Acadian Peninsula.

Baymount Outdoor Adventures

GUIDED TOURS | **FAMILY** | This outfitter leads easy 90-minute sea-kayaking tours around and between the Hopewell Rocks in the Bay of Fundy, both at high tide and midtide, after which you can wait for low tide and walk around the rocks, too—a fine way to experience the world's highest tides. ✉ *Hopewell Rocks Park, Rocks Rd., Hopewell Cape* ☎ *506/734–2660* ⊕ *www.baymountadventures. com* ✍ *$61.99–$70.25* ⊙ *Closed early Sept.–mid-June* ☞ *Reservations open mid-December.*

Golf New Brunswick

SPECIAL-INTEREST TOURS | A resource for 45 golf courses in the province, all with carts and clubs to rent. The website has an interactive map locating all the courses. ✉ *500 Beaverbrook Ct., Suite 440, Fredericton* ☎ *506/451–1324* ⊕ *www. golfnb.ca.*

Uncorked Tours

SPECIAL-INTEREST TOURS | Hugely popular escorted tours to New Brunswick wineries and breweries (with tastings) follow scenic routes, and some include cheese sampling, lunch or dinner, or visits to artisan studios. Tours, with departures from Saint John, Moncton, Fredericton, and St. Andrews, are usually half- or full-days, but can be customized, and include transportation and pickup from area hotels. Walking tours of Saint John combine wine, beer, and food sampling with historic sights. The company also has a tasting room in the Saint John Market where you can sample local drinks and food. ✉ *Saint John* ☎ *506/324–4644* ⊕ *www.uncorkednb.com.*

Visitor Information

CONTACTS **Tourism New Brunswick.** ☎ *800/561–0123* ⊕ *www.tourismnew-brunswick.ca.*

Saint John

Like any seaport worth its salt, Saint John is a welcoming place, even before 1785, when it became the first city in Canada to be incorporated. The natives of Saint John welcomed explorers Samuel de Champlain and Pierre Du Gua, Sieur de Monts when the Frenchmen landed here on St. John the Baptist Day in 1604. Nearly two centuries later they opened their rocky, forested land to 3,000 British Loyalists fleeing the United States after the American Revolutionary War, and then to an influx of Irish families,

thousands who came after the Napoleonic Wars in 1815 and later many thousands more during the Irish potato famine of 1845 to 1852. Today, Saint John's shores bring in visitors from around the world on the increasing number of cruise ships (95 in 2020) that dock at its revitalized waterfront; such is the demand that the city now has two cruise terminals, has dredged them to accommodate larger ships and, at the time of writing, is set to install a container village and a stage for live music to welcome passengers ashore.

All the comings and goings over the centuries have exposed Saint Johners to a wide variety of cultures and ideas, creating a characterful Maritime city with a vibrant artistic community. Visitors will discover rich and diverse cultural products in its urban core, including a plethora of art galleries and antiques shops. In the summer of 2018, eight artists from four countries took part in an international sculpture symposium in the city, creating sculptures in New Brunswick granite on the waterfront that were later moved to locations on the International Sculpture Trail that runs between Maine and the town of Sussex, New Brunswick, joining the 22 sculptures created during two previous symposia. It was the fourth of a planned five-biennial symposia, which will eventually place 38 large-scale granite art works along the trail (⊕ *www.sculpturesaintjohn.com*). As of 2021, there were 34 in place. Saint John also has a growing collection of salmon sculptures, dotted around the city, by local artists.

Industry and salt air have combined to give parts of Saint John a weather-beaten quality, but you'll also find lovingly restored 19th-century wooden and redbrick homes as well as modern office buildings, hotels, and stores. A 20-foot Celtic cross on Partridge Island at the entrance to Saint John Harbour stands as a reminder of the hardships and suffering the Irish immigrants endured. Their descendants make Saint John Canada's most Irish city, a fact that's celebrated in grand style each March with a week-long St. Patrick's Day celebration.

The St. John River, its Reversing Falls Rapids, and Saint John Harbour divide the city into eastern and western districts. The historic downtown area (locally known as "uptown") is on the east side, where an ambitious urban-renewal program started in the early 1980s, has transformed the downtown waterfront. Older properties have been converted into trendy restaurants and shops, while glittering new apartment buildings and condos will take full advantage of the spectacular view across the bay. Harbour Passage, a redbrick walking and cycling path with benches and interpretive information, begins downtown at Market Square and winds along the waterfront all the way to the Reversing Falls Rapids. A shuttle boat between Market Square and the falls means you have to walk only one way. On the lower west side, painted-wood homes with flat roofs—characteristic of Atlantic Canadian seaports—slope to the harbor. Industrial activity is prominent on the west side, which has stately older homes on huge lots.

Regardless of the weather, Saint John is a delightful city to explore, as so many of its key downtown attractions are linked by enclosed overhead pedways known as the "Inside Connection." Its annual festivals on the waterfront include a mid-July event called Buskers on the Bay, featuring acrobats, musicians, comedy troupes and more, and an August event, Area 506, that celebrates the province's culture and music.

GETTING HERE AND AROUND

Saint John Airport receives flights from Halifax, Montréal, Ottawa, and Toronto, all of which provide connections to international flights; Saint John Transit Bus No. 32 will get you into the city on weekdays, otherwise you'll need to take a taxi; the fare to downtown is C$30. There is no rail service to Saint John, but Maritime Bus provides long-distance bus service to the city from Montréal, Québec City, Halifax, and Charlottetown, and numerous towns and cities within Atlantic Canada. If you arrive in the downtown area by car, park and proceed on foot for full enjoyment. Parking costs C$2 per hour, up to a maximum of C$10 for the day, and is free after 6 pm. If it's just a day trip, you might consider using Saint John Transit's Parcobus park-and-ride service (C$4), which has three parking lots on the outskirts. The city bus network is quite extensive, with a fare of C$2.75, but bear in mind that some city sights, such as Rockwood Park and the Cherry Brook Zoo or Irving Nature Park, are beyond the downtown area, and you might need your car. Additionally, Saint John Transit offers two-hour sightseeing bus tours of historic areas from June to October on days when a cruise ship is in port, with two departures daily at 10 am and 12:30 pm. Times may be adjusted to suit cruise ship arrival times, but the tours are not restricted to cruise passengers. The pickup and drop-off point is just up the street from the cruise ship terminal. Tickets, which can be purchased from the driver (cash only), cost C$30 for adults.

CONTACTS Maritime Bus. ☎ *506/672–2055, 800/575–1807* ⊕ *maritimebus.com.* **Saint John Airport.** ✉ *4180 Loch Lomond Rd.* ✛ *About 18 km (11 miles) northeast of downtown Saint John* ☎ *506/638–5555* ⊕ *www.saintjohnairport.com.* **Saint John Transit.** ✉ *55 McDonald St.* ☎ *506/658–4700* ⊕ *www.saintjohntransit.com.*

VISITOR INFORMATION
CONTACTS Visitor Information Centre. ✉ *City Hall, 15 Market Sq.* ☎ *866/463–8639* ⊕ *discoversaintjohn.com.*

This 19th-century country shop in the heart of Saint John now serves as a museum showcasing items sold in its 1860s heyday.

Sights

Barbour's General Store

STORE/MALL | Now serving as a fascinating museum, this authentic and picturesque 19th-century country shop sits in a prominent location in the heart of the city, near the site where Barbour's factory once stood. It contains some 2,000 artifacts that would have been sold here in its 1860s heyday. The store also doubles as a retail outlet for modern local merchandise, some of which make good souvenirs, and there's a tearoom, a visitor information center, and a tour desk, where you can book various city tours and harbor cruises. The amusing figures on the walkway outside make for a popular photo op. ⊠ *St. Andrews Bicentennial Green, 10 Market Slip* ☎ *506/658-2990* ⌨ *Free* ☉ *Closed Mon.–Wed.*

Carleton Martello Tower

MILITARY SIGHT | **FAMILY** | The four-level tower, a great place from which to survey the harbor and Partridge Island, was built during the War of 1812 as a precaution against an American attack. Guides portray the spartan life of a soldier living in the stone fort, and an audiovisual presentation in the visitor center outlines the tower's role in the defense of Saint John during World War II. The Sunday afternoon "Saint John Privateers" program in July and August, included in admission fee and available in English and French, brings the era to life for families with children ages 6 to 11 (call to reserve space). ⊠ *454 Whipple St.* ☎ *506/636–4011* ⊕ *www.pc.gc.ca/en/lhn-nhs/nb/carleton* ⌨ *C$3.90* ☉ *Closed Oct. 9–mid-June and Mon.–Tues. early Sept.–early Oct.*

Irving Nature Park

NATURE SIGHT | **FAMILY** | The marine ecosystems of the southern New Brunswick coast are preserved in this lovely 600-acre park on a peninsula close to downtown, where a salt-marsh boardwalk, eight walking trails, a seal observation deck, and a lookout tower make bird- and nature-watching easy. Many shorebirds breed here, and it's a staging site on the flight path of shorebirds

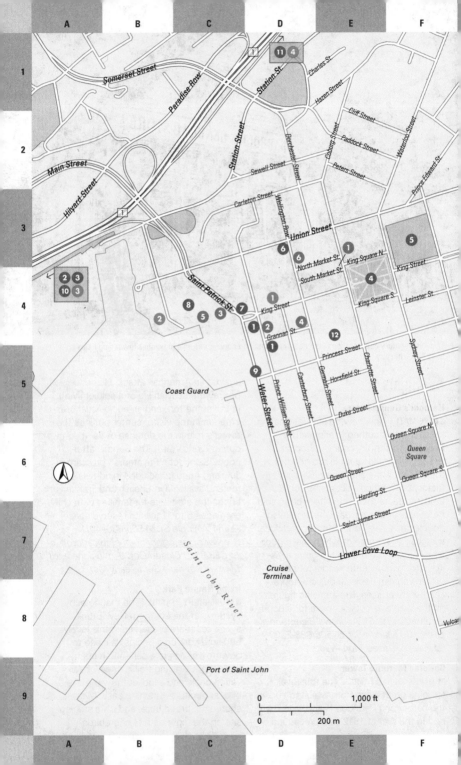

Saint John

Sights ▼

Restaurants ▼

Quick Bites ▼

Hotels ▼

KEY

1 *Exploring Sights*
1 *Restaurants*
1 *Quick Bites*
1 *Hotels*

migrating between the Arctic and South America—a wildlife tracking system here feeds data to Bird Studies Canada as part of an important research and conservation project. The Children's Forest has a playground and there are picnic sites and gas barbecues. Various educational programs, guided walks, and activities are offered. Motor vehicles are excluded on Saturday before noon. ⊠ *1790 Sand Cove Rd.* ⊹ *From downtown take Hwy. 1 west to Exit 119A (Catherwood Rd.) south; follow Sand Cove Rd. 4½ km (3 miles)* ☎ *506/653–7367* ⊕ *www.jdirving. com* ✉ *Free.*

King's Square and King Street

PLAZA/SQUARE | Laid out in a Union Jack pattern, King's Square is a green refuge in the heart of the city, with a number of monuments and a two-story bandstand that hosts summer concerts. The mass of metal on the ground in the northeast corner is actually a great lump of melted tools from a neighboring hardware store that burned down in Saint John's Great Fire of 1877, in which hundreds of buildings were destroyed. It's a great place to picnic on food bought at the City Market across the street, but you might not want to linger here after dark. From the west side of the square, King Street, the steepest, shortest main street in Canada, heads down toward the waterfront, with a variety of shops and restaurants along the way. ⊠ *King's Sq., Between Charlotte and Sydney Sts.*

Loyalist Burial Ground

CEMETERY | Established soon after the United Empire Loyalists arrived in 1783, the cemetery features a magnificent beaver-pond fountain, created to depict the hard work and tenacious spirit of the city's founders and those who followed them. Brick and granite walkways lead from the memorial gates through the restored gravestones—the oldest is that of Coonradt Hendricks, dated 1784—and crypts amid shady trees and flowers. Closed in 1848, the cemetery was sadly neglected until 1995, when the Irving family restored it as a gift to the people of Saint John. ⊠ *Sydney St., between King E and Union Streets* ✉ *Free.*

Loyalist House

HISTORIC HOME | The former home of the Merritt family, wealthy Loyalist merchants, this imposing Georgian structure was built in 1817 and, as one of the few survivors of the great fire of 1877, is a designated National Historic Site. It is furnished with authentic period pieces, including a working piano organ and the original kitchen equipment. Visitors can explore on their own or join a guided tour, and visits may be possible by appointment during the closed season. ⊠ *120 Union St.* ☎ *506/652–3590 July–Aug., 506/650–8293 Sept.–June* ⊕ *loyalisthouse.com* ✉ *C$5* ⌕ *Open by appointment.*

Market Square

MARINA/PIER | The waterfront area at the foot of King Street is where the Loyalists landed in 1783. Today it's a lively and appealing area—the site of restaurants, pubs, and a venue for festivals and street performers—but it still conveys a sense of the city's maritime heritage. There's access to the Harbour Passage Trail; a floating wharf accommodates boating visitors to the city and those waiting for the tides to sail up the St. John River; and there's a beach area with imported sand and volleyball nets. ⊠ *Market Sq.* ⊕ *marketsquaresj.com.*

★ New Brunswick Museum

HISTORY MUSEUM | FAMILY | Imaginative and engaging in its approach, the provincial museum has fascinating displays covering the history, geology, and culture of New Brunswick and a large and outstanding collection of art in the galleries. The popular whale exhibit includes Delilah, a full-size young right whale skeleton, suspended from the ceiling. You can also watch the phenomenal Bay of Fundy tides rise and fall in a glass tidal tube connected to the harbor and find out why

The Secrets of the Stonehammer ◉

In 2010, a great swathe of southern New Brunswick became North America's first designated, UNESCO-supported Global Geopark. Here, the rocks have given up secrets of our planet's development throughout its lifetime, intriguing the curious among us. Encompassing rocks from all geological ages except the Jurassic, Paleogene and Neogene periods, the 2,500-square-km (964-square-mile) park stretches roughly from Lepreau to Norton and from the Fundy Trail to the Kingston Peninsula.

Of the park's more than 60 significant sites, a dozen can be visited, and are interpreted either by information panels or through outfitters who can guide you on foot or by kayak. Even if you're not among the geologists and paleontologists who would find a lifetime's fascination within what to the rest of us are just rocks, there's much to excite the imagination—the birthplace of the Atlantic Ocean, land that was once joined to what is now Africa, and terrain where some of the planet's earliest creatures have left visible evidence of their existence. When you need to give your cerebral side a break, there are also physical activities from ziplining to rock climbing.

Saint John itself holds many of these sites, and a good place to start is the **New Brunswick Museum**, for some background information and to pick up free pamphlets. Then head out to see the **Reversing Falls Rapids**, where two continents collided; **Irving Nature Park**, with its Ice-Age stories to tell; **Rockwood Park** and **Dominion Park**, with their geology on show.

For more information, visit ⊕ *stonehammergeopark.com*.

the nearby Stonehammer Geopark has global importance. The Family Discovery Gallery has fun and educational games for all ages. Admission is free on certain holidays and notable dates. ⊠ *1 Market Sq.* ☎ *506/643–2300, 888/268–9595* ⊕ *www.nbm-mnb.ca* ⊠ *C$10* ⊘ *Closed Mon., Nov.–mid-May.*

Prince William Streetscape National Historic Site of Canada

HISTORIC SIGHT | Off King Street one block back from the waterfront, this street is full of historic buildings, particularly around Princess and Duke streets, preserving some of the city's finest late 19th-century architecture. The Old Post Office, at No. 115, is a particularly fine example. This is no frozen-in-time monument, though—these buildings now hold shops, galleries, and restaurants so good and plentiful that the site has become a dining destination. The triple-bulb lamp known as the Three Sisters, at the far end of Prince William Street, was erected in 1848 to guide ships into the harbor. Next to it is a replica of the Celtic cross on nearby Partridge Island, where many immigrants landed and were quarantined. ⊠ *Prince William St.*

★ Reversing Falls Rapids and Skywalk

VIEWPOINT | The strong Fundy tides rise higher than the water level of the river, so twice daily, at the Reversing Falls Rapids, the tidewater pushes the river water some 90 km (56 miles) back upstream and the rapids appear to reverse themselves. When the tide ebbs, the river once again flows downstream over the rock ledges and on into the bay. You can see the rapids from Fallsview Park, or get an overhead view from the cliff top on Bridge Road. Here, you can also venture

The unique phenomenon where rapids appear to reverse themselves is due to the colliding waters of the St. John River and the Bay of Fundy.

out onto the Skywalk, featuring five glass panels for a straight-down view. An excellent introductory film details the fascinating geology and uniqueness of the phenomenon, and docents are on hand to answer questions and offer further insights. It takes time to fully appreciate the Reversing Falls Rapids; you need to visit at high, slack, and low tides—the website, or any visitor information office, has tide times—and to allow for this, Skywalk tickets are valid for the whole day. ⊠ *200 Bridge Rd.* ☎ *506/642–4400* ⊕ *skywalksaintjohn.com* ⊡ *Free; Skywalk and film C$15.*

Rockwood Park

CITY PARK | FAMILY | Encompassing 2,200 acres, this is one of the largest urban parks in Canada and is also one of the dozen or so highlighted elements of the Stonehammer Geopark, designated as such by UNESCO for its global geological importance. There are more than 55 hiking trails and paths through the forest, 13 lakes, several sandy beaches, a campground, and a golf course with an aquatic driving range. There are art and yoga sessions and many summer and winter activities available. Equipment rentals are at the Inside Out Nature Centre, and the Interpretation Centre organizes guided nature walks; it also has trail maps and information on events, which include open-air movie screenings and concerts. ⊠ *55 Fisher Lake Dr. S, off Mt. Pleasant Ave.* ☎ *506/658–4455* ⊕ *www.rockwood-park.ca* ⊡ *Free.*

Trinity Church

CHURCH | The present church dates from 1880, when it was rebuilt after the Great Fire. Inside, over the west door, is a coat of arms—a symbol of the monarchy—rescued from the council chamber in Boston by a British colonel during the American Revolution. It was deemed a worthy refugee and given a place of honor in the church. Guided tours are available during July and August, and there's a self-guided tour at other times. ⊠ *115 Charlotte St.* ☎ *506/693–8558* ⊡ *Free; donations accepted.*

🍴 Restaurants

★ Billy's Seafood Company
$$$$ | **SEAFOOD** | It's a restaurant, it's an oyster bar, and it's a fish market, where the fresh fish selection is impressive and everything is cooked to perfection, making for delicious meals (there are choices for nonfish fans, too). You can also enjoy divine desserts for the finale. **Known for:** impeccable service; the on-site fish market will ship anywhere; huge, succulent lobsters. [$] *Average main: C$35* ✉ *Saint John City Market, 51 Charlotte St., Downtown* ☎ *506/672–3474, 888/933–3474* 🌐 *billysseafood.com* 🕒 *Closed Sun.*

★ East Coast Bistro
$$$ | **BISTRO** | Take a good look at the surroundings when you arrive—exposed brick walls, artworks, hardwood floors—because once the food appears, it will have your full attention. Artfully plated dishes, like local goat cheese terrine and house-smoked salmon, lead into main courses that might include yogurt-and-coriander-roasted chicken breast or pan-seared sustainable blue trout with chorizo, caramelized onion rösti, and sautéed greens. **Known for:** good range of vegan and gluten-free food; inventive salads and vegetarian dishes; everything is made in-house. [$] *Average main: C$25* ✉ *60 Prince William St.* ☎ *506/696–3278* 🌐 *eastcoastbistro.com* 🕒 *Closed Sun. and Mon., no lunch Sat.*

Lemongrass Thai Fare
$$$ | **THAI** | If you shy away from Thai food because of its reputation for spicy hotness, do not hesitate to try this stylish restaurant that caters to all tastes and will prepare your pad thai to match your preference for heat, or lack thereof. Thai stir-fries, noodle dishes, and curries, many featuring ginger and coconut, share the menu with both mild and fiery Indian dishes, and are enjoyed indoors or on the patio. **Known for:** patio dining; great value lunch menu; delicious noodle dishes. [$] *Average main: C$30* ✉ *1 Market Sq., Downtown* ☎ *506/657–8424* 🌐 *lemongrasssaintjohn.com* 🕒 *Closed Sun. and Mon.*

Port City Royal
$$ | **CANADIAN** | In this innovative little restaurant where everything is cooked to order (so be prepared to wait—it's worth it), the talented chef's commitment to locally sourced ingredients might extend to delicacies foraged from the wild by dedicated staffers. Hand-crafted snacks, available throughout the day, offer an irresistible temptation to return after 5:30 to dine on dishes such as pan-seared tenderloin and molasses-butter-poached mushrooms. **Known for:** memorable combinations of flavors; celebrated acclaim from critics; genuine staff enthusiasm for the cuisine. [$] *Average main: C$18* ✉ *45 Grannan St.* ☎ *506/631–3714* 🌐 *www.portcityroyal.com* 🕒 *Closed Mon.*

★ Saint John Ale House
$$$ | **CANADIAN** | This gastropub is one of the best places to eat in the city—proven by its slew of awards and two appearances on the "You Gotta Eat Here" TV show—and it couldn't have a better location, with a great patio overlooking the downtown waterfront. Drawing on supplies from local farmers, fishermen, and food producers, the menu presents "progressive pub food," and the beer menu includes 35 varieties on tap and 56 bottled options. **Known for:** live entertainment some nights; superior treatment of pub food favorites; patio offers prime people-watching. [$] *Average main: C$25* ✉ *1 Market Sq., Downtown* ☎ *506/657–2337* 🌐 *www.saintjohnalehouse.com.*

Vegolution
$$ | **VEGETARIAN** | As the name suggests, this is a great choice for vegetarians and vegans, but it's popular with nonvegetarians too, particularly for the beautifully presented and tasty salads—many people come specifically for the incredible carrot cake. Beverages include vegan wines and beer from local microbreweries. **Known for:** licensed, and

Tastes of New Brunswick

Seafood is plentiful all year (lobsters, oysters, crabs, mussels, clams, scallops, and salmon) and prepared in as many ways as there are chefs, and just about anywhere in New Brunswick you'll find some kind of fish-and-chips. Try snacking on dulse, a dried purple seaweed as salty as potato chips and as compelling as peanuts.

A spring delicacy is fiddleheads—emerging ferns that look like the curl at the end of a violin. These emerald gems are picked along riverbanks, then boiled and sprinkled with lemon juice, butter, salt, and pepper.

The big boys of the beer world are Moosehead, brewed in Saint John, Alexander Keith's (originally a Nova Scotia brewery, now owned by Labatt, a subsidiary of Anheuser-Busch) and, of course, the various Molson brews. They are being robustly challenged these days by a growing number (45 at the time of writing) of excellent local craft breweries, and Fredericton is the epicenter, home to no less than ten microbreweries. Moncton has six,

including the Pump House Brewery and the Tide & Boar Gastropub, which brews its own beer on-site, and the rest are scattered around smaller communities. Look for the blue road sign representing a mug full of suds, visit beerocracymovie.com to see their craft breweries map and a trailer for their documentary film, and check listings for beer festivals.

New Brunswick also has nine distilleries and 20 wineries, so ask what's available in stores and restaurants. A good introduction would be to take one of the Uncorked Tours out of Saint John, Fredericton, Moncton, or St. Andrews; the tours specialize in local wineries and artisan breweries and the company also has a tasting room in Saint John City Market.

New Brunswick's maple products are sought the world over, and chocolates made by Ganong Bros. Limited of St. Stephen, who have been in the candy business for nearly a century and a half, are a popular treat.

has vegan wines; vegetarian and vegan options; grab-and-go items to take out. $ *Average main: C$16* ⊠ *26 Germain St.* ☎ *506/643–8401* ⊕ *www.vegolution.ca* ⊗ *Closed Sun.–Tues.*

☕ Coffee and Quick Bites

JavaMoose

$ | BAKERY | A relatively small, locally owned chain, JavaMoose has its own small-batch roasting facility in Saint John and a small chain of cafés, where locals flock for the great-tasting coffee and quick bites such as muffins and breakfast sandwiches. The main branch is on Prince William Street, and they are

also in Saint John City Market and the McAllister Place Shopping Centre on Westmorland Road. **Known for:** muffins; locally owned; small-batch roastery. $ *Average main: C$8* ⊠ *84 Prince William St.* ☎ *506/657–7283* ⊕ *javamoose.com.*

🛏 Hotels

Delta Hotels by Marriott Saint John

$$ | HOTEL | FAMILY | Right in the heart of the city, this modern and stylish hotel is within the Brunswick Square mall and linked to other shopping and entertainment venues by an indoor walkway, making it perfect for a winter visit. **Pros:** very friendly staff; room key needed in

elevator to access room floors; near all downtown attractions. **Cons:** a bit uphill from the waterfront; first-time arrival by car can be confusing; most rooms have a street view only. $ *Rooms from: C$149* ✉ *39 King St.* ☎ *506/648–1981* ⊕ *deltahotels.marriott.com* ↪ *250 rooms* ❍ *No Meals.*

Hilton Saint John

$$$ | HOTEL | FAMILY | This stunning hotel is sleek and very stylish, with open-aspect public areas flooded with natural light, spacious rooms, and an unbeatable city-center waterfront location. **Pros:** adjoining rooms for families; in the hub of the city's action; wonderful views. **Cons:** not easy to find the parking garage; some rooms could do with a face-lift; atmosphere can be affected by conventioneers. $ *Rooms from: C$179* ✉ *1 Market Sq.* ☎ *506/693–8484, 800/561–8282 in Canada* ⊕ *www. hilton.com* ↪ *197 rooms* ❍ *No Meals.*

★ Homeport Historic Bed & Breakfast Inn

$$ | B&B/INN | Graceful arches, fine antiques, Italian marble fireplaces, Oriental carpets, and a maritime theme distinguish this pair of mansions overlooking the harbor. **Pros:** close to the Reversing Falls Rapids; hospitable, well-versed owners; great sense of history. **Cons:** quite a lot of stairs up to the rooms; not a pretty walk to downtown; the amazing view is sometimes obscured by fog. $ *Rooms from: C$134* ✉ *80 Douglas Ave.* ☎ *506/672–7255, 888/678–7678* ⊕ *www.homeportinn.ca* ↪ *10 rooms* ❍ *Free Breakfast.*

Shadow Lawn Inn

$$$ | B&B/INN | In an affluent suburb with tree-lined streets, palatial homes, tennis, golf, and a yacht club, this inn fits right in, with its clapboards, columns, antiques, and original artwork. **Pros:** historic character is balanced by elegant style; great food, includes superior continental breakfast; hospitable service. **Cons:** weddings are sometimes hosted here; dinner not available on Sunday; a bit far from town. $ *Rooms from: C$200* ✉ *3180 Rothesay Rd., 12 km (7 miles) northeast of Saint John, Rothesay* ☎ *506/847–7539, 800/561–4166* ⊕ *www.shadowlawninn. com* ↪ *9 rooms* ❍ *Free Breakfast.*

⏁ Nightlife

Happinez

WINE BARS | With a welcoming laid-back atmosphere, exposed stone and brick walls, an interesting wine list, and knowledgeable staff, this intimate wine bar is a pleasant place to spend an evening. Two-ounce tasters are available, along with cheese and charcuterie plates. Various tasting events include featured wines from global destinations. It's open Wednesday through Saturday from 4 or 5 pm. ✉ *42 Princess St.* ☎ *506/634–7340* ⊕ *happinezwinebar.com* ⏲ *Closed Sun.–Tues.*

Hopscotch

BARS | In three small rooms of a historic building, with bare brick walls and subdued lighting, you'll find a massive selection of the finest whiskeys in the world. The focus is mainly on Scotch, with all the famous (and some lesser-known) Scottish distilleries represented, but there's also an interesting selection from other parts of the world, including Ireland, Japan, France, the United States, and—of course—Canada. Currently, there are two from Atlantic Canada distilleries (Signal Hill from Newfoundland and Gin Thuya from New Brunswick), with plans to bring in more as their whiskeys mature sufficiently. If whiskey isn't your thing, there are other options, including a lengthy selection of cocktails. ✉ *45 Canterbury St.* ☎ *506/642–3371* ⊕ *www. hopscotchbar.ca* ⏲ *Closed Sun. and Mon.*

O'Leary's Pub

PUBS | In the downtown historic district, this pub lives up to its name with old-time Irish fun, including a weekly live traditional music session in a room at the back. In the main bar on Wednesday, Brent Mason, a well-known neofolk artist, starts the evening and then turns the mike over to the audience, and Friday and Saturday (and some Thursdays) it's mostly live cover bands, starting at 10 pm. ⊠ *46 Princess St.* ☎ *506/634–7135* ⊕ *www.olearyspub.ca.*

Punch Lines Comedy Club

COMEDY CLUBS | Two-hour shows here bring some well-known touring comedians to Saint John as well as showcasing local and regional talent. ⊠ *9 Sydney St.* ☎ *506/647–8338* ⊕ *www.punchlinescomedyclub.ca* ☞ *Shows several times a month. Check website for details.*

Performing Arts

★ Imperial Theatre

CONCERTS | Saint John's theater, opera, ballet, and symphony productions, along with touring bands and comedians, take place at this beautifully restored theater—and the 1912 vaudeville venue offers the most comprehensive programming in Atlantic Canada. Tours (C$2) are available from May through August during regular business hours, or by appointment September through April. ⊠ *12 King's Sq. S* ☎ *506/674–4100, 800/323–7469, 506/674–4111 for tours* ⊕ *imperialtheatre.ca.*

Saint John Arts Centre

ARTS CENTERS | Occasional classical musical events include a Summer Classics Series and an Early Music Festival in May. The center also houses several art galleries and runs arts and crafts workshops for all ages. ⊠ *20 Peel Plaza* ☎ *506/633–4870* ⊕ *www.sjartscentre.ca.*

TD Station

CONCERTS | This hockey arena, home of the Sea Dogs, also hosts musical events, including big-name rock acts like Aerosmith and Guns N' Roses; comedians such as Jerry Seinfeld and John Cleese; shows like *Riverdance* and *Mamma Mia!*; and shows for children, such as *Paw Patrol Live!*. ⊠ *99 Station St.*

☎ *506/657–1234, 800/267–2800* ⊕ *www.harbourstation.ca.*

Shopping

Handworks Gallery

ART GALLERIES | Some of the best professional crafts and fine art created in New Brunswick are carried by this lively gallery, which represents more than 60 Saint John artists and artisans. The historic building was the home of 19th-century painter J.C. Miles. ⊠ *12 King St.* ☎ *506/631–7626* ⊕ *www.handworks.ca.*

Queen Square Farmers Market

MARKET | Local vendors set up their stands on this leafy square every Sunday in summer, and it's a great place to wander, soak up the atmosphere, view the crafts and foods displayed for sale, chat to the farmers and artisans, and maybe hear some live music. ⊠ *Queen Sq. S.*

★ Saint John City Market

MARKET | This is the oldest continuously operating farmers' market in Canada, dating from 1876, and the building occupies a whole city block between Germain and Charlotte streets. Inside, it's a lively and bustling shoppers' dream-come-true, with a wide range of temptations—fresh and organic produce from local farms, live and fresh-cooked lobsters, artisan cheeses, dulse, international foods, craft beers, local wine, and tasty, inexpensive snacks. Local artists and artisans are also represented, making this a great stop for souvenirs and arts and crafts. ⊠ *47 Charlotte St.* ☎ *506/658–2820* ⊕ *sjcitymarket.ca.*

Activities

Osprey Adventures

CANOEING & ROWING | Northeast of Saint John, the beautiful Kennebacasis River is a calm and peaceful haven of wildlife, and Osprey's experts lead informative guided kayaking trips. Also available are excursions in the Hampton-based outfitter's superb Voyageur canoe, built by the local Oromocto First Nation and which can accommodate up to 10 paddlers (a minimum of five is required). Or you can rent a kayak, canoe, or stand-up paddleboard to explore on your own. It's advisable to reserve tours and rentals. ⊠ *Lighthouse River Centre, 1075 Main St., Hampton* ☎ *506/566–0727* ⊕ *www.ospreyadventures.net* 🎟 *Tours from C$23; rentals from C$25.*

TimberTop Adventures

ZIP LINING | FAMILY | Clambering through the treetops with the aid of ladders, platforms and ziplines is a fun way to relive your childhood and get in touch with the sights, sounds, and smells of nature. Various sessions of up to three hours are available for ages 8 and up, and may include the free-fall (for a while) Flying Squirrel Jump, and a "starter" course is available for ages 5 to 7. ⊠ *730 Dominion Park Rd.* ☎ *506/657–6060* ⊕ *timbertop.ca* 🎟 *C$44.99.*

St. Andrews by-the-Sea

102 km (63 miles) west of Saint John.

A designated National Historic District on Passamaquoddy Bay, St. Andrews by-the-Sea is one of North America's prettiest resort towns. It has long been a summer retreat of the affluent, and mansions ring the town. Of the town's 550 buildings, 280 were erected before 1880, and 14 of those have survived from the 1700s. When the American Revolution didn't go their way, some Loyalists even brought their homes with them piece by piece across the bay from Castine, Maine. Pick up a walking-tour map at the visitor information center and follow it through the pleasant streets. Water Street, by the harbor, has eateries, gift and craft shops, and artists' studios. The harbor has a cluster of whale-watching boats and outfitters for other activities.

GETTING HERE AND AROUND

There is no public transportation to St. Andrews by-the-Sea. By road, it's about 100 km (60 miles) west of Saint John via Highway 1 then Route 127. If you're crossing the border from Calais, Maine, it's about a half-hour drive via Route 127 north, then Route 170 west. From the Trans-Canada Highway, go south on Highway 3. Once there, the Water Street and harbor area is delightfully walkable, but a car will be needed to get to some of the attractions.

ESSENTIALS

VISITOR INFORMATION St. Andrews. ⊠ *24 Reed Ave., St. Andrews* ☎ *506/529–3556, 800/563–7397* ⊕ *www.townof-standrews.ca.*

◉ Sights

Charlotte County Courthouse and Old Gaol

GOVERNMENT BUILDING | Active since 1840 and a National Historic Site since 1983, the courthouse is an exceptionally fine example of 19th-century Greek Revival architecture—one of the finest in Canada. The adjacent Old Gaol, on the other hand, is a grim reminder of the conditions that awaited local wrongdoers. The courthouse is also the home of Charlotte County Archives, whose volunteers offer free tours of the courthouse and the Old Gaol (June to September). Ask about their Ghost Walks, too. ⊠ *123 Frederick St., St. Andrews* ☎ *506/529–4248* ⊕ *www.ccarchives.ca* 🎟 *C$2.*

Chocolate Museum

OTHER MUSEUM | FAMILY | The Ganong family has been making chocolates in St. Stephen since 1873 and their original candy factory now houses this museum. It explores the sweet history of candy making with hand-dipping videos, a collection of antique chocolate boxes, and hands-on exhibits. A Heritage Chocolate Walking Tour, available Monday to Saturday, July through mid-August, includes a guided tour of the museum and a stroll

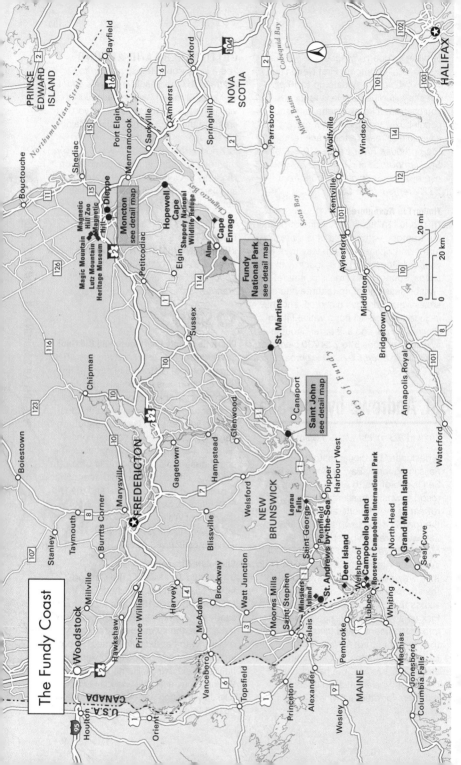

The Fundy Coast

around town, where the guide points out buildings associated with the chocolate industry. There are occasional activities for children and a chocolate festival in early August. After all that chocolate talk and those tempting displays, there's a sweet finale: an on-site, year-round retail outlet selling the indulgent treats. ✉ *73 Milltown Blvd., St. Stephen* ☎ *506/466–7848* ⊕ *www.chocolatemuseum.ca* ✉ *From C$10* ⊗ *Closed early Dec.–early Mar. Closed Mon. and Tues. early Mar.–May. Closed Sun. Sept.–Nov.*

Greenock Church

CHURCH | After a remark was made at an 1822 dinner party about the "poor" Presbyterians not having a church of their own, Captain Christopher Scott took exception to the insult and spared no expense on this building. The church is decorated with a carving of a green oak tree in honor of Scott's birthplace, Greenock in Scotland. ✉ *135 Montague St., St. Andrews.*

Huntsman Fundy Discovery Aquarium

AQUARIUM | **FAMILY** | This small but interesting aquarium, established in 1969, is at the Huntsman Marine Science Centre, a private not-for-profit research and education institution. Marine exhibits include a huge two-story tank with indicators showing the varying levels of the Fundy tides, teeming touch tanks that delight children (and adults), rare wolffish, sea horses, squid, salmon, and a pair of very entertaining harbor seals (fed at 11 and 4 daily), as well as free movies and slide shows. A trail leads to the beach on the Saint Croix River (depending on tides). Check the website for other feeding times, behind-the-scenes tours, and sleepover opportunities. Also consult the website or call for driving directions—it's not easy to find. ✉ *1 Lower Campus Rd., St. Andrews* ☎ *506/529–1200* ⊕ *www.huntsmanmarine.ca* ✉ *C$15.*

★ Kingsbrae Garden

GARDEN | **FAMILY** | Horticulture and art combine in this spectacular public garden. Nearly 2,500 varieties of trees, shrubs, and plants cover the 27 acres, with woodland trails and many theme gardens, including one specially designed for touch and smell, a rose garden, a bird and butterfly garden, and a gravel garden. A children's fantasy garden offers child-centered activities, and there are daily programs for kids under 12 (1:30 pm in July and August). One of the oldest and rarest trees in the world, a Wollemi pine, named Pericles, is a big attraction, as is the opportunity to participate in a ladybug release program every morning at 10:30. The Sculpture Garden features works by Don Pell, exhibits on loan from the Beaverbrook collection, and many other established and emerging artists, including winners of the annual Kingsbrae Garden Canadian Sculpture Competition. Kingsbrae also has an art gallery, an artists-in-residence series, a café (with live music on Wednesday evenings in July and August), and the superb Savour in the Garden restaurant. ✉ *220 King St., St. Andrews* ☎ *506/529–3335, 866/566–8687* ⊕ *www.kingsbraegarden.com* ✉ *From C$16.*

Lepreau Falls Provincial Park

NATURE SIGHT | These beautiful falls within a park inside the Stonehammer Geopark tumble over ancient rocks and near a fossil of a rare tetrapod trackway. The park provides visitors with tantalizing views of the falls from the boardwalk in the wooded surroundings, where there are picnic tables and hiking trails. At the right time of year, you can pick wild strawberries here. ✉ *Lepreau Falls Rd., Lepreau* ✛ *40 km (25 miles) west of Saint John via Hwy. 1 and Hwy. 175* ☎ *866/672–0770* ⊕ *stonehammergeopark.com/geosite/lepreau-falls-provincial-park* ✉ *Free.*

Ministers Island

ISLAND | This huge island estate, once completely self-sufficient, was the summer home of Sir William Van Horne, chairman of the Canadian Pacific Railway from 1899 to 1915. Tours of the property include Covenhoven, Sir William's 50-room summer home; a tidal swimming pool; a livestock barn; a cottage; an old windmill; and the 1790 Minister's House from which the island takes its name. To get to the island you drive, walk, or bike at low tide; be sure to leave the island before the tide comes in or you will be stuck for another six hours. The website gives details of accessible hours for each open day. ✉ *St. Andrews* ✣ *Via Bar Rd., off Rte. 127, 5 km (3 miles) north of St. Andrews* ☎ *506/529–5081* 🌐 *www.ministersisland.net* 🎟 *C$15 in advance or C$17 on arrival (cash only), includes guided tour.*

Ross Memorial Museum

HISTORIC HOME | A U.S. couple who had a summer home in St. Andrews for 40 years established this museum. The Rosses donated the trappings of that home and an extensive collection of 19th-century New Brunswick furniture and decorative artwork to the town and purchased this 1824 Georgian mansion to house them. The Christmas Open House, over five days in late November/early December, is a popular event. ✉ *188 Montague St., St. Andrews* ☎ *506/529–5124* 🌐 *rossmemorialmuseum.ca* 🎟 *By donation.*

Beaches

New River Beach

BEACH | **FAMILY** | Unlike most Bay of Fundy beaches, this one is sandy and great for swimming, especially if you wait until the tide is coming in. The sun warms the sand at low tide, and the sand warms the water as it comes in. There are quite a lot of steps down to the beach, and the toilets, canteen, and picnic tables are at the top. It's part of the New River Beach Provincial Park that also has a boardwalk through a bog, a playground, interpretive programs, hiking trails, kayak rentals, and campsites. The annual Sand Sculpture Competition in late July is a popular event. **Amenities:** food and drink; parking; toilets; water sports. **Best for:** swimming; walking. ✉ *78 New River Beach Rd.* ✣ *Lepreau, off Hwy. 1, 50 km (30 miles) west of Saint John* 🌐 *www.parcsnbparks.info/en/parks/13/new-river-beach-provincial-park* 🎟 *C$10 vehicle entrance to park (May–Oct.).*

Restaurants

The Gables

$$$ | **SEAFOOD** | A relaxing meal with breathtaking harbor views (and fleece blankets available in case the wind comes up) on the outdoor deck of this friendly harborside eatery is the perfect way to end a day of whale-watching or craft shopping. The hearty seafood chowder will warm the heart and soul on a foggy Fundy night, and the lobster club sandwich is a favorite; there are also non-fish dishes on the menu such as steaks—and, of course, the house-made desserts. **Known for:** child-friendly; great location by the water; lines to get in at busy times. [$] *Average main: C$23* ✉ *143 Water St., St. Andrews* ☎ *506/529–3440* 🕒 *Closed Tues.–Wed., and Nov.–mid-Apr.*

Harbour Front

$$$ | **SEAFOOD** | **FAMILY** | Right on the water's edge near the harbor, this restaurant in a beautifully restored building is a great spot for a casual meal, and the large covered deck makes it deservedly popular when the weather's right. The long menu focuses on seafood, such as lobster, sole almandine, and seafood casserole in a creamy sauce, but there also are steaks, chicken dishes, salads, and sandwiches, along with a children's menu. **Known for:** waterside deck; steamed mussels in a richly flavored broth; friendly and efficient service. [$] *Average main: C$24* ✉ *225 Water St., St. Andrews* ☎ *506/529–4887* 🌐 *harbourfrontrestaurant.ca* 🕒 *Closed late Oct.–mid-May.*

Niger Reef Tea House

$$$ | **CANADIAN** | Overlooking the bay with seating inside or out on a rustic deck, this 1926 former meetinghouse now houses a fine restaurant. Everything is top quality, from the simple but expertly produced lunchtime options—seafood chowder, sandwiches, frittata—to more substantial dinner selections such as traditional cedar-planked salmon with a ginger glaze, steak bavette with chipotle hollandaise sauce, or herb-crusted lamb loin chops. **Known for:** water views away from downtown tourist traps; mural painted by American artist Lucille Douglass; Hammond River Brewing Company beers on tap. $ *Average main: C$25* ⊠ *1 Joe's Point Rd., St. Andrews* ☎ *506/529–8005* ⊘ *Closed Nov.–Apr. No dinner May and Oct.*

★ Savour in the Garden

$$$$ | **CANADIAN** | Within the lovely Kingsbrae Garden, one of Canada's finest chefs, Alex Haun, offers creative tasting menus—consisting of three or six courses—based on available fresh local ingredients, some of which come right from the garden. One example, Six Wings to Fly, features duck ragout, seared quail breast and braised leg, partridge terrine, roasted potato shell, mushroom demiglace, sautéed carrots, sugar snap peas, chanterelles, and beet ketchup—yes, that's just one dish. **Known for:** pump nights on the lawn, with live music; culinary art on the tasting menus at dinner; dedication to sustainability and local ingredients. $ *Average main: C$80* ⊠ *Kingsbrae Garden, 220 King St., St. Andrews* ☎ *506/529–4055* ⊕ *www.kingsbraegarden.com* ⊘ *Closed Mon.–Wed.*

☕ Coffee and Quick Bites

Honeybeans

$ | **BAKERY** | A local institution in the heart of town, Honeybeans serves coffee so good that there's a regular early morning line of locals stretching out of the door. There's a long coffee menu, including Fair Trade and decaf, more than 30 types of tea, and house-baked treats including sweet pastries, cheese croissants, and gluten-free items. **Known for:** fabulous coffee; cheese croissants; local favorite. $ *Average main: C$10* ⊠ *180 Water St., St. Andrews* ☎ *405/529–4888* ⊕ *www. facebook.com/honeybeanscafe* ⊘ *Closed Tues.*

🛏 Hotels

★ The Algonquin Resort

$$$$ | **RESORT** | **FAMILY** | This iconic resort has been meticulously restored to perfectly recapture the historic elegance that made it legendary, with every architectural detail inside and out preserved and black-and-white photographs throughout recalling the hotel's earlier heyday—yet every modern comfort has been provided. **Pros:** spacious studio rooms with kitchenettes; luxurious surroundings; indoor pool has a three-story waterslide. **Cons:** not all rooms have a view of the bay; fire-pits are near rooms so can get noisy; a bit of a walk from the waterfront hub. $ *Rooms from: C$320* ⊠ *184 Adolphus St., St. Andrews* ☎ *506/529–8823, 855/529–8693* ⊕ *algonquinresort.com* ⇨ *233 rooms* ⦿ *No Meals.*

Inn on Frederick

$$ | **B&B/INN** | Within easy walking distance of the main attractions in downtown St. Andrews, this wonderful country inn was originally built in the 1840s by the Pheasant family, and the current owners have carefully renovated the property to preserve its historic authenticity. **Pros:** very thoughtful and helpful owners; full home-cooked breakfasts are different every day; well-equipped rooms, including mini-refrigerator. **Cons:** old-fashioned decor not to everyone's taste; deluxe suite has kitchen so no breakfast included; a bit pricey. $ *Rooms from: C$130* ⊠ *58 Frederick St., St. Andrews* ☎ *506/529–2603, 877/895–4400* ⊕ *www. innonfrederick.ca* ⇨ *9 rooms* ⦿ *Free Breakfast.*

The historic Algonquin Resort takes pride of place in the charming seaside town of St. Andrews by-the-Sea.

★ Kingsbrae Arms

$$$$ | **HOTEL** | **FAMILY** | Expect excellent service from the hosts and staff at this restored 1897 estate, where eclectic antiques fill the rooms, and pampering touches include plush robes and daily afternoon tea. **Pros:** delicious local food prepared by creative chef; lovely grounds; kid- and pet-friendly. **Cons:** no elevator; no stove in the carriage house kitchen; in winter the only meal offered is breakfast. $ *Rooms from: C$349* ✉ *219 King St., St. Andrews* ☎ *506/529–1897* ⊕ *www.kingsbrae.com* ↩ *10 rooms* ¶⊙ *Free Breakfast.*

Montague Rose B&B

$$ | **B&B/INN** | Two blocks back from the harbor, this lovely French Empire-style home offers a warm welcome and individually styled, comfortable bedrooms. **Pros:** open year-round; friendly hosts; good location close to all downtown attractions. **Cons:** all bathrooms are private, but not all are en suite; fixed time for breakfast, at 8:30 am; bathrooms have either a tub or shower, not both.

$ *Rooms from: C$160* ✉ *258 Montague St., St. Andrews* ☎ *506/529–8963, 778/875–2204* ⊕ *www.themontague-rose.com* ↩ *4 rooms* ¶⊙ *Free Breakfast.*

Rossmount Inn Hotel Restaurant & Bar

$$ | **HOTEL** | Surrounded by 87 acres at the base of Chamcook Mountain, this inn is renowned for hospitality and outstanding food and is particularly convenient for visiting Ministers Island. **Pros:** peacefully secluded at the end of a long driveway; impeccable surroundings and details; individual heat and air-conditioning in rooms. **Cons:** located 6½ km (4 miles) from town; stairways are steep; some rooms are very small. $ *Rooms from: C$148* ✉ *4599 Rte. 127, St. Andrews* ☎ *506/529–3351* ⊕ *www.rossmountinn. com* ⊗ *Closed Jan.–mid-Apr.* ↩ *18 rooms* ¶⊙ *No Meals.*

🛍 Shopping

Crocker Hill Store/Steven Smith Designs

ART GALLERIES | Owner-artist Stephen Smith's art—on framed prints, T-shirts, tote bags, and note cards—focuses on local birdlife. The shop, which also has gardening and nature products, is in an 1837 heritage building within a garden, with some interesting features inside. Call to check off-season opening hours. ✉ 45 King St., St. Andrews ☎ 506/529-4303, 888/255-4251 ⊕ www.crockerhill. com.

Garden by the Sea

SKINCARE | This aromatic shop specializes in all-natural body products made in New Brunswick, including Bay of Fundy sea salts and ecoflowers (made from various recycled materials including wood, paper, and fabric), as well as fresh flowers and 130 varieties of ethical, fair trade, and organic teas. ✉ 217 Water St., St. Andrews ☎ 506/529-8905 ⊕ gardenbytheseanb.com.

★ Marée

JEWELRY & WATCHES | Owner Pam Vincent's sense of style is reflected in the artsy and quirky range of jewelry, gifts, handbags, clothing, greetings cards, homewares, and irresistible chocolate truffles in this upscale boutique. ✉ 147 Water St., St. Andrews ☎ 506/529-4040 ⊕ shopmaree.com.

Oven Head Salmon Smokers

FOOD | Regulations no longer allow tours of the smokehouse, but the friendly owners will explain the process of producing some of New Brunswick's best cold-smoked Atlantic salmon, and you can buy the finished product. You'll also see it for sale in local grocery stores and on the menu at many regional restaurants. ✉ 101 Oven Head Rd., Bethel ⊕ Off Hwy. 1 at Exit 45 onto Hwy. 760, signed Bethel, Elmsville ☎ 506/755-2507, 877/955-2507 ⊕ www.ovenheadsmokers.com.

Serendipin' Art

CRAFTS | Fine art, handblown glass, hand-painted silks, jewelry, woodturning, and other crafts by more than 100 New Brunswick artists are sold here, and the "little big art gallery" next door has works produced elsewhere in the Maritimes. ✉ 168–170 Water St., St. Andrews ☎ 506/529-8955 ⊕ www.serendipinart. com.

🏃 Activities

A variety of physical activities and tours allow you to experience the outdoors in St. Andrews by-the-Sea. Golf, kayaking, nature cruises, and whale-watching are particularly popular. Whale-watching season is from June or July through late October. Whale and nature cruises all begin at the town wharf, heading out into the Bay of Fundy for sightings of several species of whale, plus dolphins, porpoises, seals, and other marine life. Birdlife includes bald eagles, ospreys, puffins, and sheerwaters. Sightings can't be guaranteed, but the success rate averages between 95% and 100%. All outfitters supply flotation devices, and some provide drinks and snacks while others suggest you bring your own. All recommend warm clothing, regardless of the onshore temperature. You should arrive at the wharf up to 45 minutes before sailing time, and be aware that tours depend on weather conditions.

GOLF

★ Algonquin Golf Club

GOLF | In July 2018, this beautifully landscaped historic signature course reopened after a major links-style redesign by course architect Rod Whitman, with new greens, holes, and bunkers and a new par-3 course. The holes on the back 9—especially the 12th—have beautiful sea views, as does the Clubhouse Grill, within Canada's oldest clubhouse. Part of the Algonquin resort, it's also open to nonguests and has a "traditional golf" dress code. ✉ 465 Brandy Cove Rd., off Rte. 127, St. Andrews ☎ 506/529-8165 ⊕ algonquinresort.com/golf ⚑ C$55–C$125 ⚑ 18 holes, 7135 yards, par 72.

WHALE-WATCHING

Fundy Tide Runners

WILDLIFE-WATCHING | FAMILY | A 24-foot Zodiac will zip you out into the bay on a two-hour whale-watching or nature-viewing trip. ☒ *16 King St., St. Andrews* ☏ *506/529–4481* ⊕ *www.fundytiderunners.com* ☒ *C$78 (a fuel surcharge may apply).*

Jolly Breeze Whale Adventures

WILDLIFE-WATCHING | FAMILY | The *Jolly Breeze* is an elegant (and quiet) sailing vessel, and particularly good for families—in addition to watching the whales, children can dress in pirate costumes, steer the ship, hoist sails, learn a sea shanty, and dabble in the marine touch tank. Breakfast is included on morning sailings, hot soup is served on later sailings. The 3½-hour tours run daily from June through mid-October. The company also offers trips on a high-speed jet boat. ☒ *4 King St., St. Andrews* ☏ *506/529–8116, 866/529–8116* ⊕ *www.jollybreeze.com* ☒ *Tall ship C$75; Zodiac jet boat $80.*

Quoddy Link Marine

WILDLIFE-WATCHING | FAMILY | Whale- and wildlife-watching tours lasting 2½–3 hours are on a powered catamaran that takes up to 46 passengers. ☒ *20 King St., St. Andrews* ☏ *506/529–2600, 877/688–2600* ⊕ *www.quoddylinkmarine.com* ☒ *C$79.*

Grand Manan Island

48 km (30 miles) east of St. Andrews by-the-Sea to Blacks Harbour, then 1½ hrs by car ferry.

Grand Manan, the largest of the three Fundy Islands, is also the farthest from the mainland. You might see whales, seals, or the occasional puffin on the way over. Circular herring weirs dot the island's coastal waters, and fish sheds and smokehouses lie beside long wharfs that reach out to bobbing fishing boats.

Place-names are evocative: Swallowtail, Southern Head, Seven Days Work, and Dark Harbour. It's easy to get around; only about 32 km (20 miles) of road lead from the lighthouse at Southern Head to the one at North Head. John James Audubon, that human encyclopedia of birds, visited the island in 1831, attracted by the more than 240 species of seabirds that nest here. The puffin may be the island's symbol, but whales are the stars. Giant finbacks, right whales, minkes, and humpbacks feed in the rich waters. With only 2,700 residents, it may seem remote and quiet, but there is plenty to do including birding, kayaking, whale-watching, and beachcombing. You can visit lighthouses, hike a heritage trail, or just hang around the busy wharves and chat with the fishermen. A day trip is possible, but you'll wish you had planned to stay at least one night.

GETTING HERE AND AROUND

Ferry service to Grand Manan is provided by Coastal Transport, which leaves the mainland from Blacks Harbour, off Route 1, and docks at North Head on Grand Manan Island. If you haven't made a reservation online, plan to be at the ferry early for the best chance of getting on. There are four crossings daily year-round, at 9:30, 1:30, 5:30, and 9, and seven daily (additional crossings at 7:30, 11:30, and 3:30) between late June and mid-September. Rates are C$35.80 for a car, excluding the driver, C$12 for adults and $5.95 for ages 5–12 years, payable on return passage from Grand Manan. Cash, debit, or credit cards (Visa, MasterCard, or American Express) are accepted, and the same credit cards are accepted for online and phone reservations.

CONTACTS Coastal Transport. ☏ *506/662–3724, 855/882–1978* ⊕ *www.coastal-transport.ca.*

ESSENTIALS

VISITOR INFORMATION Grand Manan Tourism Association and Chamber of Commerce. ✉ *Grand Manan* ☎ *506/662–3442* 🌐 *www.grandmanannb.com/index.html.*

Hotels

Marathon Inn

$$ | B&B/INN | FAMILY | This mansion with a large deck sits on a hill with lovely views over the harbor; built by a sea captain, the home on 10 acres of grounds has been an inn since 1871. **Pros:** free Wi-Fi; lovely views; discounts available on kayaking and whale-watching trips. **Cons:** if other guests make a noise, you'll hear them; lots of stairs; rooms are of various sizes. [$] *Rooms from: C$139* ✉ *19 Marathon La., North Head, Grand Manan* ☎ *506/662–8488, 888/660–8488* 🌐 *www.marathoninn.com* 🛏 *23 rooms* 🍴 *No Meals.*

Whale Cove Cottages

$$$ | B&B/INN | These rental properties include the former bed-and-breakfast Main House, which dates back to 1816 and has a living room with a fireplace and library, a dining room, a well-equipped kitchen and four traditional, country-style bedrooms with en-suite bathrooms. **Pros:** Wi-Fi available throughout; great rustic feel; lovely property for wandering. **Cons:** Coopershop bathroom is downstairs, with shower only; only one bathroom in Main House has both tub and shower; no on-site restaurant. [$] *Rooms from: C$1200–1500 per week* ✉ *26 Whale Cottage Rd., off Whistle Road, Grand Manan* ☎ *506/662–3181* 🌐 *www.whalecovecottages.ca* 🛏 *6 units* 🍴 *No Meals.*

Activities

A whale-watching cruise from Grand Manan takes you well out into the bay. Dress warmly, but some boats have winter jackets, hats, and mittens onboard for those who don't heed this advice. While focused on kayaks, Adventure High also rents bikes to explore the trails along the coastline.

KAYAKING

Adventure High

ADVENTURE TOURS | FAMILY | Kayaking tours on the Bay of Fundy range from two hours to weeklong trips, and some include a lobster dinner on the beach, as long as there's a minimum of four people. You can rent bicycles here, too. ✉ *83 Rte. 776, Grand Manan* ☎ *800/732–5492, 506/662–3563* 🌐 *www.adventurehigh.com* 🎟 *From $27.50.*

WHALE-WATCHING

Sea Watch Tours

RAFTING | FAMILY | Interpreters on these tours are very knowledgeable about the birds, whales, and other marine life you might encounter on your cruise. They also offer trips to Machias Seal Island to view Atlantic puffins, either on land or from the skiff. Trips are 4 to 5½ hours and run from late June through the end of July for the Machias Seal Island tour and early July to late September for whale-watching. ✉ *2476 Rte. 776, Grand Manan* ☎ *877/662–8552, 506/662–8552* 🌐 *seawatchtours.ca* 🎟 *From C$60.*

Deer Island

52 km (32 miles) east of St. Andrews-by-the-Sea to Letete, 30 minutes by free ferry from Letete.

One of the pleasures of Deer Island is walking around the fishing wharves like those at Chocolate Cove. Exploring the island takes only a few hours; it's a mere 12 km (7 miles) long, varying in width from almost 5 km (3 miles) to a few hundred feet at some points.

GETTING HERE AND AROUND

From Saint John travel west on Highway 1 and take the St. George exit, then take Route 172 south, a total distance of about 85 km (53 miles). The ferry is free, and runs every 30 minutes from 6:30 am to 5 pm, then hourly, with the last one back to the mainland leaving at 10 pm. There is no public transportation or bike rental on the island, so all but avid hikers will need a car.

Sights

Deer Point

VIEWPOINT | A walk through this small nature park is always pleasant, and a great way to pass the time while waiting for the ferry to Campobello Island. Just a few feet offshore in the Western Passage, the Old Sow, the second-largest whirlpool in the world, is visible, but its intensity depends on the state of the tide–it is at its most dramatic three hours before high tide. The water is always highly active, though, and porpoises can often be seen. ✉ *Deer Island Point Rd., Deer Island* 🌐 *www.deerislandpointpark.com* 🎟 *Free.*

Restaurants

45th Parallel Restaurant

$$$ | **SEAFOOD** | Seafood is an integral part of the home cooking at this casual and friendly motel restaurant overlooking Passamaquoddy Bay. The lobster roll is renowned, but you can't go wrong with other country-diner options like fresh panfried haddock, scallops, or the old-fashioned chicken dinners—baked chicken, stuffing, real gravy, mashed potatoes, veggies, and cranberry sauce. **Known for:** they'll pack up a picnic for you; fish-and-chips; nice patio for outside dining. [$] *Average main: C$30* ✉ *941 Hwy. 772, Fairhaven* ☎ *506/747–2222 year-round, 506/747–2231 May–Oct.* 🌐 *www.45thparallel.ca* 🕒 *Closed Nov.–Mar. and weekdays Apr., May, and Oct.*

Hotels

Deer Island Inn

$ | **B&B/INN** | Set in well-kept gardens, this grand Victorian building has been lovingly restored to provide modern amenities while keeping its historic character and features. **Pros:** pet-friendly if arranged in advance; discounts available for single use of double room; bedroom at front overlooks the water. **Cons:** no TV in rooms; late check-in not available; evening meal must be preordered. [$] *Rooms from: C$90* ✉ *272 Rte. 722, Lord's Cove, Deer Island* ☎ *506/321–0150* 🌐 *diinn.com* 🛏 *5 rooms* 🍴 *Free Breakfast.*

Activities

Seascape Kayak Tours

KAYAKING | Quality sea-kayaking experiences and responsible adventure tourism are provided May to October by this outfitter, which has received international recognition for its sustainable tourism practices and was among *Outside* magazine's "30 Most Incredible Trips to Take in 2015." Half-day and full-day tours, and two-hour sunset paddles, usually include sightings of wildlife, including seals, porpoises, whales, and bald eagles. ✉ *40 N.W. Harbour Branch Rd., Richardson, Deer Island* ☎ *506/747–1884, 866/747–1884* 🌐 *www.seascapekayaktours.com* 🎟 *From C$65.*

Campobello Island

40 minutes by ferry (June to September) from Deer Island; 90 km (56 miles) southeast of St. Stephen via bridge from Lubec, Maine.

Neatly manicured, preening itself in the bay, Campobello Island has always had a special appeal for the wealthy and the famous.

GETTING HERE AND AROUND

From Saint John, follow the directions for Deer Island. Once on Deer Island, drive 12 km (7 miles) to its southern tip for the East Coast Ferries service to Campobello (C$22 for car and driver, C$5 for each

Campobello's Island Head Harbour Lightstation was built in 1829 to help sailors navigate the Bay of Fundy's infamous high tides.

passenger 13 years and over), a journey of around 30 minutes. Ferries from Deer Island run hourly from 8:30 am to 5:30 pm. The company also runs a ferry from Eastport, Maine, to Campobello (C$13 for car and driver, C$4 for each adult passenger). Once there, a car is essential.

The ferry from Campobello to Deer Island departs on the hour, every hour, until 6 pm.

CONTACTS East Coast Ferries Ltd.. ✛ *Route 172 from St George to L'etete, New Brunswick* ☎ *506/747–2159, 877/747–2159* ⊕ *www.eastcoastferriesltd.com.*

👁 Sights

Herring Cove Provincial Park
STATE/PROVINCIAL PARK | FAMILY | The 425-hectare (1,049-acre) park has camping, a restaurant, playgrounds, a 9-hole, par-36 Geoffrey Cornish golf course, a sandy beach 1.6 km (1 mile) long, and six hiking trails, one of which follows a carriage and logging trail once used by the Roosevelts. ✉ *136 Herring Cove Rd.,*

Welshpool, Campobello ☎ *506/752–7010, 800/561–0123* ⊕ *parcsnbparks.ca* ✉ *Free.*

Roosevelt Campobello International Park
HISTORIC HOME | The 34-room rustic summer cottage of the family of President Franklin Delano Roosevelt is now part of a nature preserve, Roosevelt Campobello International Park, a joint project of the Canadian and U.S. governments. The miles of trails here make for pleasant strolling, many incorporating observation decks with stunning views and marine life sightings. Roosevelt's boyhood summer home was also the setting for the 1960 movie *Sunrise at Campobello.* Twice-daily Tea with Eleanor events include a talk about her life on the island. As an alternative to the ferry from Deer Island, Canada-based visitors can drive across the border into Maine from St. Stephen, go down Route 1, and take Route 189 to Lubec, Maine, then cross the bridge to the island. ✉ *459 Rte. 774, Welshpool, Campobello* ☎ *506/752–2922, 877/851–6663* ⊕ *fdr.net* ✉ *Free* ⊘ *Closed mid-Oct.–late May.*

Hotels

An Island Chalet

$$ | HOUSE | With stunning coastal views from their windows and front porches, and enough beds for four people, these log cottages (in spite of the singular name, there are five of them) offer great value. **Pros:** a real bargain for a party of four; close Roosevelt-Campobello International Park; plenty of space for the price. **Cons:** Wi-Fi connectivity not always reliable; beach rather difficult to reach; cell-phone reception can be unreliable. [$] *Rooms from: C$145* ✉ *115 Narrows Rd., Welshpool, Campobello* ☎ *506/752–2971* 🌐 *www.anislandchalet.com* 🛏 *5 rooms* 🍴 *No Meals.*

The Owen House

$ | B&B/INN | With glorious sea views, this 1835 house is full of antiques and original artwork by the owner, Joyce Morrell. **Pros:** several large sitting rooms; a really peaceful haven, free of everyday distractions; many original features. **Cons:** not everyone likes a communal breakfast table; the only TV is set up for video; two rooms share a bathroom. [$] *Rooms from: C$104* ✉ *11 Welshpool St., Welshpool, Campobello* ☎ *506/752–2977* 🌐 *www.owenhouse.ca* 🛏 *9 rooms* 🍴 *Free Breakfast.*

St. Martins

54 km (34 miles) east of Saint John.

The fishing village of St. Martins has a rich shipbuilding heritage, whispering caves, miles of lovely beaches, spectacular tides, and a cluster of covered bridges, as well as several heritage inns and a couple of restaurants right on the beach. It's also the gateway to the spectacular Fundy Trail Parkway, which now combines with the Connector Road to Alma to link all of southern New Brunswick, cutting the driving time by about an hour.

GETTING HERE AND AROUND

There is no public transportation to St. Martins. From Saint John drive north on Route 1, then head east on Route 111, past the airport, following signs for St. Martins. Coming from the Trans-Canada Highway (Route 2), exit onto Route 1 or Route 10 southbound via Sussex; both will get you to Route 111, signposted St. Martins.

ESSENTIALS

VISITOR INFORMATION Visitor Information Center. ✉ *Lighthouse, 424 Main St., St. Martins* ☎ *506/833–2006* 🌐 *stmartinscanada.com.*

Sights

Fundy Trail Parkway

SCENIC DRIVE | The scenic Fundy Trail Parkway extends for 30 km (18.6 miles) along the cliff tops through previously inaccessible wilderness with stunning views, and you can stop along the way at a number of lookouts. These include the stunning Walton Glen Gorge, the "Grand Canyon of New Brunswick"–1,000 feet across, 525 feet deep, and 550 million years old. Once a difficult eight-hour round-trip hike, it is now an easy 2-km (1-mile) round-trip walk to an observation deck with spectacular views across the towering rock face cliffs. Also along the Parkway make a stop at the Interpretive Centre at Big Salmon River. Various Stonehammer Geopark activities are offered here, including walks with an interpreter. The road closely parallels the cycling/walking Fundy Trail along the shore. There are lots of places to park and many accessible scenic lookouts. The 49-km (30-mile) Fundy Footpath, for expert hikers, continues through to the national park. The parkway portion operates mid-May through mid-October. In 2020 a new road linked the parkway to Sussex, and in 2021 a new Connector Road to Alma opened, both improving access to this highly scenic area. ✉ *St.*

Fundy National Park—New Brunswick's first park to be designated as such—is located on the shores of the Bay of Fundy and is brimming with beaches, unspoiled wilderness, and rocky headlands.

Martins ☎ 506/833–2019, 866/386–3987 🌐 www.fundytrailparkway.com 🎫 C$10.

Hotels

St. Martins Country Inn
$$ | **B&B/INN** | High on a hill overlooking the Bay of Fundy, the appeal of this restored sea captain's home comes from both its Victorian interiors, including antiques, quilts, and old-fashioned wallpaper, and the accomplished cuisine. **Pros:** restaurant open for breakfast, lunch, and dinner; breakfast available until 11 am; good food. **Cons:** reservations required for dinner; decoration may seem a little too "busy" to some; some rooms are small. [$] *Rooms from: C$139 ✉ 303 Main St., St. Martins ☎ 506/833–4534, 🛏 16 rooms 🍴 Free Breakfast.*

Tidal Watch Inn
$ | **B&B/INN** | This luxurious property is situated just a mere 150 feet away from where the highest tides in the world sweep in and out each day. **Pros:** fireplace rooms available; comfortable style and atmosphere; good food, including choice at breakfast. **Cons:** Wi-Fi not reliable in some rooms; not all rooms have good views; some rooms are in newer additions. [$] *Rooms from: C$115 ✉ 16 Beach St., St. Martins ☎ 888/833–4772 🌐 www.tidalwatchinn.ca 🛏 15 rooms 🍴 Free Breakfast.*

Fundy National Park

135 km (84 miles) northeast of Saint John.

Preserving a unique wilderness on the shores of the Bay of Fundy, this national park is the province's top attraction, with areas of true wilderness, beaches, rocky headlands, sea caves and inlets, wildlife, and stunning vistas. In recent years the federal government has undertaken a multimillion dollar investment in the park to improve access roads, the trails network, and visitor amenities. This included the completion of the Fundy Trail Parkway in 2018, construction of a connector road

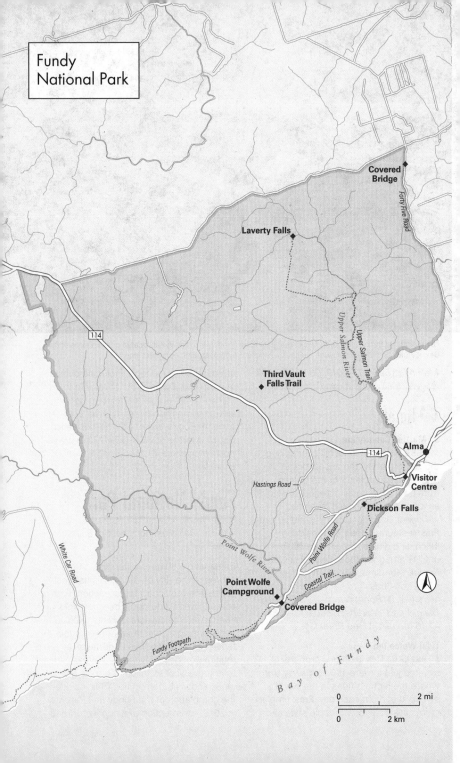

north to Sussex Corner in 2020, and, in 2021, another connector road linking the Parkway to Alma. Eventually there will be a spectacular coastal route—the Fundy Coastal Drive—stretching all the way from St. Stephen in the west to Sackville in the east.

GETTING HERE AND AROUND

Fundy National Park is bisected by Route 114, which loops down from just east of Sussex, leaves the park at Alma, and follows the coast, via Riverview, to Moncton. From the Trans-Canada Highway (Route 2), exit onto Route 10 to Sussex. Here you can take Route 1 east for a short distance (signposted Moncton) before exiting onto Route 114 south. New roads in 2020 and 2021 provided links to the scenic Fundy Trail Parkway, one from Sussex Corner and another via the Connector Road from Alma, the latter cutting about an hour off the previous journey time. There are a number of parking places within the park.

Sights

Alma

TOWN | The small seaside village of Alma services Fundy National Park with restaurants that serve good lobster, a bakery that sells sublime sticky buns, and motels. There's plenty to do around here—from bird-watching and kayaking to horseback riding. Around Canada Day, events may include performances at the Alma Activity Centre and a (plastic) duck race on the Salmon River. In 2021 a new Connector Road opened, linking Alma directly with the Fundy Trail Parkway and reducing the driving time to get there by about an hour. ✉ *Alma* 🌐 *www.villageofalma.ca.*

★ Fundy National Park

NATIONAL PARK | **FAMILY** | This incredible 206-square-km (80-square-mile) park—New Brunswick's first national park—is a microcosm of New Brunswick's inland and coastal climates, and has been designated a Dark Sky Preserve by the Royal Astronomical Society of Canada. The park has 100 km (60 miles) of hiking and mountain-biking trails, plus a playground, a heated saltwater pool, tennis courts, and a 9-hole golf course. Among the most scenic of the trails is Laverty Falls, a 2½-km (1½-mile) trail that ascends through hardwood forests to the beautiful Laverty waterfall. At Third Vault Falls, a 3.7-km (2.3-mile) trail from the Laverty Auto Trail Parking Lot, hikers can take a refreshing dip in the pool. On the way to the Coppermine Trail, visitors wind around a steep curve and through a bright-red covered bridge, a favorite spot for photographers. At a dozen scenic spots around the park, two or more red Adirondack chairs have been placed for visitors to sit and admire the view. Park naturalists offer daily programs, including beach walks and hikes that explore the forests (and even find and enjoy nature's edibles along the way). In the evening there are interactive programs in the amphitheater and campfires. Campsites range from full-service to wilderness, and yurts and "oTENTik" accommodations. ✉ *Rte. 114, Alma* ☎ *506/887–6000* 🌐 *www.pc.gc.ca/en/pn-np/nb/fundy* 🎫 *C$6.44* 🕐 *Visitor Reception Centre closed Nov.–May; closure of campgrounds varies.*

Hotels

Falcon Ridge Inn

$$ | **B&B/INN** | **FAMILY** | Perched high above the village and the ocean, every window (and there are many) in this modern property affords a spectacular view and eliminates any need for air-conditioning. **Pros:** electric vehicle charging available; amazing view of the fishing boats of Alma and shale cliffs of Fundy; full breakfast served at individual tables. **Cons:** nightlife is sparse in this area; village is walkable, but it's a steep slope back up; Fundy fog can unexpectedly block the vista. [$] *Rooms from: C$135* ✉ *24*

Falcon Ridge Dr., Alma ☎ 506/887–1110, 888888/321–9090 🌐 www.falconridge-inn.nb.ca 🛏 4 rooms 🍴 Free Breakfast.

Parkland Village Inn

$$ | B&B/INN | FAMILY | Right on the water, next to the fishermen's wharf in the heart of the bustling village, this long-established inn also has a very good restaurant. **Pros:** children stay for free; view of the Bay of Fundy is extraordinary; overnight guests have guaranteed seating in the busy restaurant. **Cons:** standard "parkview" rooms overlook the main street; breakfast not included in July and August rates; can be hard to get a room or table in peak season. [$] *Rooms from: C$135 ✉ 8601 Main St., Alma ☎ 506/887–2313, 866/668–4337 🌐 www.parklandvillageinn.com ⏲ Closed Nov.–Apr. 🛏 15 rooms 🍴 No Meals ☞ A continental breakfast is included April–June and September.*

Activities

GOLF

Fundy National Park Golf Club

GOLF | This is one of the province's most beautiful and challenging 9-hole courses, near cliffs overlooking the restless Bay of Fundy. Designed by course architect Stanley Thompson, it has some interesting hazards—the 6th green is particularly tricky—and quite taxing elevations (but carts are available), not to mention the distraction of the wonderful views. ✉ *Fundy National Park, near Alma entrance, 47 Fundy Park Chalet Rd., Alma ☎ 506/887–2970 🌐 www.pc.gc.ca/en/pn-np/nb/fundy/activ/golf 🎫 C$16–C$19 for 9 holes; daily rate C$28–C$34 ⛳ 9 holes, 6168 yards, par 70 ⏲ Closed early Oct.–mid-May.*

SEA KAYAKING

Kayak Fundy

KAYAKING | Bay of Fundy sea-kayaking excursions last from a half day to three days. Guides, instruction, park fees, and equipment are provided, including camping gear and meals for multi-day trips. ✉ *16 Fundy View Dr., Alma ☎ 506/887–2249, 800/545–0020 🌐 www.freshairadventure.com 🎫 From C$74 ⏲ Closed mid-Sept.–early May.*

Cape Enrage, Hopewell Cape, and Nearby

15 km (9 miles) east of Alma to Cape Enrage; 40 km (25 miles) from Alma to Hopewell Cape.

Rocky Cape Enrage juts more than 7 km (4½ miles) out into the bay, with a 6-km (4-mile) driftwood-cluttered beach, a lighthouse, and spectacular views, as well as an adventure center with a restaurant. Farther east along the coast, Hopewell Cape has the remarkable phenomenon of the Hopewell Rocks—tiny islands at high tide that reveal themselves as lofty columns rising from the dry beach at low tide. Between the two capes there are internationally significant nature reserves, an enclave of artists and artisans with studios and galleries to visit, and opportunities for outdoor activities.

GETTING HERE AND AROUND

From Alma, Route 114 follows a scenic route through Riverside-Albert, around Hopewell Cape and all the way to Moncton. There is no public transportation and the only option is to drive. For Cape Enrage, branch off via Route 915 then take Cape Enrage Rd.

ESSENTIALS

VISITOR INFORMATION Cape Enrage Interpretive Centre. ✉ *650 Cape Enrage Rd., Waterside ☎ 506/887–2273, 888/423–5454 🌐 www.capeenrage.ca.*

Sights

Cape Enrage

NATURE SIGHT | FAMILY | If the name of the cape isn't enough of a hint, the

At low tide in the Bay of Fundy you can walk amid the famous Hopewell Rocks.

140-year-old (still-working) lighthouse perched on the end of its rocky promontory says much about the nature of the waters here. Add tides that rise as much as 16 vertical meters (53 feet) and this becomes a must-see. If the ziplining, rappelling, and rock-climbing opportunities represent too much excitement, you can walk the boardwalk to a viewing platform below the lighthouse, and from there head down to the long "wilderness" beach below (check tide times and leave at least two hours before high tide; staff can advise). ⊠ *Cape Enrage Rd., Waterside* ☎ *506/887–2273* ⊕ *www. capeenrage.ca* ☒ *C$6 mid-May–mid-Oct.*

★ Hopewell Rocks

NATURE SIGHT | **FAMILY** | These famous "giant flowerpots" have been carved by the Bay of Fundy tides, and though a major rockfall in 2016 robbed the one they call 'the elephant' of its distinctive profile, walking among them at low tide remains a remarkable experience. At high tide, all you see is the very top, crowned with vegetation and appearing as tiny islands. There are also trails, an interactive visitor center, a café-restaurant, a gift shop, and a children's play area. Guided tours are available. It's about a 15-minute walk from the visitor center to the rocks, but there's also a shuttle service (C$2 each way). The tide comes in very quickly, so check tide tables, keep an eye on your watch, and exit the beach with time to spare. ⊠ *131 Discovery Rd., Hopewell Cape* ☎ *877/734–3429* ⊕ *www.thehopewellrocks.ca* ☒ *C$14 (valid for 2 consecutive days)* ☉ *Closed mid-Oct.–mid-May.*

Shepody National Wildlife Area

NATURE PRESERVE | The three main areas of this freshwater preserve—Germantown Marsh, Mary's Point, and New Horton—comprise an important habitat for species, including the American bittern, sora, and pied-billed grebe, and are also a staging point for tens of thousands of migrating shorebirds, such as American black duck, green- and blue-winged teal, and ring-necked duck. Most notable, perhaps, is the fact that 98 percent of the world population of sandpipers stop to feed on the mud shrimp in the Bay of Fundy on their way south. The mammal population includes moose, bobcats, white-tailed deer, coyotes, otters, and mink. The shoreline at Mary's Point—a Ramsar-designated conservation site—offers spectacular sightings during the peak season from July 20 through mid-August and also has an interpretation center. Shepody is a great place for hiking, and at Mary's Point you can follow the shoreline and stroll through forests for land-bird sightings, which include bald eagles and peregrine falcons. The area, now a bird sanctuary and interpretive center, is near Riverside-Albert. ✉ *Riverside-Albert* ✣ *Germantown Marsh is on Hwy. 114; Mary's Point and New Horton are off Rte. 915 near Riverside-Albert* ☎ *800/668–6767* 🌐 *www.canada.ca/en/environment-climate-change/services/national-wildlife-areas/locations/shepody.html* 🎫 *Free.*

Hotels

Florentine Manor Heritage B&B

$$ | **B&B/INN** | With beautiful antique furniture and handmade quilts on the beds, this restored shipbuilder's house is a haven for honeymooners and romantics, and the Fundy Coast is close by. **Pros:** good breakfasts; comfortably decorated, but not overstuffed rooms; abundant birdlife. **Cons:** some rooms are small; breakfast fixed at 8 am; minimum two-night stay. [$] *Rooms from: C$125* ✉ *356 Rte. 915, Harvey* ☎ *800/665–2271* 🌐 *www.florentinemanor.com* 🛏 *8 rooms* 🍴 *Free Breakfast.*

Innisfree Bed and Breakfast

$$ | **B&B/INN** | An 1847 farmhouse just minutes from Hopewell Rocks now provides stylish and comfortable accommodations in rooms furnished with antiques and quilts. **Pros:** vegetarian, vegan, and gluten-free food options; closest bed-and-breakfast to Hopewell Rocks; friendly, helpful hosts. **Cons:** seven-day cancellation policy; not for those traveling with children; may be too quiet for some. [$] *Rooms from: C$145* ✉ *4270 Hwy. 114, Lower Cape, Hopewell Cape* ☎ *506/734–3510* 🌐 *www.innisfreebandb.com* 🛏 *5 rooms* 🍴 *Free Breakfast.*

Shopping

Albert County Clay Company

CRAFTS | In a large converted community hall, Judy Tait makes beautiful and stylish pottery from local clay, many pieces imprinted with the forms of leaves and wildflowers. ✉ *900 Albert Mines Rd., Curryville* ✣ *Off Rte. 114 near Hopewell* ☎ *506/734–2851.*

Farm Life Studio

ART GALLERIES | Normand Brandford's paintings and prints reflect his affinity with farm animals—some living examples of the subject matter look on from the surrounding pastures—as well as local wildlife, landscapes, and nostalgic scenes. ✉ *474 Albert Mines Rd., Albert Mines, Hopewell Cape* ☎ *506/734–3493.*

Studio on the Marsh

ART GALLERIES | In a perfect setting for wildlife art, this studio sells prints by the late Lars Larsen. His New Brunswick scenes in particular make excellent souvenirs. ✉ *255 Marys Point Rd., off Rte. 915* ☎ *506/882–2917* 🌐 *www.studioonthemarsh.com.*

Activities

HORSEBACK RIDING

Broadleaf Guest Ranch

HORSEBACK RIDING | **FAMILY** | Horseback trail rides go through lowland marshes or woodland, or a combination of the two, and options include four- and six-hour excursions with lunch. Other activities including cycling, canoeing, hiking, rappelling are offered, and in winter there's cross-country skiing, snowshoeing, sleigh rides, and other pursuits. Packages, including accommodations at the ranch, and youth summer camps are also available. ✉ *5526 Rte. 114, Hopewell Hill* ☎ *506/882–2349, 800/226–5405* ⊕ *broadleafranch.ca* ✐ *From C$35; from C$130 for 4 hrs, including lunch.*

SEA KAYAKING
Baymount Outdoor Adventures

KAYAKING | This company provides guided sea kayaking tours at Hopewell Rocks Provincial Park and also offers hiking and biking tours on the Bay of Fundy. ✉ *131 Discovery Rd., Hopewell Cape* ☎ *506/734–2660, 877/601–2660* ⊕ *www. baymountadventures.com* ✐ *From C$61.99.*

ZIPLINING
Cape Enrage Adventures

ZIP LINING | Activities includes rappelling, rock climbing, and ziplining, and prices, which start at C$52 for three zipline runs, C$98 for rappelling, and C$135 for both, include admission to the cape. There are also guided fossil tours (C$5) on the beach, where there are fossils of trees, plants, and insects that are 350 million years old. The zipline is usually open daily in the season, but reservations are required for other activities. Weight restrictions for the zipline are 75–275 pounds, which may be adjusted due to weather conditions. A restaurant and a gift shop are on-site. ✉ *650 Cape Enrage Rd., off Rte. 915, Cape Enrage* ☎ *506/887–2273, 883/796–2273* ⊕ *www. capeenrage.ca* ☉ *Closed mid-Sept.–June.*

Moncton and Dieppe

80 km (50 miles) northeast of Alma.

Metro Moncton—the second-largest city in Atlantic Canada (after Halifax, Nova Scotia)—is attractive and welcoming, with several family-friendly attractions, some world-class restaurants, a splendid modern museum, and an ongoing calendar of festivals throughout the year.

The World Wine and Food Expo and the annual Santa Claus Parade of Lights draw more than 100,000 people in November, as do the HubCap Comedy Festival in February and the Northrop Frye Festival, the largest bilingual literary festival in Canada, in April. Outdoor summer concerts at Magnetic Hill, by the likes of the Rolling Stones, U2, Nickelback, and AC/DC, seem to have gone into a hiatus, but the smaller River Glen Amphitheatre is planning to take up the slack, and the 8,800-seat Avenir Centre, the state-of-the-art hockey arena, is also a major entertainment venue. Year-round entertainment is provided at the historic Capitol Theatre, the casino's concert hall, and smaller venues.

Two natural attractions are the main draws here: the Tidal Bore and the Magnetic Hill. The latter is often derided, but the optical illusion does create a very strange sensation and it's worth experiencing. The Tidal Bore, once justifiably described as the other kind of bore, was restored to its former glory after riverbank erosion was addressed, and the bore can be several feet high, depending on the tides. As a result, the city has made the most of its downtown riverside, with a park and boardwalk and a small amphitheater overlooking the best place to view the tidal bore sweep around a bend in the river. In summer, buskers often take advantage of this "stage."

Moncton is an agreeable, lively place, home to two universities and a center for information technology and communications. It is often called the Gateway to Acadia because of its equal mix of English and French and its proximity to the Acadian shore, though it also has a large Irish population and a growing Korean community. The renovated downtown has unique shops and restaurants and such beautiful flower displays that it has won national "Communities in Bloom" awards.

With its twin city of Dieppe—the join is almost imperceptible—Moncton is considered the shopping mecca of Atlantic Canada. Moncton's big chain stores are mostly strung out along Mountain Road, Mapleton Road, and the Trinity Power Centre, while Dieppe is home to Champlain Place, the province's biggest shopping mall. Both cities have good Saturday farmers' markets, and other retail opportunities.

GETTING HERE AND AROUND

Moncton is one of the few places in the province accessible by rail, on VIA Rail's Montréal—Halifax route known as "The Ocean," which runs three times a week. Dieppe is home to Greater Moncton Roméo Leblanc International Airport, one of the province's major airports. Maritime Bus provides long-distance bus service from points all along the Trans-Canada Highway between Québec and Nova Scotia, from Saint John, and down the Acadian Coast from Campbellton. By road, the Trans-Canada Highway (Route 2) loops around the city, with several exit points.

Moncton and Dieppe have an excellent bus system, operated by Codiac Transit; the fare is C$2.50, or you can buy a 10-trip pass for C$21 or a 20-day pass for C$39, available from the bus station at 140 Millennium Boulevard or Shoppers Drug Marts (535 Edinburgh Dr. or 860 Mountain Rd.). Free transfers, valid for 60 minutes, are available from the driver if you need to change buses to get to a single destination. Buses are equipped with bike racks.

CONTACTS Codiac Transpo. ⊠ *140 Millennium Blvd., Moncton* ☎ *506/857–2008* ⊕ *www.codiactranspo.ca.* **Greater Moncton Roméo LeBlanc International Airport.** ⊠ *777 Aviation Ave., Dieppe, Moncton* ✈ *Off Hwy. 15 about 10 km (6 miles) northwest of central Moncton* ☎ *506/856–5444* ⊕ *cyqm.ca.* **Maritime Bus.** ⊠ *77 Canada St., Moncton* ☎ *506/854–2023* ⊕ *www.maritimebus.*

com. **VIA Rail.** ⊠ *77 Canada St., Moncton* ☎ *888/842–7245 toll-free in North America, 506/857–9830 Moncton* ⊕ *www.viarail.ca.*

ESSENTIALS

VISITOR INFORMATION Moncton Visitor Information Centre. ⊠ *Resurgo Place, 20 Mountain Rd., Moncton* ☎ *800/856–4383* ⊕ *www.moncton.ca.*

◉ Sights

Aberdeen Cultural Centre

OTHER ATTRACTION | The halls of the Aberdeen Cultural Centre ring with music and chatter. The converted schoolhouse is now home to theater and dance companies, a framing shop, artists' ateliers, and several galleries, and concerts and artist talks are also hosted here. Galerie 12 represents leading contemporary Acadian artists. Galerie Sans Nom is an artist-run co-op supporting avant-garde artists from throughout Canada. The artist-run IMAGO Inc. is the only print-production shop in the province. Guided tours are available by appointment. ⊠ *140 Botsford St., Moncton* ☎ *506/857–9597* ⊕ *centreculturelaberdeen.com* ✉ *Free.*

Acadian Museum

HISTORY MUSEUM | On the campus of the University of Moncton, this museum has one of the world's largest collection of Acadian artifacts reflecting 400 years of Acadian life in the Maritimes and covering culture and beliefs, domestic life, politics, and more. Additionally, a fine art gallery showcases contemporary works by local and national artists.

■ TIP→ **The university is also home to several pieces of public art, so look out for these as you drive through** ⊠ *Clement-Cormier Bldg., 405 University Ave., Moncton* ☎ *506/858–4088* ⊕ *www.umoncton.ca/umcm-maum* ✉ *C$7.*

Lutz Mountain Heritage Museum

OTHER MUSEUM | If you love antiques and would thrill at the notion of discovering an old barn or attic crammed with centuries-old furniture, household items, and miscellaneous other artifacts, it's worth the short trip out here from downtown Moncton. Within a restored 1883 meetinghouse, there are authentic household, work-related, schoolroom, and even military items of the area's non-Acadian pioneer settlers, including the Lutz family, from as far back as 1766. Ignore your first impression—there's more than immediately meets the eye when you enter; more than 3,000 artifacts are crammed into the upper floor and basement areas as well as the main level, and guided tours tell fascinating stories behind the objects. The museum hosts a Canada Day Farmfest and occasional theater, tea, and supper events. ⊠ *3143 Mountain Rd., Moncton* ☎ *506/384–7719* ⊕ *www. lutzmtnheritage.ca* ⛁ *C$2 suggested donation.*

Magic Mountain
THEME PARK | FAMILY | This is an excellent theme park, adjacent to Magnetic Hill. It includes the SplashZone water park with a huge wave pool, thrill-ride body slides, including the 60 km/hour (37 mph) Kamikaze and three giant twister slides. The FunZone has plenty of thrill rides as well as rides for younger children, including battery-powered Bumper Boats with built-in squirters, while video games in the TekZone and four 9-hole golf courses round out the attractions. ⊠ *2875 Mountain Rd., Moncton* ⊕ *Off Trans-Canada Hwy. Exit 450 (Mountain Rd.) on outskirts of Moncton* ☎ *506/857–9283* ⊕ *www.magicmountain.ca* ⛁ *Fun-zone C$20; SplashZone C$30; Golf Zone $6.50 for 9 holes, $11.50 for 18 holes.*

★ Magnetic Hill
NATURE SIGHT | FAMILY | A bizarre optical illusion has been attracting visitors since the days of horse-drawn wagons. If you park your car in neutral at the designated spot, you seem to be coasting uphill without power. Don't be tempted to turn the vehicle around; the effect is most pronounced when you are going backward. Get out and try it on foot and it seems harder to walk downhill than up. There are shops and a restaurant within the attached Wharf Village, designed to resemble a traditional coastal village (⊕ *www.magnetichillwharfvillage.ca*). ⊠ *Moncton* ⊕ *North of Moncton via Mountain Rd., or off Trans-Canada Hwy. Exit 450 (Mountain Rd.); watch for signs* ☎ *506/384–9527* ⛁ *C$6 per car.*

Magnetic Hill Zoo
ZOO | FAMILY | This is the largest zoo in Atlantic Canada, covering 40 acres and housing 575 animals in more than 70 species, including a Big Cat exhibit housing endangered Amur tigers (which produced three cubs in 2018) and a leopard in a replication of a Siberian landscape (the New Brunswick climate is also similar to that of Siberia). In addition to imaginative viewing areas, the cats are fed from a zipline, which encourages them to chase and jump. There's no shortage of other exotic species, including lemurs, lions and other big cats, zebras, and ostriches, plus around 80 bird species are represented, both Indigenous and exotic. A tropical house has reptiles, amphibians, birds, and primates, and at Old MacDonald's Barnyard, children can pet domestic animals or ride a pony in summer. Check feeding times on the way in. ⊠ *125 Magic Mountain Rd., Moncton* ⊕ *Off Trans-Canada Hwy. Exit 450 (Mountain Rd.), on outskirts of Moncton* ☎ *506/877–7720* ⊕ *www. new-brunswick.net/new-brunswick/ moncton/zoo.html* ⛁ *C$9-C$16* ⊙ *Closed early Jan.–Mar.*

★ Resurgo Place
HISTORY MUSEUM | FAMILY | In a bright modern building, this imaginative and highly engaging museum relates the history of Moncton from its earliest settlement, through its various ups and downs (*Resurgo,* the city's motto, means "I rise again"), to the present day. Rather than just a collection of old stuff in glass

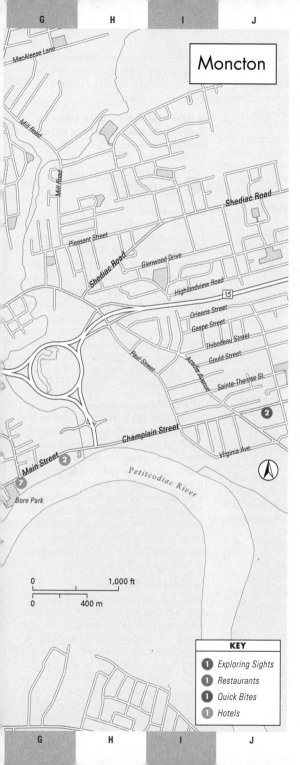

Moncton

Sights ▼

1 Aberdeen Cultural Centre **E6**
2 Acadian Museum.................. **D3**
3 Lutz Mountain
   Heritage Museum **A1**
4 Magic Mountain................... **A1**
5 Magnetic Hill....................... **A1**
6 Magnetic Hill Zoo................. **A1**
7 Resurgo Place **F6**
8 Thomas Williams House **D6**
9 Tidal Bore and Riverfront Park **F8**

Restaurants ▼

1 Café Archibald **E5**
2 Calactus
   Vegetarian Restaurant............. **E6**
3 Little Louis' Oyster Bar **A5**
4 St. James' Gate **E7**
5 Tide and Boar **F7**
6 Windjammer **F7**

Quick Bites ▼

1 Café Cognito....................... **F6**
2 Café La Lieto **J5**

Hotels ▼

1 Casino Hotel........................ **A1**
2 Château Moncton
   Hotel & Suites..................... **G6**
3 Crowne Plaza **E7**
4 Delta Beauséjour **F7**
5 Hotel St. James.................... **E7**
6 Magnetic Hill
   Winery and B&B................... **A1**
7 Rodd Moncton **G6**

KEY

- ❶ *Exploring Sights*
- ❶ *Restaurants*
- ❶ *Quick Bites*
- ❶ *Hotels*

cases, the museum seeks to conjure up a feeling of the age, and technology is used to involve visitors in their discoveries—in one of the Transportation Discovery Centre galleries, push-carts fitted with iPads connect with various points on the floor, allowing you to explore each subject on the screen before rolling along to the next. The museum also has a great area for kids, where learning through fun activities is taken to a new level to help develop their thought processes. The historic Free Meeting House, next door to the museum, can be visited by request at the museum's admissions desk. But before you leave the museum, ask if you can try the "Backward Brain Bicycle"—good luck! ✉ *20 Mountain Rd., Moncton* ☎ *506/856–4383* 🌐 *www.resurgo.ca* 🎟 *C$10 (C$5 Thurs. 5–8 pm)* 🕑 *Closed Mon.*

Thomas Williams House

HISTORIC HOME | Built in 1883, this beautiful house was the home of an Intercolonial Railway executive and gives more than just an idea of how a prosperous Victorian family would have lived. It also hosts exhibitions and events. After touring certain rooms of the house, you can get refreshments in the Verandah Tearoom, but check the closing time—you might need to take your afternoon tea first, before your tour. ✉ *103 Park St., Moncton* ☎ *506/857–0590 summer, 506/856–4383 off-season* 🌐 *www.resurgo.ca/our-heritage-landmarks* 🎟 *Free* 🕑 *Closed late Aug.–late June.*

Tidal Bore and Riverfront Park

CITY PARK | When the world's highest tides come in on the Bay of Fundy, the surge of water pushes far upstream on the Petitcodiac River, reversing the flow with a wall of water up to a meter high and raising the overall river level. It is an incredible sight when tides are at their highest. With its terraced seating and positioning, Bore Park on Main Street is the best vantage point; viewing times are posted. In summer, there's an introductory talk about the tides. The park is part of the larger Riverfront Park, with 5 km (3 miles) of multiuse trails along the banks of the river.

■ TIP→ Entering the water is extremely dangerous because of the deep, soft mud that lines the river. ✉ *Main St., Moncton* 🎟 *Free.*

🍴 Restaurants

Café Archibald

$$ | **ECLECTIC** | This is a great little place for a quick bite or bistro meal in pleasant surroundings. There's a huge range of coffees and teas as well as hot chocolate, house-made lemonade, juice, wine and beer, and the open kitchen serves good crepes, pizzas, salads, sandwiches, and desserts. **Known for:** imaginative pizza toppings and crepe fillings; sweet and savory crepes; huge drink menu. [$] *Average main: C$12* ✉ *221 Mountain Rd., Moncton* ☎ *506/853–8819* 🌐 *www.cafearchibald.com.*

Calactus Vegetarian Restaurant

$$ | **VEGETARIAN** | **FAMILY** | Tempting aromas fill this inviting restaurant, emanating from the world of flavors offered on the menu. Specialties include Oaxaca Deep Dish (black beans, grilled veggies, and spicy tomato sauce, baked with cheese), a classic vegetarian lasagna, and vegan desserts. **Known for:** popular with non-vegetarians, too; kids' menu has healthy options; Taj Mahal Thali. [$] *Average main: C$17* ✉ *125 Church St., Moncton* ☎ *506/388–4833* 🌐 *calactus.ca.*

★ **Little Louis' Oyster Bar**

$$$$ | **MODERN FRENCH** | So much more than just oysters, this stylish, sophisticated dining room with impeccable service is one of the finest restaurants in Atlantic Canada, despite its unlikely location on a predominantly industrial street. The modern French menu offers complex but perfectly balanced creations based on local seafood, beef, lamb, and poultry, and the daily tasting menu is a delicious and artistic culinary adventure—plus there's a first-rate wine list. **Known for:** elegant surroundings; chef Pierre Richard; the entire experience. $ *Average main: C$50* ✉ *245 Collishaw St., Moncton* ☎ *506/855–2022* 🌐 *www.littlelouis.ca* 🕒 *Closed Sun. No lunch.*

St. James' Gate

$$$$ | **ECLECTIC** | Named after the Guinness brewery in Dublin, this is by no means your standard Irish-theme pub. The menu is wide-ranging, including mussels, oysters, and other interesting seafood dishes, as well as meat dishes such as bacon-wrapped pork tenderloin or chicken carbonara. **Known for:** live music five nights a week; good selection of beers and cocktails; streetside patio. $ *Average main: C$35* ✉ *14 Church St., Moncton* ☎ *506/388–4283, 888/782–1414 reservations* 🌐 *www.st-jamesgate.ca* 🕒 *No dinner Sun.*

Tide and Boar

$$$ | **ECLECTIC** | The name of this classy gastropub is a fun play on words, referencing the proximity of Moncton's tidal bore and the seafood and boar on the menu, but it takes its food very seriously, earning a very loyal local following and a place on *Maclean's Magazine*'s list of Canada's Top 50 restaurants. The menu includes upscale pub favorites and inventive combinations, and the drinks menu is long, focusing mainly on draught and bottled craft beers. **Known for:** Sunday brunch; braised boar poutine; can get very busy. $ *Average main: C$21* ✉ *700 Main St., Moncton* ☎ *506/857–9118* 🌐 *www.tideandboar.com.*

★ Windjammer

$$$$ | **INTERNATIONAL** | Lists of Canada's top restaurants all include the Windjammer, where a memorable, pampering dining experience is assured and the setting creates an equally rarified atmosphere without being stuffy. Executive chef Stefan Mueller's menus feature seasonal ingredients from land and sea and some vegetables, herbs, and edible flowers come from the hotel's roof garden, which also supplies honey from its working beehives. **Known for:** excellent service; a very special occasion destination; chef's tasting menu. $ *Average main: C$55* ✉ *Delta Beauséjour Hotel, 750 Main St., Moncton* ☎ *506/877–7137* 🌐 *deltahotels.marriott.com* 🕒 *Closed Sun. and Mon.*

Coffee and Quick Bites

Café Cognito

$$ | **CAFÉ** | A nice modern spot serving good East Coast coffee and food that includes soups, sandwiches, St-Viateur bagels, and house-made scones, date squares, and muffins. There are vegan options, too. **Known for:** pavement seating on Main Street; very good Down East brand coffee selections; friendly and efficient service. $ *Average main: C$20* ✉ *581 Main St., Moncton* ☎ *506/854–4888* 🌐 *cafecognito.ca* 🕒 *Closed Sun.*

Café La Lieto

$$ | **CAFÉ** | This is a nice little café in the Dieppe area, serving 14 varieties of coffee, five unusual teas, hot chocolate, and hand-made soy milk. There are sweet treats, too, plus soups, sandwiches, and healthy lunches such as a quinoa salad. **Known for:** good coffee; outdoor seating; fireplace in winter. $ *Average main: C$15* ✉ *200 Champlain St., Dieppe* ☎ *506/388–3872* 🌐 *www.cafelalieto.com.*

Hotels

Casino Hotel

$$$ | **HOTEL** | This five-story hotel is part of the Casino New Brunswick complex and is linked to the gaming rooms and entertainment center via an interior walkway. **Pros:** regular special offers on room prices are good value; friendly and helpful staff; convenient for the Trans-Canada Highway. **Cons:** it's quite a walk from rooms to the restaurant; not in walking distance to downtown; food service is in the casino (minimum age 19 years). $ *Rooms from: C$179* ✉ *21 Casino Dr., Moncton*

☎ *506/859–7770, 877/859–7775* 🌐 *www.casinonb.ca* 🛏 *126 rooms* 🍴 *No Meals.*

Château Moncton Hotel & Suites

$$$ | **HOTEL** | Alongside the Petitcodiac River, this modern hotel with a distinctive red roof has a great view of the tidal bore, an extensive riverfront trail right out back, and Champlain Place shopping mall across the road. **Pros:** hot and cold buffet breakfast included in the price; some rooms have rain and jet showers; friendly and helpful staff. **Cons:** rooms on street side may suffer from traffic noise; no on-site restaurant, but spacious breakfast room; geared to business travelers. [$] *Rooms from: C$185* ✉ *100 Main St., Moncton* ☎ *506/870–4444, 800/576–4040* 🌐 *www.chateaumoncton.ca* 🛏 *105 rooms* 🍴 *Free Breakfast.*

Crowne Plaza

$$ | **HOTEL** | **FAMILY** | This upscale, modern hotel is in a great downtown location, particularly convenient for the new event center. **Pros:** views extend across downtown and the river; stylish makeover has been completed; very friendly and helpful staff. **Cons:** need to park first and haul luggage upstairs to check-in desk; not right in the hub of downtown bar and restaurant area; limited parking. [$] *Rooms from: C$142* ✉ *1005 Main St., Moncton* ☎ *506/854–5340, 866/854–4656 reservations* 🌐 *www.cpmoncton.com* 🛏 *191 rooms* 🍴 *No Meals.*

★ **Delta Beauséjour**

$$$ | **HOTEL** | **FAMILY** | In a great downtown location, this is one of Moncton's finest and friendliest hotels, catering equally to business travelers, vacationers, and families, who particularly enjoy the 125-foot indoor waterslide that is connected to the indoor pool. **Pros:** exceptionally warm welcome and friendly service; right in the hub of downtown; some rooms overlook the river, with good tidal bore viewing. **Cons:** no concierge; rooms near pool can be noisy; parking not free and in a busy public lot at rear. [$] *Rooms from: C$175* ✉ *750 Main St., Moncton* ☎ *506/854–4344, 888/351–7666* 🌐 *delta-hotels.marriott.com* 🛏 *304 rooms* 🍴 *No Meals.*

Hotel St. James

$$ | **HOTEL** | Moncton's first boutique hotel is in the heart of downtown, just off Main Street, and has chic and spacious rooms above a highly regarded pub-restaurant. **Pros:** very comfortable; good central location; stylish design. **Cons:** elevator only goes up to the hotel lobby; gets noisy when there's a band in the pub; everything, including reception, is upstairs. [$] *Rooms from: C$161* ✉ *14 Church St., Moncton* ☎ *888/782–1414* 🌐 *www.st-jamesgate.ca/boutique-hotel-moncton* 🛏 *9 rooms* 🍴 *Free Breakfast.*

Magnetic Hill Winery and B&B

$$ | **B&B/INN** | On Lutz Mountain, with a panoramic view over Moncton, this delightful bed-and-breakfast offers warm and friendly personal service from a wine-making family. **Pros:** intimate; price includes wine tastings; near Magnetic Hill attractions. **Cons:** not for those who aren't sociable in the morning; not ideal for small children; some distance out of town. [$] *Rooms from: C$149* ✉ *860 Front Mountain Rd., Moncton* ✣ *North of Hwy. 2, Exit 450. After turning off Mountain Rd. onto Front Mountain Rd., ignore Magnetic Hill B&B on left; Winery B&B is a little farther on right* ☎ *506/384–9463* 🌐 *www.magnetichillwinery.com* 🛏 *2 rooms* 🍴 *Free Breakfast.*

Rodd Moncton

$$ | **HOTEL** | **FAMILY** | In an ideal location right next to Bore Park, the riverfront trail, and many downtown restaurants, this is a gem of a hotel that's run by the friendliest staff you could wish to meet. **Pros:** free on-site parking; great river views from some rooms; free Wi-Fi and local calls. **Cons:** outdoor pool is nice but quite small; no on-site restaurant; soundproofing could be better. [$] *Rooms from: C$145* ✉ *434 Main St., Moncton* ☎ *506/382–1664* 🌐 *www.roddvacations.*

com/rodd-moncton ➣ 97 rooms ❚○❚ Free Breakfast.

ⓨ Nightlife

Casino New Brunswick

LIVE MUSIC | Along with its gaming tables and slots, the casino has a large, state-of-the-art concert hall with a mixed lineup ranging from tribute bands to clairvoyants. Lesser-known local acts entertain for free in the pub on weekends. The casino is open from 7 am to 3 am (24 hours on weekends), with table games from noon. ✉ *21 Casino Dr., Moncton* ☎ *506/859–7770, 877/859–7775* ⊕ *www.casinonb.ca.*

Navigators Pub

BARS | An antidote to the trendy Rouge next door, Navigators Pub is a no-frills downtown watering hole offering live music every night. It has a particularly nice (and sheltered) patio. It's open until 2 am, and music starts at 10. ✉ *191 Robinson Ct., Moncton* ☎ *506/854–8427.*

The Old Triangle Irish Alehouse

PUBS | A good re-creation of the quintessential Dublin pub, this place has a buzzing atmosphere, good food, and live music Wednesday through Saturday—a mix of Irish, rock, and easy listening. On some weekend afternoons, except in summer, local Celtic musicians get together here for an informal *seisun* (jam). ✉ *751 Main St., Moncton* ☎ *506/384–7474* ⊕ *www.oldtrianglemoncton.com.*

Pump House Brewpub & Restaurant

BREWPUBS | In addition to the list of house brews, which have won a whole slew of awards and are now sold internationally, and a long and varied food menu, you can enjoy live music Saturday night (mostly classic rock and oldies). The pub is also a venue for the HubCap Comedy Festival in February. ✉ *5 Orange La., Moncton* ☎ *506/855–2337* ⊕ *www.pumphouse-brewery.ca.*

🎭 Performing Arts

Avenir Centre

ARTS CENTERS | Moncton's C$100-million-plus downtown events center is home to the Wildcats ice hockey team, and a variety of events, including concerts and comedy shows, are held in the 8,800-seat arena. The box office is open 9–6 weekdays year-round and additionally from 10 to noon Saturday from September through April. Tickets also may be purchased via Ticketmaster.ca. ✉ *150 Canada St., Moncton* ☎ *506/962–4545 box office, 855/985–5000 Ticketmaster* ⊕ *www.avenircentre.com.*

Capitol Theatre

THEATER | A restored 1920s vaudeville stage, the opulent Capitol Theatre is a beautiful attraction in itself as well as a venue for plays, musicals, ballets, stand-up comedy, and concerts. Free tours are given when guides are available; call ahead. ✉ *811 Main St., Moncton* ☎ *506/856–4379, 800/567–1922* ⊕ *www.capitol.nb.ca.*

🛍 Shopping

Dieppe's Champlain Place shopping mall and Moncton's downtown boutiques and big-box stores on Mountain Road and the Trinity/Mapleton area make the twin cities one of New Brunswick's major shopping destinations—a lot of people come over from Prince Edward Island to shop here, too. There's also quite a network of secondhand clothing stores with some amazing designer bargains and some interesting independent shops and galleries. Farmers' markets in both cities focus on quality foods, arts, and crafts from local producers.

Apple Art Gallery

ART GALLERIES | Representing around 20 local artists and artisans, this gallery covers a range of works, including fine art, crafts such as ceramics and jewelry, and books. Shipping can be arranged.

The gallery also exhibits paintings at Moncton's airport. ✉ *333 St. George St., 2nd fl., Moncton* ☎ *506/533–0672* ⊕ *www.appleart.co.*

Dieppe Market

CRAFTS | Every Friday from 4 to 6 pm and every Saturday, from 8 am to 1 pm, this weekly market brims with fresh produce, baked goods, ethnic cuisine, crafts, and live music. They also fill online orders for drive-through pickup, though hours are limited. ✉ *232 Gauvin Rd., off Acadie Ave., Dieppe* ☎ *506/317–0321* ⊕ *www. marchedieppemarket.com.*

Gifts Galore

CRAFTS | This friendly store has an incredible range of arts and crafts, jewelry and other accessories, souvenirs, fashions, books, and collectibles, with strong support for local artisans as well as Canadian brands like Ganz and Webkinz toys. ✉ *569 Main St., Moncton* ☎ *506/857–9179* ⊕ *www.giftsgalorenb.ca.*

Marché Moncton Market

MARKET | The weekly market buzzes on Saturday from 8 am to 2 pm, with more than 130 vendors selling fresh produce, meat and deli foods, baked goods, and crafts. Vendors serve delicious Asian, Mediterranean-Canadian, and Latin-American food here Monday through Saturday. ✉ *120 Westmorland St., Moncton* ☎ *506/389–5969* ⊕ *www. marchemonctonmarket.ca.*

Second Edition

WOMEN'S CLOTHING | This resale boutique has gently worn designer and brand-name clothing, footwear, and accessories for women at a fraction of the new price. ✉ *215 Park St., Moncton* ☎ *506/855–6300* ⊕ *secondedition.ca.*

 Activities

GOLF

The Moncton area is home to two of New Brunswick's four signature golf courses.

Fox Creek Golf Club

GOLF | This is an exceptional course, fast becoming famous for its architectural and natural beauty. Play begins with an uphill shot to the first and ends with a long par 5 at the 18th, with some unique challenges in between—watch out for some high hills, sloped greens, and water and front guard bunkers on the par-3 fourth hole. ✉ *200 Golf St., Dieppe* ☎ *506/859–4653* ⊕ *www.foxcreekgolfclub.ca* ▧ *C$79– C$99* ⅄ *18 holes, 6925 yards, par 72.*

Royal Oaks Golf Club

GOLF | This PGA Championship course was the first Canadian course designed by the U.S. golf course architect Rees Jones. Its bent grass fairways, strategic bunkering, and plenty of water hazards present a rewarding challenge, and you'll need to be aware of prevailing winds in some areas. There's a dress code and only soft-spiked shoes are permitted. Club and cart rentals are available. ✉ *401 Royal Oaks Blvd., Moncton* ✛ *5 km (3 miles) north of Trans-Canada Hwy. off Elmwood Dr.* ☎ *506/388–6257* ⊕ *www. royaloaks.ca* ▧ *C$79; twilight C$50* ⅄ *18 holes, 7103 yards, par 72.*

ZIPLINING

TreeGO Moncton

ZIP LINING | **FAMILY** | With courses for children, teens, and adults, anyone can clamber through the treetops of Centennial Park, negotiating swinging rope-suspended logs, rope ladders, and ziplines, all while safely harnessed. Parents can watch their kids' progress from the ground. Adults embark on four courses, each more challenging than the last. Check the website for tips on suitable clothing and footwear. ✉ *Centennial Park, 45 Centennial Beach La., Moncton* ☎ *506/363–4440* ⊕ *www. treegomoncton.com* ▧ *C$38.*

Dorchester and Memramcook

Memramcook is 24 km (15 miles) south-east of Moncton; Dorchester is 14 km (9 miles) south of Memramcook.

Memramcook and Dorchester are on opposite sides of a marsh, each surrounded by gentle, rolling landscape filled with colorful native grasses. Acadian roots run deep in Memramcook, while Dorchester was a center of British culture and industry long before the Loyalists landed and is home to some of the province's oldest buildings.

GETTING HERE AND AROUND
There is no public transportation to Memramcook and Dorchester, which are 24 km (15 miles) and 38 km (24 miles) southeast of Moncton via Route 106 through Dieppe. From the Trans-Canada Highway (Route 2), take Exit 488 for Memramcook and Exit 482 (Renaissance Street) for Dorchester. Route 106 (Royal Road) links the two towns.

ESSENTIALS
VISITOR INFORMATION Visitor Information Center. ⊠ *Keillor House Museum, 4974 Main St., Dorchester* ☎ *506/379–6633* ⊕ *www.dorchester.ca.* **Visitor Information Center.** ⊠ *480 Centrale St., Memramcook* ☎ *506/758–4078* ⊕ *www.memramcook.com.*

◉ Sights

Keillor House Museum
HISTORIC HOME | This museum is composed of several buildings: Keillor House, an early Regency stone house built in 1813 that contains thousands of artifacts relating to mid-19th-century life and where docents are in costume; Coach House, which contains a fascinating collection of artifacts from the Dorchester Penitentiary; and, just a minute away on foot, the St. James Museum, set

in a former church and containing the Beachkirk Collection of equipment used in the manufacturing of textiles, including antique looms; you can sometimes see demonstrations of carding, spinning, and weaving, and there are also blacksmiths' and carpenters' tools. Special events are held at the museum throughout the year. ⊠ *4974 Main St., Dorchester* ☎ *506/379–6633 early June–early Sept.* ⊕ *keillorhousemuseum.com* ⊠ *C$5.*

Monument Lefebvre National Historic Site
HISTORIC SIGHT | Overlooking the marshes, fields, and birding sites of the lovely Memramcook Valley, this historic site commemorates the survival of the Acadians and celebrates the renaissance of Acadian culture. This monument is in the original home of St. Joseph's College, the first degree-granting French-language institution in Atlantic Canada, founded by Father Camille Lefebvre in 1864. A permanent interactive exhibit, "Reflections of a Journey—the Odyssey of the Acadian People," provides an excellent overview. Guided tours are available. ⊠ *480 Central St., Memramcook* ☎ *506/758–9808* ⊕ *www.pc.gc.ca* ⊠ *C$3.90.*

Activities

Johnson's Mills Shorebird Reserve
BIRD WATCHING | The beaches here, which are on the Ramsar list of Wetlands of International Importance, are a staging area for some two million migratory shorebirds. These include semipalmated sandpipers—more than 98 percent of the world population of these webbed shorebirds stop in New Brunswick on their way south. Bird numbers are most impressive in July and August, when as many as 140,000 may be present on a single day. A Nature Conservancy interpretive center is open to coincide with high tides. Tide times are posted on the website, which also has a time-lapse film. ⊠ *Rte. 935, Dorchester* ✛ *About 8 km (5 miles) south of Dorchester*

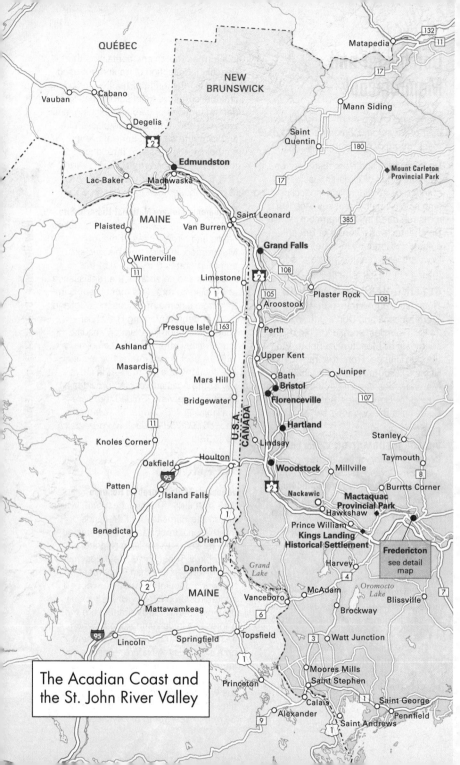

The Acadian Coast and
the St. John River Valley

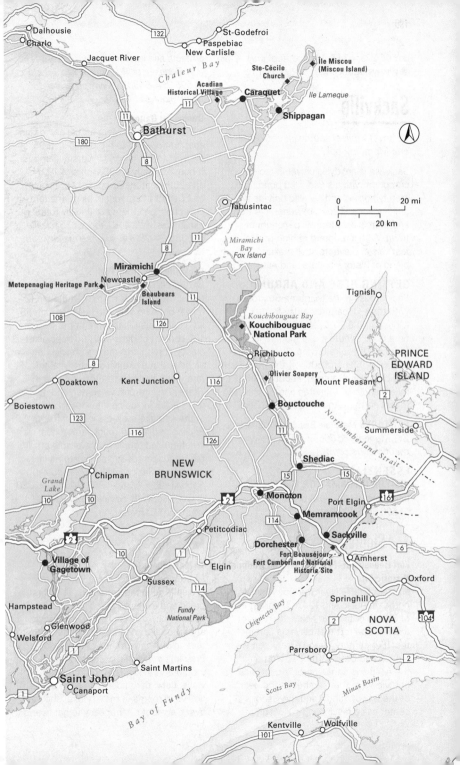

✆ 506/379–6347 July and Aug. only
⊕ www.natureconservancy.ca.

Sackville

22 km (14 miles) southeast of Dorchester and Memramcook.

Sackville is an idyllic university town complete with a swan-filled pond. Its stately homes and ivy-clad university buildings are shaded by venerable trees, and there's a waterfowl park right in town. With a program of high-profile festivals and events, it all makes for a rich blend of history, culture, and nature.

GETTING HERE AND AROUND

Sackville is on the Maritime Bus route, with three departures a day from Moncton at 9:20, 2, and 6. The journey time is 40 minutes, and the fare is C$20.15. If you're driving, Sackville has two exits (504 and 506) off the Trans-Canada Highway (Route 2), about 50 km (31 miles) south of Moncton and 17 km (10½ miles) north of Amherst, Nova Scotia.

CONTACTS Maritime Bus. ✉ *77 Canada St., Moncton* ✆ *506/854–2023* ⊕ *www. maritimebus.com.*

ESSENTIALS

VISITOR INFORMATION Visitor Information Center. ✉ *34 Mallard Dr., Sackville* ✆ *506/364–4967.*

◉ Sights

Fort Beauséjour–Fort Cumberland National Historic Site

MILITARY SIGHT | Near the Nova Scotia border in Aulac and 12 km (7 miles) east of Sackville, the site holds the ruins of a star-shape fort that played a part in the 18th-century struggle between the French and British. The Deportation of the Acadians began here. The fort has fine views of the marshes at the head of the Bay of Fundy, and the visitor center has a fascinating collection of artifacts and interpretive exhibits. ✉ *111 Fort Beauséjour Rd., Aulac, Sackville* ✆ *506/364–5080* ⊕ *www.pc.gc.ca/ beausejour* 🎫 *C$3.90.*

Owens Art Gallery

ART GALLERY | The oldest art gallery in Canada, first opened to the public in 1895, is on the Mount Allison University campus. It houses nearly 4,000 works of 19th- and 20th-century European, American, and Canadian artwork in its permanent collection, and there are usually rotating exhibits as well. ✉ *61 York St., Sackville* ✆ *506/364–2574* ⊕ *owensartgallery.com* 🎫 *Free.*

Sackville Waterfowl Park

NATURE PRESERVE | In the heart of the town, the park has more than 3½ km (2 miles) of boardwalk and trails through 55 acres of wetlands that are home to some 160 species of birds and 200 species of plants. Throughout the marsh, viewing areas and interpretive signs reveal the rare waterfowl species that nest here. There's an interpretive center, and guided tours (C$6, including info kit and a snack at the end) are available in French and English mid-May through late August. A self-guided tour is also available at the visitor center and some stores in downtown Sackville. ✉ *34 Mallard Dr., Sackville* ✆ *506/364–4967, 800/249–2020* ⊕ *www.sackville.com/visit/attractions/ waterfowl* 🎫 *Free.*

🛏 Hotels

★ Marshlands Inn

$ | B&B/INN | A list of celebrity guests is displayed in the entrance hall of this grand and elegant inn, including Queen Elizabeth II, who once stopped in for afternoon tea and left the signed portrait that now hangs on the upstairs landing. **Pros:** lots of historic character; the good food draws in locals; nice art on the walls. **Cons:** third-floor rooms are small; no TVs in rooms in main house; shower over claw-foot tub not easy to get in and out. 💲 *Rooms from: C$120* ✉ *55 Bridge St., Sackville* ☎ *506/536–0170* ⊕ *www. marshlands.nb.ca* ⇨ *18 rooms* ⦿ *No Meals.*

👜 Shopping

Fog Forest Gallery
ART GALLERIES | Small, friendly, and reputable, this commercial gallery represents around 50 Atlantic Canadian artists, with works including fine art, prints, sculpture, crafts, and photography. Exhibitions change every three to five weeks. ✉ *14 Bridge St., Sackville* ☎ *506/536–9000* ⊕ *www.fogforestgallery.ca.*

🏃 Activities

Canadian Wildlife Service
BIRD WATCHING | Without a doubt, bird-watching is the pastime of choice in this region, and these are the people to call for information. ✉ *17 Waterfowl La., Sackville* ☎ *506/364–5044.*

Cape Jourimain Nature Centre
BIRD WATCHING | FAMILY | The National Wildlife Area here covers 1,800 acres of salt and brackish marshes, and large numbers of waterfowl, shorebirds, and other species can be seen. The outstanding interpretive center includes a museum and exhibit hall with displays on natural and human history, a restaurant specializing in local fare, and a boutique with nature art and fine crafts. You will also find a viewing tower, 11 km (6.8 miles) of trails (come prepared to deal with insects, and wear long pants and enclosed footwear), and daily guided tours in July and August. This is the best location to photograph the striking architecture of the 13-km (8-mile) Confederation Bridge that links New Brunswick to Prince Edward Island. ✉ *5039 Rte. 16, at Exit 51, Bayfield* ☎ *506/538–2336* ⊕ *www.capejourimain.ca* ▣ *Free.*

Shediac

25 km (16 miles) northeast of Moncton.

Shediac is the self-proclaimed Lobster Capital of the World, and it has a giant lobster sculpture to prove it, plus a five-day lobster festival each July. Beautiful Parlee Beach also draws people to this pleasant fishing village/resort town.

GETTING HERE AND AROUND
If you're planning to stay overnight and want to visit by bus, Maritime Bus has a daily departure from Moncton, at 4 pm, and the journey takes 30 minutes; buses back to Moncton depart at 1:05 pm Monday through Thursday and 11:40 am Friday through Sunday. The one-way fare is C$12.25, and the trip must be booked at least three hours in advance. By car from Moncton, take Route 15 east to Exit 31B onto Route 11, then almost immediately exit onto Route 133 and follow signs into the town. The town is great for strolling, but a car is necessary to get to the beaches.

CONTACTS Maritime Bus. ✉ *77 Canada St., Moncton* ☎ *506/854–2023* ⊕ *www. maritimebus.com.*

ESSENTIALS
VISITOR INFORMATION Visitor Information Center. ✉ *229 Main St., Shediac* ☎ *506/532–7788, 506/532–7000 off-season* ⊕ *www.shediac.ca.*

🏖 Beaches

★ **Parlee Beach Provincial Park**
BEACH | FAMILY | The warmest salt water in Canada and a 3-km (2-mile) stretch of glistening sand has earned Parlee Beach the title of the best beach in Canada by several surveys, and it has a Blue Flag international eco-certification. It is a popular vacation spot for families, with a campground, and plays host to beach-volleyball and touch-football tournaments; an annual sand-sculpture contest and a triathlon are among a

Acadian Culture

History

French settlers arrived in the early 1600s and brought with them an efficient system of dikes called *aboiteaux* that allowed them to farm the salt marshes around the head of the Bay of Fundy. In the 1700s they were joined by Jesuit missionaries who brought the music of Bach, Vivaldi, and Scarlatti, along with their zeal. In 1713, England took possession of the region, and authorities demanded that Acadians swear an oath to the English crown. Only those who fled into the forests escaped Le Grand Dérangement—the Expulsion of the Acadians, mostly during the Seven Years' War—which dispersed them to Québec, the eastern seaboard, Louisiana (where they became known as Cajuns), France, and even as far as the Falkland Islands. It was a devastating event that profoundly affected Acadian expression—mobility remains a pervasive theme in the art, literature, and music of Acadian people.

Whether they were hiding deep in Maritime forests or living in exile, Acadians clung tenaciously to their language and traditions. Within 10 years of their deportation, they began to return, building new communities along coasts and waterways in the northeastern part of the province, remote from English settlement. In the 1850s Acadians began to think

"nationally." By 1884 there was an Acadian national anthem and a flag, essentially the French tricolor with a bright yellow star on the blue section.

Acadians Today

The Acadian national holiday, on August 15, provides an official reason to celebrate Acadian culture. Le Festival Acadien de Caraquet stretches the celebration out for the two preceding weeks, with music and cultural events. Caraquet is also home to Théâtre Populaire d'Acadie, which mounts original productions for French communities throughout the Maritimes and encourages contemporary Acadian playwrights. Books by Acadian authors, including internationally renowned Antonine Maillet, circulate in Québec, France, and Belgium.

Modern Acadian artisans create pottery and baskets. Handmade wooden spoons are doubly beautiful—in pairs they keep time for the music at kitchen parties, where Acadian families have traditionally sung their history around the kitchen fire. But it isn't necessary to have a party to enjoy "music de cuisine." Clearly, the love of music endures—ringing clear in churches; the cotillion and quadrille are danced at soirees; and Acadian sopranos and jazz artists enjoy international renown.

schedule of summer events. **Amenities:** food and drink; lifeguards; parking (fee 9 am–5 pm); showers; toilets. **Best for:** sunrise; swimming; walking. ✉ *Exit 37 off Rte. 133, Shediac* ☎ *506/533–3363, 800-561-0123.*

Plage de l'Aboiteau
BEACH | FAMILY | On the western end of Cap-Pelé, this fine, sandy Blue Flag beach slopes gently into the warm waters of the Northumberland Strait, so it's very popular with families. A boardwalk runs through the adjacent salt marshes where waterfowl nest. The

The giant lobster sculpture in the town of Shediac makes for a great photo op.

beach complex includes a restaurant and lounge with live music in the evening, and cottages are available for rent year-round. **Amenities:** food and drink; parking (fee); showers; toilets. **Best for:** sunrise; swimming; walking. ✉ *150 Allée du Parc, Cap-Pele* ✣ *Exit 53 off Rte. 15* 🌐 *plageaboiteau.ca.*

🍴 Restaurants

Le Menu Acadien

$$ | **CANADIAN** | Don't expect any frills here, but don't expect any processed food either—this diner and takeout, far removed from the touristy center of town, is the place to taste some authentic and delicious Acadian dishes. Try the *fricôt* (a hearty chicken soup), *poutine rappé* (a potato dumpling stuffed with ground pork), fish cakes, or traditional baked beans. **Known for:** convivial conversations with locals; great nostalgia value for Acadians; fast foods made from scratch. [$] *Average main: C$13* ✉ *55 Ohio Rd., Shediac* ✣ *From downtown Shediac, drive east on Main St. and turn right at lights by Ultramar gas station* ☎ *506/532–6366* 🌐 *www.menuacadien.ca* 🕓 *Closed Jan.–May.*

Le Petit Paris

$$$$ | **FRENCH** | This little restaurant serves authentic French cuisine—the chef is from France—on a well-balanced menu based on organic and natural ingredients. The menu changes with the season, but if you're looking for a classic *escargots à la bourguignonne* (snails in garlic butter) or local specialties like Magdalen Islands charcuterie or scallops, you won't be disappointed. **Known for:** good French wines are well chosen; delightful atmosphere and good service; a new dessert every day. [$] *Average main: C$34* ✉ *562 Main St., Shediac* ☎ *506/533–8805* 🌐 *www.lepetitparis.ca* 🕓 *No lunch Sat.–Mon.*

☕ Coffee and Quick Bites

Adorable Chocolat

$$ | **CAFÉ** | **FAMILY** | Not surprisingly, chocolate features heavily on the menu here, including hot chocolate drinks, and

there's good coffee too, including latte and iced coffee. They also serve freshly baked croissants and chocolate treats containing nothing but healthy natural ingredients. **Known for:** hot chocolate; freshly baked treats; chocolates to go. $ *Average main: C$22* ⊠ *395 Main St., Shediac* ☎ *506/351-0367* ⊕ *www.adora-blechocolat.ca* ⊘ *Closed Sun. and Mon.*

🛏 Hotels

Nowak's Own B&B
$ | B&B/INN | FAMILY | An unusual find in New Brunswick, this charming little bed-and-breakfast has a German theme, which is hardly surprising since the couple who run it are from Germany. **Pros:** pleasant rural surroundings; good coffee and breakfasts; quality linens and towels. **Cons:** out-of-town location; 7 km (4.3 miles) from Shediac; shared bathroom. $ *Rooms from: C$115* ⊠ *2999 Hwy. 134, Shediac* ☎ *506/351-1628* ⊕ *nowaksweb. de* ⊃ *2 rooms* ⦿ *Free Breakfast.*

Bouctouche

35 km (22 miles) north of Shediac.

This idyllic, bustling town on the sandy shores of Bouctouche Bay is famous for pristine beauty and for Le Pays de la Sagouine, a theme park based on an Acadian novel. The K.C. Irving Riverside Park and Monument honors the New Brunswick businessman born in 1899, whose descendants are still very prominent in the province's business community. The 12-km (7½-mile) dune of Bouctouche is one of the few remaining on the east coast of North America and is bordered by a 2-km (1¼-mile) boardwalk along the Irving Eco-Centre.

GETTING HERE AND AROUND
Bouctouche is 58 km (36 miles) northeast of Moncton via Route 15 east. From Route 15 take Exit 31B onto Route 11

north, then take Exit 32B for Bouctouche. A car is essential to reach all of the attractions.

ESSENTIALS
VISITOR INFORMATION Visitor Information Center. ⊠ *14 Acadie St., Bouctouche* ☎ *506/743-8811, 866/444-2411* ⊕ *www. villedebouctouche.ca/en/visitors/ visitor-information-center.*

👁 Sights

Irving Eco-Centre: La Dune de Bouctouche
NATURE PRESERVE | FAMILY | The center preserves a superb example of a coastal ecosystem that protects the exceptionally fertile oyster beds in Bouctouche Bay, a salt marsh, and an important 12-km (7½-mile) sand dune. Hiking trails and an 800-meter (½-mile) boardwalk with ramps and stairs to the beach make it possible to explore sensitive areas without disrupting the environment of one of the few remaining great dunes on the northwest coast of the Atlantic Ocean, and electric vehicles provide tours for visitors with mobility issues. An outstanding interpretive center puts the ecosystem in perspective with nature exhibits, a film presentation, a saltwater aquarium and seasonal special events. The staff regularly conducts guided walks. Swimming is allowed. ⊠ *1932 Rte. 475, Bouctouche* ☎ *888/640-3300, 506/743-2600* ⊕ *www. jdirving.com/jd-irving-sustainability-na-ture-parks-irving-eco-centre.aspx* ⊠ *Free.*

Le Pays de la Sagouine
MUSEUM VILLAGE | FAMILY | This Acadian culture theme park re-creates the world of La Sagouine, an old charwoman-philosopher created by celebrated Acadian author Antonine Maillet. It's a make-believe island community that comes to life (in French) in daylong musical and theatrical performances, with dinner theater/musical evenings July through September. There are also four performances in English Wednesday to Sunday, from June

to September. Tours are available in English and French, and the Friday-night jam sessions are accessible to English-speaking visitors, too. ✉ *57 rue Acadie, Exit 32 A or B off Hwy. 11, Bouctouche* ☎ *506/743–1400, 800/561–9188* 🌐 *www.sagouine.com* 🎟 *Free; presentations $5–10; shows various prices.*

The Olivier Soapery
FACTORY | FAMILY | A working artisan soapery, Olivier includes a museum with a fascinating array of bathtime memorabilia, from old bars of soap and soap-making equipment to tubs and basins. There's a skin-care art gallery, featuring paintings commissioned for soap labels throughout the years, and, naturally, plenty of soap and other skin-care products are for sale. By far the best attraction, however, is the soap-making demonstration, late June to early September at 10, 11:30, 2, and 4. ✉ *851 Rte. 505, 10 km (6 miles) north of Bouctouche, Ste.-Anne-de-Kent* ☎ *506/743–8938* 🌐 *www.oliviersoaps.com* 🎟 *Free.*

Hotels

Auberge Bouctouche Inn & Suites
$ | MOTEL | Renowned for its friendly and helpful staff, this inn has a range of rooms and suites, including family suites and wheelchair-accessible rooms. **Pros:** drinks available in the evening in the breakfast room; helpful and bilingual staff; within walking distance of town center. **Cons:** no elevator; sometimes hosts business conferences; need to drive to get to the beach. [$] *Rooms from: C$95* ✉ *50 rue Industrielle, Bouctouche* ☎ *506/743–5003, 888/450–2244* 🌐 *aubergebouctoucheinn.ca* 🛏 *38 rooms* 🍴 *Free Breakfast.*

Kouchibouguac National Park

40 km (25 miles) north of Bouctouche; 100 km (62 miles) north of Moncton.

On the warm east coast, you'll enter through old-growth forest laced with trails before emerging on glorious golden sands, with dunes and lagoons sheltered by barrier islands and a boardwalk that extends through the salt marshes to the sands.

GETTING HERE AND AROUND

Kouchibouguac National Park is off Route 11. Take Exit 75 onto Route 117 and follow the signs. An alternative route is on the scenic Acadian Coastal Drive, following the starfish road signs.

Sights

★ **Kouchibouguac National Park**
NATIONAL PARK | FAMILY | The word Kouchibouguac (Kou-she-boo-gwack) means "river of the long tides" in the Mi'Kmaq language, and this natural wilderness park consists of sandy beaches, dunes, bogs, salt marshes, lagoons, and freshwater, and is home to an abundance of birds. It is also a Dark Sky Preserve, so when the bird-watching is over for the day, stargazing can take over. The visitor center (open mid-May–mid-October) features information and interpretive exhibits. Kellys Beach is supervised and has facilities. There are more than 60 km (37 miles) of trails for biking and hiking in summer and for cross-country skiing, snowshoeing, snow walking, and kick sledding in winter. The forests and peat bogs can be explored along 10 nature trails, each of which has a parking lot. There are lots of nature-interpretation programs, and you can canoe, kayak, and picnic or rent bikes and boats. In summer there are Voyageur Canoe trips, paddling to a seal colony while your interpreter

In addition to beaches, lagoons, and salt marshes, Kouchibouguac National Park offers ample birding opportunities.

recounts tales of Mi'Kmaq and Acadian culture. Other programs include storytelling, Mi'Kmaq dances, and outdoor theater. Reserve ahead for one of the 311 campsites. ⊠ Rte. 117 ✛ 60 km (37 miles) north of Bouctouche, off Hwy. 11 ☎ 506/876–2443 ⊕ www.pc.gc.ca/kouchibouguac ⊠ C$7.90 mid-June–early Sept.; C$3.90 Apr.–late June and early Sept.–Nov.

Miramichi

40 km (25 miles) northwest of Kouchibouguac; 150 km (93 miles) northwest of Moncton.

Celebrated for salmon rivers that reach into some of the province's richest forests, and the ebullient nature of its residents (Scottish, English, Irish, and a smattering of First Nations and French), this is a land of lumber kings, ghost stories, folklore, and festivals. Sturdy wood homes dot the banks of Miramichi Bay. The city of Miramichi incorporates the former towns of Chatham and Newcastle and several small villages and is where the politician and British media mogul Lord Beaverbrook grew up and is buried.

GETTING HERE AND AROUND

Miramichi is 175 km (109 miles) northeast of Fredericton via Route 8 (also designated the scenic "Miramichi River Route"). From Moncton, Maritime Bus has a daily service, departing at 1:55, but it's not a practical choice; a car is necessary to see all the attractions. Take Route 15 east, then Route 11 north.

CONTACTS Maritime Bus. ⊠ 77 Canada St., Moncton ☎ 506/854–2023 ⊕ www.maritimebus.com.

ESSENTIALS

VISITOR INFORMATION Visitor Information Center. ⊠ 21 Cove Rd., Miramichi ☎ 506/778–8444 ⊕ www.discovermiramichi.com.

Sights

Beaubears Island

ISLAND | FAMILY | Formerly a thriving shipbuilding center, this is one of Miramichi's most interesting outdoor spots. Start at the museum-style interpretive center, with interactive audio-visual displays. A short boat trip will then take you to the island to see two historic sites, staffed by characters who love to share their colorful island stories and adventures. There are also guided tours and trips around the island in a 26-foot traditional Voyageur canoe, and regular special events are another attraction. ✉ *35 St. Patrick's Dr., Nelson* ☎ *506/622–8526* 🌐 *www.beaubearsisland.com* 🎫 *Interpretive center C$5; ferry to island $10; tours from C$20; Voyageur canoe experience (call for information).*

Metepenagiag Heritage Park

INDIGENOUS SIGHT | Two important First Nations archaeological sites, the Augustine Mound and Oxbow national historic sites, are at the heart of this park, "Where Spirits Live"—where the Mi'kmaq have lived for more than 3,000 years. In the museum, enthusiastic and knowledgeable staff are on hand to answer questions about the exhibits, and there's a good film about the history of the site. Outside, there are a number of walking trails to explore, and events include drumming circles, traditional dancing, and the annual powwow in June. First Nations experiences on offer include traditional foods, tipi retreats, storytelling from Mi'Kmaq elders around the firepit, and guided walks. ✉ *2156 Micmac Rd., Red Bank* ✣ *36 km (22 miles) west of Miramichi* ☎ *506/836–6118, 888/380–3555* 🌐 *www.metpark.ca* 🎫 *C$8* 🕒 *mid-Oct.–mid-May.*

Ritchie Wharf Park

CITY PARK | FAMILY | This waterside public park recalls the area's former shipbuilding industry. It has a nautical-theme playground complete with a "Splash Pad" that sprays water from below and dumps it from buckets above. Shops sell local crafts, and there are several restaurants and docking facilities. An amphitheater showcases local entertainers most evenings and on Sunday afternoon in summer. ✉ *84 Norton's La., Newcastle* 🎫 *Free.*

Restaurants

Namaste Bistro

$$ | INDIAN | Delicious and authentic Indian cuisine is expertly cooked and artistically presented here and gets rave reviews. The long menu includes vegetarian and vegan dishes as well as chicken, beef, lamb, and seafood–all prepared using traditional recipes, with varying degrees of spiciness. **Known for:** various degrees of spiciness to suit all tastes; lots of choice on the menu; traditional regional recipes of India. [$] *Average main: C$20* ✉ *12 Henderson St., Chatham, Miramichi* ☎ *506/773–3131* 🌐 *namastebistro.ca* 🕒 *Closed Mon.*

Hotels

Metepenagiag Lodge

$$$ | HOTEL | Overlooking the Little Southwest Miramichi River in unspoiled countryside, this lovely cedar lodge is run by members of the local Mi'Kmaq First Nations and is close to the Metepenagiag Heritage Park. **Pros:** surrounded by nature; friendly service; you can immerse yourself in First Nations culture. **Cons:** a continental breakfast only is included; can be overrun by business conference excursions; it's a 20-minute drive from Miramichi. [$] *Rooms from: C$175* ✉ *2202 Micmac Rd., Red Bank* ☎ *506/836–6128, 800/570–1344* 🌐 *www.met-lodge.com* 🔑 *10 rooms* 🍴 *Free Breakfast.*

Rodd Miramichi River

$$ | HOTEL | In a great riverside location in the downtown Chatham area, this is a good choice for both business travelers and vacationers. **Pros:** well-equipped meeting and conference spaces; indoor pool, whirlpool, and fitness center; next to a small riverside park. **Cons:** breakfast is not included; some bathrooms only have a shower (no tub); many business conventions and weddings. $ *Rooms from: C$165* ✉ *1809 Water St., Miramichi* ☎ *506/773–3111* ⊕ *www.roddvacations. com* ⇛ *79 rooms* ⦿ *No Meals.*

Shippagan

37 km (23 miles) north of Tracadie-Sheila.

Shippagan is an important fishing and marine education center as well as a bustling town with lots of amenities and the gateway to the idyllic islands of Lamèque and Miscou.

GETTING HERE AND AROUND

Shippagan is about 110 km (68 miles) northeast of Miramichi via Route 11, taking Exit 217 onto Route 113 for the final 12 km (7½ miles). The town is very walkable, but a car is necessary to visit the islands.

ESSENTIALS

VISITOR INFORMATION Visitor Information Center. ✉ *200 Hôtel-de-ville Ave., Shippagan* ☎ *506/336–3900* ⊕ *www. shippagan.ca.*

 Sights

Aquarium NB

AQUARIUM | FAMILY | This wonderful aquarium has a serious side and a fun side, with labs that are the backbone of marine research in the province and more than 1,000 specimens to see in more than 31 indoor exhibition areas, outdoor touch tanks, and the harbor seal pool. Feeding time for the seals (at 11 and 4) is always popular, as are the touch tanks, containing such species as sea stars, clams, sea cucumbers, and rare blue lobsters. Another exhibit illustrates the underwater world of the Acadian Peninsula and how fishing is carried out there, and there

are various educational activities and a documentary film to see. ✉ *100 rue de l'Aquarium, Shippagan* ☎ *506/336–3013* ⊕ *www.aquariumnb.ca* ⛶ *C$9.15* ⊗ *Late Sept.–late May.*

Île Miscou (Miscou Island)

ISLAND | FAMILY | Accessible by bridge from Île Lamèque, Miscou, on the northeastern tip of New Brunswick between the Bay of Chaleurs and the Gulf of St. Lawrence, has white sandy beaches, and the dunes and lagoons are good places to see migrating bird species. ✉ *Rte. 113, Shippagan* ☎ *506/344–7203* ⊕ *ilemiscou-island.webs.com.*

Ste-Cécile Church

CHURCH | Across a causeway from Shippagan is Île Lamèque and Ste-Cécile Church. Although the church is plain on the outside, every inch of its interior is decorated with folk art, painted in the late 1960s by the priest and two students. Each July, the International Festival of Baroque Music takes place here. ✉ *8166 Rte. 313, Petite-Rivière-de-l'Île, Shippagan* ☎ *506/344–5626.*

Caraquet

40 km (25 miles) west of Shippagan.

Perched on Caraquet Bay, along the beautiful Baie des Chaleurs, with Québec's Gaspé Peninsula beckoning across the inlet, Caraquet is rich in French flavor and is the acknowledged Acadian cultural capital. Its beaches are also a draw, and it has begun to attract the attention of the cruise lines that ply the waters of the Atlantic Provinces. It is also a great destination for cycling, with its 610-km Acadian Peninsula Veloroute, split into 22 circuits and mostly hugging the lovely coastline. Bikes can be rented from the Visitor Information Centre.

GETTING HERE AND AROUND

Caraquet is 113 km (70 miles) north of Miramichi on Route 11. A car is necessary to get around its scattered attractions. In August each year, Caraquet hosts the Acadian Festival, and other festivals celebrate art, comedy, song and wine.

ESSENTIALS

VISITOR INFORMATION Visitor Information Center. ✉ *39 St-Pierre Blvd. W, Caraquet* ☎ *506/726–2676* 🌐 *www.caraquet.ca.*

Sights

Acadian Historical Village

MUSEUM VILLAGE | FAMILY | More than 40 restored buildings here re-create Acadian communities between 1770 and 1949. There are modest homes, a church, a school, and a village shop, as well as an industrial area with a lobster hatchery, a cooper, and a tinsmith shop. The bilingual staff tells fascinating stories and provides demonstrations; visitors are invited to take part. You can also enjoy dinner and entertainment during the evening and stay overnight in the grand Hôtel Château Albert, an authentic re-creation of a 1907 hotel. ✉ *5 rue du Pont, Bertrand, 10 km (6 miles) west of Caraquet, Rivière-du-Nord* ☎ *506/726–2600* 🌐 *www.villagehistoriqueacadien.com* 🎫 *C$22* 🕒 *Closed early Oct.–early June.*

Founding Cultures Museum

OTHER MUSEUM | The former Pope's Museum now explores the peoples and cultures that shaped the area—First Nations, French, Irish, Scottish, and English, with a room dedicated to each—and how they formed the inclusive society they enjoy today. One exhibit that remains from the previous museum is the scale model of St. Peter's in Rome. ✉ *184 Acadie St., Grande-Anse* ☎ *506/732–3003* 🌐 *museedescultures.ca* 🎫 *Donation* 🕒 *May be closed in winter.*

Restaurants

Grains de Folie

$$ | BISTRO | This artisan bakery-café with a shaded streetside terrace is a great place to drop in for a quick bite, with an inviting aroma of fresh-baked bread and freshly brewed coffee to greet you. There's a deli counter with a great range of cheeses plus quick counter service for delicious soups, sandwiches, omelets, panini, pizzas, salads, and tempting pastries; table-service breakfasts run until 1 pm on weekends. **Known for:** staff appreciates visitors ordering in French; mouthwatering range of cakes and pies; art exhibitions and live music. [$] *Average main: C$15* ✉ *171 Blvd. Saint-Pierre O, Caraquet* ☎ *506/727–4001* 🌐 *grainsdefolie.ca* 🕒 *Closed Mon. and Tues. and Jan.–late Feb. No dinner.*

Hotels

Hotel Chateau Albert

$ | HOTEL | Once upon a time people managed to be perfectly happy without all our modern luxuries, and this hotel within the historic village is a true lodging experience for those who can go without them and enjoy the ensuing tranquility. **Pros:** total peace and quiet; free Wi-Fi (the one modern-era concession); can explore after day-trippers have left. **Cons:** need to pay admission fees to the historic village; not all bathrooms are en suite; no elevator and all rooms accessed by stairs. [$] *Rooms from: C$100* ✉ *5 Du Pont St., Caraquet* ☎ *506/726–2600, 877/721–2200* 🌐 *www.villagehistoriqueacadien.com/en/hotel-chateau-albert* 🕒 *Closed mid-Sept.–mid-June* 🛏 *15 rooms* 🍴 *Free Breakfast.*

Activities

Sugarloaf Provincial Park

BIKING | FAMILY | Eight trails on the 507-foot drop at Sugarloaf Provincial Park accommodate skiers and snowboarders of all levels in winter—a snow-making machine makes for an earlier start and longer season—and mountain bikers in summer; a chairlift operates in both seasons. There are also more than 25 km (16 miles) of bike trails, cross-country ski trails, hiking trails, a summer alpine slide, and other recreational amenities. Instruction and equipment rentals are available, including GPS for geocaching, there's a summer welcome center and a campground, and the lodge operates a lounge and restaurant year-round. ⊠ *596 Val d'Amour Rd., 180 km (112 miles) northwest of Caraquet, Atholville* ☎ *506/789–2366, 506/753–6825 for ski/snowboard rentals, 800/561–0123 for campsite reservations* ⊕ *parcsugarloafpark.ca* ⊠ *Bike park from C$5. Alpine skiing/snowboarding from C$14; cross-country skiing/snowshoeing season pass from C$30.*

Edmundston

275 km (171 miles) northwest of Fredericton.

Edmundston, the unofficial capital of Madawaska County, has always depended on the wealth of the deep forest around it—the legend of Paul Bunyan was born in these woods. Even today the town looks to the pulp mills of the Twin Rivers Paper Company as the major source of employment. Each summer, the town celebrates with the lively event Foire Brayonne, the largest Francophone festival in Canada outside Quebec.

GETTING HERE AND AROUND
Edmundston is on the Trans-Canada Highway (Route 2) about 16 km (10 miles) southeast of the Québec border—Exit 18 is best for downtown—and just across the river from Madawaska, Maine. Maritime Bus operates long-distance service via the Trans-Canada Highway from many towns and cities in New Brunswick, Nova Scotia, and Prince Edward Island. A car is

necessary to visit the Botanical Garden, on the northern edge of the city.

CONTACTS Maritime Bus. ⊠ *77 Canada St., Moncton* ☎ *506/854–2023* ⊕ *www.maritimebus.com.*

ESSENTIALS
VISITOR INFORMATION Edmundston–Madawaska Tourism. ⊠ *121 Victoria St., Edmundston* ☎ *506/737–1850, 866/737–6766* ⊕ *tourismedmundston.com.*

◉ Sights

New Brunswick Botanical Garden
GARDEN | FAMILY | In the Edmunston suburb of St-Jacques, roses, rhododendrons, alpine flowers, medicinal plants, and dozens of other annuals and perennials bloom in 10 gardens. Khronos: The Celestial Garden has an astronomical theme, complete with a contemporary stone circle. The music of Mozart, Handel, Bach, and Vivaldi often plays in the background. Two arboretums have coniferous and deciduous trees and shrubs. Mosaiculture plantings on metal frames placed throughout the gardens illustrate legends and cultural themes. Children (and adults) enjoy the phasmids (stick insects) and beekeeping exhibits. ⊠ *15 boulevard Isidore-Boucher, St-Jacques, Edmundston* ☎ *506/737–4444* ⊕ *www.jardinnbgarden.com* ⊠ *C$18, C$10 for phasmids exhibit only* ⊗ *Closed Oct.–early June.*

◉ Restaurants

Valley View Restaurant
$$$ | CANADIAN | Even if you don't go for the gambling, it's worth going to the Grey Rock Casino's Valley View Restaurant for dinner. The lengthy menu, which changes with the seasons, ranges from fast food to filet mignon to vegetarian stir-fries and much more, and prices are very reasonable. Ⓢ *Average main: C$25* ⊠ *Maliseet First Nation, 100 Chief Joanna Blvd, Saint-Basile, Edmundston*

☎ *506/735–2820* 🌐 *greyrockcasino.com* 🕒 *No lunch.*

Hotels

Four Points by Sheraton

$$$ | HOTEL | Linked to both the convention center and the shopping mall in downtown Edmundston, this is a super stylish hotel, with the clever use of natural stone, old barn boards, and industrial relics in public areas imparting a sleek and modern look. **Pros:** convenient for downtown shopping; very comfortable and well equipped; free coffee and bottled water. **Cons:** soundproofing could be better; needs more luggage carts; no nice views. [$] *Rooms from: C$197* ✉ *100 Rice St., Edmundston* ☎ *506/739–7321, 800/576–4656* 🌐 *www.fourpoints.com/edmundston* 🛏 *103 rooms* 🍴 *No Meals.*

Activities

Kasakayak

KAYAKING | FAMILY | Canoe and kayak rentals and tours are available from Kasakayak in Saint-Joseph-de-Madawaska. Rentals cost from C$40 to C$60 per day and include taxes, life jackets, paddles, and transportation back to your vehicle. ✉ *189 Rang 8 Rd., Saint-Joseph-de-Madawaska, Edmundston* ☎ *506/739–6255* 🌐 *kasakayak.com* 🎟 *Rentals C$40–C$60 per day* ☞ *Rentals include taxes, life jackets, paddles and transportation back to your vehicle.*

Petit Témis Biking Trail

BIKING | From Edmundston, you can access a section of the Petit Témis trail, which forms part of the Trans-Canada Trail. It would be an out-and-back bike ride, but it makes for a nice trip on a well-surfaced and fairly level track. Bikes can be rented at the Edmundston Visitor Information Centre. ✉ *Edmundston Visitor Information Centre, 121 Victoria St., Edmundston* ☎ *506/737–6766 bike rentals.*

Grand Falls

65 km (40 miles) southeast of Edmundston.

The St. John River rushes over a 75-foot-high cliff, squeezes through a narrow rocky gorge, and emerges as a wider river at the town of Grand Falls. The result is a magnificent cascade whose force has worn strange round wells in the rocky bed, some as large as 16 feet in circumference and 30 feet deep.

GETTING HERE AND AROUND

Grand Falls is just off the Trans-Canada Highway (Route 2), at Exit 77 or 79, and is served by Maritime Bus from points along the TCH north and south. From Edmundston, an alternative (and about the same distance) is on Route 144, the River Valley Scenic Drive. There's not much to see in town, other than the falls and gorge, but it's an easy walk across the bridge along Broadway Boulevard to cafés and restaurants.

CONTACTS Maritime Bus. ✉ *77 Canada St., Moncton* ☎ *506/854–2023* 🌐 *www.maritimebus.com.*

ESSENTIALS

VISITOR INFORMATION La Rochelle Tourist Information Centre. ✉ *1 Chapel St., Grand Falls* ☎ *877/475–7769 Ext. 2* 🌐 *www.grandfallsnb.com.* **Malabeam Tourist Information Center.** ✉ *25 Madawaska Rd., Grand Falls* ☎ *877/475–7769 Ext. 2* 🌐 *www.grandfallsnb.com/malabeam.*

Sights

Gorge Walk

NATURE SIGHT | FAMILY | Starting at the Malabeam Tourist Information Center, the walk covers the full length of the gorge and is dotted with interpretive panels and monuments. Nearby, you can descend the nearly 250 steps to the wells, holes worn in the rocks by the swirling water. Guided walking tours are also available. According to native legend,

See a spectacular waterfall in the town of Grand Falls, just off the Trans-Canada Highway.

a young woman named Malabeam led her Mohawk captors to their deaths over the foaming cataract rather than guide them to her village. The bodies of the Mohawks were found the following day, but Malabeam was not found. The view over the gorge from the center is breathtaking, particularly at snowmelt time or after heavy rain. ⊠ *Malabeam Tourist Information Center, 25 Madawaska Rd., Grand Falls* ☎ *506/475–7769 ext 2 information center* ⌨ *Walk free; steps to wells C$5; guided walks C$10* ◷ *Closed early Oct.–May.*

Grand Falls Museum

HISTORY MUSEUM | Pioneer and early Victorian artifacts are the basis of a collection that includes memorabilia of Ron Turcotte, the jockey who rode Secretariat to Triple Crown victory in 1973, a wedding cake made in 1940, and the balance beam used by daredevil Van Morrell, who crossed the falls on a tightrope in 1904. ⊠ *68 Madawaska Rd., Suite 100, Grand Falls* ☎ *506/473–5265* ⌨ *Free; donations accepted* ◷ *Closed Sept.–May.*

Mount Carleton Provincial Park

MOUNTAIN | The most remote of New Brunswick's nine provincial parks is a vast area of unspoiled wilderness. It is centered on Mount Carleton, at 2,690 feet the highest point in all of the Maritimes. From its summit you can look out over 10 million trees, and it is particularly worth the climb in the fall for the dazzling patchwork of colors below. Rich in wildlife, including moose, white-tailed deer, lynx, marten, and porcupines, the park is also a Dark Sky Preserve, so an overnight camping trip on a clear night would be well rewarded. Most people come to hike the trails or mountain-bike on old logging roads, and there's canoeing on several lakes. Check out guided hikes and other park events ⊠ *7612 Rte. 385, Saint-Quentin* ☎ *800/561–0123* ⊕ *parcsnbparks.ca* ⌨ *C$10 per vehicle.*

🏃 Activities

Grand Falls Golf Club

GOLF | The undulating 18-hole championship course has a well-designed layout, including water hazards and bunkers, and there are scenic views of the St. John River Valley along the way. ✉ *803 Main St., Grand Falls* ☎ *506/473–4494* 🌐 *www.grandgolf.ca* 🎟 *C$20–25 for 9 holes, C$30–45 for 18 holes* ⛳ *6648-yard par 72* ☞ *power cart rentals are available.*

Florenceville-Bristol

81 km (50 miles) south of Grand Falls.

The title "French Fry Capital of the World" does nothing to convey how pretty Florenceville is, with its Main Street running right along the riverside, but there's no getting away from the fact that it's also the home of McCain's, the frozen food giant, which, along with other products, produces one-third of all the frozen french fries sold worldwide. The main factory is north of town, various ancillary buildings are dotted around, and vast potato fields spread out in all directions. The town is also home to the Andrew and Laura McCain Art Gallery, well worth a visit, and the Second Wind Music Centre, which hosts occasional concerts in a former church building. There's also good walking on trails in the area.

GETTING HERE AND AROUND

Both towns are right on the River Valley Scenic Route (Route 105), with the Trans-Canada Highway running parallel at a discreet distance. Maritime Bus stops on Main Street, Florenceville, but you'll need a car to reach Potato World and the Visitor Information Centre.

CONTACTS Maritime Bus. ✉ *77 Canada St., Moncton* ☎ *506/854–2023* 🌐 *www.maritimebus.com.*

ESSENTIALS

VISITOR INFORMATION Florenceville-Bristol Visitor Information Centre. ✉ *Potato World, 385 Centreville Rd., Florenceville-Bristol* ☎ *506/392–1955* 🌐 *www.florencevillebristol.ca.*

👁 Sights

Andrew and Laura McCain Art Gallery

ART GALLERY | This lively gallery hosts an eclectic series of exhibitions each year, showcasing Atlantic Canadian artists working in traditional and experimental media, as well as art and craft workshops, seasonal festivals, and children's events. ✉ *8 McCain St., Unit 1, Florenceville-Bristol* ☎ *506/392–6769* 🌐 *www.mccainartgallery.com* 🎟 *Free* 🕒 *Closed Sun. and Mon., by appointment Tues.*

Potato World

OTHER MUSEUM | **FAMILY** | In the "French Fry Capital of the World" (aka the location of McCain's HQ) it's hardly surprising that this humble vegetable, which fills fields for miles around and keeps many folks employed hereabouts, is celebrated—but you may be surprised by how interesting it is. Run by the community as a nonprofit enterprise, Potato World has some fascinating displays related to the history, industry, and science of the potato, plus hands-on exhibits; and, when the café is open, you'll have the chance to munch on some hot fries. ✉ *385 Centreville Rd., Florenceville-Bristol* ☎ *506/392–1955* 🌐 *www.potatoworld.ca* 🎟 *C$5* 🕒 *Closed early Oct.–May and weekends June and Sept.*

☕ Coffee and Quick Bites

On the Boardwalk

$$ | **CAFÉ** | Open for snacks, breakfast, lunch, and dinner, with brunch available on weekends, this is a nice casual spot for a bite to eat during a scenic drive along the St. John River via Route 105. **Known for:** casual atmosphere; scenic location; weekend brunch. [$] *Average main: C$15* ✉ *8754 Main St., Florenceville-Bristol* ☎ *506/595–0120* 🌐 *www.on-the-boardwalk.ca* 🕒 *Closed Mon. and Tues.*

Hotels

Shamrock Suites

$$ | **B&B/INN** | In a converted 19th-century home, the elegant suites have been designed to suit business and leisure travelers for short or long stays, with access to a fully equipped kitchen and guest laundry. **Pros:** full breakfast included; lovely setting, on 6 acres of heritage gardens; high levels of comfort and good amenities. **Cons:** have to share kitchen and laundry; may be a lot of business guests; rooms vary in size. [$] *Rooms from: C$129* ✉ *8 Curtis Rd., Florenceville-Bristol* ☎ *506/392–8801, 506/391–5274 cell* 🌐 *www.shamrocksuites.ca* 🛏 *5 rooms* 🍴 *Free Breakfast.*

Nightlife

A. C. Sharkey's

MUSIC | There's occasional live music at this pub, including rock bands, acoustic acts, and singer-songwriters—and the food's good, too. On St. Patrick's Day there's often traditional Celtic music. ✉ *2 Curtis Rd., Florenceville-Bristol* ☎ *506/392–6675* 🌐 *www.acsharkeyspub.ca.*

Performing Arts

Second Wind Music Centre

CONCERTS | A lovely converted church building is a popular venue for touring and local musicians, including some bigger names than you might expect in such an out-of-the-way place. There may only be one or two concerts a month, but they are worth checking out, and there are occasional community events and kids' musical activities, too. The center doesn't have a website, but it lists its events on its Facebook page. ✉ *18 Curtis Rd., Florenceville-Bristol* ☎ *506/425–4999.*

Hartland

19 km (12 miles) south of Florenceville-Bristol.

Hartland is best known for having the longest covered bridge in the world, still carrying traffic across the wide St. John River. A sleepy little town for much of the year, Hartland is deluged with busloads of camera-toting tourists in summer, but doggedly avoids the kind of tourist trappings that can be detrimental. You can also visit the Covered Bridge Potato Chip company, just across the highway, for a tour and tasting of the still warm chips straight off the production line.

GETTING HERE AND AROUND

The town of Hartland is on Route 105 (the River Valley Scenic Route) and has an exit off the Trans-Canada Highway, which runs a short distance to the east. There's no public transportation. The reason to come here is simple: to experience its star attraction—the world's longest covered bridge.

ESSENTIALS

VISITOR INFORMATION Hartland Visitor Information Centre. ✉ *365 Main St., beside bridge, Hartland* ☎ *506/375–4075* 🌐 *www.town.hartland.nb.ca.*

Sights

Longest Covered Bridge

BRIDGE | New Brunswick has its fair share of superlatives, but this Hartland attraction may be the most surprising. In what is otherwise a rather sleepy little town, the St. John River is spanned by the longest covered bridge in the world—1,282 feet long. A national and provincial historic site, the bridge opened in 1901 and is still used by traffic crossing the river between Routes 103 and 105—maximum vehicle height is 13 feet 9 inches; maximum weight 10 tons. Through the openings in the side walls, passengers can enjoy nice river views in both directions.

The town of Hartland is believed to have the world's longest covered bridge—it's total length is 1,282 feet.

There also is a safely separated walkway that you can walk across. A fun fact is that of the total 131 covered bridges in Canada, New Brunswick has 58.

■ TIP → There's only room for traffic going one way at a time across the bridge, and there are no traffic lights; so stop and check whether there's anything coming the other way and wait your turn if necessary, then turn on your headlights before driving across. ✉ *Hartland Bridge Rd., Hartland.*

🍴 Restaurants

Covered Bridge Golf & Country Club Restaurant

$$ | CANADIAN | FAMILY | You don't have to play golf to come and eat at the restaurant in the clubhouse, and it features big windows with nice views. They serve pub-style food, including fresh clams, traditional fish-and-chips, and a range of panini, salads, wraps, and burgers. **Known for:** views out over the golf course; unpretentious menu, including kids' menu; reasonable prices. $ *Average*

main: C$18 ✉ *190 Golf Club Rd., Hartland* ☎ *506/375–1110* ⊕ *coveredbridgegolf. nb.ca* ⊗ *Closed Sun.*

Woodstock

93 km (58 miles) northwest of Fredericton.

New Brunswick's first incorporated town (in 1856), Woodstock still preserves many fine old buildings on its leafy downtown streets. A focal point of the town is the meeting of its two rivers, the St. John and the Meduxnekeag, with riverside walks, a nature reserve, a floating dock in summer, and a small marina. The big (for Woodstock) celebrations are Old Home Week and the Dooryard Arts Festival, both in August. Other than that, it's a laid-back town with understated charm.

GETTING HERE AND AROUND

Woodstock is off the Trans-Canada Highway (Route 2) at Exits 188 and 185. Coming from the United States, Interstate 95 becomes Route 95 as it crosses the U.S. border near Houlton, Maine, and continues the short distance to Woodstock. The town is on the Maritime Bus route along the Trans-Canada, but the set-down/pickup point is near the box stores, quite a walk from the center (and a steep climb back up). Downtown is easily explored on foot, though it's quite an uphill trudge from the riverside to some of the finest old residential streets off Main Street, and a car is necessary to visit the Old County Court House in Upper Woodstock.

CONTACTS Maritime Bus. ✉ *77 Canada St., Moncton* ☎ *506/854–2023* 🌐 *www.maritimebus.com.*

ESSENTIALS

VISITOR INFORMATION Provincial Visitor Information Centre. ✉ *109 Tourist Bureau Rd., Richmond Corner, Woodstock* ☎ *506/325–4427.*

Sights

Connell House

HISTORIC HOME | A fine example of Greek Revival architecture, this is the former home of Honorable Charles Connell (1810–73), a politician active in many areas of public life, but perhaps best remembered for putting his own image on the five-cent stamp instead of that of the Queen when he was Postmaster General. The largely restored house, home to the Carleton County Historical Society, contains fine furniture, artifacts, musical instruments, and the Tappan Adney Room, honoring the man who is credited with saving the birch-bark canoe. His grave is in the Upper Woodstock Cemetery. Temporary exhibitions and occasional concerts are added attractions, and a Victorian High Tea buffet (C$20) is served from 11:30 am to 2 pm every Thursday in July and August. ✉ *128 Connell St., Woodstock* ☎ *506/328–9706* 🌐 *www.cchs-nb.ca* 🎫 *C$5* ⏲ *Closed Sun. and Mon.*

Nackawic

OTHER ATTRACTION | For a quick stop for something quirky, from Woodstock you can take Route 105 along the St. John River toward Nackawic—known as the Forestry Capital of Canada—to see "the world's biggest axe." The 60-foot-tall axe is lodged in a concrete stump in a small park by the river. ✉ *Nackawic* 🌐 *www.nackawic.com.*

Old County Court House

NOTABLE BUILDING | Dating from 1833, this splendid galleried former court house was restored after years of neglect and misuse and was opened to the public by H.R.H. Princess Anne in 1986. Guided tours are available in summer, and occasional special events include an annual Christmas concert. ✉ *19 Court St., Upper Woodstock, Woodstock* ☎ *506/328–9706* 🌐 *www.cchs-nb.ca* 🎫 *C$2 donation requested* ⏲ *Closed Sept.–June and Mon., Thurs., and Sun. July and Aug.*

Restaurants

Creek Village Gallery and Café

$$ | **CAFÉ** | Organic, vegetarian, and gluten-free food is the specialty of this café-art gallery just off Main Street in the downtown area, including nourishing soups with organic Red Fife bread, and panini, wraps, and sandwiches. More substantial options are served in the evening, and drinks include wine, cocktails, and local brews. **Known for:** a welcome alternative to fast-food joints; art and crafts on display; occasional live music and art reception events. [$] *Average main: C$15* ✉ *119 Connell St., Woodstock* ☎ *506/328–3232* ⏲ *No dinner Sat.–Wed.*

Hotels

Best Western Plus Woodstock Hotel & Conference Centre

$$ | **HOTEL** | Conveniently located just off the Trans-Canada Highway and Highway 95 from the U.S. border at Houlton, this

The Kings Landing Historical Settlement is a living history museum of a Loyalist settlement circa 1790 to 1900.

hotel is very friendly and welcoming and well suited to both business and leisure guests. **Pros:** above-average hotel breakfast; convenient for the highway; nice indoor pool. **Cons:** in a commercial area on the edge of town; out of walking distance to downtown; only casual restaurants nearby. [$] *Rooms from: C$169* ✉ *123 Gallop Ct., Woodstock* ☎ *506/328–2378, 888/580–1188 reservations* 🌐 *www.bestwestern.com* 🛏 *105 rooms* 🍴 *Free Breakfast.*

Kings Landing Historical Settlement

72 km (45 miles) east of Woodstock; 30 km (19 miles) west of Fredericton.

New Brunswick became home to many Loyalists who headed north across the border after the American Revolution, and this 300-acre site charmingly replicates their lifestyle beside the St. John River. Around 70 historic buildings from that era have been relocated here to form a complete settlement, including agricultural, industrial, and social exhibits, and it is populated by costumed characters portraying day-to-day life as it would have been.

GETTING HERE AND AROUND

There's no public transportation to Kings Landing. By car, it's just off the Trans-Canada Highway (Route 2), but the River Valley Scenic Drive (Route 102) is a more pleasant option; it's well signposted from both.

Sights

★ **Kings Landing Historical Settlement**
MUSEUM VILLAGE | **FAMILY** | When the Mactaquac Dam was created in the 1960s, a number of historically important buildings were saved and moved to a new shore, later to be joined by more rescued buildings from elsewhere in New Brunswick. Restored and furnished, they created a living-history museum in the form of a typical Loyalist settlement

of 1790 to 1900. The winding country lanes and meticulously restored homes reflect the society and lifestyles of the era. It's interesting to compare the life of the wealthy owner of the sawmill to that of an immigrant farmer. Hearty meals and heritage ales are served at the Kings Head Inn. ✉ *5804 Rte. 102, Exit 253 off Trans-Canada (Hwy. 2), Prince William* ☎ *506/363–4999* ⊕ *kingslanding.nb.ca* 🎫 *C$24* ⊘ *Closed early Oct.–early June except for special events.*

Mactaquac Provincial Park

25 km (16 miles) west of Fredericton.

Just a short distance from the provincial capital, this 525-hectare (1,300-acre) park alongside the St. John River is geared up for all kinds of summer and winter outdoor pursuits. Highlights include the sandy beaches (with volleyball nets), the viewpoint and information panel overlooking the natural beaver ponds, many trails, one of which is suitable for wheelchairs, and a MOCO restaurant.

GETTING HERE AND AROUND
The park is on Route 105, west of Fredericton and off the Trans-Canada Highway (Route 2) at Exit 258, via Routes 102 then 105. There are two main entrances: on the northern edge opposite the intersection of Routes 105 and 615, and midway down the western side off Route 105 near the golf course. A third, southern entrance only leads to Walinaik Cove marina.

◉ Sights

Mactaquac Provincial Park
STATE/PROVINCIAL PARK | FAMILY | Surrounding the giant pond created by the Mactaquac Hydroelectric Dam on the St. John River is Mactaquac Provincial Park. Its facilities include an 18-hole championship golf course, two beaches, two marinas (one for powerboats and one for sailboats), supervised crafts activities, myriad nature and hiking trails, and a restaurant. There are also guided walks on summer Wednesdays through a nature reserve to beaver ponds. Reservations are advised for the more than 300 campsites in summer. Winter is fun, too, with trails for cross-country skiing and snowshoeing, and sleigh rides are available by appointment (*506/328–7030*). The toboggan hills and skating/ice hockey ponds are even lighted in the evening. There's a TreeGO attraction (☎ *877/707–4646;* ⊕ *www.treegomactaquac.ca*) in the adjacent Centennial Park. ✉ *1265 Rte. 105, Mactaquac* ☎ *506/363–4747* 🎫 *C$10 per vehicle, mid-May–mid-Oct.; no entrance fee in winter.*

Fredericton

The small inland city of Fredericton, New Brunswick's provincial capital, occupies a broad point of land jutting into the wide St. John River and is a gracious and beautiful place. It's especially interesting to visit if history is your passion, with some fine old buildings and the Historic Garrison District in the downtown area.

Fredericton's predecessor, the early French settlement of Pointe-Sainte-Anne (Ste. Anne's Point), was established in 1642 during the reign of the French governor Joseph Robineau de Villebon, who made his headquarters at the junction of the Nashwaak and St. John rivers. Settled by Loyalists and named for Frederick, second son of George III, the city serves as the seat of government for New Brunswick's nearly 777,000 residents. Wealthy and scholarly Loyalists set out to create a gracious and beautiful place, and even before the establishment of the University of New Brunswick, in 1785, and St. Thomas University, in 1910, the town served as a center for liberal arts and sciences.

Fredericton holds several summer festivals: the New Brunswick Highland Games and Scottish Festival in late July, the New Brunswick Summer Music Festival in August, and the Harvest Music Festival for six days in September.

Fredericton was the first city in Canada to offer free Wi-Fi throughout downtown. To learn more check out ⊕ *www.gofred.ca.*

GETTING HERE AND AROUND

Fredericton is a little way north of the Trans-Canada Highway (Route 2), with four exits to choose from. Coming from the west, Exit 280 onto Route 8 is best; from the east take Exit 294 onto Route 7. Fredericton can also be reached by air or bus. Within town, Fredericton has an excellent bus service, Fredericton Transit, operating 12 routes Monday to Saturday 6:15 am to 11 pm; fares are C$2.75 or 10 trips for C$25, and exact change is required.

Downtown Queen Street runs parallel to the river and has several historic sights and attractions. Most major sights are within walking distance of one another. The city has a network of trails through parks and along and across the river for those who want to explore by bike.

CONTACTS Fredericton International Airport. ✉ *2570 Rte. 102* ⊹ *About 10 min east of downtown Fredericton* ☎ *506/460–0920* ⊕ *yfcfredericton. ca.* **Fredericton Transit.** ✉ *Fredericton* ☎ *506/460–2200* ⊕ *www.fredericton. ca/en/transit.* **Maritime Bus.** ✉ *77 Canada St., Moncton* ☎ *506/854–2023* ⊕ *www. maritimebus.com.*

ESSENTIALS

VISITOR INFORMATION Fredericton Visitor Information Centre. ✉ *City Hall, 397 Queen St.* ☎ *506/460–2129* ⊕ *www.tourismfredericton.ca.*

TOURS

Calithumpians Theatre Company
SPECIAL-INTEREST TOURS | FAMILY | Haunted Hikes (C$15, cash only) are conducted

from early July to early September, Tuesday through Saturday, departing from the Amphitheatre of the Beaverbrook Art Gallery (✉ *703 Queen St.*) for a 90-minute walk. Arrive at 8:45 pm for the 9 pm departure. ☎ *506/457–1975* ⊕ *www. calithumpians.com.*

Wolastoq Boat Tours
BOAT TOURS | Hop aboard, right in the heart of downtown Fredericton (just behind the lighthouse), for a sightseeing cruise on the St. John River that offers a unique perspective on city sights. Tours depart Tuesday through Sunday at 2, 4, 6, and 8 pm, and last around two hours. ✉ *Regent St. Wharf* ☎ *506/471–8680* ⊕ *wolastoqboattours.com* ⌷ *C$21.*

◉ Sights

★ Beaverbrook Art Gallery
ART GALLERY | This already exceptional gallery continues to grow—following on from its 5,000 square-foot expansion in 2017, it is set to open another new building, the Harrison McCain Pavilion, in 2022. The Beaverbrook's international collection is a remarkably broad and important one that one might not expect to find in a relatively small provincial city. The foundation on which this has been built is the lasting gift of the late Lord Beaverbrook, born and raised in New Brunswick before building his U.K. media empire. It contains a significant collection of Canadian, American, British, and other European masterworks that rivals many major Canadian galleries. Salvador Dalí's gigantic painting *Santiago el Grande* has always been the star, but a rotation of avant-garde Canadian paintings now shares pride of place. The current McCain "gallery-within-a-gallery" is devoted to the finest Atlantic Canadian artists. Larger spaces employ the artful use of dividers to create an intimate exerience, and in the 2017 extension, the art is enhanced by a stunning view of the river. Various special events and an artist-in-residence program add to the

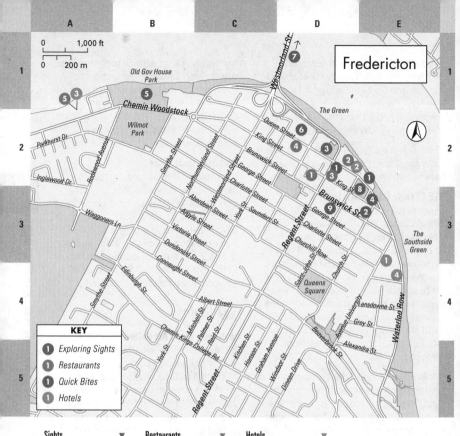

Fredericton

Scale: 0 — 1,000 ft / 0 — 200 m

Sights ▼

1. Beaverbrook Art Gallery **E2**
2. Christ Church Cathedral **E3**
3. Fredericton Region Museum **D2**
4. Gallery 78 .... **E3**
5. Government House..... **B1**
6. Historic Garrison District **D2**
7. Marysville **D1**
8. Provincial Legislature ... **E3**
9. Science East **D3**

Restaurants ▼

1. Brewbakers **D2**
2. Isaac's Way **D2**
3. MOCO Downtown **D2**
4. The Palate Restaurant & Café...... **D2**
5. STMR.36 BBQ & Social............ **A2**

Quick Bites ▼

1. The Muse............... **D2**

Hotels ▼

1. Carriage House Inn...... **E3**
2. Crowne Plaza Fredericton- Lord Beaverbrook **D2**
3. Delta Fredericton Hotel...................... **A2**
4. Quartermain House B&B **E4**

enjoyment. There's a great café with a terrace on the lower level, and a sculpture garden outside links to the riverside path. ⊠ *703 Queen St.* ☎ *506/458–2028, 506/458–8545* ⊕ *beaverbrookartgallery. org* ⊠ *C$10; by donation during last half-hour and 5–9 pm Thurs.* ⊘ *Closed Mon. Oct.–Apr.*

Christ Church Cathedral

CHURCH | This gray-stone building, completed in 1853, is an excellent example of decorated neo-Gothic architecture. The cathedral's design was based on an English medieval architectural style, and the cathedral became a model for many American churches. Inside is some fine carved marble and a clock known as "Big Ben's little brother"—it was the prototype for London's famous timepiece, designed by Lord Grimthorpe. ⊠ *168 Church St.* ☎ *506/450–8500* ⊠ *Free.*

Fredericton Region Museum

HISTORY MUSEUM | FAMILY | The Officers' Quarters in the Historic Garrison District house a museum that presents a living picture of the community from the time when only First Nations peoples inhabited the area through the Acadian and Loyalist days to the immediate past. Its World War I trench puts you in the thick of battle, and the shellacked remains of the giant Coleman Frog, a Fredericton legend, still inspire controversy. There is also an artists' co-op store featuring locally produced art and crafts. If you're visiting outside the summer months, wear warm clothing—the historic site has no heating or insulation. ⊠ *Officers' Sq., 571 Queen St.* ☎ *506/455–6041* ⊕ *www.frederictonregionmuseum.com* ⊠ *C$6* ⊘ *Closed Dec.–early Apr.*

Gallery 78

ART GALLERY | In a distinctive historic house, the oldest private gallery in New Brunswick has original works by more than 100 Atlantic Canadian artists, including painters, printmakers, ceramicists, sculptors, jewelers, and photographers. ⊠ *796 Queen St.* ☎ *506/454–5192,*

Fredericton Arts

The **Downtown Art Walk** takes place on certain Thursdays, from June to September. You can visit up to 15 of the art galleries, craft studios, and shops in the downtown area, all within walking distance of each other (all stay open until 8 pm). It's free, and information and maps are available at City Hall Visitor Information Centre.

888/883–8322 ⊕ *www.gallery78.com* ⊘ *Closed Sun. and Mon. except by appointment.*

Government House

GOVERNMENT BUILDING | This imposing 1828 Palladian mansion on the south bank of the St. John River is the official residence and office of New Brunswick's lieutenant governor. Guided tours take in elegantly restored state rooms and art galleries exhibiting New Brunswick art and crafts. The 11-acre grounds, once a 17th-century Acadian settlement, border an early Maliseet burial ground. It's also the venue for a number of festivals and other events every year. ⊠ *51 Woodstock Rd.* ☎ *506/453–2505* ⊕ *www2.gnb.ca/ content/gnb/en/lgnb/house.html* ⊠ *Free* ⊘ *Closed Sept.–mid-May; galleries closed weekends.*

★ Historic Garrison District

MILITARY SIGHT | FAMILY | The restored buildings of this British and Canadian military post is a National Historic Site and one of New Brunswick's top attractions. It extends two blocks along Queen Street and includes soldiers' barracks, a guardhouse, and a cellblock. Local artisans operate studios in the casemates below the soldiers' barracks on Barracks Square. In July and August free guided tours run throughout the day, and there

Wander amid restored soldier's barracks, a guardhouse, and a cellblock in the Historic Garrison District in Fredericton.

are regular outdoor concerts on Officers' Square. Redcoat soldiers have long stood guard on the square, and a formal changing-of-the-guard ceremony takes place July and August at 11 am and 4 pm daily, with an additional ceremony at 7 pm on Tuesday and Thursday. It's even possible for children (ages 4 to 12) to live a soldier's life for a while: each summer at 1:15 (or 11:15 for the French version) at the Guardhouse, would-be Redcoats get their own uniforms, practice drilling, and take part in a "mission" (C$10 per child). The square hosts a number of festivals, there's nightly entertainment in summer, and on Sunday evenings in July and August, free classic movies are shown under the stars in Barracks Square at approximately 9 pm. A summertime Garrison Night Market features arts, crafts, local produce, live music, and more. ⊠ *Queen St. at Carleton St.* ☎ *506/460–2041* ⊕ *historicgarrisondistrict.ca* ⊠ *Free.*

Marysville

TOWN | A National Historic Site of Canada, Marysville is one of the country's best-preserved examples of a 19th-century mill town, centered on the large, brick, 1883–85 cotton mill on River Street. Its architecture and social history are amazing and can be appreciated with the help of a self-guided walking-tour booklet available at the Fredericton Regional Museum. Marysville itself is on the north side of the St. John River, about 10 km (6 miles) from downtown Fredericton via Route 8. ⊠ *Fredericton.*

Provincial Legislature

GOVERNMENT BUILDING | The interior chamber of this imposing building, where the premier and elected members govern the province, reflects the taste of the late Victorians. The chandeliers are brass, and some of the prisms are Waterford. Replicas of portraits by Sir Joshua Reynolds of King George III and Queen Charlotte hang here. There's a freestanding circular staircase, and the library *(506/453–2338)* owns a complete four-volume set of hand-color copper engravings of Audubon's *Birds of America,* one of only five sets in Canada. Wander in for a look around, or call ahead to arrange a tour. ⊠ *706 Queen St.* ☎ *506/453–2527* ⊕ *www.gnb.ca* ✉ *Free* ☉ *Closed Sat. and Sun.*

Science East

SCIENCE MUSEUM | FAMILY | This hands-on science center, in the former York County Jail, is all about family fun, with more than 150 hands-on exhibits on its three floors. You can test your reflexes in the Batak Reaction Tester, have fun with flying machines in the wind tunnel, set off the rocket launcher, walk into a giant kaleidoscope, create a mini-tornado, and explore the museum in the dungeon. The Hurricane Simulator is a current favorite. Outside is Atlantic Canada's only outdoor science playground with a giant ship and human gyroscope (C$2 extra) among the learn-through-play structures. Various special programs are also offered. ⊠ *668 Brunswick St.* ☎ *506/457–2340* ⊕ *www. scienceeast.nb.ca* ✉ *C$10* ☉ *Closed Sun. and Mon.*

🍴 Restaurants

Brewbakers

$$$$ | ECLECTIC | Popular with the business community and with a loyal local following, this upscale lunch and dinner spot above the King Street Ale House has a cool urban interior and a rooftop garden patio. The menu includes pasta and flatbreads, seafood and vegetarian choices, and dishes such as house-brined chicken breast with arborio rice, raita, and naan bread; Wagyu rib eye; and pork tenderloin with Parmesan-whipped potatoes and vegetables. **Known for:** very obliging staff and kitchen; bold, well-defined flavors and very tender meat; wide ranges of choices and prices to suit all budgets. $ *Average main: C$33* ⊠ *546 King St.* ☎ *506/459–0067* ⊕ *brewbakers.ca* ☉ *No lunch Sat.–Sun.*

Isaac's Way

$$$ | CANADIAN | FAMILY | Not only will you taste delicious food in this old courthouse building, you can almost feel yourself being nourished by the top-quality ingredients, most of which are sourced locally. On the varied dinner menu, you might find chili molasses–glazed pork ribs, maple curry chicken, or roasted cauliflower ragu, while lunchtime options include gourmet sandwiches, salads, house-made soups, and a kids' menu. **Known for:** periodic silent auctions raise money for children's art project charity; lovely old building with original art (for sale) on the walls; a go-to place for its gluten-free menu and vegetarian options. $ *Average main: C$25* ⊠ *649 Queen St.* ☎ *506/474–7222* ⊕ *isaacsway.ca.*

★ MOCO Downtown

$$$ | ITALIAN | You won't find a warmer welcome or a more tender and delicious beef tenderloin anywhere in town, and chef Brian Foster offers an interesting menu that presents the finest local ingredients in very generous portions. In an inviting interior of bare brick, barn boards, and pale walls dotted with trendy accoutrements, you can feast on dishes such as a wonderful chicken fettuccine Alfredo, the rich Sunday pasta with three-beast meatballs, or rack of lamb, and all the tasty little extras. **Known for:** the pleasant waitstaff; everything, including the pasta, is made in-house; stylish but decidedly unstuffy atmosphere. $ *Average main: C$27* ⊠ *100 Regent St.* ☎ *506/455–6626* ⊕ *www.mocodowntown.ca* ☉ *No lunch Sun.*

The Palate Restaurant & Café

$$$ | MEDITERRANEAN | From the colorful, spacious interior, hung with local art, the open kitchen reveals enthusiastic chefs in action, preparing the interesting combinations of flavors, as in the lemon meringue salmon, with lemon, Parmesan, and chive aioli; or New York–style steak with a sriracha caramel glaze. The vegetarian option might be an oriental treatment of sautéed vegetables, tofu, and noodles, while lunch focuses on creative sandwiches, panini, stir-fries, and naan pizzas; brunch is served on Saturday. **Known for:** extensive brunch menu; local art; loyal band of regulars. [$] *Average main: C$23* ✉ *462 Queen St.* ☎ *506/450–7911* 🌐 *www.thepalate.com* ⏲ *Closed Sun.*

STMR.36 BBQ & Social
$$$ | **BARBECUE** | The restaurant in the Delta Hotel has views across the poolside patio to the St. John River, knowledgeable and enthusiastic staff, and a nice atmosphere. Specializing in barbecue, the kitchen turns out delicious dishes like smoked pulled pork with a maple spice rub, bacon-wrapped tenderloin, and house-made bratwurst. **Known for:** buttermilk biscuits; barbecue specialties; patio seating. [$] *Average main: C$25* ✉ *225 Woodstock Rd.* ☎ *506/451–7950* 🌐 *stmr36bbqsocial.com.*

☕ Coffee and Quick Bites

The Muse
$ | **CAFÉ** | You won't find a better cup of coffee in the city than at this cool spot, where photography exhibitions and live music on some evenings add to the enjoyment. Even the craft pottery mugs that your coffee comes in reflect the café's dedication to creativity in all its forms. **Known for:** central location; good coffee; Montréal bagels. [$] *Average main: C$8* ✉ *86 Regent St.* ☎ *506/454–8779* 🌐 *www.tipsymusecafe.ca* ⏲ *Closed Mon. and Tues. after 1.30 pm.*

🛏 Hotels

★ **Carriage House Inn**
$$ | **B&B/INN** | Originally the 1875 home of Fredericton's mayor, this beautiful pre-Victorian mansion—a Provincial Historic Site—is as authentic as they come, and it's in the loveliest part of the city. **Pros:** variety of room sizes; excellent location near everything; scenic 10-minute walk to downtown. **Cons:** some bathrooms may not be en suite; some rooms are on the third floor and are smaller; not for those who favor a more modern style. [$] *Rooms from: C$129* ✉ *230 University Ave.* ☎ *506/452–9924, 800/267–6068* 🌐 *www.carriagehouse-inn.net* 🔑 *11 rooms* 🍴 *Free Breakfast.*

Crowne Plaza Fredericton–Lord Beaverbrook
$$$ | **HOTEL** | This historic hotel has a great location, overlooking the river at the back and fronting some of the city's most important landmarks, and a renovation has given it a fresh, modern style. **Pros:** own parking lot; amenities you'd expect from a large chain hotel; convenient downtown location. **Cons:** parking not free; corridors to some areas are a bit of a warren; some rooms are small. [$] *Rooms from: C$219* ✉ *659 Queen St.* ☎ *506/455–3371, 866/444–1946* 🌐 *www.cpfredericton.com* 🔑 *168 rooms* 🍴 *No Meals.*

★ **Delta Fredericton Hotel**
$$ | **RESORT** | **FAMILY** | This is a chic urban resort where the superfriendly staff create a lively modern atmosphere and the riverside location is fully utilized—an expansive split-level terrace alongside the outdoor pool has its own open-air café and a riverside walk links into the city's trail system (bikes can be rented at the hotel). **Pros:** wonderful riverside location; exceptionally friendly atmosphere; indoor and outdoor pools. **Cons:** café's piped pop music not to everyone's taste; outdoor pool can get busy in summer; outside the downtown area. [$] *Rooms from: C$169* ✉ *225 Woodstock Rd.* ☎ *506/457–7000* 🌐 *deltahotels.marriott.com* 🔑 *222 rooms* 🍴 *No Meals.*

Quartermain House B&B
$ | **B&B/INN** | An extraordinarily pretty Gothic Revival heritage home, Quartermain House offers an exceptional bed-and-breakfast experience in leafy surroundings. **Pros:** vegetarian and gluten-free breakfast options; river views;

coffeemakers and home-baked cookies provided. **Cons:** nearly 20-minute walk to downtown shopping areas; only one bathroom is en suite; no children or pets. *$ Rooms from: C$110 ⊠ 92 Waterloo Row ☎ 506/206-5255, 855/758-5255 ⊕ www.quartermainhouse.com ⇩ 3 rooms ⁝⊘⁝ Free Breakfast.*

▼ Nightlife

Dolan's Pub
LIVE MUSIC | This Irish-themed pub is a great place to see live rock and blues bands from all over Eastern Canada on Thursday, Friday, and Saturday night from about 10:30 pm. St. Patrick's Day here is a wild daylong party. ⊠ *349 King St.* ☎ *506/454-7474 ⊕ www.dolanspub.ca ⊘ Closed Sun. and Mon.*

Grimross Brewery
LIVE MUSIC | An eclectic roster of live music is hosted in this bar, with a backdrop of the massive vats where the beer is brewed. Local bands, comedians, and touring acts on their way through the Maritimes provide the entertainment, and there are open mike and trivia nights, and other events. ⊠ *600 Bishop Dr., Unit 2* ☎ *506/454-4810 ⊕ www.grimross. com.*

Lunar Rogue
PUBS | An old-world-pub atmosphere and a bar with more than 400 whiskey options are the main attractions here, and the patio is lively in summer. ⊠ *625 King St.* ☎ *506/450-2065 ⊕ www.lunarrogue.com.*

◉ Performing Arts

Calithumpians Theatre Company
THEATER | **FAMILY** | For more than 40 years, Calithumpians has continued to delight family audiences with its shows about local history, folklore, and legend as well as modern social and environmental issues, always tinged with humor. Free outdoor performances run daily July through early September (12:15 pm weekdays, 2 pm weekends) in Officers' Square, and at 4:30 outside the Guard House. ⊠ *Fredericton* ☎ *506/457-1975 ⊕ www.calithumpians.com.*

★ Playhouse
CONCERTS | A wide range of entertainment is staged at this fine theater next door to the provincial legislature, including international comedians and musicians, tribute bands, and cultural performances by Symphony New Brunswick, Theatre New Brunswick, and traveling ballet and dance companies. ⊠ *686 Queen St.* ☎ *506/458-8344 ⊕ www.theplayhouse. ca.*

🛍 Shopping

Downtown shopping is focused on Queen, King, and York streets west of Regent, the latter having an interesting range of fashion and specialty stores. At the top of Regent Street, south of downtown, you'll find the Regent Mall, the big-box stores of the Corbett Centre, and Prospect Street ("Uptown Fredericton"). Shopping north of the river is more workaday, but the relatively new Northside Market on St. Mary's Street (weekends only) gets good reviews. In addition to the year-round Boyce Farmers' Market downtown, mammoth indoor crafts markets are held in the fall and run-up to Christmas, and a Labor Day–weekend outdoor crafts fair (the New Brunswick Fine Crafts Festival) is held on Officers' Square. You can find pottery, blown glass, pressed flowers, turned wood, leather, and other items, all made by members of the New Brunswick Craft Council.

Aitkens Pewter
CRAFTS | The owners of this shop design, produce, and sell pewter jewelry and belt buckles, goblets, candlesticks, and other home decor pieces, made in the on-site workshop. ⊠ *698 McLeod Ave.* ☎ *506/453-9474 ⊕ www.aitkenspewter. com.*

Art Jewel Designs by Gallagher and Tremblay

CRAFTS | Sparkling wearable works of art are produced here, and you can often see the jewelers at work. ✉ *Isaac's Way Restaurant, 649 Queen St.* ☎ *506/799–1398* ⊕ *www.artjeweldesigns.ca.*

The Barracks Fine Craft Shops

CRAFTS | Pottery, jewelry, paintings, and other crafts are made and sold in this shop in the converted soldiers' barracks of the Historic Garrison District, and there's a schedule of art and craft demonstrations. ✉ *Barracks Sq., 485 Queen St., corner of Carleton St.* ☎ *506/460–2129.*

Eloise

WOMEN'S CLOTHING | This women's fashion boutique specializes in Canadian clothing lines, footwear, and accessories. ✉ *69 York St.* ☎ *506/453–7715* ⊕ *eloiseltd.com.*

Endeavours and ThinkPlay

CRAFTS | **FAMILY** | Artistic endeavors are catered to here, with all kinds of art and craft supplies and stationery, funky toys (some of which are hand-made), science kits, and games that appeal to all ages. ✉ *141 Brunswick St.* ☎ *506/455–4278* ⊕ *www.endeavoursthinkplay.com.*

Fredericton Boyce Farmers' Market

MARKET | It's hard to miss this Saturday-morning market because of the crowds. It's one of the finest markets in Canada, operating since 1951, with the building and surrounding space housing more than 200 local suppliers. Local and organic meat and produce, cheeses, baked goods, maple syrup, crafts, and seasonal items such as wreaths and garden furniture are on offer. Good ready-to-eat food is available as well, from German sausages to tasty samosas. Good luck finding a parking spot, here or on surrounding streets! ✉ *665 George St.* ☎ *506/451–1815* ⊕ *frederictonfarmersmarket.ca.*

Urban Almanac General Store

HOUSEWARES | An eclectic collection of household gifts, furniture, loose-leaf teas, organic coffee, gadgets, and gizmos of exemplary design will keep you browsing here. ✉ *75 York St.* ☎ *506/450–4334* ⊕ *www.urbanalmanac.com.*

🏃 Activities

BIKING
Radical Edge

BIKING | **FAMILY** | This outlet sells a variety of gear, from snowshoes to bikes to camping equipment to hiking poles. Fat bikes can be rented for C$50 per day and hybrids can be rented by the half day (C$15), full day (C$25), or week (C$100) from their other location at 386 Queen Street. ✉ *129 Westmorland St.* ☎ *506/459–3478* ⊕ *radicaledge.ca.*

Savage's

BIKING | **FAMILY** | In business since the 1890s, Savage's sells and rents bikes, including trail bikes and children's bikes. Rentals are C$15 half day, C$25 full day or C$120 for the week. ✉ *441 King St.* ☎ *506/457–7452* ⊕ *www.sbcoutlet.com.*

CANOEING AND KAYAKING
Second Nature Outdoors

CANOEING & ROWING | **FAMILY** | Canoes, kayaks, stand-up paddleboards, and bicycles can be rented by the hour (C$20–C$30), and the center also runs a free shuttle service to Hartt Island on weekends, from where you can paddle back downstream with the current to help you. Guided paddling tours and activities such as mid-stream yoga on a standup paddleboard (C$45) and city bicycle tours (with food and drink along the way) are also offered. The center has two locations, in Fredericton and Oromocto, open daily from noon, mid-June through early September. ✉ *Small Craft Aquatic Center, 63 Brunswick St.* ☎ *506/460–2260.*

GOLF
Kingswood Park

GOLF | The 18-hole championship Signature Course and 9-hole Executive Course, designed by Cooke-Huxham International, offer a rewarding game amid beautiful scenery. The Signature course includes a 30-foot waterfall on the 14th hole and a tricky long par 4 on the 18th. Marshes, rocks, and well-placed bunkers and water hazards add to the challenge of a course that was *Golf Digest's* "Best New Course" when it opened. (Non-golfing members of the family will appreciate the Kingswood Entertainment Centre, with indoor play facilities, a bowling alley, skating rink, and arcade games.) ⊠ *31 Kingswood Park* ☎ *506/443–3334, 800/423–5969* ⊕ *www.kingswoodpark. ca* ⊠ *Signature Course, C$39–C$89; Executive Course, C$15–C$25* ⚑ *Signature Course: 18 holes, 6601 yards, par 72; Executive Course: 9 holes, 2060 yards, par 27.*

SKIING

Many of Fredericton's 70 km (44 miles) of walking trails, especially those along the river and in Odell and Wilmot parks, are groomed for cross-country skiing.

Ski Crabbe Mountain

SKIING & SNOWBOARDING | The 21 downhill trails here have a vertical drop of 853 feet, and there are three good terrain parks, plus trails for Nordic skiing, snowshoeing, and snowmobiling. Other amenities include lifts, snowboard and ski rentals, a ski shop, instruction, a skating pond, babysitting, and a lounge and restaurant. Check the website for details of offers and special events. ⊠ *50 Crabbe Mountain Rd., Central Hainesville* ✛ *55 km (34 miles) west of Fredericton, off Trans-Canada Hwy. at Exit 231, via Nackawic* ☎ *506/463–8311 snow phone, 902/896–1205* ⊕ *www.crabbemountain. com* ⚑ *Lift tickets: C$38 full day, C$28 night; lift ticket plus equipment rental: C$58 full day.*

WALKING

Fredericton has a fine network of nonmotorized (but motorized wheelchairs are permitted) multiuse trails totaling more than 115 km (70 miles), one of which follows the river from the Delta Hotel, passing behind Government House and the Beaverbrook Art Gallery, and in front of the Victorian mansions on Waterloo Row, before crossing the river via the Bill Thorpe Walking Bridge, a former railroad bridge, and continuing along the north side of the river. This also forms part of the Fredericton section of the Trans-Canada Trail. Other trails include Odell Park and the University of New Brunswick campus. The Visitor Information Centre can provide details.

Village of Gagetown

50 km (31 miles) southeast of Fredericton.

The historic riverside Village of Gagetown—seperate from the Gagetown military base at Oromocto—bustles in summer, when artists welcome visitors, many of whom arrive by boat and tie up at the marina, to their studios and galleries. It also has several small restaurants with interesting menus.

GETTING HERE AND AROUND

If you're driving from Fredericton, the Trans-Canada Highway (Route 2) is fast and direct, leaving at Exit 330, signposted "Village of/de Gagetown" (do not follow the earlier signs for "Gagetown," which lead to the military base). Route 102 from Fredericton is the scenic option. Once there, the village is great for strolling.

ESSENTIALS

VISITOR INFORMATION Visitor Information Centre. ⊠ *Tilley House, 69 Front St., Gagetown* ☎ *506/488–2966.*

Sights

CFB Gagetown Military Museum

MILITARY SIGHT | Oromocto, off Highway 2, east of Fredericton, is the site of the Canadian Armed Forces base Camp Gagetown, the largest military base in Canada (not to be confused with the pretty Village of Gagetown farther downriver), where Prince Charles completed his helicopter training. The interesting museum here traces Canada's military history back to the 18th century and includes regimental, naval, and air force exhibits. ✉ *Bldg. A5, off Walnut St., Camp Gagetown* ☎ *506/422–1304* 🌐 *www.nbmilitaryhistorymuseum.ca* 🎫 *Free.*

Queens County Museum

HISTORY MUSEUM | Expanding by leaps and bounds, the museum's original building, Tilley House (a National Historic Site), was the birthplace of Sir Leonard Tilley, one of the Fathers of Confederation. It displays Loyalist and First Nations artifacts, early-20th-century medical equipment, Victorian glassware, and more. The nearby Queens County Courthouse (✉ *16 Courthouse Rd.*) is part of the museum and has archival material and courthouse furniture as well as changing exhibits. The third site is Flower House in Cambridge Narrow (✉ *2270 Lower Cambridge Rd.*), built in 1818 by artist Anthony Flower. It relates his family history and contains a collection of his art, alongside works by other New Brunswick artists. Another building, the historic Loomcrofters Studio, dating back at least to 1761, has now been moved onto the grounds of Tilley House. ✉ *69 Front St., Gagetown* ☎ *506/488–2483 seasonal* 🌐 *www.queenscountyheritage.com* 🎫 *From C$3.*

Restaurants

Gulliver's World Café

$$$ | **INTERNATIONAL** | Chef Thane Mallory trained at the Institut Paul Bocuse in France and studied classic Italian food in Italy. Now he brings his expertise to this lovely riverside spot in Gagetown with a regularly changing menu reflecting availability of fresh local ingredients. **Known for:** chef Thane Mallory's cuisine; pretty spot by the river; local ingredients. [$] *Average main: C$25* ✉ *17 River Run La., Gagetown* ☎ *50/506–429–4156* 🌐 *gullivers.ca* 🕒 *Closed Mon.–Thurs.* ☞ *By reservation only.*

Hotels

Steamers' Bed & Breakfast

$ | **B&B/INN** | Not just a lovely bed and breakfast, Steamers is also a coffee/tea house and a pub—and it's right by the riverside with a long covered veranda from which to enjoy the views. **Pros:** patchwork quilts made by the owner; convivial pub on-site; lovely riverside location. **Cons:** owners have cats (bad for those with allergies); small bathrooms; no cribs or child beds. [$] *Rooms from: C$100* ✉ *74 Front St., Gagetown* ☎ *506–488–3009, 506–262–0666* 🌐 *steamers-bed-breakfast.business.site* 🔑 *4 rooms* 🍴 *Free Breakfast.*

Shopping

Grieg Pottery

CRAFTS | Grieg's Pottery carries superior pottery made on the premises. Budding potters can attend off-season weekend workshops (call for details). ✉ *36 Front St., Gagetown* ☎ *506/488–2074.*

Juggler's Cove

CRAFTS | This studio-gallery features the pottery of Peter Thomas, ceramics instructor at the New Brunswick College of Craft and Design in Fredericton. ✉ *27 Front St., Gagetown* ☎ *506/488–2574.*

PRINCE EDWARD ISLAND

Updated by
Penny Phenix

⊙ Sights	🕽 Restaurants	🛏 Hotels	💼 Shopping	🍸 Nightlife
★★★★☆	★★☆☆☆	★★☆☆☆	★☆☆☆☆	★☆☆☆☆

WELCOME TO PRINCE EDWARD ISLAND

TOP REASONS TO GO

★ **Anne of Green Gables.** The orphan nobody wanted has been adopted by the world. She's everywhere on the Island, but Cavendish's Green Gables farmhouse is ground zero.

★ **Beaches.** Even the most jaded, jet-setting beach bum will still be dazzled by the parabolic dunes at Prince Edward Island National Park in Greenwich.

★ **Golf.** A concentration of championship courses—among them the Links at Crowbush Cove, Dundarave, and Brudenell River—make PEI a top choice for golfers.

★ **Cycling the Confederation Trail.** Even "I haven't ridden a bike in ages" types can cover the stunning 10-km (6-mile) waterside stretch between Morell and St. Peter's Bay.

★ **Fresh seafood.** Forget the frozen fish sticks of your childhood. The local seafood here—whether served in a classy restaurant or community hall—is sensational.

1 Charlottetown. PEI's historic capital city is an excellent base for exploring the island.

2 Prince Edward Island National Park. Discover beaches, dunes, and wetlands.

3 Brackley Beach. Top beach with miles of pristine sands.

4 Cavendish. Ground zero for Anne of Green Gables fans.

5 Malpeque. Famed for its world-class oysters.

6 Victoria. A historic fishing village.

7 Georgetown. Expect sea views and Victorian buildings.

8 Souris. A pretty coastal spot with beaches.

9 St. Peter's Bay. Lighthouses are one of the big draws here.

10 Summerside. PEI's second-largest city.

11 O'Leary. A low-key potato farming community.

12 West Point. Home to PEI's tallest functioning lighthouse.

13 North Cape. A remote spot on the island's northwest tip.

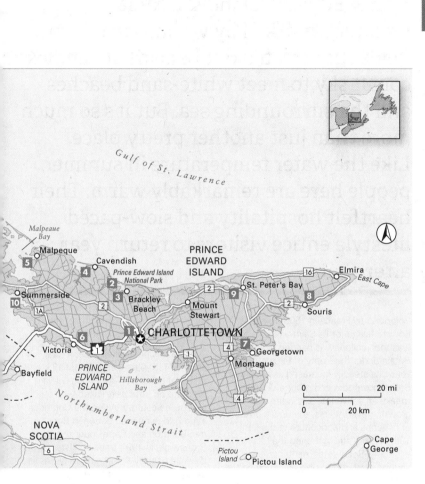

Gulf of St. Lawrence

Malpeque Bay

Malpeque

Cavendish

PRINCE EDWARD ISLAND

Prince Edward Island National Park

5

4

Summerside

10

1A

2

3

Brackley Beach

2

Mount Stewart

St. Peter's Bay

9

16

Elmira

East Cape

2

8

Souris

6

Victoria

1

1

CHARLOTTETOWN

PRINCE EDWARD ISLAND

Bayfield

Hillsborough Bay

1

4

7

Georgetown

Montague

Northumberland Strait

4

0   20 mi
0   20 km

NOVA SCOTIA

6

Pictou Island

Pictou Island

Cape George

Prince Edward Island is a camera-ready landmass marked by verdant patchwork fields that stretch out beneath an endless cobalt sky to meet white-sand beaches and the surrounding sea. But it's so much more than just another pretty place. Like the water temperature in summer, people here are remarkably warm. Their heartfelt hospitality and slow-paced lifestyle entice visitors to return year after year.

Colonized by France in 1603, Prince Edward Island (or Île Saint-Jean, as it was then called) was handed over to Britain under the Treaty of Paris in 1763. Tensions steadily increased as absentee British governors and proprietors failed to take an active interest in the area's growth; nevertheless, the development of fisheries and agriculture in the early 19th century strengthened the local economy. Soon settlement increased, and those willing to take a chance on the Island prospered.

As relations between emboldened tenants and their distant landlords continued to worsen, heated talk about uniting with other colonies in British North America began. (The Civil War, then raging in the United States, made the idea of forging a peaceable alliance all the more appealing.) So in 1864, the Island's capital city hosted the Charlottetown Conference, a milestone in this nation's history, which ultimately led to the creation of the Dominion of Canada in 1867.

Despite this political alliance, it took another 130 years—and almost 13 km (8 miles) of concrete—for Prince Edward Island to be *physically* linked with the rest of the country. When the Confederation Bridge opened between Borden-Carleton and Cape Jourimain, New Brunswick, in 1997, traditionalists feared it would destroy PEI's tranquillity. (As you explore the villages and fishing ports, it's easy to see why they cherish it so.) Yet outside the tourist hub of Cavendish, the Island still seems like an oasis of peace in an increasingly busy world.

Prince Edward Island was named for the fourth son of King George III (the monarch who lost America in the War of Independence). A rather run-of-the-mill royal, Edward seemed destined to be little more than a historical footnote until he was saved from obscurity by Britain's convoluted rules of succession. Because none of Edward's older siblings had living heirs (at least not legitimate ones), his daughter took the throne by default when she was just 18 years old. Her name? Victoria.

In summer, thanks to the relatively shallow Gulf of St. Lawrence and circulating Gulf Stream, Prince Edward Island beaches have the warmest saltwater north of the Carolinas. (Temperatures can reach 70°F in July and August.) Factor in sandy strands and the result is fine swimming conditions. Best of all, the Island's 1,760-km (1,100-mile) coast means a beach is always close by. Basin Head Beach, near Souris, has miles of singing sands. Often less populated, and with fine ocean sunsets, is West Point. At Greenwich, near St. Peter's Bay, a boardwalk stroll brings you to an endless empty beach. Each is supervised in season. Remember: this is the ocean, so choosing a life-guarded beach is important. Changing tides, breaking waves, and the occasional rip current can put even strong swimmers in peril.

Planning

When to Go

PEI is generally considered a summer destination—in July and August the beaches have the warmest water north of the Carolinas—but don't overlook the shoulder seasons. May, June, September, and October usually have fine weather and few visitors. In late spring, those famous farm fields look especially green, and bright wildflowers blanket the roadsides. Autumn, too, is multihued thanks to the changing fall foliage. If white is your color, come in winter for cross-country skiing, snowmobiling, and ice-skating. Bear in mind that many

sights and services close in mid-October; however, you won't have any problem finding food, lodging, and fun things to do year-round in Charlottetown.

Planning Your Time

Covering 5,656 square km (2,184 square miles), PEI is roughly the size of Delaware; and the fact that its area is small is a big advantage for visitors. First-timers will want to concentrate on the central section, which includes not only the capital city (Charlottetown), but also the province's most popular beaches, key portions of the Confederation Trail, plus must-see Anne sites. If you've already covered those bases, travel west or east to enjoy the quiet charms of the adjoining regions.

Getting Here and Around

AIR

Scheduled air service operates in and out of Charlottetown Airport (YYG), 5 km (3 miles) north of the capital. Air Canada runs direct service year-round from Halifax, Montréal, and Toronto, with seasonal service from Ottawa usually from June to September, but sometimes the season is extended. Connections from other destinations worldwide can be made via Toronto and Montréal. WestJet provides year-round service from Toronto. At the airport you can rent a car or grab a cab for the C$16 drive into town.

CONTACTS Air Canada. ☎ *888/247–2262* ⊕ *www.aircanada.ca.* **Charlottetown Airport.** ⊠ *250 Maple Hills Ave., Charlottetown* ☎ *902/566–7997* ⊕ *www.flypei. com.* **WestJet.** ☎ *888/937–8538* ⊕ *www. westjet.com.*

BUS

Maritime Bus offers daily scheduled service from many towns and cities in Nova Scotia and New Brunswick, via Confederation Bridge. On the Island, service runs between Summerside, Borden-Carleton, Crapaud, Cornwall, and Charlottetown.

CONTACTS Maritime Bus. ☎ 800/575–1807 ⊕ www.maritimebus.com.

CAR OR MOTORCYCLE

Due to limited public transport, having your own wheels is almost a necessity on the Island. Motorists can come via the 13-km (8-mile) Confederation Bridge, which connects Cape Jourimain, New Brunswick, with Borden-Carleton, PEI. The crossing takes about 10 minutes, and the toll is C$19.50 for motorcycles, C$48.50 for cars, and, for larger vehicles, C$8.25 per each additional axle. On the Island, there are more than 3,700 km (2,300 miles) of paved roads, including three scenic drives: North Cape Coastal Drive, Central Coastal Drive, and Points East Coastal Drive. Designated Heritage Roads offer an old-fashioned alternative. Surfaced with red clay (the local soil base) and often arched with a canopy of trees, they meander through rural, undeveloped areas where you're likely to see lots of wildflowers and birds. A four-wheel-drive vehicle isn't necessary, but in spring and inclement weather the mud can get quite deep, making narrow, unpaved roads impassable. A highway map of the province is available from Tourism PEI and at visitor centers on the Island.

■ TIP→ **Don't get too excited about crossing over to the Island without purchasing a ferry ticket or paying the bridge toll. Fares are only collected when you leave PEI—giving you further incentive to stay.**

CONTACTS Confederation Bridge. ✉ Borden-Carleton ☎ 902/437–7300 ⊕ www.confederationbridge.com.

FERRY

Weather permitting, Northumberland Ferries sails between Wood Islands, PEI, and Caribou, Nova Scotia, from May to late December. The crossing takes about 75 minutes, and there are three to nine per day depending on the season. For crossings to the island from Caribou, payment is made on the return journey. If you're taking your car over, round-trip rates depend on vehicle length; those up to 20 feet long cost C$82; those up to 40 feet long and under seven feet high cost C$112; and those more than seven feet high are C$132. Foot passengers aged 13 and over are C$21, cyclists C$21, and motorcyclists C$43.

CONTACTS Northumberland Ferries. ☎ 877/762–7245 ⊕ www.ferries.ca.

Restaurants

An island that's world famous for its mussels and renowned for its rich soil is certainly not going to disappoint when it comes to eating out, while first-rate craft breweries, wineries, and distilleries provide excellent liquid accompaniments. From humble mom-and-pop spots and creative cafés that give classic dishes a contemporary twist, to splurge-worthy bastions of gourmet dining, there is no shortage of places to eat on Prince Edward Island. In Charlottetown especially, the restaurant scene is booming. The ambience tends to be casual across the board, and reservations are seldom necessary—though at popular waterfront fish shacks, you may be in for a lengthy wait.

At every price point, the best eateries offer seasonally inspired menus that emphasize local ingredients. So when you see lobster, mussels, and oysters listed, they're likely from the neighborhood. Ditto for fresh produce: after all, those bucolic fields you drive by aren't just for show. If dining is your true raison d'être, be sure to investigate the PEI Flavours Culinary Trail (⊕ *canadasfoodisland.ca/culinary-trail*). It pinpoints locally owned restaurants that take advantage of the area's edible bounty; plus it shows you where to find farmers' markets, fishmongers, flavorful festivals, and fun "culinary adventures" like clambakes and lobster-dinner cruises. Culinary experiences await, in which you can work with chefs, fishermen, and food producers to find out exactly how those delicious ingredients make it onto your plate.

Restaurant reviews have been shortened. For full information, visit Fodors. com.

Hotels

Full-service resorts, boutique hotels, vintage motels, and waterside vacation rentals are just some of your lodging options on PEI, and the province operates a reliable inspection and star-rating system. Beyond the capital, inns and B&Bs—sometimes with cottage colonies attached—dominate and, design-wise, almost all of them favor the historic and traditional over the hip and trendy. Rodd Hotels & Resorts is a local and reliable small chain, headquartered in Charlottetown, with four locations on the Island. Whatever you choose, it's wise to book three to six months in advance— either directly or through the province's tourism website (⊕ *www.tourismpei. com*)—especially if you are planning to arrive in July or August. Note that all accommodations here are nonsmoking and precious few have elevators. Due to the sandy composition of the land, it's too expensive to lay the necessary foundations for them (we note only when a hotel *does* have an elevator). Heavy packers shouldn't panic, though. Most

lodgings are low-rise anyway and the staff is always ready to help lift luggage. Because so many reviewed properties are still family operated, friendly service is pretty much guaranteed.

Hotel reviews have been shortened. For full information, visit Fodors.com.

What It Costs In Canadian Dollars			
$	$$	$$$	$$$$
RESTAURANTS			
under C$12	C$12–C$20	C$21–C$30	over C$30
HOTELS			
under C$125	C$125–C$174	C$175–C$250	over C$250

Visitor Information

Well-staffed, well-stocked visitor information centers are strategically positioned throughout Prince Edward Island. Provincially operated ones can be found at the Island's main points of entry (Borden-Carleton, near the Confederation Bridge; Wood Islands, at the ferry terminal; and Charlottetown, at the airport) as well as in Cavendish, Souris, and West Prince; has complete details. Municipally run centers are located in Charlottetown, Summerside, Cavendish, and St. Peter's. For help with advance planning, click PEI's official tourism website (⊕ *www. tourismpei.com*) or call the office (☎ *800/463–4734; 902/437–8570*) to order a free printed copy of the comprehensive Island Visitor's Guide. Regional tourism websites, like ⊕ *www.centralcoastalpei. com*, are also helpful.

Charlottetown

Designated as the Island capital in 1765, Charlottetown is both PEI's oldest and largest urban center. However, since the whole "metropolitan" area only has a population of about 65,000, a pleasing small-town atmosphere prevails. The city's appearance is a winner as well, whatever the season. Fall brings seasonal pops of vibrant color from the many trees within the downtown core, there's nothing more magical than seeing Charlottetown dressed in her wintery best, and the summer season sees the historic city alive with energetic festivals, live music, public art, and outdoor dining. Colorful Victorian homes, converted warehouses, striking churches, and monumental government buildings, reflect its historic importance as the "Birthplace of Confederation".

GETTING HERE AND AROUND

The city center is compact, so walking is the way to go. If you drive in for a day of sightseeing, you can park at an on-street meter or in garages like those on Pownal, Queen, and Fitzroy streets. From June through September, there's also a parking lot at Peakes Wharf that's convenient for waterfront activities. When driving downtown, be aware that Great George Street is in two sections and it is not possible to drive the entire length of it without making a detour around Province House. One-way streets are an added complication, so be sure to pick up a map.

Alternately, you can rent a bike at Outer Limit Sports or MacQueen's Bike Shop. Rentals start around C$40 per day, including a helmet, and there are various options, including tandems, child trailers, and electric-assist bikes. T3 Transit operates city bus service as part of a public-private partnership (some cover the surrounding communities of Cornwall and Stratford, too). Most have their hub

Authentic Experiences 👁

Eager to haul a lobster trap or learn First Nations traditional cooking techniques? Prefer to paint a watercolor or turn PEI's signature red clay into a piece of pottery? How about trying your hand at fiddling or deep-sea fishing? Click ⊕ *www.tourismpei.com/pei-experiences* for complete listings.

downtown at the Confederation Centre of the Arts, and the fare is C$2 in exact change. Prefer a guided tour? Options include the Confederation Players tours, the Harbour Hippo and its dry-land alternative, the Hippopotabus, and Prince Edward Tours (a Gray Line affiliate).

BICYCLE RENTALS MacQueen's Bike Shop. ✉ *430 Queen St.* ☎ *902/368–2453* ⊕ *www.macqueens.com.* **Outer Limit Sports.** ✉ *330 University Ave.* ☎ *902/569–5690* ⊕ *ols.ca.*

BUS CONTACTS T3 Transit. ☎ *902/566–9962* ⊕ *www.t3transit.ca.*

VISITOR INFORMATION

CONTACTS Charlottetown Visitor Information. ✉ *Founders Hall, 6 Prince St.* ☎ *902/368–4444* ⊕ *www.tourismpei.com.*

TOURS

Confederation Players Walking Tours
WALKING TOURS | Costumed guides from the Confederation Players troupe lead history-themed walks on Tuesday through Saturday from early July to mid-August as part of the Charlottetown Festival. The 75-minute Great George Street Tour departs from the Visitor Info Centre at Founders Hall at 3:30, and the 45- to 60-minute Historic Queen Square Tour departs from the soldiers' monument on

The Confederation Centre of the Arts in Charlottetown is the island's leading cultural venue.

the north side of Province House at 2:30 pm. ⊠ *Charlottetown* ☎ *800/565–0278* ⊕ *confederationcentre.com/heritage/con-federation-players* 🎫 *From C$10.*

Harbour Hippo

GUIDED TOURS | FAMILY | Tour the sights by land and sea in an amphibious vehicle, departing from in front of the Confederation Centre of the Arts. The 55-minute tours run daily June through September. If you'd rather stay on dry land, the Hippopotabus, an open-top double-decker, offers an hour-long tour. ⊠ *Lower Prince St. Wharf* ☎ *902/628–8687 June–Sept.* ⊕ *www.harbourhippo.com* 🎫 *C$35.*

Peake's Wharf Boat Tours

BOAT TOURS | FAMILY | Departing from Peake's Wharf, this company operates cruises aboard a 45-foot vessel, including 1½-hour-long sunset cruises from June to September, 1½-hour harbour tours from July to early September, and 2½-hour seal-watching trips in July and August. Some include lobster-trap hauling.

⊠ *1 Great George St., Peake's Wharf* ☎ *902/394–2222* ⊕ *www.peakeswharf-boattours.com* 🎫 *From C$29.*

Prince Edward Tours

DRIVING TOURS | The City Highlights double-decker bus tour lasts about an hour and departs from the Visitor Information Centre at Founders Hall daily at 10, 11:30, and 1, July through September and on certain days in May, June, and October. Local guides provide an entertaining and informative commentary. ⊠ *Charlottetown* ☎ *902/566–5259, 877/286–6532* ⊕ *www.princeedwardtours.com* 🎫 *C$24.*

◉ Sights

Beaconsfield Historic House

HISTORIC HOME | FAMILY | Designed by W.C. "Willy" Harris in 1877 for shipbuilder James Peake Jr., this gracious mansion near the entrance to Victoria Park is one of the Island's finest historic homes. The 11 furnished rooms have rich architectural details and accents—little wonder the

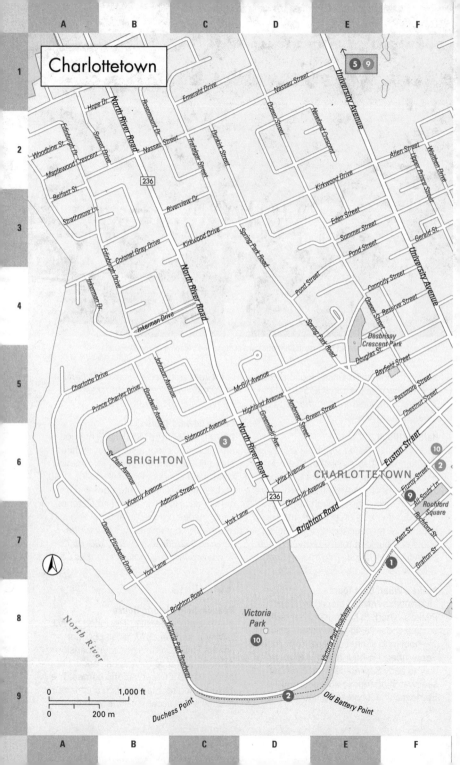

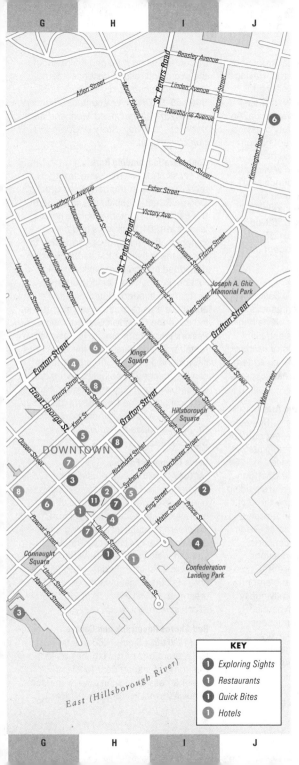

Sights ▼

1 Beaconsfield Historic House...... **F7**
2 Boardwalk........................... **D9**
3 Confederation
Centre of the Arts................. **G6**
4 Confederation Landing Park....... **I7**
5 Cows Creamery Factory **E1**
6 Red Shores
Racetrack and Casino............. **J2**
7 St. Dunstan's Basilica **H7**
8 St. Paul's Anglican Church **H6**
9 St. Peter's Cathedral............... **F6**
10 Victoria Park....................... **D8**
11 Victoria Row....................... **H6**

Restaurants ▼

1 The Brickhouse
Kitchen & Bar **H7**
2 Claddagh Oyster House........... **H7**
3 The Dining Room.................. **G8**
4 The Gahan House
Pub & Brewery..................... **H7**
5 Leonhard's.......................... **H6**
6 The Pilot House **G7**
7 Sims Corner
Steakhouse and Oyster Bar **H7**
8 Splendid Essence.................. **H5**

Quick Bites ▼

1 Kettle Black **H7**
2 Receiver Coffee Company......... **I6**

Hotels ▼

1 Delta Prince Edward **H7**
2 Dundee Arms Inn **F6**
3 Elmwood Heritage Inn **C6**
4 Fairholm National Historic
Inn and Carriage House.......... **G5**
5 The Great George.................. **H6**
6 Hillhurst Inn **H5**
7 The Holman Grand Hotel......... **G6**
8 The Hotel on Pownal **G6**
9 Rodd Royalty **E1**
10 Shipwright Inn B&B **F6**

once-wealthy Peake went bankrupt soon after his house was completed. Having taken a tour of the first and second floors, pause to enjoy a view of Charlottetown Harbour from the veranda. An on-site bookstore has a variety of Island publications, and special events (such as musical performances and history-themed lectures) are held year-round. A carriage house on the grounds also hosts a Celtic music and dance show on Tuesday evenings (for an additional charge). ⊠ *2 Kent St.* ☎ *902/368–6603* ⊕ *www.peimuseum.com* ✉ *C$5* ☾ *Closed Sun. and Mon., except on cruise ship days.*

Boardwalk

PROMENADE | Charlottetown's boardwalk extends from Confederation Landing to Victoria Park, wending its way along the water past historic sites and leafy picnic spots, providing views of sailboats and cruise ships en route. As an added bonus, it's lit at night for romantic strolls. ⊠ *Charlottetown.*

★ Confederation Centre of the Arts

ARTS CENTER | **FAMILY** | With a 1,100-seat main stage theater, a 1,000-seat outdoor amphitheater, and several studio stages, this block-long building—opened in 1964 to mark the centennial of the Charlottetown Conference—is the Island's leading cultural venue. From late June through September it hosts the Charlottetown Festival, which includes *Anne of Green Gables—The Musical,* plus concerts, comedy acts, and other productions. Weather permitting, there are free lunchtime performances in the amphitheater and on the plaza from Monday to Saturday. Off-season, a dynamic mix of touring and local productions, choral concerts, and special events is scheduled. A provincial art gallery has more than 15,000 works and around 20 exhibitions of Canadian art each year. The upper lobby has a replica of the Confederation Chamber, where the Fathers

of Confederation met, and a film about the event and related historical themes. ⊠ *145 Richmond St.* ☎ *902/566–1267, 800/565–0278* ⊕ *www.confederationcentre.com* ☾ *Gallery closed Mon. and Tues. mid-Oct.–mid-May; Story of Confederation closed Sun.*

Confederation Landing Park

CITY PARK | **FAMILY** | This waterfront recreation area at the bottom of Great George Street occupies the site where the Fathers of Confederation famously landed in 1864. Walkways and park benches offer plenty of opportunities to survey the activity of the harbor, with the added attraction of banks of wild rosebushes behind. During summer, performers in period costume stroll about the area re-creating the events that led up to the Canadian Confederation. **Peake's Wharf,** right next to it, has casual restaurants and bars, souvenir and crafts shops, and a marina where boat tours can be arranged. It hosts its own outdoor concert series in July and August. Featuring local talent, the free shows start at 2 and 6 daily, weather permitting. ⊠ *Water St. between Queen and Hillsborough Sts.* ✉ *Free.*

Cows Creamery Factory

FACTORY | **FAMILY** | Just outside Charlottetown, the Cows Creamery Factory offers self-guided tours that teach you everything you need to know about ice-cream production. Following a film (shown in the "Milky Whey Theater"), you can watch staff make waffle cones, whimsical T-shirts, cheddar cheese, and, of course, that award-winning ice cream. ⊠ *12 Milky Way* ☎ *902/628–3614* ⊕ *cowscreamery.ca* ✉ *Free.*

Red Shores Racetrack and Casino

SPORTS VENUE | Since 1888 this track at the eastern end of the city has been the home of a sport dear to islanders—harness racing. An on-site theater simulcasts racing from other tracks, while slot machines and Texas Hold'em provide further gambling options. If you'd rather save your dollars for dinner, there is excellent dining at the Top of the Park Dining Room, too. In August, during **Old Home Week**, Eastern Canada's best harness horses converge here for 10 days of races. Old Home Week also brings the provincial agricultural exhibition and a family-friendly midway to Red Shores. ⊠ *58 Kensington Rd.* ☎ *902/620–4222, 877/620–4222* ⊕ *redshores.ca* 🖃 *Free.*

St. Dunstan's Basilica

CHURCH | One of Canada's largest churches, St. Dunstan's is the seat of the Roman Catholic diocese on the Island. The church is known for its fine Italian carvings and twin Gothic spires. ⊠ *45 Great George St.* ☎ *902/894–3486* ⊕ *www.stdunstanspei.com.*

St. Paul's Anglican Church

CHURCH | Erected in 1896, this is actually the third church building on the same site. The first was erected in 1769, making this parish the Island's oldest. Large sandstone blocks give it a heavy exterior. However, the interior seems to soar heavenward, largely because of the vaulted ceilings: a common architectural feature of churches designed by W.C. "Willy" Harris. It seats only 450 but appears much larger. Harris is reputed to be the Island's finest architect, and St. Paul's will give you an idea why. Some of the stained glass dates back to the 19th century. ⊠ *101 Prince St.* ☎ *902/892–1691* ⊕ *www.stpaulschurch.ca.*

St. Peter's Cathedral

CHURCH | The glorious murals adorning this Anglican edifice's **All Souls' Chapel** were painted by artist Robert Harris, and the chapel itself was designed in 1888 by his brother W.C. Harris, the most celebrated Island architect. (It is attached to the side of the cathedral. If it isn't open, just ask.) Within the main sanctuary, free summer organ recitals are given Thursday at noon. ⊠ *Rochford Square, All Souls' Lane and Rochford St.* ☎ *902/566–2102* ⊕ *www.stpeter.org/cathedral.*

Victoria Park

CITY PARK | FAMILY | At the southern tip of the city, overlooking Charlottetown Harbour, sit 40 serene acres that provide the perfect place to stroll, picnic, or cool off on a hot day. Next to the park, on a hill between groves of white birches, is the white Georgian-style **Government House.** Built in 1834 as the official residence for lieutenant governors (the Queen's provincial representatives), it's open weekdays in July and August from 10 to 4 for free guided tours. The collection of antique cannons that still "guard" the city's waterfront is a play area for children, though there is also an actual playground, inclusive to both able-bodied children and those with disabilities. A pool is open daily in summer from 11 to 8, and there is a water-play area at the northwest entrance to the park. Runners and walkers can take advantage of woodland trails and a boardwalk that edges the harbor. ⊠ *Lower Kent St.* ☎ *902/368–1025* 🖃 *Free.*

★ Victoria Row

STREET | The section of Richmond Street between Queen and Great George streets is home to a variety of shops (Island crafts, art, hand-knitted sweaters, chocolates, antiques, and glassware are just some of the options), together with eateries, cafés, and a dance club. This vibrant, compact stretch of road really comes alive in summer, when traffic is blocked off and you'll frequently see musicians perform at lunchtime or in the evenings. For more shopping, head around the corner to Queen Street or Water Street. ⊠ *Charlottetown.*

🍴 Restaurants

The Brickhouse Kitchen & Bar

$$$ | **ECLECTIC** | In a converted warehouse downtown, this is the sort of place that could pull in a trendy crowd based solely on its exposed brick and wood-beam interior, but the open kitchen also delivers. Local ingredients are used to create dishes with international appeal (think trout with a ginger chili glaze, New York strip with mustard-and-pepper crust, or coconut chicken curry). **Known for:** bustling atmosphere; unique seafood concoctions; huge house burger. [$] *Average main: C$25* ✉ *125 Sydney St.* ☎ *902/566–4620* 🌐 *www.brickhousepei.com.*

Claddagh Oyster House

$$$ | **SEAFOOD** | Urban style meets rural delicacies at this upscale restaurant, which occupies a handsome brick building downtown. Not surprisingly, given the name and location, seafood is a specialty here—the local oysters, mussels, and lobsters are all memorable. **Known for:** great nonseafood options; world-famous Malpeque oysters; live music upstairs. [$] *Average main: C$30* ✉ *131 Sydney St.* ☎ *902/892–9661* 🌐 *www.claddaghoysterhouse.com* 🕒 *No lunch.*

The Dining Room

$$$ | **CONTEMPORARY** | Chefs at this restaurant, part of the acclaimed Culinary Institute of Canada at Holland College, are second-year students working under the supervision of master-chef instructors; service is provided by hospitality students. It's an opportunity to enjoy ambitious dishes that combine local ingredients with international influences, like grilled leg of lamb with Israeli couscous. **Known for:** open kitchen or harbor view seating options; high-quality cooking by future top chefs; sophisticated menu. [$] *Average main: C$30* ✉ *4 Sydney St.* ☎ *902/894–6868* 🌐 *www.hollandcollege.com* 🕒 *Closed late Apr.–early Oct.*

The Gahan House Pub & Brewery

$$ | **CANADIAN** | Housed in an 1880 brick building downtown, this pub clearly takes pride in its 10 handcrafted ales and craft cider, prominently displayed on the menu. Beer reappears in several dishes as well, including the signature brown-bag fish-and-chips with honey wheat ale–battered haddock, and a specific brew is recommended to accompany each dish. **Known for:** beer-battered brown-bag fish-and-chips; variety of award-winning craft beers; atmospheric historic building. [$] *Average main: C$17* ✉ *126 Sydney St.* ☎ *902/626–2337* 🌐 *charlottetown.gahan.ca.*

Leonhard's

$$ | **CAFÉ** | Alexandra and Axel Leonhard have gone from humble beginnings selling homemade bread at a local farmers' market to running a full-fledged café where food is made from scratch without additives, preservatives, or artificial flavorings. The room is bright and cheerful, and the devoted clientele keeps coming back for breakfast, casseroles, hearty gluten-free soups, sandwiches, and delicious desserts. **Known for:** closing early at 5 pm; freshly baked bread and sweet treats; support of local farmers and food producers. [$] *Average main: C$15* ✉ *142 Great George St.* ☎ *902/367–3621* 🌐 *www.leonhards.ca* 🕒 *No dinner.*

The Pilot House

$$$ | **CANADIAN** | In the 19th-century Roger's Hardware building, this restaurant has both fine dining and casual fare. A pub menu features upscale sandwiches, fish-and-chips, and more, while quality PEI-raised beef and fresh seafood dominate the dinner menu. **Known for:** award-winning One-Eyed Jack burger; top-quality locally sourced steaks and seafood; lively pub atmosphere. [$] *Average main: C$28* ✉ *70 Grafton St.* ☎ *902/894–4800* 🌐 *thepilothouse.ca.*

Seafood in Prince Edward Island 🍴

Prince Edward Island shellfish has a reputation for being among the world's best. Mollusks and crustaceans are harvested all along the coast, so you can spot fishermen in shallow boats scooping up oysters with what look like giant salad servers. Moreover, you can see rows of buoys in bays and estuaries holding up lines covered with mussels, plus solo buoys securing the lobster traps that wait to be hauled offshore. Obviously, you'll see shellfish on almost every Island menu, too, as well as on many activity rosters: tour operators are taking increasing numbers of visitors out to trap, haul, tong, and shuck. Shellfish also pops up on festival calendars.

Sims Corner Steakhouse and Oyster Bar

$$$$ | STEAKHOUSE | The farm-to-plate focus helped this place earn accolades from the Prince Edward Island Restaurant Association, while the custom-cut, Island-raised beef (it's aged 45 days for richer taste) has earned kudos from patrons. Seafood selections start with a wide range of oysters at the raw bar, and divine desserts are made in-house. **Known for:** extensive wine list and climate-controlled cellar; flavorsome steaks; accommodating to dietary requirements. $ *Average main: C$42* ⊠ *86 Queen St.* ☎ *902/894–7467* ⊕ *www. simscorner.ca.*

Splendid Essence

$$ | VEGETARIAN | Sharing a pretty house with a Buddhist prayer hall, this little eatery serves vegetarian and vegan fare with Asian flair. Aside from the expected noodles, dumplings, and stir-fries, Splendid Essence has a fine selection of hot and cold teas, which you can enjoy outdoors on the porch in fine weather. **Known for:** great dim sum; eco-friendly credentials; authentic Chinese dishes. $ *Average main: C$18* ⊠ *186 Prince St.* ☎ *902/566–4991* ⊕ *www.splendidessence.com* 🕑 *Closed Sun.*

☕ Coffee and Quick Bites

Kettle Black

$ | VEGETARIAN | Trained baristas brew up a great cup of coffee from house-roasted beans, along with a wide selection of espresso-based drinks and chemical-free decaf. They also have a good variety of locally blended organic loose-leaf teas and a menu of locally sourced food, including sandwiches, fresh pastries, and desserts. **Known for:** environmentally sound credentials; locally sourced food ingredients; friendly atmosphere. $ *Average main: C$10* ⊠ *45 Queen St.* ☎ *902/892–9184, 902/370–0776* ⊕ *www. kettleblack.com.*

Receiver Coffee Company

$ | CANADIAN | In one of the oldest buildings in the city, known as the Brass Shop from its days as a brass polishing shop for locomotives, you can enjoy a great cup of coffee and some enticing food, including breakfast and lunch. **Known for:** strawberry sundae crepes; interesting old building; bakery items cooked on the premises. $ *Average main: C$8* ⊠ *128 Richmond St.* ☎ *902/367–3436* ⊕ *www. receivercoffee.com.*

Hotels

Delta Prince Edward
$$$ | **HOTEL** | Right on the waterfront boardwalk next to Peake's Wharf, and ideal for exploring downtown on foot, this beautifully renovated high-rise hotel has wonderful views and good amenities for leisure and business travelers. **Pros:** complimentary electric car–charging station; modern lobby area; upper category rooms have Jacuzzis. **Cons:** lots of business guests; soundproofing could be better; parking costs C$19 per day. [$] *Rooms from: C$219* ✉ *18 Queen St.* ☎ *902/566–2222* 🌐 *www.marriott.com/hotels/travel/yygdp-delta-hotels-prince-edward* 🛏 *211 rooms* 🍴 *No Meals.*

Dundee Arms Inn
$$$ | **B&B/INN** | A 1903 Queen Anne mansion and modern annex make up this attractive inn just minutes from downtown. **Pros:** in-room perks include Paya Organic bath products; relaxed setting; free Wi-Fi. **Cons:** annex rooms lack historic style; breakfast not included in high season; rooms vary widely in size and quality. [$] *Rooms from: C$225* ✉ *200 Pownal St.* ☎ *902/892–2496, 877/638–6333* 🌐 *www.dundeearmspei.com* 🛏 *22 rooms* 🍴 *No Meals.*

Elmwood Heritage Inn
$$ | **B&B/INN** | Tranquil and retaining its historic elegance, this 1889 inn, once the home of a provincial premier, sits at the end of a tree-lined lane in a residential neighborhood and claims, with some justification, to be the inspiration for a house described in *Anne of Green Gables.* **Pros:** friendly family atmosphere; gorgeous historical grounds; beautiful dining room. **Cons:** shower is old-fashioned in some rooms; a 15-minute walk to downtown; rather flowery for some tastes. [$] *Rooms from: C$158* ✉ *121 N. River Rd.* ☎ *902/368–3310, 877/933–3310* 🌐 *www.elmwoodinn.pe.ca* 🛏 *8 rooms* 🍴 *Free Breakfast.*

★ **Fairholm National Historic Inn and Carriage House**
$$$ | **B&B/INN** | The Fairholm, a designated National Historic Site, is a prime Maritime example of the architectural Picturesque movement. **Pros:** free parking and Wi-Fi; lovely gardens; superb breakfast coffee. **Cons:** breakfast not included in the room rate; check-in and breakfast are at Hillhurst Inn; lots of wallpaper. [$] *Rooms from: C$229* ✉ *230 Prince St.* ☎ *902/892–5022, 888/573–5022* 🌐 *www.fairholminn.com* 🛏 *10 rooms* 🍴 *No Meals.*

★ **The Great George**
$$$ | **HOTEL** | This centrally located boutique hotel is fashioned from 20 heritage buildings, and history is clearly in the air (some Fathers of Confederation stayed in them during the Charlottetown Conference), but it's nicely balanced by the contemporary style and 21st-century touches. **Pros:** free Wi-Fi and access to hotel gym; excellent staff; comfy beds topped with duvets and premium linens. **Cons:** parking can be difficult; separate buildings can mean issues on rainy days; street noise is sometimes audible. [$] *Rooms from: C$239* ✉ *58 Great George St.* ☎ *902/892–0606, 800/361–1118* 🌐 *www.thegreatgeorge.com* 🛏 *50 rooms* 🍴 *Free Breakfast.*

Hillhurst Inn
$$$ | **B&B/INN** | In the heart of downtown, this grand, renovated 1897 Georgian Revival mansion has tasteful guest rooms. **Pros:** big, bright rooms; close to the Confederation Trail; gorgeous decor. **Cons:** breakfast is only meal on-site; operates seasonally; small bathrooms. [$] *Rooms from: C$179* ✉ *181 Fitzroy St.* ☎ *902/894–8004, 888/573–5022* 🌐 *www.fairholminn.com/hillhurst-inn* ⏲ *Closed Nov.–May* 🛏 *8 rooms* 🍴 *Free Breakfast.*

The Holman Grand Hotel

$$$$ | HOTEL | Sitting atop the Confederation Court Mall, the 10-story structure's upper floors provide sensational views (being a larger sized hotel it does have an elevator); lower ones, connected to both the mall and Confederation Centre of the Arts, offer indoor access to city amenities. **Pros:** nice pool; eco-friendly geothermal heating; some suites have kitchenettes. **Cons:** lower rooms lack harbor views; comparatively pricey; standard rooms have no tubs. $ *Rooms from: C$285 ✉ 123 Grafton St. ☎ 902/367–7777, 877/455–4726 ⊕ www.theholmangrand.com ⇨ 80 rooms* ❖ *No Meals.*

The Hotel on Pownal

$$$ | HOTEL | This is a contemporary lodging option with high-end atmosphere and high standards of service. **Pros:** free home-baked treats available 24/7; on-site gym; free Wi-Fi and buffet breakfast. **Cons:** no views; no on-site restaurant; some room are accessed from the outside. $ *Rooms from: C$189 ✉ 146 Pownal St. ☎ 902/892–1217, 800/268–6261 ⊕ thehotelonpownal.com ⇨ 45 rooms* ❖ *Free Breakfast.*

Rodd Royalty

$$$ | HOTEL | FAMILY | Just off the highway, this friendly modern hotel, part of a small Island-based chain, is handy both for getting into the heart of the city, for zipping off to other island destinations, and for shopping opportunities at Charlottetown Mall. **Pros:** convenient edge of city location; good-value golf and family packages; indoor pool with waterslide. **Cons:** need to drive to get into the city; no views; no historic character. $ *Rooms from: C$189 ✉ 14 Capital Dr. ☎ 902/894–8566, 800/031-5667 ⊕ www.roddvacations.com/hotels/rodd-royalty ⇨ 119 rooms* ❖ *Free Breakfast.*

Shipwright Inn B&B

$$ | B&B/INN | The name of this cottage-y 1860s inn is a nod to the first owner's occupation, and its charming accommodations further attest to his seafaring ways (the Captain's Quarters, the Navigator's Retreat—you get the picture). **Pros:** off-street private parking; downtown location with pretty garden; some rooms have balconies and fireplaces. **Cons:** decor can be a bit old-fashioned; five rooms are not original; lots of knick-knacks. $ *Rooms from: C$169 ✉ 51 Fitzroy St. ☎ 902/368–1905, 888/306–9966 ⊕ www.shipwrightinn.com ⇨ 9 rooms* ❖ *Free Breakfast.*

🍸 Nightlife

The nightlife scene in PEI centers around the city's pubs, some of which offer live music and/or DJs and dance floors. For complete and current listings of entertainment events check *The Buzz*; you can pick up a free copy at most hotels, restaurants, and newsstands or view it online at ⊕ *buzzpei.com.*

Baba's Lounge

LIVE MUSIC | It's not a late-night venue (it closes at 11 pm on Friday and Saturday and 10 pm the rest of the week), but it's the place to come for quality bands playing original material in a cozy setting. There's live music at least six nights a week, plus open mike, comedy and trivia nights. ✉ *181 Great George St. ☎ 902/892–7377 ⊕ www.cedarseatery.ca.*

The Factory Cookhouse and Dancehall

DANCE CLUBS | When dinner is over—and that's worth going for, too, for meats smoked on the premises—the dance floor heats up on Saturday night, with DJs on two floors playing a mix of classic rock and country on some nights, '80s dance parties on others. ✉ *189 Kent St. ☎ 902/370–3663 ⊕ www.thefactorycookhouse.com.*

A view of the harbor in Charlottetown with the twin Gothic spires of St. Dunstan's Basilica in the background.

Olde Dublin Pub

LIVE MUSIC | This pub has been a top spot for entertainment for more than 30 years, with something going on every weekend, mostly in the form of live traditional Maritimes music or rock. It draws a mixed crowd of all ages and is open until 2 am. ⊠ *131 Sydney St.* ☎ *902/892–6992* ⊕ *oldedublinpub.com.*

🎭 Performing Arts

Benevolent Irish Society Hall

CONCERTS | **FAMILY** | Friday night ceilidhs with Celtic dancing, fiddling, and a few stories thrown in for good measure, run weekly May through October. It's worth checking out the winter concert series, too. ⊠ *582 N. River Rd.* ☎ *902/892–2367* ⊕ *benevolentirishsocietyofpei.com* 🎫 *C$15.*

The Guild

THEATER | One of Charlottetown's major cultural centers, the Guild hosts plays, musicals, comedy and other performances, and a variety of exhibits throughout the year. ⊠ *111 Queen St.* ☎ *902/620–3333, 866/774–0717* ⊕ *www. theguildpei.com.*

The Homburg Theatre

THEATER | **FAMILY** | This is the city's main theater, at the Confederation Centre of the Arts. With more than 1,100 seats on two levels, it has hosted the famous *Anne of Green Gables—The Musical* for more than 55 seasons. ⊠ *145 Richmond St.* ☎ *902/566–1267, 800/565–0278* ⊕ *www.confederationcentre.com.*

The Mack

THEATER | An intimate little theater, The Mack has just 200 seats, arranged cabaret-style around tables. Some evening performances have liquor service (so no under-19s are admitted). ⊠ *128 Great George St.* ☎ *902/566–1267, 800/565–0278* ⊕ *www.confederationcentre.com/ venues/the-mack/.*

🛍 Shopping

The most interesting shops in Charlottetown are on Peake's Wharf, in Confederation Court Mall (off Queen Street), along Victoria Row (the section of Richmond Street between Queen and Great George streets), and on Water Street. There are also factory outlet stores along the Trans-Canada Highway at North River Causeway near the western entrance to the city, next to Cows Creamery (try their ice cream), and the Charlottetown Mall, on the outskirts just north of the university.

Anne of Green Gables Chocolates
CANDY | FAMILY | This local chocolatier sells old-fashioned chocolates, peanut brittle, and assorted candy—all made on the premises. (For a double dose of local flavor, try chocolate-coated PEI potato chips.) Sweet treats for those who can't get enough of the Island's sweetest fictional orphan are available at this location year-round. Other outlets, open seasonally, are at Cows Creamery, in Avonlea Village, at Gateway Village in Borden-Carleton, and on the Cavendish Boardwalk. ☒ 100 Queen St. ☎ 902/368–3131 ⊕ annechocolates.com.

Anne of Green Gables Store
SOUVENIRS | FAMILY | Anne fans can buy memorabilia from this store, owned by an actual relative of author Lucy Maude Montgomery. Everything is carefully curated here to preserve the family legacy through licensed products only, from the classic straw hats with braids attached to dolls to ornaments and copies of the book. There are other branches at Cavendish and Park Corner. ☒ 110 Queen St. ☎ 902/368–2663, 800/665-2663 ⊕ annestore.ca.

Charlottetown Farmers' Market
MARKET | Along with the expected array of local produce, artisanal cheeses, organic meats, craft beer, and tasty baked goods, you'll find a fine array of Island-made crafts and natural, organic skin-care products here. The market runs from 9 until 2 on Saturday year-round as well as on Wednesday 9 until 2, mid-June through early October. ☒ 100 Belvedere Ave. ☎ 902/626–3373 ⊕ charlottetownfarmersmarket.com.

Moonsnail Soapworks and Aromatherapy
CRAFTS | The vegetable-based soaps sold here are handcrafted and scented with essential oils, and the production area is open to view so the aromas fill the store. The expanding inventory also includes sublime bath and body-care products, a pet-care line, and crafts by local artisans. ☒ 85 Water St. ☎ 902/892–7627, 888/771–7627 ⊕ www.ilovemoonsnail.com.

Northern Watters Knitwear
MIXED CLOTHING | This shop carries its own line of chill-chasing knitted sweaters, along with fine locally sheared and spun alpaca and merino yarn, and a wide range of other Island-made products. They also run the Tartan Shop next door. ☒ 150 Richmond St. ☎ 902/566–5850, 800/565–9665 ⊕ www.nwknitwear.com ⏱ Closed Sun.

🏃 Activities

GOLF
Clyde River Golf Club
GOLF | About 10 minutes west of Charlottetown, this beautiful public course on the Clyde River has stunning water views on most holes. The 18-hole parkland and woodland course is linked to the 9-hole links course, making for a varied and interesting game. The natural land provides some tricky elements: the

green on the 8th is completely surrounded by water, and the 15th requires a very accurate tee shot. ✉ *472 Clyde River Rd., Rte. 247, Clyde River* ☏ *902/675–2585* ⊕ *clyderivergolf.ca* ✐ *C$30–C$35 for 18 holes, C$20–C$25 for 9 holes* ⚡ *18 holes, 5781 yards, par 71; 9 holes, 2982 yards, par 36* ⊙ *Closed Nov.–Apr.*

Fox Meadow Golf and Country Club

GOLF | This club is a mere five minutes southeast of the city and is a challenging championship course, designed by Rob Heaslip. In a delightful rural landscape, it overlooks Charlottetown Harbour and the community of Stratford, and, apparently, it lives up to its name—resident foxes have been known to steal golf balls in play (which can be replaced without penalty). ✉ *167 Kinlock Rd., Stratford* ☏ *902/569–4653, 877/569–8337* ⊕ *www. foxmeadow.pe.ca* ✐ *18 holes C$50–C$89, 9 holes C$30–C$45* ⚡ *18 holes, 6836 yards, par 72.*

WATER SPORTS

Saga Sailing Adventures

SAILING | June to October, you can sail away on a 36-foot sloop and, with space for just 12 passengers, there's the chance to take the helm or help with adjusting the sails. You can also do some diving, snorkeling, or swimming—or just relax and enjoy the ride. The trips last 2½-hours and depart daily at 10 am, 1 pm, and 5 pm June–October. Charter tours are also available. ✉ *Charlottetown Yacht Club, 1 Pownal St.* ☏ *902/672–1222* ⊕ *www.sagasailing.com* ✐ *From C$70.*

Top Notch Lobster Tours

FISHING | FAMILY | For an authentic lobster-fishing experience that's fun and informative, hop aboard the 45-foot *Top Notch* for a 1½- or 2½-hour trip with Captain Mark Jenkins. The tour, available morning, afternoon, or evening in July and August, includes taking a turn at the wheel, learning about on-board technology, hauling traps and banding a lobster claw, hearing about Mark's

own lobster-fishing experiences, and a lobster dinner (or chicken if ordered when booking the trip). ✉ *2 Prince St.* ☏ *902/626–6689* ⊕ *www.markscharters. com* ✐ *From C$50.*

Prince Edward Island National Park

Touched with nature's boldest brushstrokes, at Prince Edward Island National Park, sky and sea meet red sandstone cliffs, woodlands, wetlands, rolling dunes, and long stretches of sand. The park encompasses 40 km (25 miles) of the north shore of the Island and is separated into three regions: Cavendish to North Rustico, Brackley to Dalvay, and Greenwich. Diverse habitats are home to a variety of plants and animals, including more than 300 species of birds and the marram grass that's vital to the survival of the dunes. Boardwalks and carpeted footpaths are the only places where human feet should venture, opening up spectacular vistas. The park's Cavendish

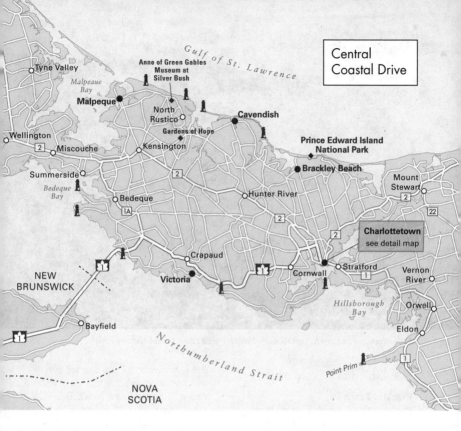

Destination Centre and Greenwich Interpretation Centre are both open early June through mid-September.

GETTING HERE AND AROUND

There are several entrances to the park system off Routes 6, 13, 15, and 313. If you're not on a guided tour, you'll need a car to visit the park; vehicles must be parked in designated parking lots or you'll risk being towed or receiving a fine.

◉ Sights

★ Prince Edward Island National Park

NATIONAL PARK | FAMILY | Numerous beaches can be enjoyed between Cavendish and Greenwich, but boardwalks and stairs to reach them are only in place from mid-May to the end of September. Brackley, Cavendish, and Stanhope beaches are accessible to those with

mobility issues, and beach wheelchairs are available. A relaxing alternative to the beaches is to picnic in the titular grove, accompanied by a soundtrack of songbirds and honking Canada geese that call the nearby pond home. A full slate of cultural and ecological interpretive programs aimed at all ages is also available. More active types can bike or hike on the park's scenic trails. If you'd rather be out on the water, kayaking and canoeing opportunities abound. Winter visitors will find snow cleared from parking lots and can enjoy cross-country skiing and snowshoeing, but should be aware that Parks Canada does not provide emergency services in winter. ⊠ *Cavendish* ☎ *902/672–6350* ⊕ *www.pc.gc.ca/en/ pn-np/pe/pei-ipe* ⊠ *C$7.90 July and Aug.; C$3.90 Sept.–June.*

The picturesque Oceanview Lookoff located within Prince Edward Island National Park.

 Beaches

Brackley Beach

BEACH | FAMILY | Less crowded than Cavendish, Brackley Beach, within Prince Edward Island National Park, stretches for miles along the north shore, so it's easy to find a secluded spot to enjoy the fine sands and clear water. It's a great place for beach walks, and there's also a cycle track a little way back from the shore. It can get very windy here, which is good news for windsurfers. A boardwalk leads from the parking lot to the beach, and there's access to the Gulf Shore Way East trail, with four-wheel pedal-powered Coastal Cruisers for rent from the Stanhope campground. In summer, a Discovery Dome tent has interactive activities, and you can learn sand-sculpting techniques on Monday afternoons. To access the beach you have to pay the entrance fee to the national park. Pets are not allowed on the beach from April through mid-October. **Amenities:** food and drink; lifeguards; parking (free); showers; toilets. **Best for:** swimming; walking; windsurfing. ⊠ *Gulfshore Pkwy., Brackley Beach* ☎ *902/672–6350 weekdays 8:30–4:30* ⊕ *www.pc.gc. ca/eng/pn-np/pe/pei-ipe/index.aspx* ✉ *C\$7.90, mid-May–Sept.*

★ Cavendish Beach

BEACH | FAMILY | Close to—but far enough from—the tourist hot spots of Cavendish, and protected within the Prince Edward Island National Park, this wonderful beach has a long stretch of clean, soft sand backed by dunes, low cliffs, a boardwalk, and a bike trail. Various access points (with boardwalks and stairs in place mid-May through September 30) add to its popularity, but it's big enough to provide plenty of space for all, and beach wheelchairs are available for those with mobility issues. Organized activities include lessons in sand sculpting on Wednesday afternoons and there are trails through the dunes with interpretive panels along the way. Don't head for home when the sun starts to set—the glow of its final rays on the rich red cliffs is an unforgettable sight. **Amenities:** food and drink; lifeguards; parking (free); showers; toilets. **Best for:** sunrise; sunset; swimming; walking. ✉ *Graham's La., Cavendish* ☎ *902/672–6350 weekdays 8:30–4:30* 🌐 *www.pc.gc.ca/eng/pn-np/pe/pei-ipe/index.aspx* 🎫 *Park entrance fee C$7.90.*

★ Greenwich Beach

BEACH | Seclusion and stunning scenery is your reward for taking the walk to the beach here, and there are various access points involving varying amounts of walking (the shortest is from the parking lot at the end of Wild Rose Road). But take a longer hike along one of the Greenwich Dune Trail loops and along the way you'll enjoy wonderful views across the parabolic dune system (a rare occurrence in North America) and ponds, including sightings of the rich birdlife. Once there, the beach is an unspoiled expanse of fine pink sand that makes a curious sound beneath your feet. It's well worth stopping in at the Interpretation Centre at the entrance, too. Note: the dunes are extremely fragile, so keep to the beach, boardwalks, and marked trails. **Amenities:** lifeguards; parking (free); showers; toilets. **Best for:** solitude; walking. ✉ *Wild Rose Rd., Greenwich* ⊕ *Via Rte. 313, 6 km (4 miles) west of St. Peters Bay* ☎ *902/961–2514* 🌐 *www.pc.gc.ca* 🎫 *C$7.90 July and Aug; C$3.90 other times.*

🍴 Restaurants

★ Richard's Fresh Seafood

$$ | **SEAFOOD** | This down-home dockside eatery serves common fare in an uncommonly good way. Befitting its location, the seafood is *very* fresh: expect lobster rolls, scallop sandwiches, steamed clams, and such served with fries that are twice-cooked for added crispness, plus house-made sauces and slaws. **Known for:** PEI craft beers on tap; generously loaded lobster rolls; stunning location. [$] *Average main: C$15* ✉ *9 Covehead Wharf Rd., Stanhope* ☎ *902/672–3030* 🌐 *www.richardsfreshseafood.com* 🕒 *Closed Oct.–May.*

🛏 Hotels

Dalvay-by-the-Sea

$$$$ | **B&B/INN** | Built in 1895 as the summer retreat for a U.S. oil tycoon, this sprawling Queen Anne Revival "cottage" on the east edge of Prince Edward Island National Park is filled with antique furnishings, giving guest rooms a lovely period look. **Pros:** free Wi-Fi; elegant vintage vibe; 328 feet from the beach. **Cons:** no kitchens in cottages; lot of weddings and conferences; no air-conditioning and no TVs in guest rooms. [$] *Rooms from: C$299* ✉ *16 Cottage Cres., just off Rte. 6, near Dalvay Beach, Stanhope* ☎ *902/672–2048, 888/366–2955* 🌐 *www.dalvaybythesea.com* 🕒 *Closed Nov.–Apr.* 🛏 *33 rooms* 🍽 *No Meals.*

🏃 Activities

BIKING

Dalvay Bike Rentals

BIKING | FAMILY | The Dalvay-by-the-Sea resort rents bikes suitable for all members of the family to guests and nonguests alike. ✉ *Rte. 6, near Dalvay Beach, Stanhope* ☎ *902/672–2048* 🌐 *www.dalvaybythesea.com* 🎫 *C$25 per day.*

FISHING

Richard's Deep-Sea Fishing

FISHING | Captains Pat Gaudet and Nick Watts take eager anglers out on a 45-foot boat three times per day in summer, at 8 am, 1 pm, and 6 pm. Fishing gear is supplied and whatever you catch will be cleaned and filleted. ✉ *5 Wharf Rd., Covehead Bay* ☎ *902/672–2376.*

GOLF

Stanhope Golf and Country Club

GOLF | The links-style course at Stanhope Golf and Country Club is among the most challenging and scenic on the Island, with greens that can be hard to read. Ocean breezes can help or hinder, and there are great sea views from most holes, particularly on the back nine. The course is a couple of miles west of Dalvay, along Covehead Bay. ✉ *2961 Bayshore Rd., Stanhope* ☎ *902/672–2842, 888/672–2842* 🌐 *www.stanhopegolfclub.com* 🎫 *C$40–C$72 for 18 holes, C$25–C$35 for 9 holes* ⛳ *18 holes, 6600 yards, par 74.*

Brackley Beach

15 km (9 miles) northwest of Charlottetown.

Brackley Beach, located within Prince Edward Island National Park, has sand in ample supply. Since the hinterland is a low-key farming community, the beach here offers considerably fewer amenities than Cavendish and activities are refreshingly simple. Water sports, for example, tend to be the nonmotorized kind, and gentle pursuits like bird-watching are popular (area waterways attract many migratory species). Nevertheless, lodgings such as Shaw's have been in business for generations, so clearly there is enough here to warrant guests' return.

GETTING HERE AND AROUND

Lying along Route 15, just north of Route 6, Brackley Beach is meant for motorists.

🍴 Restaurants

★ The Dunes Café

$$$$ | **ECLECTIC** | Located within the excellent Dunes Studio Gallery, this café has wood ceilings that soar above the indoor dining room and a deck overlooking the dunes and marshlands of Covehead Bay. Like the view, the food offered by chef Norman Day is amazing, showcasing local ingredients with an international twist and some inspired combinations. **Known for:** interesting pizza-of-the-day toppings; excellent seafood chowder; beautiful setting, amid art and craft displays. [$] *Average main: C$37* ✉ *3622 Brackley Point Rd., Rte. 15, Brackley Beach* ☎ *902/672–1883* 🌐 *www.dunesgallery.com* 🕑 *Closed mid-Oct.–early June. No dinner Oct.*

🛏 Hotels

Barachois Inn

$$ | **B&B/INN** | Rustico, just below Brackley Beach, is one of the oldest communities on the Island—and this 1880 inn's Victorian elegance blends right in with the historic surroundings. **Pros:** includes passes to tourist sights in the area; thoughtful hosts; on-site gym. **Cons:** two-night minimum stay in high season; gable ceilings not great for tall guests; pretty far from civilization. [$] *Rooms from: C$169* ✉ *2193 Church Rd., Rte. 243, North Rustico* ✥ *Off Rte. 6, 8 km (5 miles) west of Brackley Beach* ☎ *902/963–2194, 800/963–2194* 🌐 *www.barachoisinn.com* 🛏 *8 rooms* 🍽 *Free Breakfast.*

Shaw's Hotel and Cottages

$$ | **RESORT** | **FAMILY** | Canada's oldest family-operated inn has been winning a faithful following since opening in 1860, and the homey rooms in the three-story lodge are attractive enough. **Pros:** family-friendly; next to the national park; chalets have full kitchens and propane barbecue. **Cons:** additional charge for dogs in cottages and chalets; air-conditioning in deluxe inn rooms only; may be mosquitoes in the air or jellyfish in the water. [$] *Rooms from: C$157* ✉ *99 Apple Tree Rd., Rte. 15, Brackley Beach* ☎ *902/672–2022* 🌐 *www.shawshotel.ca* 🕑 *Closed early Oct.–May; some cottages open in shoulder months* 🛏 *43 rooms* 🍽 *Free Breakfast.*

🎭 Performing Arts

Brackley Drive-In Theatre

FILM | FAMILY | Brackley Drive-In Theatre gives visitors in this neck of the woods a reason to stay up past dark. It shows a pair of first-run flicks nightly at 9 pm, from late April to October; gates open at 8 pm. Onion rings and other classic snacks from the canteen complement the experience. There's limited RV parking (arrive by 8:30 pm). Bring bug spray and, if possible, a bug screen for the car window(s); and if there's no way to turn off car headlights, bring a blanket to cover them (battery booster cables are available if necessary). ⊠ *3164 Brackley Point Rd., Rte. 15, Brackley Beach* ☎ *902/672–3333* ⊕ *drivein.ca* ⊠ *C$12* ⊙ *Closed Nov.–late Apr.* ☞ *cash only.*

🛍 Shopping

★ The Dunes Studio Gallery and Café

CRAFTS | This enticing gallery sells an array of cool Canadian-made goods, much of it from local artists and artisans. Some come with an unmistakable Indonesian influence, including pottery (you can watch it being crafted in the on-site studio), Island art, clothing, funky furniture, fine jewelry, contemporary glassware, and other one-of-a-kind items. It also has a beautiful garden and views to the water. ⊠ *3622 Brackley Point Rd., Rte. 15, Brackley Beach* ☎ *902/672–2586* ⊕ *www.dunesgallery.com.*

The Great Canadian Soap Co.

SKINCARE | This shop produces dozens of types of hand-milled goat's milk soap at its home base near Brackley Beach. (That explains the gamboling goats you'll encounter near the shop). Other all-natural bath, beauty, and household cleaning products are available as well. ⊠ *4224 Portage Rd., Rte. 6, Brackley Beach* ☎ *902/672–2242, 800/793–1644* ⊕ *www. greatcanadiansoap.com.*

🏃 Activities

Northshore Bike Rentals

BIKING | Run by Shaw's Hotel, this shop can equip you with bicycles for C$9 per hour or C$26 per day; weekly rates are also available. ⊠ *Shaw's Hotel, 99 Apple Tree Rd., Rte. 15, Brackley Beach* ☎ *902/672–2022.*

Cavendish

21 km (13 miles) west of Brackley Beach.

Cavendish is the most visited Island community after Charlottetown. The proximity of Prince Edward Island National Park, with its promise of summertime sun and sand, is one reason for the heavy influx of vacationers. The crop of amusement park-style attractions that has sprung up on Route 6 as a counterpoint to the pristine park is another. However, it all began with *Anne of Green Gables.* Thousands of Anne-ites flock to the Cavendish area every year to visit the homes associated with Lucy Maud Montgomery, who was born and buried in the area, and to explore the places so lovingly described in her books.

GETTING HERE AND AROUND

Most visitors drive themselves to Cavendish, either via Highway 13, which branches north from the two cross-island Highways 1 (the Trans-Canada) and 2, or via Highway 6 that loops along the north coast. Once you're in Cavendish, the main attractions are within easy walking distance, and it's only a 1-km (½-mile) stroll to the beach in the national park.

ESSENTIALS

VISITOR INFORMATION Cavendish Visitor Information Centre. ⊠ *7591 Cawnpore La., intersection of Rtes. 13 and 6, Cavendish* ☎ *902/963–7830, 800/463–4734* ⊕ *www. cavendishbeachpei.com.*

This green-and-white 19th-century farmhouse served as the inspiration for the Cuthbert place in Lucy Maud Montgomery's *Anne of Green Gables*.

TOURS
Prince Edward Tours
BUS TOURS | The scenic four-hour "Island Drive and Anne of Green Gables" tour from Charlottetown includes brief stops along the way and a tour of Green Gables House. The bus departs from Charlottetown Visitor Information Centre at 6 Prince St. at 11:30 am on certain days May to mid-October, including cruise ship days. ⊠ *Charlottetown* ☎ *902/566–5259, 877/286–6532* ⊕ *princeedwardtours.com* ⊠ *C$64.*

◉ Sights

Gardens of Hope
GARDEN | Need a break from those Cavendish crowds? Gardens of Hope, part of the PEI Preserve Company property, is located about 8 km (5 miles) south of town in the Island's most beautiful river valley. The garden covers more than 12 acres and includes a butterfly house. With 2 km (1 mile) of walking trails that thread past fountains and groomed flower beds, then through natural woodland, it provides ample opportunity for quiet contemplation. ⊠ *2841 New Glasgow Rd., New Glasgow* ⊹ *Off Rte. 13, 10 km (6 miles) south of Cavendish, at intersection of Rtes. 224 and 258* ☎ *902/964–4300, 800/565–5267* ⊕ *preservecompany.com/gardens-of-hope* ⊠ *By donation.*

★ Green Gables
HISTORIC HOME | **FAMILY** | Green Gables, ½ km (¼ mile) west of Lucy Maud Montgomery's Cavendish Home, is the green-and-white 19th-century farmhouse that served as the inspiration for the Cuthbert place in *Anne of Green Gables*. The house, outbuildings, and grounds, all of which belonged to cousins of the author's grandfather, re-create some of the settings found in the book. The same goes for short walking trails dubbed the Haunted Wood and Lovers Lane/Balsam Hollow. If you're well acquainted with the novel, you'll spy lots of evocative details on-site (say, a broken slate or amethyst

Anne of Green Gables

In Lucy Maud Montgomery's 1908 novel, Marilla Cuthbert and her brother Matthew live on a PEI farm. Getting on in years, the pair decides to adopt an orphan boy to help out with the chores. It's with some surprise, then, that Matthew comes back from the train station with a feisty, 11-year-old, redheaded girl. But it's not long before Anne—and her adventures and mishaps and friends—becomes an essential part of Marilla and Matthew's lives. An immediate hit, the book made Anne an essential part of readers' lives as well. Even Mark Twain, who called her "the dearest and most lovable child in fiction since the immortal Alice [in Wonderland]," was smitten.

Montgomery went on to write a total of eight volumes in the series. In 1985, the original was made into a two-part TV movie, which was a huge success, airing first on the CBC in Canada and then on PBS in the United States. That was followed by a series that ran from 1990 to 1996, and a newer series, launched by CBC and Netflix in 2017, is ongoing. Anne has also become a stage staple thanks to theatrical productions like *Anne of Green Gables—The Musical* (a must-see at the Confederation Centre in Charlottetown) and *Anne and Gilbert* (a melodious sequel that debuted in 2005). Of course, for the millions of modern-day Anne fans, Cavendish is hallowed ground because the top Green Gables sites and experiences are all in the area. These include **Green Gables,** the **Site of Lucy Maud Montgomery's Cavendish Home,** the **Lucy Maud Montgomery Birthplace,** and the **Anne of Green Gables Museum at Silver Bush.**

brooch). An audiovisual presentation on Montgomery's life shares space with a café in the barn nearby. This National Historic Site has been part of Prince Edward Island National Park since 1937 and hosts daily events throughout July and August such as guided tours, puppet shows, and old-fashioned games. ⊠ *8619 Rte. 6, Cavendish* ☎ *902/963–7874* ⊕ *www. pc.gc.ca/en/lhn-nhs/pe/greengables* ⊠ *C$3.90–C$7.90.*

Lucy Maud Montgomery Birthplace
HISTORIC HOME | FAMILY | The cottage-y white house with green trim overlooking New London Harbour, 11 km (7 miles) southwest of Cavendish, is where the *Anne* author was born in 1874, and the interior has been furnished with antiques to conjure up that era. Among memorabilia on display are a replica of Montgomery's wedding gown and personal scrapbooks filled with many of her poems and stories. ⊠ *Intersection of Rtes. 6 and 20, Cavendish* ☎ *902/886–2099 summer, 902/836–5502 winter* ⊕ *www.lmmontgomerybirthplace.ca* ⊠ *C$5.*

Sandspit Amusement Park
AMUSEMENT PARK/CARNIVAL | FAMILY | The largest amusement park on PEI kicks things up a notch with midway rides and go-cart tracks that appeal to tots and tweens alike. Thrill rides include the Cyclone rollercoaster, the longest in Atlantic Canada, and the Cliffhanger, with a 52-foot drop. Single-ride coupons, park passes, and multiattraction passes are available. ⊠ *8986 Rte. 6, Cavendish* ☎ *877/963–3939, 902/963–3939* ⊕ *www. sandspit.com* ⊠ *Day pass C$26.50; coupon book C$33.*

Shining Waters Family Fun Park

AMUSEMENT PARK/CARNIVAL | FAMILY | Topping the list of irresistibly cheesy amusements operating seasonally along the Route 6 tourist corridor, Shining Waters Family Fun Park is aimed at younger children, with a waterpark with pools and slides, a kiddy splash pool, pirate pedal boats, petting zoo, and small-scale rides. Weekly and season passes, and multi-attraction passes, are available. ✉ 8885 Rte. 6, Cavendish ☎ 877/963–3939, 902/963–3939 ⊕ www.shiningwaterspei.com 🖃 Day pass C$25.

Site of Lucy Maud Montgomery's Cavendish Home

HISTORIC SIGHT | FAMILY | The Site of Lucy Maud Montgomery's Cavendish Home is where the writer lived with her maternal grandparents after the untimely death of her mother. Though the foundation of the house where Montgomery wrote *Anne of Green Gables* is all that remains, the homestead's fields and old apple-tree gardens are lovely. A bookstore and small museum are also on the property, which is operated by descendants of the family and, together with neighbouring Green Gables, is a National Historic Site of Canada. ✉ 8521 Rte. 6, Cavendish ☎ 902/963–2231, 888/733–8888 ⊕ www.pc.gc.ca/en/lhn-nhs/pe/cavendish 🖃 C$6.

🍴 Restaurants

★ New Glasgow Lobster Suppers

$$$$ | SEAFOOD | FAMILY | Established in 1958, New Glasgow Lobster Suppers brings fresh lobster direct from a pound on the premises to your plate. Scallops, roast beef, salmon, chicken, haddock, ham, and even a vegetarian dish are other choices if you've already had your fill of crustaceans, or you can choose to have just an appetizer and dessert. **Known for:** house-made desserts; classic PEI lobster; always busy but rarely a wait. $ *Average main: C$37* ✉ 604 Rte. 258, New Glasgow ☎ 902/964–2870 ⊕ www.peilobstersuppers.com ⊗ Closed early Oct.–early June. No lunch.

Prince Edward Island Preserve Company

$$ | CANADIAN | One of the best spots on the Island to stop for a bite, the café at this preserve company has a soaring ceiling and two walls of windows looking over the Clyde River. Everything served is noted for freshness—even the ice cream is house-made. **Known for:** very popular, so there may be a wait for a table; wide range of preserves made on-site; good breakfasts served until 11 am. $ *Average main: C$17* ✉ 2841 New Glasgow Rd., New Glasgow ✛ Off Rte. 13 ☎ 902/964–4300, 800/565–5267 ⊕ www.preserve-company.com ⊗ Closed Tues. and late Sep.–late May.

☕ Coffee and Quick Bites

Samuel's

$ | BAKERY | FAMILY | Avonlea Village may be all about Anne of Green Gables, but the branch of Samuel's Coffee House in this historic setting is all about good coffee and house-made treats such as muffins, scones, soups, salads and a delectable raspberry cream cheese pie. It's in a nice old clapboard building with a few tables out on the sidewalk. **Known for:** great breakfasts; nice outdoor seating for sunny days; Avonlea location. $ *Average main: C$15* ✉ 8619 Rte. 6, Cavendish ☎ 902/963–3330 ⊕ www.samuelscoffeehouse.ca.

🛏 Hotels

Accommodations in the Cavendish area are often booked a year in advance for July and most of August. If you're late in planning, don't despair—hotels in Charlottetown and elsewhere in the central region are still within easy driving distance of "Anne's Land."

The Confederation Trail

In the 1980s, new life was given to the ground once covered by the Prince Edward Island Railway, when the abandoned track was converted into a recreational route dubbed the Confederation Trail. Gorgeous, well groomed, and generally flat, its 410 km (255 miles) are ideal for hiking and, above all, biking. Serious cyclists can race through it in 17 hours. But most pedal pushers opt for a more leisurely pace that allows them to stop and smell the lupines. If you're short on time, rent a bike from any cycle shop and just do a single section. Plum-color access gates are near roadways at many points, and food and lodging are available at villages along the way. Tourism PEI provides details on rental locations and touring tips, and the website has interactive and downloadable maps. You can also pick up the "Confederation Trail Cycling Guide" that includes maps, itinerary highlights, and accommodations that are part of the Cyclists Welcome Program. Just a heads-up: properly certified helmets are compulsory in PEI while riding bicycles on the highway, regardless of age.

Bay Vista Motel and Cottage

$ | HOTEL | FAMILY | This straightforward, spotlessly clean motel has real family appeal, including a playground, a heated swimming pool, and water views. **Pros:** close to tourist sights; friendly staff; picnic areas and swimming pool. **Cons:** shared barbecues in picnic areas; dated decor; looks like a motel inside and out. *[$] Rooms from: C$99 ✉ 9517 Rte. 6, Cavendish ☎ 902/963–2225, 800/846–0601 🌐 www.bayvista.ca 🕒 Closed late Sept.–early June 🛏 34 rooms 🍴 Free Breakfast.*

Cavendish Country Inn and Cottages

$$ | B&B/INN | FAMILY | The family atmosphere of this 9-acre cottage complex is a big draw for some folks; there are several playgrounds on-site, as well as a pair of heated pools, hot tubs, fire pits, and outdoor games (complimentary movies help on rainy days). **Pros:** plenty of activities on-site; choice of accommodations for the budget-conscious; free Wi-Fi. **Cons:** if you want a quieter holiday, this isn't the place; dated decor; no air-conditioning. *[$] Rooms from: C$125 ✉ 8405 Cavendish Rd., Rte. 6, Cavendish ☎ 902/963–2181, 800/454–4853 🌐 www.cavendishpei.com 🕒 Closed late Sept.–mid-May 🛏 11 rooms, 35 cottages 🍴 No Meals.*

Kindred Spirits Country Inn and Cottages

$ | B&B/INN | FAMILY | Named in a nod to Anne, this lovely 6-acre property is just a short walk from Green Gables. **Pros:** laundry facilities; national park passes provided; some cottages have private hot tubs. **Cons:** 20-minute walk to the beach; breakfast not included in cottage rates; style is a bit twee for some tastes. *[$] Rooms from: C$115 ✉ Memory La., off Rte. 6, Cavendish ☎ 902/963–2434, 800/461–1755 🌐 www.kindredspirits.ca 🕒 Closed early Oct.–late May 🛏 25 rooms, 20 cottages 🍴 Free Breakfast.*

Activities

GOLF

Andersons Creek Golf Club

GOLF | Designed by Graham Cooke, this rolling parkland course features some tricky terrain and water hazards on nine holes. The third hole is one to watch out for, with a steep downward slope to the green. Proud of the game's Scottish roots, the championship course employs its own bagpiper. ✉ *68 North Rd., Rte. 240, Stanley Bridge* ☎ *902/886–2222* ⊕ *www.andersonscreek.com* 🖭 *C$60–C$90 daily rate* 🏌 *18 holes, 6651 yards, par 72* ⊙ *Closed late Sept.–Apr.*

Eagles Glenn Golf Course

GOLF | FAMILY | Graham Cooke was the designer behind this course, reminiscent of a Scottish links course, with 18 walkable holes in a stunning setting. This championship course is a testing one, but five sets of tees allow for various skill levels and family and beginner nights are offered. ✉ *374 Eagles Glenn Blvd., Rte. 6, Cavendish* ☎ *902/963–3600, 866/963–3600* ⊕ *eaglesglenn.com* 🖭 *C$55–C$90* 🏌 *18 holes, 6785 yards, par 72* ⊙ *Closed Nov.–Apr.*

Glasgow Hills Resort and Golf Club

GOLF | About five minutes southeast of Cavendish, this course wins high praise for its challenging Les Furber–designed layout and killer clubhouse views. Kept in superior condition, it utilizes the natural, undulating landscape, with views of the River Clyde and the Gulf of St. Lawrence. It's popular with many top players, although every hole has multiple tee boxes to suit all levels of play. ✉ *98 Glasgow Hills Dr., New Glasgow* ☎ *902/621–2201* ⊕ *www.glasgowhills.com* 🖭 *C$69–C$89* 🏌 *18 holes, 6915 yards, par 72* ⊙ *Closed Oct.–Apr.*

Green Gables Golf Course

GOLF | This classic Stanley Thompson-designed course, located within Prince Edward Island National Park, was restored by Thomas McBroom in 2007. The result reflects many of Thompson's original features. With great views, including the coastline and Green Gables House, four tee decks, and ocean breezes tickling your shot, it's a good choice for both aspiring and avid golfers. The clubhouse lounge serves refreshments and light meals. The course is open for play May through October. ✉ *8727 Rte.*

6, Cavendish ☎ *902/963–4653* ⊕ *www. greengablesgolf.com* 🖭 *C$60–C$100* 🏌 *18 holes, 6874 yards, par 72* ⊙ *Closed Nov.–Apr.*

WATER SPORTS
Inn at the Pier

WATER SPORTS | FAMILY | You can splash out in rented kayaks or on stand-up paddleboards, and shallow waters make it ideal for beginners. ✉ *9796 Cavendish Rd., Rte. 6, Stanley Bridge* ☎ *902/886–3126* ⊕ *www.innatthepier.com/watersports.*

Malpeque

32 km (20 miles) west of Cavendish.

There are two good reasons why motorists make the drive to Malpeque. Some do it to cram in one last Anne shrine—specifically Silver Bush at Park Corner. Others continue westward to stuff themselves full of oysters. Named for the bay from which many are drawn, the Malpeque variety has had a huge cachet since earning the "best in show" title at the 1900 Paris World's Fair. Eating them is a time-honored tradition. The same goes for harvesting them: traditional methods are still employed (tongs are used, not dredgers) despite the fact that Prince Edward Island sells about 300,000 tons of oysters annually.

GETTING HERE AND AROUND

Malpeque is best accessed—and appreciated—by car. To reach it, turn right off Route 6 at New London onto Route 20.

Sights

Anne of Green Gables Museum at Silver Bush

HISTORIC HOME | FAMILY | This was once home to Lucy Maud Montgomery's aunt and uncle. The writer also lived here for a time and was married in the parlor in 1911—in fact, that room serves as a wedding venue for modern-day

A Bridge Too Far?

Gephyrophobiacs (people with an extreme fear of bridges) had best avoid the Confederation Bridge. Linking Borden-Carleton to Cape Jourimain, New Brunswick, it is the longest in the world spanning ice-covered water. But for anyone else intent on driving to or from PEI, the so-called fixed link is the way to go. Even if you're merely passing by while doing the Central Coastal circuit, this 13-km (8-mile) engineering marvel is worth a look. To construct it, massive concrete pillars—each 65 feet across and 180 feet high—were sunk into

waters more than 110 feet deep. The cost? A cool billion.

First-time traversers invariably want to stop on the bridge itself to take a picture. Don't—it's illegal. You must maintain a speed of 80 kph (50 mph). The best angles are from the Prince Edward Island side anyway. For an up-close perspective, pull into Gateway Village at the foot of the bridge. In addition to a 3-acre park where you can take in the bridge view, it has a plethora of souvenir shops where you can buy postcards of said view.

couples. Inside the house, which is still owned by Montgomery descendants, are mementos such as photographs and a quilt Montgomery worked on. The site includes a gift shop jam-packed with licensed *Anne of Green Gables* goodies, and there is a Matthew Cuthbert look-alike on hand to take visitors on buggy rides around the pastoral 110-acre property. Trips for up to five passengers cost C$75 for a half-hour, C$125 for one hour. ⊠ *4542 Rte. 20, Park Corner* ☎ *902/886–2884, 800/665–2663* ⊕ *www.annemuseum.com* ⊠ *C$6* ⊗ *Closed mid-Oct.–mid-May, except by reservation.*

⊛ Beaches

Cabot Beach Provincial Park

BEACH | FAMILY | In addition to a popular campground, 360-acre Cabot Beach Provincial Park has fine day-use facilities—particularly for families. In summer, the sandy beach is supervised, plus there's a playground and children's programming. Naturalist-led walks are also available. Surf conditions can sometimes deter swimmers, and alerts are issued if it becomes dangerous, but when it's calm,

it's very calm. **Amenities:** lifeguards; parking (free); showers; toilets. **Best for:** sunset; surfing; swimming; walking. ⊠ *449 King St., Rte. 20, Malpeque* ☎ *902/836–8945, 877/445–4938* ⊗ *Closed Oct.–May.*

Darnley Beach

BEACH | FAMILY | Just north of Darnley (on Route 20, about halfway between Park Corner and Malpeque), this long stretch of sands includes Thunder Cove Beach, weather-sculpted sea stacks, and a number of sandstone caves. There are no developed facilities here, other than a campground, and the beach is often almost entirely deserted except for the seabirds—so it's perfect for those seeking a "castaway" experience. **Amenities:** none. **Best for:** solitude; sunset; walking. ⊠ *Off Lower Darnley Rd.*

⊛ Restaurants

Malpeque Oyster Barn

$$$ | SEAFOOD | There's nowhere better to enjoy world-famous Malpeque oysters than this casual, family-run wharf-side eatery right at the source—you can see their beds right outside the window. Oysters can be prepared several ways, but purists should just order a dozen una-dorned (with a cold beer as an accompa-niment), then slurp away. **Known for:** limit-ed choices for children; top-quality fresh oysters; picturesque setting. $ *Average main: C$25* ⊠ *10 Malpeque Wharf Rd., off Rte. 105, Malpeque* ☎ *902/836–3999* ⊗ *Closed mid-Sept.–mid-June.*

Hotels

Noble House

$$$ | **B&B/INN** | Staying at this cheery yel-low heritage farmhouse with its welcom-ing front porch and gingerbread trim, you might feel like you have stepped into a Norman Rockwell painting—save for the fact that, back in the day, guests wouldn't have been able to book into well-equipped rooms that pair period charm with contemporary amenities like Jacuzzi tubs, cable TV, and high-speed Internet. **Pros:** ocean views; Jacuzzis in all bath-rooms; off-season rates available. **Cons:** bathrooms are all private, but only one is en suite; resident pets may not appeal to those with allergies; no air-conditioning. $ *Rooms from: C$190* ⊠ *187 Taylor Rd., RR No. 1, Malpeque* ☎ *902/836–4380* ⇆ *3 rooms* ❤ *Free Breakfast.*

🎭 Performing Arts

St. Mary's Church

CONCERTS | Built in 1902 by Island archi-tect W.C. Harris, this French Gothic-style church hosts performances by visiting artists from mid-June to mid-September as part of the Indian River Festival of classical and other music. The church has exceptionally good acoustics, plus a beautiful pastoral setting, and the concerts here are often broadcast nationally by the Canadian Broadcasting Corporation. ⊠ *1374 Hamilton Rd., Rte. 104, Indian River* ✛ *6 km (3½ miles) south of Malpeque* ☎ *902/836–4933, 866/856–3733* ⊕ *www.indianriverfestival. com* ⊠ *From C$20.*

🏃 Activities

Malpeque Bay Kayak Tours

KAYAKING | **FAMILY** | Malpeque is a French corruption of the Mi'Kmaq word for "big water." You can go out and explore it in summer with these informative, half-day interpretive trips. The company also rents kayaks, stand-up paddleboards, and bicycles. And if you overdo the activi-ties, there's an infrared sauna on-site. ⊠ *Rte. 20, Malpeque* ☎ *902/439–7885, 866/836–3784* ⊕ *www.peikayak.ca* ⊠ *Tours from C$45; kayak rentals from C$30; paddleboard lessons from C$30.*

Victoria

45 km (28 miles) south of Malpeque.

Cross-country from the Green Gables Shore is the Red Sands Shore where charming, understated villages await. The jewel in this coastal crown is Victoria, known locally as Victoria-by-the-Sea. It's peaceful, lovingly preserved, and popular with artsy types who come to escape the hectic pace of modern life. Browse the shops; admire the architecture; then kick back on a nearby beach that's washed by the warm waters of Northumberland Strait.

GETTING HERE AND AROUND

Victoria—sitting just off the Trans-Canada Highway, 22 km (14 miles) east of the Confederation Bridge—is most easily reached by car. When you arrive in the village, park by the wharf and set out on foot. It's only two blocks wide and two blocks long, so you won't get lost.

🍴 Restaurants

Landmark Oyster House

$$$ | **SEAFOOD** | In addition to the excellent oysters, this nice little restaurant has an eclectic menu that includes other sea-food such as charred haddock, along with

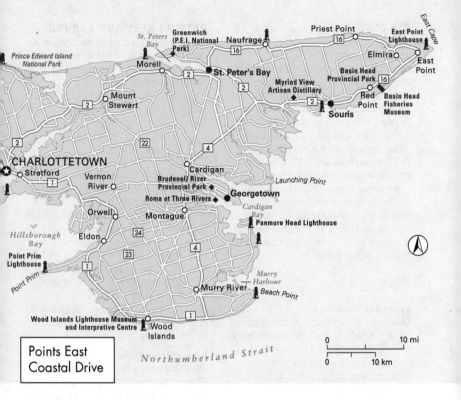

Points East Coastal Drive

slow-roasted PEI beef, jerk chicken, and salads. Vegetarian, vegan, and gluten-free options are also available. **Known for:** small space so reservations are helpful; Cajun-style jumbo shrimp and scallop stir-fry; wide range of drinks. $ *Average main: C$25* ⊠ *12 Main St., Victoria* ☎ *902/658–2286* ⊕ *www.landmarkcafe. ca* ⊗ *No lunch Mon. and Tues.*

Hotels

Orient Hotel Bed and Breakfast

$ | **B&B/INN** | Cozy guest rooms and suites that are individually decorated lend this vintage B&B a comforting grandma's-house vibe. **Pros:** free Wi-Fi and bicycle storage; some rooms have water views; lovely hosts. **Cons:** exterior is in need of some paint; no air-conditioning; some rooms are small. $ *Rooms from: C$100* ⊠ *34 Main St., Victoria*

☎ *902/658–2503, 800/565–6743* ⊕ *www. theorienthotel.com* ⊗ *Closed Oct.–May* ⇥ *7 rooms* ⏿⃝ *Free Breakfast.*

🎭 Performing Arts

Victoria Playhouse

CONCERTS | Offering a renowned professional program with a focus on contemporary Canadian theater and music, this place may only have 150 seats but it has big talent and a huge heart. It operates year-round, and in the peak season, July through mid-September, the circa-1914 venue operates daily, offering four theater productions plus assorted concerts. ⊠ *Howard and Main Sts., Victoria* ☎ *902/658–2025, 800/925–2025* ⊕ *www. victoriaplayhouse.com* ⌸ *From C$30.*

🛍 Shopping

Island Chocolates

CHOCOLATE | FAMILY | A family-run chocolate factory in a 19th-century store, Island Chocolates sells sweets handmade with Belgian chocolate, fresh fruit, nuts, and liqueurs. Espresso, teas, and decadent desserts are also available, and there is a nice deck to sit on while you munch. Willy Wonka wannabes will enjoy the chocolate-making workshops held on Wednesday. Sunday brunches feature chocolate waffles and fresh fruit, and special events include music, literary soirées, and Wine & Chocolate pairings. ⊠ 7 Main St., Victoria ☎ 902/658–2320 ⊕ www.islandchocolates.ca.

🏃 Activities

By-the-Sea Kayaking

KAYAKING | June through September, you can join kayaking tours, including sunrise, sunset, full-moon, and full-day tours, with the opportunity to do some clam digging on the beach. Kayaks, stand-up paddleboards, and bicycles are also available for rent, and picnic lunches can be provided. ⊠ Victoria Wharf, Victoria ☎ 902/658–2572, 877/879–2572 ⊕ www.bytheseakayaking.ca ☜ Tours from C$60, rentals from C$25.

Georgetown

52 km (32 miles) northeast of Charlottetown.

The pint-size capital of Kings County, at the tip of a peninsula jutting into Cardigan Bay, was a major shipbuilding center in the 19th century. Thanks to its location—and early settlers' vocation—the town has both wraparound sea views and a collection of charming, Victorian-era buildings. Georgetown is also a mere five minutes from Brudenell River Provincial Park (the county's largest such facility).

GETTING HERE AND AROUND

Georgetown is a drive-to destination. To get here from Charlottetown or the Wood Islands Ferry, follow the signs for the well-marked Points East Coastal Drive. Alternately, you can save time by cutting cross-country from Charlottetown on Route 3.

👁 Sights

Brudenell River Provincial Park

STATE/PROVINCIAL PARK | FAMILY | From late June to late August, the park promises interpretative programs, plus a wealth of outdoor opportunities—including boating, hiking, and horseback riding. There's also a heated swimming pool from July through early September. Two championship golf courses (Brudenell River and Dundarave) are the icing on its proverbial cake. ⊠ 283 Brudenell Island Blvd., Rte. 3, Georgetown ☎ 902/652–8966, 877/445–4938.

Roma at Three Rivers

HISTORIC SIGHT | FAMILY | This National Historic Site, about 2 km (1 mile) outside Georgetown, commemorates the trading post that French merchant Jean Pierre Roma established here in 1732. Costumed staffers offer interpretive programs and guided tours daily (there are trails with informational panels if you'd prefer to explore independently). Heritage lunches with sustaining soup and brick-oven-baked bread are also served on-site. ⊠ 505 Roma Point Rd., Brudenell Pt. ⊕ Off Rte. 319 ☎ 902/838–3413 ⊕ www.roma3rivers.com ☜ C$5 ⊘ Closed late Sept.–June.

🍴 Restaurants

Clam Diggers Beach House Restaurant

$$$ | SEAFOOD | FAMILY | It's worth making the 6 km (4-mile) drive from Georgetown to Cardigan to this restaurant in a lovely waterside location, where the big dining room has windows all around with great

views over the water. There's a patio too. **Known for:** long menu with lots of options; friendly and efficient service; wheelchair accessible. $ *Average main: C$23* ⊠ *6864 Water St., Cardigan* ☎ *902/583–3111* ⊕ *clamdiggerspei.com.*

Wheelhouse

$$$ | SEAFOOD | FAMILY | There's a lovely view from this waterfront spot, especially if you choose to sit out on the deck, and the food is attractively presented too, featuring plenty of the bounty from the ocean that you're looking at—one of the deepest harbors in North America. **Known for:** attentive service; wonderful waterside location; nice dessert options and specialty coffees. $ *Average main: C$28* ⊠ *7 West St., Georgetown* ☎ *902/652–2474* ⊕ *www.wheelhouseingeorgetown. com* ⊙ *No lunch Mon.–Thurs.*

🛏 Hotels

Rodd Brudenell River

$$ | RESORT | FAMILY | If you've come to eastern PEI to golf, this resort is *the* place to stay because the provincial park that shares its name is home to two 18-hole championship courses. **Pros:** kids stay free, eat free May–October; many rooms and all cottages have private decks; cottages have fireplaces and full kitchens. **Cons:** not all rooms have a river view; fine dining available July–September only; tired decor. $ *Rooms from: C$164* ⊠ *Brudenell River Provincial Park, 86 Dewars La., Georgetown* ☎ *902/652–2332, 800/565–7633* ⊕ *www. roddvacations.com* ⊙ *Closed Nov.–Apr.* ⤳ *99 rooms, 16 cottages.*

📷 Performing Arts

Kings Playhouse

CONCERTS | In summer months, the Kings Playhouse stages lighthearted comedies on Sunday and Wednesday evening. On Tuesday, the venue is turned over to fiddlers and dancers during the weekly

ceilidh, and other productions include dinner theater, comedy shows, and concerts. ⊠ *65 Grafton St., Georgetown* ☎ *902/652–2053, 888/346–5666* ⊕ *kingsplayhouse.com.*

🏃 Activities

GOLF

Brudenell River Golf Course

GOLF | One of the best in the country and arguably the most popular on the Island, the Brudenell course hosts professional matches and numerous Canadian Tour events. Broad fairways and manicured greens are dotted with lakes, ponds, and gardens, adding to the pleasure of playing a round here. Blind shots and doglegs present a good challenge. Four sets of tees vary the distances. ⊠ *Brudenell River Provincial Park, 82 Dewars La., Georgetown* ☎ *800/235–8909* ⊕ *peisfinestgolf.com/brudenell/* 🏌 *C$65–C$85, twilight C$55–C$65* 🏌. *18 holes, 6542 yards, par 72* ⊙ *Closed Oct.–late June (may vary).*

Dundarave Golf Course

GOLF | With its striking red-sandstone bunkers, set out in equally striking patterns, the Dundarave Golf Course is Brundenell River's beautiful younger sister. Its wide fairways are lined by pine trees and the Brudenell River winds through, making for a stunning landscape. Watch out for the thick rough, though, and be prepared for some challenging moments. ⊠ *Brudenell River Provincial Park, 82 Dewars La., Georgetown* ☎ *800/235–8909* ⊕ *www.golfpei.ca/course/dundarave* 🏌 *C$59–C$89, twilight C$49–C$69* 🏌. *18 holes, 7089 yards, par 72* ⊙ *Closed Oct.–late June (may vary).*

WATER SPORTS

Outside Expeditions

KAYAKING | FAMILY | Kayak rentals and kayak tours are offered here, in more sheltered waters than those at sea. The tours include everything from easy

90-minute paddles appropriate for any level of expertise to full-day trips to the mouth of the Brudenell River to view seals, including a picnic lunch. Rental bikes and stand-up paddleboards are also available. ⊠ *Brudenell River Provincial Park, 283 Brudenell Island Blvd., Rte. 3, Georgetown* ☎ *902/652–2434 Canada Day–Labor Day, 800/207–3899* ⊕ *getoutside.com* 🖃 *From C$55 for tours; from C$30 for kayak rentals* ⊗ *Closed early Sept.–June.*

Tranquility Cove Adventures

BOAT TOURS | FAMILY | One way to experience PEI like a native is to sign up for a half day of clam digging on an offshore island, complete with cooking up your finds. Another option is to set out for two hours of starfish hunting or deep-sea fishing. The experiences are both fun and informative. In winter, if you have your own snowmobile, a guided tour along the Confederation Trail is available. ⊠ *1 Kent St., Georgetown* ☎ *902/969–7184* ⊕ *www.tcapei.com* 🖃 *From C$45* ⊗ *Closed Oct.–mid-June.*

Souris

Souris is 46 km (29 miles) northeast of Georgetown.

A pretty town perched on the water, Souris (pronounced "Surrey") gives easy access to PEI's essential sights and sounds. The seascape includes harbors, lighthouses, and bountiful beaches with the famous "singing sands." There's music in the salt air, too, thanks to the seasonal ceilidhs and outdoor concerts Souris hosts, including performances at the town's theater and concert venue, the Souris Show Hall, and at the Centre Stage (formerly St. James United Church). You'll hear more five minutes away in Rollo Bay, which holds the PEI Bluegrass and Old Time Music Festival (*902/566–2641*) in early July and the

Rollo Bay Fiddle Festival during the third weekend (⊕ *rollobayfiddlefest.ca*).

GETTING HERE AND AROUND

The East Connection Shuttle (☎ *902/393–5132; 902/892–6760*), which operates from mid-June through mid-October, carries passengers from Charlottetown to Souris and other Kings County communities. The fare is C$75 one-way; advance reservations are required and a pickup location can be arranged anywhere around the Charlottetown area. You'll want your own vehicle, however, to properly see outlying areas. To drive here from Georgetown, follow signs for the Points East Coastal Drive or head out of town on Route 3, then go right on Route 321 to join Route 4 east, which merges with Route 2 at Dingwells Mills.

◉ Sights

Basin Head Fisheries Museum

OTHER MUSEUM | Overlooking the Northumberland Strait, this small museum depicts the ever-changing nature of PEI's inshore fishing industry through artifacts, exhibits, and dioramas. The museum also hosts events, including demonstrations, music, food sampling, and art exhibitions. ⊠ *336 Basin Head Rd., Souris* ☎ *902/368–6600 during off-season, 902/357–7233* ⊕ *www.peimuseum.ca* 🖃 *C$5* ⊗ *Closed Oct.–mid-June.*

Basin Head Provincial Park

BEACH | FAMILY | This park, 13 km (8 miles) east of Souris, is noted for an expanse of exquisite silvery sand that's backed by grassy dunes. The beach (accessible via a boardwalk and supervised in peak months) is well worth visiting, and not only because it's one of the Island's most beautiful. If you scuff your feet in the sand here, you can hear it squeak and squawk. The so-called singing sand is a rare phenomenon produced by the sand's high silica content. For visitors with mobility issues a floating wheelchair is available when conditions are safe. ✉ *336 Basin Head Rd., Souris* ✣ *Off Rte. 16* ☎ *902/357–7230, 877/445–4938* 🌐 *www.tourismpei.com/provincial-park/basin-head* 🎫 *Free.*

Myriad View Artisan Distillery
DISTILLERY | In Rollo Bay, just west of Souris, handcrafted spirits like vodka, gin, rum, whiskey, brandy, and pastis are produced; the brandy is made with grapes from their own vineyard, and the Physike's Garden Gin is infused with 20 herbs grown on the island. Tours (for up to 10 people at a time) and tastings are offered May through September. Tours are free, but any voluntary donations are passed on to the local hospital. Products can be purchased on-site or online. ✉ *1336 Rte. 2, Rollo Bay* ☎ *902/687–1281* 🌐 *www.straitshine.com* 🎫 *Free* ⏲ *Closed Oct.–Apr., weekends in May, and Sun. in Sept.*

🍴 Restaurants

★ Inn at Bay Fortune
$$$$ | **MODERN CANADIAN** | Celebrity chef Michael Smith's first ever career experience was working in the kitchen here, and now he's back as its owner. Many of the ingredients come from the inn's own organic farm, and when chef Michael has worked his magic it makes for a memorable experience. **Known for:** convivial open-air dining experience; one of the country's finest chefs; organic ingredients from the inn's onsite farm. [$] *Average main: C$175* ✉ *358 Rte. 310, Souris* ☎ *902/687–3745, 888/687–3745* 🌐 *innatbayfortune.com.*

21 Breakwater Restaurant
$$ | **INTERNATIONAL** | **FAMILY** | A welcome find in a town where dining options are thin, this eatery overlooking Colville Bay stays true to its rural roots yet presents a menu with some international charm. Try the mussels in lime butter or the herby fish-and-chips that are baked Portuguese-style. **Known for:** convenient to the ferry terminal; interesting takes on traditional favorites; nice waterfront views from the deck. [$] *Average main: C$20* ✉ *21 Breakwater St., Souris* ☎ *902/687–2556* 🌐 *www.21breakwater.com* ⏲ *Closed Sun.–Tues.*

🛏 Hotels

Inn at Spry Point
$$$ | **B&B/INN** | **FAMILY** | Hugging the end of a 110-acre peninsula a few kilometers east, this inn benefits from both an attractive shoreline and a 1-km (½-mile) sandy beach. **Pros:** breakfast is available until 10 am; ocean sounds lull you to sleep; comfy beds. **Cons:** the inn hosts a lot of weddings; TV only in shared lounge; relatively remote. [$] *Rooms from: C$199* ✉ *222 Ark La., Little Pond* ✣ *Off Spry Point Rd.* ☎ *902/583–2400* 🌐 *www.innatsprypoint.com* ⏲ *Closed early Oct.–mid-June* 🛏 *15 rooms* 🍽 *Free Breakfast.*

🏃 Activities

The Souris area is rich in birdlife, so much so that the town's website has a downloadable checklist that birders can consult and record their sightings. According to the list, Prince Edward Island birders have recorded 353 species, including migratory birds and there's further information at 🌐 *www.gov.pe.ca/birds* and 🌐 *www.parkscanada.gc.ca/pei.*

St. Peter's Bay

28 km (17 miles) northwest of Souris.

St. Peter's Bay won the location lottery—at least that's what folks who love quiet, outdoorsy destinations think. The nearby Greenwich portion of Prince Edward Island National Park has dunes that draw beachgoers, hikers, and bird-watchers (so many avian species flock here that the park runs themed programs). If you'd rather pursue a different kind of birdie, the Links at Crowbush Cove are a short drive west. St. Peter's Bay, meanwhile, provides a sublime backdrop for cycling. On the waterside leg of the Confederation Trail between the village and Morell, you pedal past idyllic coves dotted with boats and buoys an can cross the river on a 235-ft long bridge.

GETTING HERE AND AROUND

Driving independently is the best way to get here. From Souris continue along the Points East Coastal Drive or take a cross-country shortcut on Route 2. Alternately, the East Connection Shuttle (☎ 902/892–6760) will bring you here from Charlottetown for C$75 one-way.

◉ Sights

The Points East Coastal area is rich for lighthouse lovers. PEI has more than 50 of the navigational aids, but many of the highlights (literally) are right here. For further details, grab a copy of the themed brochure produced by the PEI Lighthouse Society (⊕ www.peilighthousesociety.ca).

East Point Lighthouse

LIGHTHOUSE | Ships from many nations have been wrecked on the reef running northeast from here, necessitating the installation of the East Point Lighthouse in 1867. Guided tours of the towering edifice are offered mid-June through Labor Day. Books about life at sea, as well as local crafts, are available at the on-site gift shop, and there's a café. Because of the erosion, caution should be used when approaching the high cliffs overlooking the ocean here. ⊠ 404 Lighthouse Rd., East Point ✛ Off Rte. 16 ☎ 902/357–2718 ⊕ www.eastpointlighthouse.ca ⊇ C$6.90.

★ Greenwich (P.E.I. National Park)

BEACH | FAMILY | The west end of the Greenwich Peninsula, known for its superior beach and shifting sand dunes, was federally protected in 1998 when a 6-km (3½-mile) section was incorporated into Prince Edward Island National Park. Because the dunes are still moving, gradually burying the nearby woods, here and there bleached tree bits thrust up through the sand like wooden skeletons. The road in ends at an interpretive center (open daily early June to mid-September) where displays, hands-on activities, and themed programs teach visitors about the ecology of this unique land formation. Walking trails let you follow the progression from forest to dune to beach, and include a photogenic boardwalk over Bowley Pond. ⊠ Greenwich Rd., off Rte. 313, Greenwich ✛ 10 km (6 miles) west of St. Peters Bay ☎ 902/672–6350 ⊕ www.pc.gc.ca ⊇ C$7.90 July and Aug.; C$3.90 other times.

Panmure Head Lighthouse

LIGHTHOUSE | FAMILY | Marking the entrance to Georgetown Harbour, it stands more than 60 feet tall. You can ascend to the top; then catch your breath browsing the on-site gift shop. ⊠ 62 Lighthouse Rd., Rte. 347, Panmure Island ☎ 902/969–9380 ⊇ C$6 ⊙ Closed mid-Oct.–mid-June.

Point Prim Lighthouse

LIGHTHOUSE | Erected in 1845, Point Prim is PEI's oldest lighthouse, a circular brick structure designed by the same architect (Isaac Smith) as Province House in Charlottetown. Knowledgeable guides will tell you the history of the lighthouse while you climb to the top. ⊠ 2147 Point Prim Rd., Rte. 209, 11 km (7½ miles) west of Belfast, Belfast ☎ 902/659–2768 ⊕ www.pointprimlighthouse.com ⊇ C$5 ⊙ Closed Oct.–mid-June and weekends in Sept.

Wood Islands Lighthouse Museum and Interpretive Centre

LIGHTHOUSE | This lighthouse by the ferry terminal contains exhibits on local history and marine lore—like the Burning Phantom Ship of Northumberland Strait and stories of the rumrunners—along

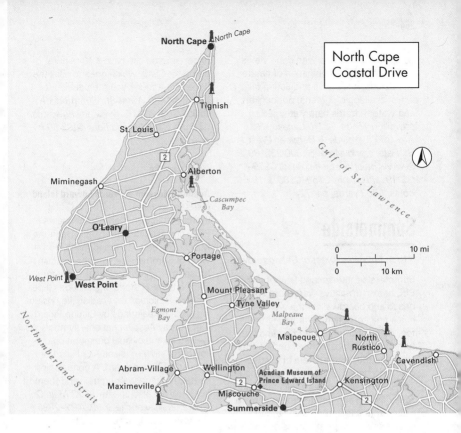

with period room settings, a craft shop showcasing island artisans, and an interpretive center. There is, of course, a great view from the top of the tower. ⊠ *173 Lighthouse Rd., Rte. 1, Wood Islands* ☎ *902/962–3110* ✎ *C$6* ⊗ *Closed Sun.*

🎭 Performing Arts

St. Peters Courthouse Theatre

THEATER | In summer, local musical acts perform and amateur actors mount plays several times a week at the St. Peters Courthouse Theatre. It's also the venue for the three-day Frank Ledwell Storytelling and Comedy Festival each July, and shows old-release movies. During certain days in summer, it hosts the "Escape of the Courtroom," a game in which intrepid participants have to solve various tasks to get out. Logically enough, the venue

is a restored courthouse that dates back to 1874. ⊠ *5697 St. Peters Rd., Rte. 2, St. Peters Bay* ☎ *902/961–3636* ⊕ *www. courthousetheatre.ca* ✎ *From C$15.*

🏃 Activities

Confederation Trail Bike Rentals

BIKING | FAMILY | This outfitter has cycles and accessories, including tag-along kid carriers. It's open daily late June through mid-September, and weekdays in mid-to-late June and mid-September to early October. ⊠ *15465 Northside Rd., St. Peters Bay* ✛ *Junction of Rte. 2 and Rte. 16* ☎ *902/367–7900* ✎ *From C$30 per hr* ⊗ *Closed mid-Oct.–mid-May.*

The Links at Crowbush Cove

GOLF | Designed by Thomas McBroom, the Links at Crowbush Cove is a

Scottish-style course with dune views. With a pleasing combination of nature and design, it features undulating fairways, challenging greens, pot bunkers, and water hazards hardly affected by prevailing winds. ✉ *710 Canavoy Rd., Rte. 350, Lakeside* ✛ *Between West St. Peter's and Morell* ☎ *800/235–8909* ⊕ *www.peisfinestgolf.com* ✉ *C$79–C$119; after 3 pm C$59–C$89* ⚲ *18 holes, 6903 yards, par 72.*

Summerside

71 km (44 miles) west of Charlottetown.

Summerside, the second-largest city on PEI, has an attractive waterfront with a beach and boardwalk in the west end. It has a fine collection of heritage homes, too, many of them erected around the turn of the 20th century when Summerside was the headquarters of a virtual gold rush based on silver-fox ranching (a small municipal museum tells that tale). Today fishing and potato processing are more profitable enterprises—though good fish-and-chips spots are curiously in short supply. Happily, lobster is plentiful in early July during the 10-day **Summerside Lobster Festival.**

GETTING HERE AND AROUND
Summerside can be accessed by car, bus, or shuttle. Maritime Bus can get you here from Charlottetown or from the mainland (Saint John or Moncton) via Confederation Bridge. Once here, you're best off exploring on foot. Biking is another option: the Confederation Trail passes through the city, and the former train station makes an excellent starting point for cycling excursions.

TOURS
PEI Segway Tours
GUIDED TOURS | These waterfront tours put a different spin on two-wheeling fun. One- and two-hour tours depart daily from the Scooter Depot. If you are uncertain, you can have a 10-minute demo for C$10, which goes toward the price of the tour if you then decide to take it. ✉ *433 Water St., Summerside* ☎ *902/303–7049* ⊕ *www.peisegway.com* ✉ *From C$68 for one hour, $102.50 for two hours.*

◉ Sights

Acadian Museum of Prince Edward Island
(*Musée Acadien*)
HISTORY MUSEUM | Many descendants of PEI's first French settlers still live in the Miscouche area, 10 km (6 miles) northwest of Summerside, and the Acadian Museum commemorates their history. This National Historic Site includes a permanent exhibition on Acadian life, including six large paintings by Claude Picard that portray Acadian national symbols, as well as an audiovisual presentation outlining the story of Island Acadians from the early 1700s onward. A genealogical center, heritage walking trail, and themed gift shop are also on-site. ✉ *23 Main Dr. E, Rte. 2, Miscouche* ☎ *902/432–2880* ⊕ *www.museeacadien.org* ✉ *C$5.50* ⊙ *Closed Sat. in Sept.–June.*

Eptek Art and Culture Centre
ART GALLERY | On the waterfront, this center has rotating exhibits of PEI history and fine arts on display in the main gallery: the variety of the exhibitions is one of the center's hallmarks. It also hosts art and craft demonstrations in July and August and lunchtime films on winter Thursdays. ✉ *130 Heather Moyse Dr., Summerside* ☎ *902/888–8373* ⊕ *www.peimuseum.com* ✉ *$3 suggested donation.*

International Fox Museum and Armoury
OTHER MUSEUM | Housed in a 1911 armory used by local militia until 1992, the museum recounts the days when fox fur was the height of fashion and fox "farming" was a thriving Summerside industry, and also charts its eventual decline. The

heritage building also has a seasonal art gallery upstairs. ✉ *33 Summer St., Summerside* ☎ *902/432–1332, 902/432–1298* 🌐 *culturesummerside.com/international-fox-museum/* 🎟 *By donation* 🕒 *Closed Sun. and Oct.–late June.*

Spinnakers' Landing
PROMENADE | The cornerstone of Summerside's waterfront revitalization project is this collection of cheery little structures that are linked by a boardwalk and designed to evoke a seaside fishing village. The development offers a good blend of craft, clothing, and souvenir shopping, history, and entertainment; plus you can climb a lighthouse lookout for panoramic views of Bedeque Bay and the city. In summer, weather permitting, there's often free weekend entertainment (usually starting at 6 pm, earlier on Canada Day) on the outdoor stage over the water. ✉ *150 Heather Moyse Dr., Summerside* ☎ *902/432–6531* 🌐 *www.spinnakerslanding.com* 🕒 *Shops closed Oct.–May.*

★ **Wyatt Historic House Museum**
HISTORIC HOME | Built in 1867 (the year Canada was "born"), the restored, heirloom-filled home of a prominent local family feels like a Summerside time capsule. Guided interpretive tours last about 50 minutes. There are concerts in the garden on Wednesdays, and this is also a venue during the Summerside Lobster Carnival and Summerside Arts Festival. The entry fee also admits you to another of the Wyatt Heritage Properties: the Lefurgey Cultural Centre at 205 Prince Street. ✉ *85 Spring St., Summerside* ☎ *902/432–1332* 🌐 *www.culturesummerside.com/wyatt-historic-house-museum* 🎟 *C$10* 🕒 *Closed Sun., Mon. and Oct.–late June.*

🍴 Restaurants

The Deckhouse Pub & Eatery
$$ | CANADIAN | FAMILY | Generous portions of traditional pub grub are supplemented here by a range of tasty seafood dishes. Its location at Spinnakers' Landing means that water views are an added bonus, and there are a few tables on an upper-level deck. **Known for:** great deck, but it can get too breezy; excellent seafood chowder; family-friendly atmosphere. [$] *Average main: C$15* ✉ *150 Heather Moyse Dr., Summerside* ☎ *902/436–0660* 🌐 *www.facebook.com/deckhousepub* 🕒 *Closed early Sept.–mid-June.*

☕ Coffee and Quick Bites

Holman's Ice Cream Parlour
$ | CANADIAN | FAMILY | In this historic house-turned-ice-cream-parlor, delicious gourmet ice cream is made from scratch, using fresh natural ingredients. They offer all the classic flavors and more—and even the crisp, light waffle cones are handmade on-site. **Known for:** outside garden to enjoy your ice cream; the five-flavor sampler, for those who can't decide; soda floats. [$] *Average main: C$6* ✉ *286 Fitzroy St., Summerside* ☎ *902/436–5675* 🌐 *www.holmansicecream.com* 🕒 *Closed Sun.*

Samuel's Coffeehouse
$ | CAFÉ | Everything is made in-house at this artsy converted space inside a handsome 1895 building, with locally sourced and organic ingredients creating the tasty house-made soups, sandwiches, and panini. Tempting sweet treats and baked goods are also available. **Known for:** pleasant and efficient service; interesting sandwich fillings; extensive range of teas and coffee blends. [$] *Average main: C$11* ✉ *4 Queen St., Summerside* ☎ *902/724–2300* 🌐 *samuelscoffeehouse.ca.*

Hotels

Clark's Sunny Isle Motel

$ | **HOTEL** | PEI may be one of the last places in Canada where motels are plentiful and worth recommending, and Clark's Sunny Isle is a case in point, because it has managed to stay in business for more than 50 years by providing affordable, whistle-clean rooms and unwaveringly pleasant service. **Pros:** safe storage for bicycles; beautifully kept grounds; each room has a mini-refrigerator. **Cons:** closed from early December to late April; not in walking distance of downtown area; free continental breakfast served May–October only. [$] *Rooms from: C$75* ✉ *720 Water St. E, Summerside* ☎ *902/436–5665, 877/682–6824 reservations only* 🌐 *www.sunnyislemotel.com* 🕒 *Closed Dec.–late Apr.* 🛏 *21 rooms* 🍴 *Free Breakfast.*

Hub 223 Micro Suites

$$ | **APARTMENT** | If you want a downtown location, a modern vibe, and total privacy, these self-contained mini-apartments will likely fit the bill. **Pros:** OpenEats restaurant is right next door; free parking; freedom to rise and shine at your own pace. **Cons:** minimum two-night stay; not very cozy; no staff on the premises outside check-in hours. [$] *Rooms from: C$155* ✉ *223 Water St., Summerside* ☎ *902/724–7755* 🌐 *www.hub223.com* 🕒 *Closed early Oct.–early June* 🛏 *24 apartments* 🍴 *No Meals.*

★ **Summerside Inn Bed and Breakfast**

$ | **B&B/INN** | **FAMILY** | Located on one of Summerside's leafy historic streets, this beautifully converted old house, former home of two island premiers, offers superior accommodations, wonderful breakfasts, and a delightfully friendly and unstuffy atmosphere. **Pros:** parking available; interesting decor; charming owner is a great breakfast cook. **Cons:** no pets allowed; kids need to be watched near fine china on display; it's a bit of a walk to Water Street. [$] *Rooms from: C$120* ✉ *98 Summer St., Summerside* ☎ *905/467–1265, 905/278–2787* 🌐 *summersideinnbandb.com* 🛏 *4 rooms* 🍴 *Free Breakfast.*

Performing Arts

College of Piping and Celtic Performing Arts of Canada

CONCERTS | An energetic revue—featuring more than 30 bagpipers, Highland dancers, step dancers, and fiddlers—is hosted in the 290-seat theater here several nights a week, along with a few matinees, in July and August. During the same months, miniconcerts also run five times daily weekdays, and the C$7 tab can be credited toward the price of evening show tickets. Other events include piping contests and a Robbie Burns Dinner on the Scottish bard's birthday in January. ✉ *619 Water St. E, Summerside* ☎ *902/436–5377, 877/224–7473* 🌐 *www.collegeofpiping.com* 🎟 *From C$25.*

Feast Dinner Theatre

THEATER | **FAMILY** | For more than 40 years, this company has served up musical comedy with a buffet meal Tuesday through Saturday. ✉ *Brothers 2 Restaurant, 618 Water St., Summerside* ☎ *902/436–7674* 🌐 *www.brothers2.ca* 🎟 *From C$63* 🕒 *Closed Sept.–mid-June.*

Harbourfront Theatre

CONCERTS | Sharing space with the Eptek Art and Culture Centre (but accessed through a different entrance), this 527-seat theater stages dramatic and musical productions year-round. Touring musicians and comedians routinely drop by, too. ✉ *124 Heather Moyse Dr., Summerside* ☎ *902/888–2500, 800/708–6505* 🌐 *www.harbourfronttheatre.com* 🎟 *From C$25.*

Club Hopping—Island Style

Great golf clubs are par for the course on PEI, where green gables and green fields are complemented by challenging golf greens. There are more than 30 courses, both 9- and 18-hole, open to the public from May through October, with top choices including—from west to east—Mill River, Andersons Creek, Eagles Glenn, Green Gables, Glasgow Hills, Stanhope, Fox Meadow, Links at Crowbush Cove, Brudenell River, and Dundarave. All are within a 45-minute drive of one another, which means ambitious golfers can play 27 or 36 holes a day. Contact Golf PEI (☎ 866/465–3734 ⊕ www.golfpei. ca) for details on courses, events, and play-and-stay packages, or to book tee times.

🏃 Activities

The Paddle Shack
BIKING | FAMILY | Bikes, including big-wheeled beach bikes, can be rented here, and organized bike tours are also offered. They also rent out single and double kayaks, single and family-size paddleboards, kite-surfing boards, and electric one-wheels, with courses run by professional instructors. There are paddleboard yoga sessions and tours too. ⊠ 368 Water St., Summerside ☎ 902/388–7873 ⊕ www.suppei.ca ⌑ Rentals from C$20, tours C$100.

O'Leary

37 km (23 miles) northwest of Summerside.

Central Prince County is composed of a loose network of small communities set amid green fields. In the tradition of their forebears, most residents are farmers, and those in O'Leary are no exception. In terms of preferred crops, the potato is big here—literally. A giant fiberglass one that looms outside the PEI Potato Museum is the town's distinguishing feature. After eating potatoes prepared every possible way, you can work off the calories in nearby Mill River Provincial Park with golfing and other outdoor activities.

GETTING HERE AND AROUND
You'll need a car to explore O'Leary and the surrounding area. To get here from Summerside, follow Route 2 west; then transfer onto Route 142.

👁 Sights

Canadian Potato Museum
FARM/RANCH | The potato is one terrific tuber: that's the message delivered by this museum. Earnest and intriguing, it has exhibits devoted to the "Amazing Potato," displays of antique potato-farming equipment, a Potato Hall of Fame, even a gift shop selling potato-themed goods. The museum also runs fun add-on tours, which include a guided spin through the facility, plus a trip out to a potato farm, a potato fudge-making lesson, and a lunch of (you guessed it) potato-based dishes. ⊠ 1 Dewar La., O'Leary ☎ 902/859–2039 mid-May–early Oct., 844/849–1470 tour bookings, 902/853–2312 early Oct.–mid-May ⊕ www.peipotatomuseum.com ⌑ C$10; farm tours C$79 or C$65 each for three or more adults 🕑 Closed Sat., Sun., and early Oct.–mid-May.

Hotels

Mill River Resort
$$ | RESORT | FAMILY | Since full-blown resorts are so rare in this portion of the province, Mill River Resort provides a welcome change of pace. **Pros:** beautiful location; good base for exploring western PEI; golf packages are frequently available. **Cons:** relatively long drive from city shopping and entertainment; rooms near golf course may suffer from morning noise; steps along upper level corridor impede luggage carts. [$] *Rooms from: C$155* ✉ *180 Mill River Resort Rd., Woodstock* ✥ *Off Rte. 136, 5 km (3 miles) east of O'Leary* ☎ *902/859–3555, 800/565–7633* 🌐 *www.roddvacations.com* 🛏 *90 rooms* 🍴 *Free Breakfast.*

Shopping

MacAusland's Woollen Mills
OTHER SPECIALTY STORE | The mills, 5 km (3 miles) west of O'Leary, have been producing their famous MacAusland 100% pure virgin wool blankets since 1932 and are the only mills of their kind in Atlantic Canada. ✉ *38317 Hwy. 2, Bloomfield* ☎ *902/859–3005* 🌐 *www.macauslandswoollenmills.com.*

Activities

Mill River Golf Course
GOLF | This is among the most scenic and challenging courses in Eastern Canada, with mature woodland, many lakes and streams, well-placed bunkers, and doglegs that call for accurate shots. It has been the site of several championship tournaments, and a season of the golf reality show *The Big Break* was filmed here. Book in advance. ✉ *Mill River Provincial Park, 180 Mill River Resort Rd., Woodstock* ✥ *Off Rte. 2* ☎ *902/859–3555, 844/375–3555* 🌐 *millriver.ca/golf* 🎟 *C$40–C$80* ⛳ *18 holes, 6,840 yards, par 72* ⏲ *Closed late Oct.–early May.*

West Point

24 km (15 miles) south of O'Leary.

West Point, on the southern tip of the western shore, may be tiny (there are only about 700 residents), but it is home to PEI's tallest functioning lighthouse. After admiring the handsome structure, you can stroll the 4,921-foot beachfront boardwalk; then cool off with a swim at Cedar Dunes Provincial Park.

GETTING HERE AND AROUND

Easily accessible by car from O'Leary via Route 14, West Point is usually viewed as a day trip. The presence of the West Point Lighthouse Inn, however, gives lighthouse-loving motorists an incentive to stay overnight.

Sights

★ **West Point Lighthouse Museum**
OTHER MUSEUM | FAMILY | Built in 1875, lit in 1876, manned until 1963, and still operating today, the West Point Lighthouse is a certifiable PEI icon. A gracefully tapered shape and eye-popping black-and-white stripes make the 69-foot structure very photogenic. Inside, displays and assorted artifacts relating to lighthouses provincewide make it educational, too. Be sure to climb the 72 steps to the top for panoramic views. Beautiful any time of day, they are especially glorious at sunset because the lighthouse faces west. ✉ *364 Cedar Dunes Park Rd., Rte. 14, West Point* ☎ *902/859–3605* 🌐 *www.westpointlighthouse.com* 🎟 *C$5* ⏲ *Closed Oct.–mid-June.*

Hotels

West Point Lighthouse Inn
$$$ | B&B/INN | Few people can say they've spent the night in a lighthouse—or at least in a guest room adjacent to one—so take the opportunity when

you're here. **Pros:** some pets allowed; unique lodgings; original rooms full of character. **Cons:** lighthouse equals bright flashing light; books up quickly; dearth of area dining options. [$] *Rooms from: C$189* ✉ *364 Cedar Dunes Park Rd., Rte. 14, West Point* ☎ *902/859–3605, 800/764–6854* 🌐 *www.westpointlighthouse.com* ⏲ *Closed mid-Oct.–mid-June* 🛏 *13 rooms* 🍴 *Free Breakfast.*

Activities

Cedar Dunes Provincial Park
STATE/PROVINCIAL PARK | FAMILY | Encompassing the lighthouse site, this park boasts blissful beaches and supervised swimming (late June to early September), plus children's activities in summer. Recreational programs—including guided walks of the park's nature trails—are also available seasonally. ✉ *265 Cedar Dunes Park Rd., Rte. 14, West Point* ☎ *902/859–8785* 🎟 *Free* ⏲ *Closed Oct.–June.*

North Cape

47 km (29 miles) north of O'Leary.

Mother Nature meets modern technology at PEI's northwest tip. The Gulf of St. Lawrence and Northumberland Strait converge at North Cape's reef (the longest rock reef in North America) creating a popular hangout for seals, seabirds, and other forms of marine life. But it's the wind sweeping over the water and the meeting of the waves tumbling from opposite directions that makes this place really stand out. Scores of windmills—some of them 262 feet high—dot the site. Part of the Atlantic Wind Test Site and Wind Farm, they were built to make the "Gentle Island" even greener. Trails wind around and across the headland, including a path to a point where it's possible to stand right beneath one of the turbines.

GETTING HERE AND AROUND

North Cape is another drive-to destination. To reach it, take Route 14 along the strait or Route 12 along the gulf.

Sights

North Cape Wind Energy Interpretive Centre
FACTORY | FAMILY | Exhibits here explain how turbine technology channels wind power to produce "clean" electricity for Islanders. It also includes hands-on displays pertaining to wind energy, local history (including the story of the infamous "ghost ship"), and a touch tank with lobster, crabs, and starfish that kids will enjoy. (A staff member will lift one out so you can get a real feel for these aquatic creatures.) ✉ *21817 Rte. 12, North Cape* ☎ *902/882–2991* 🌐 *www.northcape.ca* 🎟 *C$6* ⏲ *Closed early Oct.–mid-May.*

Restaurants

Wind & Reef Restaurant
$$$ | SEAFOOD | Dining options are few and far between in this remote corner of PEI, so it's a blessing that the airy eatery above the North Cape Wind Energy Interpretative Centre offers more than mere sustenance. The Island seafood—including oysters, mussels, and lobster—is fresh and well prepared. **Known for:** reservations usually needed; incredible views; good mussels. [$] *Average main: C$30* ✉ *21817 Rte. 12, North Cape* ☎ *902/882–3535* 🌐 *www.northcape.ca/wind-and-reef-restaurant.*

Hotels

La Petite France B&B
$ | B&B/INN | Built in the 1890s, this heritage home with its plentiful gables and pretty bay windows has a classic Island look with a lovely French theme inside. **Pros:** free Wi-Fi; attentive hosts; near a popular biking trailhead. **Cons:** traditional

bedding rather than duvets; the largest room is in a newer addition; two rooms share a bathroom. [$] *Rooms from: C$70* ✉ *441 Church St., Alberton* ☎ *902/853–3975* 🌐 *www.lapetitefrance-pei.com* 🕓 *Closed Nov.–Apr.* 🛏 *4 rooms* 🍴 *Free Breakfast.*

Northport Pier Inn

$$$ | B&B/INN | FAMILY | Conveniences like air-conditioning and Wi-Fi set this spot a notch above many rural inns, but it's the view that guests really rave about. **Pros:** wheelchair-accessible rooms; restaurant and marina next door; roomy kitchenette suites work well for families. **Cons:** not within walking distance of local shopping in Alberton; early morning harbor traffic in May and June; interior style is basic. [$] *Rooms from: C$189* ✉ *298 Rte. 152, Northport* ✣ *33 km (21 miles) south of North Cape* ☎ *902/853–4900, 855/844–243–1553* 🌐 *northportpier.ca* 🕓 *Closed Oct.–May* 🛏 *14 rooms* 🍴 *Free Breakfast.*

Activities

Black Marsh Nature Trail

HIKING & WALKING | FAMILY | One of the best ways to see North Cape's natural and man-made assets is by hiking this out-and-back trail. The 5½-km (3½-mile) walk passes tidal pools, whirring windmills, and the cape's 1908 lighthouse, taking in a pretty bog crossed via a boardwalk; there are 25 interpretive panels along the way. ✉ *21817 Rte. 12, North Cape.*

Jacques Cartier Provincial Park

HIKING & WALKING | FAMILY | South of North Cape, this park was named for the famed French explorer who came ashore nearby in 1534, an event that's celebrated each July. In July and August, you can take naturalist-led hikes on park trails or swim on the supervised (from late June through August) Gulf of St. Lawrence beach. ✉ *16448 Rte. 12, Kildare Capes* ☎ *902/853–8632* 🎟 *Free.*

Chapter 6

NEWFOUNDLAND

Updated by
Lynette Adams

◉ Sights	🍴 Restaurants	🛏 Hotels	🛍 Shopping	🍸 Nightlife
★★★★★	★★☆☆☆	★★☆☆☆	★☆☆☆☆	★☆☆☆☆

WELCOME TO NEWFOUNDLAND

TOP REASONS TO GO

★ **UNESCO World Heritage sites.** The mountains of Gros Morne National Park offer hiking and sweeping vistas. L'Anse aux Meadows National Historic Site boasts the only authenticated Viking settlement in North America. The Bonavista Peninsula is home to the geologically significant Discovery Geopark, while Mistaken Point showcases preserved fossils of earth's first large-bodied, multicellular organisms displayed on rock cliffs above a crashing deep blue sea.

★ **Wildlife.** Watch pods of humpbacks dive and breach alongside your boat tour, and see puffins, caribou, moose, and more in bird sanctuaries and ecological reserves.

★ **Icebergs.** Newfoundland is one of the easiest places to see these 10,000-year-old beauties of the ocean. See them from St. Anthony to St. John's.

★ **The arts.** From traditional accordion concerts to art-house cinema and award-winning plays, the local and touring talent should not be missed.

1 St. John's.

2 **Witless Bay Ecological Reserve.**

3 **Ferryland.**

4 **Salmonier Nature Park.**

5 **Brigus and Cupids.**

6 **Harbour Grace.**

7 **Placentia.**

8 **Cape St. Mary's Ecological Reserve.**

9 **Clarenville.**

10 **Terra Nova National Park.**

11 **Trinity.**

12 **Bonavista.**

13 **Grand Bank.**

14 **St-Pierre and Miquelon.**

15 **Gander.**

16 **Fogo and Change Islands.**

17 **Boyd's Cove.**

18 **Twillingate.**

19 **Deer Lake.**

20 **Gros Morne National Park.**

21 **L'Anse aux Meadows National Historic Site.**

22 **St. Anthony.**

23 **Corner Brook.**

24 **Stephenville.**

25 **Port aux Basques.**

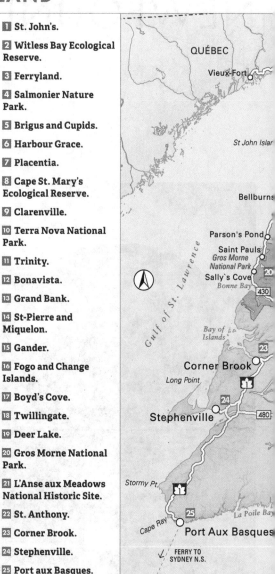

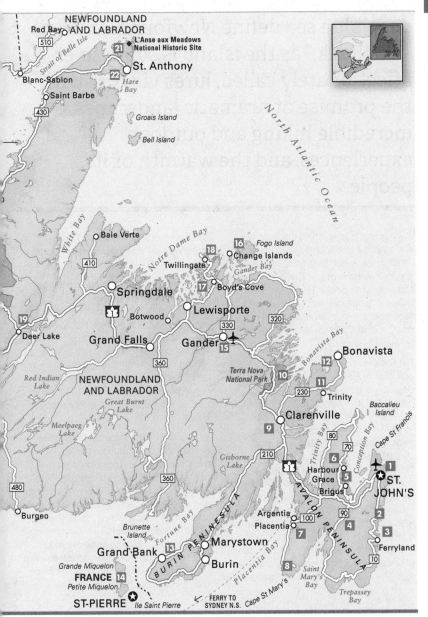

Magnificent mountains, sweeping vistas, colorful wooden houses perched on rocky sea cliffs, hidden fjords, and the deep blue sea define Newfoundland. "The Rock," as the island is sometimes affectionately called, lures visitors with the promise of dramatic landscapes, incredible hiking and outdoor experiences, and the warmth of its people.

Canada starts here, from the east, on the island of Newfoundland in the North Atlantic. Labrador, to the northwest, is on the mainland bordering Québec. Along the province's nearly 17,699 km (11,000 miles) of coastline, humpback whales feed near shore, millions of sea birds nest, and 10,000-year-old icebergs drift by fishing villages.

Off the east coast of Canada, the province of Newfoundland and Labrador, as it is officially called, is a bit of a contradiction in terms: it's the youngest province—it joined the Confederation in 1949—but its European timeline stretches back to AD 1000, when Vikings made first landfall on the Great Northern Peninsula. They assembled a sod-hut village at what is now L'Anse aux Meadows National Historic Site, calling their new home Vinland. They stayed less than 10 years and then disappeared into the mists of history. Preceding the Vikings were the Maritime Archaic people who lived in that region as long ago as 6,000 years. In southern Labrador, an 8,500-year-old burial site at L'Anse Amour is the oldest-known cemetery in North America.

When explorer John Cabot arrived at Bonavista from England in 1497, he reported an ocean so full of fish they could be caught in a basket lowered over the side of a boat. Within three decades, the harbor in St. John's would receive fishing vessels from Normandy, Brittany, and Portugal. Soon, European fishing boats vied for Newfoundland's lucrative cod, which would shape the province's history up to the present day.

At one time, 700 outports dotted Newfoundland's coast, devoted to the world's most plentiful fish. Today, only about 400 of these settlements survive. By 1992, cod had become scarce from overfishing and the federal government called a moratorium on fishing, throwing thousands of citizens out of work. The moratorium is still in place, forcing generations of people to retrain for other industries or to leave, and the fishing industry has since diversified into other species, mainly shrimp and crab. Mining in Labrador, thanks to the development of one of the world's richest and largest nickel deposits at Voisey's Bay, now makes up a substantial portion of the economy, along with tourism and the offshore oil and gas industry.

Despite Newfoundland and Labrador's more than 70 years as a Canadian province, its people remain resolutely independent and maintain a unique language and lifestyle. E. Annie Proulx's Pulitzer Prize–winning novel *The Shipping News* (1993) brought the province to the world's attention, and Newfoundland writers such as Wayne Johnston (*The Colony of Unrequited Dreams, The Navigator of New York*), Michael Crummey (*River Thieves* and *Galore*), and Lisa Moore (*February* and *Caught*) continue to introduce international audiences to the province.

Visitors to Newfoundland find themselves straddling the centuries. Old Irish, French, and English accents and customs still exist in small towns and outports despite television and the Internet, but the cities of St. John's in the east and Corner Brook to the west are very much part of the 21st century. Wherever you travel in the province, you're sure to meet some of the warmest, wittiest people in North America. No matter how remote the spot, no one is ever bored in Newfoundland.

Planning

When to Go

Seasons vary dramatically in Newfoundland and Labrador. Most tourists visit between June and September, when the bogs and meadows turn into a colorful riot of wildflowers and greenery and the province is alive with festivals, fairs, and concerts. Daytime temperatures may hover between 18°C (64°F) and 25°C (77°F) in July and August. June can be quite cold and foggy, what is known locally as "capelin weather," as these small fish come ashore in droves. In spring, icebergs float down from the north, and in late spring, whales arrive to hunt for food along the coast, staying until August. Fall is also popular: the weather is usually fine, hills and meadows are loaded with berries, and the woods are alive with moose, caribou, partridge, and rabbits. In winter, ski hills attract downhillers and snowboarders, forest trails hum with snowmobiles, and cross-country ski trails in various communities and provincial and national parks are oases of quiet.

This rocky island perched on the edge of the cold North Atlantic Ocean might be the only place in the world where you can have four seasons blow through in one day and where the saying "If you don't like the weather out your front door, go look out the back door" rings true. St. John's is a weather champion in Canada. It holds the distinctions of being the foggiest, snowiest, wettest, windiest, and cloudiest of all major Canadian cities.

When packing for the trip, remember it's all about layers in Newfoundland. You'll need aspirational shorts and short-sleeve shirts in case it's warm and sunny. Pack a fleece jacket or a hoodie for when the temperature drops. A windbreaker might be the most important piece of clothing; you'll need it to keep the chill out when the winds are up. To top off your ensemble, you'll need rain gear, like a slicker. You may want a scarf, hat, and gloves too, but local craftspeople make beautiful pieces for you to purchase. May the sun shine on your holidays, but when it doesn't, you'll be dressed for it.

Planning Your Time

Many visitors to Newfoundland and Labrador arrive in St. John's, the provincial capital, and a great place to get a sense of the region's history. Spend a few days touring downtown, including Water Street, the oldest street in North America, or hike part of the East Coast Trail right from town. A half-hour's drive south of St. John's, you can see whales, icebergs, and huge seabird colonies in Witless Bay. Continue driving down Route 10 (known as the "Irish Loop") to Mistaken Point, a UNESCO World Heritage Site, to see some of the oldest fossils on the planet. The next day, extend your loop and take a side trip to Cape St. Mary's, one of the best places in the world to see gannets up close—you can even walk within 10 yards of their nests.

Travelers with more time often drive across the island. Twillingate, 444 km (276 miles) from St. John's (a five-hour journey), is an especially scenic destination, and Fogo Island is gaining acclaim for its unique artists' studios, artist-in-residence programs, and the architecturally groundbreaking Fogo Island Inn. The ferry to Fogo Island takes about an hour each way. You could enjoy a marvelous three-day interlude touring the Bonavista Peninsula in eastern Newfoundland with its visually stunning coastline and settlements such as picturesque Trinity.

Allow at least three days to appreciate western Newfoundland's dramatic mountains and rugged shoreline. One fly-and-drive option is through Deer Lake Regional Airport. An alternative would be to take the car ferry from Nova Scotia, which arrives in Port aux Basques on the southern coast of Newfoundland. Corner Brook, this region's main city, makes a fine base for exploring the picturesque Bay of Islands. You won't want to miss the glacier-carved fjords and magnificent

Time Zones ◉

Newfoundland has its own time zone (Newfoundland Standard Time is UTC-3:30), a half hour ahead of the rest of Labrador and the other Atlantic provinces. When time zones were established, the Dominion of Newfoundland was an independent country with its own time zone. The government tried to make the province conform to Atlantic Time in 1963, 14 years after it became part of Canada. The measure was quashed by public outcry, so Newfoundlanders remain the first people in Canada to welcome the new year.

mountains at Gros Morne National Park, a UNESCO World Heritage Site. Take a boat tour, go hiking or sea kayaking, and visit an interpretation center to learn more about what you've seen. Many people spend at least a couple of days here—if you're a hiker, you could easily spend a week exploring the multitude of trails. Farther up the peninsula, at L'Anse aux Meadows National Historic Park, another UNESCO World Heritage Site, you can visit the only authenticated Viking settlement in North America.

Getting Here and Around

AIR
The province's main airport is St. John's International Airport on the east coast of the island, and there is also a much smaller international airport in Gander. Domestic airports are at Stephenville, Deer Lake, and St. Anthony on the island, and at Goose Bay and Wabush in Labrador.

■TIP→ **If you plan to fly in and rent a car, book as far in advance as possible; rental vehicles are in limited supply, and in peak season they go quickly.**

BOAT AND FERRY

Marine Atlantic operates a car ferry from North Sydney, Nova Scotia, to Port aux Basques, Newfoundland (crossing time is about 7 hours) year-round, and from North Sydney to Argentia (crossing time is about 16 hours) June to September.

CONTACTS Marine Atlantic. ☎ *902/794–5254, 800/341–7981* ⊕ *www.marineatlantic.ca.*

CAR

Newfoundland has a decent highway system, and most secondary roads are paved, but some are winding. Most roads, including the highways and main roads into St. John's, suffer seasonal damage and potholes from the frequent freeze-thaw cycles through the winter, which will require you to moderate your speed. Bear this in mind when deciding how far to travel in a day. Also remember that summer is road-mending season, and speed limits are reduced to 50 kph (31 mph) in construction areas. Allowing time for breaks, it takes about 11 hours to drive along the Trans-Canada Highway (Route 1) from Port aux Basques to St. John's. The trip from Corner Brook to St. Anthony, at the northernmost tip of the island, takes about five-and-a-half hours. Driving from St. John's to Grand Bank, on the Burin Peninsula, takes about four hours. If you're heading for the southern coast of the Avalon Peninsula, pick up Route 10 (the "Irish Loop") just south of St. John's and follow it toward Trepassey.

■TIP→ **More than 110,000 moose live in Newfoundland, and most highways run through their habitats. If possible, avoid night driving, as most moose-related vehicle accidents (about 600 a year) happen between dusk and dawn. Watch for vehicles that slow down or stop on the side of the road; the driver may have spotted a moose. Pay attention to the caution signs indicating where moose cross frequently.**

In winter, some highways close during and after severe snowstorms. Year-round, the Department of Transportation's website has up-to-date information on road conditions and closures. The website of the province's tourism board has a handy Road Trips page (⊕ *www.newfoundlandlabrador.com/trip-ideas/road-trips*) listing itineraries—categorized by region and then by areas of interest—all over Newfoundland.

CONTACTS Department of Transportation & Works. ⊕ *www.roads.gov.nl.ca.*

CRUISE SHIP

Today's cruise passengers join the flow of centuries of seafarers who have docked in St. John's, the most easterly port in North America. Each cruise ship to arrive in the downtown harbor is greeted by flag-waving, cannon fire (friendly, of course) by "soldiers" in 19th-century uniform, and onshore ceremonies accompanied by a fife band, mounted police, and both Newfoundland and Labrador dogs. Passengers disembark within walking distance of the main shopping streets and city sights, though it's an uphill climb to some of them. The visitor information center is just a short, level walk along Water Street. (Some ships have on-board information kiosks, and right at the dock local volunteer "ambassadors" are on hand to answer questions and offer advice.)

Public buses cost C$2.50 to ride, C$22.50 for a 10-ride pass. Taxis are metered, and rates start at C$3.75. Some taxi companies offer city tours that generally cost about C$50/hour for up to four passengers. Bus tours, including some tailored to cruise-ship passengers' interests and schedule, start at C$64 for three hours.

Outdoor Activities

Fishing the unpolluted waters of Newfoundland is an angler's dream, and many outfitters are available to make the dream come true. The website of the Newfoundland & Labrador Outfitters Association contains a list of members, with contact details and online links.

Many provincial parks and both national parks have hiking and nature trails. Coastal and forest trails radiate out from most small communities. The East Coast Trail, on the Avalon Peninsula, covers 336 km (208 miles) of coastline and is a beautifully maintained international destination for hikers. The system passes through dozens of communities and along cliff tops that provide ideal lookouts for icebergs, whales, and seabirds. The East Coast Trail Association has a detailed website. On the west coast of the island, Gros Morne Adventures runs guided day and multiday hikes in Gros Morne National Park.

★ East Coast Trail Association

TRAIL | FAMILY | This organization is a helpful resource for those who like to hike in groups or on their own. Volunteers lead free scheduled day hikes along all sections of the breathtaking East Coast Trail. If you would rather hike without a guide, you can purchase their printed trail maps, which are detailed, easy to navigate, and list interesting information about each leg to make sure you know "what to look for" so you get the most out of a hike even if you are new to the area. Their website lists, and links to, community resources for food, supplies, overnight camping, or other accommodations for any extended hiking trips. ☎ 709/738–4453 ⊕ www.eastcoasttrail.com.

CONTACTS Gros Morne Adventures. ☎ 709/458-2722, 800/685-4624 ⊕ grosmorneadventures.com. **Newfoundland & Labrador Outfitters Association.** ☎ 709/639–5926, 866/470–6562 ⊕ www.nloa.ca.

Restaurants

A decade ago, eating out in Newfoundland was all about cod. Today, Newfoundland cuisine fuses tradition and serious talent with a fierce locavore movement focused on taking full advantage of the diverse bounty of ocean, bluff, bog, and pasture. In St. John's, the culinary scene is a bounty and a treat. Towns outside the capital city may lack its concentration of excellent dining options. But talented chefs live and work beyond St. John's, and many of them are committed to using fresh, local, and organic ingredients. Some unique dining experiences unfold well off the main roads. For example Lightkeepers Seafood Restaurant in St. Anthony stages a Great Viking Feast inside a sod hut, where diners tuck into moose stew. If you must grab something from a basic roadside stop, turkey club sandwiches are the safe bet as most places will have fresh baked turkey.

Local seafood includes cod, cold-water shrimp, snow crab, lobster, steelhead trout, salmon, mussels, and sea scallops.

Unlike elsewhere in Atlantic Canada, you'll find moose meat on restaurant menus here. It's very lean, very tasty, somewhat similar to beef, and certainly worth ordering if you get the chance.

In July and August, Newfoundland's wild berries ripen. Blueberries, bakeapples (also called cloudberries), and partridge berries (also called mountain cranberries, cowberries, and lingonberries) are used for pies, jams, cakes, pancakes, and in sauces for meat.

You won't find much in the way of local wines, with just two or three small-scale operations making artisanal wines from grapes and wild berries. You can, however, find good craft beers, ciders, and spirits, including varieties made using water from icebergs and local seaweed for gin.

Restaurant reviews have been shortened. For full information, visit Fodors.com.

Hotels

Most hotels in Newfoundland are casual, friendly, and with the kind of amenities, standards, and room styles you'd expect elsewhere in North America. Wi-Fi is widespread, and you won't have to search hard to find a room with a view. Recognizable brands—Alt, Sheraton, Marriott, Ramada, and Holiday Inn among them—do business in St. John's, in historic buildings or standard modern structures. Lodgings outside the city are more varied. You'll find motels, bed-and-breakfasts, timber-frame lodges, inns comprised of one or more heritage houses, and all kinds of rental properties. There's also the unique Fogo Island Inn, a cutting-edge architectural marvel atop a rugged cliff on a remote offshore island.

To experience Newfoundland's world-renowned hospitality close up, try to spend at least one night in a bed-and-breakfast. You'll likely be treated to a wonderful home-cooked breakfast, and you'll probably leave feeling like family. B&B owners here are very knowledgeable about their areas and are often generous with advice and directions, which may enhance your travels as well. Newfoundland & Labrador Tourism provides general information about the province's lodgings.

Hotel reviews have been shortened. For full information, visit Fodors.com.

What It Costs In Canadian Dollars

	$	$$	$$$	$$$$
RESTAURANTS				
	under C$12	C$12–C$20	C$21–C$30	over C$30
HOTELS				
	under C$125	C$125–C$174	C$175–C$250	over C$250

Tours

Local operators offer sea kayaking, ocean diving, canoeing, wildlife viewing, mountain biking, white-water rafting, hiking, and interpretive walks in summer. In winter, snowmobiling expeditions are popular. In spring and early summer, a favored activity is iceberg watching. Maxxim Vacations in St. John's organizes packaged adventure and cultural tours. McCarthy's Party in St. John's arranges guided bus tours, learning vacations, and charter services. The luxurious Tuckamore Lodge, in Main Brook, on the Great Northern Peninsula, is a base for winter snowmobile excursions and for viewing caribou, seabird colonies, whales, and icebergs. Wildland Tours in St. John's operates weeklong guided tours to view wildlife and visit historically and culturally significant sites.

Maxxim Vacations
DRIVING TOURS | Offering a range of self-drive vacations, they provide tour options ranging from six days to two weeks for the island of Newfoundland and coastal Labrador. You choose a theme or a destination, they'll plan your custom trip and book the rental car and accommodations. Then, you enjoy the road trip unescorted. ☎ 709/754–6666, 800/567–6666 ⊕ www.maxximvacations.com ✉ From C$2399.

McCarthy's Party
BUS TOURS | Specializing in bus tours, the guides are never a letdown; they show

intimate knowledge of the area and with plenty of humor. Offering everything from three-hour tours of St. John's to 12-day tours of the entire province, they will handle all aspects of your trip including luggage handling. ☎ *709/579–4444, 888/660–6060* ⊕ *www.mccarthysparty. com* ✉ *Half-day tours from C$60; week-long tours from C$2445.*

Tuckamore Lodge

SPECIAL-INTEREST TOURS | Choose your adventure with activity packages specializing in the outdoor experience. Choose from experiences built around wilderness adventures, cultural and historical experiences, fishing and hunting expeditions, and women's wellness. ✉ *Main Brook* ☎ *709/865–6361, 888/865–6361* ⊕ *www. tuckamorelodge.com* ✉ *From C$799/day.*

Wildland Tours

SPECIAL-INTEREST TOURS | These are full-week escorted holidays for small groups of no more than 18 people. Tour packages focus on various parts of Newfoundland or Labrador. The tours include all accommodations but not airfare. ✉ *St. John's* ☎ *709/722–3123, 888/615–8279* ⊕ *www.wildlands.com* ✉ *From C$3300.*

Visitor Information

Newfoundland and Labrador Tourism distributes brochures from its offices. The province maintains a 24-hour tourist-information line year-round that can help with accommodations and reservations.

A network of visitor information centers dots the province. These centers have information on events, accommodations, shopping, and crafts stores in their areas. The airports in Gander and St. John's operate in-season visitor-information booths. The city of St. John's operates an information center at 348 Water Street.

CONTACTS Newfoundland and Labrador Tourism. ☎ *709/729–2830, 800/563–6353* ⊕ *www.newfoundlandlabrador.com.*

St. John's

Old meets new in the province's capital (metro-area population just more than 200,000 people), with modern office buildings surrounded by heritage shops and colorful row houses. St. John's mixes English and Irish influences, Victorian architecture and modern convenience, and traditional music and rock and roll into a heady brew. The arts scene is lively, but overall the city moves at a relaxed pace.

For centuries, Newfoundland was the largest supplier of salt cod in the world, and the harbor in St. John's was the center of the trade. As early as 1627, the merchants of Water Street—then known as the Lower Path—were doing a thriving business buying fish, selling goods, and supplying alcohol to soldiers and sailors.

The city of St. John's encircles St. John's Harbour, expanding past the hilly, narrow streets of old St. John's. Downtown has the most history and character. The city was destroyed by fire many times, and much of its row housing was erected following the last major blaze, known as the Great Fire, in 1892. Heritage houses on Waterford Bridge Road, winding west from the harbor along the Waterford River, and on Rennies Mill Road and Circular Road to the east (backing onto Bannerman Park) were originally the homes of sea captains and merchants. Duckworth Street and Water Street, which run parallel to the harbor, are lined with shops and restaurants. Explore the narrow lanes and paths as you get farther from the harbor to get the best sense of the city's history.

Signal Hill at the east end of downtown, with its distinctive Cabot Tower, is the city's most prominent landmark. The hill rises up from the Narrows, the appropriately named entrance to St. John's Harbour. Standing at Cape Spear and looking back toward St. John's, you will

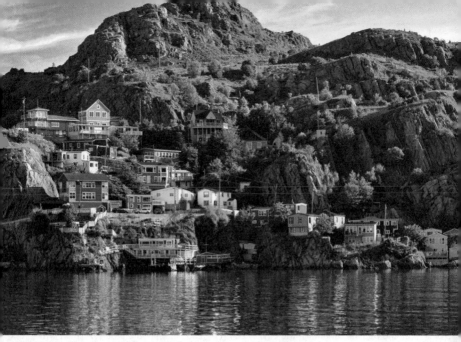
Colorful waterside homes along St. John's harbor make for a postcard-perfect panorama.

see Cabot Tower atop Signal Hill, but you'll scarcely believe there's a city there, because the entrance to the port is narrow and almost hidden.

GETTING HERE AND AROUND
The only direct ways to get to St. John's are to fly in or arrive by cruise ship. The nearest ferry route from the mainland docks at Argentia, a drive of about one-and-a-half hours from the city. From the airport, it's a 15-minute taxi ride to downtown. There are no direct public transit routes or private shuttle buses between the downtown and the airport, but the Route 14 Metrobus picks up passengers at the airport and will get you as far as Memorial University (MUN) where you can transfer to Route 10 to downtown. Cabs from the airport are exclusively operated by City Wide Taxi, with fixed rates to certain hotels, ranging from C$12.50 to C$30 plus C$3 for every extra passenger. For other destinations, fares are metered, with a C$3.50 basic charge.

Metrobus Transit operates more than 20 bus routes in St. John's with cash fares of $2.50 per ride (be sure to have correct fare). The transit company also operates a seasonal hop-on, hop-off trolley serving downtown, major hotels, and visitor attractions. For rides within the city, taxis carry a flag rate of C$3.75, with increments of C$0.25 for every 0.166 km (0.1 miles) and C$0.25 for each 30 seconds of stop time. Downtown is walkable, but you'll want a car to explore farther afield because public-transit options are limited.

BUS AND TAXI CONTACTS City Wide Taxi. ☎ 709/722–7777 ⊕ www.citywidetaxi.ca. **Metrobus Transit.** ✉ St. John's ☎ 709/722–9400 ⊕ www.metrobus.com.

TOURS
An alternative to driving yourself around is to take a sightseeing jaunt with a local guide, who can offer an insider's perspective.

Cod Sounds

ADVENTURE TOURS | FAMILY | A provincial treasure, Cod Sounds offers tours that share traditional knowledge and a deep love of the region. Known for her oceanside walks focusing on edible plant identification, founder and owner Lori McCarthy and her team offer half-day tours/courses on foraging, many of which culminate in an incredible "boil-up" of food harvested on the spot and cooked on the beach. ⊠ *St. John's* ☎ *709/749– 4946* ⊕ *www.codsounds.ca.*

Legend Tours

BUS TOURS | This company provides knowledgeable guides and comfortable motorcoach tours of St. John's and the surrounding areas. It's a good way to see multiple sites in one day without struggling on the steep hills that separate all the best landmarks in the city. ⊠ *284 Water Street* ☎ *709/753–1497* ⊕ *www. legendtours.ca.*

St. John's Haunted Hikes

WALKING TOURS | FAMILY | When you are the oldest city in North America, you contain your fair share of ghoulish histories, both real and mythological. This walking tour explores them all as your guide spins tales of murder most foul and famous ghost sightings associated with the darkened alleys and streets you tread. ⊠ *Church Hill* ☎ *709/685–3444* ⊕ *www. hauntedhike.com* ☜ *From C$10.*

VISITOR INFORMATION

CONTACTS City of St. John's Visitor Information Centre. ⊠ *348 Water St.* ☎ *709/576– 8106, 844/570–2009* ⊕ *www.stjohns.ca.*

 Sights

DOWNTOWN

Anglican Cathedral of St. John the Baptist

CHURCH | Designed by Sir George Gilbert Scott, this fine example of Gothic Revival architecture was erected in the mid-1800s, with major additions in the 1880s, but it had to be rebuilt after the 1892 fire. Free lunchtime organ recitals take place on Wednesday afternoon at 1:15. From mid-July through August, you can slip into the crypt for a cup of tea and homemade tea biscuits and cookies (C$8). Tea service, run by the women of the parish, operates from 2:30 to 4:30 pm on weekdays except Wednesday, when it starts at 2. ⊠ *16 Church Hill* ☎ *709/726–5677* ⊕ *www.ourcathedral.ca* ☜ *Free.*

Basilica Cathedral of St. John the Baptist

CHURCH | Consecrated in 1855 after 14 years of construction, this Romanesque-style Roman Catholic cathedral holds a commanding position above Military Road, overlooking the older section of the city and the harbor. The Irish sculptor John Hogan carved the sanctuary's centerpiece, *Dead Christ,* out of Carrara marble in the mid-19th century. Also note the many stained-glass windows, side altars, and statuary. A museum with vestments and religious objects is next door in the Episcopal Library of the Archbishop's Palace. Every December, the Basilica hosts Handel's *Messiah* performed by the Newfoundland Symphony Orchestra and Choir. ⊠ *200 Military Rd.* ☎ *709/754–2170* ⊕ *www.thebasilica.net.*

Circular Road

STREET | After the devastating fire of 1846, the business elite of St. John's moved to Circular Road. The street contains some very fine Victorian houses and shade trees. ⊠ *Circular Rd.*

Commissariat House

NOTABLE BUILDING | FAMILY | The residence and office of the British garrison's supply officer in the 1830s has been restored to reflect that era. Interpreters sometimes dress in period costume, and the videos and labels are engaging and informative. Guided tours and child-friendly activities are offered during the summer and fall. Visitors are welcome to use the green space on the grounds to enjoy a picnic. ⊠ *11 Kings Bridge Rd.* ☎ *709/729–6730* ⊕ *www.seethesites.ca* ☜ *C$6 including access to Newman Wine Vaults* ☉ *Closed Oct.–May.*

Duckworth Street

STREET | Once called the Upper Path, this has been the "second street" of St. John's for centuries, Water Street being the main street. Stretching from the bottom of Signal Hill in the east to near City Hall in the west, Duckworth Street has restaurants, bars, antiques and crafts shops, as well as lawyers' offices and a yoga studio. A few blocks east of City Hall, the Newfoundland Supreme Court is housed in a late-19th-century building with an eccentric appearance: each of its four turrets is in a different style. If you take the time to go through security and wander the halls, you will see a unique collection of artwork from the provincial artbank on the walls. Lanes and stairways between Duckworth Street and Water Street or George Street give access to some of the city's most popular pubs. ✉ *Duckworth St.*

Government House

GOVERNMENT BUILDING | The lieutenant governor—the Queen's representative in Newfoundland—lives at Government House, which was built in the 1830s. Myth has it that the 12-foot ditch surrounding the structure was intended to keep out snakes, though Newfoundland is one of the few regions in the world to have no snakes. The original governor, so the story goes, was expecting a warmer colony where serpents might be a problem. In fact, the moat was designed to allow more light into the basement rooms. House tours (free) can be arranged by appointment. The marvelous garden is open all year for you to explore on your own. ✉ *50 Military Rd.* ☎ *709/729–2669 tour reservations* ⊕ *www.govhouse.nl.ca* ✉ *Free.*

Gower Street United Church

CHURCH | FAMILY | This 1896 church has a redbrick facade, green turrets, about 40 stained-glass windows, and a massive Casavant pipe organ. The church itself is on a sort of concrete island, the lone occupant of a small tract of land surrounded by four streets. The home of a community band and choirs for adults and youth, this acoustically pleasing venue hosts musical performances throughout the year. ✉ *99 Queen's Rd.* ✛ *Queen's Rd. at Gower St.* ☎ *709/753–7286* ⊕ *www.gowerunited.com* ✉ *Free.*

Harbourside Park

CITY PARK | FAMILY | This is the spot where Sir Humphrey Gilbert claimed Newfoundland for Britain in 1583, much to the amusement of the French, Spanish, and Portuguese fishermen in port at the time. They thought him a fool, a judgment borne out a few days later when he ran his ship aground and drowned. The small park is a good vantage point to watch the boats come and go and a nice spot to stop for a rest. Kids love the bronze Newfoundland and Labrador dog statues you can sit on. With benches placed among the greenery in an amphitheater-style formation, this is a pleasant place to enjoy family-friendly concerts. Enjoy free lunchtime and afternoon performances by some of the best musicians in the city through July and August. ✉ *Queens Cove* ✛ *Enter on Water St. by Queens Cove* ⊕ *www.stjohns.ca/living-st-johns/arts-and-culture/music-concert-series* ✉ *Free.*

Newman Wine Vaults

NOTABLE BUILDING | This 200-year-old building with stone barrel vaults is where the renowned Newman's Port was aged. According to legend, a Newman and Company vessel loaded with port wine was driven off course by pirates in 1679 and forced to winter in St. John's. Upon its return to London, the cargo was found to have improved in flavor, and after that the company continued to send port to be matured in these wine cellars. The vaults are now a historic site, with guides who interpret the province's long and unique association with port. A small taste of port comes with admission. ✉ *436 Water St.* ☎ *709/729–2627* ⊕ *seethesites.ca* ✉ *C$6 includes admission to Commissariat House.*

St. John's

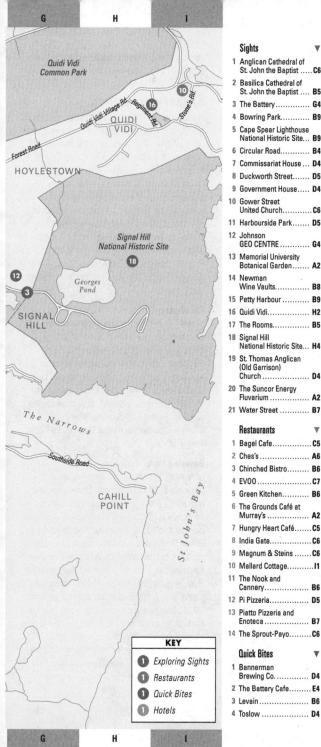

Sights ▼

1 Anglican Cathedral of
St. John the Baptist **C6**

2 Basilica Cathedral of
St. John the Baptist **B5**

3 The Battery **G4**

4 Bowring Park **B9**

5 Cape Spear Lighthouse
National Historic Site ... **B9**

6 Circular Road **B4**

7 Commissariat House ... **D4**

8 Duckworth Street **D5**

9 Government House **D4**

10 Gower Street
United Church **C6**

11 Harbourside Park **D5**

12 Johnson
GEO CENTRE **G4**

13 Memorial University
Botanical Garden **A2**

14 Newman
Wine Vaults **B8**

15 Petty Harbour **B9**

16 Quidi Vidi **H2**

17 The Rooms **B5**

18 Signal Hill
National Historic Site ... **H4**

19 St. Thomas Anglican
(Old Garrison)
Church **D4**

20 The Suncor Energy
Fluvarium **A2**

21 Water Street **B7**

Restaurants ▼

1 Bagel Cafe **C5**

2 Ches's **A6**

3 Chinched Bistro **B6**

4 EVOO **C7**

5 Green Kitchen **B6**

6 The Grounds Café at
Murray's **A2**

7 Hungry Heart Café **C5**

8 India Gate **C6**

9 Magnum & Steins **C6**

10 Mallard Cottage **I1**

11 The Nook and
Cannery **B6**

12 Pi Pizzeria **D5**

13 Piatto Pizzeria and
Enoteca **B7**

14 The Sprout-Payo **C6**

Quick Bites ▼

1 Bannerman
Brewing Co. **D4**

2 The Battery Cafe **E4**

3 Levain **B6**

4 Toslow **D4**

Hotels ▼

1 Blue on Water **B7**

2 Courtyard St. John's
Newfoundland **D5**

3 Delta Hotels by Marriott
St. John's
Conference Centre **B7**

4 DoubleTree by Hilton
St. John's
Harbourview **D4**

5 Holiday Inn—St. John's
Convention Centre **B1**

6 JAG **B8**

7 Murray Premises
Hotel **C7**

8 Sheraton Hotel
Newfoundland **D4**

KEY

1 Exploring Sights

1 Restaurants

1 Quick Bites

1 Hotels

★ The Rooms

HISTORY MUSEUM | FAMILY | An eye-catching feature of the cityscape, this lively space celebrating the arts and cultures of Newfoundland and Labrador has a design inspired by traditional "fishing rooms," shacks by the waterside where fishing families would process their catch. Multimedia and hands-on exhibits explore the region's cultural heritage, archaeology, and ecology, while the art gallery presents contemporary and older works from the permanent art collection and mounts temporary and traveling art exhibitions. Displays at the Provincial Archives include historical photos and documents. The facility's observation deck has awe-inspiring views over St. John's, even in bad weather. ⊠ *9 Bonaventure Ave.* ☎ *709/757–8090* ⊕ *www.therooms.ca* ✉ *$10.*

St. Thomas Anglican (Old Garrison) Church

CHURCH | This wooden building, the oldest church in the city, is painted blue and trimmed in white in a style consistent with the "jellybean" houses in the neighborhood. The primary section was built in 1836 and, while it escaped damage by the fire of 1846, it is believed to have shifted by six inches in a storm that took place that same year. This led to the further construction of wings to stabilize the original structure. English soldiers used to worship at this church during the early and mid-1800s. ⊠ *8 Military Rd.* ☎ *709/576–6632* ⊕ *www.st-thomaschurch.com* ✉ *Free.*

Water Street

STREET | Originally called the Lower Path, Water Street has been used by St. John's residents since the 1520s. The older architecture resembles that of seaports in southwest England and Ireland. If you do nothing else in St. John's, take a walk down Water Street. This is the center of the downtown universe, and on a sunny day it will be packed with smiling locals. Sections may be closed to car traffic during the summer, allowing for a lively pedestrian space with outdoor restaurant service. ⊠ *Water St.*

GREATER ST. JOHN'S

A number of must-see attractions can be found a short drive from the downtown core of St. John's. When you stand with your back to the ocean at Cape Spear National Historic Site—the easternmost point of North America—the entire population of the continent is to your west. Cape Spear Lighthouse National Historic Site and the surrounding coastal trails are excellent places to see icebergs and whales in spring and early summer. Plan to spend a full day exploring Greater St. John's to give yourself some time at each spot.

The Battery

TOWN | This tiny fishing village perches precariously at the base of steep cliffs between Signal Hill and St. John's Harbour. Narrow lanes snake around the houses, so it's a good place to get out of the car and walk. A public access to the North Head walking trail that winds around Signal Hill crosses the doorstep of a private home in the Battery! ⊠ *Battery Rd.*

Bowring Park

CITY PARK | FAMILY | An expansive Victorian park west of downtown, Bowring was modeled after the famous city parks of London. Dotting the grounds are ponds and rustic bridges; the statue of Peter Pan just inside the east gate was cast from the same mold as the one in Kensington Park in London. The wealthy Bowring family, which made its money in trade and shipping, donated the park in 1914. There is a swimming pool, a splash pad (both open July and August), a large playground, and walking trails. ⊠ *305 Waterford Bridge Rd.* ✛ *Parking at 399 Waterford Bridge Rd.* ⊕ *www.bowringpark.com* ✉ *Free.*

★ Cape Spear Lighthouse National Historic Site

LIGHTHOUSE | At the easternmost point of land on the continent, songbirds begin chirping in the dim light of dawn, and whales in early summer feed directly below the cliffs, providing an unforgettable start to the day. From April through July, you might see icebergs floating by. Cape Spear Lighthouse, Newfoundland's oldest such beacon, has been restored to its original form and furnishings. There is a visitor center and souvenir shop open in the summer. The historic gun batteries can be viewed up close from the walking trail whenever weather conditions allow.

■ **TIP➔** The cliffs surrounding the lighthouse are beautiful but dangerous. Rogue waves and slippery rocks have caused fatal accidents in recent years. It is important to heed the warnings and avoid getting close to the edge, as there are no barriers and no rangers on duty during the popular sunrise hour. ⊠ *Blackhead Rd.* ✛ *Drive to the end of Rte. 11* ☎ *709/772–2191* ⊕ *www. pc.gc.ca/capespear* ⊠ *Site free; lighthouse from C$4* ⊘ *Gift shop and visitor center closed Nov.–May, closed Fri. and Sat. Sept. and Oct., May.*

Johnson GEO CENTRE

NATURE SIGHT | **FAMILY** | Built deep into the earth with only the entryway protruding aboveground, this geological shrine is literally embedded in Signal Hill, itself made up of 550-million-year-old rocks. (The province's oldest rocks date back 3.87 billion years.) There are exhibits on the solar system and how Earth took form. *The Titanic Story*, a multimedia exhibition, includes fascinating artifacts and video footage from the wreck site. Step on an oil platform in the ExxonMobil Oil & Gas Gallery, and learn about how oil and gas are formed. ⊠ *175 Signal Hill Rd.* ☎ *709/864–3200, 866/868–7625* ⊕ *www. geocentre.ca* ⊠ *$12* ⊘ *Closed Jan.–Apr.*

Memorial University Botanical Garden

GARDEN | **FAMILY** | The gardens at this 110-acre natural area include rock gardens, a Newfoundland historic-plants bed, peat and woodland beds, an alpine house, a medicinal garden, a native plant collection, a vegetable garden, a crevice garden, a shade garden, a dried-flower garden, and a compost demonstration garden. There are also five pleasant walking trails. You can see scores of rhododendron varieties here, as well as many kinds of butterflies and the rare hummingbird hawkmoth. ⊠ *C.A. Pippy Park, 306 Mt. Scio Rd.* ☎ *709/864–8590* ⊕ *www.mun.ca/botgarden* ⊠ *C$9* ⊘ *Closed Dec.–Apr.*

★ Petty Harbour

TOWN | **FAMILY** | A fishing village that lies along the coast between Cape Spear and Route 10, Petty Harbour is a great day trip with something for everyone all around one scenic harbor. Two of the prettiest segments of the East Coast Trail start from either end of town. Island Rooms of Petty Harbour is dedicated to keeping the fishing and boating heritage of the town alive and can arrange walking, fishing, and traditional boating excursions (☎ *709/740–3474;* ⊕ *www. fishingforsuccess.org*). North Atlantic Ziplines boasts the longest zipline in Canada, with views over the hills and ocean (☎ *709/368–8681;* ⊕ *www.zip-thenorthatlantic.com*). The Petty Harbour Mini Aquarium has a touch tank and daily family programs (☎ *709/330–3474;* ⊕ *www.miniaqua.org*). To eat, there are plenty of eateries with fresh seafood and harbor views. ⊠ *St. John's* ✛ *From downtown St. John's, take Rte. 11* ⊕ *www. pettyharbourmaddoxcove.ca.*

Quidi Vidi

TOWN | No one knows the origin of the name of this fishing village, one of the oldest parts of St. John's. The town is best explored on foot, as the roads are narrow and make driving difficult. The

Cabot Tower, part of Signal Hill National Historic Site, was built to commemorate the 400th anniversary of explorer John Cabot's landing in Newfoundland.

inlet, known as the Gut, is a traditional outport in the middle of a modern city, though a recent slew of new building permits means it is changing rapidly. It's also a good place to catch sea-run brown trout in the spring. Down on the waterfront is the Quidi Vidi Village Plantation, an open arts-and-crafts studio where you can meet the artists and buy textiles, prints, handmade clothing, and more. It has parking and is a good place to start your walk around the village. The Inn of Olde, Quidi Vidi Brewery, and Mallard Cottage are great stops for food and shelter and, of course, beer and spirits to keep you warm as you explore. ⌧ *Quidi Vidi Village Road* ⊕ *qvvplantation.com.*

★ Signal Hill National Historic Site

MILITARY SIGHT | Signal Hill is emblematic of the island's military history, of early technological achievement, and ancient geology. En route to the top, the visitor center exhibits the history of St. John's. Cabot Tower, at the peak of Signal Hill, was constructed in 1897 to commemorate the 400th anniversary of explorer John Cabot's landing in Newfoundland. In 1901, Guglielmo Marconi received the first transatlantic-wire transmission near here, and today you can visit the Marconi exhibit on the top floor of Cabot Tower. The GEO Centre lets you to go literally inside Signal Hill and learn about the ancient rock. The drive to the tower along Signal Hill Road affords fine harbor, ocean, and city views, as does the tower itself. Walking trails take you to the base of the hill and closer to the ocean. In July and August every year, cadets in 19th-century-British uniforms perform military tattoos. ⌧ *Signal Hill Rd.* ☎ *709/772–5367* ⊕ *www.pc.gc.ca* ⌧ *Site and tower free; visitor center C$4; military tattoo performances C$10.*

The Suncor Energy Fluvarium

NATURE PRESERVE | FAMILY | A tributary of a nearby river was diverted here so visitors could see the life that inhabits it from underwater. See into the river through nine large windows at the only public facility of its kind in North America. In season you can observe spawning brown and brook trout in their natural habitat. There are also tanks housing other fish and amphibians and exhibits relating to the aquatic environment. Visitor capacity is decreased during feeding times, which take place at 3:30 or 4:00 pm daily. Grand Concourse Authority walking trails ring the pond just outside the Fluvarium. ✉ *C.A. Pippy Park, 5 Nagle's Pl.* ☎ *709/754–3474* 🌐 *www.fluvarium.ca* 🎟 *C$8.*

🍴 Restaurants

Bagel Cafe

$$ | **ECLECTIC** | The name belies the menu at this cozy spot on Duckworth Street where you can get excellent food for any meal of the day. Generous breakfast offerings bring local ingredients to traditional dishes. **Known for:** all-day breakfast; the "Newfoundland Benedict"; the menu has something for everyone. [$] *Average main: C$18* ✉ *246 Duckworth St.* ☎ *709/739–4470* 🌐 *thebagelcafe.ca.*

Ches's

$$ | **SEAFOOD** | **FAMILY** | This restaurant has been serving fish-and-chips to a steady stream of customers since the 1950s. They come from all walks of life to sample the flaky fish fried in a batter whose recipe the owner keeps under lock and key (literally). **Known for:** large portions; traditional fish-and-chips; battered seafood platters. [$] *Average main: C$13* ✉ *9 Freshwater Rd., Downtown* ☎ *709/722–2373* 🌐 *www.chessfishandchips.ca.*

★ **Chinched Bistro**

$$ | **SANDWICHES** | This culinary diamond shines with innovative yet hearty food, whether you're dining in the sit-down restaurant or grabbing something from the take-out deli. With so much perfect meat, seafood, and vegetables tucked into one tiny building, this is more than just a hidden gem. **Known for:** pig-ear fries; handcrafted charcuterie; house-infused spirits and cocktails. [$] *Average main: C$18* ✉ *5 Bates Hill* ☎ *709/722–3100* 🌐 *www.chinched.com* ⏲ *Closed Mon.*

EVOO

$$$ | **MEDITERRANEAN** | EVOO combines the rustic surroundings of a gastro pub with Mediterranean-influenced fare. The menu offers seafood, vegan, and meat-based options and a good wine selection. **Known for:** cozy candlelit atmosphere; excellent cocktails; attentive service. [$] *Average main: C$25* ✉ *5 Beck's Cove* ✣ *First floor of Murray Premises, with access from Duckworth Street* ☎ *709/738-1011* 🌐 *www.evoorestaurant.ca.*

Green Kitchen

$$ | **VEGETARIAN** | Enjoy your vegan meal in this relaxing atmosphere with hardwood floors and natural lighting. This casual eatery offers plant-based fare with most elements made from scratch with ethically sourced ingredients. **Known for:** cozy Sunday brunch; delicious and healthy smoothies; vegan children's menu. [$] *Average main: C$16* ✉ *47 Harvey Rd.* ☎ *709/237–2223* 🌐 *www.greenkitchennl.ca* ⏲ *Closed Mon.*

The Grounds Café at Murray's

$$ | **CONTEMPORARY** | **FAMILY** | The latest entrepreneurial turn for a sixth-generation heritage family farm, this restaurant within a garden center is the true definition of a farm-to-table experience. Enjoy seasonal cuisine in the deli-style café inside Murray's Garden Centre, bright with natural light and lively with guests of all ages. **Known for:** great vegetarian specials; ham and cheese on buttermilk biscuit; healthy green salads. [$] *Average main: C$14* ✉ *1525 Portugal Cove Rd.* ☎ *709/895–2800* 🌐 *www.murraysgardens.com* ⏲ *No dinner, reduced menu after 3 pm.*

★ Hungry Heart Café

$$ | BISTRO | Open for breakfast and lunch, this café makes the perfect spot to take a break from touring and enjoy a variety of options like shrimp pad thai, roast cauliflower soup, or any number of daily changing specials crafted by one of the most versatile chefs in Newfoundland. Under the umbrella of the nonprofit Stella's Circle, all revenue from the restaurant goes back into helping the most vulnerable in the community. **Known for:** Saturday brunch; fresh salads; house-made desserts. $ *Average main: C$15* ⊠ *142 Military Rd.* ☎ *709/738–6164* ⊕ *hungryheartcafe.ca* ☉ *Closed Sun.– Mon. No dinner.*

India Gate

$$$ | INDIAN | Consistency and quality in service and food make this one of the busiest restaurants in St. John's. This family-owned business is the oldest Indian restaurant in the city, serving food prepared to order in a classic tandoori oven. **Known for:** vegetarian dishes; generous servings; fresh-baked naan. $ *Average main: C$25* ⊠ *286 Duckworth St., Downtown* ☎ *709/753–6006* ⊕ *www. indiagatenl.ca* ☉ *Closed Mon.*

Magnum & Steins

$$$$ | INTERNATIONAL | Exposed stone walls, original paintings, and chic furnishings make for a serene (if dark) dining atmosphere in this restored heritage building right downtown. With two different menus (one for dinner, one for the bar) and a wine bar upstairs, this restaurant covers it all: the short but classic dinner menu features steak, seafood, lamb, and poultry while the bar menu displays some international influences. **Known for:** reservations usually not needed; duck confit nachos; happy-hour specials. $ *Average main: C$36* ⊠ *329 Duckworth St.* ☎ *709/576–6500* ⊕ *www. magnumandsteins.ca* ☉ *No lunch.*

★ Mallard Cottage

$$$ | MODERN CANADIAN | Roaring fires, an open kitchen, and jars of homemade pickles lining the rafters set the scene in this renovated historic building in Quidi Vidi Village. The menu changes daily based on the best ingredients available from local sources and might include spit-roasted pork shoulder or tuna tartare, always accompanied by novel and succulent vegetable dishes. **Known for:** fun beer garden; on-site sommelier; Sunday brunch with live music. $ *Average main: C$29* ⊠ *8 Barrows Rd.* ☎ *709/237–7314* ⊕ *mallardcottage.ca* ☉ *Closed Mon. and Tues. Nov.–May.*

★ The Nook and Cannery

$$ | DINER | This easygoing diner does a bustling lunch service in large part due to the personality and creativity of its owner, locally known as an innovative and improvisational chef. Enjoy casual fare with surprising ingredients in a space decorated with an eclectic mix of family photos, bottled preserves, and tabletops repurposed from old furniture and signage. **Known for:** gourmet-food quality at diner prices; friendly chats at the lunch counter; massive chicken sandwiches with fun flavor twists. $ *Average main: C$16* ⊠ *69 Harvey Rd.* ⊕ *www.facebook. com/thenookandcannery* ☉ *Closed Wed. and Thurs.*

★ Piatto Pizzeria and Enoteca

$$ | PIZZA | Following standards set by the Associazione Verace Pizza Napoletana (VPN), Piatto's pizza chefs (pizzaiolos) have been trained to prepare authentic Neapolitan pizza. The midtown location offers a contemporary setting that makes a popular lunch stop. **Known for:** pizza-and-salad lunch special; Italian-style hand-pulled coffee; decadent desserts. $ *Average main: C$18* ⊠ *60 Elizabeth Ave.* ☎ *709/726–0909* ⊕ *www.piattopizzeria.com.*

Pi Pizzeria

$$$ | PIZZA | FAMILY | This gourmet pizza shop has been winning international competitions for years with their innovative thin-crust creations in a family-friendly, eclectic atmosphere. The ingredients on their signature pizzas may sound random, but the chef has all the golden ratios down and the taste is perfect. **Known for:** tortellini in spicy sauce; unusual specialty pizzas; fantastic Caesar salads. $ *Average main: C$23* ⊠ *10 Kings Rd.* ☎ *709/726–2000* ⊕ *www.pinl.ca* ☽ *Closed Mon.–Tues.*

The Sprout–Poyo

$$ | VEGETARIAN | FAMILY | This stalwart vegetarian spot, beloved by vegetable and meat-eaters alike, offers counter service and comfortable seating by day and a lively after-hours scene by night that sees diners lining up for late-night tacos. Local artists and craftspeople display their creations on the walls, and there are plenty of gluten-free options in addition to beer, wine, and house-made sangria. **Known for:** nouvelle tacos; excellent vegetarian chili; tasty avocado sandwich. $ *Average main: C$15* ⊠ *364 Duckworth St.* ☎ *709/579–5485* ⊕ *thesproutrestaurant. com* ☽ *Closed Sun.–Mon.*

☕ Coffee and Quick Bites

★ Bannerman Brewing Co.

$$ | CAFÉ | Located in a former firehouse at the east end of Duckworth Street, this trendy beer and coffee bar makes an ideal place to chill at the end of your downtown explorations. The architecture features industrial elements like exposed beams and massive glass garage doors that open to an outdoor space in summer. **Known for:** baked treats are irresistible; friendly and engaging staff; communal tables are great for work meetups. $ *Average main: C$15* ⊠ *90 Duckworth St.* ☎ *709/747–2337* ⊕ *www. bannermanbrewing.com.*

The Battery Cafe

$ | CAFÉ | This little café has great coffee and snacks as well as a variety of fresh options for a quick breakfast or lunch. It is located perfectly to help energize you before hiking Signal Hill or to let you refresh and relax after a tour of downtown or the Battery. **Known for:** excellent smoked salmon bagel sandwiches; live music on weekend evenings; delicious baked goods. $ *Average main: C$8* ⊠ *1 Duckworth St.* ☎ *709/722–9167* ⊕ *www. batterycafe.ca* ☽ *No dinner.*

Levain

$ | BAKERY | A tiny whiff of Paris in the neighborhood of St. John's known by locals as the Fish 'n' Chips district, this bakery sells breads and pastries made in the French style. While they don't provide full barista service, you can order a coffee to go. **Known for:** artisanal breads that look like works of art; surprising flavor combinations; decadent cinnamon rolls. $ *Average main: C$10* ⊠ *77 Harvey Rd.* ⊕ *levainpastry.ca* ☽ *Closed Mon. and Tues.*

Toslow

$ | CAFÉ | A youthful place with two different energies, Toslow serves coffee and light breakfast fare in the mornings, then at night switches to a dinner menu with bar service. Whatever time of day, you're sure to get delicious offerings prepared with local, seasonal ingredients. **Known for:** gorgeous fruit pastries; hand-written menus shared daily on Instagram; a cheeky antique chesterfield. $ *Average main: C$11* ⊠ *108 Duckworth St.* ☎ *709/400–6655* ☽ *Closed Mon. and Tues.*

🛏 Hotels

Blue on Water

$$$ | HOTEL | A modern boutique hotel with stylish contemporary interiors, Blue on Water is the essence of its name—a calm, comfortable lodging with a whiff of the Atlantic. **Pros:** central location; spacious bathrooms and bedrooms; great restaurant and bar on-site. **Cons:** small hallways; no parking; street noise can sometimes be heard in rooms. *[$] Rooms from: C$199 ✉ 319 Water St. ☎ 877/431–2583 🌐 www.blueonwater.com 🛏 11 rooms 🍴 No Meals.*

Courtyard St. John's Newfoundland

$$$ | **HOTEL** | Business travelers in particular like this attractive Marriott property at the east end of Duckworth Street. **Pros:** complimentary valet parking; plenty of amenities; in-house restaurant/bar has exceptional views. **Cons:** no pool; no local character; working harbor can be noisy. *[$] Rooms from: C$229 ✉ 131 Duckworth St. ☎ 709/722–6636, 866/727–6636 🌐 www.marriott.com 🛏 86 rooms 🍴 No Meals.*

Delta Hotels by Marriott St. John's Conference Centre

$$$ | **HOTEL** | Half the rooms in this popular downtown convention hotel overlook the harbor; the others look out on the city but tend to be quieter (rooms facing New Gower Street have the best views). **Pros:** connects to Convention Centre via covered walkways; floor-to-ceiling windows in guest rooms; squash courts and pool. **Cons:** lack of local character; no views in restaurant; not in the prettiest part of downtown. *[$] Rooms from: C$239 ✉ 120 New Gower St. ☎ 709/739–6404, 888/793–3582 🌐 www.marriott.com 🛏 403 rooms 🍴 No Meals.*

Doubletree by Hilton St. John's Harbourview

$$ | **HOTEL** | In the core of downtown, directly overlooking the harbor, this hotel has friendly staffers who immediately flash welcoming smiles when you enter the tiled, sand-colored lobby. **Pros:** great views in on-site restaurant; connecting rooms available; refrigerators available on request. **Cons:** no historic architecture; you have to hike a hill if you're walking from Water Street; harbor can be noisy. *[$] Rooms from: C$139 ✉ 2 Hill O'Chips ☎ 709/383–1475, 855/610–8733 🌐 www.hilton.com 🛏 160 rooms 🍴 No Meals.*

Holiday Inn—St. John's Convention Centre

$ | **HOTEL** | **FAMILY** | The surprise at this family-friendly chain hotel is the location: walking trails from the property meander around small lakes and link with the Grand Concourse hiking trails. **Pros:** adjacent to walking/jogging trails; indoor heated pool; easy to get to via airport or Trans-Canada Highway. **Cons:** restaurant is part of a chain; rooms are fine but nothing special; a long walk to downtown. *[$] Rooms from: C$109 ✉ 180 Portugal Cove Rd. ☎ 709/722–0506, 877/660–8550 🌐 https://www.ihg.com/holidayinn 🛏 252 rooms 🍴 No Meals.*

JAG

$$$ | **HOTEL** | With triple-paned windows, this boutique hotel has brought the option of a good night's sleep into the more industrial end of downtown with stylish rooms and modern furnishings. **Pros:** fully wheelchair-accessible amenities; good on-site bar and restaurant; quiet rooms. **Cons:** industrial end of Water Street; windows do not open; harsh LED lighting in rooms. *[$] Rooms from: C$209 ✉ 115 George St. ☎ 844/564–1524, 709/738–1524 🌐 www.steelehotels.com/our-hotels/jag 🛏 84 rooms 🍴 Free Breakfast.*

Murray Premises Hotel

$$$ | **HOTEL** | Part of the Murray Premises National Historic Site near St. John's harbor front, this longstanding boutique hotel pairs original architectural features with luxury amenities. **Pros:** two restaurants in central courtyard; historic character; location close to downtown attractions. **Cons:** harbor views obstructed with development of large chain restaurants; decor slightly dated; soundproofing inconsistent. *[$] Rooms from: C$189 ✉ 5 Beck's Cove ☎ 709/738–7773 🌐 murraypremiseshotel.com 🛏 69 rooms 🍴 Free Breakfast.*

Newfoundland English

The English spoken in Newfoundland is full of words brought centuries ago, when the fertile fishing grounds lured sailors and settlers from Britain, Ireland, and elsewhere in Europe in the late 16th century. For generations, these settlers remained isolated with their words, sayings, and songs, confined not only to the island but within their individual outports. This isolation enabled accents to remain region-specific and persist well into modern speech as Newfoundland English.

Some expressions are used by young and old alike in contemporary Newfoundland parlance. When something is described as *best kind*, that means it is good. When someone says *job to know*, they mean they don't know something. A *crooked* person is not corrupt, they're just cranky; they may explain to you that they are *rotted*, which means something has made them angry.

The expression *come from away*, or *CFA*, has been immortalized by the Broadway musical, and refers to anyone who is not from the province. Mainland North America in general is referred to as *upalong*. On the island, the capital city is often called *Town*, and its residents *townies*. Those who do not live in St. John's are often dubbed *baymen*, irrespective of their proximity to water.

Newfoundlanders often identify one another by their regional variations in accents, and then engage in nostalgic wordplay as they trade off old-time expressions. Listen for Newfoundland words for food, like *scoff* (a big meal), *touton* (fried bread dough), and *duff* (a steamed pudding). Common weather-related terms are *mauzy* (foggy and damp), *sultry* (warm and humid), and *glitter* (freezing rain that forms a shiny ice covering). A sudden flurry of snow might be called a *dwigh*.

To help develop an ear for the provincial dialects, pick up a copy of the *Dictionary of Newfoundland English*, which contains more than 5,000 words.

Sheraton Hotel Newfoundland
$$$ | **HOTEL** | A local landmark, this hotel has charming rooms and gorgeous views of Signal Hill, the Narrows, and the old town. **Pros:** the garden atrium feels like an indoor park; walking distance to Signal Hill and the Battery; spa on-site. **Cons:** across downtown from Convention Centre; small swimming pool; no indoor parking. [$] *Rooms from: C$240* ✉ *115 Cavendish Sq.* ☎ *709/726–4980* 🌐 *www.marriott.com* 🛏 *301 rooms* 🍴 *No Meals.*

Nightlife

St. John's has tremendous variety and vitality considering its small population. Celtic-inspired traditional music and folk rock are the city's best-known music genres, although there's also a vibrant blues and alternative-rock scene. For theater, venues include traditional spaces, courtyards, and parks. A growing film and TV industry has added to the artistic and technical talent in recent years.

The well-deserved reputation of St. John's as a party town has been several hundred years in the making. To become an "honorary Newfoundlander," visitors can take part in the screech-in ceremony, which involves reciting the "Screecher's Creed," kissing a cod, and knocking back a shot of Screech Rum.

The Black Sheep on George

LIVE MUSIC | Known locally as a "musician's bar," this live music venue is not limited to traditional tunes, showcasing all styles of music from rockabilly to jazz. You'll find local musicians, whose work rivals any in the world. A former garage, this building is full of history, not to mention a few tall tales. ⊠ *5 George St.* ☎ *709/682–7161* ⊕ *www.theblacksheep. ca.*

George Street

GATHERING PLACES | The city's most famous street may be short and cobblestoned, but it is said to have more bars per capita than any other street in North America, approximately two dozen. Trapper John's is one of the more well known (it's also a great place to undertake the screech-in ceremony). Seasonal open-air festivals, which close off the street, include the George Street Festival in August. ⊠ *George St.* ⊕ *www. georgestreetlive.ca.*

O'Reilly's Pub

LIVE MUSIC | When Russell Crowe comes to town, he jams at O'Reilly's Pub, famous for its nightly live Irish and Newfoundland music. Starting times vary, but shows typically begin late. O'Reilly's also has a full pub-grub menu and additional options for food and pints in the attached Frugal Steins' eatery. ⊠ *13 George St.* ☎ *709/722–3735* ⊕ *www.oreillyspub. com.*

★ Ship Pub

PUBS | Traditionally this pub has served as the hangout for the local arts scene and continues to attract a hip crowd of all ages. There's live music from Wednesday through Saturday year-round, with Wednesday's folk-music night a famous staple. Good pub food and eclectic

Pink, White, and Green ◉

You won't be in St. John's long before you'll ask what's with the pink, white, and green? The tricolor flag flies from houses and buildings, and in souvenir shops the cheerful bands of color show up on everything. To quote the song "The Flag of Newfoundland": "The pink the rose of England shows, the green St. Patrick's emblem bright, while in between a spotless sheen of Andrew's cross displays the white." The 19th-century flag has gained popularity in recent years as an affectionate symbol of the "secret nation."

specials are served between noon and 8 pm Wednesday through Friday, and brunch until 4 pm on weekends. ⊠ *265 Duckworth St.* ✛ *Enter from the Solomon's Lane stairway between Duckworth and Water Streets* ☎ *709/753–3870* ☞ *Kitchen service Wed.–Sun.*

🎭 Performing Arts

Arts and Culture Centre

ARTS CENTERS | FAMILY | A main theater with just under 1,000 seats is the focal point of this center, which also houses the St. John's Public Library. It is the site of musical and theatrical events from September through June. ⊠ *95 Allandale Rd.* ☎ *709/729–3650, 709/729–3900 box office* ⊕ *artsandculturecentre.com.*

★ LSPU Hall

ARTS CENTERS | Known locally simply as The Hall, this historic building was constructed in the 1920s and served as the headquarters of the Longshoremen's Protective Union. In recent decades it has been established as an innovative theater housing the Resource Centre for the Arts Theatre Company (RCAT). It showcases professional main-stage and experimental second-space productions year-round. This theater and RCAT have been the launching pad for the province's most successful theatrical exports. ⊠ *LSPU Hall, 3 Victoria St.* ☎ *709/753–4531* ⊕ *lspuhall.ca.*

● Shopping

ARTS AND CRAFTS

Craft Council Shop & Pantry

CRAFTS | Recently relocated from its Devon House location, the Newfoundland Craft Council's retail center showcases a juried selection of fine art and crafts from the province's most accomplished artists and makers. With traditional and contemporary work in a host of media including wood, pottery, textiles and more, there's something here for every taste and budget. ⊠ *155 Water St.* ☎ *709/702–4295.*

Downhome Shoppe and Gallery

CRAFTS | With thousands of books, crafts, artwork, music recordings, and souvenirs created by Newfoundlanders and Labradorians, this shop occupying two adjacent late-1850s shopfronts is a great place to pick up a homegrown memento. ⊠ *303 Water St.* ☎ *709/722–2970* ⊕ *shopdownhome.com.*

Newfoundland Weavery

MIXED CLOTHING | FAMILY | This gift shop offers a mix of novelty gift items, clothing, housewares, as well as higher-end local handcrafts and souvenirs. ⊠ *177 Water St.* ☎ *709/753–0496* ⊕ *newfoundlandweavery.com.*

★ Quidi Vidi Village Plantation

CRAFTS | Local artists and artisans have their studios here, making this a perfect place to pick up original art and craft works, including textiles, prints, pottery, stained glass, leatherwork, and jewelry. ⊠ *10 Maple View Pl., Quidi Vidi* ☎ *709/570–2038* ⊕ *qvvplantation.com.*

GALLERIES

Christina Parker Gallery

ART GALLERIES | The gallery specializes in works by local artists, both established and new, from paintings and sculptures to drawings, prints, and other media. ⊠ *50 Water St.* ☎ *709/753–0580* ⊕ *www. christinaparkergallery.com.*

Eastern Edge Gallery

ART GALLERIES | Artists that run this center present everything from paintings and drawings to performance and video art from emerging talents. In August each year, this artists' collective puts on "Hold Fast," a contemporary arts festival with events and installations throughout the city. ⊠ *72 Harbour Dr.* ☎ *709/739–1882* ⊕ *easternedge.ca.*

Emma Butler Gallery

ART GALLERIES | Some of the province's most prominent and established artists show their works here in this peaceful space just across from the Convention Center. ⊠ *111 George St.* ☎ *709/739–7111* ⊕ *www.emmabutler.com.*

★ The Leyton Gallery of Fine Art

ART GALLERIES | In a cozy space tucked between the industry of the harbor and the commercial buzz of Water Street, this gallery invites an intimacy and comfort with art, with a range of work from affordable new artists to museum pieces. ⊠ *6 Clift's-Baird's Cove* ✛ *Off Water St.* ☎ *709/722–7177* ⊕ *theleytongallery.com.*

CLOTHING AND GIFTS

★ Johnny Ruth

MIXED CLOTHING | This large, eclectic space houses a fashionable clothing store, specialty gifts, and the signature Living Planet eco-friendly T-shirts, dresses, and baby onesies designed by local artists. ⊠ *183 Water St.* ☎ *709/722–7477* ⊕ *www.johnnyruth.com.*

NONIA

MIXED CLOTHING | FAMILY | The nonprofit shop also known as the Newfoundland Outport Nursing and Industrial Association was founded in 1920 to raise money for public health services, with the proceeds from the sale of the homespun, hand-knit clothes used to hire nurses. Today, it sells a variety of knits for all ages including the classic and much-coveted full-suit onesies for babies and toddlers. ⊠ *286 Water St.* ☎ *709/753–8062, 877/753–8062* ⊕ *nonia.com.*

★ **Posie Row & Co.**

OTHER SPECIALTY STORE | This shopping emporium is anchored on the first floor by Posie Row, a clothing and gift boutique with imported fashion items, beautiful stationery, jewelry, and more. The next three floors house a collection of local retailers selling everything from yarn and quilting fabric to house-made soaps and artist's prints. ⊠ *210 Duckworth St.* ☎ *709/722–2544* ⊕ *www.posierow.com.*

Travel Bug

TRAVEL | Whether you need travel gear to get you through your vacation or a pleasant memento for when you get home, this little shop has lots of charming finds. From travel bags to eco-friendly toothbrushes, plus locally authored books, it's worth a browse. ⊠ *197 Water St.* ☎ *709/738–2337.*

MUSIC

O'Brien's Music Store

MUSIC | This shop bills itself as the oldest store on the oldest street in the oldest city in North America. It's worth a visit just to see the accordions, tin whistles, fiddles, ukuleles, and ugly sticks (traditional Newfoundland instruments made from discarded tools and household items) on display. The shop also stocks recorded music, and you are sure to see your favorite local musicians popping in for a purchase or a chat, and occasionally to play a tune. ⊠ *278 Water St.* ☎ *709/753–8135* ⊕ *obriens.ca.*

The Irish Loop ◉

The Irish Loop (Route 10) goes around the southern shore of the Avalon Peninsula below St. John's. The highway hugs the coastline and takes you into the heart of Irish Newfoundland—to Bay Bulls, Witless Bay, Ferryland, Aquaforte, Fermeuse, Portugal Cove South, Trepassey, and Salmonier. It's a world filled with whales, caribou, and seabirds. If you keep following the loop around, you'll change from Rte. 10 to Rte. 90, then take Rte. 1 to end up back in St. John's.

🏃 Activities

HIKING

★ **The East Coast Trail**

HIKING & WALKING | A world-class destination for hikers, some segments of the East Coast Trail start in St. John's. The Sugarloaf Trail from Quidi Vidi Village to Logy Bay will give you a great workout, spectacular views, and, depending on the season, sightings of whales and icebergs and buckets of blueberries. Detailed maps are available to purchase on their website and at some downtown retailers. ⊠ *St. John's* ☎ *709/738–4453* ⊕ *eastcoasttrail.com.*

Grand Concourse

HIKING & WALKING | A well-developed and marked trail system through town, the Grand Concourse, crosses St. John's, Mount Pearl, and Paradise, covering more than 120 km (75 miles). Some trails traverse river valleys, parks, and other open areas; others are sidewalk routes. Well-maintained trails encircle several lakes, including Long Pond and Quidi Vidi Lake, both of which are great for bird-watching. Detailed maps are available at tourist information centers and many hotels. Some segments are

maintained through the winter. ✉ *St. John's* ☎ *709/737–1077* ⊕ *www.grand-concourse.ca.*

SCUBA DIVING

The ocean around Newfoundland and Labrador rivals the Caribbean in clarity, though certainly not in temperature. There are thousands of known shipwreck sites. One, a sunken whaling ship, is only several feet from the shore of the Conception Bay community of Conception Harbour. The wrecked ship and a wealth of sea life can be explored with a snorkel and a wet suit.

Ocean Quest

SCUBA DIVING | This outfitter leads "ocean safaris," which give you the opportunity to see icebergs and whales from a boat or to try a diving package for up-close underwater adventures to shipwrecks. Most tours depart out of Conception Bay South. ✉ *17 Stanley's Rd., Conception Bay South* ☎ *709/722–7234* ⊕ *www.oceanquestadventures.com.*

SEA KAYAKING

One of the best ways to explore the coastline is by kayak, which lets you visit sea caves and otherwise inaccessible beaches. There's also a very good chance you'll see whales, icebergs, and seabirds.

The Outfitters

KAYAKING | This full-service sports entity is not only a tour operator, but also runs a brick-and-mortar sports equipment and clothing store downtown. Kayak tours run out of Bay Bulls range from 30 minutes to full day. Transportation from St. John's to Bay Bulls can be arranged. ✉ *18 South Side Rd., Bay Bulls* ☎ *800/966–9658, 709/576–4453* ⊕ *www.theoutfitters.nf.ca.*

WHALE-WATCHING
Iceberg Quest Ocean Tours

RAFTING | Expect to see whales, icebergs, and intensely beautiful scenery on two-hour, fully narrated boat tours to the most easterly points in North America. You can also book a live music cruise to take in the views while local musicians perform. From late May through early September, departures take place daily at 9, 11:30, 2, and 4:30. ✉ *Pier 6, 135 Harbour Dr.* ☎ *709/722–1888* ⊕ *icebergquest.com* ✉ *$70.*

Witless Bay Ecological Reserve

37 km (23 miles) south of St. John's.

Four small islands and the water surrounding them make up the reserve, the summer home of millions of seabirds—puffins, murres, kittiwakes, razorbills, and guillemots. The birds and the humpback and minke whales that linger here before moving north to their summer grounds in the Arctic feed on capelin (a fish that belongs to the smelt family) that swarm inshore to spawn.

GETTING HERE AND AROUND

The departure point for boat trips around the reserve is Bay Bulls, about 32 km (20 miles) south of St. John's via Route 10. Gatherall's provides shuttle-bus service from St. John's if you're taking one of the company's tours.

◉ Sights

Witless Bay Ecological Reserve

NATURE PRESERVE | Besides the colonies of seabirds and pods of whales in late spring and early summer, this is an excellent place to see icebergs, which can remain in Newfoundland's waters into June and sometimes July. The loud crack as an iceberg breaks apart can be heard from shore, but a boat gets you a

Detour: En Route ◉

Although there are many pretty hamlets along the way from Witless Bay to Ferryland on Route 10, Tors Cove and Brigus South have especially attractive settings. Tors Cove boasts a small and hospitable printing press and bookshop that hosts events and readings in the summer (⊕ *www.runningthegoat.com*). Brigus South is a fishing village with a strong traditional vibe; some say its name is derived from an old French word *brigue*, meaning "intrigue."

closer look at these natural ice sculptures. Icebergs have spawned a lucrative business in Newfoundland beyond tourism. Iceberg water and iceberg vodka are now on the market, made from ice chipped from the 10,000-year-old bergs as they float by.

The best views of birds and icebergs are from the tour boats that operate here and are the only way to visit the reserve. There is no public access to the islands themselves—only management staff and scientific researchers (with a permit) are allowed to land. If you're driving down from St. John's, allow about four hours: between 30 and 45 minutes each way for the drive, about 90 minutes for the boat trip, and a bit of time to spare. ⊕ *Take Pitts Memorial Dr. (Rte. 2) from downtown St. John's and turn right onto Goulds off-ramp, then left onto Rte. 10* ⊕ *witlessbay.ca.*

🍴 Restaurants

Irish Loop Coffee House

$ | **DINER** | Just a five-minute drive from the boat-tour docks in Bay Bulls, this restaurant is affectionately know as "Judy's"

The historic Ferryland Lighthouse, with its sweeping views, is a popular picnicking spot.

to locals. Diner classics like tuna melts and BLTs are served with tea, coffee, or beer to sate hikers and tourists who have gratefully come upon this friendly beacon. **Known for:** all-day breakfast; excellent coffee; fluffy blueberry pancakes. [$] *Average main: C$8* ✉ *407 Main Hwy.* ✥ *Witless Bay* ☎ *709/334–1085* 🌐 *www.irishloopcoffeehouse.com* 🕓 *Closed Mon. and Tues.*

Activities

Gatherall's Puffin and Whale Watch

RAFTING | From early May to late September, Gatherall's conducts regularly scheduled 90-minute trips (C$70) each day into the waters of Witless Bay Reserve on a high-speed catamaran. The catamaran is stable even in rough seas, so if you're the queasy type, this one might be the right tour for you. Shuttle service (C$30 additional, round-trip) is available from hotels in St. John's. ✉ *90 North Side Rd., Bay Bulls* ☎ *709/334–2887* 🌐 *gatheralls.com.*

O'Brien's Whale and Bird Tours

BIRD WATCHING | This company offers two-hour excursions (C$65) in a 100-passenger boat to view whales, icebergs, and seabirds. You can also board a 12-passenger boat for a 90-minute tour (C$99). ✉ *22 Lower Rd., off Southside Rd., Bay Bulls* ☎ *709/753–4850* 🌐 *www.obriens-boattours.com.*

Ferryland

76 km (47 miles) south of St. John's.

The main road into Ferryland hugs the coastline, where tiny bay houses dot the steep hills. Ferryland is one of the oldest European settlements in North America; the Englishman Sir George Calvert, later Lord Baltimore, settled it in 1621. Calvert didn't stay long on this cold windswept shore—he left for a warmer destination and is more commonly credited with founding Maryland. In the summer this is a great spot to watch whales.

Snowy owls, caribou, and lynx are just a few of the animals you might spot in Salmonier Nature Park.

GETTING HERE AND AROUND

There is no public transportation to Ferryland, which is south of St. John's on Route 2 and then Route 10.

👁 Sights

Colony of Avalon

RUINS | FAMILY | A major ongoing archaeological dig at Ferryland has uncovered this early-17th-century colony founded by George Calvert, later Lord Baltimore. The highlights of a visit here include six dig sites, exhibits of artifacts uncovered at them, two period gardens, and a reconstructed 17th-century kitchen. You can watch the conservationists at work in their laboratory, examining and restoring newly discovered artifacts, and take in living-history demonstrations that provide a feel for colonial times. Admission includes access to the Visitor Centre and a fascinating guided tour. ⊠ *1 The Pool, Ferryland* ☎ *709/432–3200* ⊕ *www. colonyofavalon.ca* ⊠ *C$16* ⊗ *Closed Oct.–May.*

★ Ferryland Lighthouse

LIGHTHOUSE | This historic lighthouse, built in 1870, now signals the spot for breathtaking views, worry-free picnics, and great food such as smoked salmon and ice-shrimp sandwiches, green salads, and gooseberry fools. You bring the appetite, and the lighthouse staff packs everything else—even the blanket. Bread is baked daily here; in fact, everything is made on-site down to the desserts and freshly squeezed lemonade. Check the website for menus. Picnics start at C$27 per person and reservations are required; July and August book up especially quickly. ⊠ *Rte. 10, Ferryland* ☎ *709/363–7456* ⊕ *www.lighthousepicnics.ca* ⊗ *Closed Sept.–May and Mon. and Tues. in season.*

Mistaken Point Ecological Reserve

NATURE SIGHT | A UNESCO World Heritage Site, this is one of the most significant fossil sites in the world at 575 million years old. Fossils of more than 20 species of ancient organisms are found in the mudstones here, and almost all of them represent extinct groups unknown in our modern world. Mistaken Point is 152 km (94 miles) south of St. John's via Route 10. Access to the fossils is by guided hike only. Tours are offered daily at 1 pm from the Edge of Avalon Interpretive Centre in Portugal Cove South and include access to an exhibit at the Visitor Centre. Tours generally take from 3½ to 4 hours and include a 3-km (1.8-mile) one-way hike across the barrens toward the ocean to the fossil site. Call ahead to ensure availability and to check weather conditions. Proper footwear is required.

While you're here, travel 8 km (5 miles) farther along the road to Cape Race Lighthouse, famous for receiving one of the first SOS messages from the *Titanic.* ✉ *Portugal Cove South* ✛ *Off Rte. 10, about 16 km (10 miles) southeast of Portugal Cove South on minor roads* ☎ *709/438–1100* ⊕ *www.edgeofavalon.ca* ✉ *C$20* ⊙ *Closed Oct.–June.*

Salmonier Nature Park

88 km (55 miles) northwest of Ferryland; 11 km (7 miles) south of the Trans-Canada Hwy.

Newfoundland can often seem eerily quiet, but don't let that fool you into thinking this region is devoid of wildlife. At Salmonier Nature Park, you can see the diversity of larger wildlife that the deceptive stillness has been harboring around you.

GETTING HERE AND AROUND
There is no public transportation to the park. By road, it's off the Trans-Canada Highway (Route 1). Take Exit 35 and drive south on Route 90.

Sights

Salmonier Nature Park
NATURE PRESERVE | FAMILY | Many indigenous animal species—including caribou, lynx, owls, and otters—along with moose, which were introduced

from New Brunswick a little more than a century ago, can be seen at this 437-acre wilderness area. An enclosed 3 km (1½ mile) boardwalk that is stroller and wheelchair accessible allows up-close viewing. ✉ *Salmonier Line (Rte. 90), Ferryland* ✛ *19 km (12 miles) south of Trans-Canada Hwy. (Hwy. 1)* ☎ *709/229–7888* ⊕ *flr.gov.nl.ca/wildlife/snp.*

Brigus and Cupids

19 km (12 miles) north of the intersection of Rtes. 1 and 70.

These two historic villages on Conception Bay are highlights of the area. Brigus is compact and wonderfully walkable, with a public garden, winding lanes, and a teahouse. It's best known as the birthplace of Captain Bob Bartlett, the famed Arctic explorer who accompanied Admiral Robert Peary on polar expeditions during the first decade of the 20th century. Five km (3 miles) northwest of Brigus, Cupids is the oldest English colony in Canada, founded in 1610 by John Guy, to whom the town erected a monument in 1910. Nearby is a reproduction of the enormous Union Jack that flew during the village's 300th anniversary celebration. When the wind snaps the flag, you can hear it half a mile away. The Cupids Legacy Centre was built to house the many artifacts related to the archaeology of John Guy's settlement.

GETTING HERE AND AROUND
There is no public transportation to or around Conception Bay. By road, leave the Trans-Canada Highway (Route 1) at Exit 31, drive north on Route 70 toward Carbonear, and take the Roaches line exit toward Brigus and Cupids for the last few kilometers. For a more scenic route from St. John's, head southwest on Route 2 and pick up Route 60 heading west around the coast, a total of about 74 km (46 miles). To get to Cupids, drive west

from Brigus on Route 60 and turn right on Keatings Road.

Sights

Cupids Cove Plantation

HISTORIC SIGHT | The first English settlement in Canada (founded by John Guy in 1610) has been an active archaeological dig since 1995. Engaging tours of the site are given by archaeologists and archaeology students with specific knowledge of the dig and infectious enthusiasm for the region's history. ✉ *322 Seaforest Dr., Cupids* ☎ *709/528–1413* 🌐 *www.baccalieudigs.ca* 🎫 *C$6* ⏰ *Closed mid-Oct.–late May.*

Cupids Legacy Centre & Museum

RUINS | **FAMILY** | With interactive displays, interpretive tours, a shop, and an archaeological lab, this is a good place to learn about the English settlement founded here in 1610. The bright and modern museum traces 400 years of settlement in the area through interactive exhibits and a selection of the 153,000 artifacts recovered to date at the nearby archaeological site. These include trade beads and the oldest English coin found in Canada. ✉ *368 Seaforest Dr., Cupids* ☎ *709/528–1610* 🌐 *www.cupidslegacycentre.ca* 🎫 *C$9* ⏰ *Closed mid-Oct.–May.*

The Newfoundland Distillery Company

BREWERY | Newfoundland's first artisanal gin distillery has quickly expanded their award-winning line of local liquors and built a very cool tasting room. Located on the water in the small community of Clarke's Beach, the distillery draws a crowd on summer evenings. The seaweed, rhubarb, and bakeapple gins, along with fiery aquavit, are all worth the stop. ✉ *14 Conception Bay Hwy., Clarke's Beach* ☎ *709/786–0234 distillery, 709/786–1047 tasting room and shop* 🌐 *www.thenewfoundlanddistillery.com* ⏰ *Closed Mon.–Wed.*

Restaurants

Madrock Café

$$ | **DINER** | **FAMILY** | Down a long road jutting off from the town of Bay Roberts, you'll find this small diner that's worth tracking down. Their *toutons* (a stiff, doughy, fry bread traditionally served with molasses) are quite tasty. **Known for:** early closing time at 5 pm; heavenly and unique house-made bread; big crowds. [$] *Average main: C$12* ✉ *723 Water St., Bay Roberts* ☎ *709/786–4047* 💳 *No credit cards.*

Hotels

Skipper Ben's

$ | **B&B/INN** | This restored 1891 heritage home has wood ceilings, antique furnishings, and three spacious rooms. **Pros:** proximity to the sea; ocean views from deck and rooms; excellent meals. **Cons:** road runs between B&B and water; no air-conditioning; no private bathrooms. [$] *Rooms from: C$89* ✉ *408 Seaforest Dr., Cupids* ☎ *877/528–4436* 🌐 *www.skipperbens.ca* ⏰ *Closed Jan.–Apr.* 🛏 *3 rooms* 🍴 *Free Breakfast.*

Performing Arts

★ **Perchance Theatre**

THEATER | See classic Shakespeare, along with an inspired selection of more modern plays, performed in this rustic and intimate open-air venue based on Shakespeare's Globe Theatre in London. Theatergoers are encouraged to bring blankets or cushions to cozy-up the wooden bleacher-style seating. ✉ *169 Burnt Head Loop, Cupids* ☎ *709/771–2930* 🌐 *www.perchancetheatre.com* 🎫 *C$30* ⏰ *Closed Sept.-June.*

🛍 Shopping

Brindy Linens and Co.

OTHER SPECIALTY STORE | This whimsical country shop is filled with unique and charming hand-printed textiles (think dish towels, pillow cases, and tote bags) along with a collection of goods from local artisans including teas, beeswax candles, seaweed soaps, and salt water taffy. ✉ *27 North St., Brigus* ☎ *709/730–0357* ⊕ *www.brindylinens.com.*

Harbour Grace

About 30 km (19 miles) north of Cupids.

Harbour Grace, once the headquarters of 17th-century pirate Peter Easton, was a major commercial town in the 18th and 19th centuries. Beginning in 1919, the town was the departure point for many attempts to fly the Atlantic. Amelia Earhart left Harbour Grace in 1932 to become the first woman to fly solo across the Atlantic. The town has two fine churches and several registered historic houses. About 5 km (3 miles) north of Harbour Grace is Carbonear, with a center for shopping, fast-food chains, and a hospital.

GETTING HERE AND AROUND

Harbour Grace is off Route 75, which leaves the Trans-Canada Highway (Route 1) at Exit 31.

👁 Sights

★ Grates Cove

BODY OF WATER | Grates Cove community is 75 km (46 miles) north of Harbour Grace on Route 70. Here is a photographer's dream, with vistas of both Trinity and Conception bays from the flat rocks by the harbor. In iceberg season, you cannot find a wider field of view for the startling magnificence. The fields are covered with the remains of dry stone walls

built by the original Irish settlers. Maintained and well-marked walking paths wind through the hills, the community, and along the cliffs. A community-built museum is always open to the public. ✉ *Grates Cove* ☎ *709/587–3880* ⊕ *www. gratescovestudios.com.*

Western Bay Root Cellars

TRAIL | At the edge of Western Bay, at the end of Lighthouse Road, a boardwalk will take you to a windy point with an unmanned lighthouse. If you take a right turn before the boardwalk, you can follow a trail that brings you to a secluded grassland called Bradley's Cove, where 200-year-old root cellars still stand. This trail also affords opportunity to encounter foxes and other woodland creatures sunning themselves on the rocks. ✉ *Lighthouse Rd., Western Bay* ⊹ *From Rte. 70 at Western Bay, turn onto Bradley's Cove Rd.*

🏖 Beaches

Salmon Cove Sands

BEACH | **FAMILY** | This 1,640-foot sandy beach offers a pleasant day for families. With a river nearby, you have a choice of swimming in the very cold ocean water or in the more inviting fresh water. For nonswimmers, there's a 2-km (1.2-mile) hiking trail and beautiful views of surrounding rock cliffs. An on-site kiosk sells refreshments and snacks. **Amenities:** food and drink. **Best for:** swimming. ✉ *Beach Rd., Salmon Cove* ⊹ *Off Rte. 70 at Salmon Cove* ☎ *709/597–1724* 🎫 *C$8* 🕑 *Closed Oct.–May.*

🍽 Restaurants

Red Ochre Cafe

$$ | **DINER** | **FAMILY** | This A-frame roadside eatery prepares classic diner food with a kick. The menu is simple but with special touches, like artisanal bread for the chicken sandwich, and the rotating selection of cheesecakes. **Known for:**

incredible variety of cheesecakes; warm community atmosphere; maple bacon onion rings. $ *Average main: C$12* ✉ *2 Main Rd., Ochre Pit Cove* ✣ *On Rte. 70* ☎ *709/598-2888* 🌐 *www.redochrecafe.com* 🕒 *Closed Mon. and Tues.*

The Stone Jug
$$$ | **MODERN CANADIAN** | This gastropub is located in a three-story heritage building with an interior of exposed stone and stair railings built from wood recovered from a Russian *dacha*. The wood-fire grill creates a warm and aromatic experience. **Known for:** signature "dark and stormy" cocktail; woodfire pizzas with gourmet toppings; live music on the weekends. $ *Average main: C$30* ✉ *232 Water St., Carbonear* ✣ *Take Cathedral Street north to Carbonear* ☎ *709/596–2629* 🌐 *www.thestonejug1860.com* 🕒 *Closed Mon. and Tues.*

Coffee and Quick Bites

★ **Darkstar Coffee Roasters**
$$ | **CAFÉ** | It's rare for a coffee place to be a destination, but folks on the Avalon say this little coffee place with an ocean view is worth the drive. The brews are roasted in-house and served with fresh pies and pastries. **Known for:** small-batch house-roasted coffee; savory pies made fresh daily; incredible views both indoors and outside. $ *Average main: C$12* ✉ *179 Water St., Carbonear* ✣ *Take Cathedral Street north to Carbonear* ☎ *709/596–2234* 🌐 *www.darkstarcoffeeroasters.com* 🕒 *Closed Mon.–Weds.*

Hotels

Rothesay House Inn Bed & Breakfast
$$$ | **B&B/INN** | Built in 1855 in Brigus, then dismantled, transported, and reconstructed in the Queen Anne style in Harbour Grace in 1905, Rothesay House is a charming provincial heritage building with a lovely harbor-view porch. **Pros:** beautiful garden; excellent three-course dinner available; engaging hosts with extensive knowledge of local history. **Cons:** no off-site dining options within walking distance; resident dogs (but could be a plus for animal lovers); no air-conditioning. $ *Rooms from: C$185* ✉ *34 Water St., Harbour Grace* ☎ *709/596–2268* 🌐 *www.rothesay.com* 🕒 *Closed Nov.–Apr.* 🛏 *4 rooms* 🍴 *Free Breakfast.*

Route 100: The Cape Shore

The Cape Shore area, which includes Cape St. Mary's north to Argentia, is culturally and historically rich; the French settlers had their capital here in Placentia, and Irish influence is also strong in music and manner. Birders come to view the fabulous seabird colony at Cape St. Mary's. You can reach the Cape Shore, on the western side of the Avalon Peninsula, from Route 1 at its intersection with Route 100. The ferry from Nova Scotia docks in Argentia, near Placentia.

Placentia

42 km (26 miles) south of the Trans-Canada Hwy.

Placentia was first settled by 16th-century Basque fishermen and was Newfoundland's French capital in the 1600s. The remains of an old fort built on a hill look out over Placentia and beyond, to the placid waters and wooded, steep hillsides of the inlet.

GETTING HERE AND AROUND

The Nova Scotia–Argentia ferry docks 7 km (4½ miles) north of Placentia. From the port, head south to Route 100 and continue south to reach Placentia. If driving from the Trans-Canada Highway (Route 1), take Route 100 south.

Sights

Castle Hill National Historic Site

MILITARY SIGHT | Just north of Placentia, Castle Hill is what remains of the French fortifications. The visitor center has an exhibit that shows the life and hardships experienced by early English and French settlers in the settlement then known as "Plaisance." Performances of *Faces of Fort Royale,* a play about the French era, take place during the summer as weather allows on Monday, Tuesday, Thursday, and Friday at 1:30. There are hiking trails from the forts and many lookouts on-site. ✉ *1 Old Castle Hill Rd., Placentia* ✣ *Off Rte. 100* ☎ *709/227–2401* 🌐 *www.pc.gc.ca/en/lhn-nhs/nl/castlehill* 🎟 *$4* ⏲ *Closed Sept.–May.*

Hotels

Harold Hotel

$ | **HOTEL** | Convenient to the Argentia–Nova Scotia Ferry, just 7½ km (5 miles) away, this hotel is in the heart of Placentia and a two-minute walk from the boardwalk and the ocean. **Pros:** dining room is air-conditioned; great restaurant; minutes to ferry terminal. **Cons:** local charm does not extend to the furnishings; not directly on the water; no air-conditioning in guest rooms. [$] *Rooms from: C$99* ✉ *16 Blockhouse Rd., Placentia* ✣ *Off Rte. 100* ☎ *709/227–2107, 877/227–2107* 🌐 *placentia-accommodations.com* 🛏 *18 rooms* 🍴 *No Meals.*

★ **Rosedale Manor Bed & Breakfast**

$ | **B&B/INN** | Gorgeous rooms at this 1893 waterfront heritage home far exceed what you'd expect for the low price, and tall guests will be happy with the Blueberry Room, with its extra-long bed. **Pros:** direct waterfront views; 10 minutes by car from Argentia Ferry; free and reliable Wi-Fi. **Cons:** limited parking for larger vehicles; no air-conditioning; only six rooms so it can fill up fast. [$] *Rooms from: C$119* ✉ *40 Orcan Dr., Placentia* ☎ *877/999–3613* 🌐 *www.rosedalemanor.ca* 🛏 *6 rooms* 🍴 *Free Breakfast.*

Cape St. Mary's Ecological Reserve

64 km (40 miles) south of Placentia.

The third-largest nesting colony of gannets in North America resides here, at the most accessible seabird colony on the continent. A paved road takes you within a mile of the colony.

GETTING HERE AND AROUND

Public transit doesn't serve the cape. By road, it's about an hour from Placentia, south and then briefly east on Route 100 between St. Bride's and Branch. Alternatively, from Route 91 you can head south on Route 92 and then west on Route 100. A 1-km (½-mile) cliff-top path leads from the reserve's parking lot to an observation point. The path is not suitable for wheelchairs or strollers.

Sights

★ **Cape St. Mary's Ecological Reserve**

NATURE PRESERVE | The reserve has some of the most dramatic coastal scenery in Newfoundland and is a good place to spot whales. Most birds visit from March through August, although some will be viewable in October. You can visit the interpretation center—guides are on-site in summer for larger groups—and then walk to within 100 feet of nesting gannets, murres, black-billed kittiwakes, and razorbills. At busy times you may have to wait your turn at the observation point. Call ahead to check on weather conditions before heading out. In July and August the interpretation center presents local artists performing traditional music. ✉ *Cape St. Mary's* ✥ *Off Rte. 100, between St. Bride's and Branch* ☎ *709/277–1666* 🌐 *www.newfoundlandlabrador.com/top-destinations/cape-st-marys.*

Hotels

Capeway Motel & Efficiency Units
$$ | **HOTEL** | This former convent, built in 1968, is about a 15-minute drive from the seabird sanctuary at Cape St. Mary's. **Pros:** free Wi-Fi; unique setting; well-equipped suites with kitchenettes, tea, and coffee. **Cons:** wheelchair accessible on main level only; air-conditioning on main level only; no on-site restaurant. [$] *Rooms from: C$129* ✉ *11 Main St. (Rte. 100), St. Bride's* ☎ *709/337–2163, 866/337–2163* 🌐 *www.thecapeway.ca* 🛏 *7 rooms* 🍴 *Free Breakfast.*

Clarenville

189 km (117 miles) northwest of St. John's.

Clarenville has a marina, a small bird sanctuary, and a monument commemorating the laying of the first transatlantic telephone cable. It is also in aviation history as the landing site for the 1933 transatlantic flight of 24 seaplanes commandeered by General Italo Balboa. The town makes a convenient stop along the highway when traveling the long distances of the island. It is within one- to three-hours' drive of the Bonavista Peninsula, with its Discovery Trail and the twin communities of Trinity and Bonavista, as well as the sandy beaches around Eastport, Terra Nova National Park, and the Burin Peninsula.

GETTING HERE AND AROUND

No useful public transit serves Clarenville. To drive here from St. John's by car, a two-hour trip, take the Trans-Canada Highway (Route 1) west.

ESSENTIALS

VISITOR INFORMATION Clarenville Provincial Visitor Information Centre.
✉ *379 Trans-Canada Hwy., Clarenville* ☎ *709/466–3100.*

Sights

Discovery Trail
SCENIC DRIVE | If history and quaint towns appeal to you, follow this trail, which is accessible from the Trans-Canada Highway (Rte. 1) on Route 230 or 230A at Clarenville, or at Port Blandford on Route 233. It includes two gems: the old town of Trinity, famed for its architecture and theater festival, and Bonavista, one of John Cabot's reputed landing spots. The provincial tourism website (🌐 *www.newfoundlandlabrador.com*) has a more detailed description. Clarenville itself is largely a departure point for these more attractive destinations. ✉ *Clarenville.*

Newfoundland Cider Company Tasting Room
BREWERY | Newfoundland's first craft cidery, producing cider and *pét nat* (sparkling wine) for businesses around the province, has a tasting room where visitors can enjoy the products on-site along with a charcuterie board or seasonally appropriate pairings like grilled cheeses or hot chilli. Watch for pop-up events with visiting chefs. Visitors can sit outside in a a miniature orchard, and a weatherproof dome allows for a charming outdoor experience in summer and winter. In the off-season, the tasting room continues to open for Saturday afternoons. ✉ *7 Stringer's La., George's Brook-Milton, Clarenville* ☎ *709/427–5662* ✉ *nfcider@gmail.com* 🌐 *www.newfoundlandciderco.com* 🕓 *Closed Mon.–Wed. in summer.*

The third-largest nesting colony of gannets in North America resides in Cape St. Mary's Ecological Reserve.

🍴 Restaurants

Cabin Six Pizza

$$ | **PIZZA** | This is a little pizza shop that's made a big splash, with stone-baked pizzas with interesting toppings and locally grown or foraged ingredients. This destination eatery is a throwback to the old general store that once occupied the space with retro touches like a tiny black-and-white TV playing cartoons and industrial artifacts on the walls, alongside photos by a local photographer known as "Old Bones." Best not to try calling ahead; this two-person operation is doing a booming business. **Known for:** fun retro decor; the BBQ pulled pork pizza; the "bearded chef." [$] *Average main: C$16* ✉ *18 Trinity Dr., George's Brook-Milton, Clarenville* 🌐 *www.instagram.com/cabinsixpizza* 🕓 *Closed Sun.–Thurs.*

Milton Inn Relaxed Fine Dining

$$$$ | **FRENCH FUSION** | This hidden gem may be Newfoundland's best-kept secret. The four-course fine dining experience takes reservations months ahead, with meal pre-order placed a week in advance. **Known for:** they boast the best wine list on the island; honey butter made with honey from their own beehives; "Zaylah's sorbets" served in bowls carved from beach rocks. [$] *Average main: C$135* ✉ *20 Trinity Dr., George's Brook-Milton, Clarenville* ☎ *709/433–2395* 🌐 *milton-inn.ca/relaxed-fine-dining* 🕓 *Closed Sun.–Thurs.*

☕ Coffee and Quick Bites

Bare Mountain Coffee House

$$ | **CAFÉ** | This stone cottage offers a bright interior with both sofa and table seating and a view of Random Island in Trinity Bay. In finer weather, you can enjoy your coffee from an Adirondack chair on the patio overlooking the water. **Known for:** beautiful views; small on-site gift shop; huge windows overlooking the water. [$] *Average main: C$12* ✉ *53 Memorial Dr., Clarenville* ☎ *709/466-2888* 🌐 *www.baremountaincoffeehouse.com.*

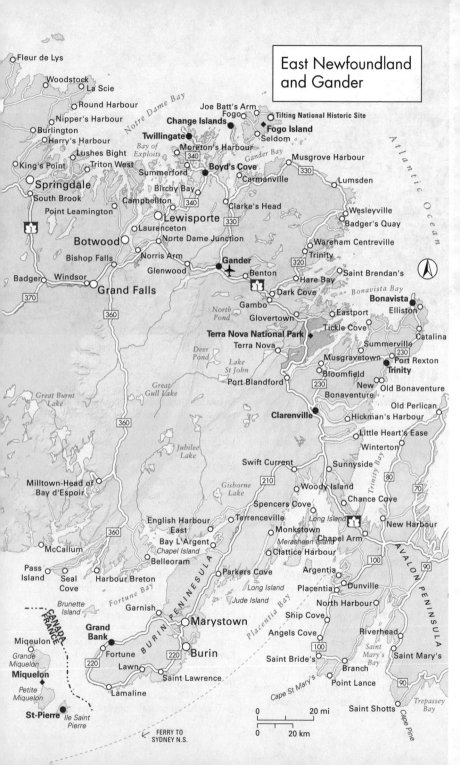

East Newfoundland and Gander

Shopping

The Barn Loft

CANDY | FAMILY | This is the kind of shop that gives you a calm feeling when you walk in. A rustic gift shop offering home decor items, unique toys, gardening items, and a candy village with imported treats and sweets you'll remember from your childhood. Don't leave without trying their house-made fudge and ice creams. ✉ *28 Harbour Dr., Clarenville* ☎ *709/466–3614.*

Mercer's Marine

GENERAL STORE | This family-run general store sells more than gear for your boat. Find quality outdoor clothing and footwear for the entire family, as well as housewares, craft supplies, and hardware. ✉ *210 Marine Dr., Clarenville* ☎ *709/466–7430* 🌐 *mercersmarine.com.*

Terra Nova National Park

About 40 km (25 miles) north of Clarenville.

Newfoundland's first national park, established in 1957, offers natural beauty, dramatic Bonavista Bay coastline, rugged woods, and many outdoor activities. Moose, black bear, and other wildlife roam freely in the forests and marshy bogs, pods of whales play in the waters within view, and many species of birds inhabit the cliffs and shores.

GETTING HERE AND AROUND

The park straddles the Trans-Canada Highway (Route 1). The southern entrance is near Port Blandford, the northern one near Glovertown at the Splash 'n' Putt waterpark.

Sights

★ **Terra Nova National Park**

NATIONAL PARK | FAMILY | Golfing, sea kayaking, fishing, camping, and canoeing are among the activities the 399-square-km (186-square-mile) park supports. You can arrange guided walks at the visitor center, which has exhibits, a small shop, and a decent snack bar–cafeteria.

■ TIP→ The visitor center can also provide connections to a local tour company for boat tours and kayaking activities while in the park. ✉ *Trans-Canada Hwy., Glovertown* ☎ *709/533–2801 National Parks Service* 🌐 *www.pc.gc.ca* 🎟 *$6.*

Hotels

Freshwater Inn

$$ | B&B/INN | On a quiet cove on Freshwater Bay, this little inn has large, well-equipped rooms and is a decent base for visiting Terra Nova National Park, 25 km (15 miles) south. **Pros:** peaceful, beautiful grounds; no stairs; snack baskets and refrigerators in-room. **Cons:** nothing within walking distance; no good restaurants nearby; bathrooms have no windows. [$] *Rooms from: C$155* ✉ *Rte. 320, Gambo* ✥ *10 km (6 miles) northeast of Trans-Canada Hwy., Exit 24* ☎ *709/674–5577, 877/674–5577* 🌐 *www.freshwaterinn.com* 🕒 *Closed Nov.–Apr.* 🛏 *6 rooms* 🍴 *Free Breakfast.*

Terra Nova Resort and Golf Community

$ | RESORT | This 220-acre oceanfront resort near Terra Nova National Park has two golf courses nestled in the picturesque Clode Sound. **Pros:** tennis and basketball courts and play area for children; heated indoor/outdoor pool; wonderful views overlooking Clode Sound. **Cons:** very golf-centric; noise from common areas can be disruptive in rooms; some rooms could use updating. [$] *Rooms from: C$119* ✉ *5-9 Muddy Brook Rd., Port Blandford* ✥ *Off Trans-Canada Hwy.* ☎ *709/543–2525* 🌐 *terranovagolfnl.com* 🕒 *Closed Oct.–Apr.* 🛏 *87 rooms* 🍴 *No Meals.*

The seaside village of Trinity charms visitors—especially when its purple lupines are in bloom.

Trinity

70 km (43 miles) northeast of Clarenville.

Trinity is one of the jewels of Newfoundland. The village's ocean views, winding lanes, and snug houses are the main attractions, and several homes have been turned into museums and inns. In the 1700s, Trinity competed with St. John's as a center of culture and wealth. Its more contemporary claim to fame, however, is that its intricate harbor was a favorite anchorage for the British navy. The smallpox vaccine was introduced to North America here by a local rector. On West Street an information center with costumed interpreters is open daily during the summer. Please keep in mind there is no grocery store, and restaurants are not open late at night. Plan ahead when traveling to small communities so you do not end up waiting until morning for a meal.

GETTING HERE AND AROUND

To get here from Clarenville, take Route 230 to Route 239.

◉ Sights

Mercantile Premises

HISTORY MUSEUM | FAMILY | At this provincial historic site you can slip back in time more than a century to the era when mercantile families ruled tiny communities. Next door the counting house has been restored to the 1820s and the retail store to the 1900s. An interpretation center traces the history of Trinity, once a hub of commerce. ⊠ *West St., Trinity* ☎ *709/464–2042* 🖃 *C$6* ⊘ *Closed mid-Oct.–early May.*

Random Passage

TOWN | The community of New Bonaventure is about 15 km (10 miles) south on Route 239 from Trinity. It has been the backdrop for two movies, *The Shipping News* and *The Grand Seduction*, and for an internationally televised miniseries based on Bernice Morgan's novel

The Eastport Peninsula

A short, pretty drive from Terra Nova National Park, part of it on a thin strip of road between two bodies of water, will take you to the Eastport Peninsula; take Route 310, at the northern boundary of the national park. There are two beautiful, sandy beaches—at Eastport and at Sandy Cove—and either is perfect to laze away an afternoon. The very old outport of Salvage and the small port of Happy Adventure are charming. B&Bs and cabins dot this agricultural peninsula, and the musical and literary festivals might convince you to stay a night or two. At Burnside, you can visit an archaeology center with Beothuk artifacts or take a boat ride to the Beaches, once the largest Beothuk settlement in Bonavista Bay. The Inn at Happy Adventure is a good choice for travelers. An all-in-one vacation stop with a restaurant, comfortable accommodations, views, boat and kayak tours, and the perfect location from which to enjoy Eastport's sandy beaches and Terra Nova National Park.

Random Passage. At the end of the road, walk a short way, and you'll reach the breathtaking cove now known as Random Passage where the set of the miniseries was constructed and eventually donated to the community as an early 19th-century outpost. You can roam the church, schoolroom, houses, and a fishing stage and flakes (where fish is dried), or sit near the vegetable garden and enjoy the quiet beauty of the cove's meadows and pastures. There are guided one-hour site tours, which include "Joe's Place," the bar featured in *The Grand Seduction.* The website is updated seasonally with frequent programming and events. The Old Schoolhouse tearoom (open from 9:30 to 4:30) serves housemade fish cakes, pea soup, and light lunches. ✉ *Rte. 239, New Bonaventure* ✥ *Off Rte. 230* ☎ *709/464–2233* 🌐 *www.randompassagesite.com* 🎟 *$10* 🕒 *Closed Sept.–late-May.*

Skerwink Trail

TRAIL | About 9,000 people a year come to hike this historic footpath, a cliff walk with panoramic vistas of Trinity and the ocean. On the trail you'll see sandy beaches, sea stacks (giant protruding rocks that have slowly eroded over time), seabirds, and, in season, whales, icebergs, and bald eagles. The 5.3-km (3¼-mile) loop trail, which begins in Port Rexton, is not for the faint of heart. It takes about two hours and can be steep in places. There are benches along the way. ✉ *Port Rexton* ✥ *Off Rte. 230* 🌐 *www.hikediscovery.com/skerwink.*

🍴 Restaurants

Port Rexton Brewery Taproom

$ | **AMERICAN** | The first opening in the microbrewery resurgence on the island is arguably the best. Oh My Cheeses, a food truck, provides the grub, like eclectic grilled cheese and other hip takes on old standards. **Known for:** amazing grilled cheese; some of the region's best brews; unique beers. [$] *Average main: C$11* ✉ *6 Ship Cove Rd., Port Rexton* ☎ *709/464–2337* 🌐 *www.portrextonbrewing.com* 🕒 *Closed Wed.*

★ Twine Loft Dining

$$$$ | **CONTEMPORARY** | Every evening, the set menu at the Twine Loft proves to be one of the region's best meals. Relax into a true fine dining experience complete with an on-site sommelier. **Known for:** reservations necessary; excellent fine dining experience; views over the water. $ *Average main: C$60* ⊠ *57 High St., Trinity* ☎ *709/464–3377* ⊕ *www.trinityvacations.com* ☉ *Closed Nov.–Apr.*

🛏 Hotels

Artisan Inn and Vacation Homes

$$ | **B&B/INN** | Six houses in the heart of Trinity make up this inn, two of which—the Campbell and Gover houses—are from the mid-1800s and are Registered Heritage Structures. **Pros:** well appointed rooms and very comfortable beds; very friendly owners; location in historic Trinity. **Cons:** only a continental breakfast included; no elevators; historical decor not for everyone. $ *Rooms from: C$150* ⊠ *57 High St., Trinity* ☎ *709/464–3377, 877/464–7700* ⊕ *www.trinityvacations.com* ☉ *Closed Nov.–Apr.* ⇥ *8 rooms* ⦿ *Free Breakfast.*

Eriksen Premises

$ | **B&B/INN** | One of Trinity's heritage structures, this two-story mansard-style building has been restored to its original elegance with modern comforts added. **Pros:** restaurant and eclectic gift shop on premises; great central location; large sitting room has cable TV, mini-refrigerator, tea, and coffee. **Cons:** dining room can get busy; no air-conditioning in some rooms; no elevator. $ *Rooms from: C$110* ⊠ *8 West St., Trinity* ☎ *709/464–3698, 877/464–3698* ⊕ *www.mytrinityexperience.com* ☉ *Closed mid-Oct.–Apr.* ⇥ *7 rooms* ⦿ *Free Breakfast.*

★ Fishers' Loft Inn

$$ | **B&B/INN** | These are without a doubt some of the best accommodations on the Bonavista Peninsula, with beautiful gardens and stunning views. **Pros:** great restaurant; beautiful decor; parking at each building. **Cons:** some hillside walking between buildings; only one dining option; no air-conditioning in some rooms. $ *Rooms from: C$160* ⊠ *Mill Rd.,*

Port Rexton ⊹ *15 km (9 miles) northeast of Trinity* ☎ *877/464–3240, 709/464–3240* ⊕ *fishersloft.com* ☉ *Closed Oct.–Apr.* ⇥ *22 rooms* ⦿ *No Meals.*

Sherwood Suites

$ | **APARTMENT** | **FAMILY** | These affordable self-service efficiency suites are spacious and have living rooms and private patios from which to enjoy tranquil views. **Pros:** Wi-Fi in all rooms; beautiful 20-acre property near Skerwink Trail; on-site laundry facilities and playground. **Cons:** basic decor; no air-conditioning; no restaurant. $ *Rooms from: C$109* ⊠ *32 Rocky Hill Rd., Port Rexton* ☎ *709/464–2130, 877/464–2133* ⊕ *www.sherwoodsuites.com* ☉ *Closed Oct.–late May* ⇥ *16 rooms* ⦿ *No Meals.*

🎭 Performing Arts

Rising Tide Theatre

THEATER | Dinner theater, local dramas, comedies, and newly commissioned plays are performed from mid-June to mid-October as part of the Bight Festival at the Rising Tide Theatre. The theater company also presents the New-Founde-Land Trinity Pageant and conducts walking tours of lanes, roads, and historical sites. More theater than tour, with actors in period costume. ⊠ *40 West St., Trinity* ☎ *709/464–3232, 888/464–3377* ⊕ *www.risingtidetheatre.com* 🎟 *From C$20.*

🏃 Activities

Rugged Beauty Boat Tours

BOATING | Experience much more than the rugged beauty of the glorious coastline on this excellent three-hour open-boat trip with a knowledgeable skipper whose family has lived here for generations. This is a historical tour, not a whale-watching trip, and you'll be moved by true stories about the lives of the fisherfolk and enjoy some local humor, too. Disembark for an informal cup of tea at the skipper's vacation cabin on a beautiful bay before heading back. Tours on the skipper's 27-foot boat, which can accommodate 12 guests, take place from May to October. ✉ *Main Rd., New Bonaventure* ✛ *Off Rte. 230* ☎ *709/464–3856* ⊕ *www.ruggedbeautyboattours.net* ✉ *$90.*

★ Sea of Whales Adventures

BOATING | Sea of Whales guides have a true passion for the ocean and the life it contains. If there are whales in the area, even in the shoulder season, you will find them with this outfit. Their knowledge of the area makes each trip out in their Zodiac one to remember. They keep the guest number between four and 11 people for each two- or three-hour tour. With guides fully versed in both boating and science, you will be thrilled and educated before returning to dry land. A break for coffee and cookies is included. ✉ *12 Ash's La., Trinity* ☎ *709/464–2200* ⊕ *www.seaofwhales.com* ✉ *C$90* ☉ *Closed Nov.–Apr.*

Bonavista

52 km (32 miles) north of Trinity.

No one knows exactly where explorer John Cabot landed when he came to Atlantic Canada in 1497, but based on his descriptions, many believe it was at Bonavista. Still a bustling industrial fishing port today, this is one of the few outport communities in Newfoundland that has maintained a steady population as the fishing industry in the region declined. A recent resurgence of economic growth is seen not only in seasonal and tourism industries, but also in year-round, sustainable manufacturing like sea salt producers (⊕ *www.newfoundlandsaltcompany. com*), soap manufacturers that specialize in products made from iceberg water (⊕ *www.eastcoastglownl.com*), and fiber mills (⊕ *www.treelinefinecraft.com*). This picturesque town is a great place to rent a bicycle that comes with a picnic lunch included (⊕ *bonavistapicnicscafe.com*).

GETTING HERE AND AROUND

Public transit doesn't serve Bonavista. From Trinity, drive north on Route 239 and continue north (turn right) on Route 230; from the Trans-Canada Highway, take the exit for Route 230A and join Route 230 north of George's Brook.

⊙ Sights

Cape Bonavista Lighthouse

LIGHTHOUSE | A provincial historic site on the point, about 1 km (½ mile) outside town, the lighthouse was built in 1843 and has been restored to the way it looked in 1870. ✉ *505 Cape Shore Rd., Bonavista* ☎ *709/468–7444* ⊕ *www. seethesites.ca* ✉ *$6* ☉ *Closed early Oct.–late May.*

Mockbeggar Plantation

HISTORIC HOME | **FAMILY** | The home of F. Gordon Bradley, a proponent of Confederation, has been restored to its 1939 appearance, the better to chronicle the days leading up to Newfoundland becoming a province of Canada a decade later. The house was built in the 1870s, when it was a fishery plantation. Interpreters lead tours of the plantation house known as the Bradley House. ✉ *Roper St., Bonavista* ✛ *Off Rte. 230* ☎ *709/468–7444* ⊕ *seethesites.ca* ✉ *C$6* ☉ *Closed Nov.–Apr.*

Ryan Premises National Historic Site

HISTORY MUSEUM | On the waterfront, this restored fish merchant's property depicts the history of the commercial cod fishery that prospered here between 1869 and the 1950s. ✉ *10 Ryan's Hill Rd., Bonavista* ✛ *Off Rte. 230* ☎ *709/468–1600* ⊕ *www. pc.gc.ca* ✉ *C$4* ☉ *Closed Sept.–May.*

🍴 Restaurants

★ Bonavista Social Club

$ | **PIZZA** | The name implies more than just a restaurant and it is: a view, a respite, a community. From a table inside, you can watch pizzas cook in a wood-fired oven while sitting on handcrafted wooden furniture. **Known for:** classic wood-fired pizza; gorgeous views; welcoming crowds. $ *Average main: C$13* ✉ *7 Longshore Rd., Bonavista* ✛ *Follow Rte. 235 to just south of Bonavista, turn at sign for Upper Amherst Cove, and follow road into Amherst Cove around to right* ☎ *709/704–6822* ⊕ *bonavistasocialclub.com* ⊗ *Closed Oct.–May.*

Boreal Diner

$$$ | CAFÉ | This diner serves a variety of dishes, all with fresh ingredients (some grown right on the front patio) along with a small but balanced selection of wine and craft beers. Salads are excellent, and they serve some of the best pies and baked goods in the area. **Known for:** support of local farmers; pies baked daily, like molasses custard pie; coffee from local roaster. $ *Average main: C$25* ✉ *61 Church St., Bonavista* ☎ *709/476–2330* ⊕ *theborealdiner.com* ⊗ *Closed Sept.–May.*

Mifflin's Tea Room

$$ | CANADIAN | FAMILY | A historic building, traditional food, and an entrepreneurial spirit make this quaint yet bustling restaurant a classic spot. The owners have turned their multigenerational family home into a business that welcomes other families with hearty standard meals and drinks served in tiny teapots and china cups. **Known for:** family-friendly atmosphere; extensive tea selection; great panfried cod. $ *Average main: C$19* ✉ *21 Church St., Bonavista* ☎ *709/468–2636* ⊗ *Closed Oct.–Apr.*

Hotels

The Harbour Quarters

$$ | B&B/INN | Overlooking Bonavista Harbour, just a few steps from the Ryan Premises, this heritage property is a great place to drop anchor for the night. **Pros:** historic ambience; easy walk to everything; sunset view from restaurant

and deck. **Cons:** breakfast not included with stays; no lunch at restaurant during the off-season; on the main road. $ *Rooms from: C$159* ✉ *42 Campbell St., Bonavista* ☎ *709/468–7982, 866/468–7982* ✉ *info@harbourquarters.com* ⊕ *www.harbourquarters.com* ⊗ *Closed Nov.–Apr.* ⇌ *12 rooms* ⦿ *No Meals.*

★ Russelltown Inn

$$ | B&B/INN | Russelltown Inn operates as a "decentralized inn," offering suites in a number of heritage properties all restored to the same luxurious standard. **Pros:** free Wi-Fi; infallible sense of design; comfortable beds. **Cons:** no air-conditioning; sound travels in certain rooms; some rooms are small. $ *Rooms from: C$169* ✉ *134 Coster St., Bonavista* ☎ *888/963–8282* ⊕ *www.russelltowninn.com* ⇌ *10 suites* ⦿ *No Meals.*

Grand Bank

226 km (140 miles) southwest of Clarenville.

One of the loveliest communities in Newfoundland, Grand Bank has a fascinating history as an important fishing center. Because of trading patterns, the architecture here was influenced more by New England than that found in the rest of Newfoundland.

GETTING HERE AND AROUND

Grand Bank is on the Burin Peninsula Highway (Route 210), which winds south and then west down the Burin Peninsula.

⊙ Sights

Provincial Seamen's Museum

NAUTICAL SIGHT | This sail-shape building contains a bright and lively museum celebrating the province's connection with both land and sea. Exhibits include boats, ship models, and artifacts from the 1800s to the present. ✉ *54 Marine Dr.,*

Grand Bank ☎ *709/832–1484* 🌐 *www.therooms.ca/PSM* 🎫 *C$3* ⏰ *Closed Oct.–Apr.*

🍴 Restaurants

Smugglers Cove

$$ | **BARBECUE** | **FAMILY** | This place is more than a restaurant, it's a whole pioneer town experience. The pub and grill deliver meals of outstanding quality in a roadhouse-style setting. **Known for:** pioneer village makes a fun photo app; fabulous food with generous portions; popular stop for cycling enthusiasts. [$] *Average main: C$20* ✉ *300-316 Church St., Burin* ☎ *709/891–2222* 🌐 *smugglerscoveroadhouse.com* ⏰ *Closed Sun. and Mon.*

🛏 Hotels

★ **Thorndyke Bed & Breakfast**

$$ | **B&B/INN** | This 1917 Queen Anne–style mansion, a former sea captain's house, is a designated historic structure with great views. **Pros:** pretty oceanfront neighborhood; fresh and healthy food; comfortable beds. **Cons:** can be a bit old-fashioned; no in-room refrigerators; no air-conditioning. [$] *Rooms from: C$165* ✉ *33 Water St., Grand Bank* ☎ *709/832–0820* 🛏 *4 rooms* 🍴 *Free Breakfast.*

St-Pierre and Miquelon

90-minute ferry ride from Fortune, which is about 7.5 km (5 miles) from Grand Bank.

The islands of St-Pierre and Miquelon, France's only territory in North America, are but a ferry ride away from Newfoundland. Be aware that you will be crossing an international border between Canada and France, so you will have to go through a customs and immigration process. Shopping and dining on French cuisine are both popular pastimes here. The bakeries open early, so there's always piping-hot fresh bread for breakfast, and bargain hunters can find reasonably priced wines from all over France. An interesting side trip via boat takes you to see seals, seabirds, and other wildlife, plus the huge sandbar (formed on the bones of shipwrecks) that now connects formerly separate Great and Little Miquelon.

GETTING HERE AND AROUND

You can fly to St-Pierre with Air Saint-Pierre from cities in Canada and France, or you can take a ferry from Fortune, which is less than 10 km (6 miles) from Grand Bank. Visitors to the islands must carry proof of citizenship—all non-Canadians must have a passport, and Canadians should have a passport or a government-issued photo ID. Because of the ferry schedule, a trip to St-Pierre means an overnight stay in a hotel or a *pension,* the French equivalent of a B&B. If you're flying, you'll need to stay longer as flights are not scheduled every day and don't allow for a one-day round-trip. St-Pierre is on French time, a half hour ahead of Newfoundland, so make sure you adjust your watch for the ferry schedule. Once you arrive in St-Pierre, everything is within a short taxi ride or walking distance.

ESSENTIALS

If you plan to stay here for any length of time, be aware that the electrical supply is the same as in France—220v, 50 Hz. Check for compatibility with your electronic equipment, and carry adapters if necessary. For other information about traveling to and within the islands, check with their tourist board.

■ **TIP→ Prices throughout are listed in euros.**

CONTACTS Air Saint-Pierre. ☎ *877/277–7765* 🌐 *www.airsaintpierre.com.*

Sights

Le Cabestan (Ferry from Fortune to St-Pierre)
TRANSPORTATION | A passenger ferry operated by this company leaves Fortune (south of Grand Bank) from late April through December. Through July and August, there is daily service (with twice-daily service some days), but the schedule thins out rapidly in the shoulder season so check the schedule and plan ahead. The crossing takes roughly an hour; one-way is about C$65 (45€), round-trip is about C$110 (73€), but rates are set in euros so check the website and exchange rate close to your travel date. ✉ *14 Bayview St., Fortune* ☎ *709/832-3455* 🌐 *www.saintpierreferry.com* 🕓 *Closed Jan.–Apr.*

Restaurants

Les P'tits Graviers
$$$ | **FRENCH** | **FAMILY** | A family-friendly spot, Les P'tits Graviers is known for a wide variety of fresh French cuisine. Using locally sourced and seasonal ingredients, they adapt their menu frequently. **Known for:** boozy desserts; tasty pizzas; great sauces on local meat dishes. [$] *Average main: €23* ✉ *2 rue Maréchal Foch* ☎ *508/41-75-28* 🕓 *Closed Wed.*

Hotels

Hôtel Robert
$$ | **HOTEL** | Convenient to the ferry, this waterfront hotel used to accommodate Al Capone when he ran rum through St-Pierre during Prohibition—you can see his hat in the mini Prohibition-era museum on-site. **Pros:** ocean views from breakfast room; on the waterfront, a five-minute walk from ferry; rental cars available. **Cons:** can get crowded with families; no room service; no elevator. [$] *Rooms from: €170* ✉ *2 rue du 11 Novembre, St-Pierre* ☎ *508/41-24-19* 🌐 *www.hotelrobert.com* 🛏 *43 rooms* 🍴 *No Meals.*

Gander

367 km (228 miles) north of Grand Bank; 331 km (207 miles) west of St. John's; 149 km (93 miles) west of Clarenville.

Gander, a busy town of 11,000 people, is notable for its aviation history. During World War II, the airport here, now called Gander International, was a major strategic air base and became a hub for civilian travel after World War II. Its international lounge, designed to receive the jet set of the mid-20th century, reflects a high-end avant-garde style. The airport gained some renown when planes destined for the United States were diverted here following the September 11, 2001, terrorist attacks. The movie *Diverted* and the Broadway musical *Come From Away* tell the heartwarming story. Today, the airport is a major air-traffic-control center.

With its central location, Gander is a good base for travel in this part of the province, including to Twillingate, the town of Change Islands, and Fogo Island.

GETTING HERE AND AROUND

Gander is on the Trans-Canada Highway (Route 1). To get to Twillingate, take Route 330 north to Route 331 north, eventually connecting to Route 340 to Twillingate. To visit Change Islands and Fogo Island, depart Route 331 at Route 335 and head northeast. You can drive on causeways to Twillingate but will need to catch the ferry in Farewell to get to Change Islands and Fogo Island. If you fly into Gander's airport, book a rental car in advance, as supplies are limited.

Sights

Gander International Airport
AIRPORT | This is a nice stop if you are interested in the more recent history of Newfoundland, regardless of whether you fly in or out from here. The International Departures Lounge was opened in 1959 by Queen Elizabeth II and

has remained a stylish, though now underused, time capsule of modernist design and the jet-setting '60s. If no flights are arriving, the Commissionaires may make time for a quick tour. However, the original furniture (some of which was designed by Arne Jacobsen), geometric terrazzo floors, and Kenneth Lochhead's singular and timeless mural can all be viewed at your leisure from a glass observation corridor. ✉ *1000 James Blvd., Gander* ☎ *709/256–6677* 🌐 *www.ganderairport.com.*

North Atlantic Aviation Museum
HISTORY MUSEUM | FAMILY | Just down the highway from the visitor information center, this museum provides an expansive view of Gander's and Newfoundland's roles in aviation. In addition to viewing the aircraft collection (including a World War II–era Lockheed Hudson and a Voodoo fighter jet) and some photographs, you can climb into the cockpit of a real DC-3. ✉ *135 Trans-Canada Hwy., Gander* ☎ *709/256–2923* 🌐 *northatlanticaviationmuseum.com* 🎟 *$8* 🕓 *Closed weekends Sept.–May.*

Silent Witness Memorial
MONUMENT | The memorial marks the spot where, on December 12, 1985, an Arrow Air DC-8 carrying the 101st Airborne Division home for Christmas crashed, killing 256 American soldiers and civilian flight crew. The site lies just off the highway on a rough gravel road, but it's a must-see. The setting, a clearing in the woods overlooking the grandeur of Gander Lake, is peaceful and moving, and the memorial sculpture, of a boy and girl holding the hands of a peacekeeper, is poignantly rendered. ✉ *Eastern side of Trans-Canada Hwy., Gander* ✣ *4 km (2½ miles) from Gander.*

🍴 Restaurants

Newfoundland Tea Co.
$$$ | BISTRO | More than a tea company, this restaurant provides lunch and dinner menus. The combination of dark wood and often whimsical local art mirrors the simple yet rich fare. **Known for:** tasty crab cake appetizers; classic dishes with a European flare; fantastic cocktails. [$] *Average main: C$28* ✉ *110 Roe Ave., Gander* ☎ *709/651–4763* 🌐 *www.thenewfoundlandteaco.com* 🕓 *Closed Sun.–Tues.*

🛏 Hotels

Quality Hotel Gander
$$ | HOTEL | FAMILY | Past its heyday but not yet "vintage" in style, the excellent service, comfortable beds, and convenient location nonetheless make this a good stopover if you're traveling from coast to coast. **Pros:** business-friendly amenities; bright, cheerful dining room; bar has outside patio. **Cons:** can get crowded with families; highway traffic makes front rooms noisy; pool sometimes closed for maintenance. [$] *Rooms from: C$155* ✉ *100 Trans-Canada Hwy., Gander* ☎ *709/256–3931, 800/563–2988* 🌐 *www.qualityhotelgander.com* 🛏 *137 rooms* 🍽 *Free Breakfast.*

Fogo and Change Islands

90 km (56 miles) north of Gander.

Tales of the famous Fogo Island Inn have revived interest in this area for travelers from around the world. While Fogo Island has begun to reinvent itself with modern artist studios, arts-residency projects, and home-built economic engines, neighboring Change Islands has remained almost frozen in time. The barren landscape and remote location of these communities are both a draw and a barrier to tourism. Once ensconced, there seems to be no end to what you can experience. The natural landscape is continually stunning, and the people are warm, creative, and entrepreneurial. See the islands from the sea from a comfortable perch with Fogo Island Boat Tours.

You can lose yourself in quiet and beauty in every cove and spit and feel like you're at the end of the earth.

GETTING HERE AND AROUND

From Gander, head north on Route 330. At Gander Bay (Clarke's Head) turn left towards Twillingate on Route 331. Keep a lookout for signs to the Fogo and Change Islands Ferry and turn right onto Route 335 heading North to Farewell. The ferry crossing to Fogo takes 45 minutes; the crossing to Change Islands is 20 minutes. Pay attention to which lane you should be in for Fogo versus Change Islands (or Change Islands versus Farewell when returning from Fogo, as there is limited to no signage, and the ferries wait for no man's mistakes!). Provincial Ferry Service charges C$25.50 for a vehicle and driver from Farewell to Fogo (return); C$10.25 for vehicle and driver to Change Islands; additional fees for other passengers. Space is limited. Plan to arrive at least one hour prior to departure. Check the website prior to travel for schedule updates (⊕ *www.gov.nl.ca/ti/ferryservices*). There are clean public restrooms at each ferry terminal.

To accommodate charter flights, Fogo Island has a provincially operated airstrip (Fogo Aerodome CDY3), suitable for aircraft such as the fixed-wing 12-passenger Beech 1900D and the 37-seat Dash 100. Evasair (⊕ *www.evasair.com*) offers flights to Fogo from Gander several times per week.

TOURS

Fogo Island Boat Tours

BOAT TOURS | With two daily scheduled departures for regular three-hour sightseeing trips and options for more personalized chartered tours, you can experience Fogo Island and its coastlines, architecture, whales, icebergs, and seabirds from the sea itself. This fully equipped boat has you covered for any whim (and most weather) with

bathrooms and indoor seating options. ⊠ *Government Wharf in Joe Batt's Arm, Fogo Island* ☎ *709/658–7374, 709/266–7081* 🖻 *C$100* ⊗ *Closed mid-Sept.–mid-May.*

◉ Sights

FOGO ISLAND
Tilting National Historic Site

TOWN | The community of Tilting, on Fogo's far end, is famous for how well they have preserved their "vernacular" architecture—small boxy wooden houses right on the water's edge with a simple and practical center-hall design broken into four small bedrooms upstairs to maximize on privacy and minimize on heating costs. The Dwyer Fishing Premises won an award for preservation of the architectural heritage of Newfoundland and Labrador, and along with the Old Irish Cemetery, the Lane House Museum, and Sandy Cove Park, make for a complete afternoon outing. If the weather is nice, a picnic or camping on Sandy Cove beach is a treat. ⊠ *Tilting, Fogo Island* ⊕ *www.townoffogoisland.ca/home/41.*

CHANGE ISLANDS
Newfoundland Pony Sanctuary

FARM/RANCH | **FAMILY** | Newfoundland ponies are a part of the Island's cultural history and heritage. Netta LeDrew, founder of the sanctuary, can tell visitors of the work this breed did hauling capelin in from the stages and plowing the fields. But the ponies under her care know no such rigors; these sturdy little beauties are a part of a rescue and breeding program. You can come and meet them and appreciate their picturesque lives with their devoted caretaker, a brand new barn, and plenty of space to graze and roam. ⊠ *Change Islands* ☎ *709/884–6953, 709/621—6381* 🖻 *Suggested donation of C$10.*

The Fogo Island Inn has garnered global attention due to its modern architecture, interior design, and breathtaking views.

Olde Shoppe Museum at Change Islands

HISTORY MUSEUM | Finding a one-room museum built and maintained by a local character is a given on most trips through small towns. Finding one that holds any interest or is meticulously well organized, with each artifact researched through painstaking tracking of oral histories, is usually akin to a snipe hunt. But Peter Porter is a curator by deep instinct if not training. His stories and anecdotes may be oft repeated and almost pat in their singsong cadence, but his respect for the history he is preserving is contagious. His accordion playing isn't shabby either. ⊠ *Change Islands* ☎ *709/621–4541.*

☕ Coffee and Quick Bites

Growler's Ice

$ | **AMERICAN** | **FAMILY** | Be sure to try the house-made ice cream at this tiny sweet shop along the main road a little ways past Fogo Island Inn. An island favorite, they offer both unique and classic flavors. **Known for:** dairy-free options; the best (and only) ice cream on the island; jam jam ice cream, a classic Newfoundland treat. $ *Average main: C$3* ⊠ *125 Main Rd., Fogo Island* ☎ *709/658–7015* 🟦 *No credit cards* ☼ *Closed Oct.–May.*

🛏 Hotels

★ Fogo Island Inn

$$$$ | **RESORT** | Everything about this place, perched on the very edge of the continent, invites superlatives—stunning modern architecture and interior design, breathtaking ocean views, exquisite cuisine, advanced technology, and renowned hospitality. **Pros:** in-house cinema and art gallery; matched with a "community host" from Fogo to show you around the island; all meals, snacks, and gratuities included in price. **Cons:** two-night minimum required; access sometimes affected by weather; very expensive. $ *Rooms from: C$2075* ⊠ *Joe Batt's Arm, Fogo Island* ☎ *709/658–3444* ⊕ *fogoislandinn.ca* 🛏 *29 rooms* ¶○¶ *All-Inclusive.*

Old Salt Box Company

$$$ | HOUSE | These traditional salt-box-style houses have been reinvigorated into luxurious and comfortable vacation rentals. **Pros:** washer and dryer; great views; full kitchen. **Cons:** interior design more "modern Scandinavian" than "local flavor"; no pets; must provide your own meals and groceries. $ *Rooms from: C$220* ⊠ *Fogo Island* ☎ *709/658–7392, 844/280–1558* ⊕ *theoldsaltboxco.com* ↪ *3 rental houses on Fogo Island* ○ *No Meals.*

Peg's

$ | B&B/INN | Clean and bright with large rooms, this B&B has an upscale-hostel vibe with a large deck to sit and meet the other visitors. **Pros:** generous breakfast included; easy walk to area attractions; shared common spaces for interaction with fellow guests. **Cons:** no unifying interior design; no air-conditioning; on the main road with no "grounds". $ *Rooms from: C$115* ⊠ *60 Main St., Fogo Island* ☎ *709/266–2392* ⊕ *www.pegsplace.ca* ↪ *6 rooms* ○ *Free Breakfast.*

💼 Shopping

Herring Cove Art Gallery and Studio

ART GALLERIES | Traditional paintings and stunning quilts along with sweet souvenirs of wooden houses and home-made pickles and preserves can all be purchased and appreciated in this homey store and gallery. The quilts display stunning originality and beauty. ⊠ *27 Herring Cove Rd., Shoal Bay, Fogo Island* ⊕ *herringcoveart.com.*

🏃 Activities

HIKING

Hiking Trails

HIKING & WALKING | The landscape is the main attraction here, and depending on the season you'll find windswept wildflower patches, carpets of bakeapples, crashing waves, or brilliant pack ice.

Many footpaths along the coasts of Fogo lead to small surprises, such as a bronze sculpture of the giant auk on a remote rock, as well as the modern architectural silhouettes of Shorefast's artist-in-residence studios (⊕ *shorefast.org*). Visit Brimstone Head, one of the four corners of the world as designated by the Flat Earth Society. ⊠ *Fogo Island.*

Squid Jiggers Trail

HIKING & WALKING | There are more than a few nice hikes on Change Islands, but this one is the most notable. It is a moderate hike of about 3½ km (about 2 miles) one way, with some steep sections. Following along the northeastern coast, it provides an alternate view of Brimstone Head on Fogo and is a peaceful vantage for whale-watching and iceberg sightings. ⊠ *Change Islands, Fogo Island* ⊹ *At northern end of Change Islands. Trail head at "Tall Boy" lookout hill just behind Olde Shoppe Museum* ☎ *709/383–0775.*

Boyd's Cove

71 km (44 miles) north of Gander.

Between 1650 and 1720, the Beothuks (an indigenous culture know as the "Red Indians" to settlers due to the use of red ocher body paint) kept their main summer camp on the northeast coast at the site that is now Boyd's Cove. The coastline in and near Boyd's Cove is somewhat sheltered by Twillingate Island and New World Island, linked to the shore by short causeways.

GETTING HERE AND AROUND

From Gander, head north on Route 330 to Gander Bay South and Harris Point. Here, turn left onto Route 331 toward Twillingate, crossing the causeway over Gander Bay, then swing right and continue north.

👁 Sights

Beothuk Interpretation Centre

INDIGENOUS SIGHT | FAMILY | Explore the lives of the Beothuk, a First Nations people who succumbed in the early 19th century to a combination of disease and battle with European settlers. A 1½-km (1-mile) trail leads to the archaeological site that was inhabited from about 1650 to 1720, when the Beothuk departed this stretch of coast as settlers moved in. Walk softly to feel *The Spirit of the Beothuk,* represented by a commanding bronze statue by Gerald Squires that stands almost hidden in the woods. Just in back of the center is a Spirit Garden, opened in consultation with First Nations in Newfoundland, which is the site of an annual "Voices on the Wind" ceremony in September. ✉ *Southside Rd., Boyd's Cove ✛ Off Rte. 340* ☎ *709/656–3114 seasonal contact, 709/729–0592* ⊕ *www. seethesites.ca* 🖃 *C$6* ⊙ *Closed early Oct.–late May.*

Twillingate

41 km (25 miles) north of Boyd's Cove.

The inhabitants of this scenic old fishing village make their living from the sea and have been doing so for nearly two centuries. Colorful houses, rocky waterfront cliffs, local museums, and a nearby lighthouse add to the town's appeal. One of the best places on the island to see icebergs, Twillingate is known to the locals as Iceberg Alley. These majestic and dangerous mountains of ice are awe-inspiring to see when they're grounded in early summer. With its range of lodging options, and live local entertainment through the summer season at the Orange Lodge on the main strip (aka the "Touton House"), Twillingate makes a good base for exploring the surrounding region.

GETTING HERE AND AROUND
From Boyd's Cove, continue north on Route 340.

👁 Sights

Long Point Lighthouse

LIGHTHOUSE | Among the few Newfoundland lighthouses you can climb (55 steps), this 1876 structure on a 300-foot cliff inspires gasps with its panoramic view, which includes whales and icebergs at the right times of year. For those who choose not to go inside, the lighthouse serves as a departure point for picturesque walking trails. The nearby Long Point Centre has a fascinating collection of local artifacts. ✉ *Lighthouse Rd., Twillingate* 🖃 *C$10.*

Prime Berth Twillingate Fishery & Heritage Centre

HISTORY MUSEUM | FAMILY | This museum pays tribute to the life and work of fishermen in Twillingate, whose livelihood was determined by annual lottery, which assigned the top fishing area or *prime berth.* Visitors are awed by actual reconstructions of two whale skeletons, as well as an underwater camera and an iceberg gallery. There's also a blacksmith shop, an aquarium, an observation tower, and a crafts studio. The facility's owner, David Boyd, aka Captain Dave (⊕ *capt-dave.ca*), conducts boat trips to fish for lobster and cod or to watch whales and icebergs. ✉ *1 Main Hwy. 340, Twillingate* ☎ *709/884–2485, 709/884–7493* ⊕ *www. primeberth.com* 🖃 *C$5.*

🍴 Restaurants

Crow's Nest Café

$ | CAFÉ | On the way to the Long Point Lighthouse, this friendly little café has a great ocean view and a deck from which to enjoy it—you might even see a passing whale or two if you're here in July or August. Light meals, including

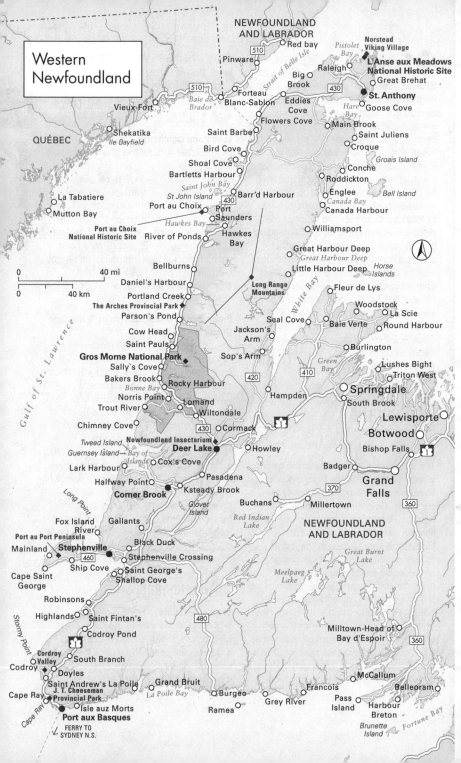

house-made soups, wraps, and chili, are served until 5 pm, or you can drop in for high-quality coffee and a delicious cinnamon bun. **Known for:** bagged lunches for hikes available; great views; excellent chili. [$] *Average main: C$8* ✉ *127 Main St., Crow Head* ☎ *709/893–2029* ⏲ *Closed Oct.–May.*

Hotels

Anchor Inn Hotel and Suites
$$ | HOTEL | Overlooking "Iceberg Alley," this hotel has a pleasant, welcoming atmosphere and large, comfortable rooms. **Pros:** friendly staff; ocean views; spacious rooms. **Cons:** style tends toward generic; no pets; rooms can get noise from pub. [$] *Rooms from: C$159* ✉ *3 Path End, Twillingate* ☎ *709/884–2777, 800/450–3950* 🌐 *www.twillingate.com/accommodations/anchor-inn-hotel-suites* ⏲ *Closed Nov.–Apr.* 🛏 *14 rooms* 🍴 *No Meals.*

Toulinguet Inn Bed & Breakfast
$$ | B&B/INN | In this 1920s-era home on the harbor front, rooms are old-fashioned, bright, and airy, and a common area balcony looks out over the Atlantic Ocean. **Pros:** away from the highway; sunroom and balcony overlook the harbor; rooms have private bath/shower. **Cons:** decor not for everyone; no air-conditioning in rooms; smoking permitted on balcony. [$] *Rooms from: C$150* ✉ *56 Main St., Twillingate* ☎ *709/884–2080* 🌐 *www.toulinguetinn.com* ⏲ *Closed Nov.–Apr.* 🛏 *7 rooms* 🍴 *Free Breakfast.*

Activities

Iceberg Man Tours
BOATING | Owner Cecil Stockley's local nickname is "Iceberg Man," and he's been leading tours for more than 30 years. Two-hour cruises (C$60) take you out to see not only icebergs, but also whales and birds. Iceberg photography is the company's specialty, helping amateur photographers to get that perfect shot. Tours depart at 9:30, 1, and 4, and sunset charters are available. The Iceberg Shop craft emporium on the harbor is under the same ownership. ✉ *50 Main St., Twillingate* ☎ *800/611–2374* 🌐 *www.icebergtours.ca* 🎟 *C$60* ⏲ *Closed Oct.–Apr.*

Twillingate Adventure Tours
BOATING | Headquartered at the docks next to its sister business, Annie's (a friendly restaurant serving classic moose soup, seafood, and other standard outport fare), these two-hour guided cruises (C$65) on the MV *Daybreak* take you to see icebergs, whales, and seabirds. ✉ *128 Main St., Twillingate* ☎ *709/884–1306, 888/447–8687* 🌐 *twillingateadventuretours.com* 🎟 *C$65* ⏲ *Closed mid-Sept.–mid-May.*

Deer Lake

214 km (133 miles) west of Grand Falls–Windsor.

Deer Lake was once just another small town on the Trans-Canada Highway, but the opening of Gros Morne National Park in the early 1970s and the construction of Route 430, a first-class paved highway passing right through to St. Anthony, changed all that.

GETTING HERE AND AROUND

Today, with an airport and car rentals available, Deer Lake is a good starting point for a fly–drive vacation, and it's open all year; it can be a cheaper option than flying into St. John's and renting a car there. There are connections from eastern and central Canada, and from St. John's. From the airport, there is a shuttle bus run by Star Taxi (☎ *709/634–4343*) into Deer Lake, Pasadena, and Corner Brook. There are major car-rental outlets, but make early reservations because stocks are limited.

Hiking trails lead to jaw-dropping scenery in Newfoundland's crown jewel, Gros Morne National Park.

ESSENTIALS

VISITOR INFORMATION Deer Lake Visitor Information Centre. ⊠ *60A Trans-Canada Hwy., Deer Lake* ☎ *709/635–2202* ⊕ *www.deerlake.ca.*

 Sights

Long Range Mountains

MOUNTAIN | Stretching all the way from the southwest coast to the Northern Peninsula, a distance of about 400 km (250 miles), the Long Range Mountains form the northernmost extent of the Appalachian Mountains. Their highest point, southwest of Corner Brook, is 2,670 feet, and the range encompasses the Gros Morne National Park and several provincial parks. Jacques Cartier, who saw them in 1534 as he was exploring the area on behalf of France, noted that their shape reminded him of the long, rectangular-shaped farm buildings of his home village in France. Among the mountains, small villages are interspersed with rivers teeming with salmon and trout.

Newfoundland Insectarium

NATURE SIGHT | FAMILY | An intriguing collection of live and preserved insects, spiders, and scorpions from six temperate zones is housed here, and there's a glass beehive with 10,000 honeybees. The verdant greenhouse is home to hundreds of live tropical butterflies. A walking trail leads through woodland to the Humber River and Rocky Brook—you have a good chance of spotting beavers and muskrats from the viewing deck. Check out the gift shop, which sometimes stocks lollipops with edible dried scorpions inside. Picnic tables provide a nice spot to stretch and rest. The insectarium is a one-minute drive off the Trans-Canada Highway at Deer Lake; turn north onto Route 430, also signed here as Bonne Bay Road. ⊠ *2 Bonne Bay Rd., Reidville* ☎ *709/635–4545, 866/635–5454* ⊕ *nlinsectarium.com* ⊡ *C$14* ☉ *Closed mid-Oct.–mid-May.*

Hotels

Deer Lake Motel
$$ | **HOTEL** | Recent renovations have perked up what was already a clean and comfortable motel, the nearest lodging to Gros Morne National Park. **Pros:** good coffee at the restaurant; at the junction of the Trans-Canada Highway and the Viking Trail; generous hours for free breakfast service. **Cons:** no elevator; highway traffic noise; restaurant more like a coffee shop. [$] *Rooms from: C$139* ✉ *15 Trans-Canada Hwy., Deer Lake* ☎ *709/635–2108, 800/563–2144* 🌐 *www.deerlakemotel.com* 🛏 *55 rooms* 🍴 *Free Breakfast.*

Gros Morne National Park

About 40 (25 miles) north of Deer Lake.

Because of its geological uniqueness and immense splendor, this park has been named a UNESCO World Heritage Site. Camping and hiking are popular activities, and boat tours are available.

To see Gros Morne properly, you should allow yourself at least two days, but once they're here, most people would appreciate having a few more. Scenic **Bonne Bay,** a deep fjord, divides the park into distinct northern and southern sections.

GETTING HERE AND AROUND

Traveling north from Deer Lake, the park's main entry point is just before the community of Wiltondale. Continue on Route 430 to Rocky Harbour for the main visitor center and Cow Head at the northern end of the park. For the southern part of the park, turn left on Route 431.

Sights

The Arches Provincial Park and Port au Choix National Historic Site
INDIGENOUS SIGHT | The Arches are a geological curiosity; the park contains rock formations made millions of years ago by wave action and undersea currents. The succession of caves through a bed of dolomite was later raised above sea level by tectonic upheaval. This is a good place to stop for a picnic.

The Port au Choix National Historic Site is 97 km (60 miles) farther north. The remains of Maritime Archaic and Dorset people have been found along this coast between the Arches Provincial Park and L'Anse aux Meadows, and this site has an interesting interpretation center with exhibits about what's been uncovered to date. Archaeologists digging in the area uncovered an ancient village. Ask at the center for directions to it. ✉ *Rte. 430, Portland Creek* ☎ *709/637–2040 Arches Provincial Park off-season, 709/458–2417 Port au Choix National Historic Site off-season* 🌐 *www.parksnl.ca/parks/arches-provincial-park* 🎫 *C$8 for historic site* 🕒 *Closed Oct.–May.*

Bonne Bay Marine Station
NATURE SIGHT | **FAMILY** | A visit here is a must, especially for kids, who often find themselves enthralled by the touch tank, the centerpiece of the 45-minute guided aquarium tours. In addition to experiencing sea stars, crabs, algae, and other marine life firsthand, participants learn about the station's past and current research projects. Tours begin every 30 minutes. ✉ *1 Clarke's Rd., Norris Point* ☎ *709/458–2874 in-season front desk, 709/458–2550 year-round administration* 🌐 *www.bonnebay.ca* 🎫 *$10* 🕒 *Closed Oct.–Apr.*

Discovery Centre
VISITOR CENTER | **FAMILY** | On the outskirts of Woody Point, a charming community of old houses and imported Lombardy poplars, this is the main center for interpreting the geology of Gros Morne National Park. Educational programs about natural history are conducted, and there's a craft shop. Learn about indigenous culture of the Mi'Kmaq in Newfoundland in an exhibition called

Miawpukek: The Middle River. At the back of the center's parking lot is the fine Lookout Hills trail, a 5-km (3-mile) trek with outstanding views of Bonne Bay, Gros Morne Mountain, and the Tablelands. ⊠ *Rte. 431, Gros Morne National Park* ✛ *Head west toward Trout River* ☎ *709/458–2417* ⊘ *Closed early Oct.–mid-May.*

Green Gardens Trail

TRAIL | As depicted beautifully in the movie *Hold Fast* (2013), this spectacular 9-km (5½-mile) round-trip hike starts at Long Pond, on Route 431, 5 km (3 miles) east of Trout River, passes through the Tablelands barrens, and descends sharply to a coastline of eroded cliffs and green meadows. Be prepared to do a bit of climbing on your return journey. A longer version of the trail includes a loop around Wallace Brook. Some parts of the cliff edges are undercut, so stick to the trail. ⊠ *Rte. 431, Gros Morne National Park* ⊕ *www.pc.gc.ca.*

★ Gros Morne National Park

NATIONAL PARK | One of Newfoundland's most treasured UNESCO World Heritage Sites, this national park showcases the beauty and splendor of this part of the world. The most popular attraction in the northern portion of Gros Morne is the hike and boat tour of Western Brook Pond. While the fjord itself remains the same, recent upgrades to the trail to the boat dock have turned a once transportive stroll into a 45 minute-slog over a gravel road with no shade. Those in good shape can tackle the 16-km (10-mile) hike up **Gros Morne Mountain,** the second-highest peak in Newfoundland at 2,644 feet. Weather permitting, the reward for your effort is a unique Arctic landscape and spectacular views. The park's northern coast has an unusual mix of sand beaches, rock pools, and trails through tangled dwarf forests. Sunsets seen from **Lobster Head Cove Lighthouse** are spectacular. In season you might spot whales here, and a visit to the lighthouse

museum, devoted to the history of the area, is rewarding. At the very north end of the park is the community of Cow Head, home to the Gros Morne Theatre Festival's popular summer program of theater and music. Also nearby, Shallow Bay Beach has a 3-km (2-mile) stretch of soft sand ready-made for beachcombing. Woody Point, a community of old houses and imported Lombardy poplars, is in the southern part of the park, on Route 431. Rising behind it are the **Tablelands,** a unique rock massif that was raised from the earth's mantle through tectonic upheaval. The Tablelands provide a remarkable exposure of mantle rock, rarely seen at the earth's surface; it's the main reason Gros Morne National Park has received UNESCO World Heritage status. ⊠ *Rocky Harbour* ⊕ *www.pc.gc. ca* ▭ *C$10.*

Gros Morne Visitor's Centre

VISITOR CENTER | A good launching-off point for your Gros Morne visit. The thoughtful displays and videos about the park make this a good place to familiarize yourself with the park and what it has to offer. ⊠ *Rte. 430, Rocky Harbour* ☎ *709/458–2417* ⊕ *www.pc.gc.ca* ⊘ *Closed Nov.–Apr.* ☞ *See website for full list of service operation dates.*

🍴 Restaurants

The Black Spruce

$$$$ | MODERN CANADIAN | The short but enticing menu here reflects the kitchen's expert touch and dedication to the concepts of sustainable farming and incorporating local ingredients. The fish dishes are always high-quality, but you'll have to wait to see what the local fishers bring in to know exactly what you're going to get. **Known for:** seafood chowder; locally caught fresh fish; views over the Bay. Ⓢ *Average main: C$34* ⊠ *Neddies Harbour Inn, 7 Beach Rd., Neddies Harbour* ☎ *709/458–3089* ⊕ *theblackspruce.ca* ⊘ *Closed Nov.–Apr.*

Fisherman's Landing

$$$ | SEAFOOD | FAMILY | The wide-ranging menu at Fisherman's Landing includes plenty of seafood as well as other options like pizza. Both the food and the service here are reliable (and the food is heavily breaded, whenever possible). **Known for:** open until 10 pm (late night for this area); classic Newfoundland seafood options; big crowds. $ *Average main: C$25* ⊠ *44 Main St., Rocky Harbour* ☎ *709/458–2060* ⊕ *www.fishermanslandingrestaurant.com.*

★ Java Jack's Restaurant and Gallery

$$$ | CANADIAN | The pleasures of this lively restaurant begin with a stroll past the meticulously kept organic garden. The dinner menu has many seafood options as well as meat dishes and vegan and vegetarian selections. **Known for:** local artwork on walls; lobster Benedict for breakfast; splendid harbor views. $ *Average main: C$28* ⊠ *88 Main St. N, Rocky Harbour* ☎ *709/458–2710 in-season number, 905/875—8590 out-of-season number* ⊕ *javajacks.ca* ☯ *Closed mid-Sept.–mid-May.*

Seaside Restaurant

$$$ | SEAFOOD | The chefs at this two-story restaurant overlooking the ocean prepare fresh seafood in traditional, innovative, Newfoundland style. A perfect meal might start with northern scallops served on greens brightened with deep burgundy partridgeberries, followed by grilled shark. **Known for:** perfectly prepared mussels; secret recipe for cod tongues; sunsets on the upper deck. $ *Average main: C$25* ⊠ *263 Main St., Trout River* ☎ *709/451–3461* ⊕ *www.seasiderestaurant.ca* ☯ *Closed Oct.–late May.*

 Hotels

Fisherman's Landing Inn

$$ | HOTEL | Although it's not on the water as the name implies, this is a spacious, bright, and well-maintained property. **Pros:** decent food; outdoor hot tub and firepit; lovely rooms. **Cons:** 2-km (1¼-mile) walk from most other eateries; away from the waterfront; no refrigerator in the rooms. $ *Rooms from: C$139* ⊠ *21-29 W. Link Rd., Rocky Harbour* ☎ *709/458–2711, 866/458–2711* ⊕ *www.fishermanslandinginn.com* ➟ *40 rooms* ○| *No Meals.*

★ Neddies Harbour Inn

$$$ | B&B/INN | In a picture-perfect location overlooking beautiful Bonne Bay, this boutique-style inn has spacious rooms and a fine restaurant. **Pros:** views from all rooms; craft shop on-site; excellent restaurant with views of sunrise and sunset. **Cons:** hot tub is in a windowless room in basement; fitness room has very limited equipment; breakfast service stops early. $ *Rooms from: C$195* ⊠ *7 Beach Rd., Neddies Harbour* ☎ *709/458–3089, 877/458–2929* ⊕ *theinn.ca* ☯ *Closed Nov.–Apr.* ➟ *17 rooms* ○| *No Meals.*

Ocean View Hotel

$$$ | HOTEL | Right on the water, this two-story hotel has good-size modern rooms and nightly entertainment in summer. **Pros:** two on-site dining options; near shopping and dining options; small strand of beach across the street. **Cons:** decor is basic; pub accessible only with cover charge; open windows bring loud music from pub. $ *Rooms from: C$199* ⊠ *38–42 Main St., Rocky Harbour* ☎ *709/458–2730, 800/563–9887* ⊕ *www.theoceanview.ca* ☯ *Closed mid-Oct.–Mar.* ➟ *52 rooms* ○| *No Meals.*

Sugar Hill Inn

$$$ | B&B/INN | The inn is quiet and relaxing; large windows throughout the building let in lots of light, and the warm color schemes and natural wood on floors and ceilings add character to the spacious, uncluttered guest rooms, most of which have a private deck. **Pros:** incredible food; cedar-lined hot tub and sauna; water comes from a spring on the property. **Cons:** not located directly on the water; limited breakfast options; exterior doesn't suggest the quality inside. $ *Rooms*

At L'Anse aux Meadows archaeological site, at the northern tip of Newfoundland, wander amid an ancient Viking settlement.

from: C$215 ✉ *115–129 Main St., Norris Point* ☎ *709/458–2147, 888/299–2147* 🌐 *www.sugarhillinn.ca* 🕓 *Closed Nov.–mid-May* 🛏 *11 rooms* 🍴 *Free Breakfast.*

Wildflowers Country Inn

$$ | **B&B/INN** | Set back from the main road on a property full of trees, this charming clapboard house overlooks the ocean. **Pros:** open year-round; pretty front veranda and beautiful landscaping; air-conditioning in all rooms. **Cons:** no refrigerator or coffee in rooms (just in common room); some rooms have showers, not baths; no breakfast served. $ *Rooms from: C$139* ✉ *108 Main St., Rocky Harbour* ☎ *709/458–3000, 888/811–7378* 🌐 *www.wildflowerscountryinn.ca* 🛏 *6 rooms* 🍴 *No Meals.*

Performing Arts

Two major festivals, the Gros Morne Summer Music and the Gros Morne Theatre Festival, make for a lively arts scene during high season.

Activities

BonTours

BOATING | This boat tour service offers a variety of options, ranging from a 15-minute shuttle service at C$10 to a 12-hour day hike at C$295. Other offerings include a sunset cruise, a cod-jigging adventure, and tours that allow participants to take part in the sailing process. ✉ *105 Pond Rd., Rocky Harbour* ☎ *709/458–2016, 888/458–2016* ✎ *info@bontours.ca* 🌐 *www.bontours.ca* 🕓 *Closed mid-Oct.–Apr.*

Gros Morne Adventures

HIKING & WALKING | Sea kayaking on Bonne Bay in Gros Morne National Park is offered by this outfitter, as well as guided coastal and mountain hiking (C$150 for a full day) in the area. Private guided hikes are also available at higher rates. Guided sea-kayaking tours are designed for various interests and include the Family Nature Paddle, the Paddle & Yoga, and the Paddle & Pint. Kayak rentals start at C$35 (single) and C$45 (double) for two hours. ✉ *9 Clarkes Rd., Norris Point* ☎ *709/458–2722, 800/685–4624* ✎ *info@grosmorneadventures.com* ⊕ *grosmorneadventures.com* ⊗ *Closed mid-Sept.–mid-June.*

L'Anse aux Meadows National Historic Site

295 km (183 miles) northeast of Arches Provincial Park.

One thousand years ago, near the northern tip of Newfoundland, Vikings from Greenland and Iceland created the first European settlement in North America. They arrived in the New World 500 years before Columbus but stayed only a few years and were forgotten for centuries. Since the settlement's rediscovery in the last century, the archaeological site has brought tourism to the area. Viking themes abound but so do views, whales, icebergs, fun dining experiences, and outdoor activities.

GETTING HERE AND AROUND
Follow Route 430 north to Route 436 and continue north for 30 km (18½ miles) more.

⊙ Sights

★ L'Anse aux Meadows National Historic Site

HISTORIC SIGHT | FAMILY | L'Anse aux Meadows is a UNESCO World Heritage Site. The Norwegian team of Helge and Anne Stine Ingstad discovered the remains of Viking settlements here in 1960. In 2021, researchers determined that the settlement had been active in 1021 AD. Parks Canada has a visitor center and has reconstructed four of the huts to give you a sense of the era and how the Vikings lived. An interpretation program introduces you to the food, clothing, and way of life of that time. The site has also turned one reconstructed hut into a very fun,

interactive escape room called the Test of Tykir. ✉ *Rte. 436, L'Anse aux Meadows* ☎ *709/623–2608 May–Oct., 709/458–2417 off-season* ⊕ *www.parkscanada.gc.ca/en/lhn-nhs/nl/meadows* 💰 *From C$12* ⊗ *Closed Nov.–May.*

Norstead Viking Village

MUSEUM VILLAGE | FAMILY | Two kilometers (1 mile) east of L'Anse aux Meadows is Norstead, a reconstruction of an 11th-century Viking port, with a chieftain's hall, church, and ax-throwing area. Interpreters in period dress answer questions as they go about their Viking business (albeit in sneakers). A highlight is the Snorri, a reconstructed viking *knarr* that sailed from Greenland to L'anse Aux Meadows in 1997, re-creating Leif Eriksson's voyage. ✉ *263 L'Anse aux Meadows, St. Lunaire-Griquet* ✛ *Off Rte. 430, 40 km (25 miles) north of St. Anthony* ☎ *709/623–2828, 877/620–2828* ⊕ *www.norstead.com* 💰 *C$12* ⊗ *Closed Oct.–May.*

⊘ Restaurants

★ Norseman Restaurant

$$$ | SEAFOOD | The high quality of the food and drink here, combined with the remoteness and spectacular view, make a meal at the Norseman one you remember. Expect traditional seafood, with a smart and extensive menu of craft beer, wine, and spirits. **Known for:** live traditional music in summer; all local seafood; classic haute cuisine meat dishes. 💲 *Average main: C$28* ✉ *Harbour Front, L'Anse aux Meadows* ✛ *Turn right at end of Rte. 436* ☎ *709/689–2126* ⊕ *www.valhalla-lodge.com/restaurant* ⊗ *Closed mid Sept.-late May.*

⊜ Hotels

Burnt Cape Cabins

$$ | HOUSE | FAMILY | These cabins are more about comfort than adventure thanks to the full kitchens, pillow-top mattresses, fine linens, and flat-screen

TVs, but step out onto your porch and be awed by the soothing, uncomplicated view over the water. **Pros:** all the convenience you might need; daily historic/botanical hikes through Burnt Cape Ecological Reserve; covered BBQ picnic area. **Cons:** limited dining options in walking distance; not a true escape thanks to Wi-Fi and television; no air-conditioning. [$] *Rooms from: C$149* ✉ *4 Main St., L'Anse aux Meadows* ✣ *Take Rte. 437 to Raleigh* ☎ *709/452–3521* 🌐 *www.burntcapecabins.com* ⏲ *Closed Nov.–May* 🛏 *7 cottages* 🍴 *Free Breakfast.*

Quirpon Lighthouse Inn B&B
$$$$ | B&B/INN | This restored 1920s lighthouse now functioning as a B&B is on the small island of Quirpon, a landmass of about 7 km (4 miles) by 1½ km (1 mile), just off the northern tip of Newfoundland. **Pros:** charming setting; indoor whale-watching station; package includes return boat trip to L'Anse aux Meadows and all meals. **Cons:** no air-conditioning; no Wi-Fi; only option is the full package. [$] *Rooms from: C$435* ✉ *Rte. 436, Quirpon Island* ✣ *Off Hwy. 436, take Quirpon Rd. to the boat dock* ☎ *709/634–2285, 877/254–6586* 🌐 *www.linkumtours.com* 🛏 *10 rooms* 🍴 *All-Inclusive.*

★ **Valhalla Lodge Bed & Breakfast**
$ | B&B/INN | On a hill overlooking "Iceberg Alley" 8 km (5 miles) from L'Anse aux Meadows, the Valhalla has quiet rooms with large windows, Scandinavian furniture, and handmade quilts. **Pros:** sitting room with fireplace and patio; view of whales, icebergs, and occasionally the Northern Lights; walking trails directly across the road. **Cons:** no breakfast served for houses, though some breakfast items provided; some bathrooms small; few services or restaurants within walking distance. [$] *Rooms from: C$129* ✉ *Rte. 436, Gunner's Cove* ☎ *709/689–2126, 877/623–2018* 🌐 *www.valhallabandb.com* ⏲ *Closed Oct.–May* 🛏 *5 rooms* 🍴 *No Meals.*

Viking Village Bed & Breakfast
$ | B&B/INN | This B&B consists of your choice of individual rooms or a saltbox by the sea, all convenient for visits to the Viking settlement at L'Anse aux Meadows. **Pros:** full hot breakfast included; proximity to L'Anse aux Meadows; bathrooms en suite. **Cons:** no air-conditioning; some rooms are small; no elevator. [$] *Rooms from: C$119* ✉ *Rte. 436, Hay Cove, L'Anse aux Meadows* ☎ *709/623–2548* 🌐 *saltboxbythesea.com* ⏲ *Closed mid-Oct–Apr.* 🛏 *9 rooms* 🍴 *Free Breakfast.*

St. Anthony

40 km (25 miles) south of L'Anse aux Meadows.

The northern part of the Great Northern Peninsula served as the setting for *The Shipping News*, E. Annie Proulx's 1993 Pulitzer Prize–winning novel. St. Anthony is built around a natural harbor on the eastern side of the Great Northern Peninsula, near its tip. If you take a trip out to the lighthouse, you may see an iceberg or two float by, and it's a good spot for whale-watching.

GETTING HERE AND AROUND

St. Anthony is the terminus of Route 430, and most travelers arrive via this highway. For variety, some return to St. John's or other destinations by heading south from St. Anthony on Route 432, which rejoins Route 430 near Plum Point, a drive of about 110 km (68 miles).

Sights

Grenfell Historic Properties
HISTORIC SIGHT | FAMILY | A museum and a nearby interpretation center document the life and inspirational work of the English-born doctor Wilfred Grenfell (later Sir Wilfred), who in the early 20th century provided much-needed medical services and transformed the lives of the people

of this remote land. ✉ *4 Maraval Rd., St. Anthony* ☎ *709/454–4010* 🌐 *www.grenfell-properties.com* 🎟 *C$10* 🕒 *Closed Sat.–Sun. Oct.–June.*

🍴 Restaurants

Lightkeepers Seafood Restaurant/Great VIking Feast

$$$$ | SEAFOOD | FAMILY | Good seafood and solid Canadian fare are served in this former lighthouse-keeper's home on a parkland site overlooking the ocean. Book the raucous Great Viking Feast dinner theater, where you can enjoy an all-you-can-eat buffet amid table-pounding, cheers, and laughter as actors perform a typical example of a Viking court of law. **Known for:** great seafood chowder; Viking-theme dinners; views of whales and icebergs. [$] *Average main: C$56* ✉ *21 Fishing Point Rd., St. Anthony* ☎ *709/454–4900, 877/454–4900* ✉ *lightkeepersinfo@gmail.com* 🕒 *Closed Sept.–late May.*

🛏 Hotels

Hotel North

$$ | HOTEL | The centrally located Hotel North might not be the most scenic spot in town, but it contains pleasant and comfortable rooms (also two self-contained cottages), all with Sealy Posturepedic mattresses. **Pros:** open throughout the year; all rooms have mini-refrigerators and coffeemakers; popular restaurant on-site. **Cons:** meals not included in price; no landscaping; parking gets crowded. [$] *Rooms from: C$149* ✉ *19 West St., St. Anthony* ☎ *709/454–3300* 🌐 *www.hotelnorth.ca/st-anthony* 🛏 *46 rooms* 🍴 *No Meals.*

Tuckamore Lodge & Country Inn

$$$ | B&B/INN | About an hour from St. Anthony, this Scandinavian-style cedar lodge with a lofty ceiling is a luxurious base from which to explore the natural bounty of the area. **Pros:** canoes available; outdoor wooden sauna; many on-site activities. **Cons:** few dining options nearby; Wi-Fi is inconsistent; meals served at communal tables. [$] *Rooms from: C$180* ✉ *1 Southwest Pond Rd., Main Brook* ☎ *709/865–6361, 888/865–6361* 🌐 *www.tuckamorelodge.com* 🛏 *12 rooms* 🍴 *Free Breakfast.*

🛍 Shopping

Grenfell Handicrafts

CRAFTS | Training villagers to become self-sufficient in a harsh environment was one of the British missionary Wilfred Grenfell's aims, and a windproof cloth that they turned into well-made parkas came to be known as Grenfell cloth. Here you can purchase it in the form of the famous parkas with fur-trimmed hoods as well as mittens and tablecloths embroidered with motifs such as polar bears and dog teams. The shop also stocks other handicrafts, most of them locally made. ✉ *4 Maraval Rd., St. Anthony* ☎ *709/454–4010* 🌐 *www.grenfell-properties.com.*

Activities

Northland Discovery Boat Tours

BOATING | Specialized 2½-hour trips (C$61) aboard a custom-built vessel will take you to see whales, dolphins, icebergs, seabirds, and sea caves. A local naturalist always accompanies the tours, which take place from mid-May through mid-September. ✉ *St. Anthony* ✣ *Off West St., behind Grenfell Interpretation Centre* ☎ *709/454–3092, 877/632–3747* 🌐 *www.discovernorthland.com.*

Corner Brook

50 km (31 miles) southwest of Deer Lake.

Newfoundland's fifth-largest municipality, and the largest city off the Avalon Peninsula, Corner Brook is the hub of the island's west coast. Hills fringe three sides of the city, which has dramatic views of the harbor and the Bay of Islands. The town is also home to a large paper mill and the Grenfell Campus of Memorial University. Captain James Cook, the British explorer, charted the coast in the 1760s, and a memorial to him overlooks the bay.

The town enjoys more clearly defined seasons than most of the rest of the island, and in summer it has many pretty gardens. The nearby Humber River is the best-known salmon river in the province, and there are many kilometers of well-maintained walking trails in the community.

GETTING HERE AND AROUND

Corner Brook is a convenient hub and point of departure for exploring the west coast. It's about a three-hour drive (allowing for traffic) from the Port aux Basques ferry. The north and south shores of the Bay of Islands have fine paved roads—Route 440 on the north shore and Route 450 on the south—and both are a scenic half-day drive from Corner Brook. Route 450 is especially lovely, and there are many well-developed hiking trails near the end of the road at Bottle Cove and Little Port. The town has two public bus routes. Bus fare is C$2.50 for one ride, C$11 for five.

Sights

Newfoundland Emporium

STORE/MALL | This store is crammed from wall to wall with Newfoundland-related stuff—reputedly more than 16,000 items. The three-level store is full of books (including rare ones by Newfoundlanders and about Newfoundland, as well as volumes about ships and sailing), art, crafts, music, antique furniture, and collectibles. ✉ *11 Broadway, Corner Brook* ☎ *709/634–9376.*

Restaurants

Newfound Sushi

$$ | **JAPANESE** | Come here to savor generous slabs of sashimi and just-sticky-enough, well-seasoned rice. Enjoy the view from the upstairs dining room overlooking the water and Corner Brook's iconic papermill or get cozy in the downstairs booths where you can watch the chef/owner at work. **Known for:** great views; best sushi in Newfoundland; house-made teriyaki sauce. [$] *Average main: C$16* ✉ *117 Broadway, Corner Brook* ☎ *709/634–6666* 🌐 *www.newfoundsushi.com* 🕓 *Closed Sun.–Mon.*

Coffee and Quick Bites

Brewed Awakening

$ | **CAFÉ** | This place has everything a favorite coffee shop should have: great coffee roasted in-house, food prepared from scratch, and a hip but welcoming atmosphere. This one is located on Bernard Street and has convenient parking. **Known for:** great sandwiches for lunch; excellent cappuccinos; homemade baked treats and granola bars. [$] *Average main: C$8* ✉ *93 Mt. Bernard Ave., Corner Brook* ☎ *709/634–1919, 709/634–7100* 🌐 *www.brewedawakening.ca* 🕓 *No dinner.*

Hotels

Glynmill Inn

$$$ | **HOTEL** | Tucked away on a treed property with a pond and a walking trail, this Tudor-style inn once housed the senior staff and visiting top brass of the local paper mill. **Pros:** restaurant serves delicious Newfoundland dishes; quiet, pleasant setting by a large park; on-site dining and small playground. **Cons:** outdoor smoking balconies directly off hallway in some wings; small windows in many rooms; hard to find from the highway. [$] *Rooms from: C$190* ✉ *1B Cobb La., Corner Brook* ☎ *709/634–5181*

🌐 *www.steelehotels.com* 🛏 *78 rooms* 🍽 *No Meals.*

Marble Villa

$$ | APARTMENT | These spotless condo-style units are meant for skiers, but they're perfect for a quiet summertime break and as a base for day trips to the Bay of Islands and Gros Morne. **Pros:** packages include ziplining and ATV tours; beautiful property with pond and walking trails; spacious, comfortable rooms. **Cons:** breakfast not included with rates; few eating options in area; cafeteria-style restaurant closed except during ski season. 💲 *Rooms from: C$169* ✉ *Dogwood Dr., Corner Brook* ✣ *Off Rte. 1, Exit 8* ☎ *709/637–7616* 🌐 *www.skimarble.com* 🛏 *29 condos* 🍽 *No Meals.*

Activities

Blow Me Down Cross-Country Ski Club

SKIING & SNOWBOARDING | FAMILY | This place is as warm and welcoming as a cold weather sport club can be. Show up with any skill level and the regulars here will help you find the right trails. Skis and snowshoes are available to rent for reasonable prices. If you make it to the very top of the mountain on a weekend, you may be rewarded with a full hot breakfast cooked by volunteers over a woodstove in a cozy hut. ✉ *Lundrigan Dr., Corner Brook* ✣ *Off Lewin Pkwy.* ☎ *709/639–2754* 🌐 *www.blowmedown.ca* 🎫 *C$20 day pass.*

Marble Mountain Ski Resort

SKIING & SNOWBOARDING | FAMILY | Here you'll find the best skiing and snowboarding in the province. With the piles of snow on the west coast every winter, this is your best bet for winter fun. In the summer, ziplining and other seasonal events are available. ✉ *2 Marble Dr., Steady Brook* ✣ *Exit 8 from the Trans Canada Hwy.* ☎ *709/637–7601, 888/462–7253* 🌐 *www.skimarble.com* 🎫 *C$45 lift tickets.*

Stephenville

82 km (51 miles) south of Corner Brook.

The former Earnest Harmon Air Force Base is in Stephenville, a town best known for its summer theater festival. To the west of town is the Port au Port Peninsula, which was largely settled by the French, who brought their way of life and language to this small corner of Newfoundland.

GETTING HERE AND AROUND

Stephenville is off the Trans-Canada Highway (Route 1). Take Exit 3, then drive southwest on Route 460 most of the way. After briefly heading southwest on Route 490, follow Minnesota Drive to get downtown.

Sights

Codroy Valley

SCENIC DRIVE | As you travel down the Trans-Canada Highway toward Port aux Basques, Routes 406 and 407 bring you into the small Scottish communities of the Codroy Valley. Some of the most productive farms in the province are nestled in the valley against the backdrop of the Long Range Mountains, from which gales strong enough to stop traffic hurtle down to the coast. Locally known as Wreckhouse winds, they have overturned tractor trailers. The Codroy Valley is great for bird-watching, and the Grand Codroy River is ideal for kayaking. Walking trails, a golf course, and mountain hikes make the area an appealing stop for nature lovers. 🌐 *https://www.newfoundlandlabrador.com/top-destinations/codroy-valley.*

Port au Port Peninsula

NATURE SIGHT | A slender isthmus tethers this peninsula to the west coast. About 20 tiny communities retain a French and First Nations heritage, but other than that it's largely undeveloped, with a wilderness interior and a rocky coastline. There are superb ocean views from

Cape St. George, and some rewarding hiking trails. ⊕ *Drive west on Rte. 460 from Stephenville to Cape St. George, at the southwestern extremity; continue north up peninsula's west side (Rte. 460 becomes Rte. 463 after about 15 km [9 miles]) and loops east back to Rte. 460. Turn left (east) to return to Stephenville.*

Port aux Basques

166 km (103 miles) south of Stephenville.

In the 1500s and early 1600s, there were seven Basque ports along Newfoundland's west coast and in southern Labrador; Port aux Basques was one of them and was given its name by the town's French successors. It's now the main ferry port connecting the island to Nova Scotia.

GETTING HERE AND AROUND

The ferry from Sydney, Nova Scotia, docks at Port aux Basques. By road, the town is at the western end of the Trans-Canada Highway (Route 1).

ESSENTIALS

VISITOR INFORMATION Port aux Basques Visitor Information Centre. ⊠ *Trans-Canada Hwy., Port aux Basques* ☎ *709/695–2262* ⊕ *www.portauxbasques.ca.*

◉ Sights

J. T. Cheeseman Provincial Park

NATURE SIGHT | FAMILY | If you are using the Port aux Basques ferry, this park is 10 km (6 miles) from the port and makes a good first or last stop, particularly if you're on a camping trip. Rich in natural flora, this is a nesting site for the piping plover. One of the hiking trails leads to waterfalls on Little Barachois River; another, with views of Table Mountain, includes fitness stations. The long, sandy Cape Ray Beach is good for swimming and sunbathing—its day-use area has

picnic tables and fireplaces, and there are about a hundred campsites. ⊠ *Trans-Canada Hwy. (Rte. 1), Port aux Basques* ⊕ *10 km east of Port aux Basques* ☎ *709/695–7222* ⊕ *www.nlcamping.ca* ⊗ *Closed mid-Sept.–mid-May.*

🛏 Hotels

St. Christopher's Hotel

$$ | HOTEL | A comfortable two-story hotel near the Nova Scotia ferry, St. Christopher's serves decent food at reasonable prices. **Pros:** free Wi-Fi; local fare, such as moose stew, served in the restaurant; waterfront boardwalk close by. **Cons:** air-conditioners sometimes loud; noise from conventions, weddings, and visiting sports teams; limited, overpriced wine list. ⑤ *Rooms from: C$140* ⊠ *146 Caribou Rd., Port aux Basques* ☎ *709/695–7034, 800/563–4779* ⊕ *www.stchrishotel.com* �){ *83 rooms* ⦿| *No Meals.*

Photo Credits

Front Cover: Sunpix Travel / Alamy Stock Photo [Description: The Battery. Houses perched under the cliffs of Signal Hill at St.Johns, Newfoundland, Canada]. **Back cover, from left to right:** Elena Elisseeva/Shutterstock, ggw/Shutterstock, Greg and Jan Ritchie/ Shutterstock. **Spine:** Matthew Jacques/Shutterstock. **Interior, from left to right:** Ken Morris/Shutterstock (1). Lightphoto/iStockphoto (2-3). **Chapter 1: Experience Nova Scotia And Atlantic Canada:** Knips Design/Shutterstock (6-7). Pi-Lens/Shutterstock (8-9). David Purchase Imagery/ Shutterstock (9). Josef Hanus/Shutterstock (9). Tourism PEI / John Sylvester (10). Tourism PEI/ John Sylvester (10). Colin D. Young/Shutterstock (10). Dani Vincek/Shutterstock (10). Pabradyphoto/iStock Editorial (11). Tourism PEI (11). ImagineGolf/iStockphoto (12). Tom Eagan/Dreamstime (12). George Burba/Shutterstock (12). Vadim.Petrov/Shutterstock (12). Jhve Photo/Shutterstock (13). Harold Stiver/ Dreamstime (13). Foodio/Shutterstock (18). Etitarenko/ Shutterstock (18). Brent Hofacker/Shutterstock (18). Chiyacat/Shutterstock (19). Sandi Cullifer/Shutterstock (19). Sergey Fatin/Shutterstock (20). Courtesy Watts Tree Farm (20). Katia1504 | Dreamstime (20). Courtesy of Maritime Salt Makers of Canada (21). Chic2view | Dreamstime (21). Tom Clausen/Shutterstock (22). Pierrette Guertin/Shutterstock (22). Andrea Quartarone/Shutterstock (22). Tom Cummins/Shutterstock (23). Russ Heinl/Shutterstock (23). Dennis Jarvis/ Flickr (24). Golasza | Dreamstime (24). Motionsense | Dreamstime (24). Rusty426 | Dreamstime (24). Doma/Shutterstock (25). Carolbsokolow | Dreamstime (25). Lightphoto | Dreamstime (25). Darryl Brooks/Shutterstock (25). **Chapter 3: Historic District:** Cworthy/Shutterstock (49). Louishenault/Dreamstime (61). Namespacerz/Dreamstime (62). Adeliepenguin/ Dreamstime (69). Sam and Brian/Shutterstock (79). Gvictoria/Dreamstime (84-85). Rndmst/ Dreamstime (91). Wangkun Jia/Shutterstock (101). Marevos imaging/Shutterstock (118). Brendan Riley/Shutterstock (122). Vadim.Petrov/ Shutterstock (131). Paulmckinnon/Dreamstime (138). Rndmst/Dreamstime (143). **Chapter 4: New Brunswick:** Lucie Kusova/Shutterstock (145).Jhve Photo/Shutterstock (155). Madscica/Dreamstime (160). Gvictoria/Dreamstime (170). Paul Reeves Photography/Shutterstock (175). Rndmst/Dreamstime (177). Guoqiang Xue/Shutterstock (181). Darlene Munro/Shutterstock (199). Mayakova/ Shutterstock (202). Alpegor/ Dreamstime (208). Gvictoria/Shutterstock (211). Jessfox/ Dreamstime (213). Adwo/Shutterstock (218). **Chapter 5: Prince Edward Island:** Elenathewise/iStockphoto (225). Prosiaczeq/Dreamstime (233). Darryl Brooks/Shutterstock (242). Ran Dembo/iStockphoto (246). Maisna/Dreamstime (250). **Chapter 6: Newfoundland:** Butlerstockphotography1/Dreamstime (271). Doug Gordon/Shutterstock (281). Ahkenahmed/Dreamstime (288). Stephen Barnes/iStockphoto (299). Grayfoxx1942/Dreamstime (300). Jtstewartphoto/iStockphoto (307). Rob Crandall/Shutterstock (310). Robert Vincelli/ Shutterstock (319). Chiyacat/Shutterstock (324). Russ Heinl/Shutterstock (328). **About Our Writers:** All photos are courtesy of the writers.

*Every effort has been made to trace the copyright holders, and we apologize in advance for any accidental errors. We would be happy to apply the corrections in the following edition of this publication.

Notes